ULTIMATE SPIDER-MAN

ULTIMATE COLLECTION
BOOK 7

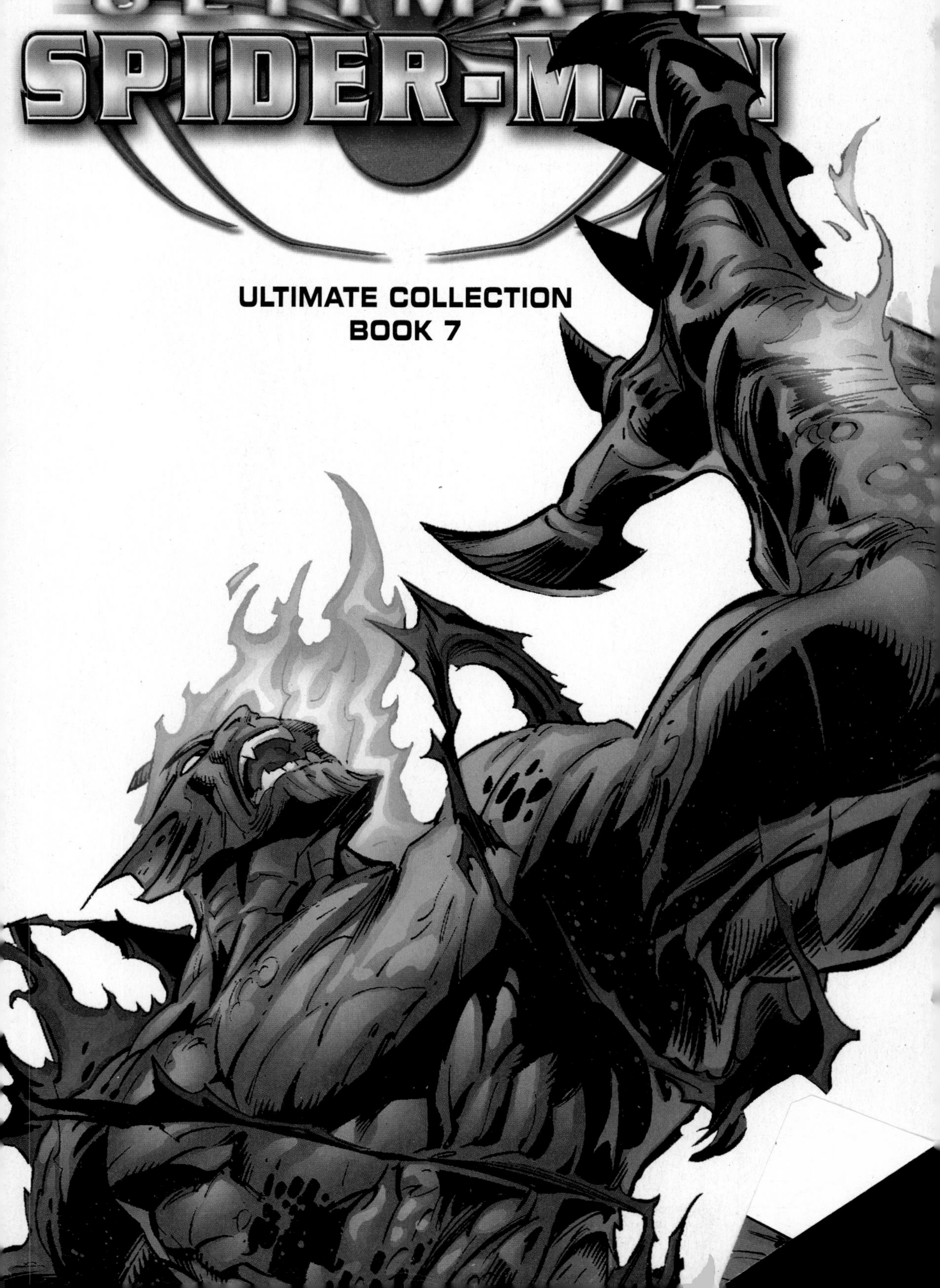

PREVIOUSLY:

Recent battles with villains Carnage and Nightmare have put Peter in an awful mental state, especially since the death of his friend Gwen Stacy at the hands of Carnage. He is doubting his role as Spider-Man and is unable to communicate with his girlfriend and confidante, Mary Jane Watson. Norman Osborn, the father of Peter's best friend, Harry, was developing a wonder drug called Oz. Testing of the mystery drug created the genetically altered spider that accidentally created Spider-Man.

In an attempt to repeat the process on himself, Osborn destroyed his life. He mutated himself into a hulking goblin figure. Driven mad by the mutation, he set out to erase any memory of his existence. He killed his wife and attempted to kill his own son. In fact, one of Spider-Man's first tests of mettle was fighting the mysterious Goblin.

Harry Osborn has been witness to all of his father's shocking and violent Goblin outbursts. Norman Osborn recently escaped from S.H.I.E.L.D. custody and tried to use Peter as part of a commando brigade against the White House. Nick Fury led the Ultimates and Spider-Man to a successful defeat of Osborn, but was forced to use Harry Osborn as a decoy. A dumbstruck Harry witnessed the violent defeat of his father. Peter tried to comfort his old friend. The only words Harry could mutter were: "I'll kill you all."

That was the last time Peter, or anyone, saw Harry.

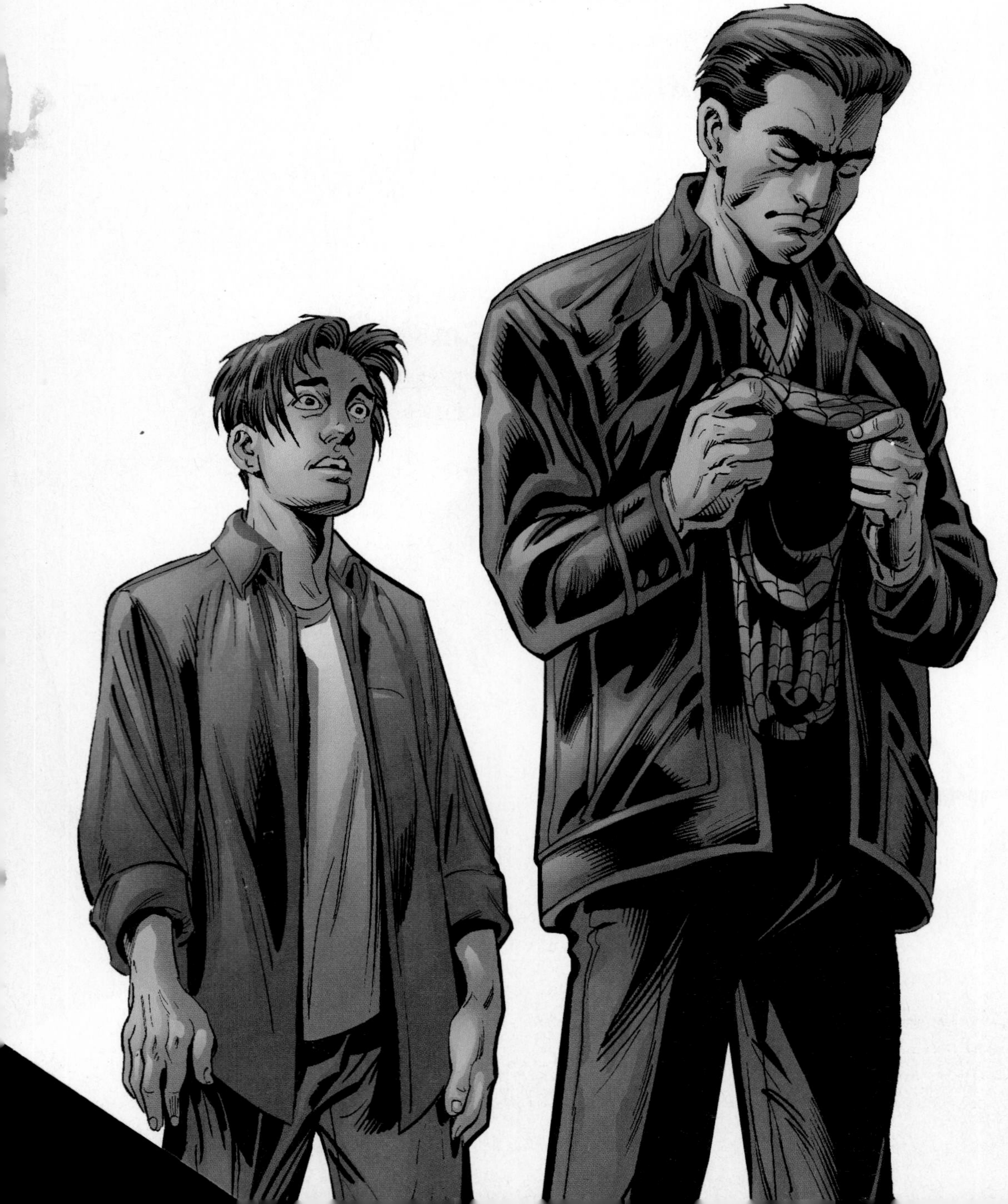

ULTIMATE COLLECTION BOOK 7

Writer: **Brian Michael Bendis**

Penciler: **Mark Bagley**

Inker: **Scott Hanna**

Colorist: **J.D. Smith**

Letterer: **Chris Eliopoulos**

Cover Art: **Mark Bagley & Richard Isanove**

Assistant Editors: **John Barber & Nicole Boose**

Associate Editor: **Nick Lowe**

Editor: **Ralph Macchio**

Spider-Man created by **Stan Lee & Steve Ditko**

Collection Editor: **Jennifer Grünwald** • Assistant Editor: **Caitlin O'Connell**
Associate Managing Editor: **Kateri Woody** • Editor, Special Projects: **Mark D. Beazley**
VP Production & Special Projects: **Jeff Youngquist** • SVP Print, Sales & Marketing: **David Gabriel**

Editor in Chief: **Axel Alonso** • Chief Creative Officer: **Joe Quesada**
President: **Dan Buckley** • Executive Producer: **Alan Fine**

ULTIMATE SPIDER-MAN ULTIMATE COLLECTION BOOK 7. Contains material originally published in magazine form as ULTIMATE SPIDER-MAN #72-85. First printing 2017. ISBN# 978-1-302-90874-4. Published
MARVEL WORLDWIDE, INC., a subsidiary of MARVEL ENTERTAINMENT, LLC. OFFICE OF PUBLICATION: 135 West 50th Street, New York, NY 10020. Copyright © 2017 MARVEL No similarity between any of the n
characters, persons, and/or institutions in this magazine with those of any living or dead person or institution is intended, and any such similarity which may exist is purely coincidental. **Printed in the U**
BUCKLEY, President, Marvel Entertainment; JOE QUESADA, Chief Creative Officer; TOM BREVOORT, SVP of Publishing; DAVID BOGART, SVP of Business Affairs & Operations, Publishing & Partnership; C
VP of Brand Management & Development, Asia; DAVID GABRIEL, SVP of Sales & Marketing, Publishing; JEFF YOUNGQUIST, VP of Production & Special Projects; DAN CARR, Executive Director of Publis
ALEX MORALES, Director of Publishing Operations; SUSAN CRESPI, Production Manager; STAN LEE, Chairman Emeritus. For information regarding advertising in Marvel Comics or on Marvel
Vit DeBellis, Integrated Sales Manager, at vdebellis@marvel.com. For Marvel subscription inquiries, please call 888-511-5480. **Manufactured between 4/7/2017 and 5/9/2017 by LSC**
SALEM, VA, USA.

10 9 8 7 6 5 4 3 2 1

72

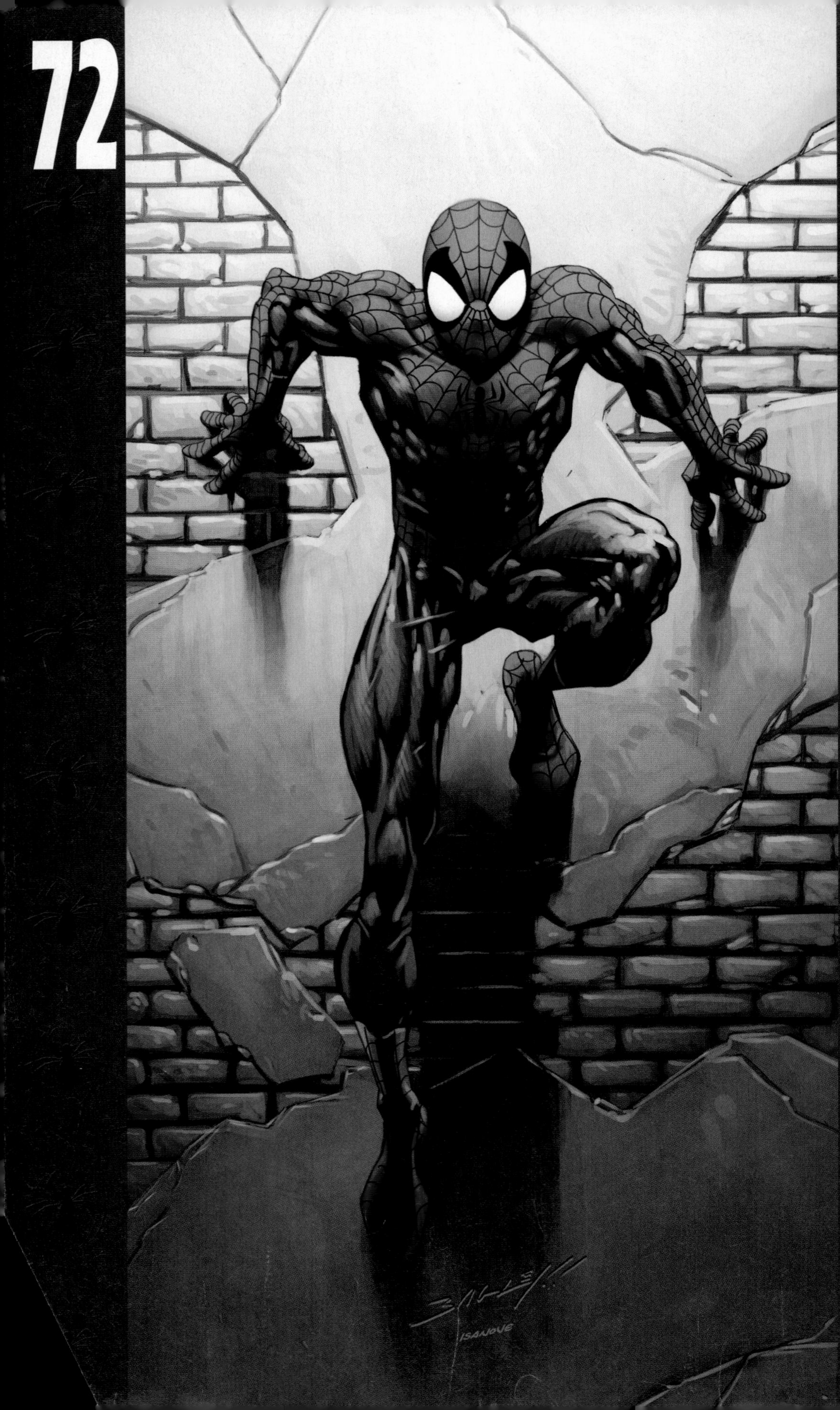

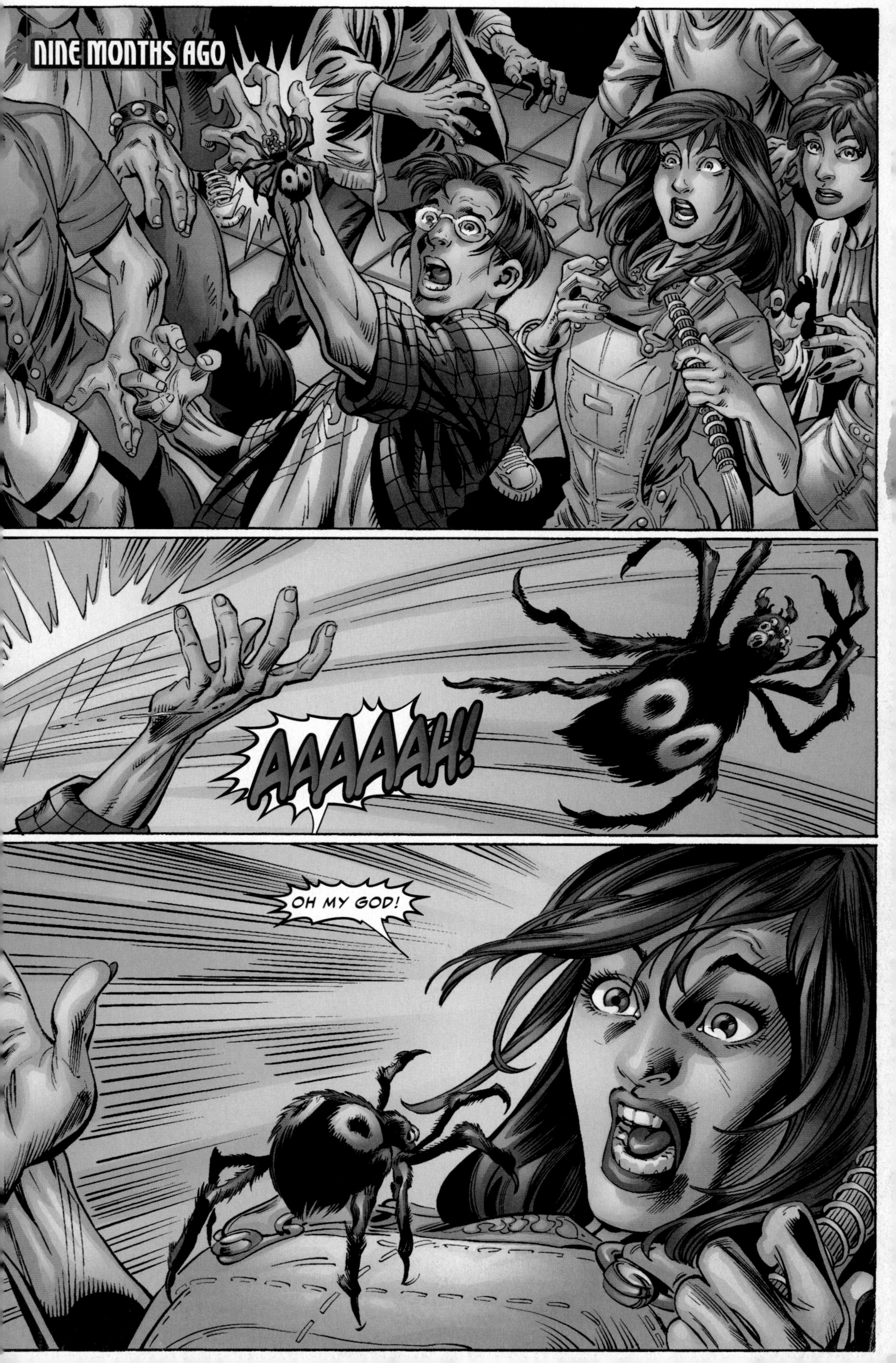
NINE MONTHS AGO
AAAAAH!
OH MY GOD!

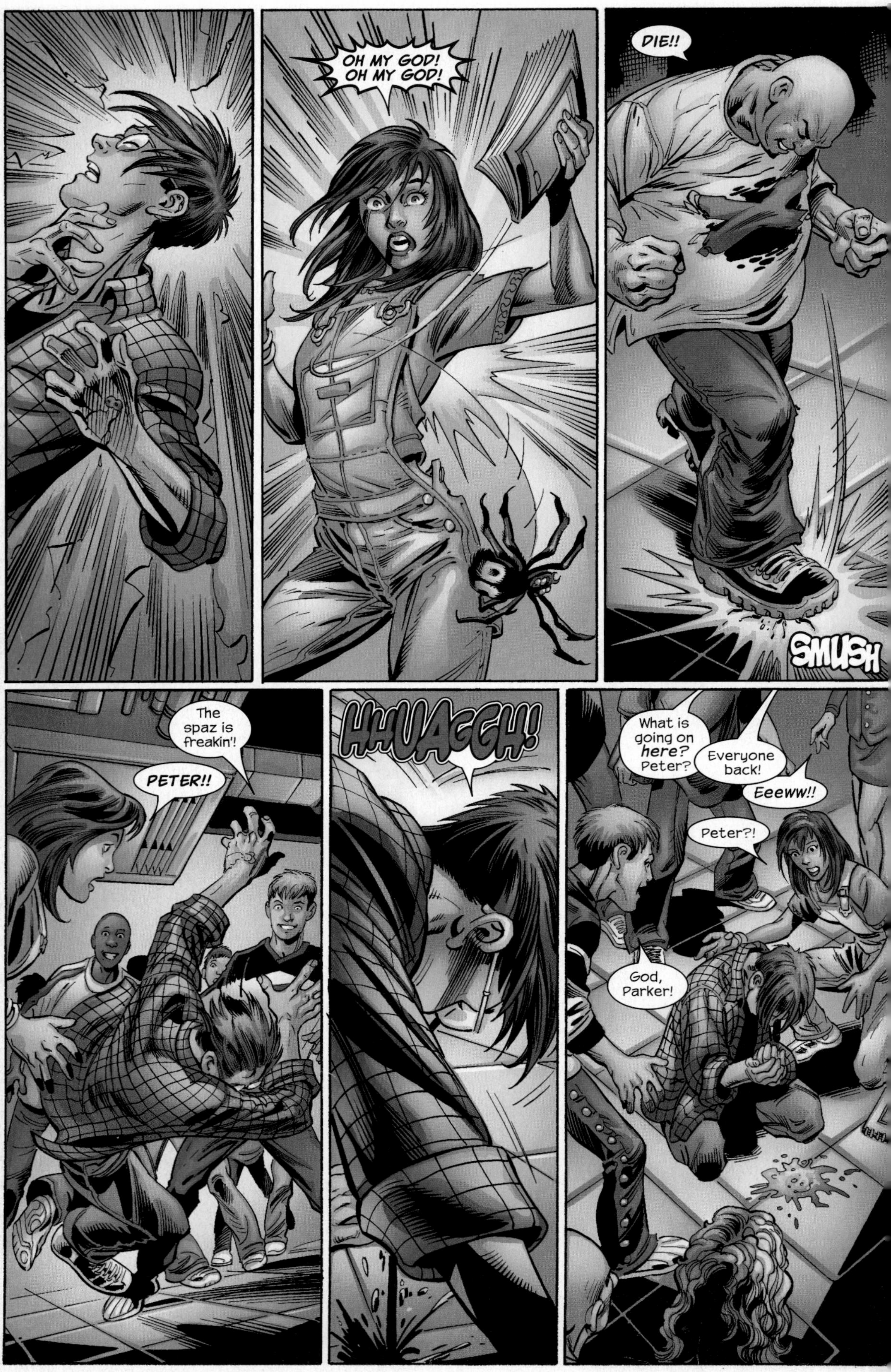

OH MY GOD! OH MY GOD!
DIE!!
SMUSH
The spaz is freakin'!
PETER!!
HHUAGGH!
What is going on *here*? Peter?
Everyone back!
Eeeww!!
Peter?!
God, Parker!

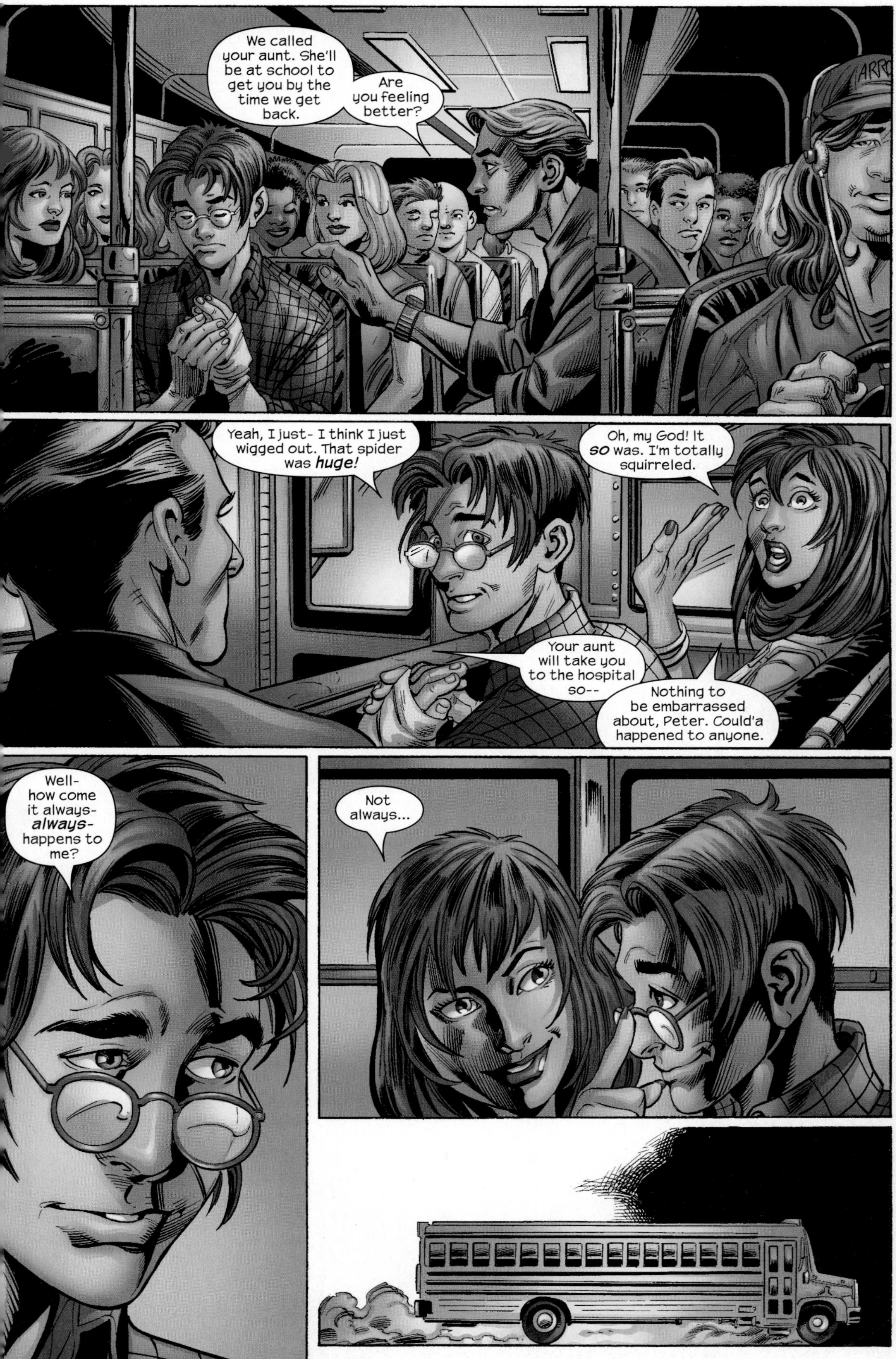

We called your aunt. She'll be at school to get you by the time we get back.
Are you feeling better?
Yeah, I just- I think I just wigged out. That spider was *huge!*
Oh, my God! It *so* was. I'm totally squirreled.
Your aunt will take you to the hospital so--
Nothing to be embarrassed about, Peter. Could'a happened to anyone.
Well- how come it always- *always*- happens to me?
Not always...

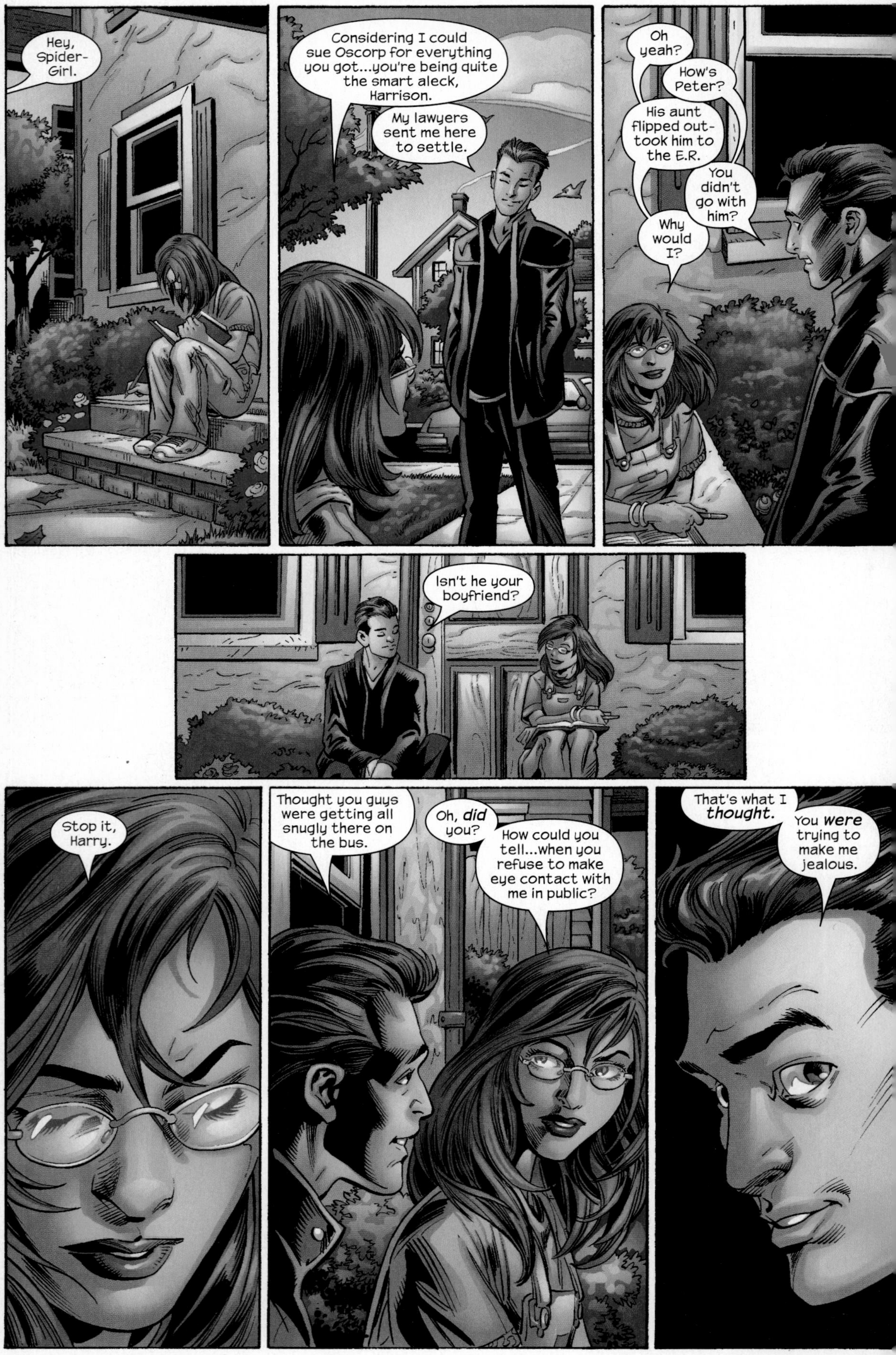
Hey, Spider-Girl.
Considering I could sue Oscorp for everything you got...you're being quite the smart aleck, Harrison.
My lawyers sent me here to settle.
Oh yeah?
How's Peter?
His aunt flipped out- took him to the E.R.
You didn't go with him?
Why would I?
Isn't he your boyfriend?
Stop it, Harry.
Thought you guys were getting all snugly there on the bus.
Oh, did you?
How could you tell...when you refuse to make eye contact with me in public?
That's what I thought.
You were trying to make me jealous.

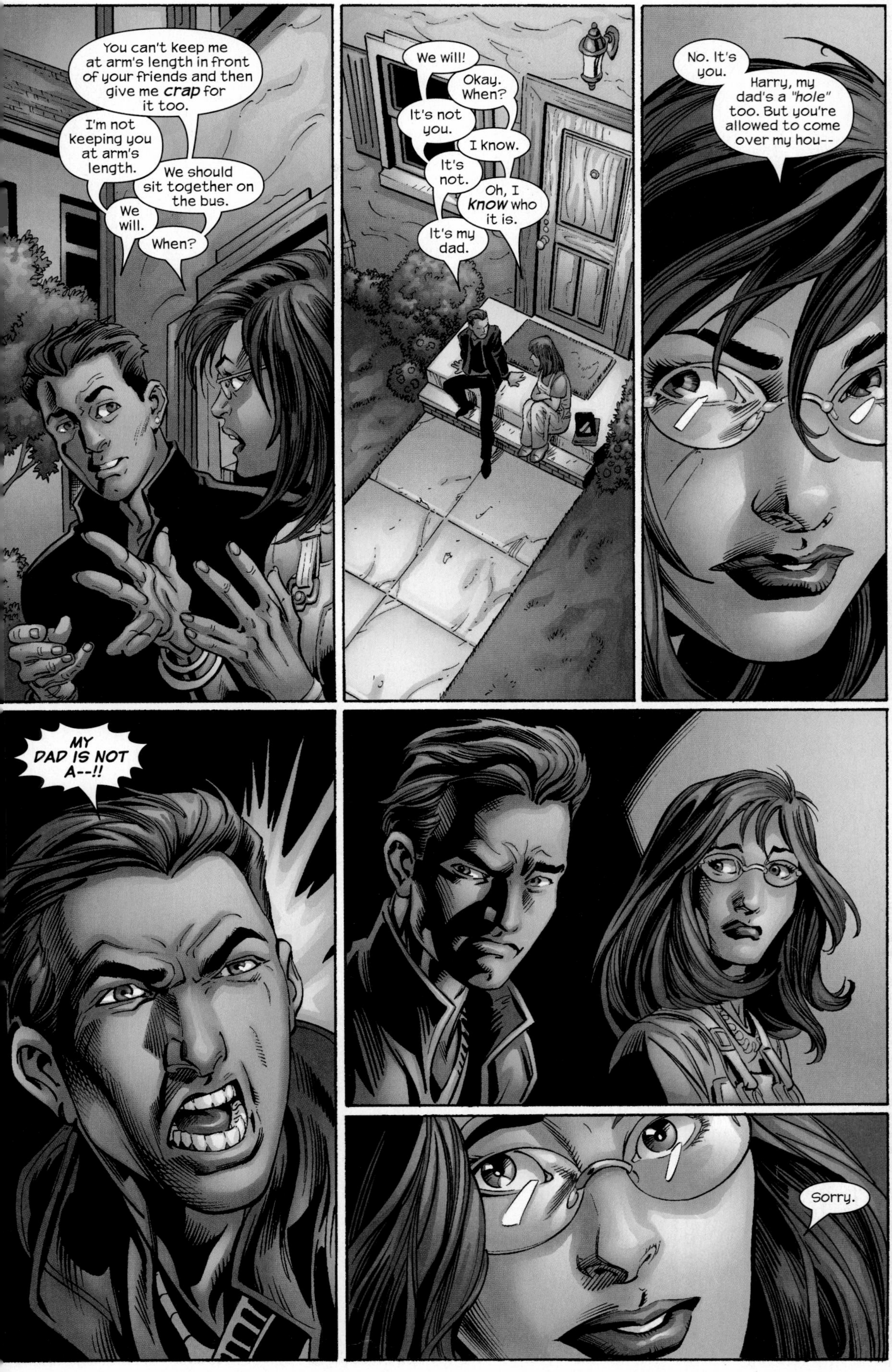
You can't keep me at arm's length in front of your friends and then give me *crap* for it too.
I'm not keeping you at arm's length.
We should sit together on the bus.
We will.
When?
We will!
Okay. When?
It's not you.
I know.
It's not.
Oh, I *KNOW* who it is.
It's my dad.
No. It's you.
Harry, my dad's a *"hole"* too. But you're allowed to come over my hou--
MY DAD IS NOT A--!!
Sorry.

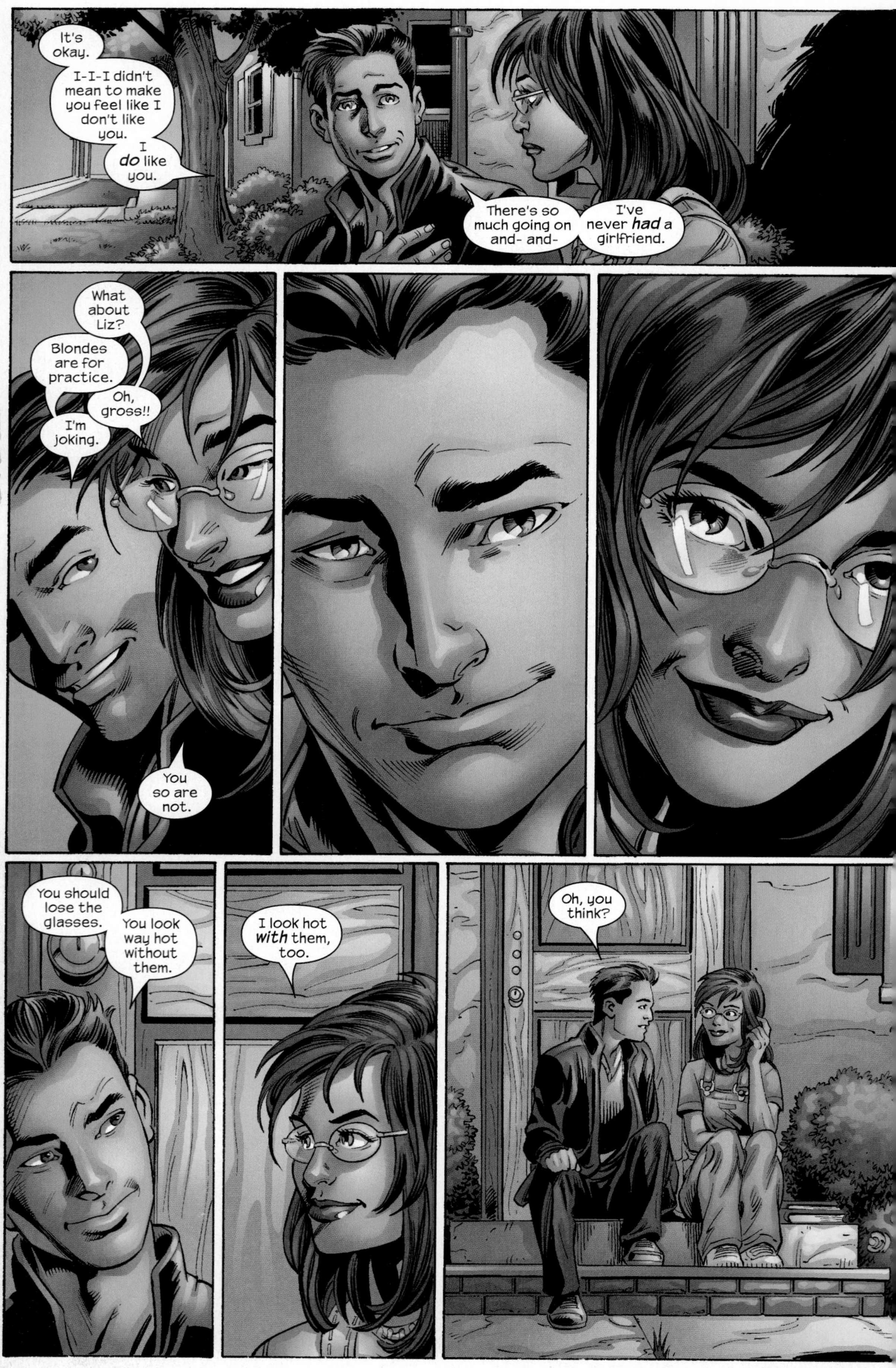
It's okay.
I-I-I didn't mean to make you feel like I don't like you.
I *do* like you.
There's so much going on and- and-
I've never *had* a girlfriend.
What about Liz?
Blondes are for practice.
Oh, gross!!
I'm joking.
You so are not.
You should lose the glasses.
You look way hot without them.
I look hot *with* them, too.
Oh, you think?

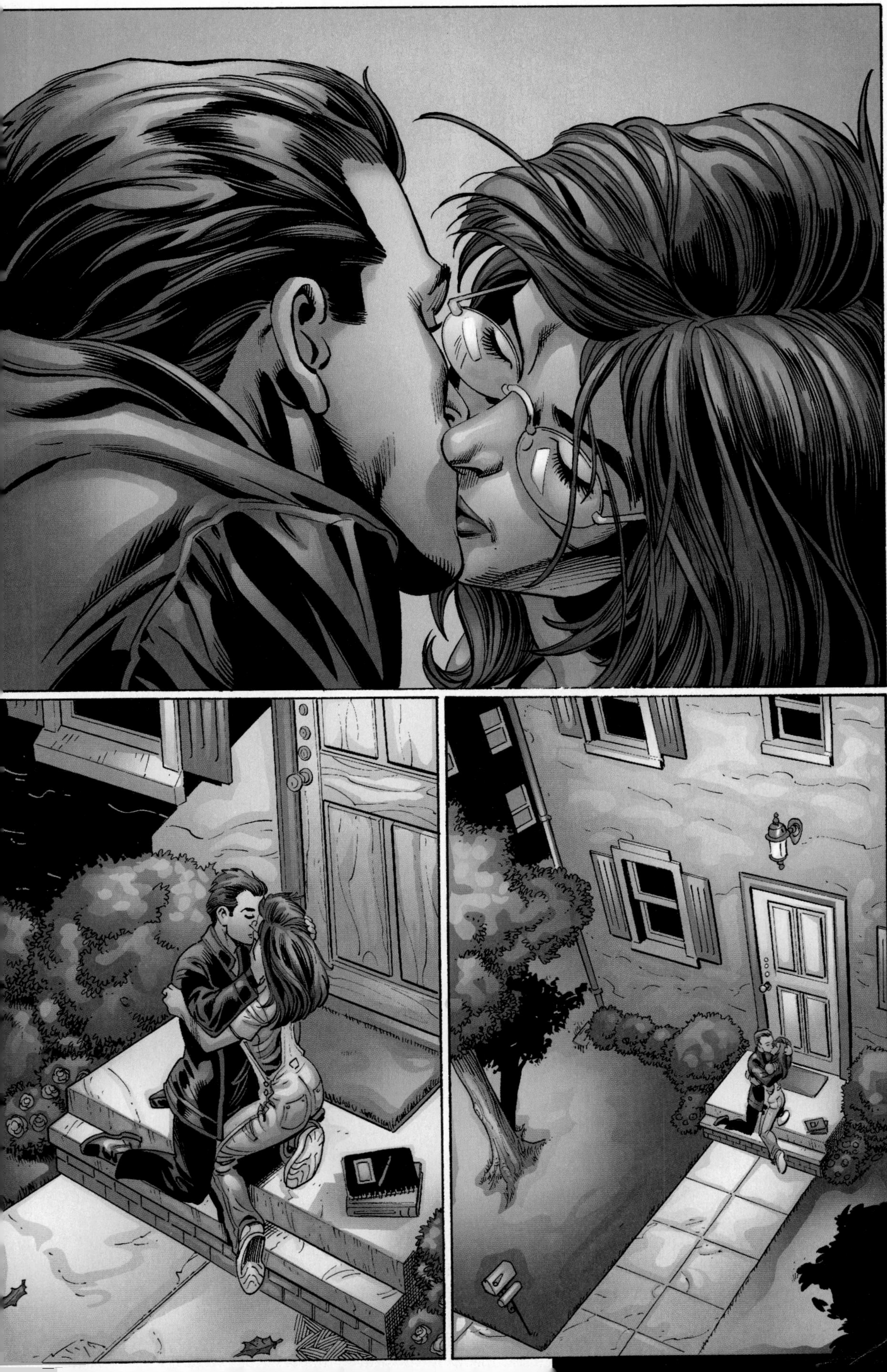

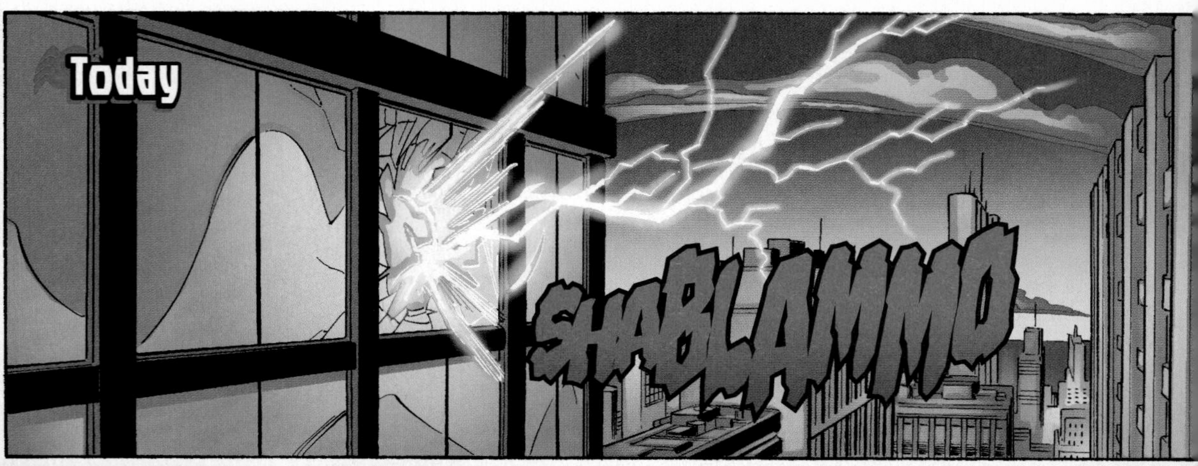
Today
SHABLAMMO

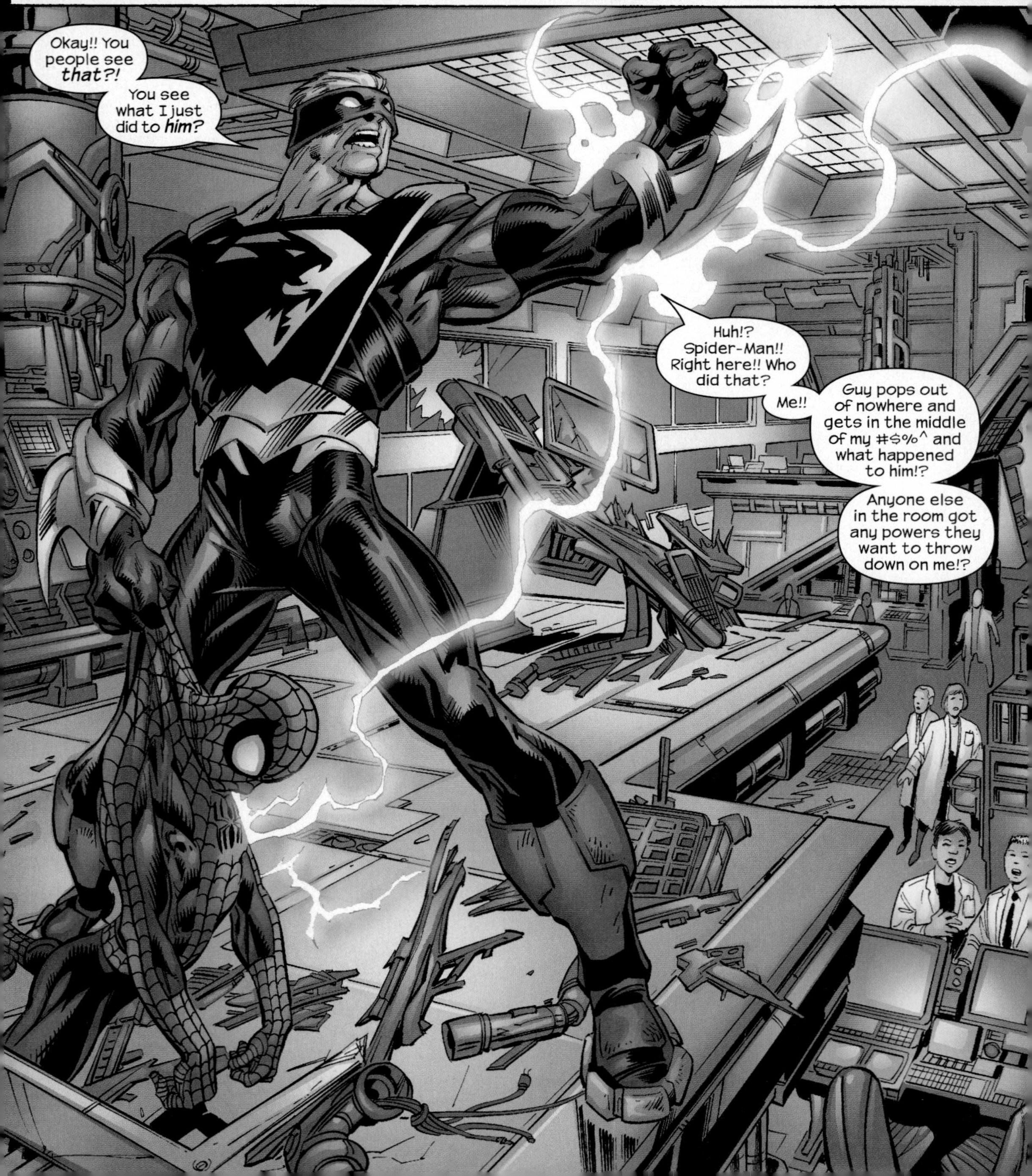
Okay!! You people see *that*?!
You see what I just did to *him*?
Huh!? Spider-Man!! Right here!! Who did that?
Me!!
Guy pops out of nowhere and gets in the middle of my #$%^ and what happened to him!?
Anyone else in the room got any powers they want to throw down on me!?

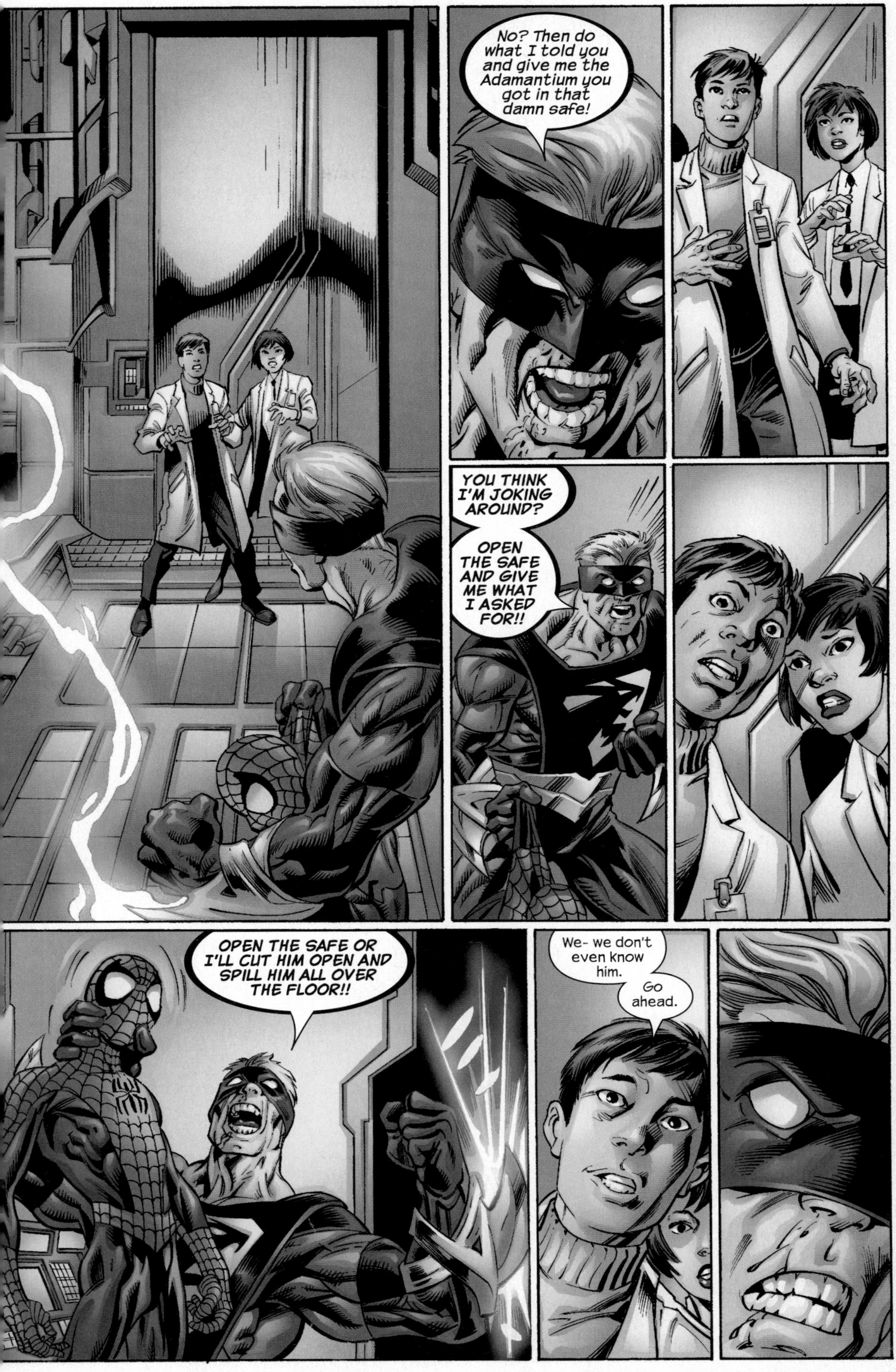
No? Then do what I told you and give me the Adamantium you got in that damn safe!
YOU THINK I'M JOKING AROUND?
OPEN THE SAFE AND GIVE ME WHAT I ASKED FOR!!
OPEN THE SAFE OR I'LL CUT HIM OPEN AND SPILL HIM ALL OVER THE FLOOR!!
We- we don't even know him.
Go ahead.

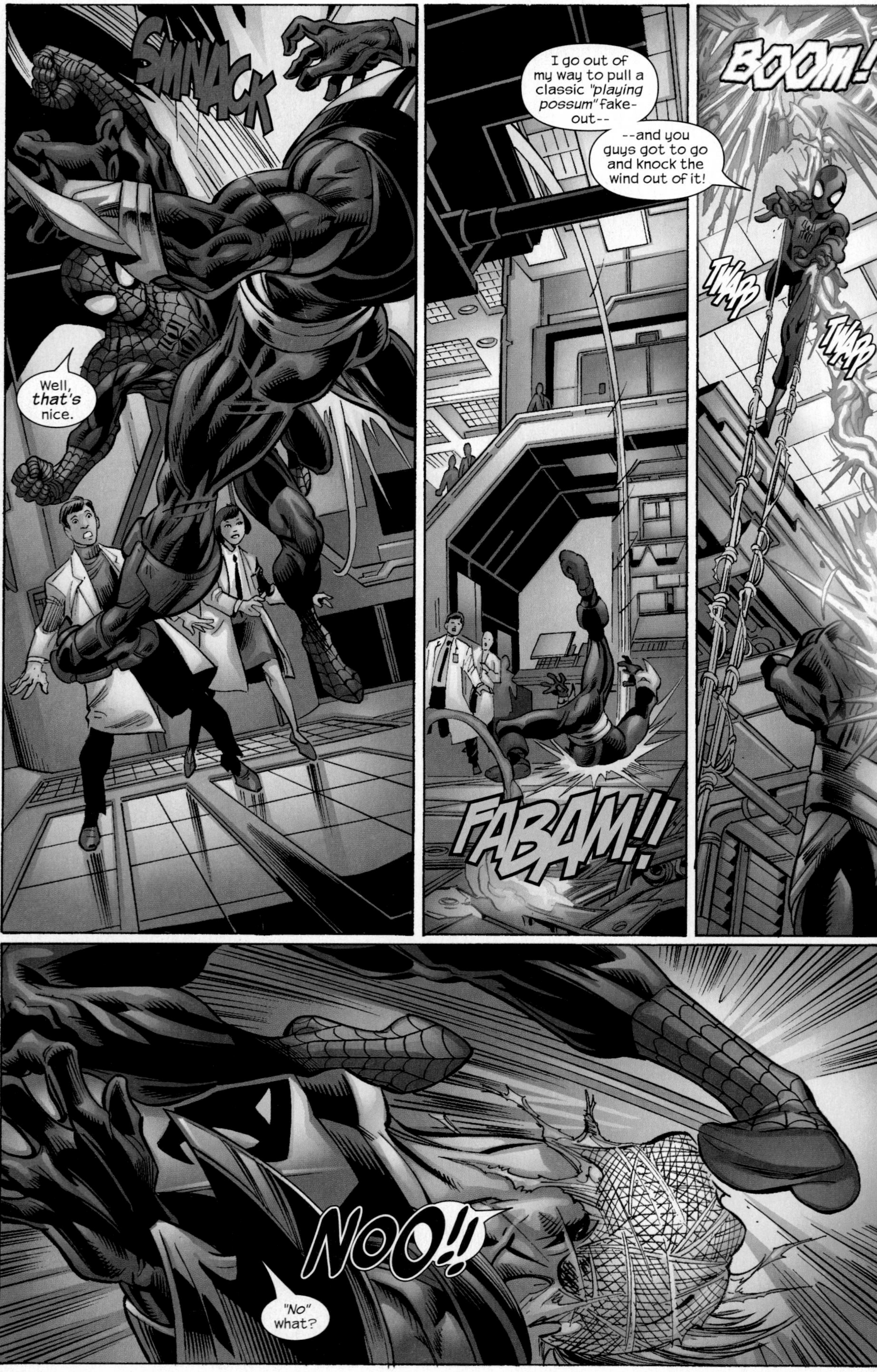
SMACK
Well, that's nice.
I go out of my way to pull a classic "playing possum" fake-out--
--and you guys got to go and knock the wind out of it!
FABAM!!
BOOM!
TWAP
TWAP
NOO!!
"No" what?

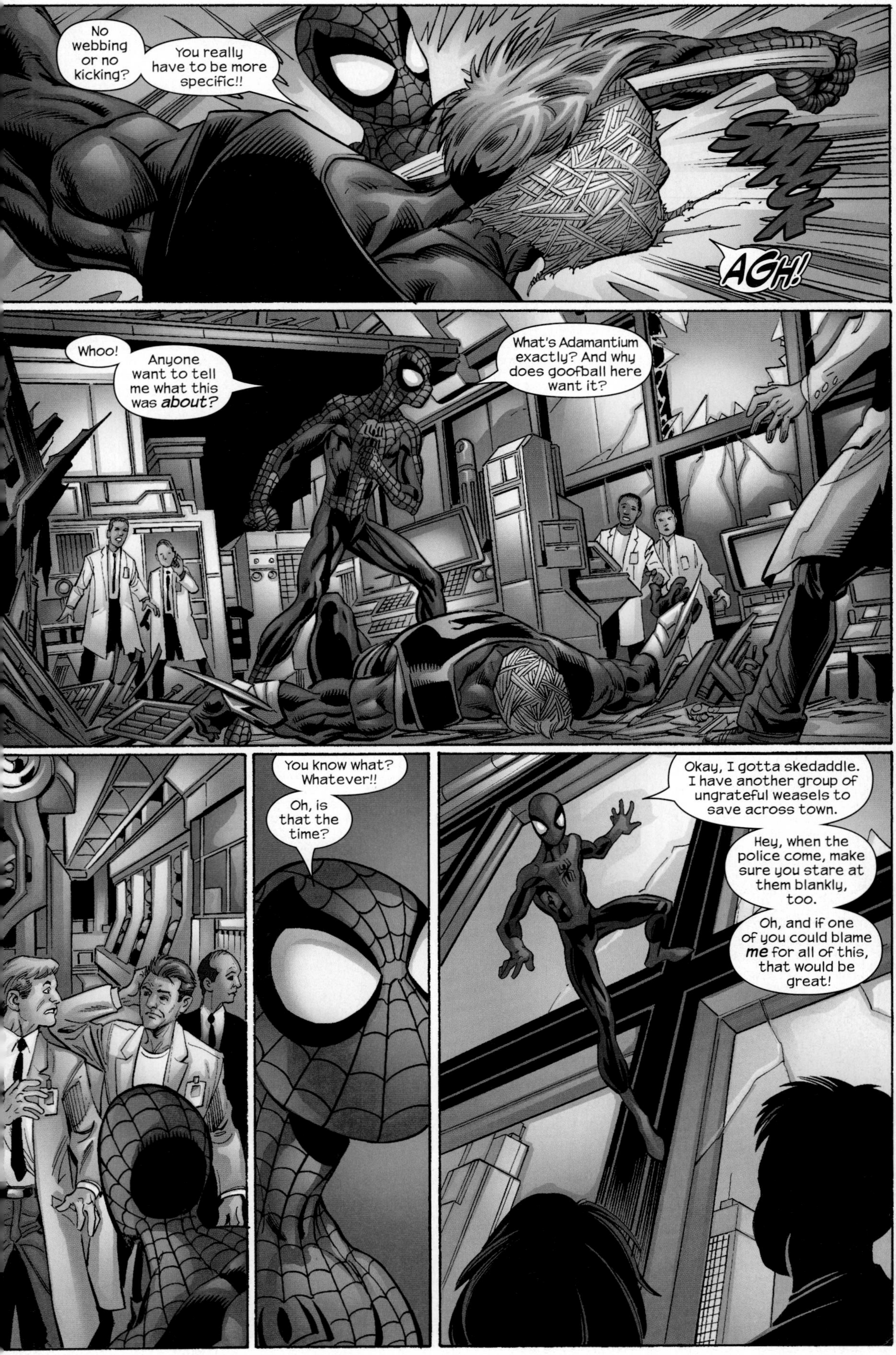
No webbing or no kicking?
You really have to be more specific!!
SMACK
AGH!
Whoo!
Anyone want to tell me what this was *about*?
What's Adamantium exactly? And why does goofball here want it?
You know what? Whatever!!
Oh, is that the time?
Okay, I gotta skedaddle. I have another group of ungrateful weasels to save across town.
Hey, when the police come, make sure you stare at them blankly, too.
Oh, and if one of you could blame **me** for all of this, that would be great!

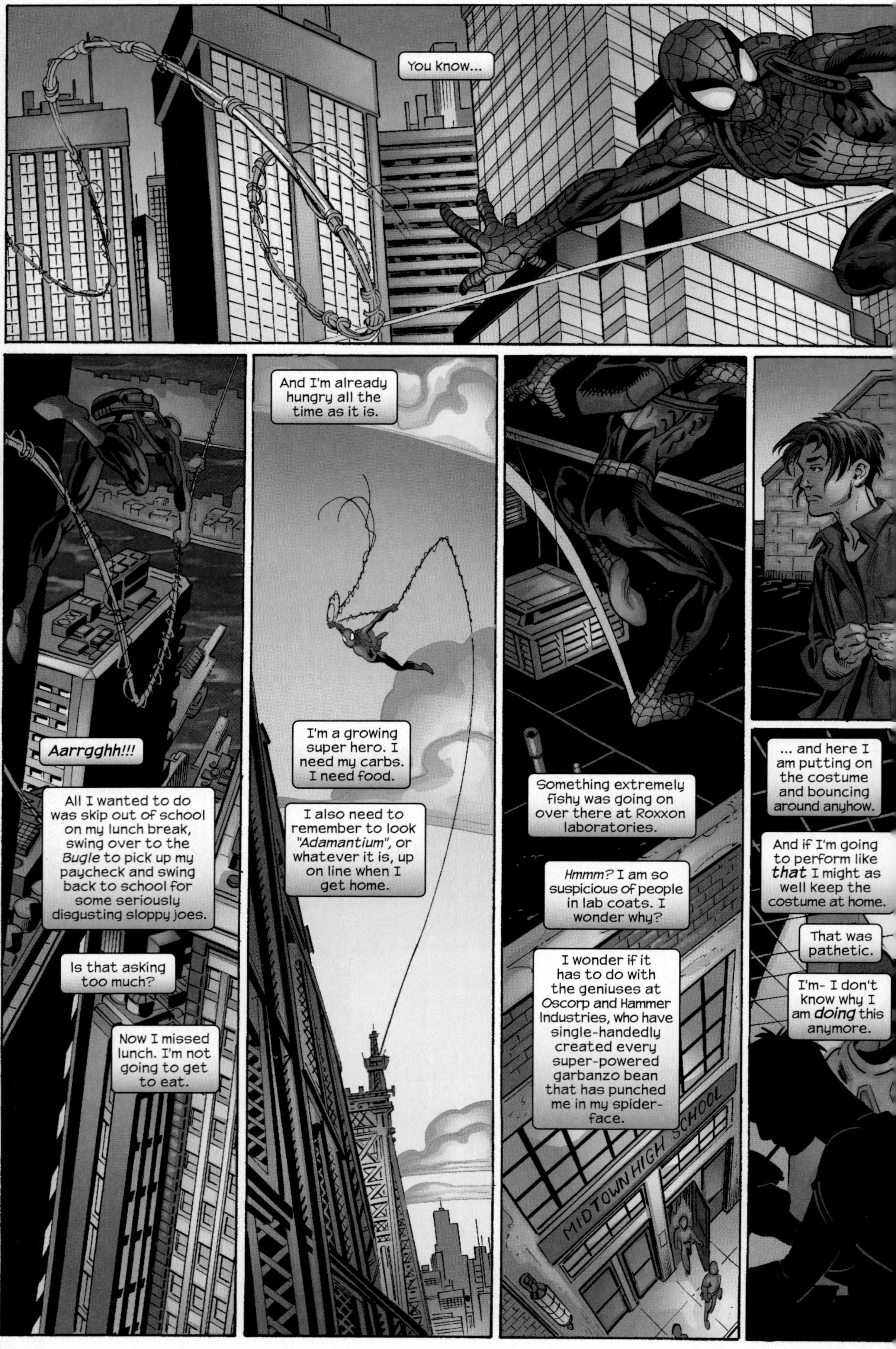
You know...
Aarrgghh!!!
All I wanted to do was skip out of school on my lunch break, swing over to the *Bugle* to pick up my paycheck and swing back to school for some seriously disgusting sloppy joes.
Is that asking too much?
Now I missed lunch. I'm not going to get to eat.
And I'm already hungry all the time as it is.
I'm a growing super hero. I need my carbs. I need food.
I also need to remember to look *"Adamantium"*, or whatever it is, up on line when I get home.
Something extremely fishy was going on over there at Roxxon laboratories.
Hmmm? I am so suspicious of people in lab coats. I wonder why?
I wonder if it has to do with the geniuses at Oscorp and Hammer Industries, who have single-handedly created every super-powered garbanzo bean that has punched me in my spider-face.
MIDTOWN HIGH SCHOOL
... and here I am putting on the costume and bouncing around anyhow.
And if I'm going to perform like ***that*** I might as well keep the costume at home.
That was pathetic.
I'm- I don't know why I am ***doing*** this anymore.

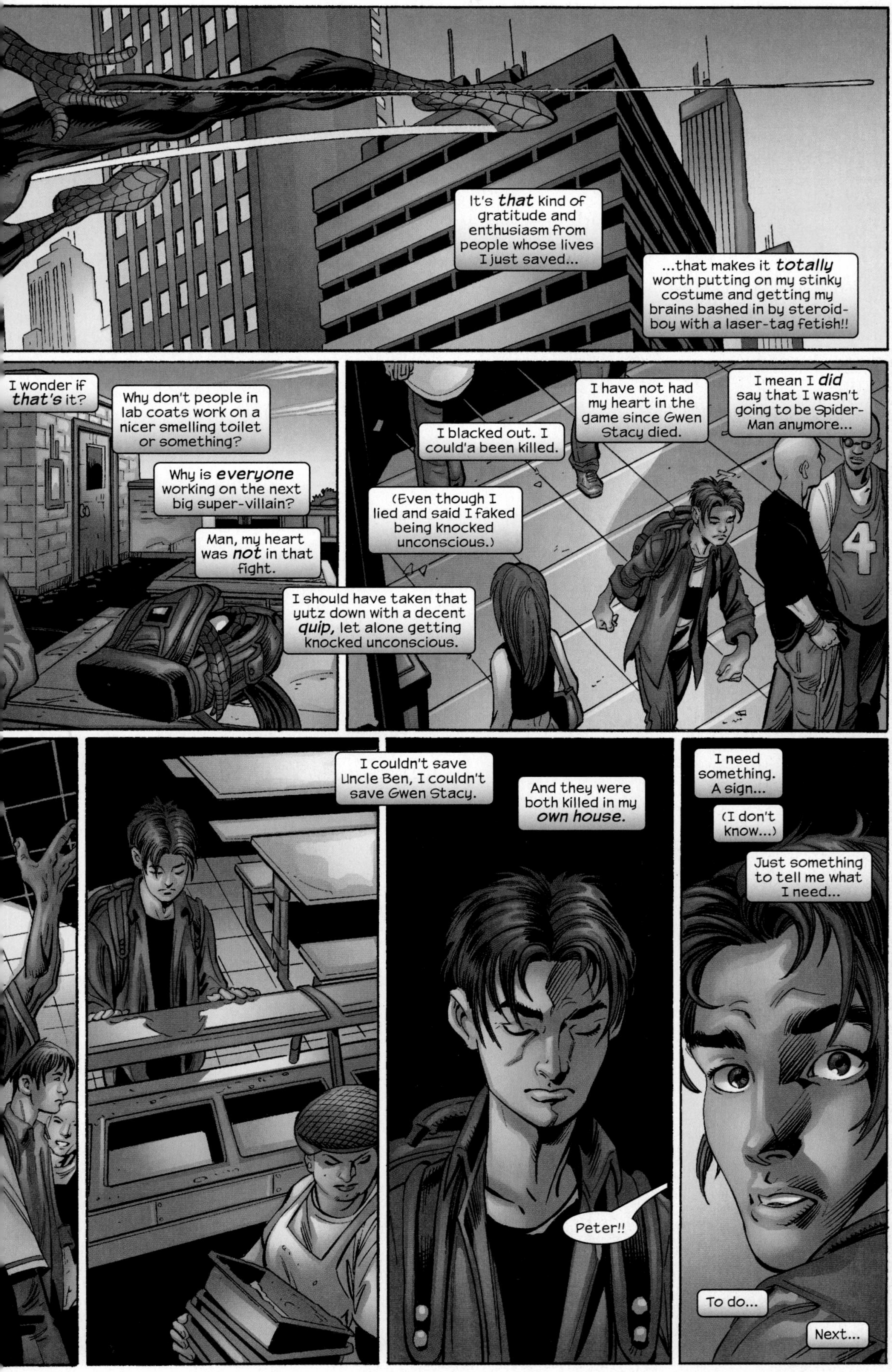
It's that kind of gratitude and enthusiasm from people whose lives I just saved...
...that makes it totally worth putting on my stinky costume and getting my brains bashed in by steroid-boy with a laser-tag fetish!!
I wonder if that's it?
Why don't people in lab coats work on a nicer smelling toilet or something?
Why is everyone working on the next big super-villain?
Man, my heart was not in that fight.
I should have taken that yutz down with a decent quip, let alone getting knocked unconscious.
I blacked out. I could'a been killed.
(Even though I lied and said I faked being knocked unconscious.)
I have not had my heart in the game since Gwen Stacy died.
I mean I did say that I wasn't going to be Spider-Man anymore...
I couldn't save Uncle Ben, I couldn't save Gwen Stacy.
And they were both killed in my own house.
Peter!!
I need something. A sign...
(I don't know...)
Just something to tell me what I need...
To do...
Next...

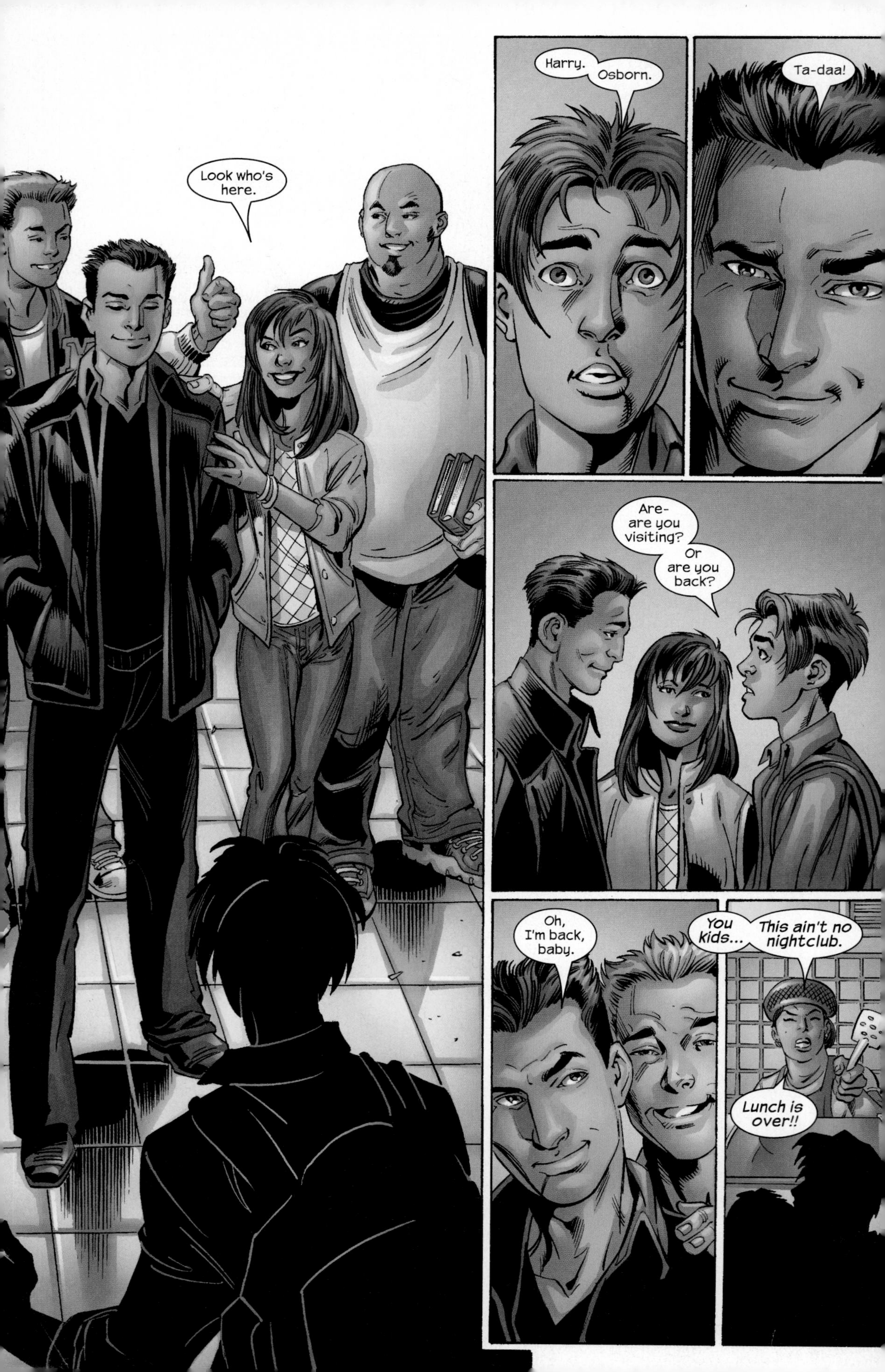
Look who's here.
Harry.
Osborn.
Ta-daa!
Are- are you visiting?
Or are you back?
Oh, I'm back, baby.
You kids...
This ain't no nightclub.
Lunch is over!!

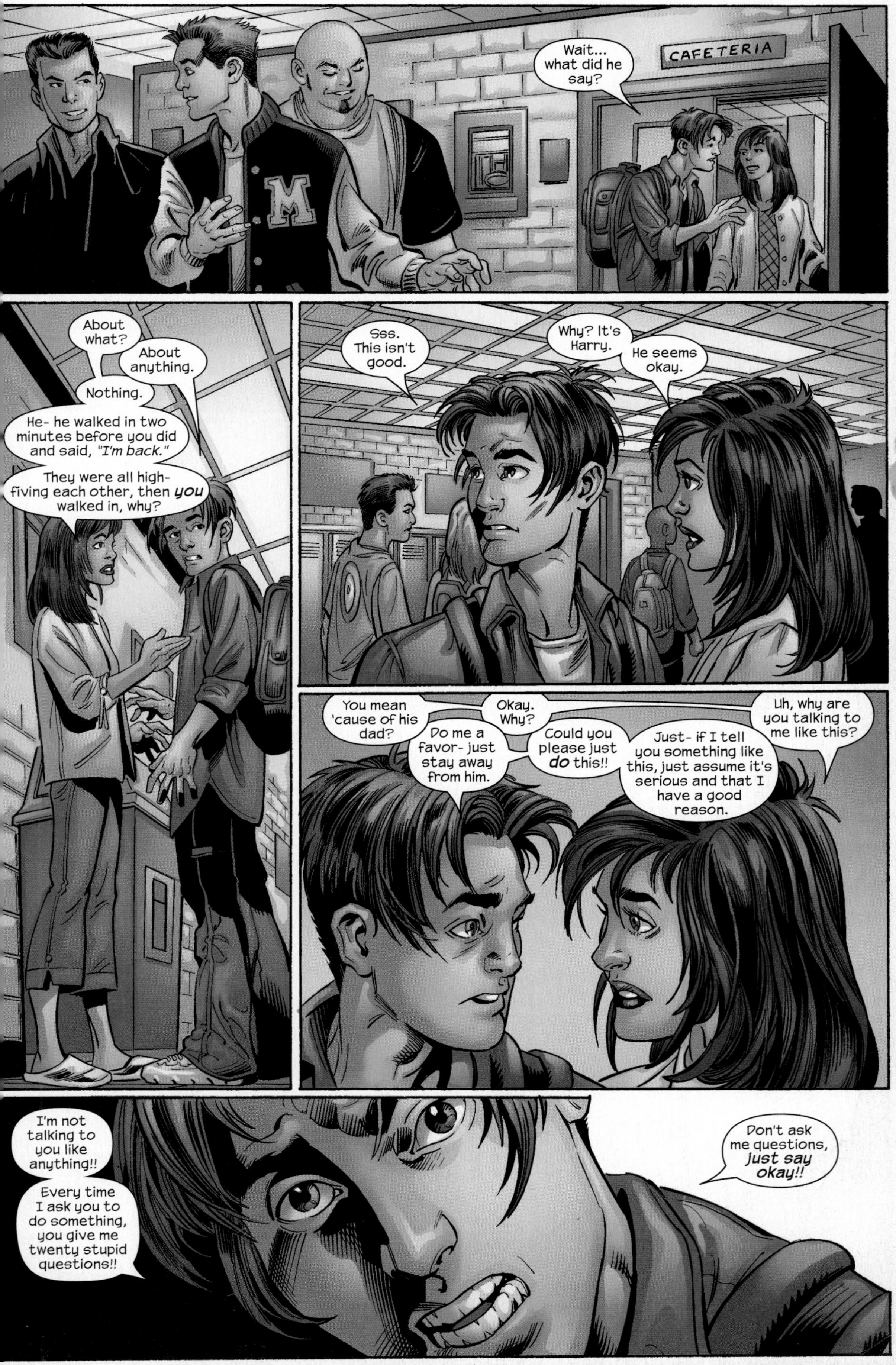
CAFETERIA
Wait... what did he say?
About what?
About anything.
Nothing.
He- he walked in two minutes before you did and said, "I'm back."
They were all high-fiving each other, then you walked in, why?
Sss. This isn't good.
Why? It's Harry.
He seems okay.
You mean 'cause of his dad?
Okay. Why?
Uh, why are you talking to me like this?
Do me a favor- just stay away from him.
Could you please just do this!!
Just- if I tell you something like this, just assume it's serious and that I have a good reason.
I'm not talking to you like anything!!
Every time I ask you to do something, you give me twenty stupid questions!!
Don't ask me questions, just say okay!!

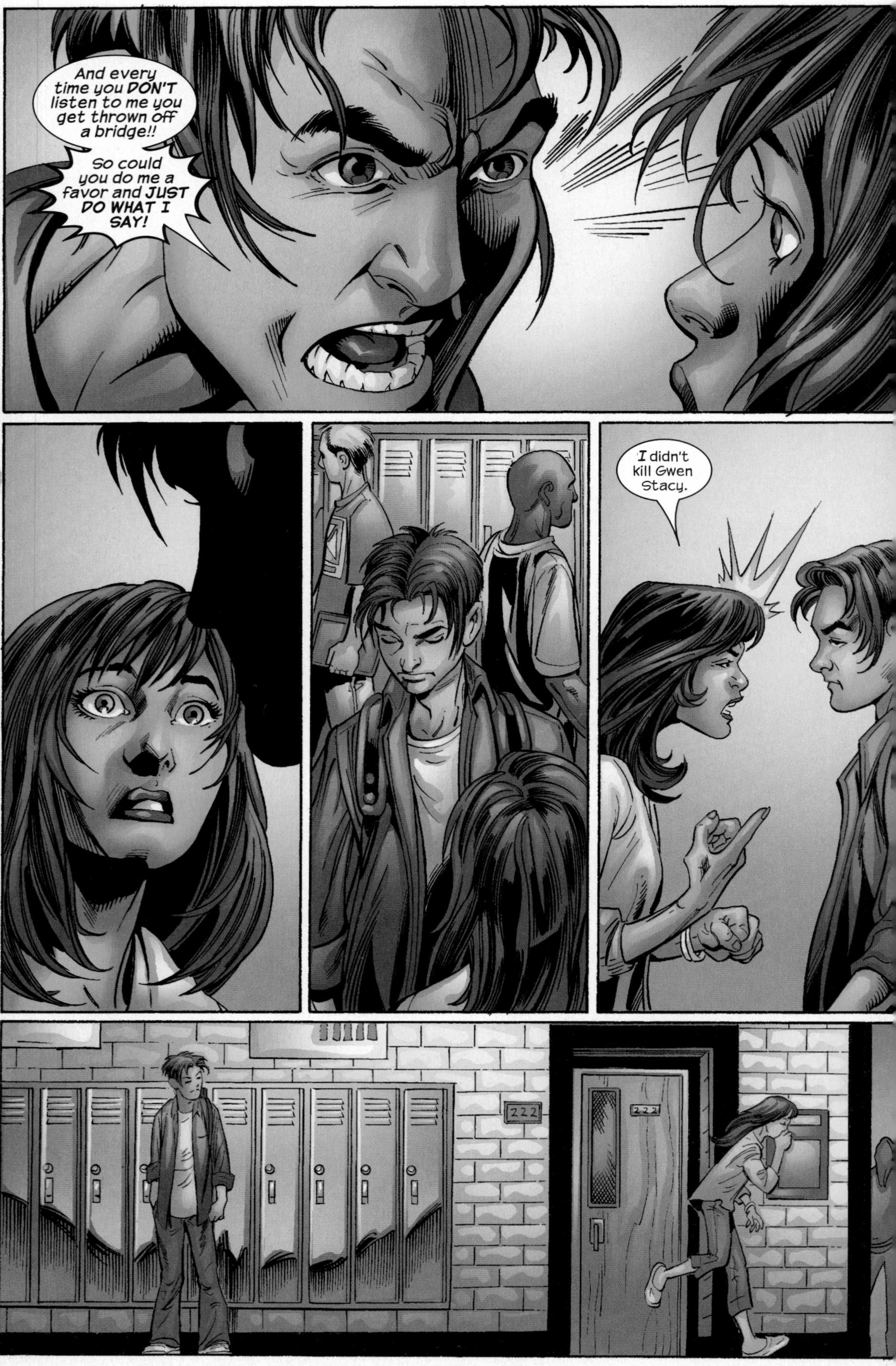

And every time you DON'T listen to me you get thrown off a bridge!!
So could you do me a favor and JUST DO WHAT I SAY!
I didn't kill Gwen Stacy.
222
222

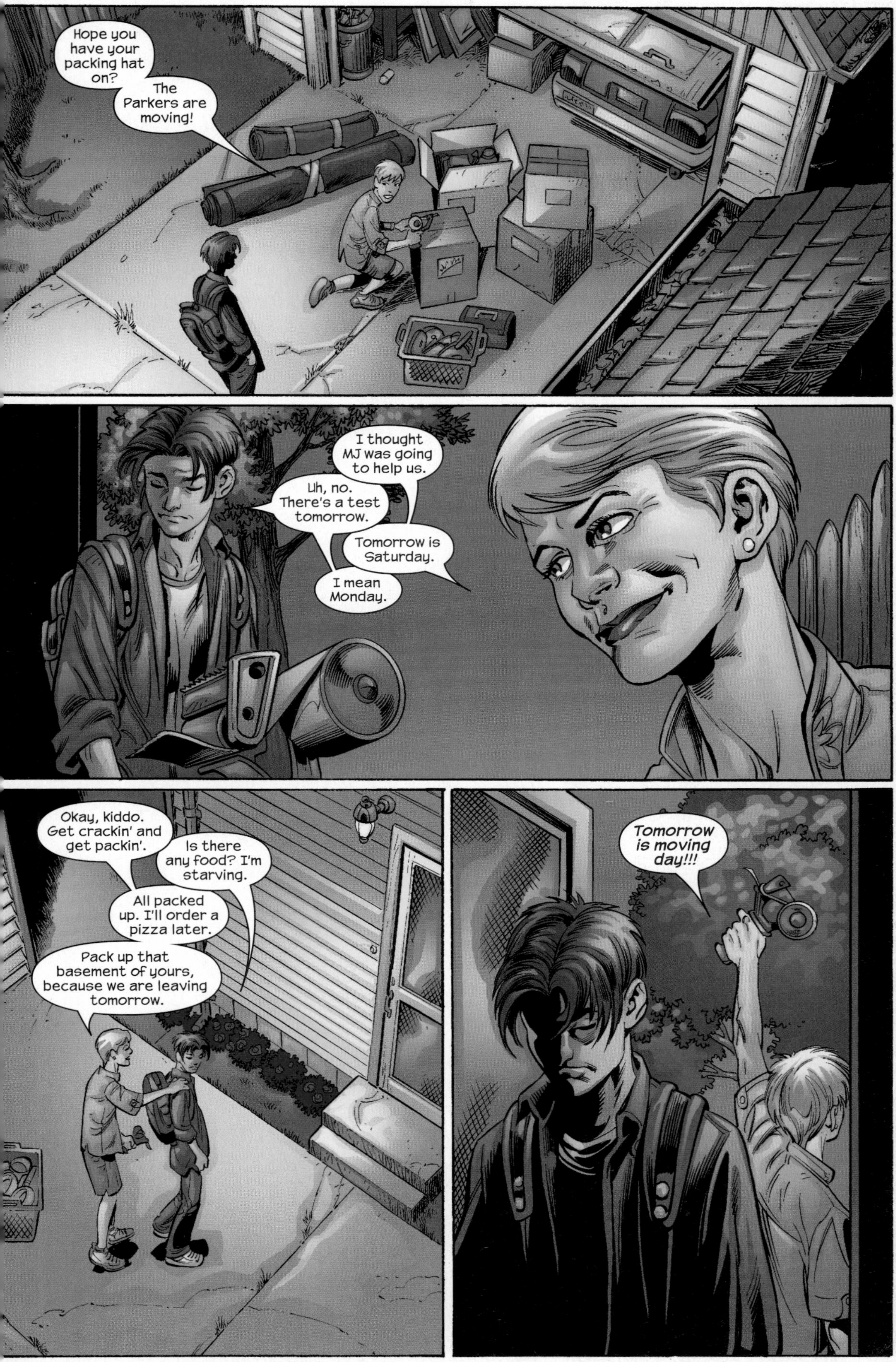
Hope you have your packing hat on?
The Parkers are moving!
I thought MJ was going to help us.
Uh, no. There's a test tomorrow.
Tomorrow is Saturday.
I mean Monday.
Okay, kiddo. Get crackin' and get packin'.
Is there any food? I'm starving.
All packed up. I'll order a pizza later.
Pack up that basement of yours, because we are leaving tomorrow.
Tomorrow is moving day!!!

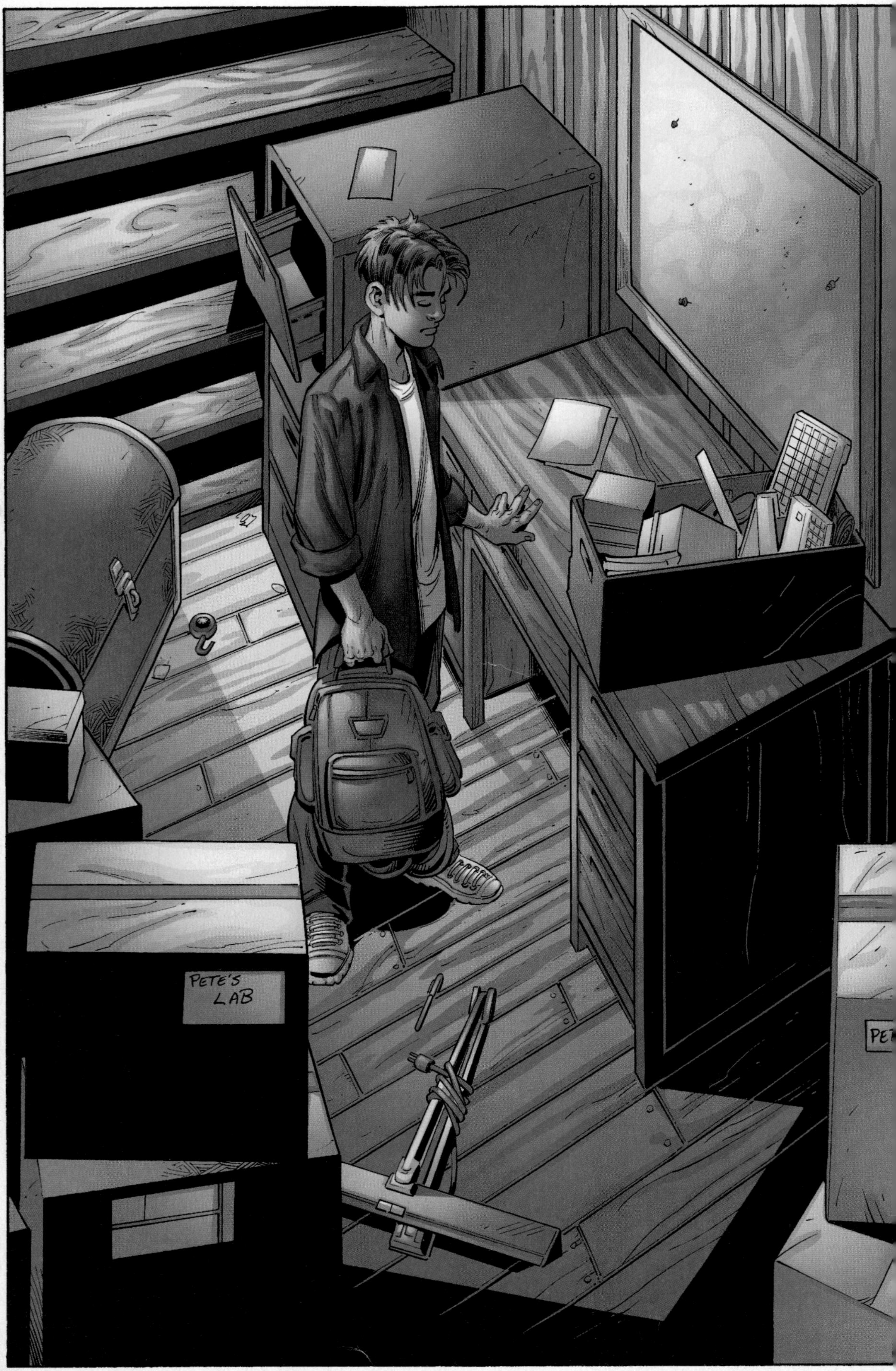
PETE'S
LAB
PET

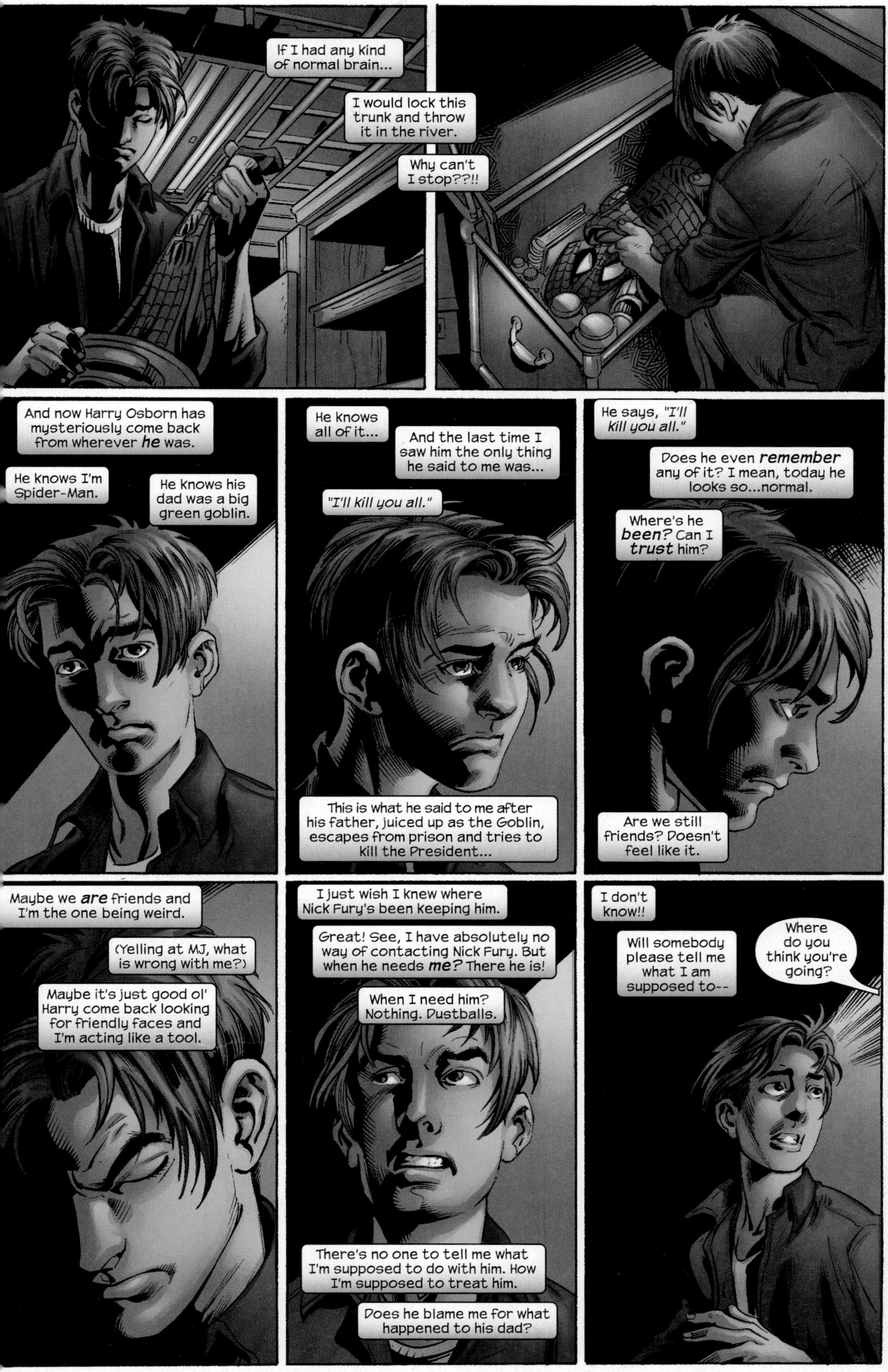
If I had any kind of normal brain...
I would lock this trunk and throw it in the river.
Why can't I stop??!!
And now Harry Osborn has mysteriously come back from wherever **he** was.
He knows I'm Spider-Man.
He knows his dad was a big green goblin.
He knows all of it...
And the last time I saw him the only thing he said to me was...
"I'll kill you all."
This is what he said to me after his father, juiced up as the Goblin, escapes from prison and tries to kill the President...
He says, *"I'll kill you all."*
Does he even **remember** any of it? I mean, today he looks so...normal.
Where's he **been?** Can I **trust** him?
Are we still friends? Doesn't feel like it.
Maybe we ***are*** friends and I'm the one being weird.
(Yelling at MJ, what is wrong with me?)
Maybe it's just good ol' Harry come back looking for friendly faces and I'm acting like a tool.
I just wish I knew where Nick Fury's been keeping him.
Great! See, I have absolutely no way of contacting Nick Fury. But when he needs ***me?*** There he is!
When I need him? Nothing. Dustballs.
There's no one to tell me what I'm supposed to do with him. How I'm supposed to treat him.
Does he blame me for what happened to his dad?
I don't know!!
Will somebody please tell me what I am supposed to--
Where do you think you're going?

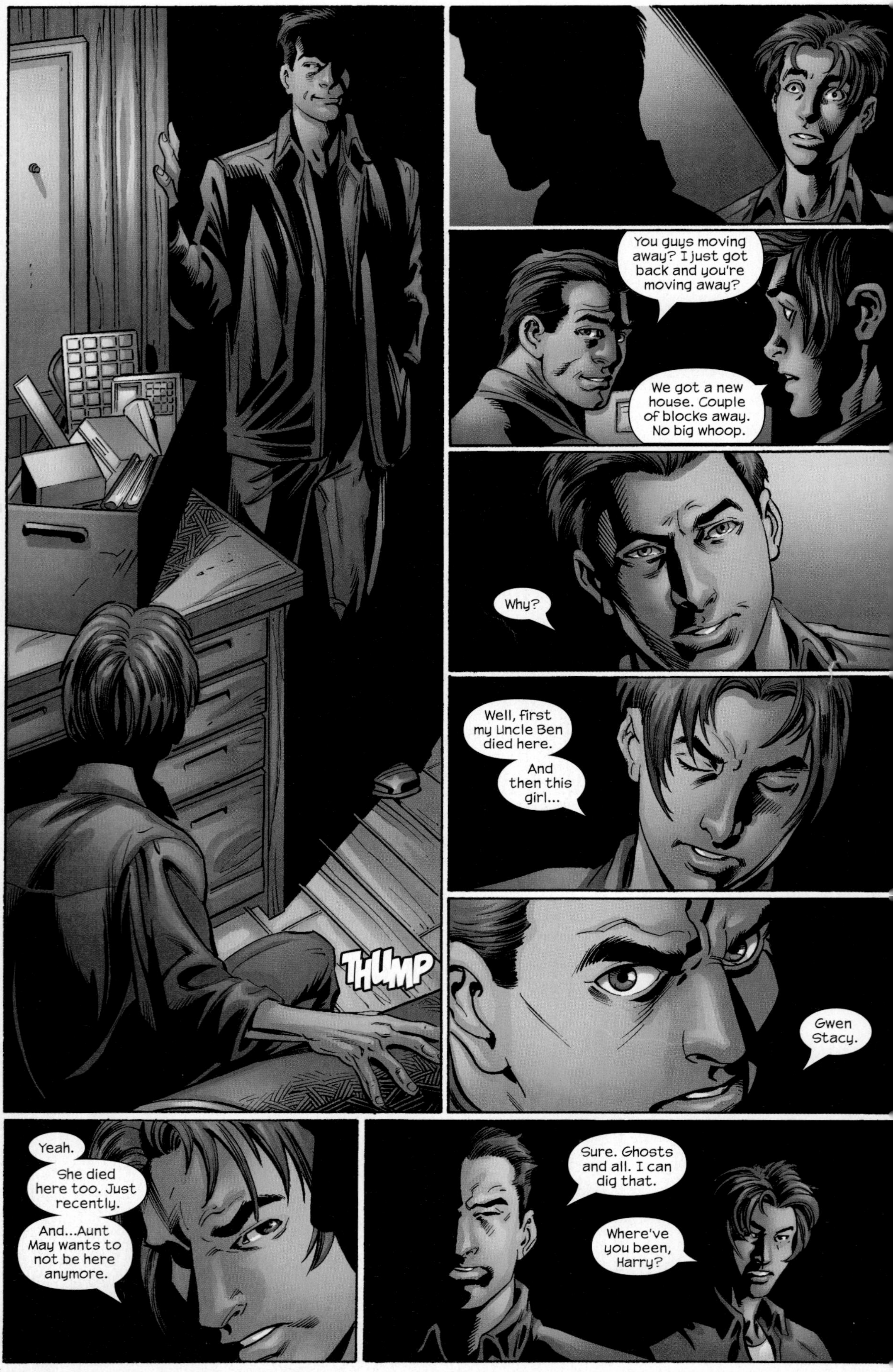
You guys moving away? I just got back and you're moving away?
We got a new house. Couple of blocks away. No big whoop.
Why?
Well, first my Uncle Ben died here.
And then this girl...
THUMP
Gwen Stacy.
Yeah.
She died here too. Just recently.
And...Aunt May wants to not be here anymore.
Sure. Ghosts and all. I can dig that.
Where've you been, Harry?

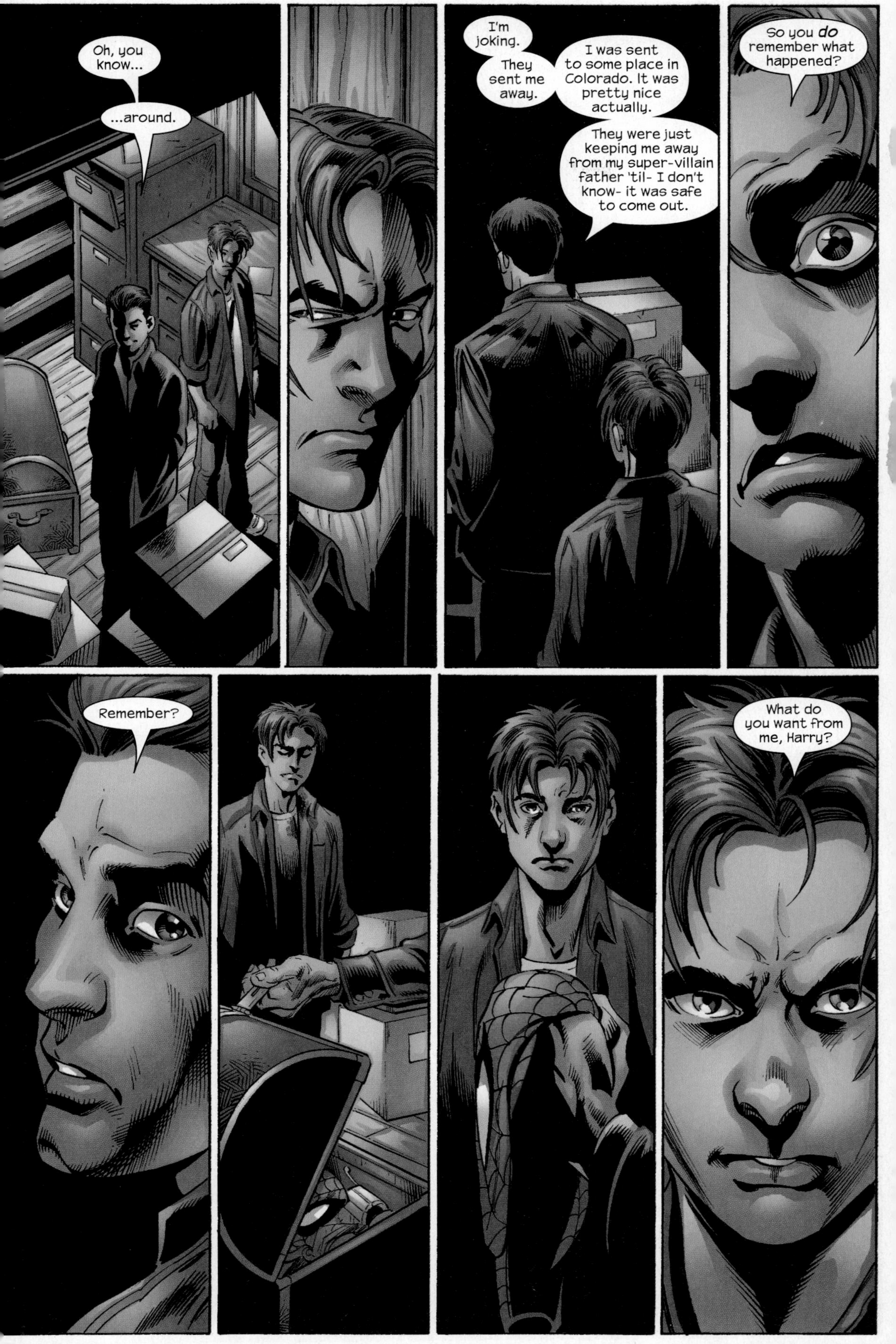
Oh, you know...
...around.
I'm joking.
They sent me away.
I was sent to some place in Colorado. It was pretty nice actually.
They were just keeping me away from my super-villain father 'til- I don't know- it was safe to come out.
So you do remember what happened?
Remember?
What do you want from me, Harry?

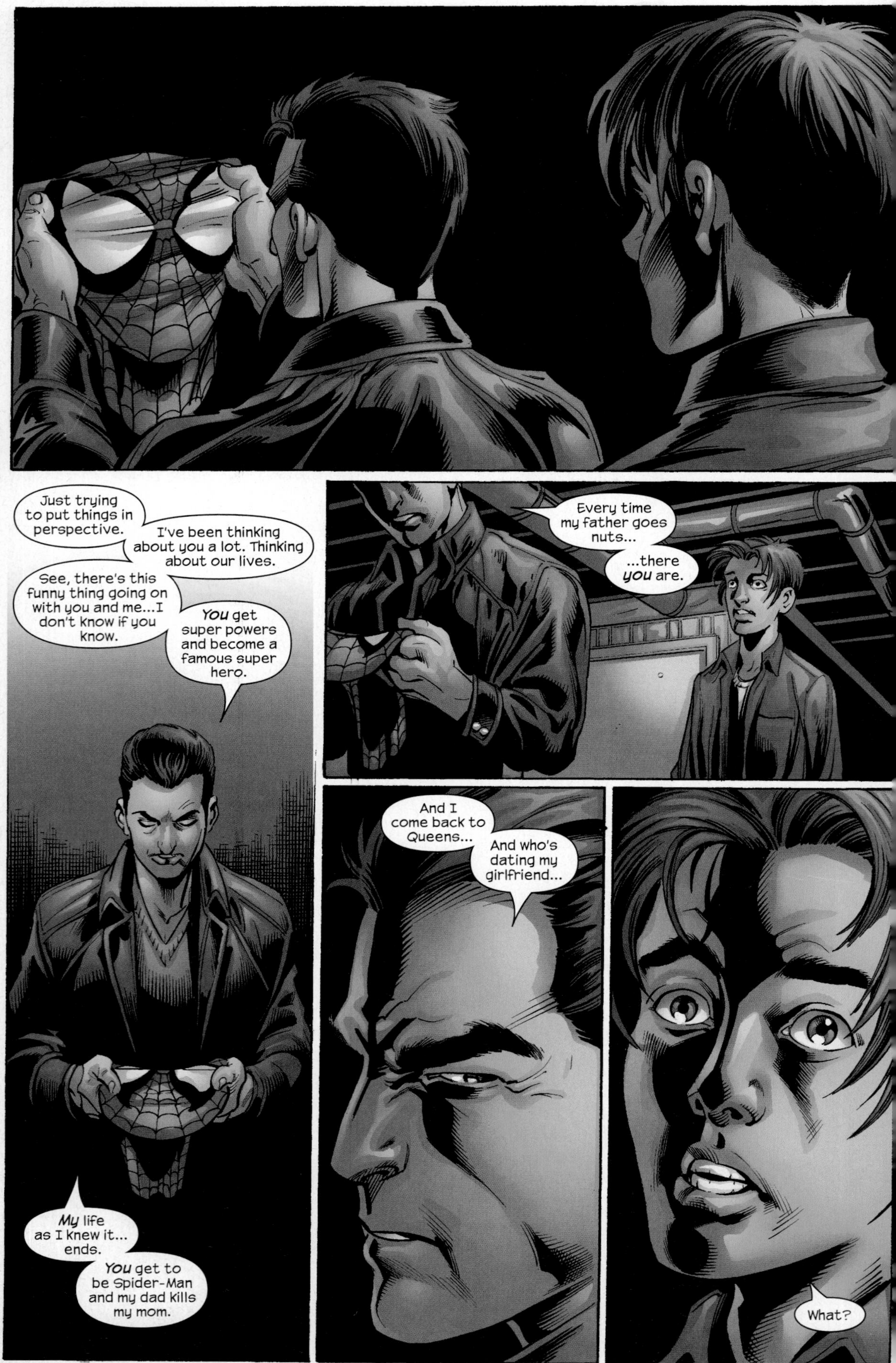
Just trying to put things in perspective.
I've been thinking about you a lot. Thinking about our lives.
See, there's this funny thing going on with you and me...I don't know if you know.
YOU get super powers and become a famous super hero.
My life as I knew it... ends.
YOU get to be Spider-Man and my dad kills my mom.
Every time my father goes nuts...
...there YOU are.
And I come back to Queens...
And who's dating my girlfriend...
What?

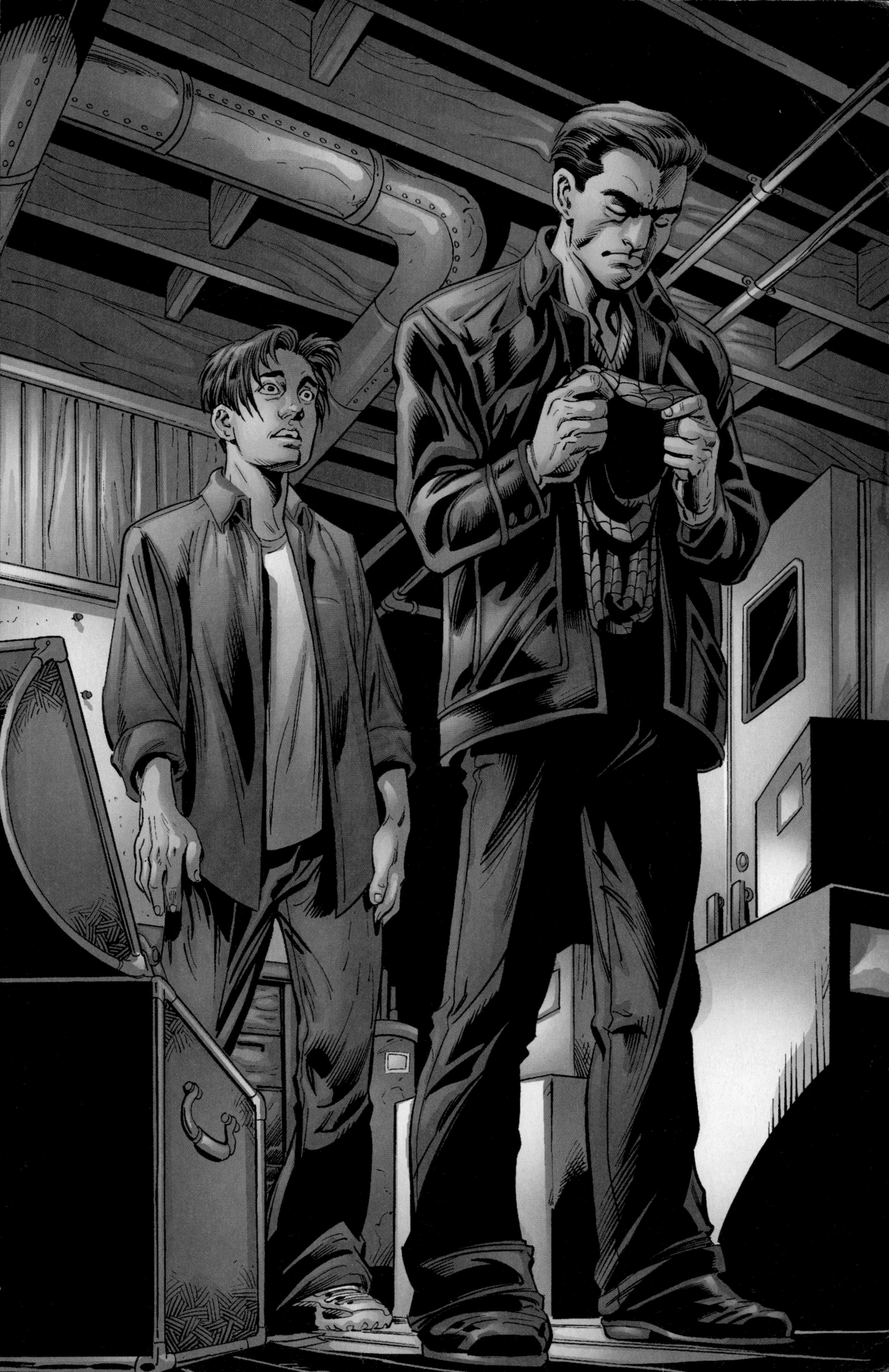

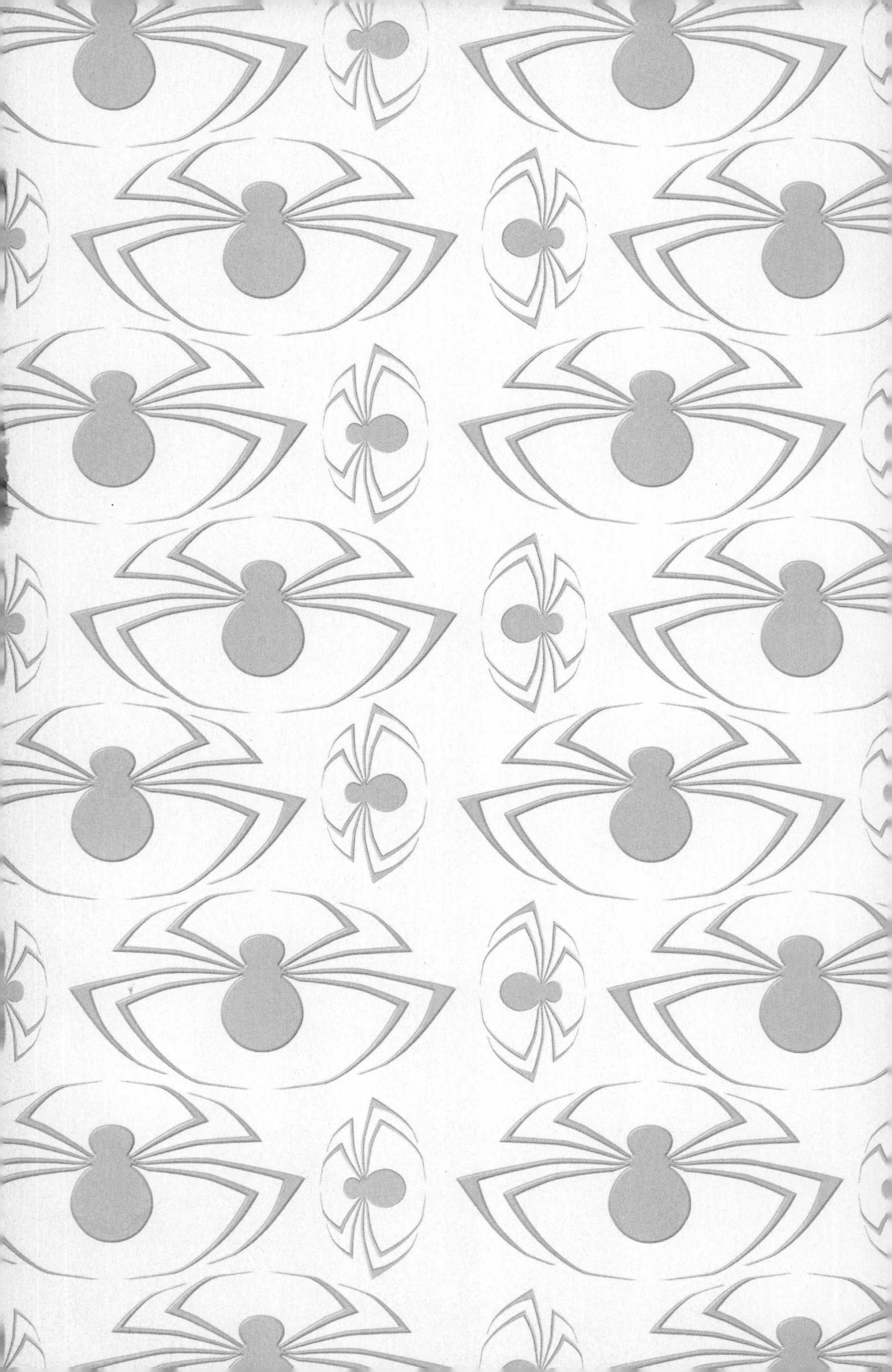

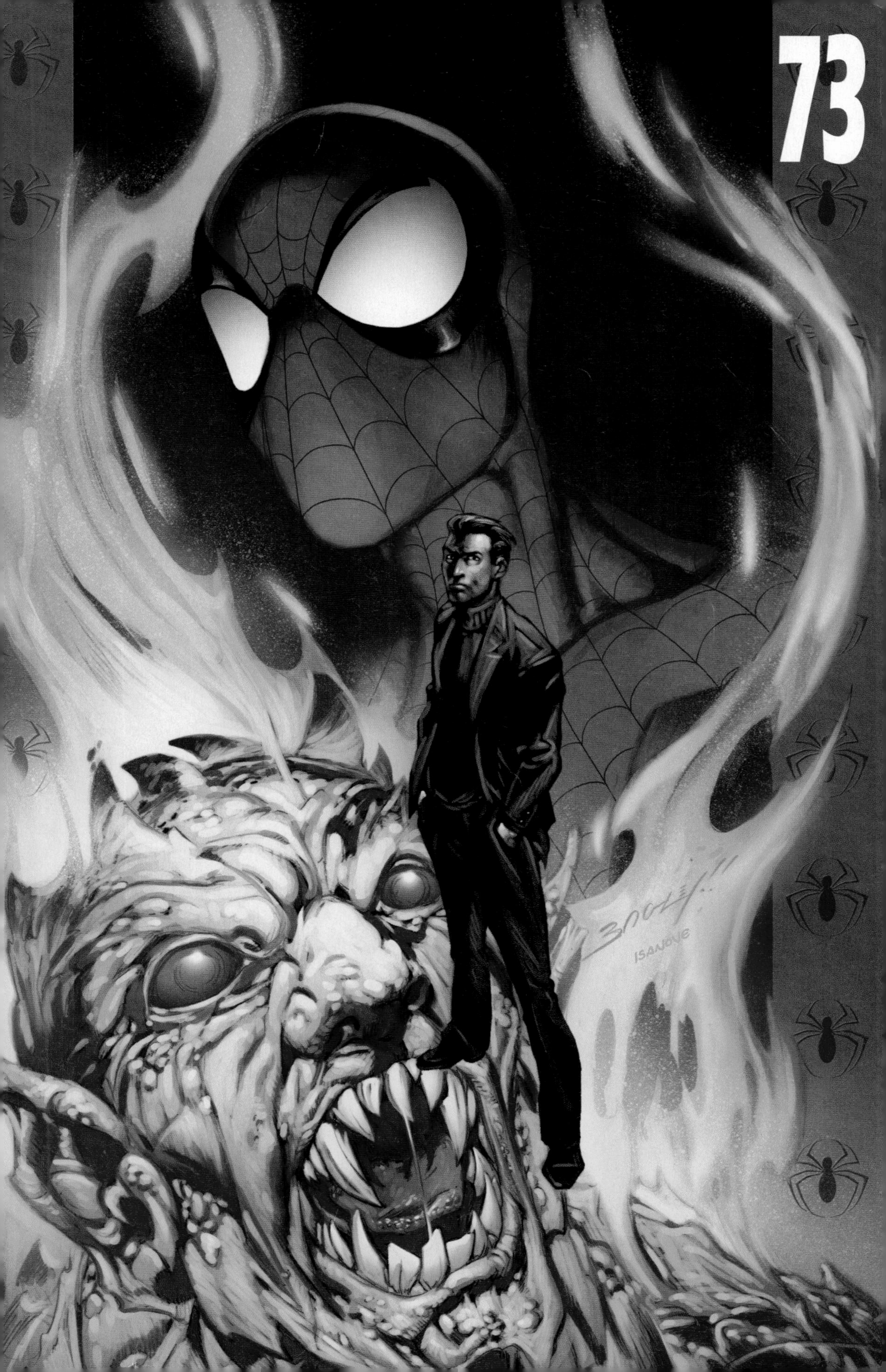
73

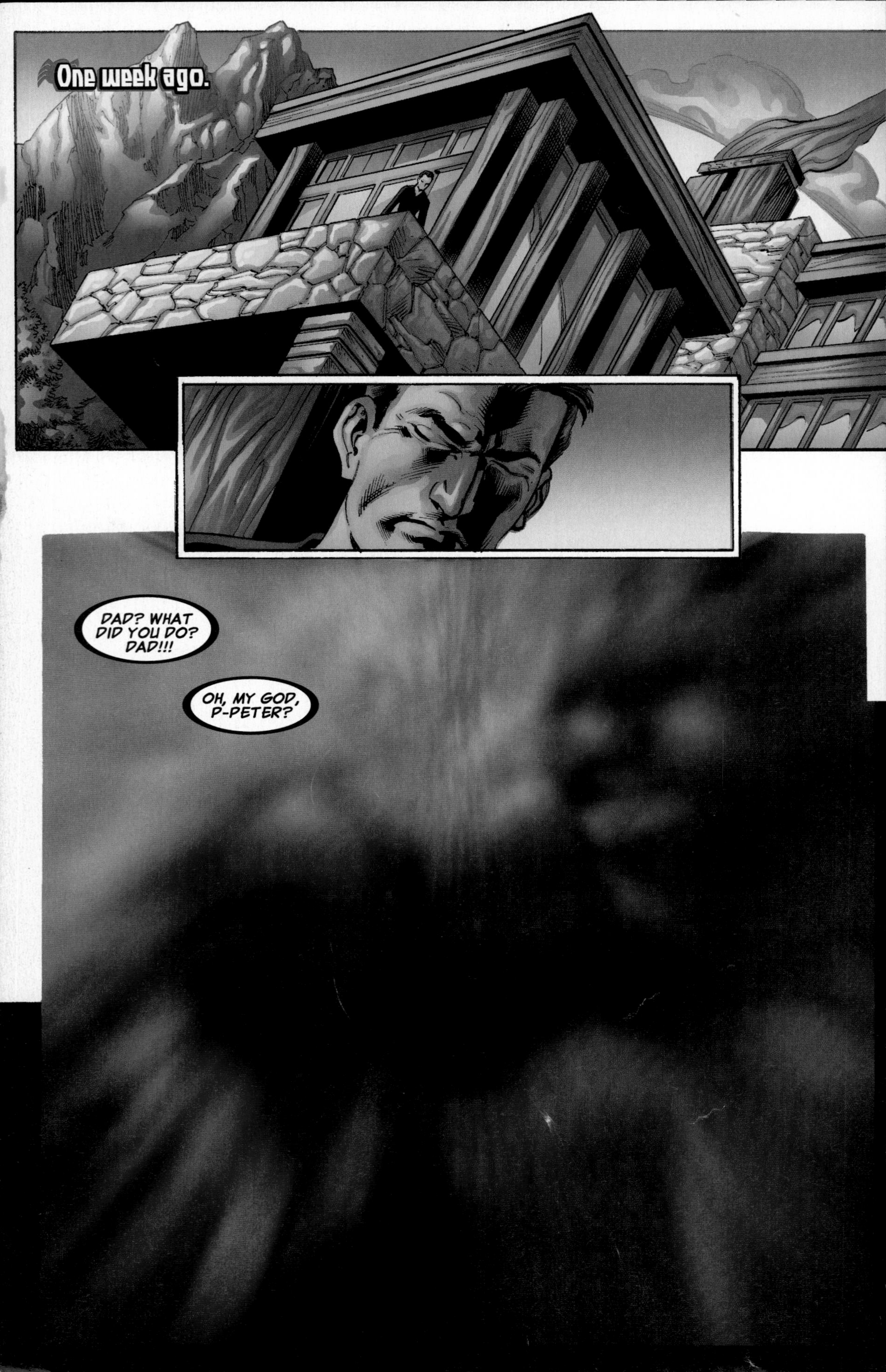
One week ago.
DAD? WHAT DID YOU DO? DAD!!!
OH, MY GOD, P-PETER?

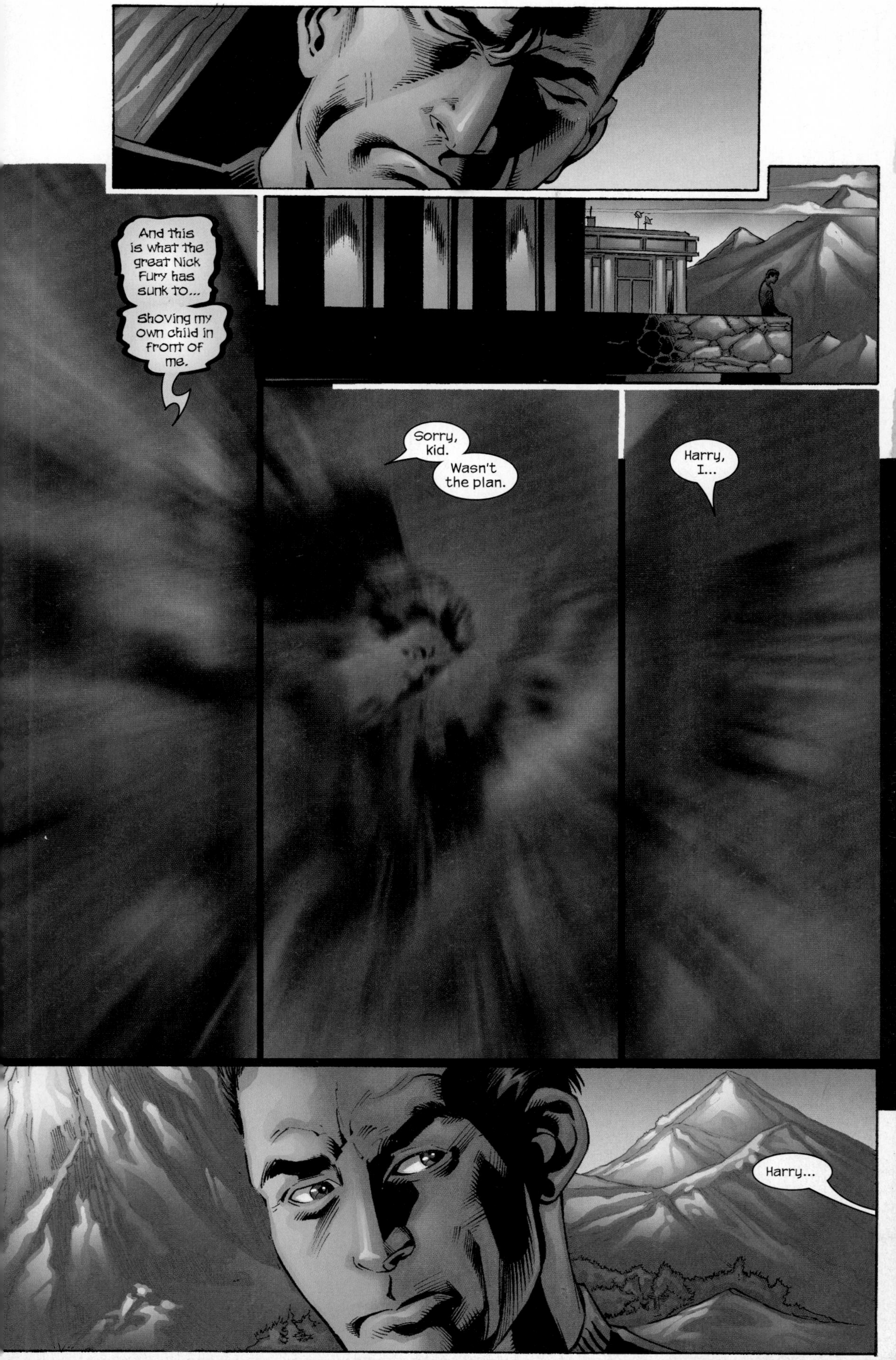

And this is what the great Nick Fury has sunk to...
Shoving my own child in front of me.
Sorry, kid.
Wasn't the plan.
Harry, I...
Harry...

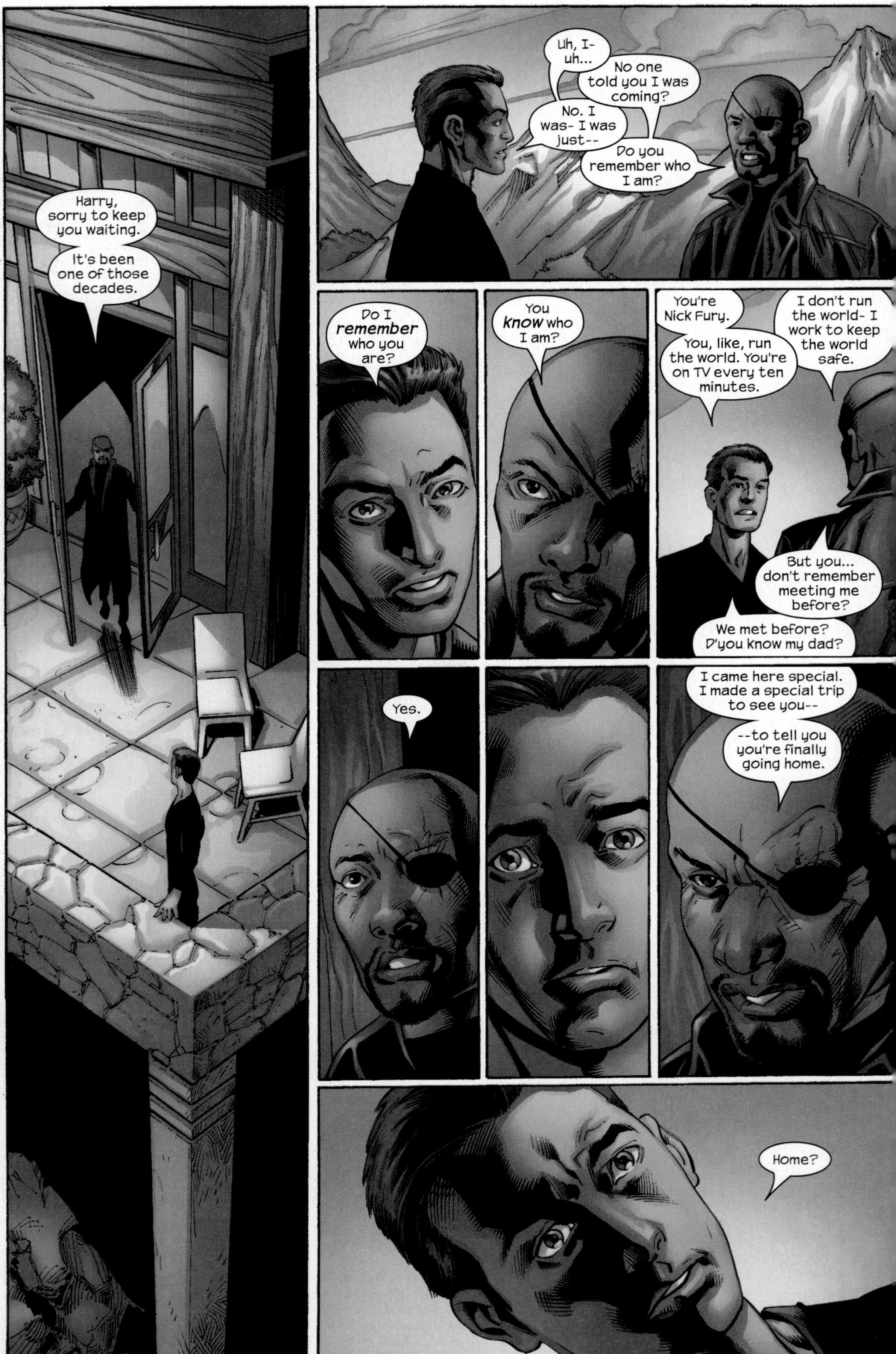
Harry, sorry to keep you waiting.
It's been one of those decades.
Uh, I- uh...
No one told you I was coming?
No. I was- I was just--
Do you remember who I am?
Do I **remember** who you are?
You ***know*** who I am?
You're Nick Fury.
You, like, run the world. You're on TV every ten minutes.
I don't run the world- I work to keep the world safe.
But you... don't remember meeting me before?
We met before? D'you know my dad?
Yes.
I came here special. I made a special trip to see you--
--to tell you you're finally going home.
Home?

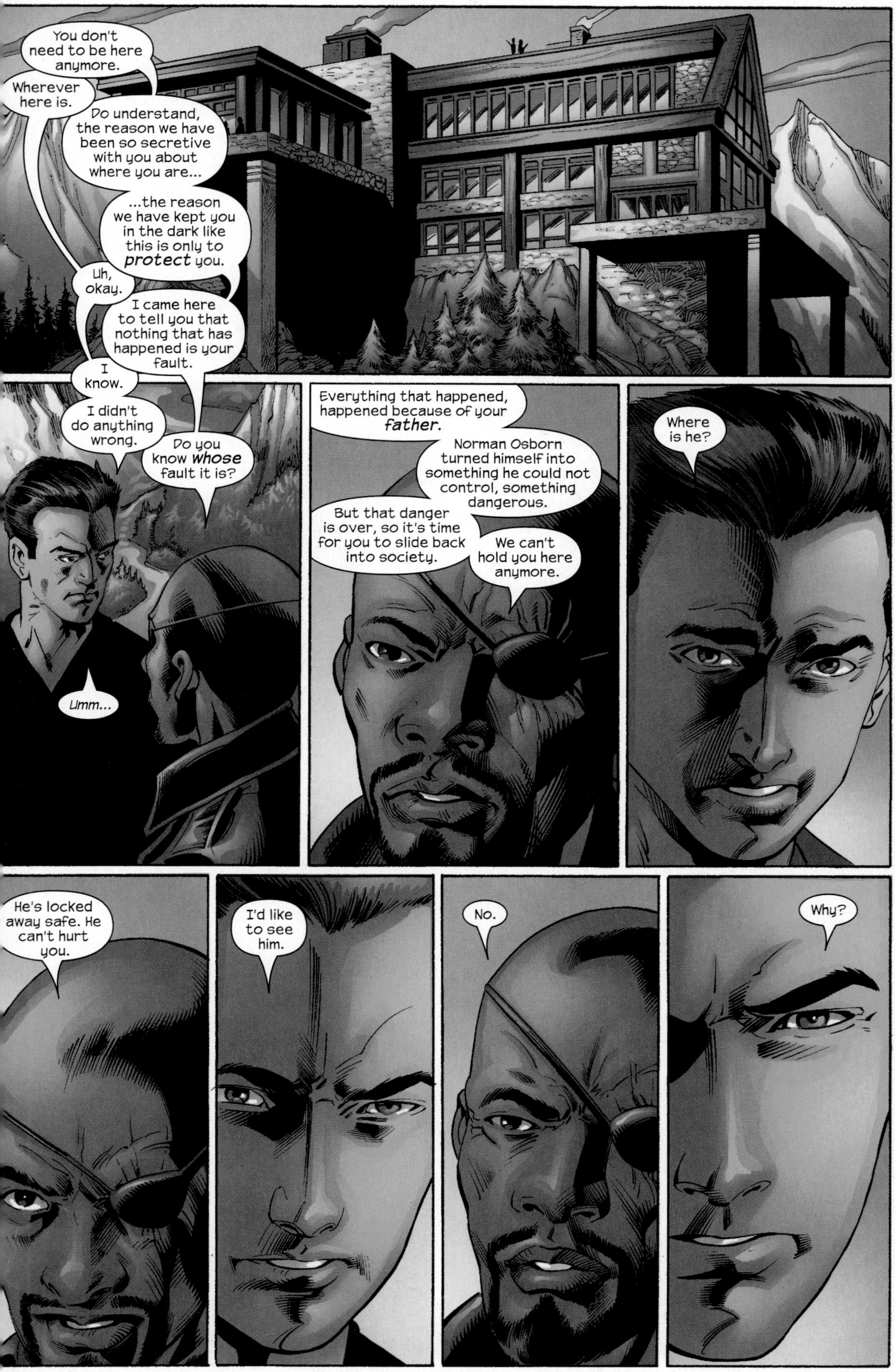
You don't need to be here anymore.
Wherever here is.
Do understand, the reason we have been so secretive with you about where you are...
...the reason we have kept you in the dark like this is only to *protect* you.
Uh, okay.
I came here to tell you that nothing that has happened is your fault.
I know.
I didn't do anything wrong.
Do you know *whose* fault it is?
Umm...
Everything that happened, happened because of your *father.*
Norman Osborn turned himself into something he could not control, something dangerous.
But that danger is over, so it's time for you to slide back into society.
We can't hold you here anymore.
Where is he?
He's locked away safe. He can't hurt you.
I'd like to see him.
No.
Why?

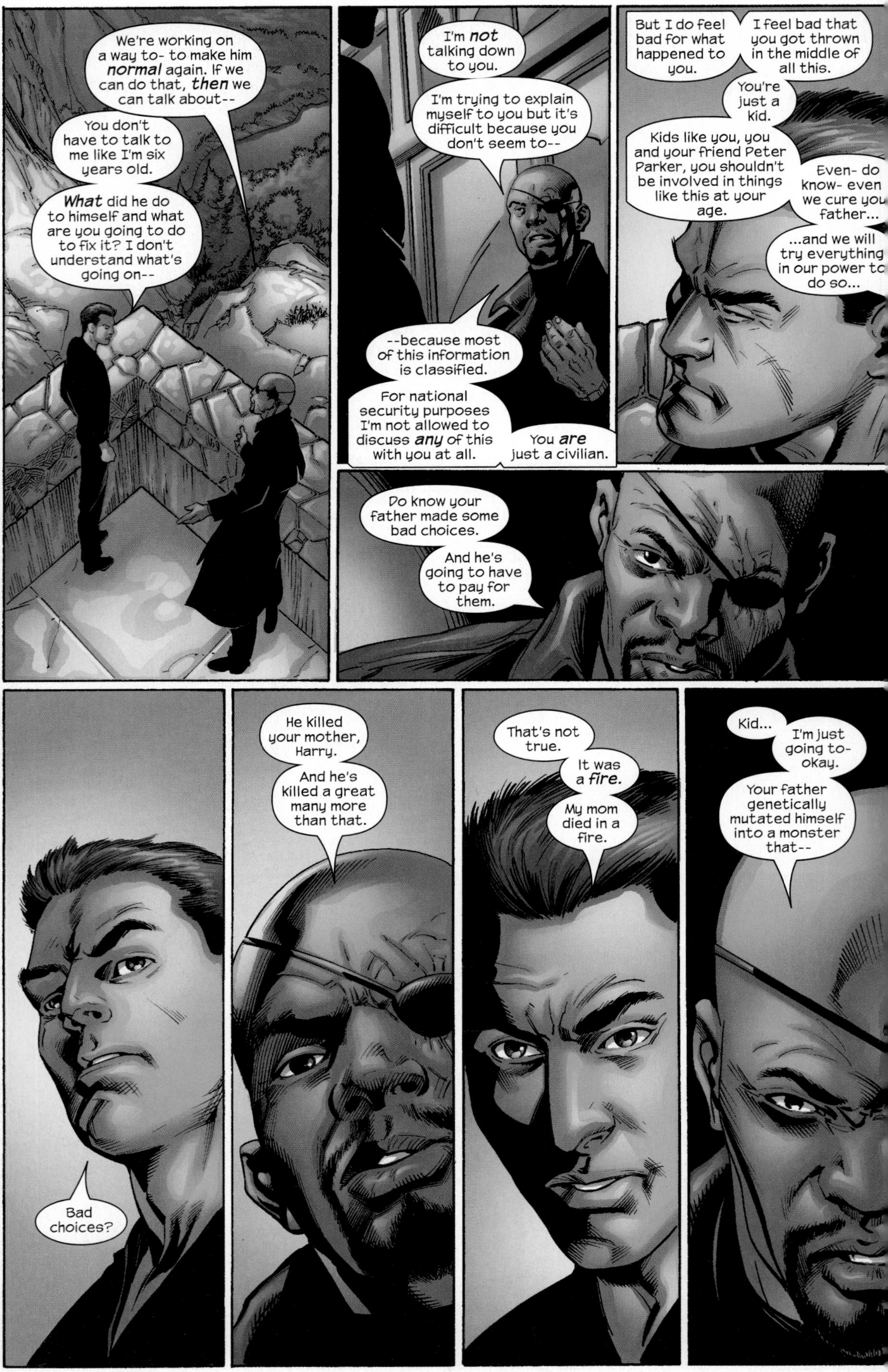

We're working on a way to- to make him *normal* again. If we can do that, *then* we can talk about--
You don't have to talk to me like I'm six years old.
What did he do to himself and what are you going to do to fix it? I don't understand what's going on--
I'm *not* talking down to you.
I'm trying to explain myself to you but it's difficult because you don't seem to--
--because most of this information is classified.
For national security purposes I'm not allowed to discuss *any* of this with you at all.
You *are* just a civilian.
But I do feel bad for what happened to you.
I feel bad that you got thrown in the middle of all this.
You're just a kid.
Kids like you, you and your friend Peter Parker, you shouldn't be involved in things like this at your age.
Even- do know- even we cure you father...
...and we will try everything in our power to do so...
Do know your father made some bad choices.
And he's going to have to pay for them.
Bad choices?
He killed your mother, Harry.
And he's killed a great many more than that.
That's not true.
It was a *fire.*
My mom died in a fire.
Kid...
I'm just going to- okay.
Your father genetically mutated himself into a monster that--

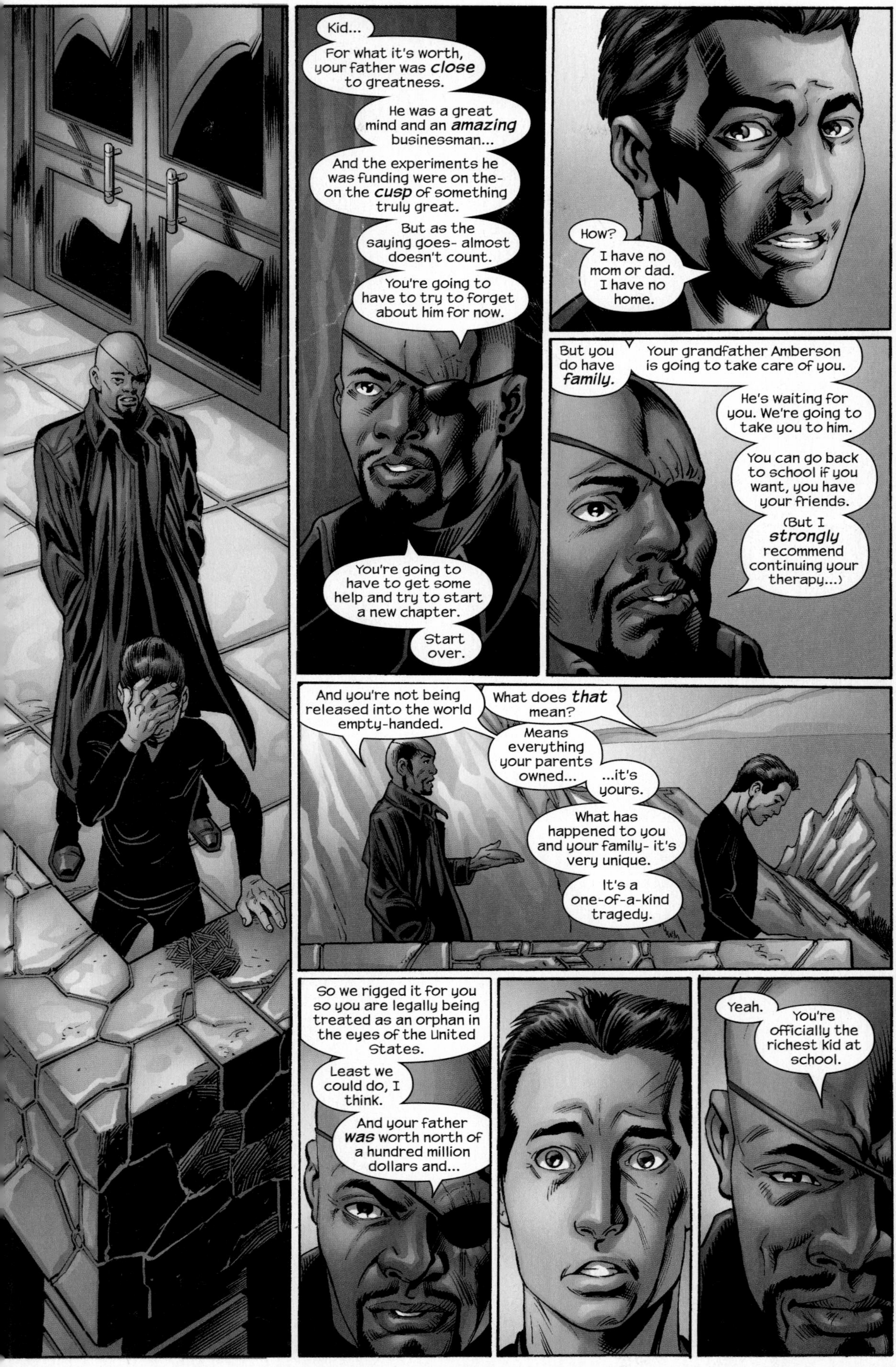

Kid...
For what it's worth, your father was *close* to greatness.
He was a great mind and an *amazing* businessman...
And the experiments he was funding were on the- on the *cusp* of something truly great.
But as the saying goes- almost doesn't count.
You're going to have to try to forget about him for now.
You're going to have to get some help and try to start a new chapter.
Start over.
How?
I have no mom or dad. I have no home.
But you do have *family.*
Your grandfather Amberson is going to take care of you.
He's waiting for you. We're going to take you to him.
You can go back to school if you want, you have your friends.
(But I *strongly* recommend continuing your therapy...)
And you're not being released into the world empty-handed.
What does *that* mean?
Means everything your parents owned...
...it's yours.
What has happened to you and your family- it's very unique.
It's a one-of-a-kind tragedy.
So we rigged it for you so you are legally being treated as an orphan in the eyes of the United States.
Least we could do, I think.
And your father *was* worth north of a hundred million dollars and...
Yeah.
You're officially the richest kid at school.

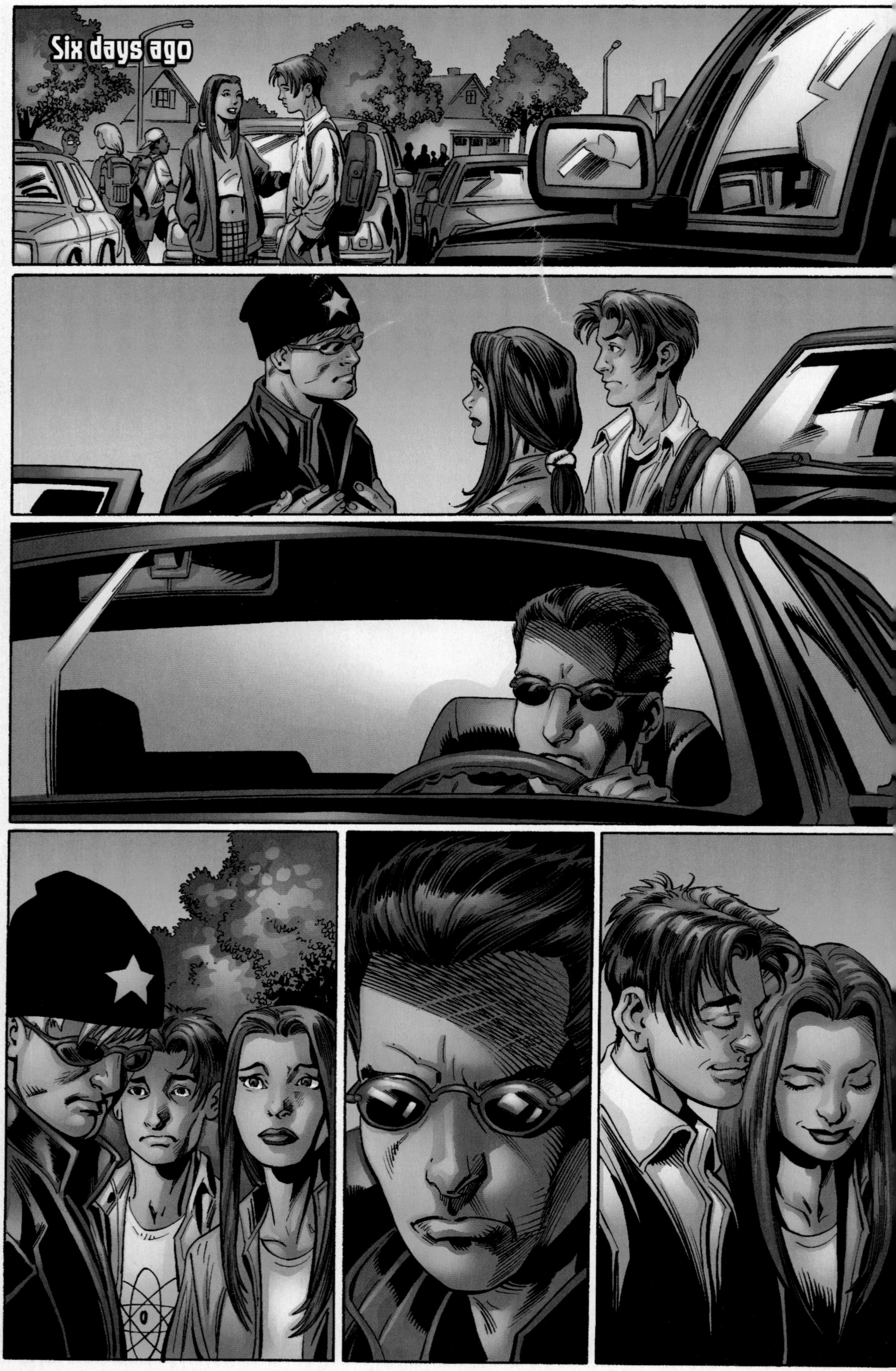
Six days ago

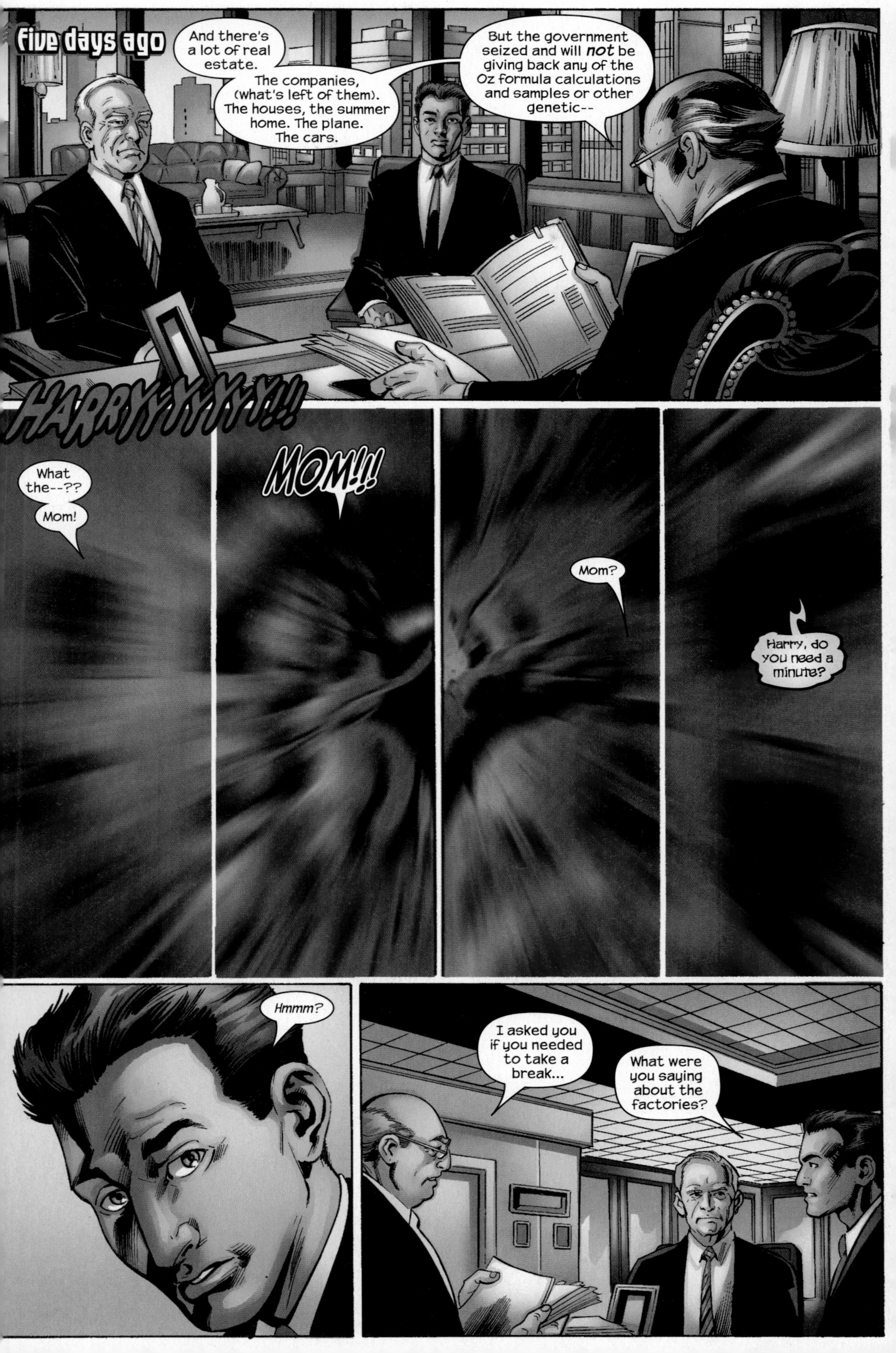
five days ago
And there's a lot of real estate.
The companies, (what's left of them). The houses, the summer home. The plane. The cars.
But the government seized and will *not* be giving back any of the Oz formula calculations and samples or other genetic--
HARRYYYYYY!!
What the--??
Mom!
MOM!!!
Mom?
Harry, do you need a minute?
Hmmm?
I asked you if you needed to take a break...
What were you saying about the factories?

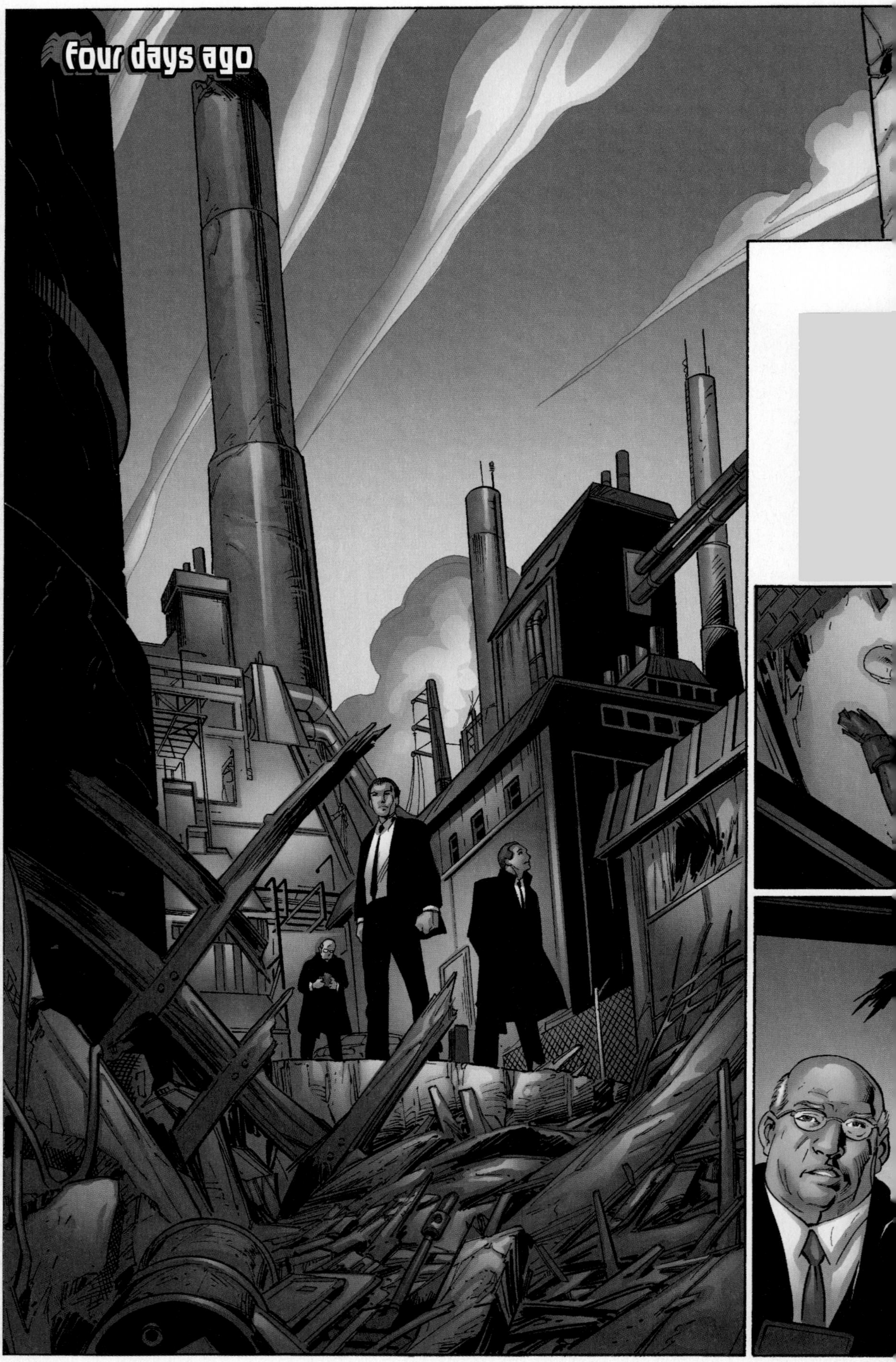
Four days ago

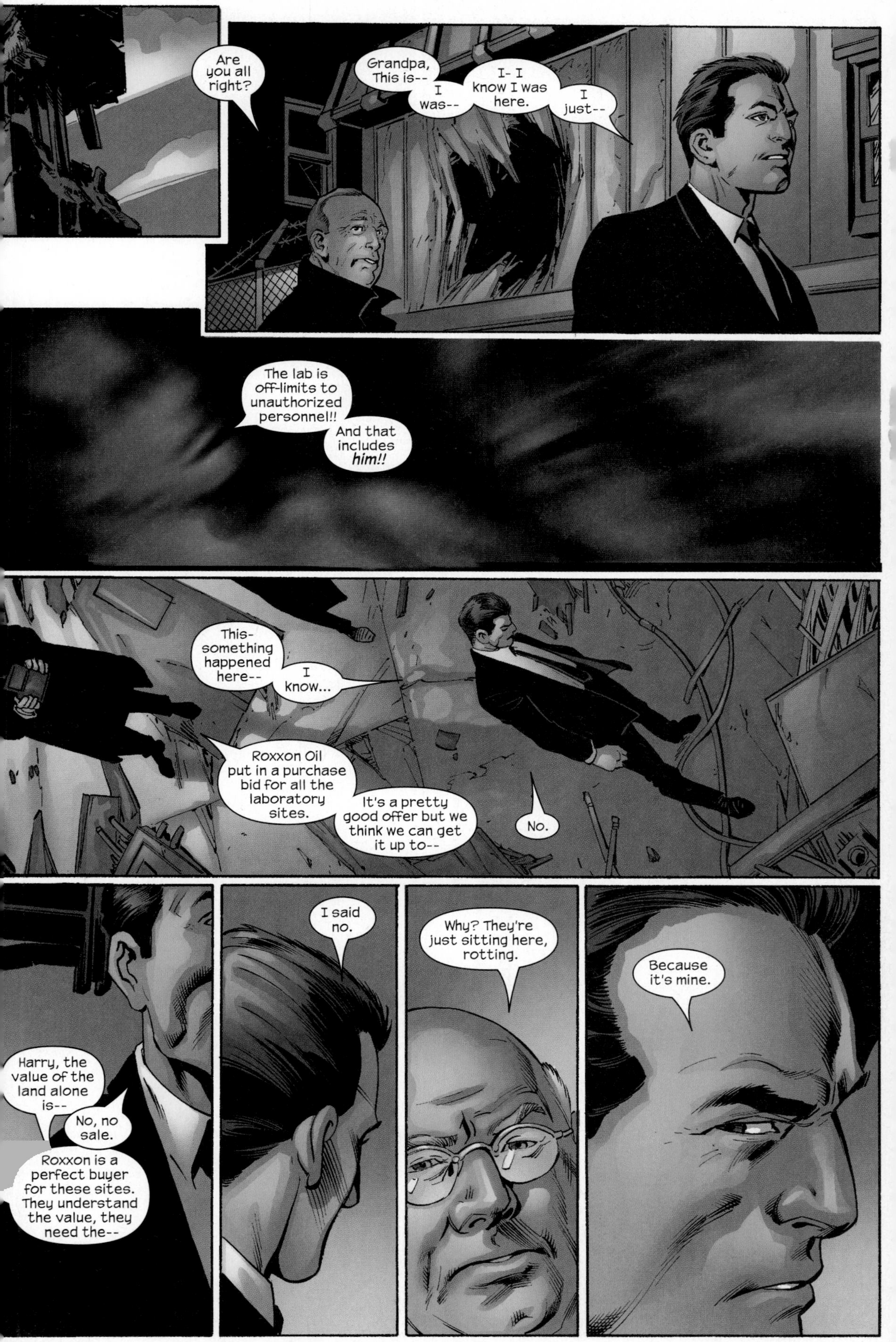
Are you all right?
Grandpa, This is--
I was--
I- I know I was here.
I just--
The lab is off-limits to unauthorized personnel!!
And that includes *him!!*
This- something happened here--
I know...
Roxxon Oil put in a purchase bid for all the laboratory sites.
It's a pretty good offer but we think we can get it up to--
No.
Harry, the value of the land alone is--
No, no sale.
Roxxon is a perfect buyer for these sites. They understand the value, they need the--
I said no.
Why? They're just sitting here, rotting.
Because it's mine.

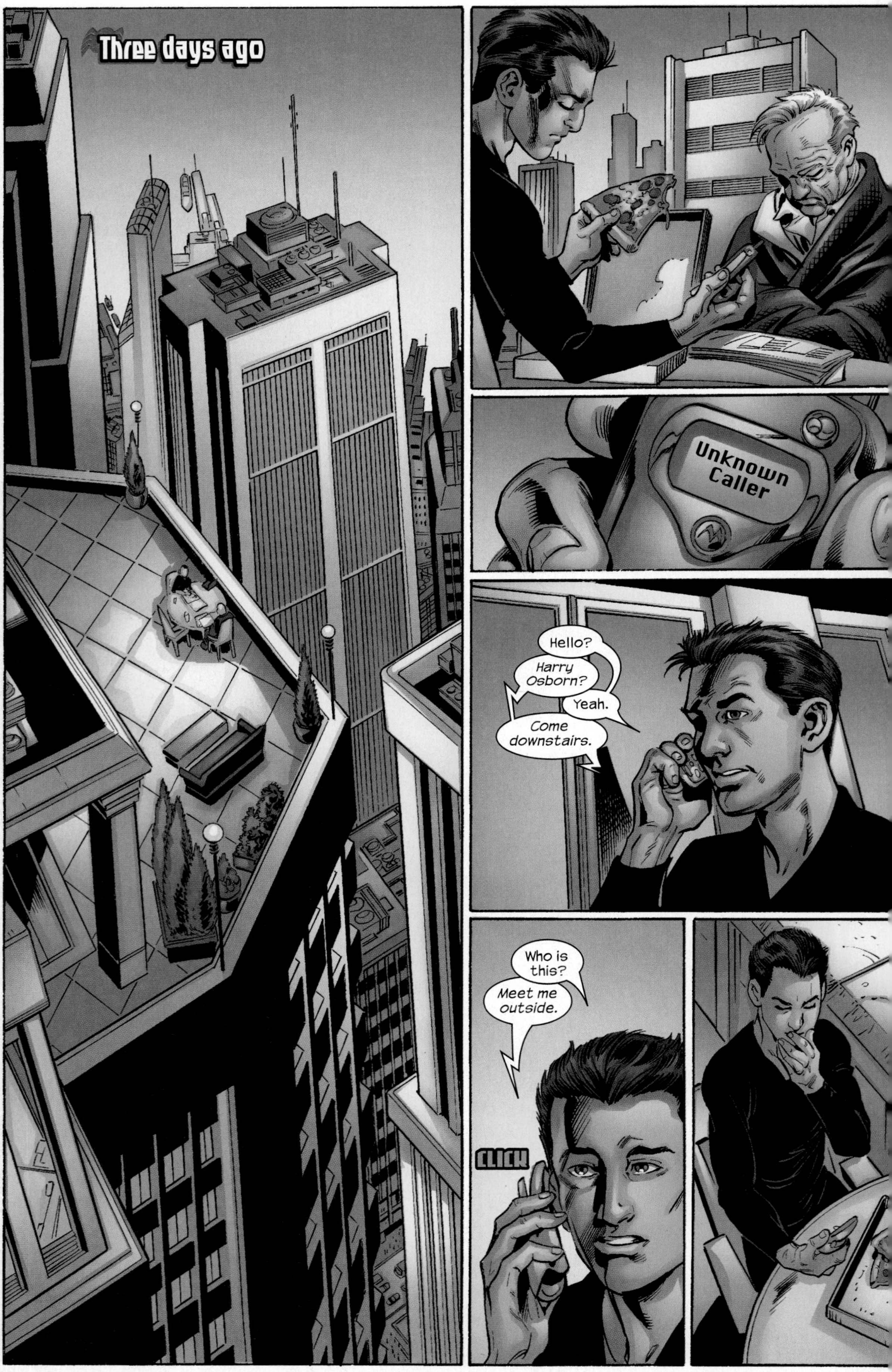
Three days ago
Unknown Caller
Hello?
Harry Osborn?
Yeah.
Come downstairs.
Who is this?
Meet me outside.
CLICK

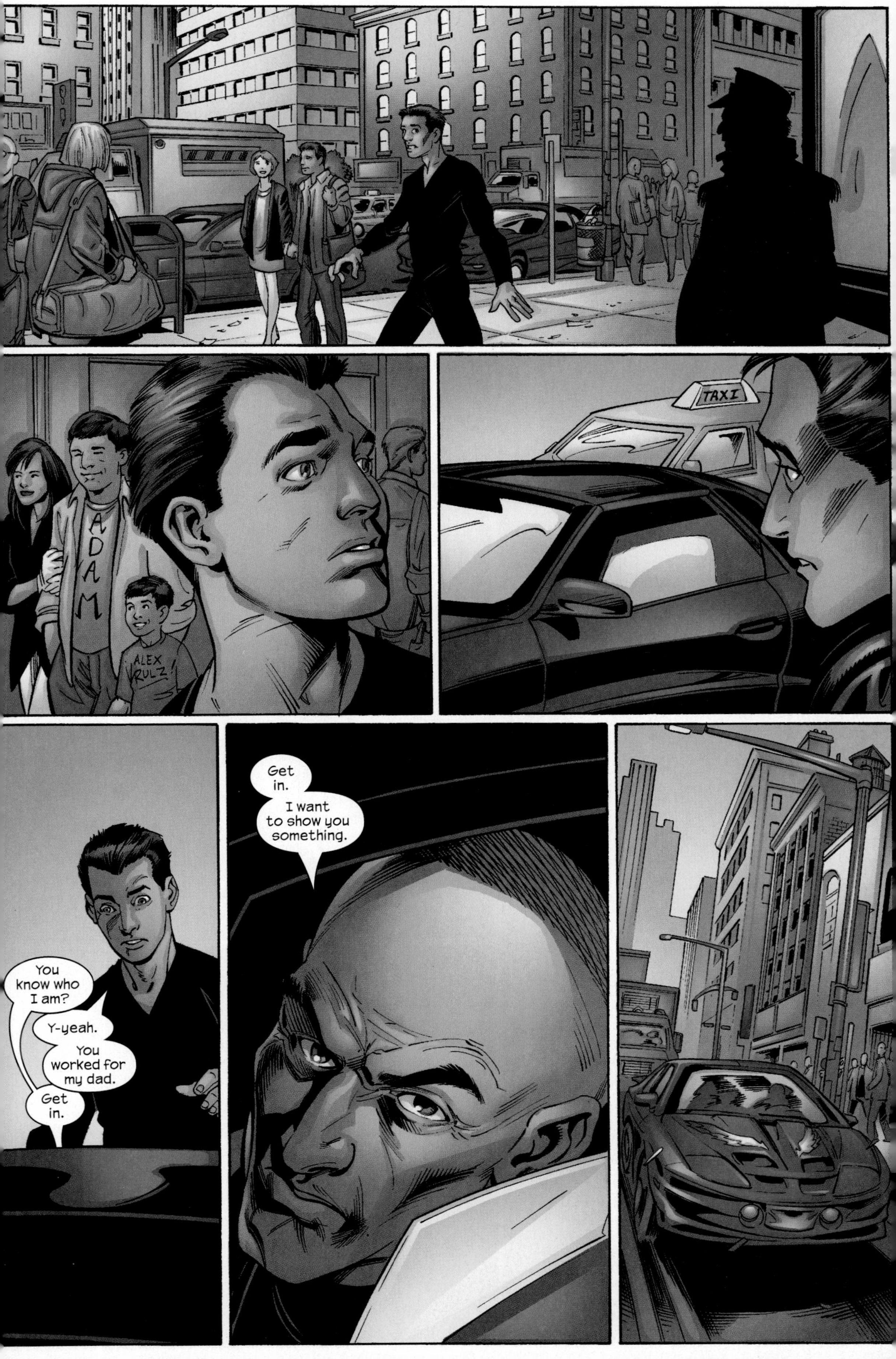
ADAM
ALEX RULZ
TAXI
You know who I am?
Y-yeah.
You worked for my dad.
Get in.
Get in.
I want to show you something.

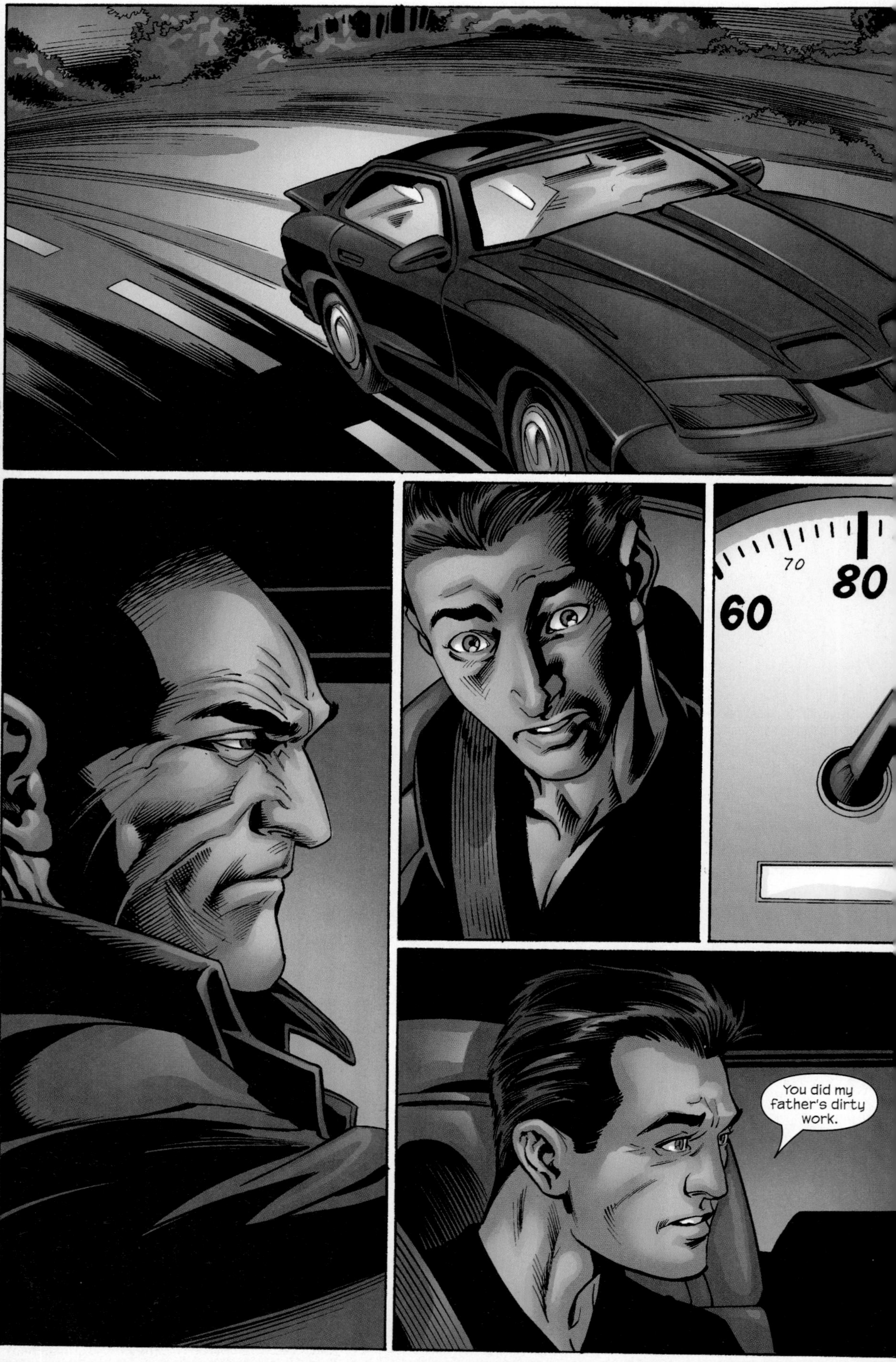
70
80
60
You did my father's dirty work.

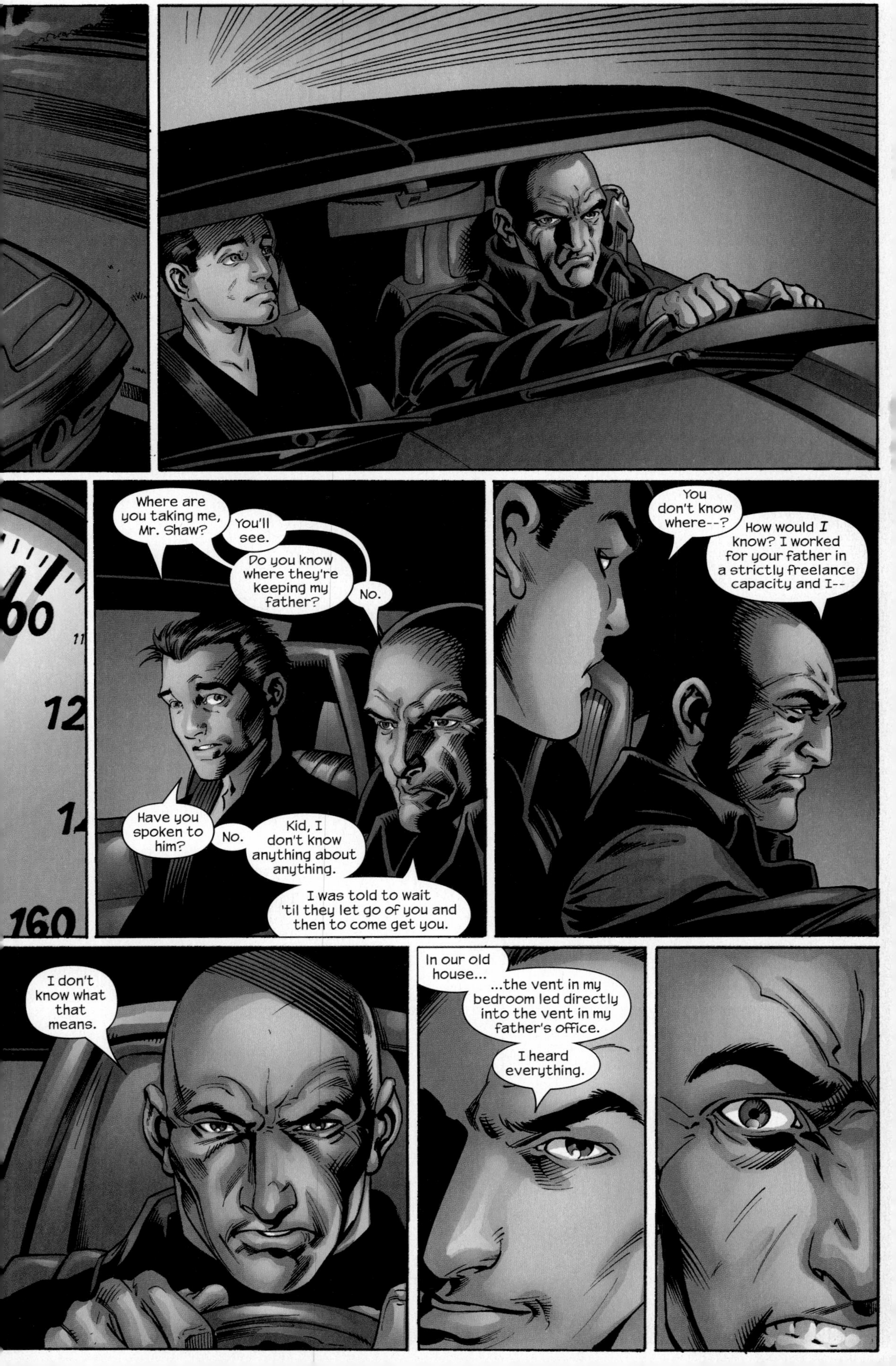

Where are you taking me, Mr. Shaw?
You'll see.
Do you know where they're keeping my father?
No.
Have you spoken to him?
No.
Kid, I don't know anything about anything.
I was told to wait 'til they let go of you and then to come get you.
You don't know where--?
How would *I* know? I worked for your father in a strictly freelance capacity and I--
I don't know what that means.
In our old house...
...the vent in my bedroom led directly into the vent in my father's office.
I heard everything.

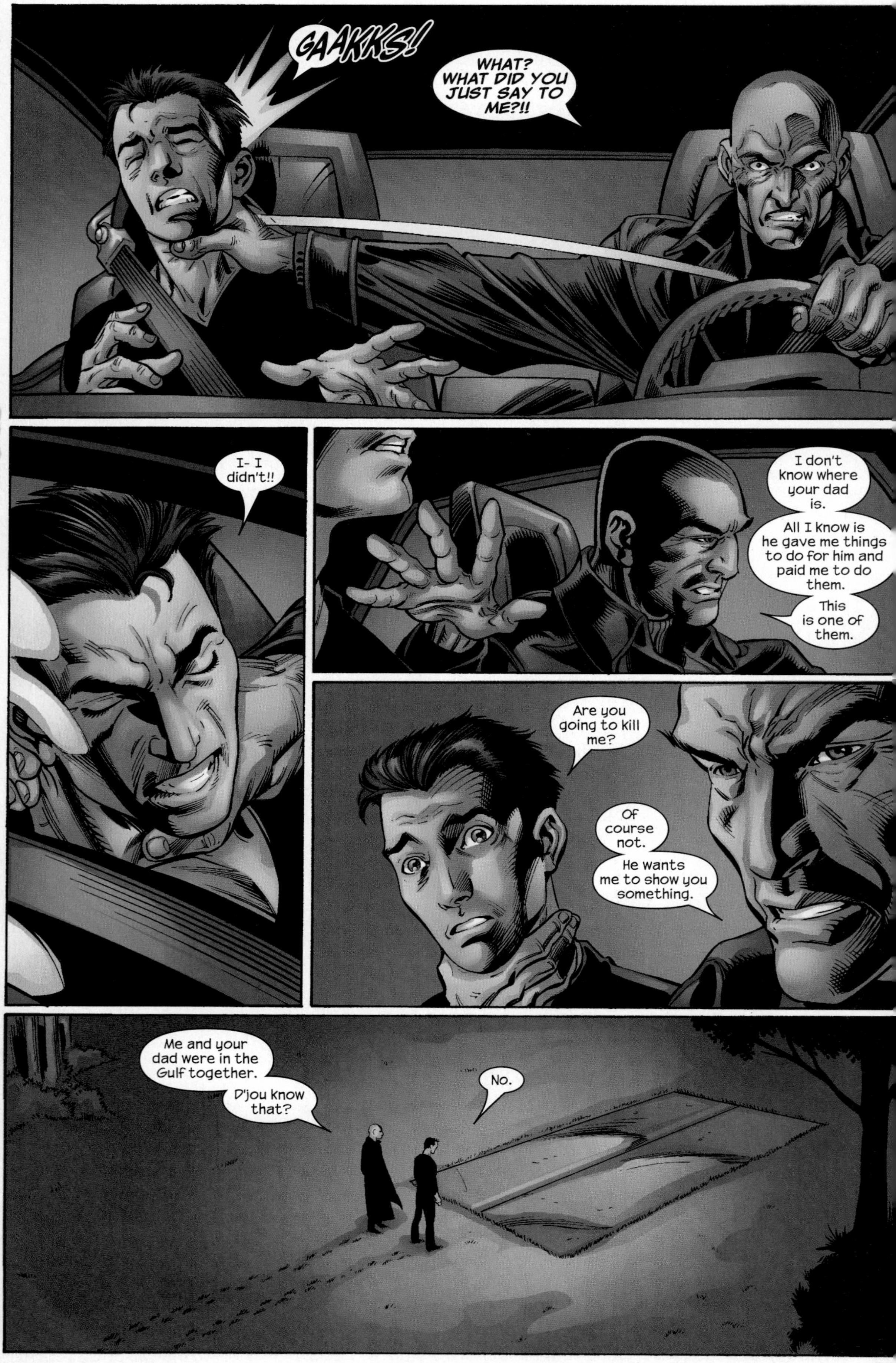
GAAKKS!
WHAT? WHAT DID YOU JUST SAY TO ME?!!
I- I didn't!!
I don't know where your dad is.
All I know is he gave me things to do for him and paid me to do them.
This is one of them.
Are you going to kill me?
Of course not.
He wants me to show you something.
Me and your dad were in the Gulf together.
D'jou know that?
No.

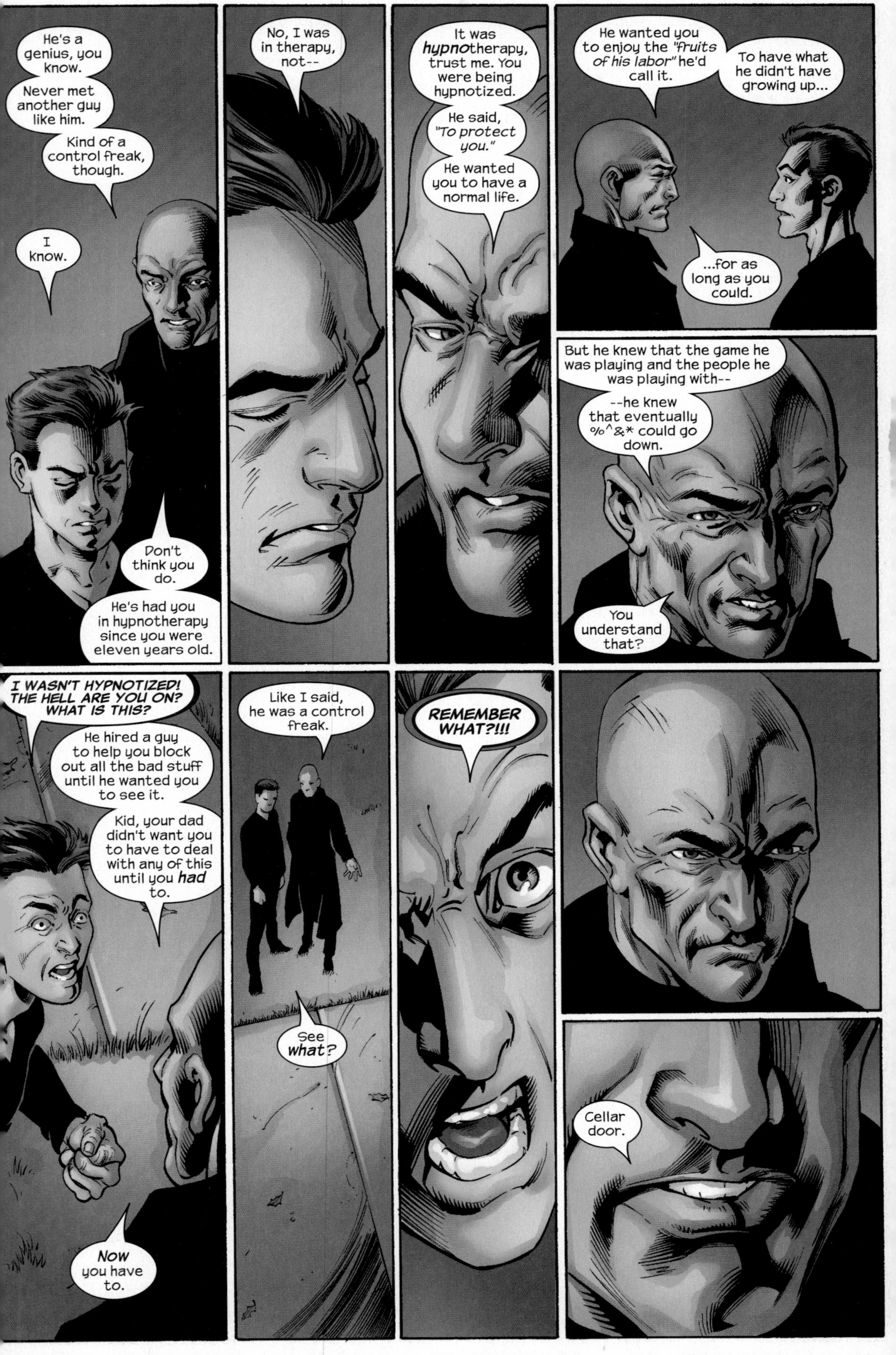
He's a genius, you know.
Never met another guy like him.
Kind of a control freak, though.
I know.
Don't think you do.
He's had you in hypnotherapy since you were eleven years old.
No, I was in therapy, not--
It was *hypno*therapy, trust me. You were being hypnotized.
He said, *"To protect you."*
He wanted you to have a normal life.
He wanted you to enjoy the *"fruits of his labor"* he'd call it.
To have what he didn't have growing up...
...for as long as you could.
But he knew that the game he was playing and the people he was playing with--
--he knew that eventually %^&* could go down.
You understand that?
I WASN'T HYPNOTIZED! THE HELL ARE YOU ON? WHAT IS THIS?
He hired a guy to help you block out all the bad stuff until he wanted you to see it.
Kid, your dad didn't want you to have to deal with any of this until you *had* to.
Now you have to.
Like I said, he was a control freak.
See *what?*
REMEMBER WHAT?!!!
Cellar door.

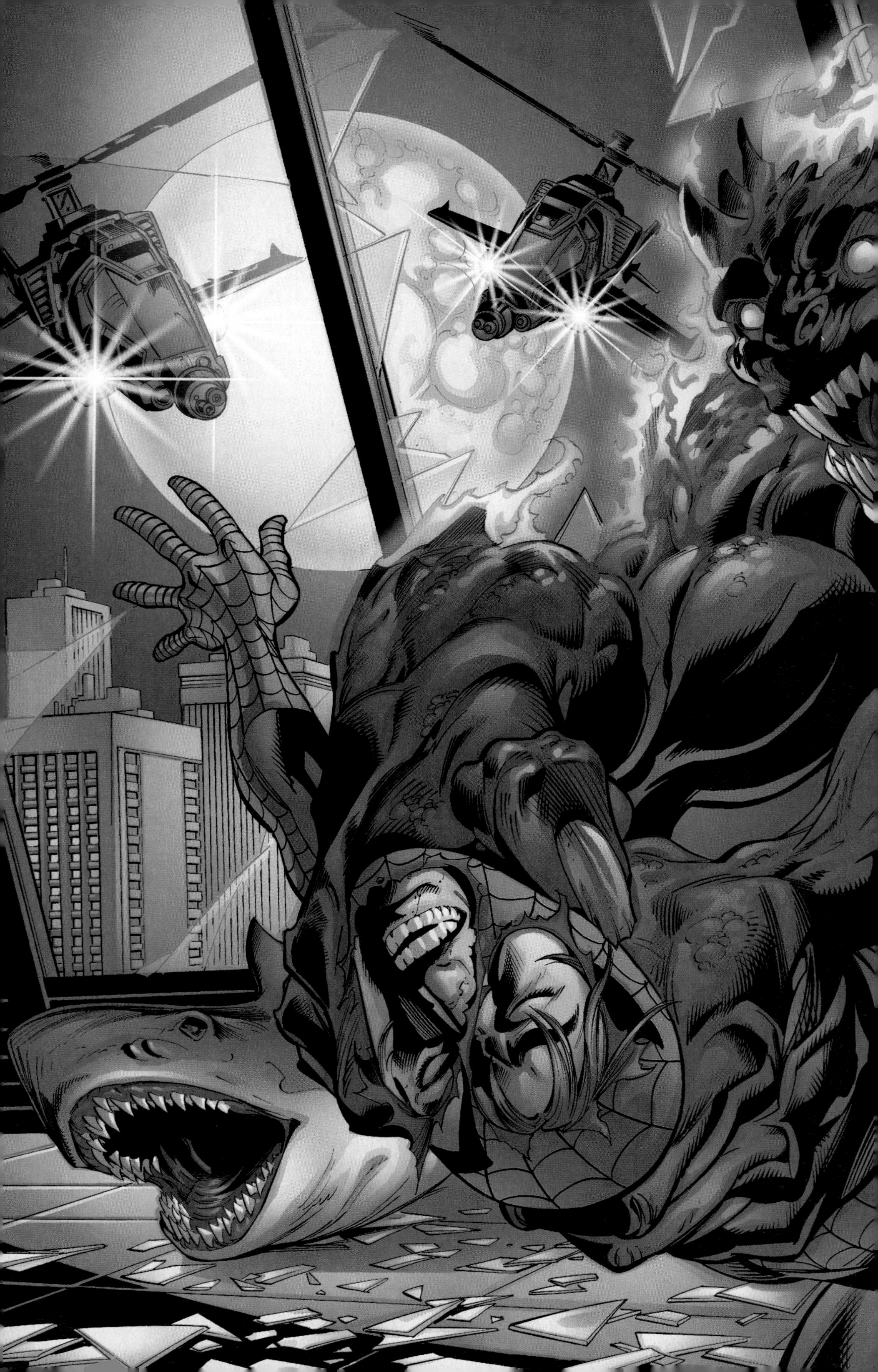

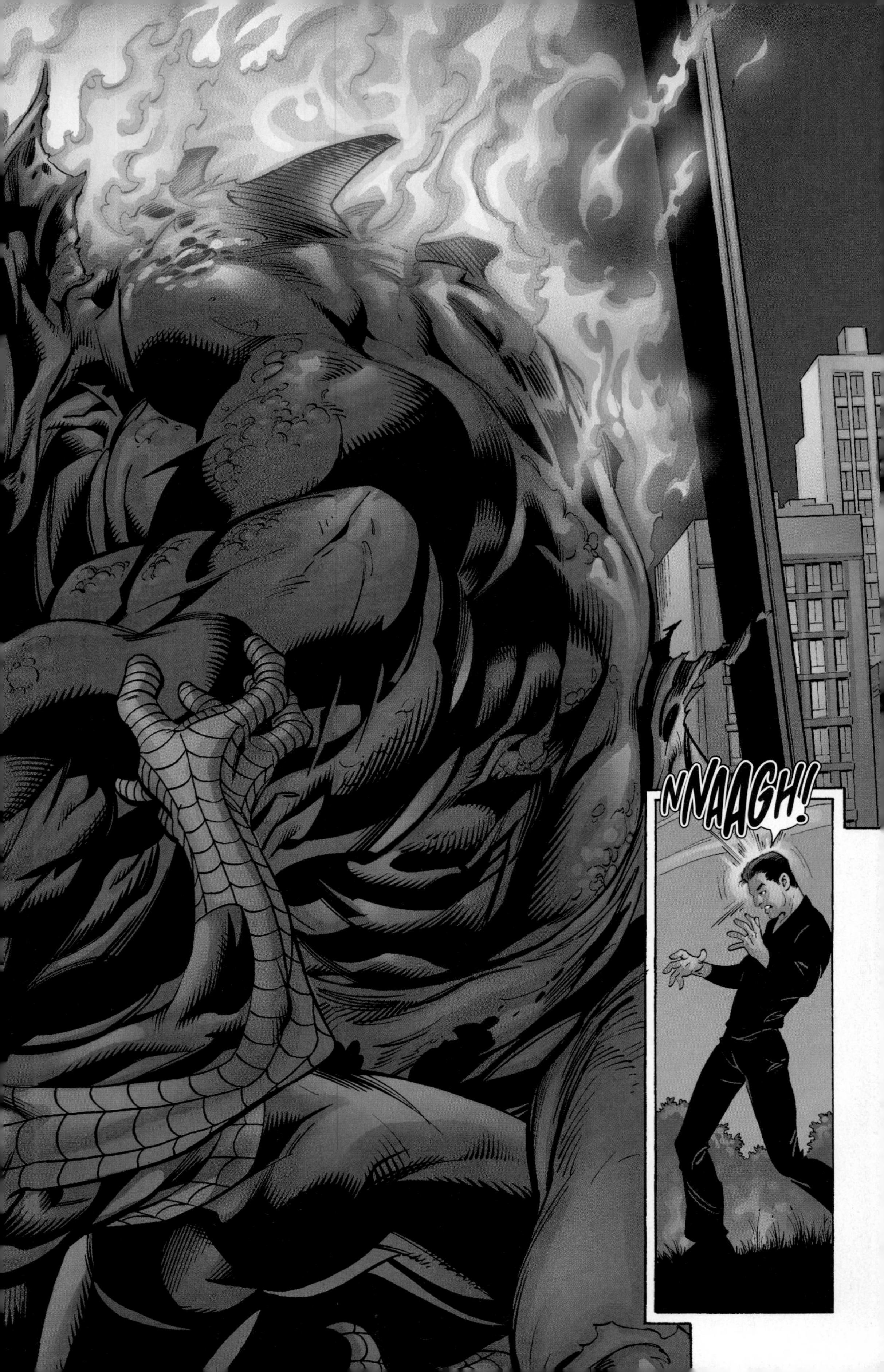
NNAAGH!

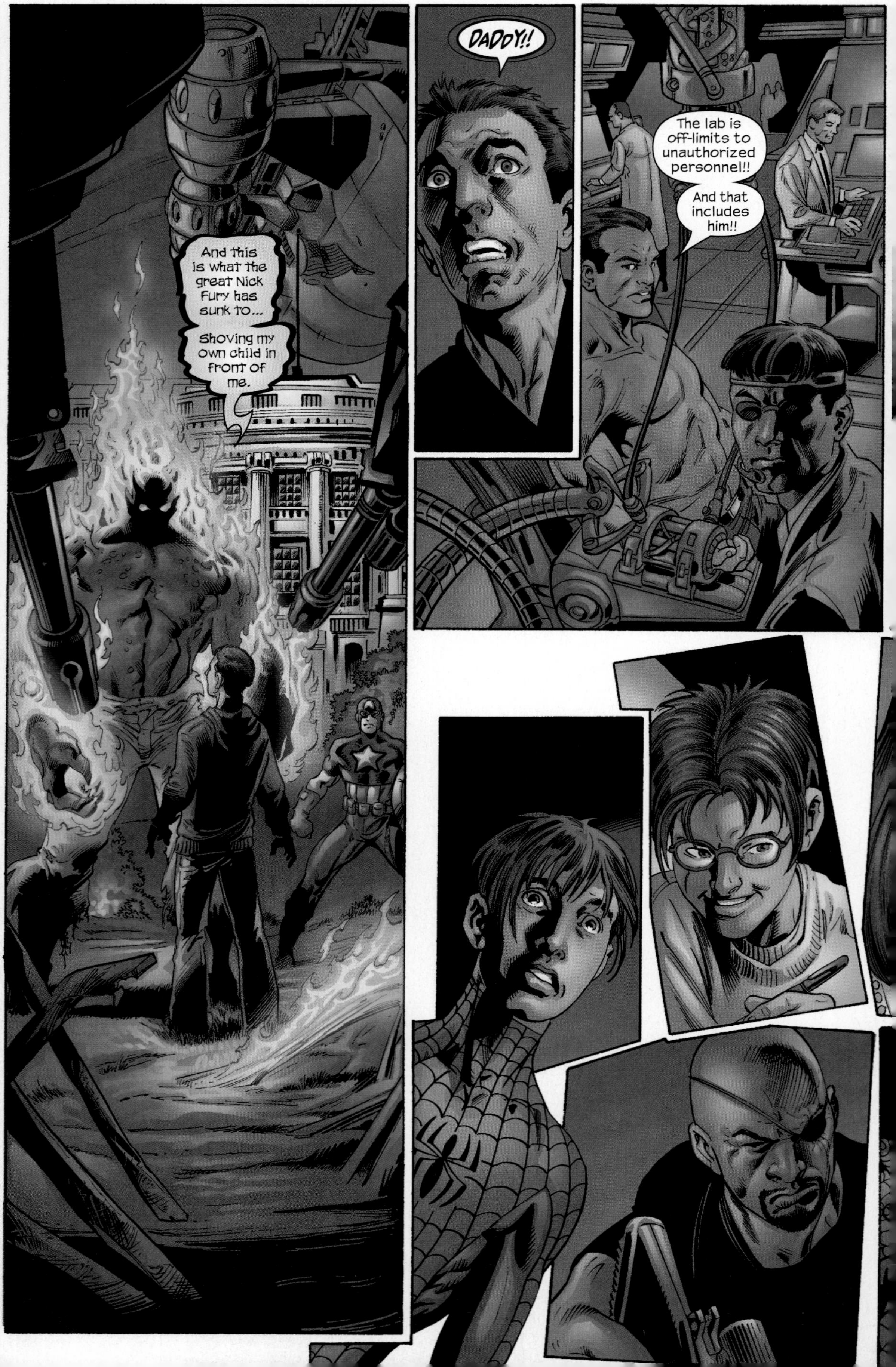
And this is what the great Nick Fury has sunk to...
Shoving my own child in front of me.
DADDY!!
The lab is off-limits to unauthorized personnel!!
And that includes him!!

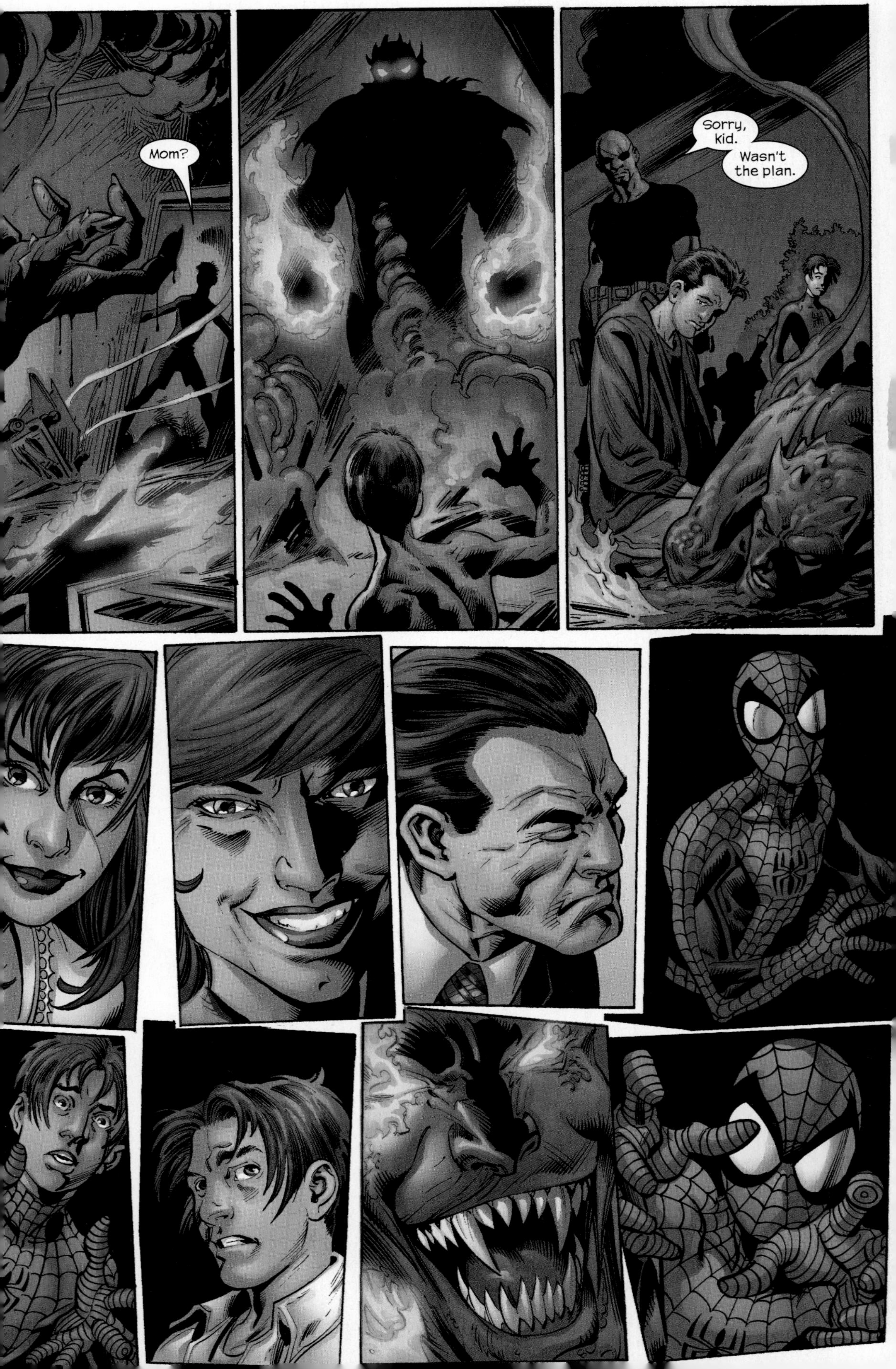
Mom?
Sorry, kid.
Wasn't the plan.

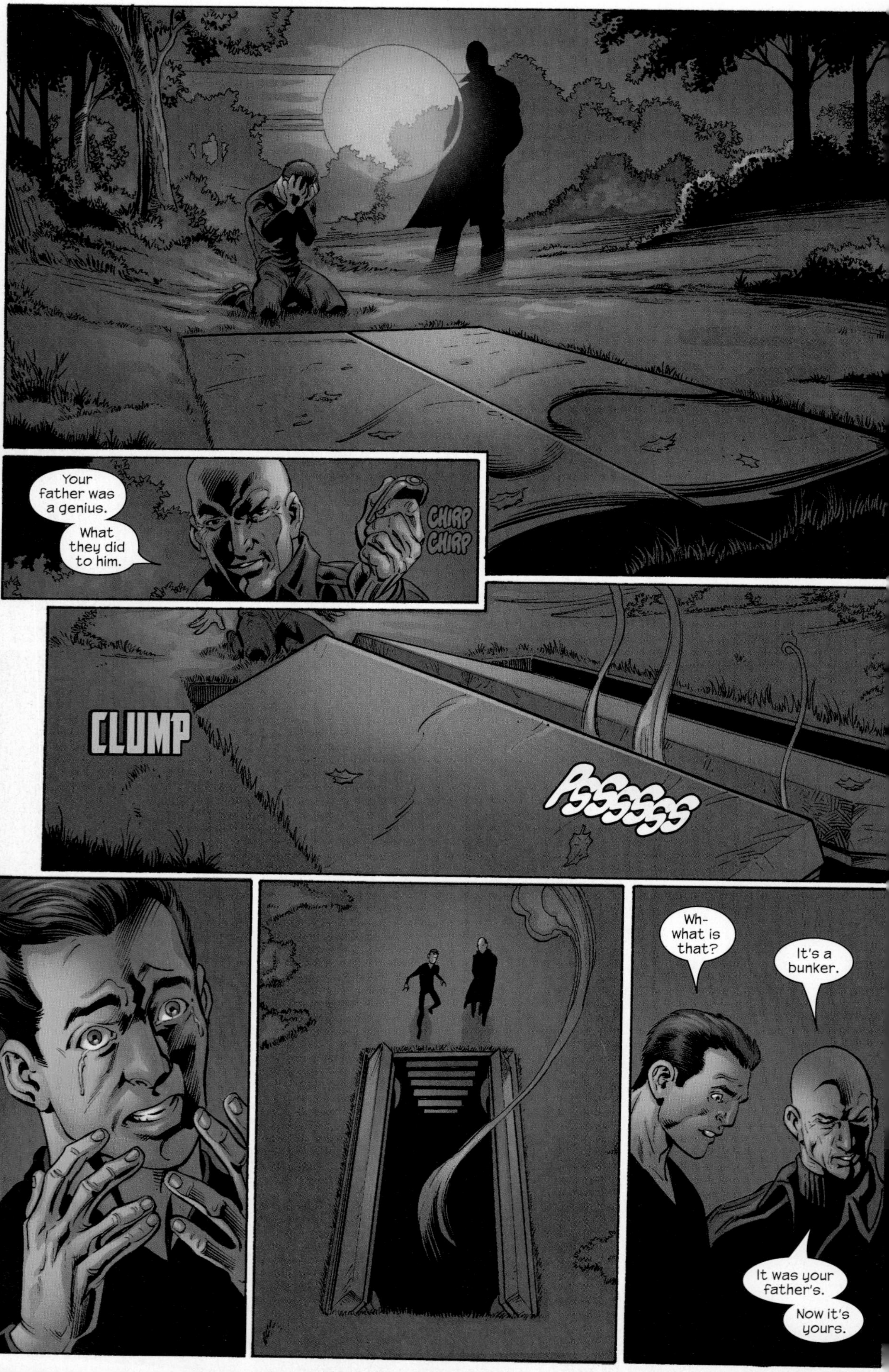
Your father was a genius.
What they did to him.
CHIRP CHIRP
CLUMP
PSSSSSS
Wh- what is that?
It's a bunker.
It was your father's.
Now it's yours.

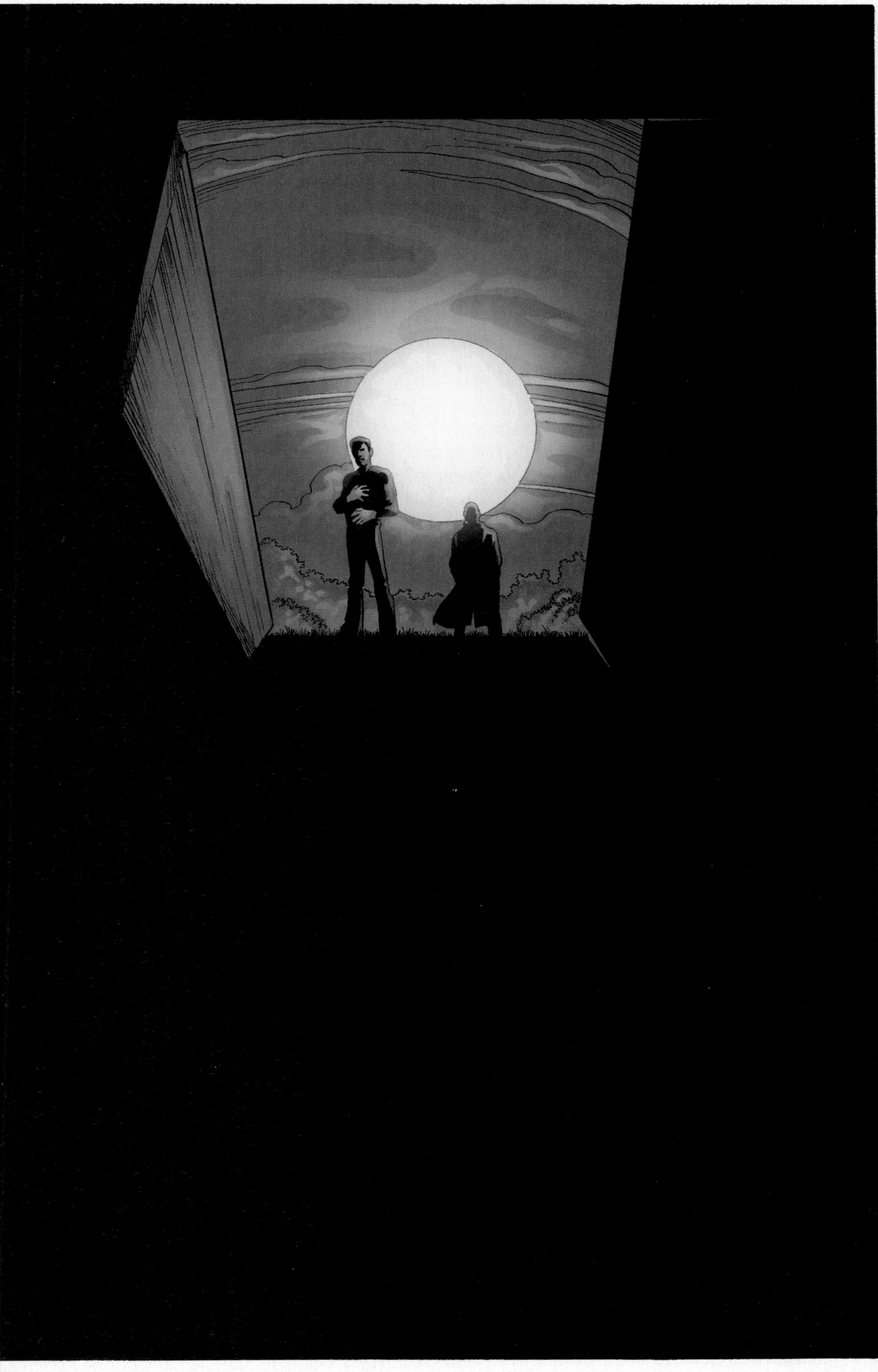

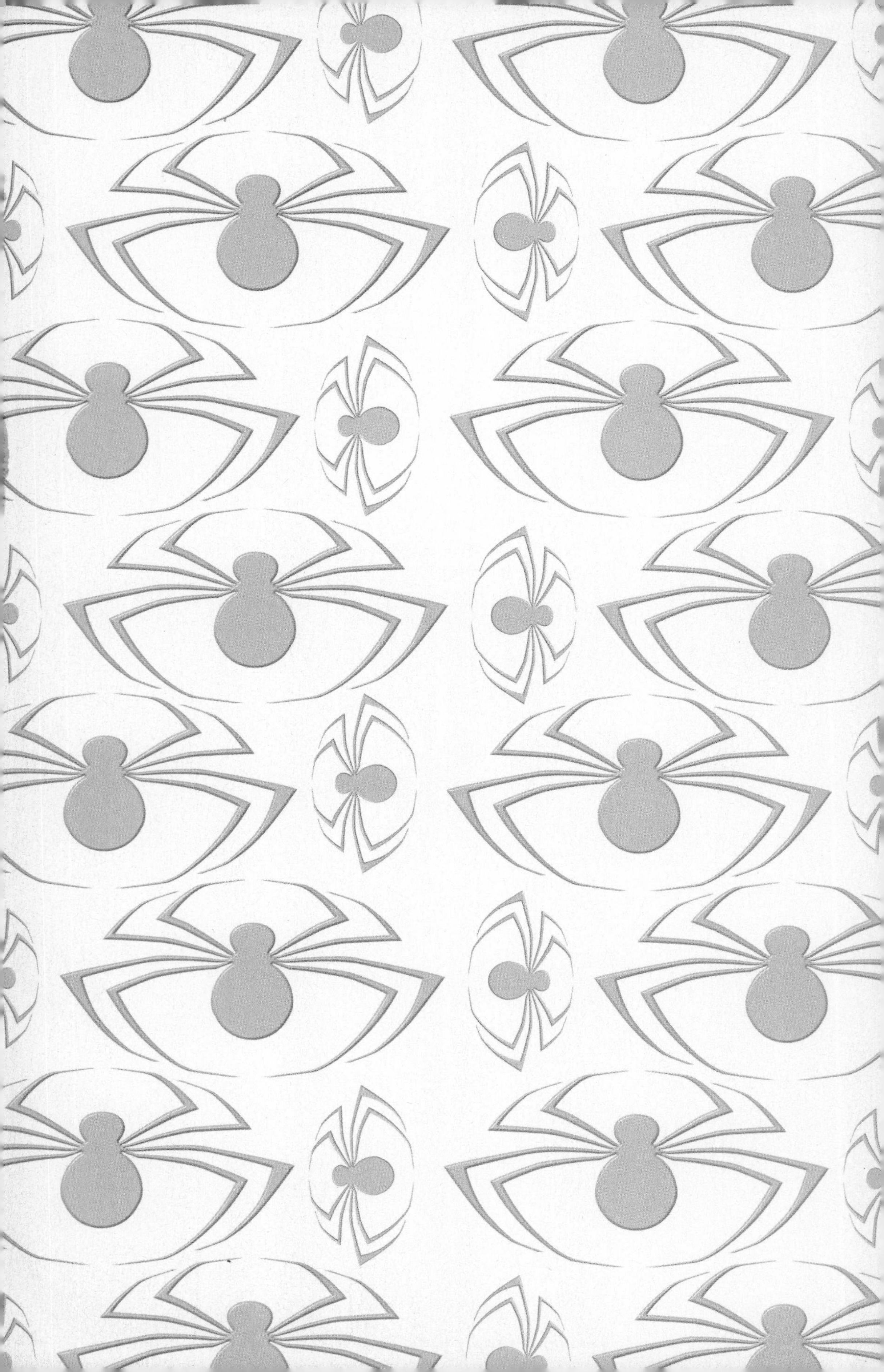

74

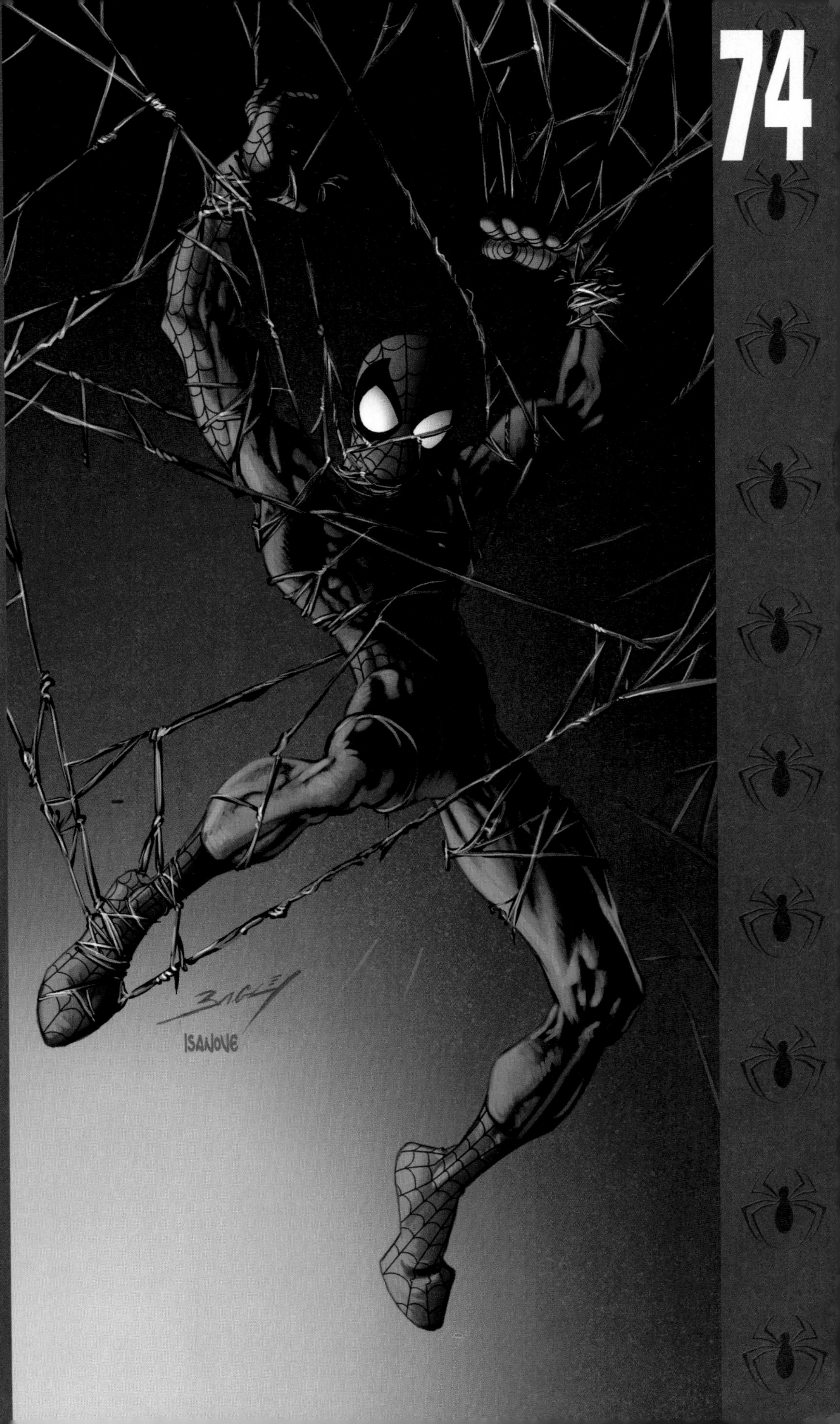
ISANOVE

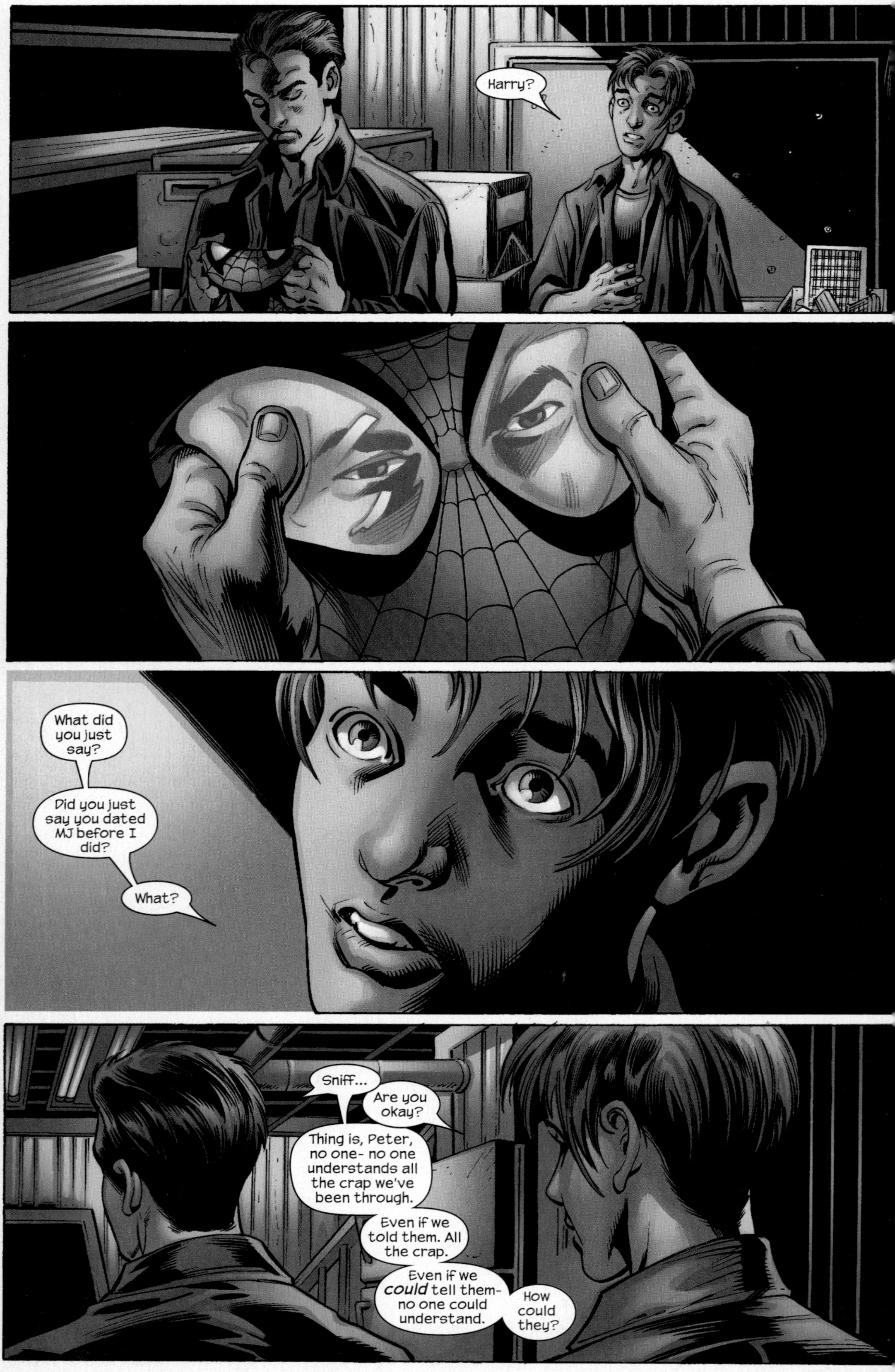
Harry?
What did you just say?
Did you just say you dated MJ before I did?
What?
Sniff...
Are you okay?
Thing is, Peter, no one- no one understands all the crap we've been through.
Even if we told them. All the crap.
Even if we *could* tell them- no one could understand.
How could they?

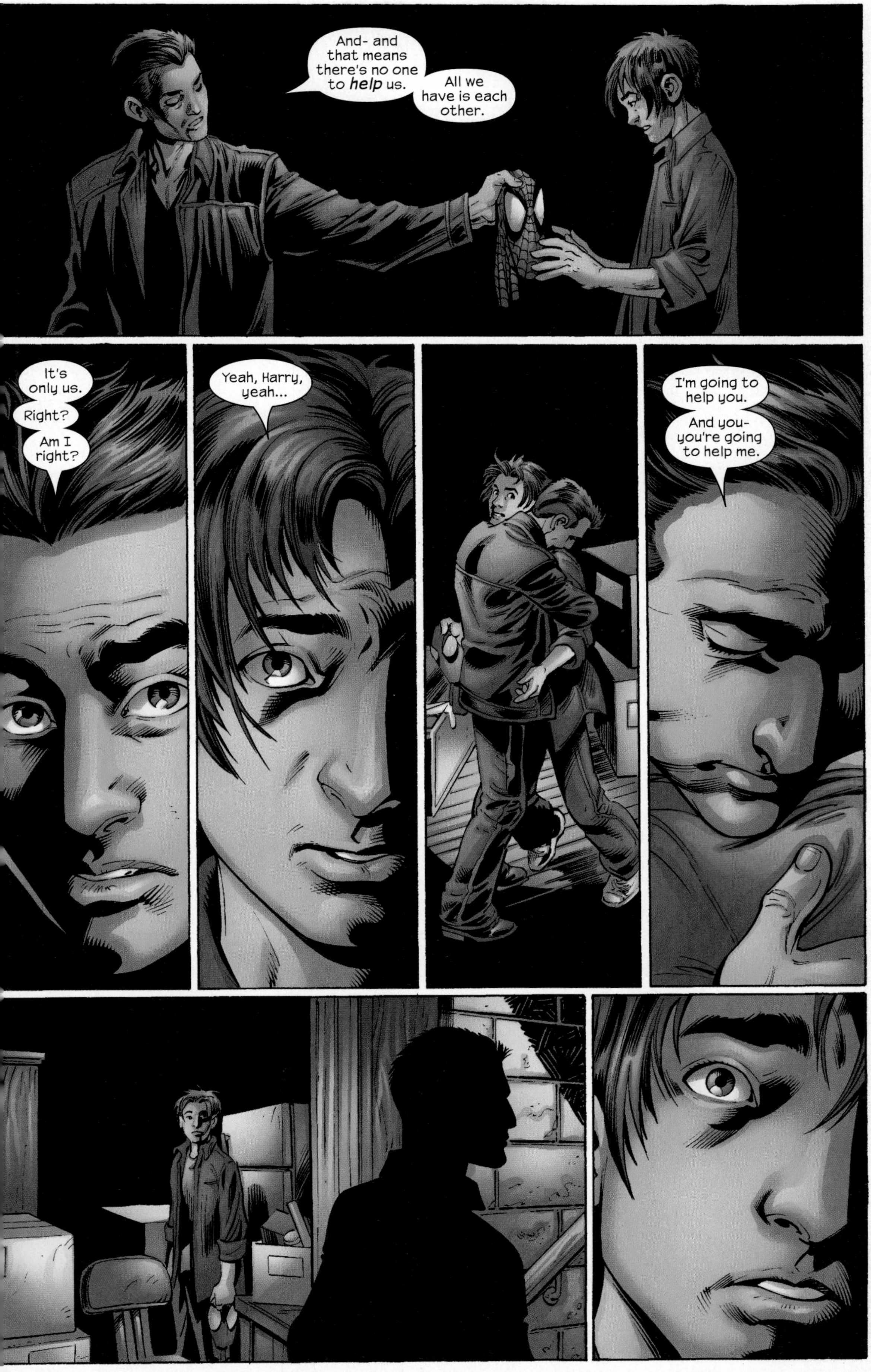
And- and that means there's no one to *help* us.
All we have is each other.
It's only us.
Right?
Am I right?
Yeah, Harry, yeah...
I'm going to help you.
And you- you're going to help me.

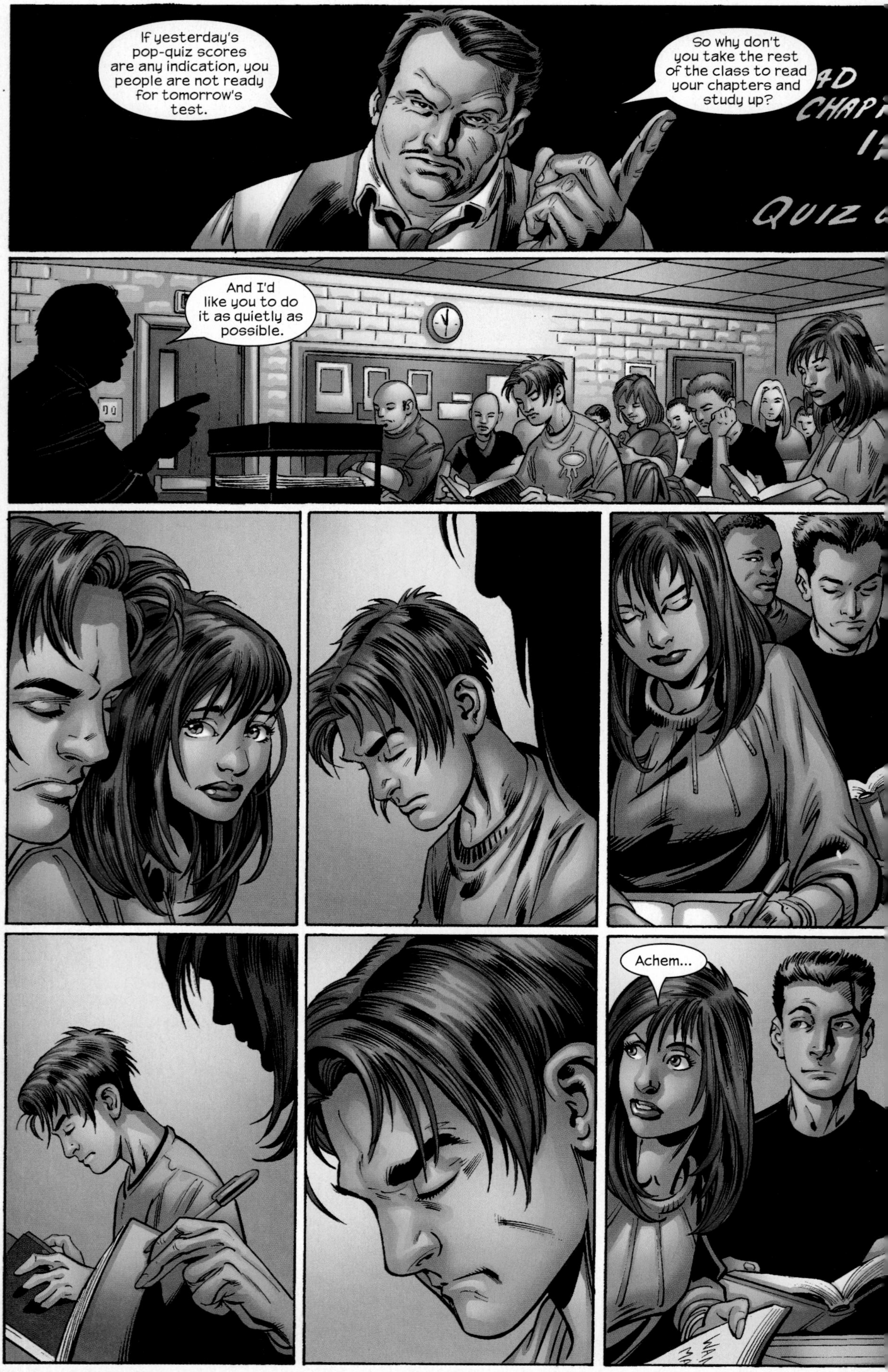
If yesterday's pop-quiz scores are any indication, you people are not ready for tomorrow's test.
So why don't you take the rest of the class to read your chapters and study up?
And I'd like you to do it as quietly as possible.
Achem...

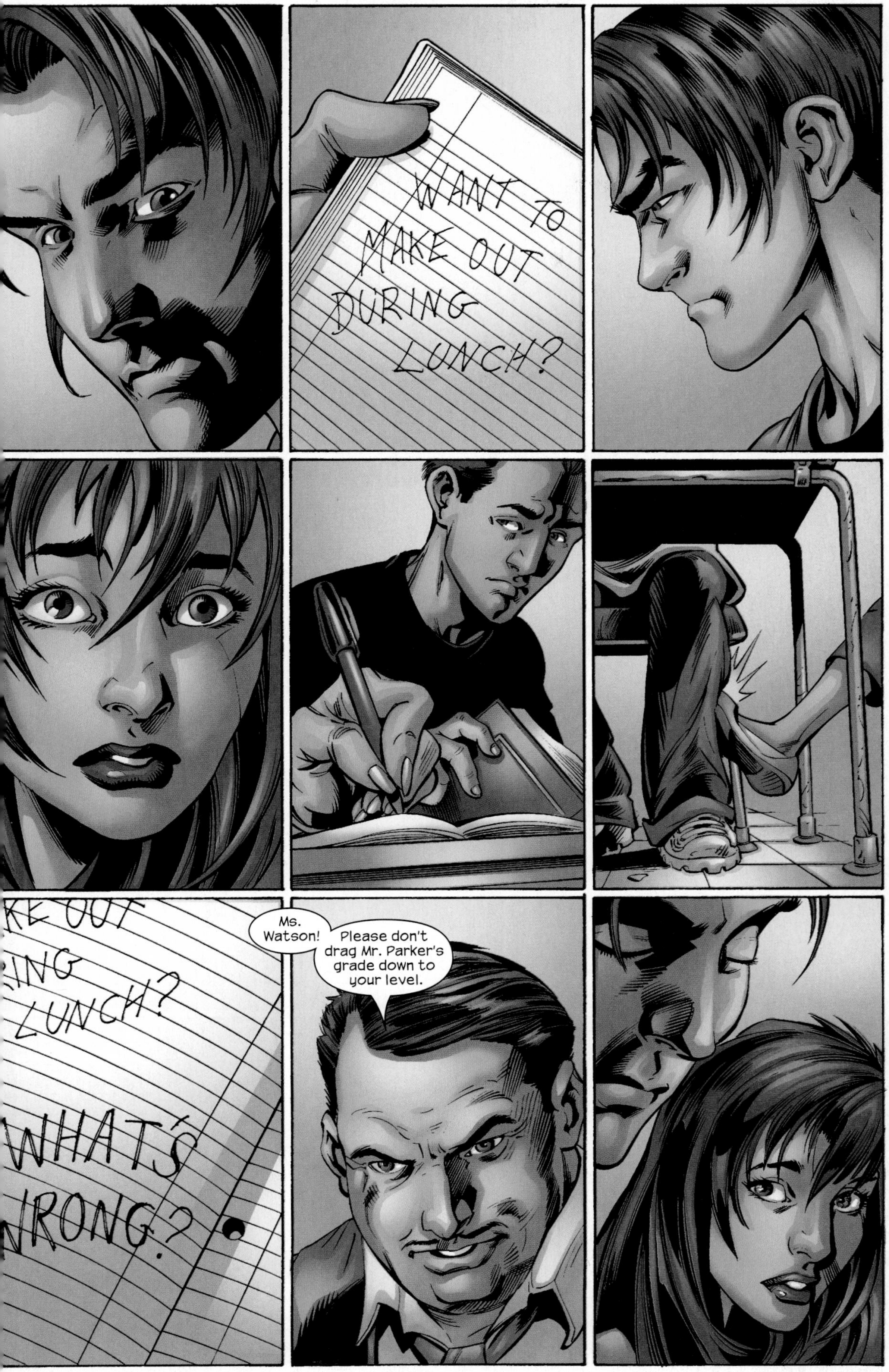
WANT TO MAKE OUT DURING LUNCH?
KE OUT
ING LUNCH?
WHAT'S WRONG?
Ms. Watson!
Please don't drag Mr. Parker's grade down to your level.

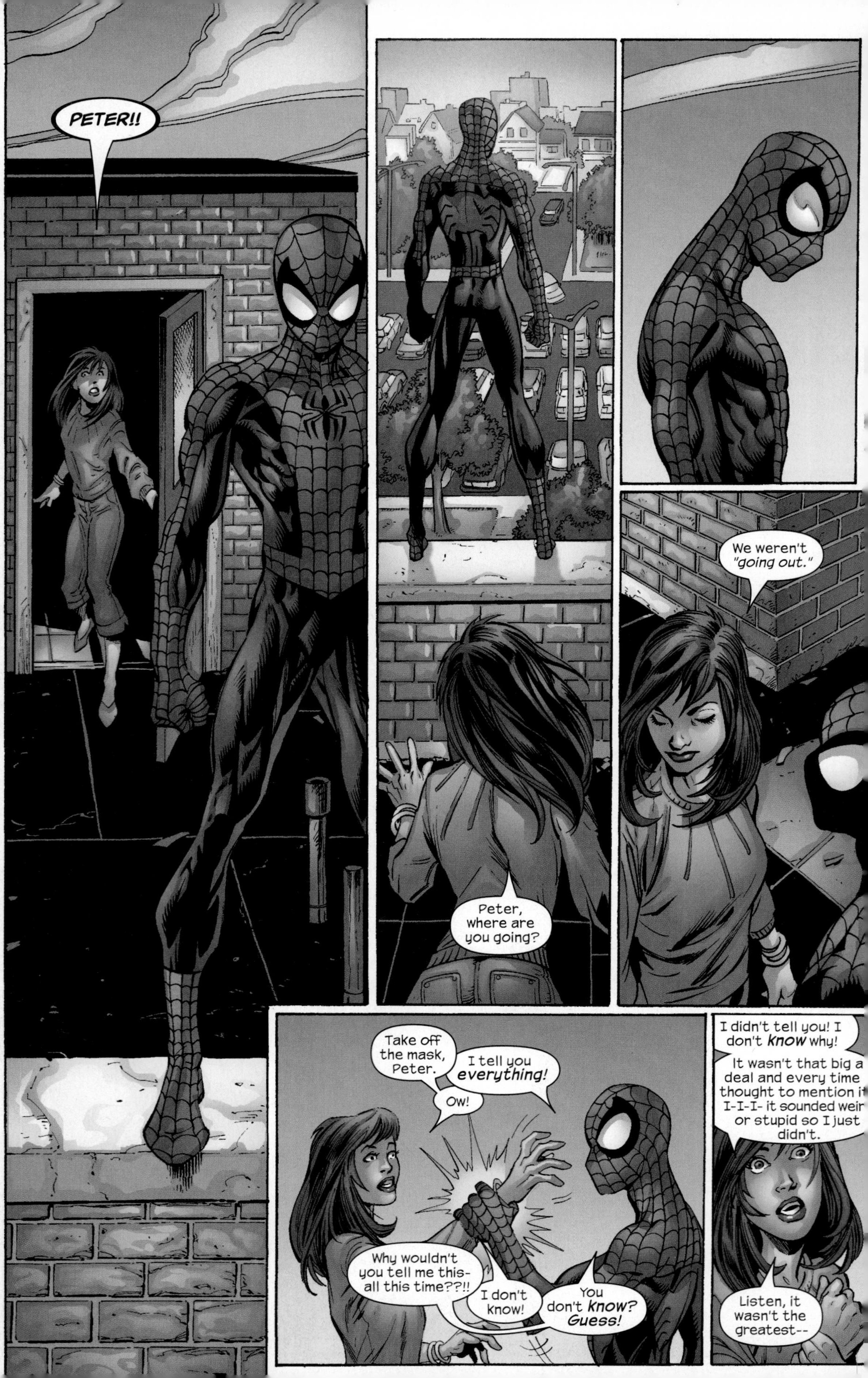
PETER!!
Peter, where are you going?
We weren't "going out."
Take off the mask, Peter.
I tell you everything!
Ow!
Why wouldn't you tell me this- all this time??!!
I don't know!
You don't KNOW? Guess!
I didn't tell you! I don't KNOW why!
It wasn't that big a deal and every time thought to mention it I-I-I- it sounded weir or stupid so I just didn't.
Listen, it wasn't the greatest--

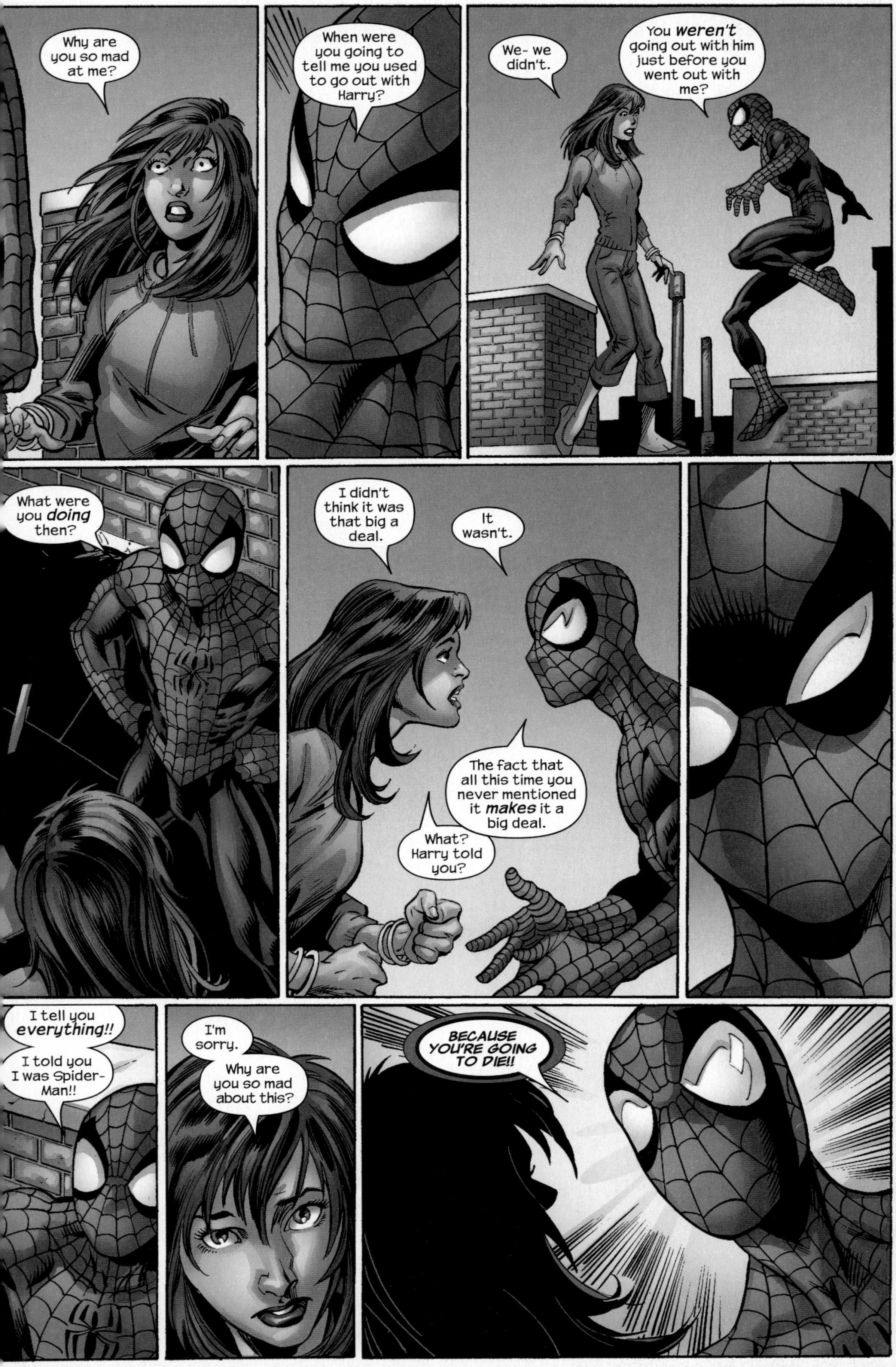
Why are you so mad at me?
When were you going to tell me you used to go out with Harry?
We- we didn't.
You *weren't* going out with him just before you went out with me?
What were you *doing* then?
I didn't think it was that big a deal.
It wasn't.
The fact that all this time you never mentioned it *makes* it a big deal.
What? Harry told you?
I tell you *everything!!*
I told you I was Spider-Man!!
I'm sorry.
Why are you so mad about this?
BECAUSE YOU'RE GOING TO DIE!!

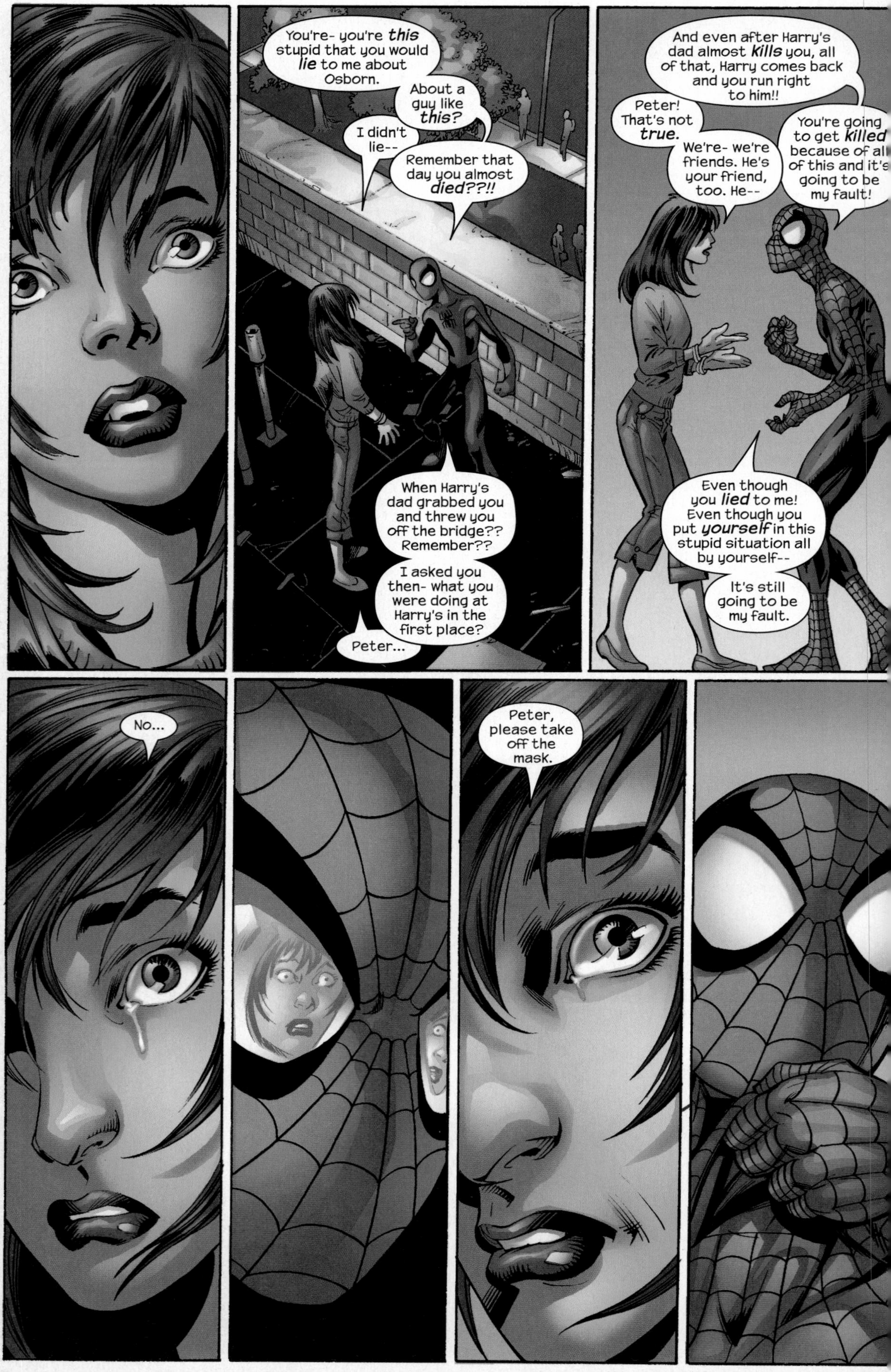

You're- you're *this* stupid that you would *lie* to me about Osborn.
About a guy like *this?*
I didn't lie--
Remember that day you almost *died??!!*
When Harry's dad grabbed you and threw you off the bridge?? Remember??
I asked you then- what you were doing at Harry's in the first place?
Peter...
And even after Harry's dad almost *kills* you, all of that, Harry comes back and you run right to him!!
Peter! That's not *true.*
We're- we're friends. He's your friend, too. He--
You're going to get *killed* because of all of this and it's going to be my fault!
Even though you *lied* to me! Even though you put *yourself* in this stupid situation all by yourself--
It's still going to be my fault.
No...
Peter, please take off the mask.

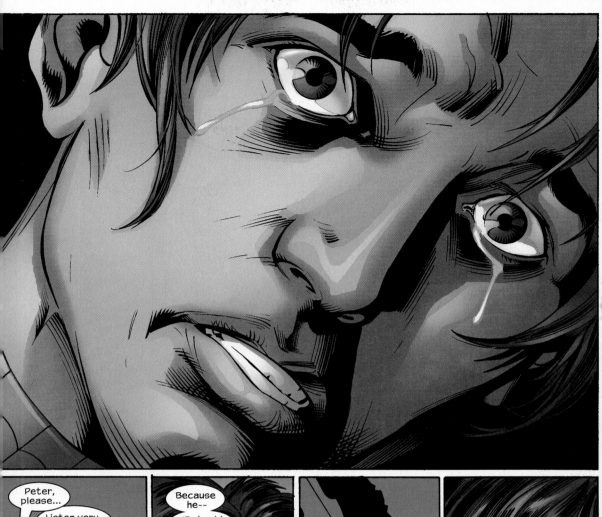

Peter, please...

Listen very carefully!

The Osborns are nuts!!

You hear what I am saying? Stay away from them. Harry is dangerous.

How is he dangerous?

Because he--

(I should never have told you who I was.)

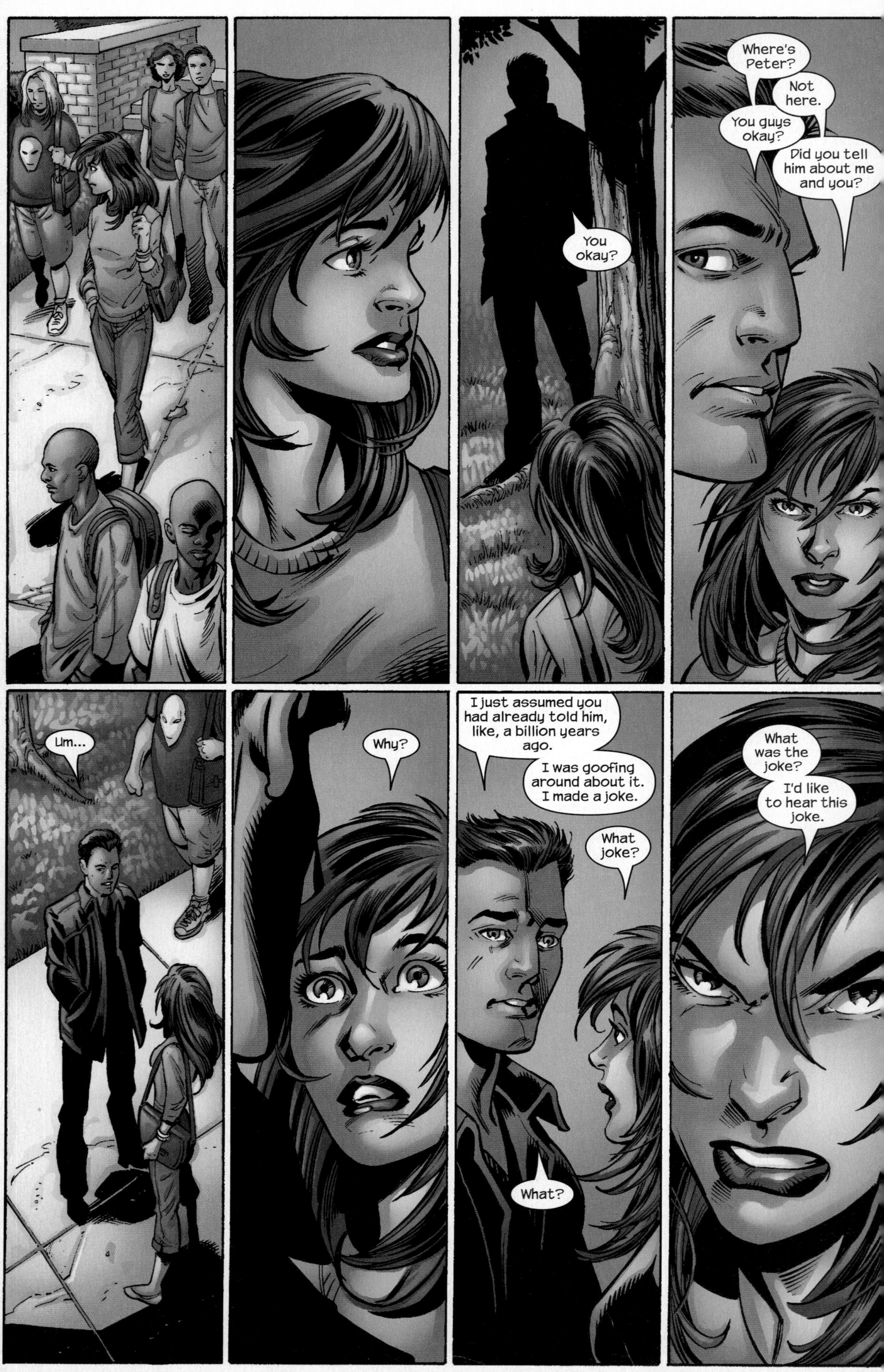
You okay?
Where's Peter?
Not here.
You guys okay?
Did you tell him about me and you?
Um...
Why?
I just assumed you had already told him, like, a billion years ago.
I was goofing around about it. I made a joke.
What joke?
What?
What was the joke?
I'd like to hear this joke.

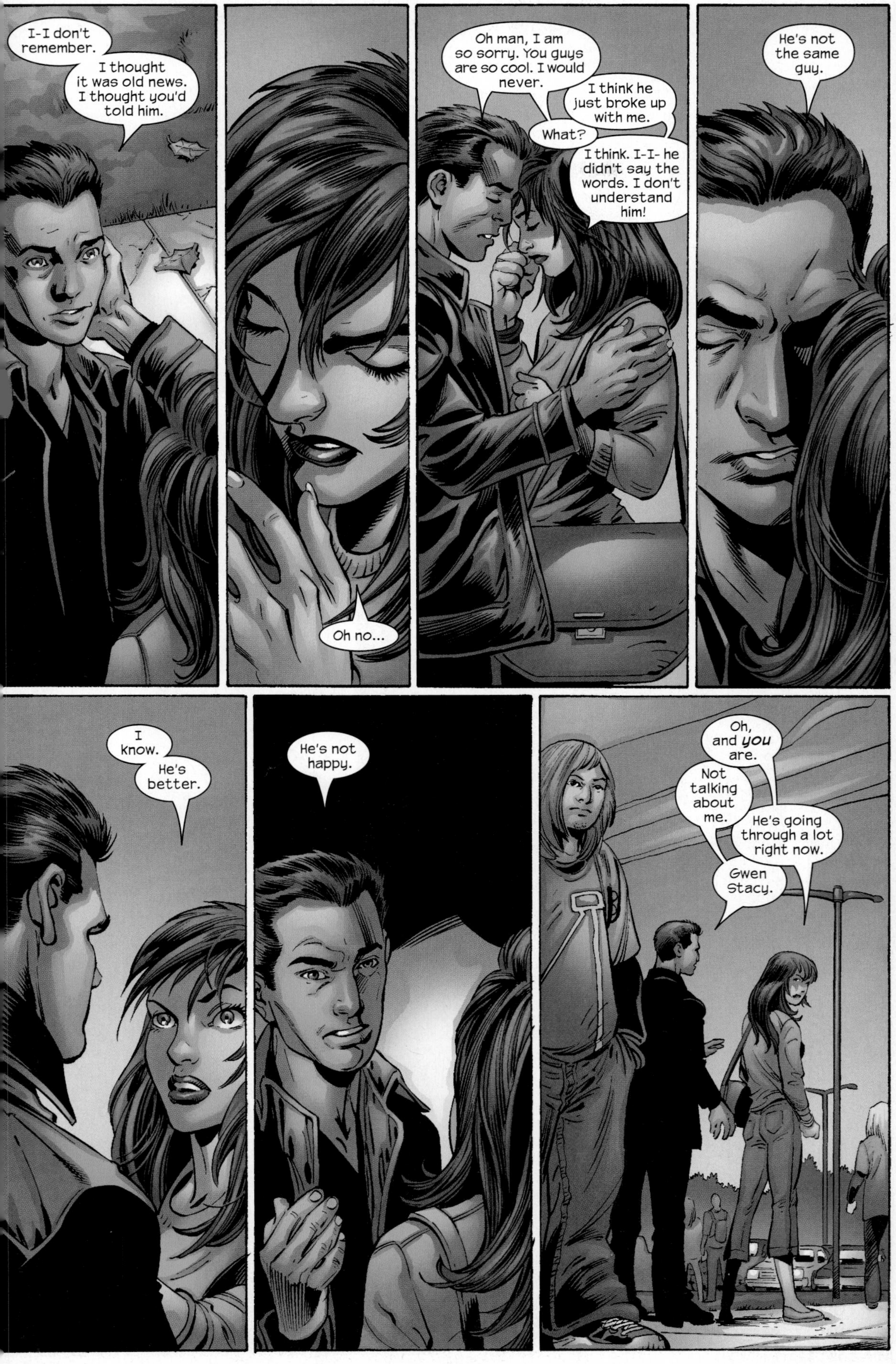
I-I don't remember.
I thought it was old news. I thought you'd told him.
Oh no...
Oh man, I am so sorry. You guys are so cool. I would never.
What?
I think he just broke up with me.
I think. I-I- he didn't say the words. I don't understand him!
He's not the same guy.
I know.
He's better.
He's not happy.
Oh, and *you* are.
Not talking about me.
He's going through a lot right now.
Gwen Stacy.

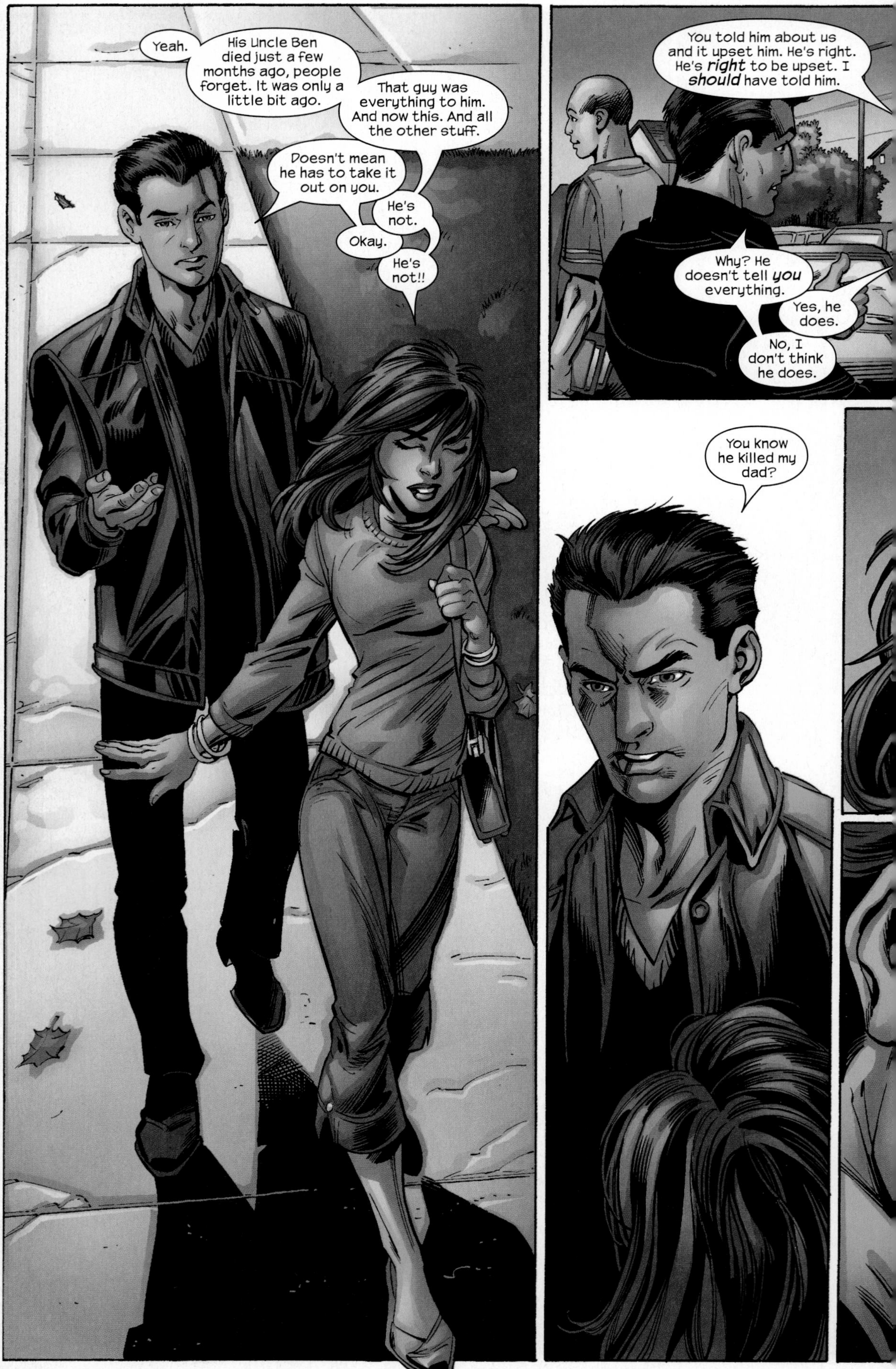
Yeah.
His Uncle Ben died just a few months ago, people forget. It was only a little bit ago.
That guy was everything to him. And now this. And all the other stuff.
Doesn't mean he has to take it out on you.
He's not.
Okay.
He's not!!
You told him about us and it upset him. He's right. He's *right* to be upset. I *should* have told him.
Why? He doesn't tell *you* everything.
Yes, he does.
No, I don't think he does.
You know he killed my dad?

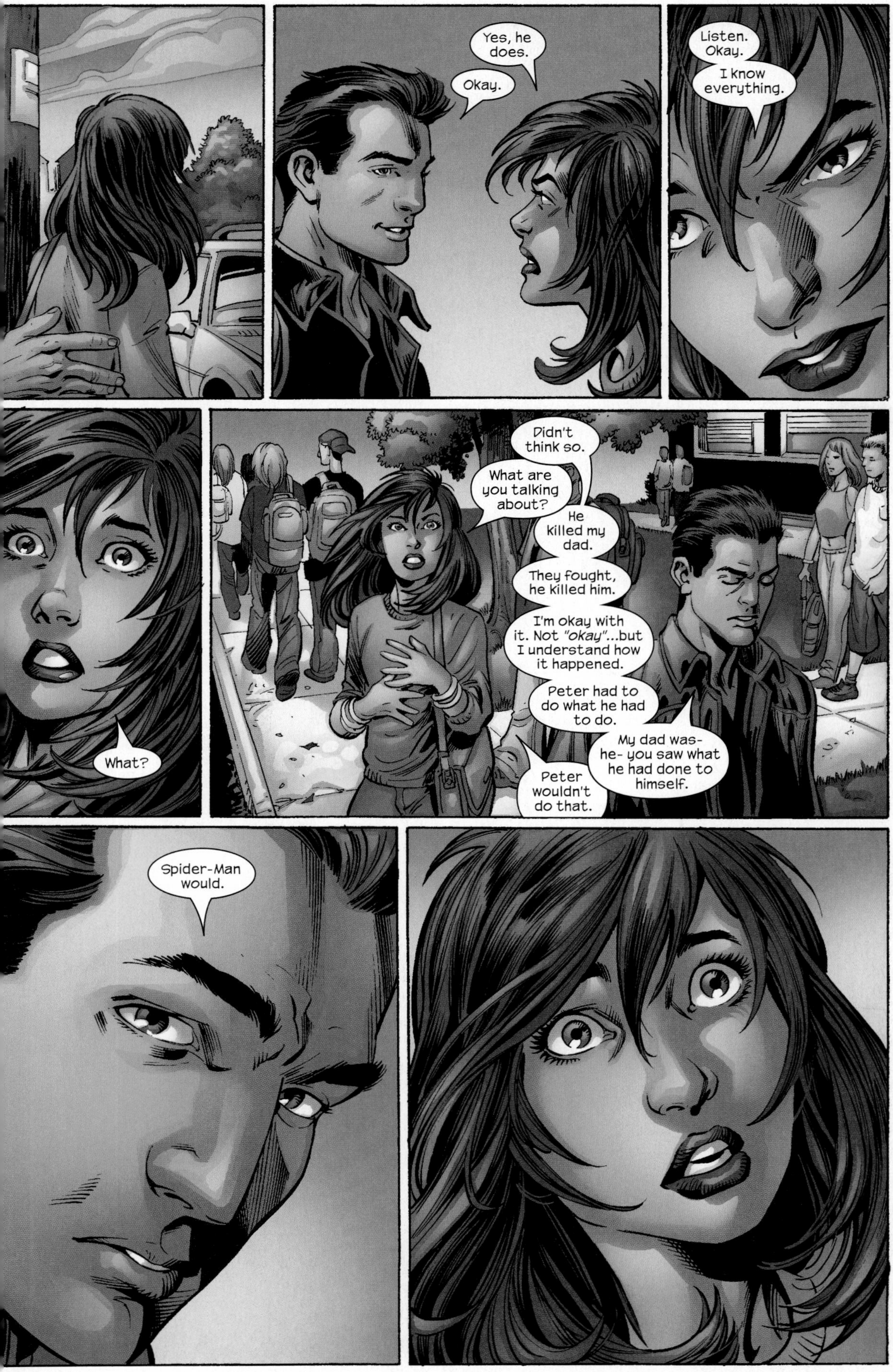
Yes, he does.
Okay.
Listen. Okay.
I know everything.
What?
Didn't think so.
What are you talking about?
He killed my dad.
They fought, he killed him.
I'm okay with it. Not "okay"...but I understand how it happened.
Peter had to do what he had to do.
My dad was- he- you saw what he had done to himself.
Peter wouldn't do that.
Spider-Man would.

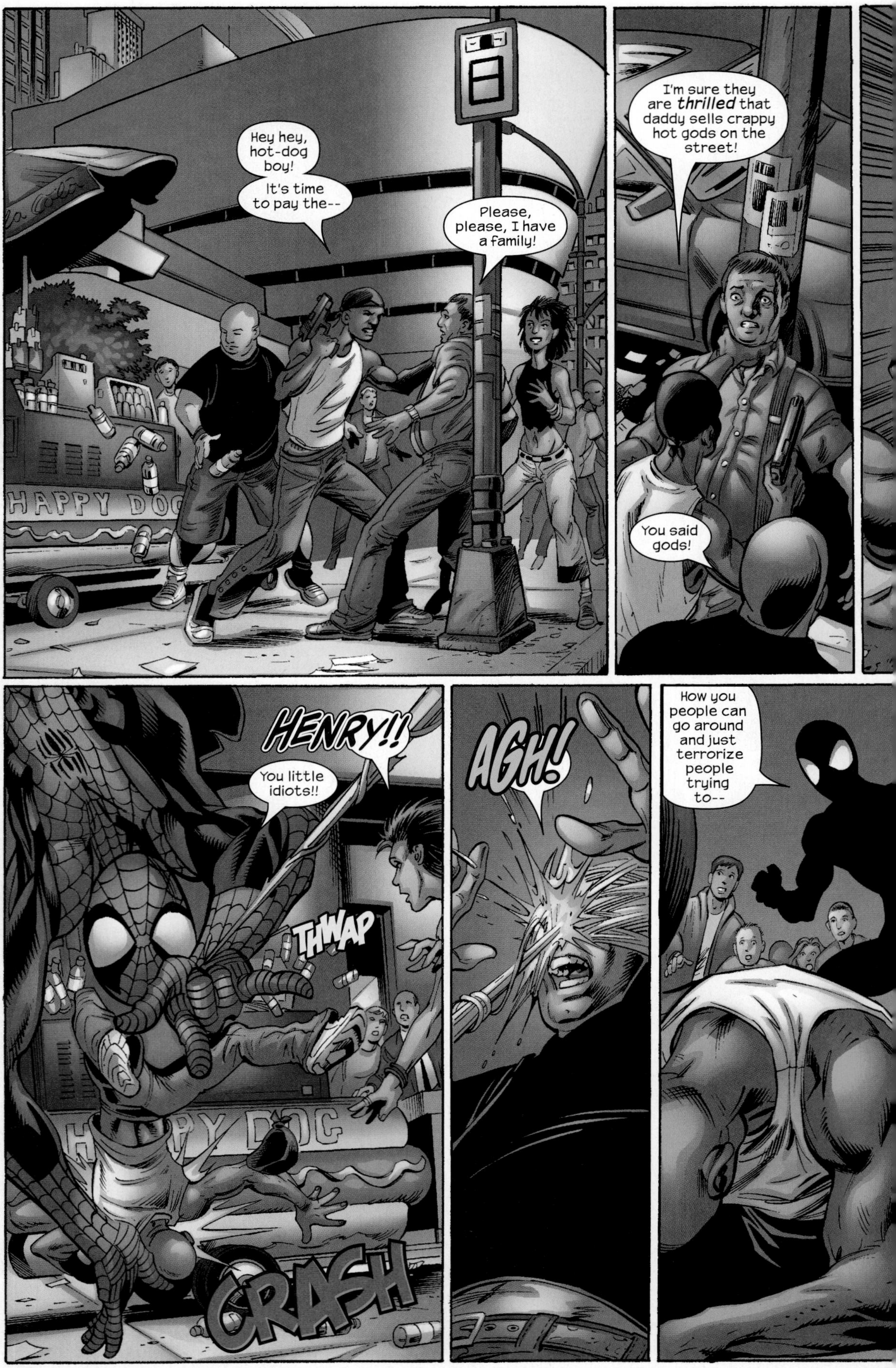

Hey hey, hot-dog boy!
It's time to pay the--
Please, please, I have a family!
HAPPY DOG
I'm sure they are *thrilled* that daddy sells crappy hot gods on the street!
You said gods!
HENRY!!
You little idiots!!
THWAP
HAPPY DOG
CRASH
AGH!
How you people can go around and just terrorize people trying to--

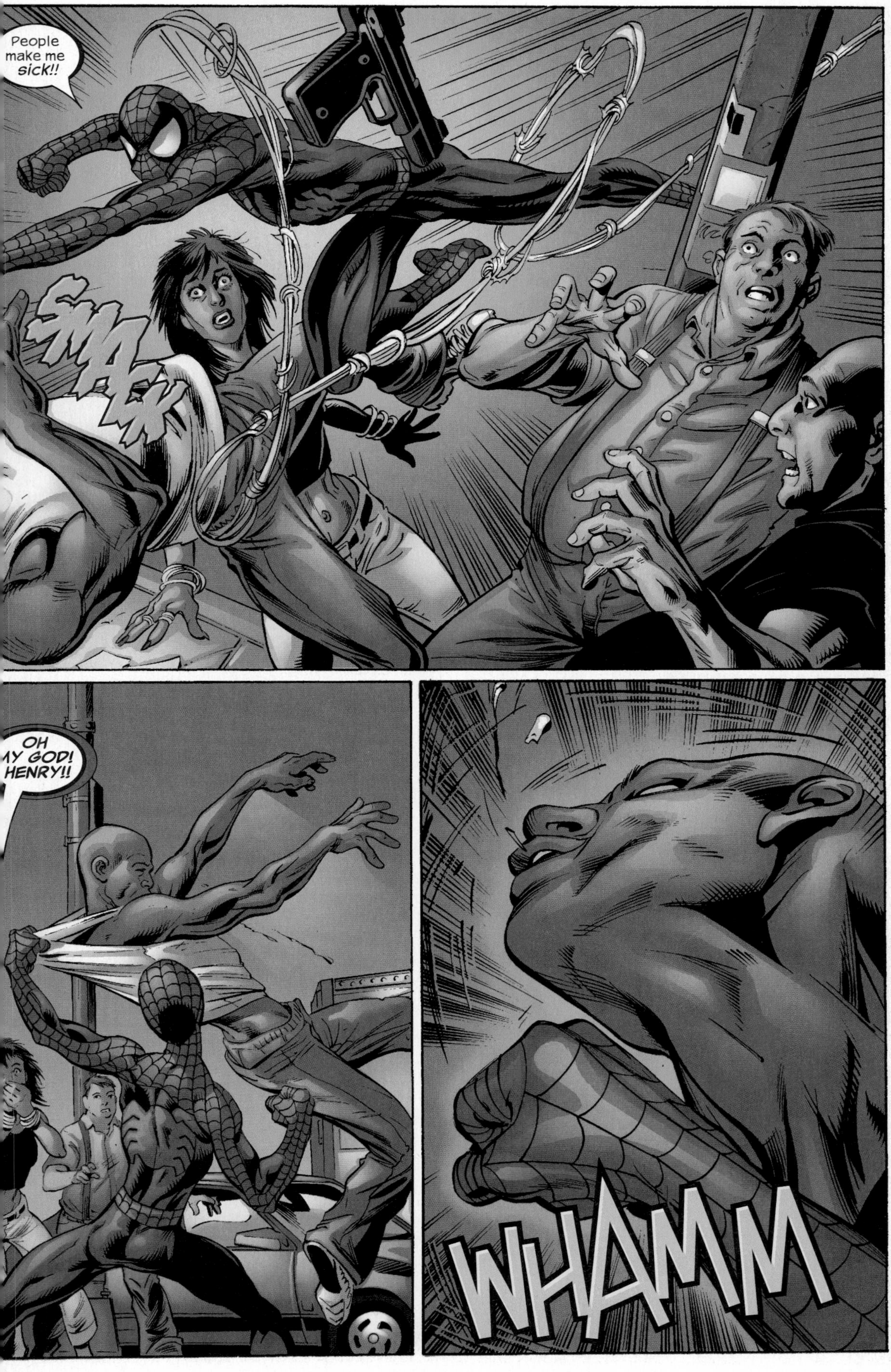
People make me sick!!
SMACK
OH MY GOD! HENRY!!
WHAMM

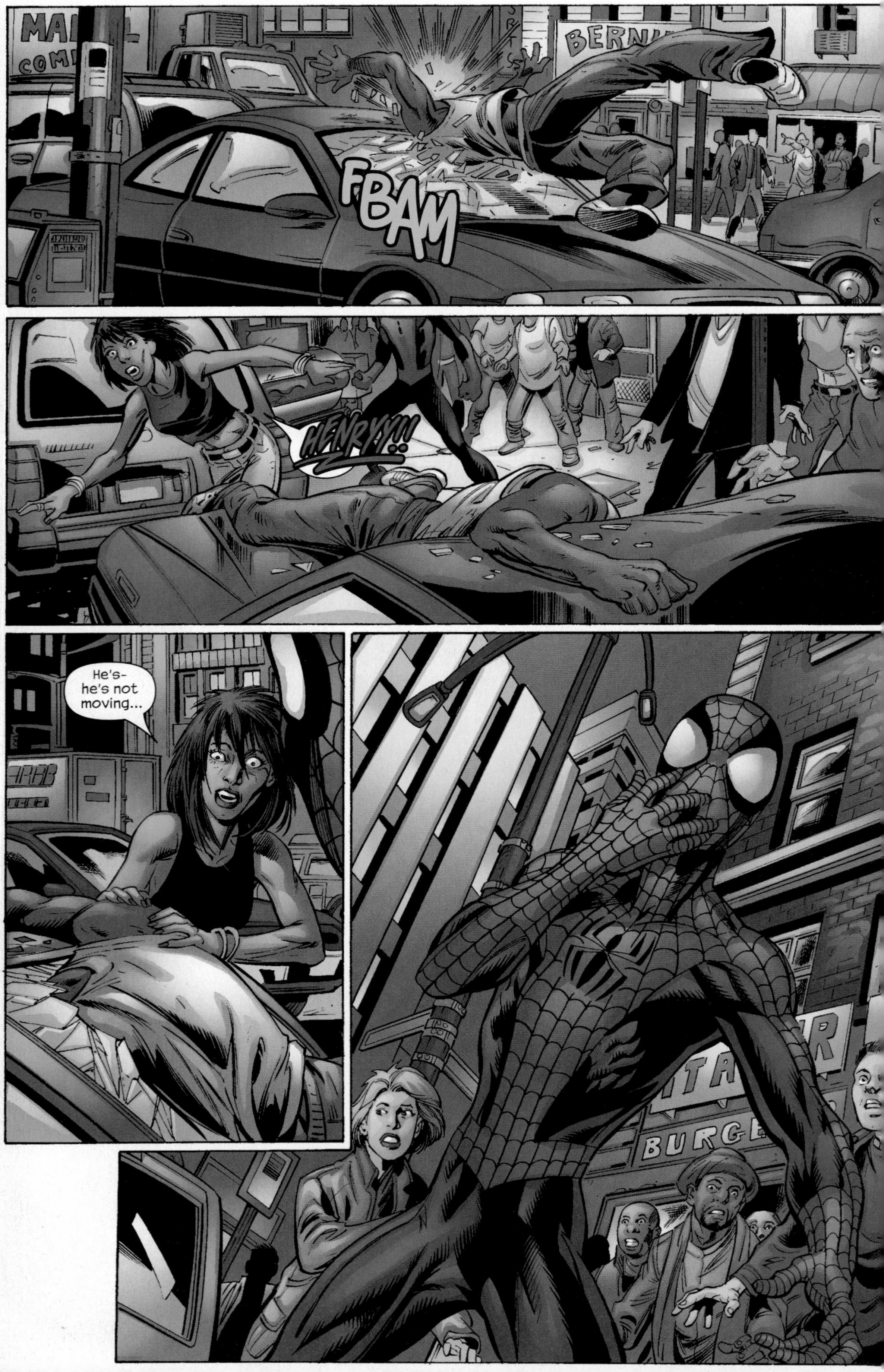
FBAM
HENRYY!!
He's- he's not moving...
BURGE

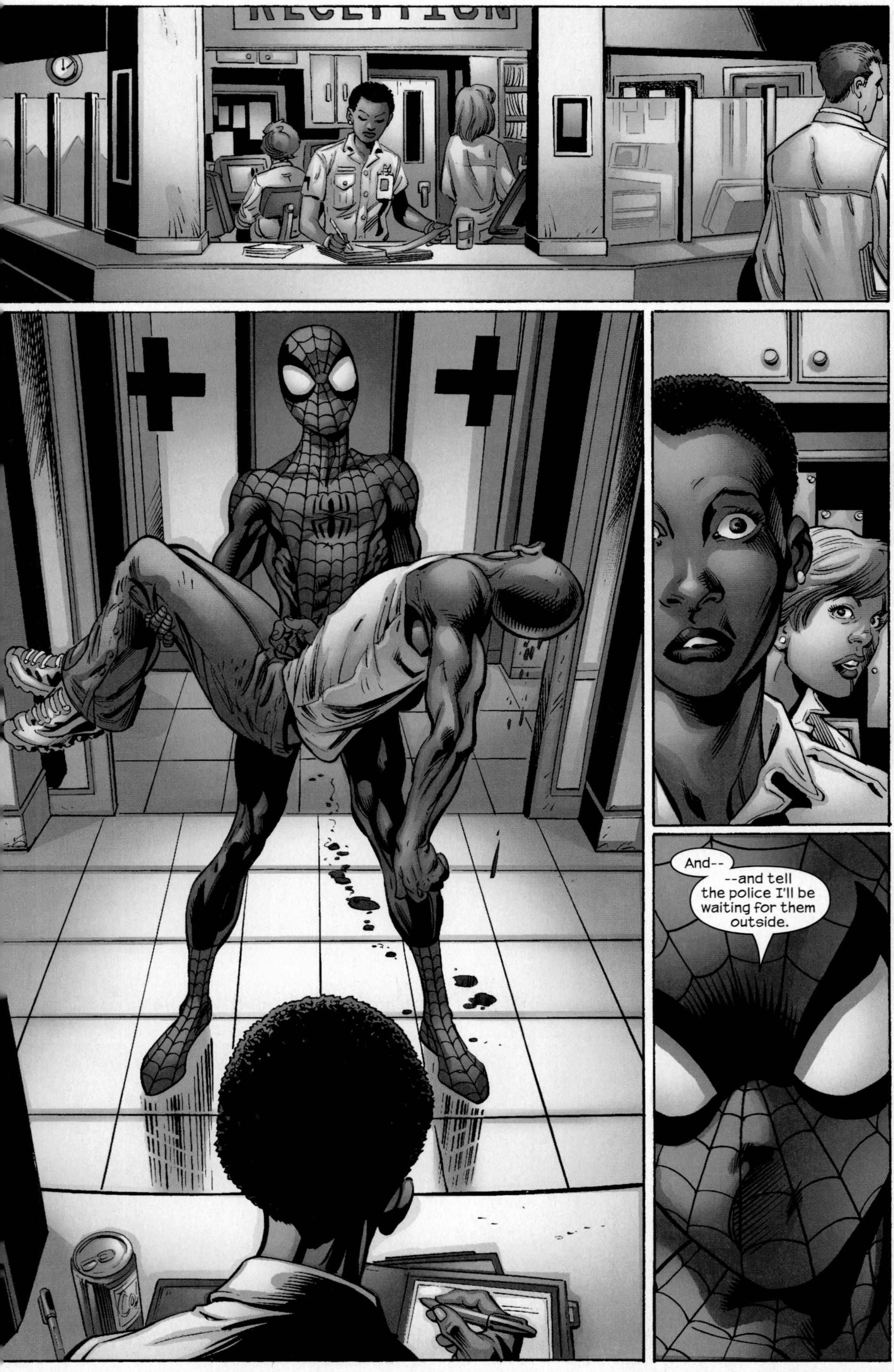

And--
--and tell the police I'll be waiting for them outside.

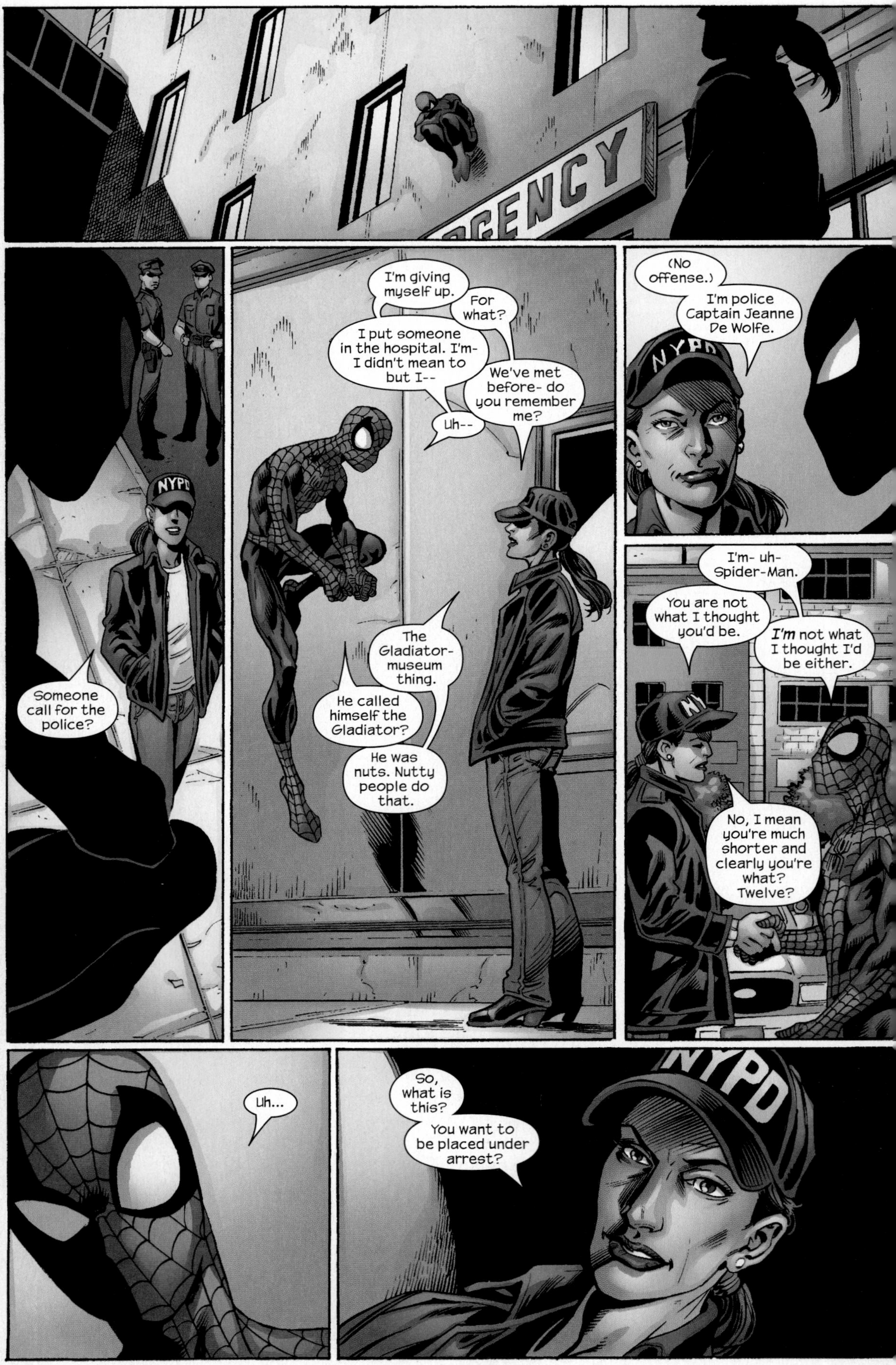
Someone call for the police?
I'm giving myself up.
For what?
I put someone in the hospital. I'm- I didn't mean to but I--
We've met before- do you remember me?
Uh--
The Gladiator-museum thing.
He called himself the Gladiator?
He was nuts. Nutty people do that.
(No offense.)
I'm police Captain Jeanne De Wolfe.
NYPD
I'm- uh- Spider-Man.
You are not what I thought you'd be.
I'm not what I thought I'd be either.
No, I mean you're much shorter and clearly you're what? Twelve?
Uh...
So, what is this?
You want to be placed under arrest?
NYPD

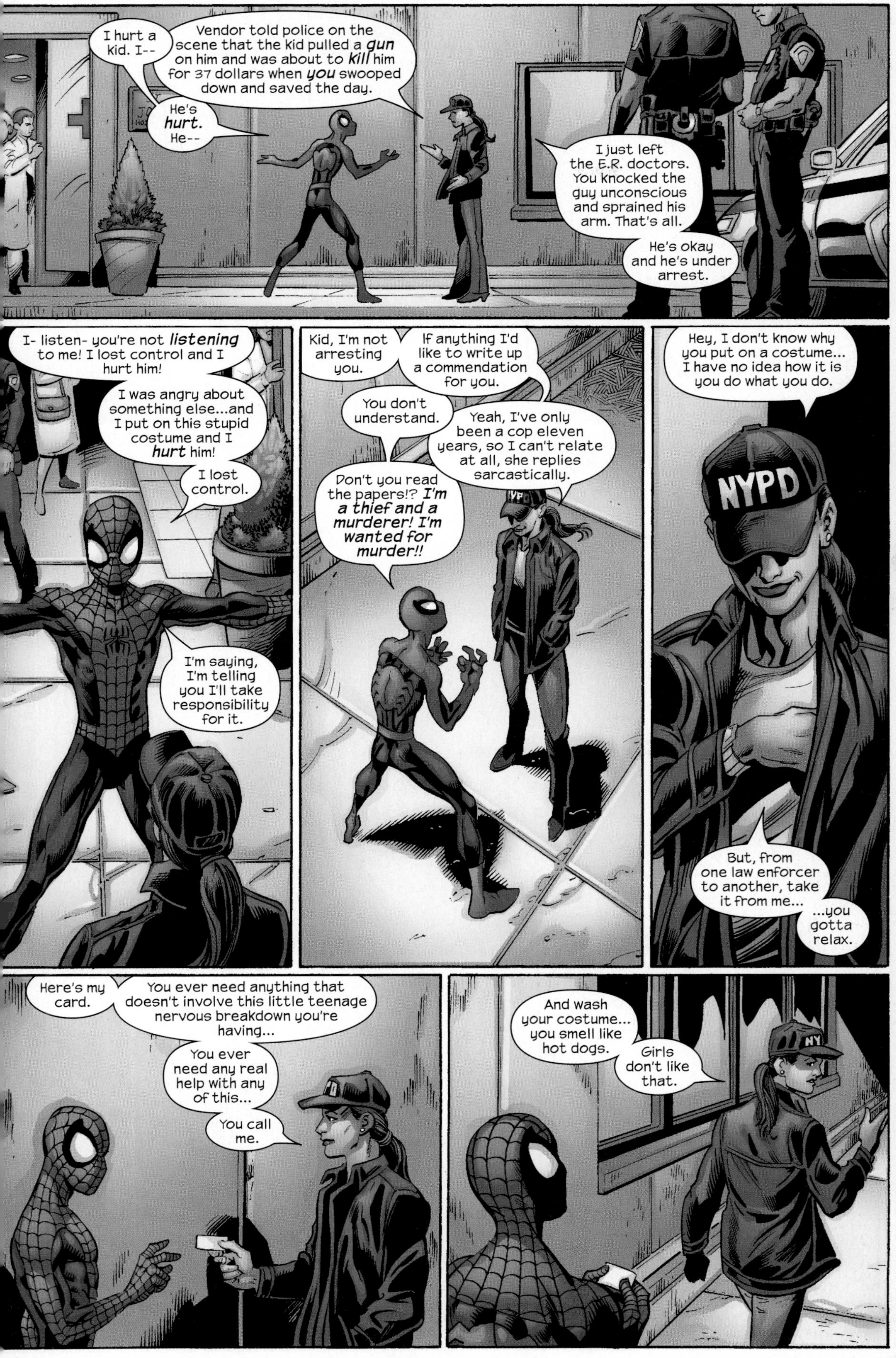
I hurt a kid. I--
Vendor told police on the scene that the kid pulled a *gun* on him and was about to *kill* him for 37 dollars when *you* swooped down and saved the day.
He's *hurt.* He--
I just left the E.R. doctors. You knocked the guy unconscious and sprained his arm. That's all.
He's okay and he's under arrest.
I- listen- you're not *listening* to me! I lost control and I hurt him!
I was angry about something else...and I put on this stupid costume and I *hurt* him!
I lost control.
I'm saying, I'm telling you I'll take responsibility for it.
Kid, I'm not arresting you.
If anything I'd like to write up a commendation for you.
You don't understand.
Yeah, I've only been a cop eleven years, so I can't relate at all, she replies sarcastically.
Don't you read the papers!? *I'm a thief and a murderer! I'm wanted for murder!!*
Hey, I don't know why you put on a costume... I have no idea how it is you do what you do.
NYPD
But, from one law enforcer to another, take it from me...
...you gotta relax.
Here's my card.
You ever need anything that doesn't involve this little teenage nervous breakdown you're having...
You ever need any real help with any of this...
You call me.
And wash your costume... you smell like hot dogs.
Girls don't like that.

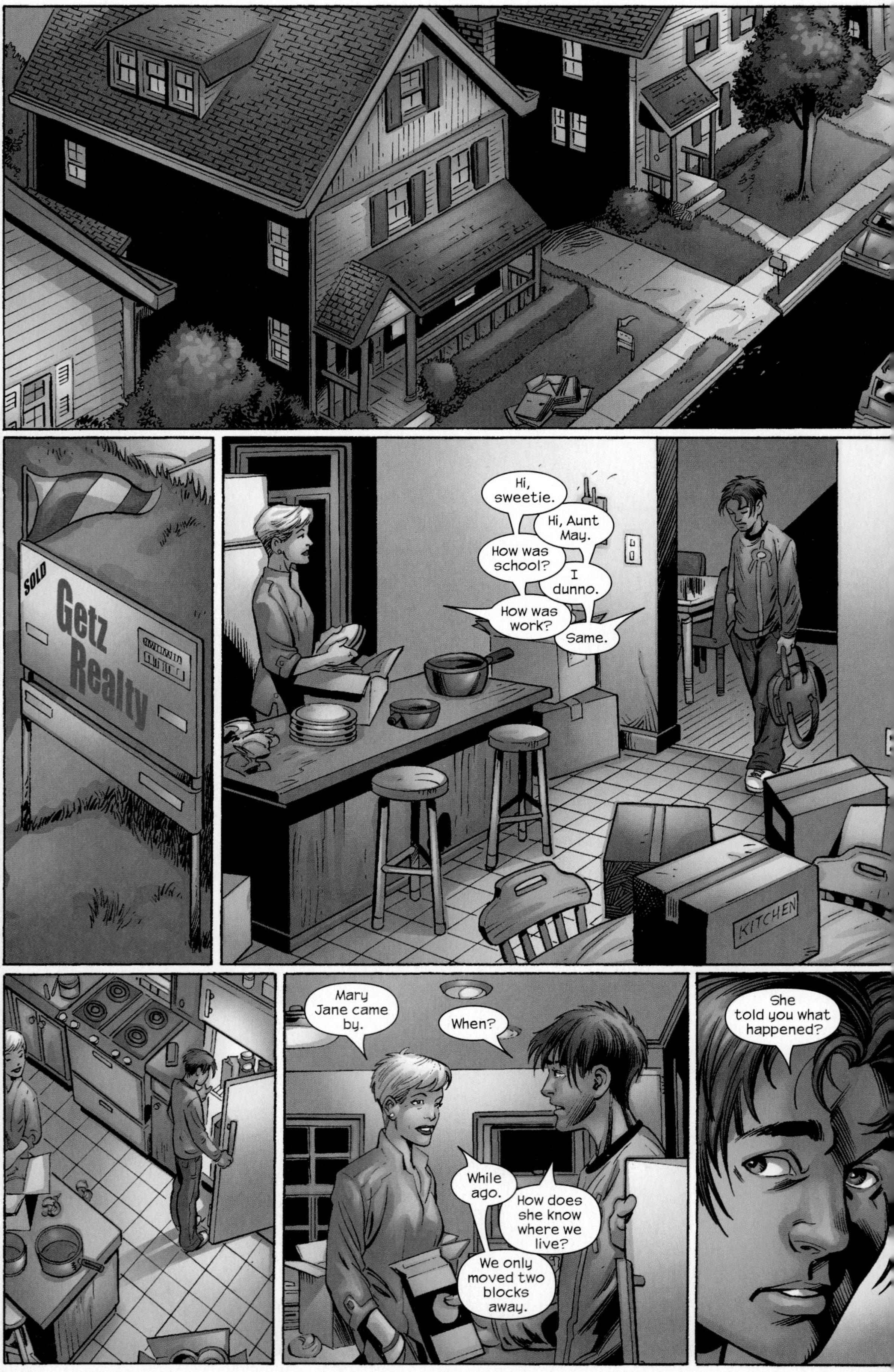
SOLD
Getz Realty
Hi, sweetie.
Hi, Aunt May.
How was school?
I dunno.
How was work?
Same.
KITCHEN
Mary Jane came by.
When?
While ago.
How does she know where we live?
We only moved two blocks away.
She told you what happened?

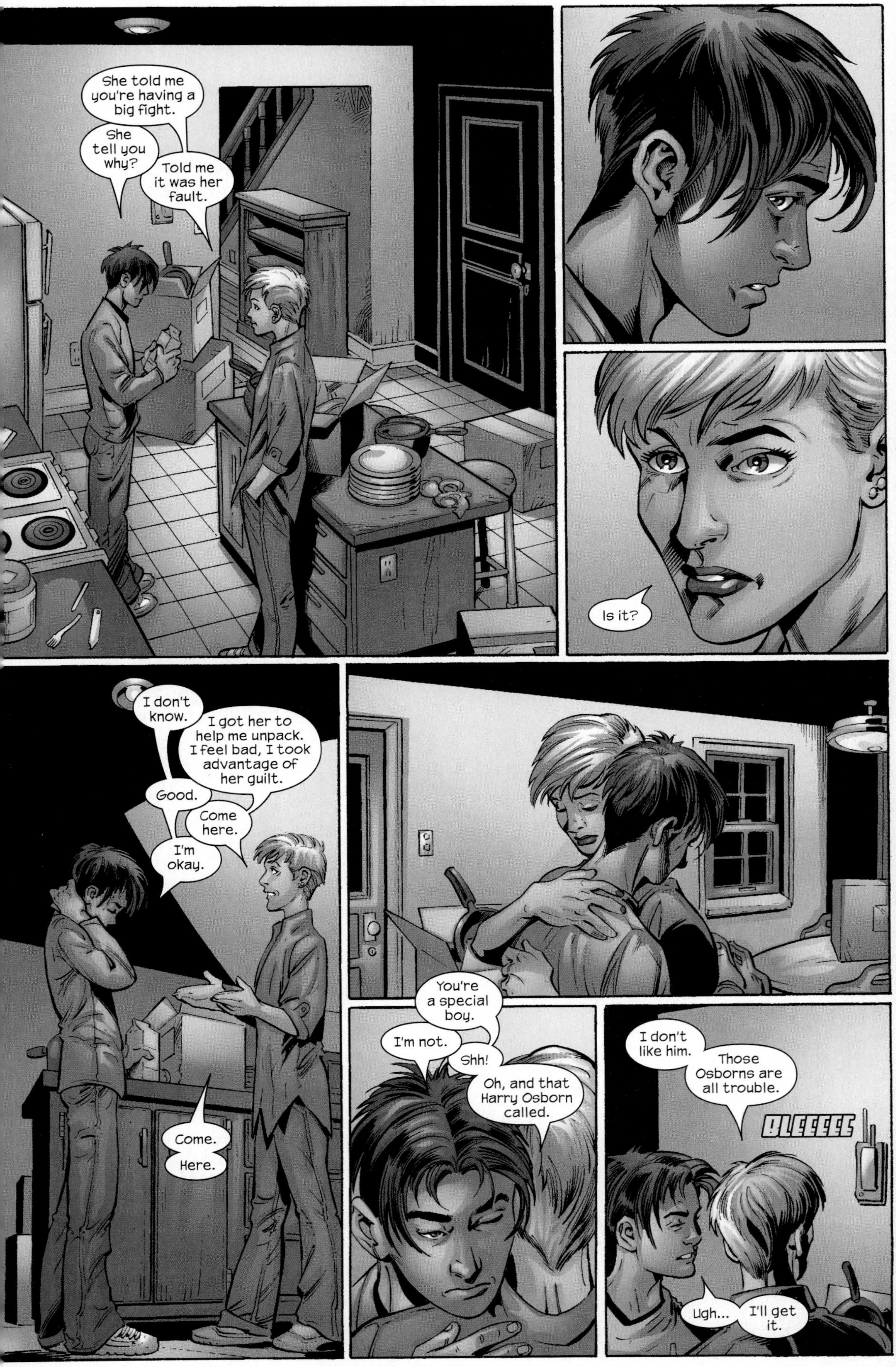
She told me you're having a big fight.
She tell you why?
Told me it was her fault.
Is it?
I don't know.
I got her to help me unpack. I feel bad, I took advantage of her guilt.
Good.
Come here.
I'm okay.
Come.
Here.
You're a special boy.
I'm not.
Shh!
Oh, and that Harry Osborn called.
I don't like him.
Those Osborns are all trouble.
BLEEEEE
Ugh...
I'll get it.

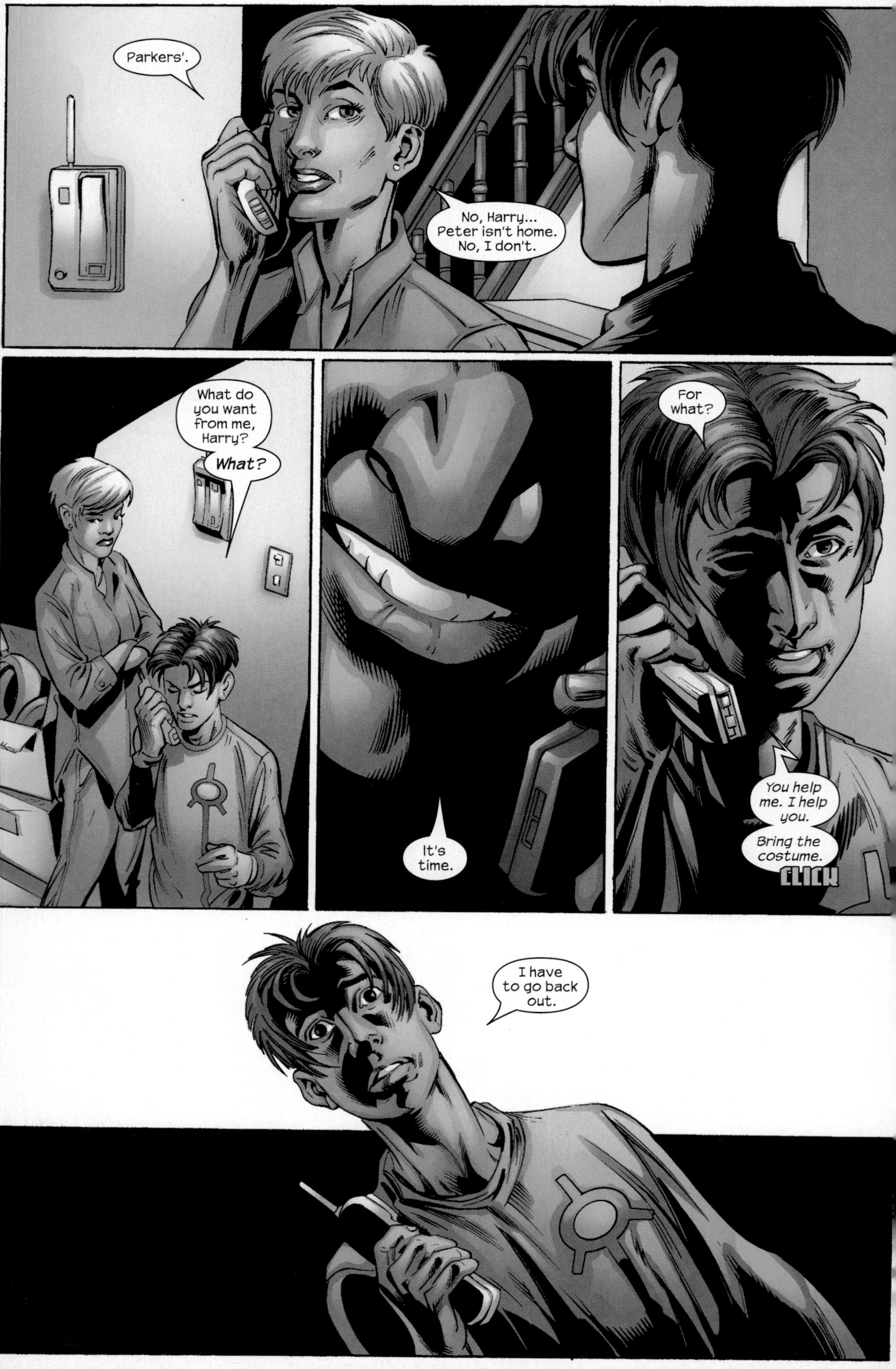
Parkers'.
No, Harry... Peter isn't home. No, I don't.
What do you want from me, Harry?
What?
It's time.
For what?
You help me. I help you.
Bring the costume.
CLICK
I have to go back out.

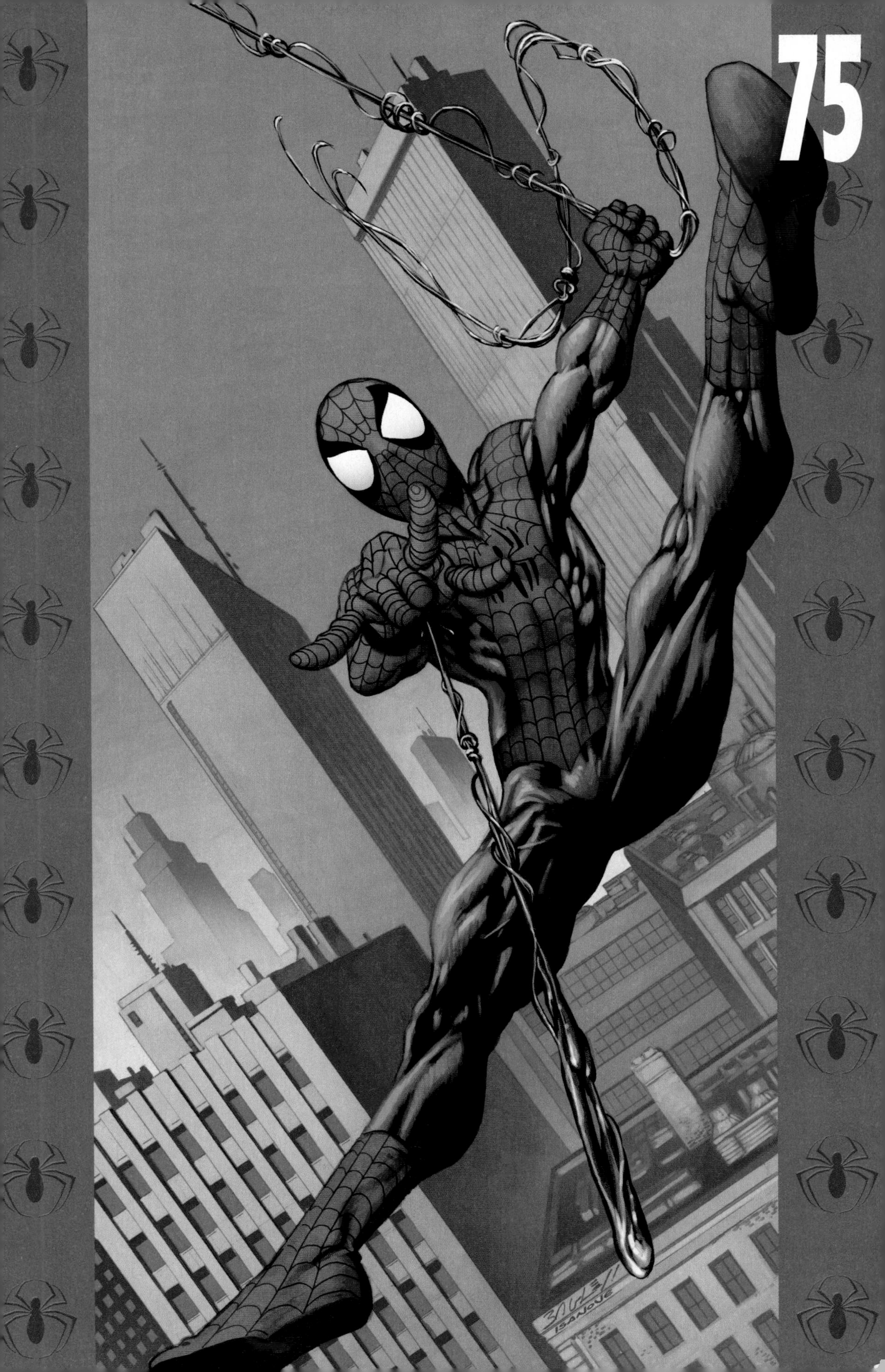
75

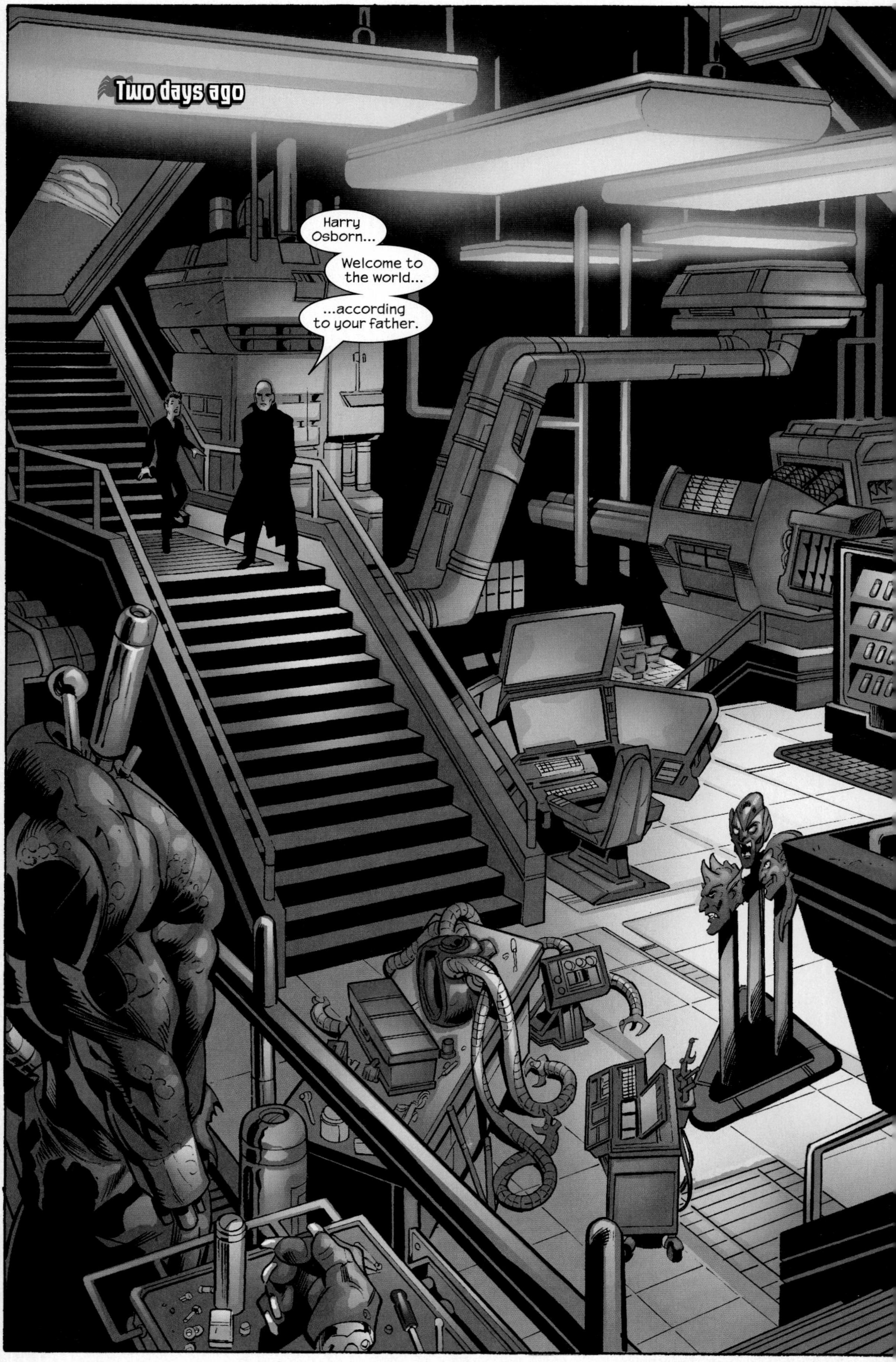
Two days ago
Harry Osborn...
Welcome to the world...
...according to your father.

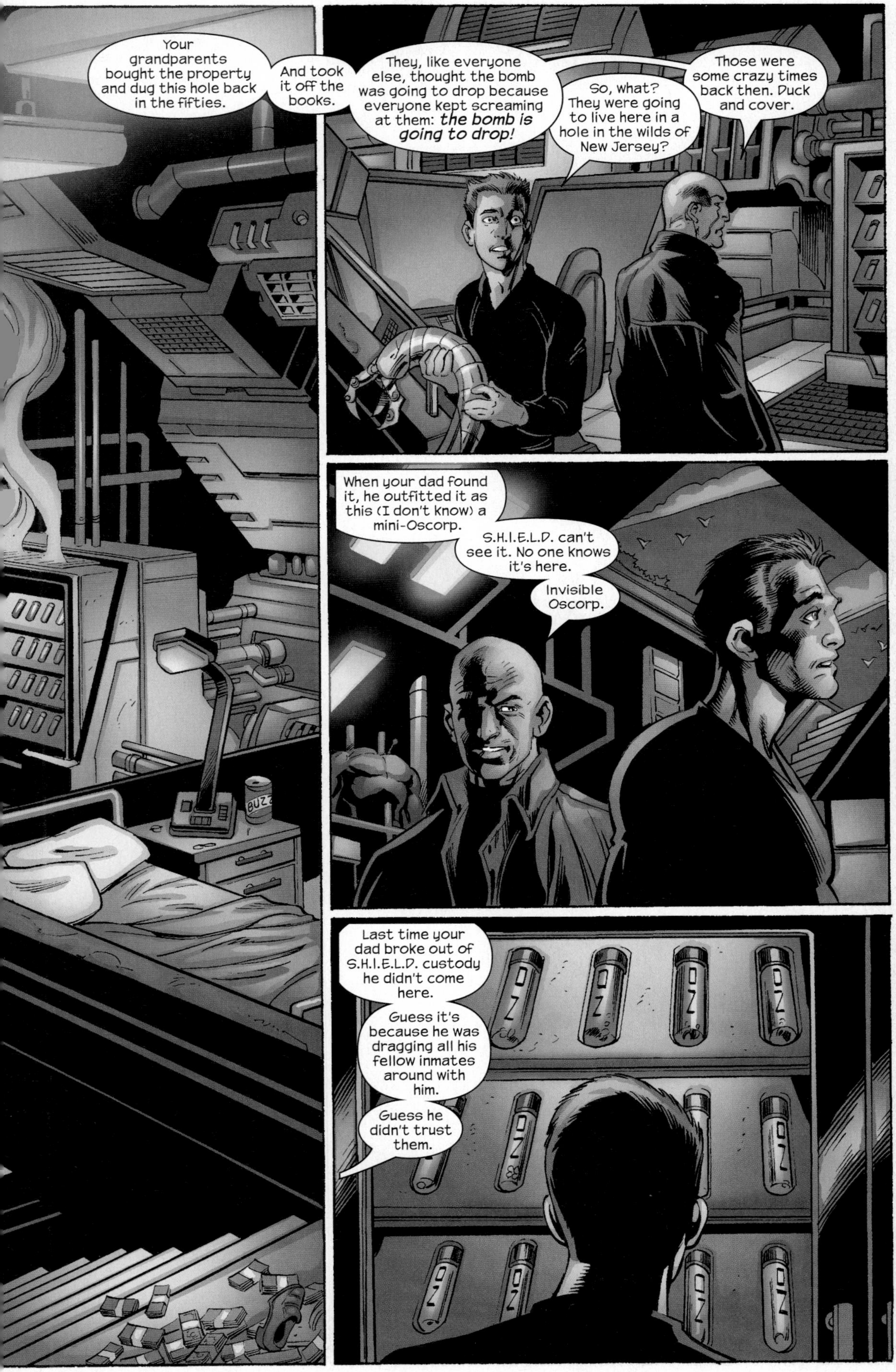
Your grandparents bought the property and dug this hole back in the fifties.
And took it off the books.
They, like everyone else, thought the bomb was going to drop because everyone kept screaming at them: *the bomb is going to drop!*
So, what? They were going to live here in a hole in the wilds of New Jersey?
Those were some crazy times back then. Duck and cover.
When your dad found it, he outfitted it as this (I don't know) a mini-Oscorp.
S.H.I.E.L.D. can't see it. No one knows it's here.
Invisible Oscorp.
Last time your dad broke out of S.H.I.E.L.D. custody he didn't come here.
Guess it's because he was dragging all his fellow inmates around with him.
Guess he didn't trust them.
BUZZ
OZ

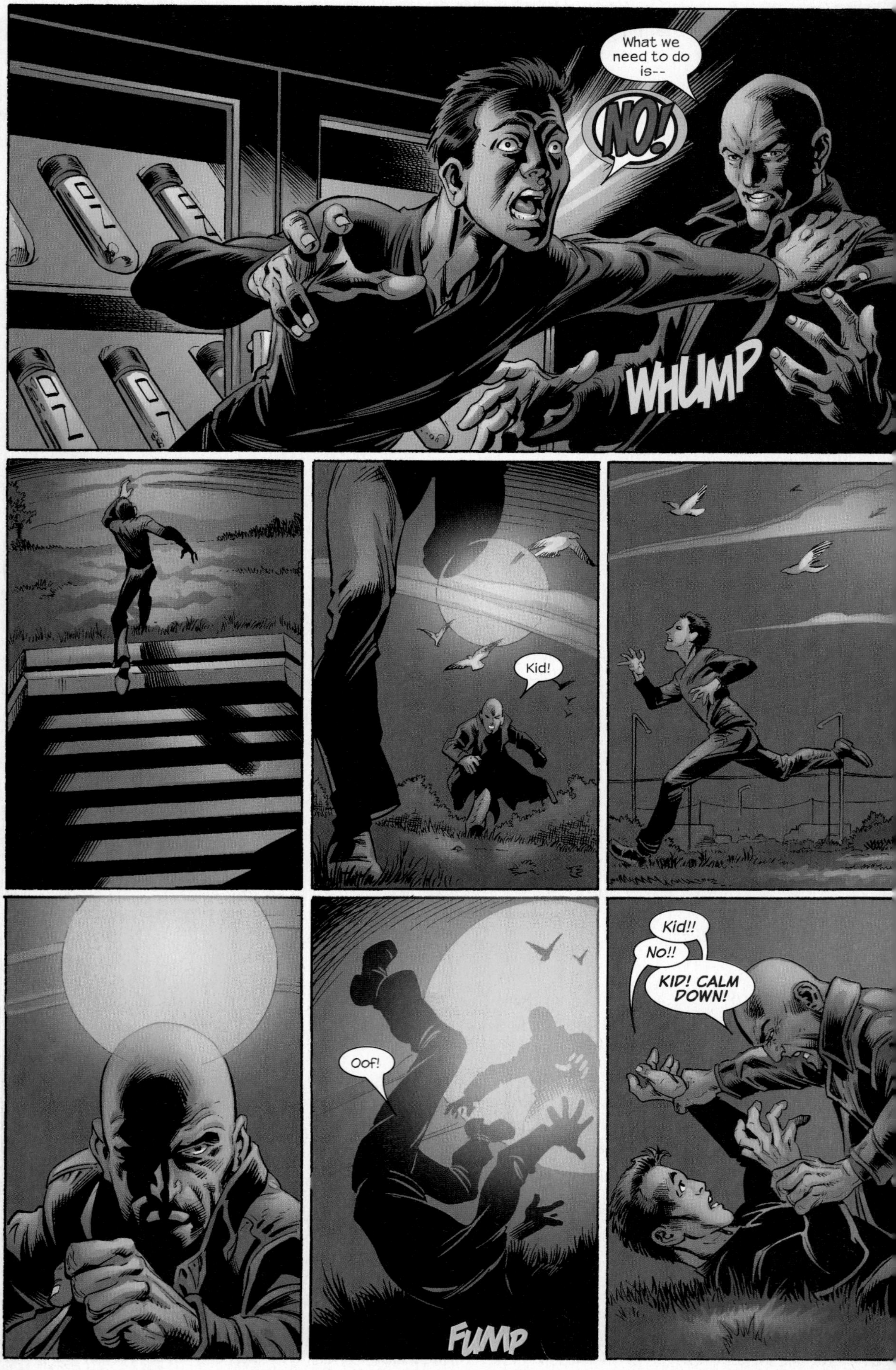
What we need to do is--
NO!
WHUMP
Kid!
Oof!
FUMP
Kid!!
No!!
KID! CALM DOWN!

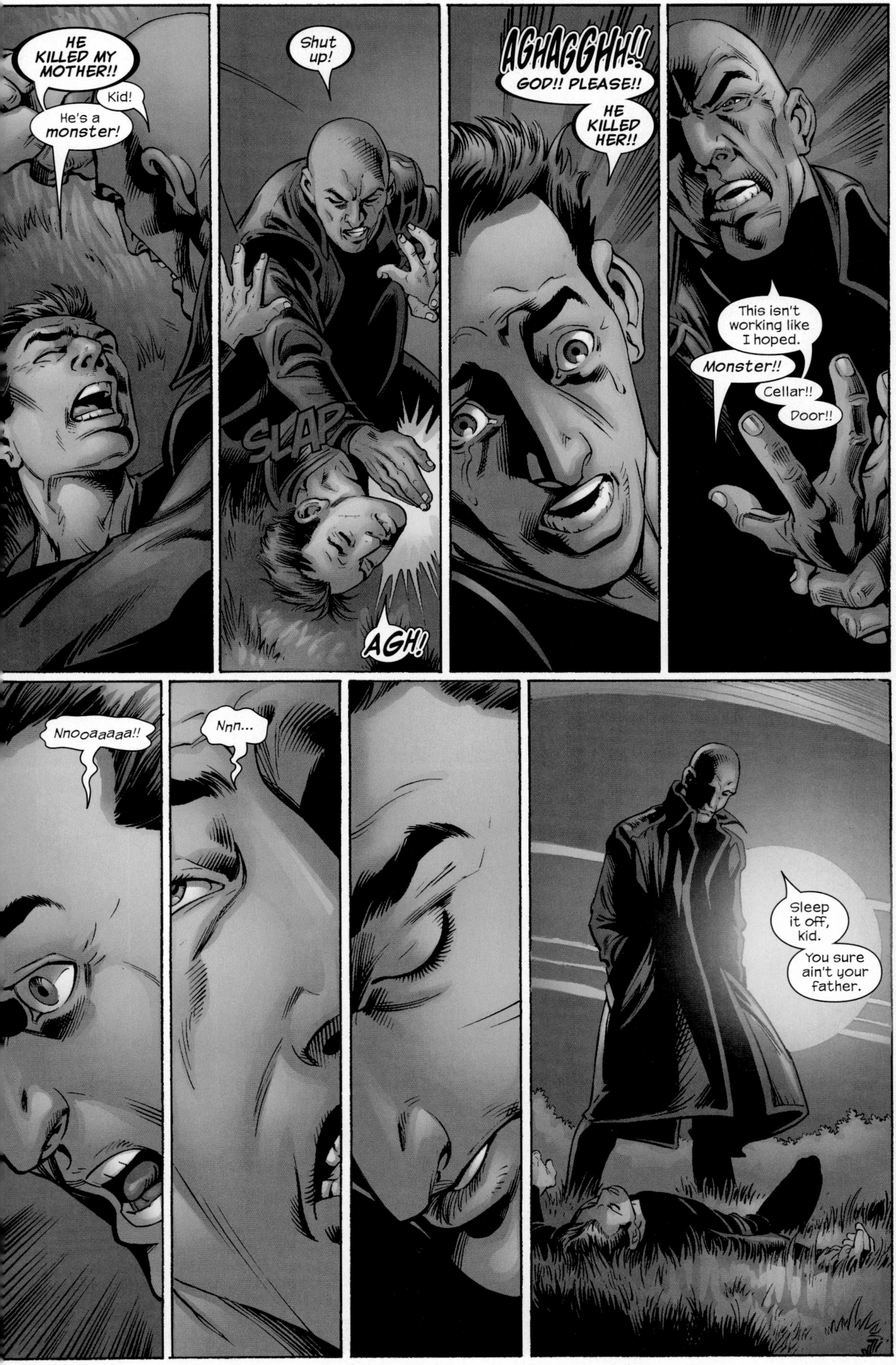
HE KILLED MY MOTHER!!
Kid!
He's a monster!
Shut up!
SLAP
AGH!
AGHAGGHH!!
GOD!! PLEASE!!
HE KILLED HER!!
This isn't working like I hoped.
Monster!!
Cellar!!
Door!!
Nnooaaaaa!!
Nnn...
Sleep it off, kid.
You sure ain't your father.

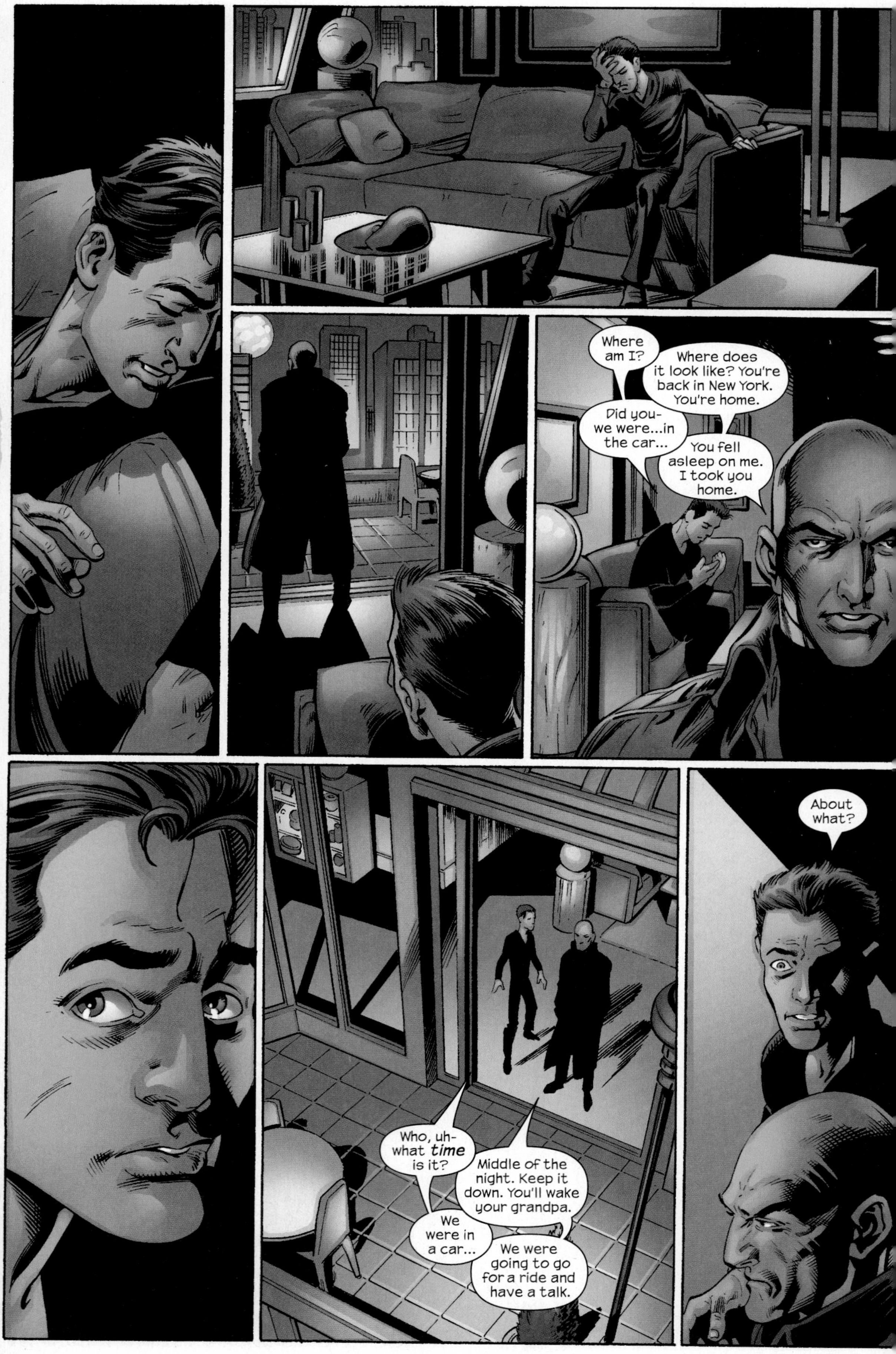
Where am I?
Where does it look like? You're back in New York. You're home.
Did you- we were...in the car...
You fell asleep on me. I took you home.
Who, uh- what *time* is it?
Middle of the night. Keep it down. You'll wake your grandpa.
We were in a car...
We were going to go for a ride and have a talk.
About what?

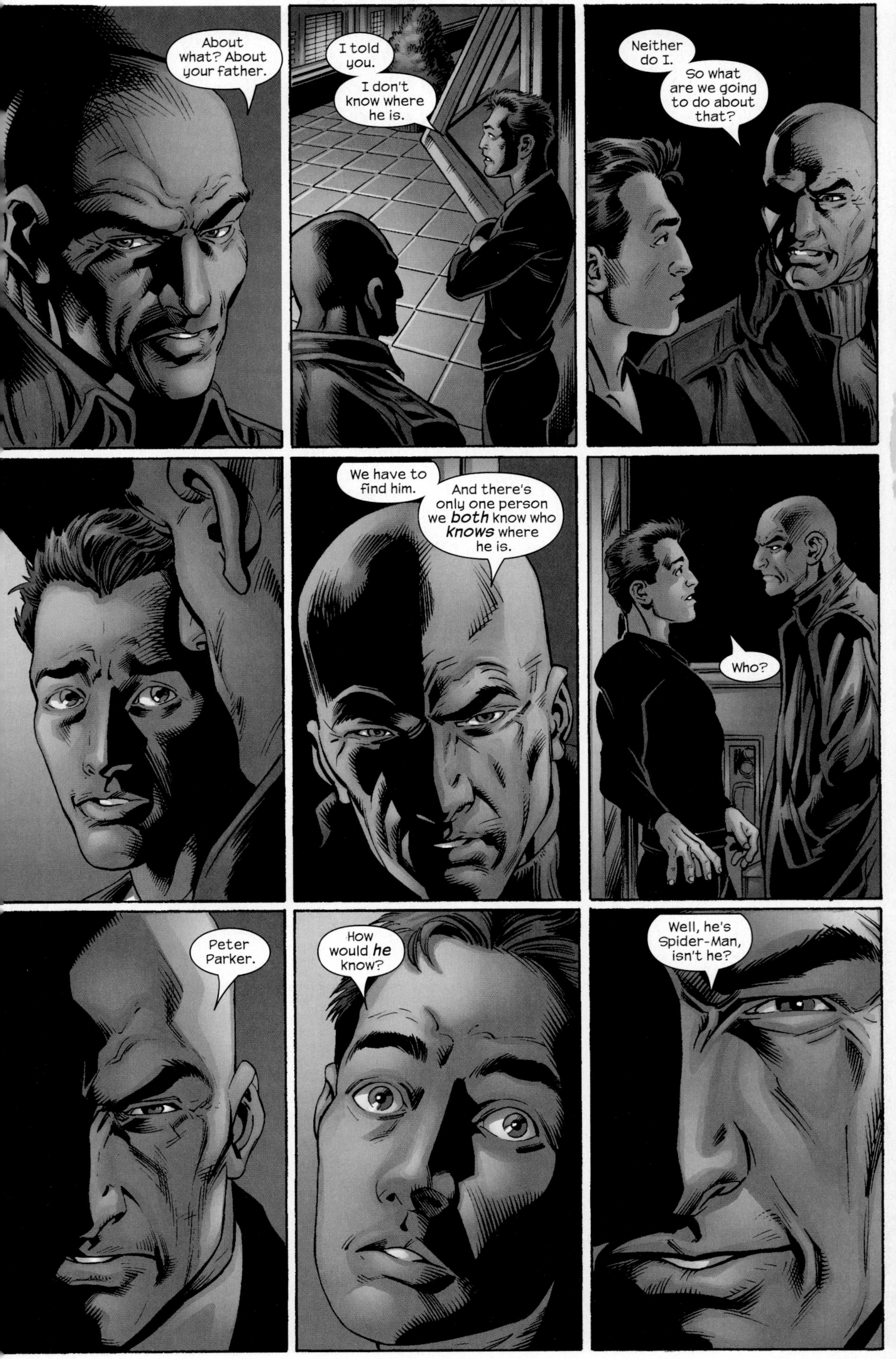
About what? About your father.
I told you.
I don't know where he is.
Neither do I.
So what are we going to do about that?
We have to find him.
And there's only one person we *both* know who *knows* where he is.
Who?
Peter Parker.
How would *he* know?
Well, he's Spider-Man, isn't he?

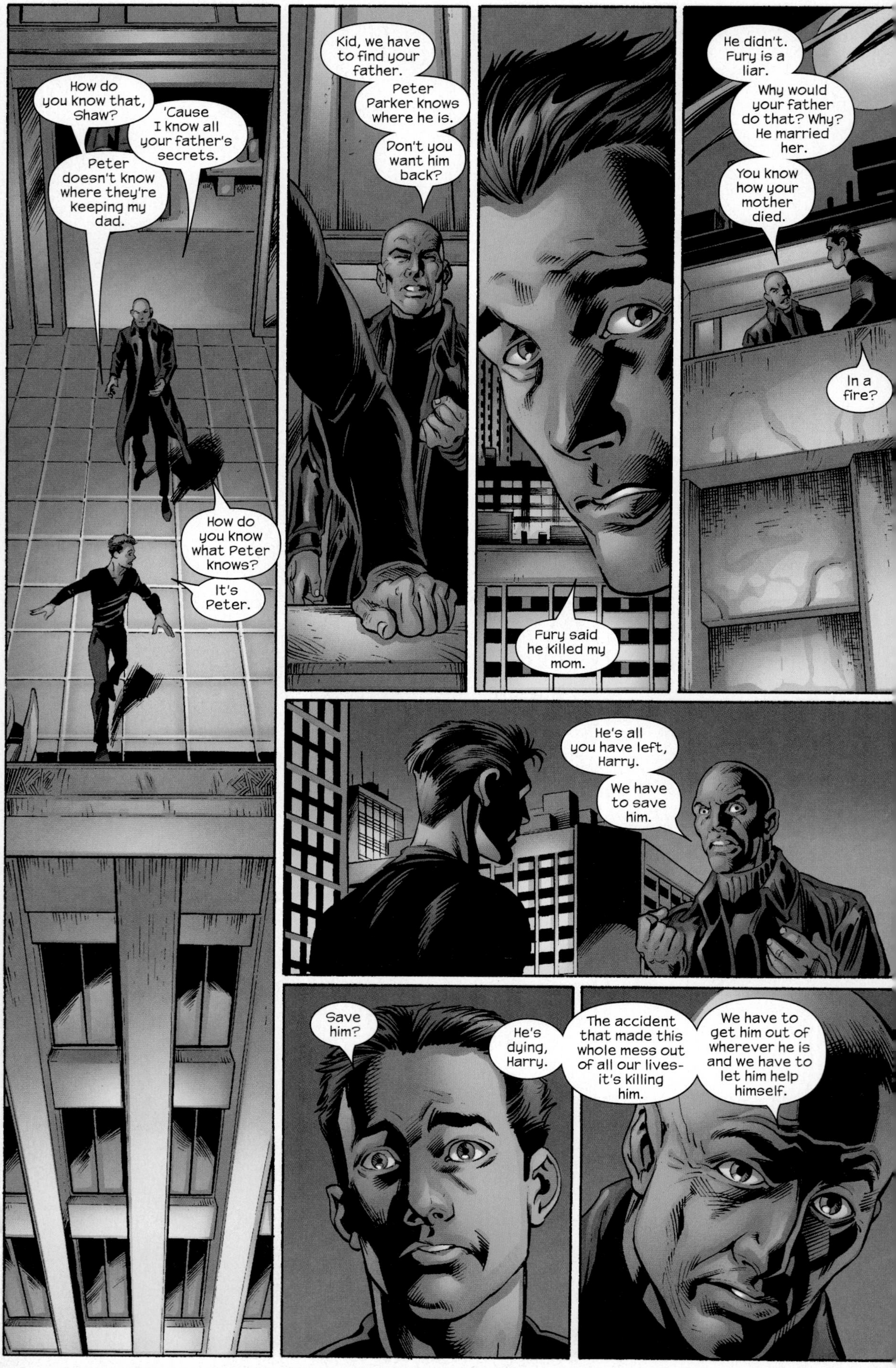
How do you know that, Shaw?
'Cause I know all your father's secrets.
Peter doesn't know where they're keeping my dad.
How do you know what Peter knows?
It's Peter.
Kid, we have to find your father.
Peter Parker knows where he is.
Don't you want him back?
Fury said he killed my mom.
He didn't. Fury is a liar.
Why would your father do that? Why? He married her.
You know how your mother died.
In a fire?
He's all you have left, Harry.
We have to save him.
Save him?
He's dying, Harry.
The accident that made this whole mess out of all our lives- it's killing him.
We have to get him out of wherever he is and we have to let him help himself.

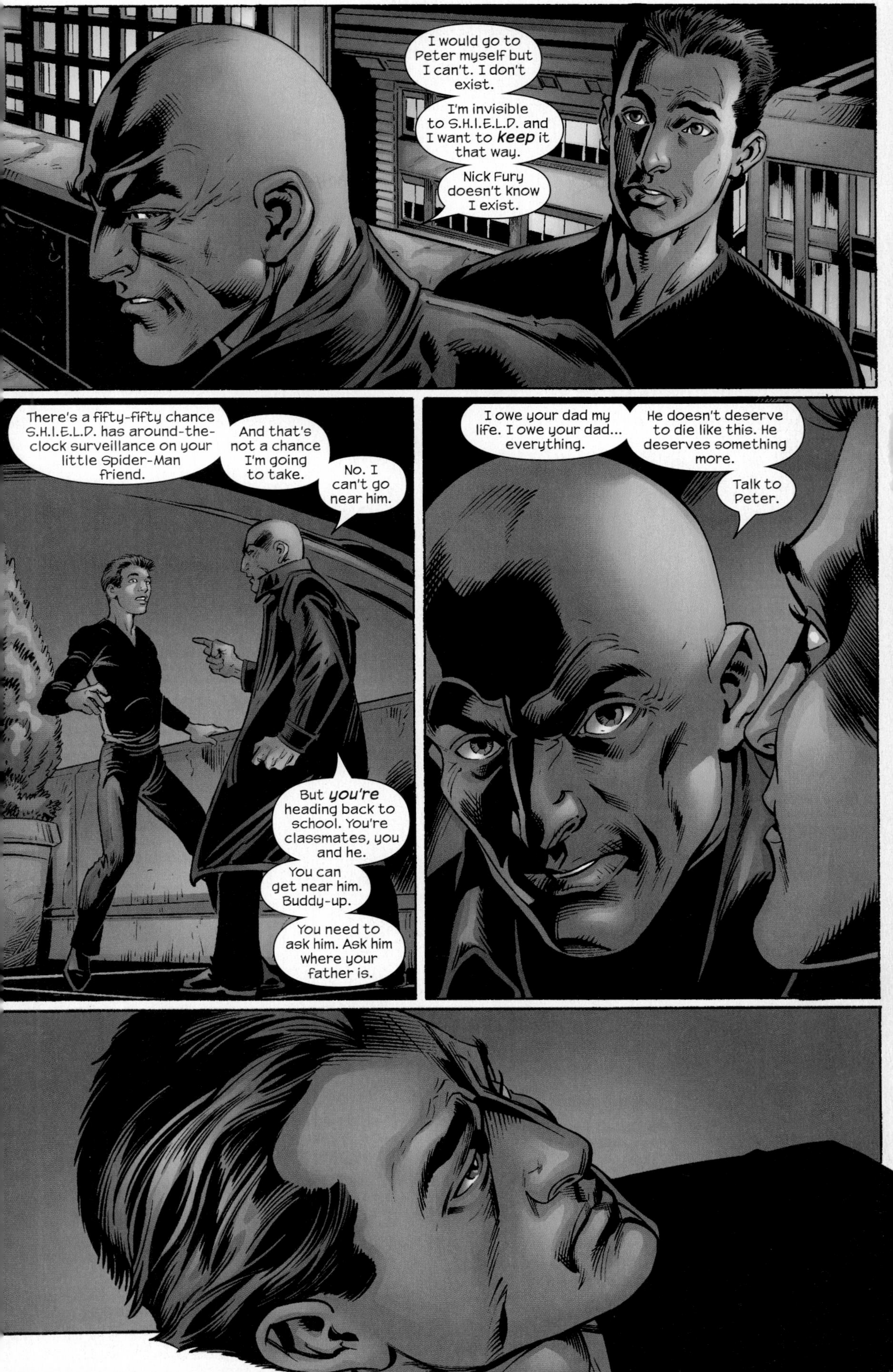
I would go to Peter myself but I can't. I don't exist.
I'm invisible to S.H.I.E.L.D. and I want to *keep* it that way.
Nick Fury doesn't know I exist.
There's a fifty-fifty chance S.H.I.E.L.D. has around-the-clock surveillance on your little Spider-Man friend.
And that's not a chance I'm going to take.
No. I can't go near him.
But *you're* heading back to school. You're classmates, you and he.
You can get near him. Buddy-up.
You need to ask him. Ask him where your father is.
I owe your dad my life. I owe your dad... everything.
He doesn't deserve to die like this. He deserves something more.
Talk to Peter.

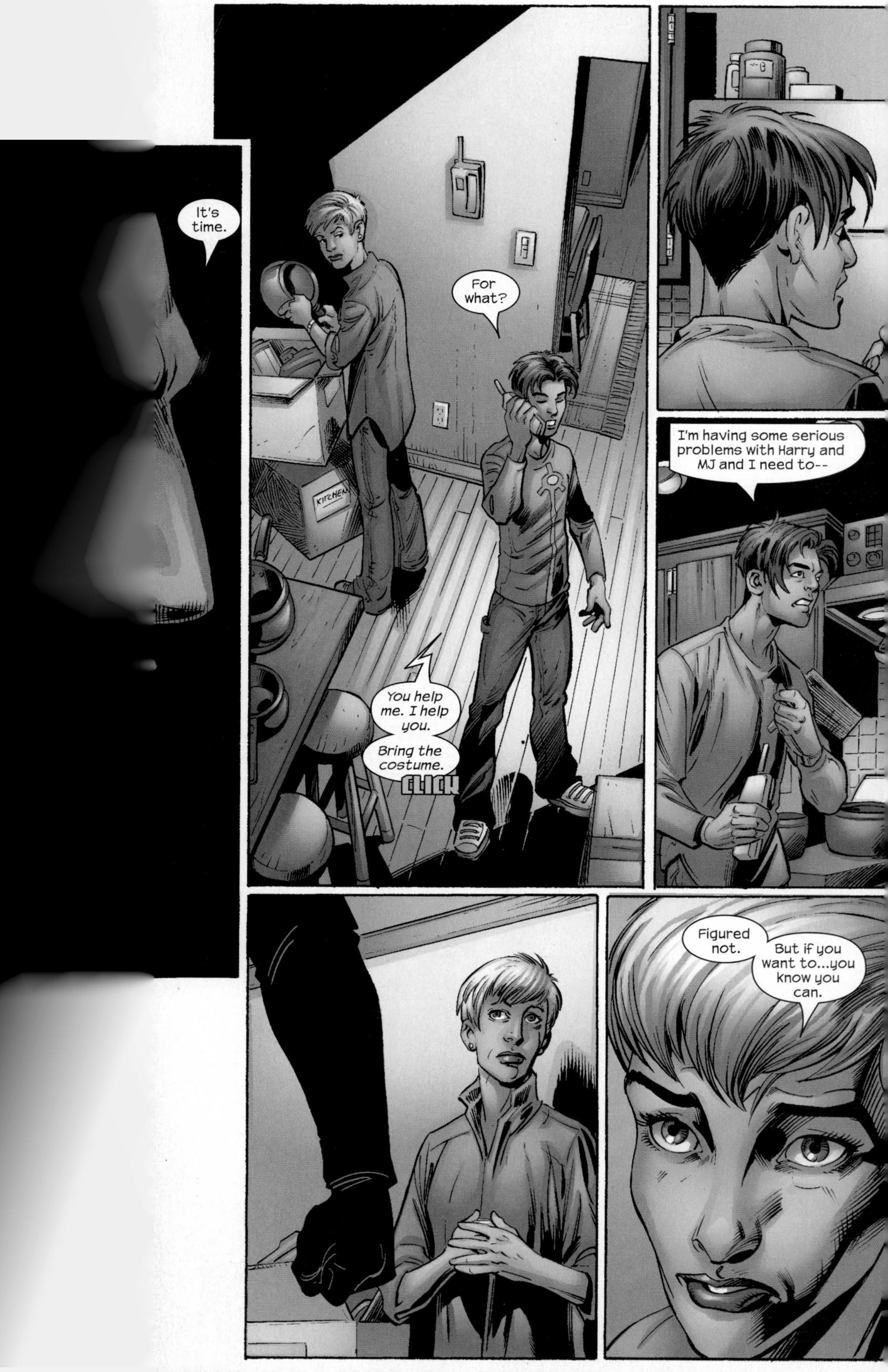
It's time.
For what?
You help me. I help you.
Bring the costume.
CLICK
I'm having some serious problems with Harry and MJ and I need to--
Figured not.
But if you want to...you know you can.

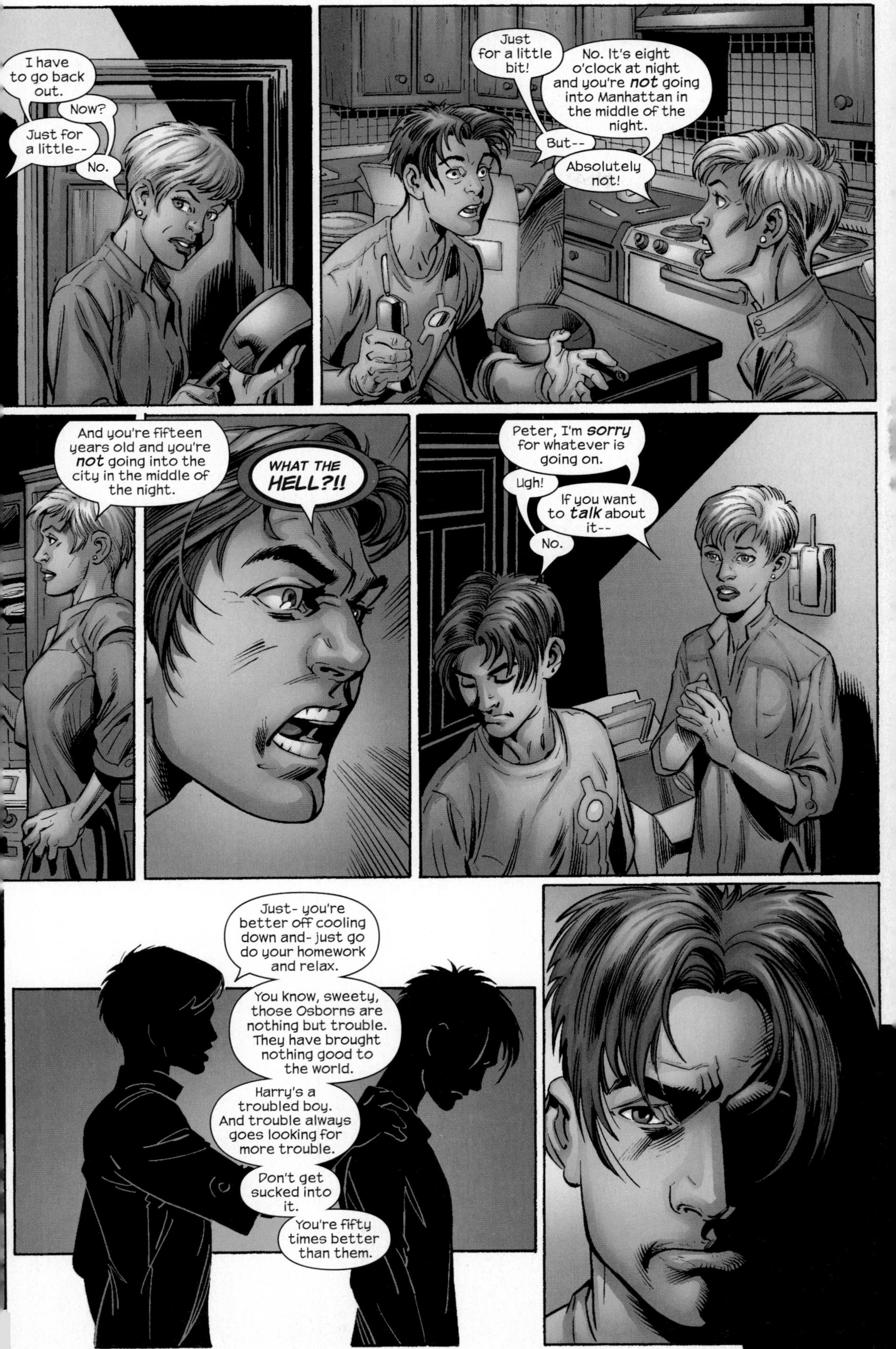

I have to go back out.
Now?
Just for a little--
No.
Just for a little bit!
No. It's eight o'clock at night and you're *not* going into Manhattan in the middle of the night.
But--
Absolutely not!
And you're fifteen years old and you're *not* going into the city in the middle of the night.
WHAT THE HELL?!!
Peter, I'm *sorry* for whatever is going on.
Ugh!
If you want to *talk* about it--
No.
Just- you're better off cooling down and- just go do your homework and relax.
You know, sweety, those Osborns are nothing but trouble. They have brought nothing good to the world.
Harry's a troubled boy. And trouble always goes looking for more trouble.
Don't get sucked into it.
You're fifty times better than them.

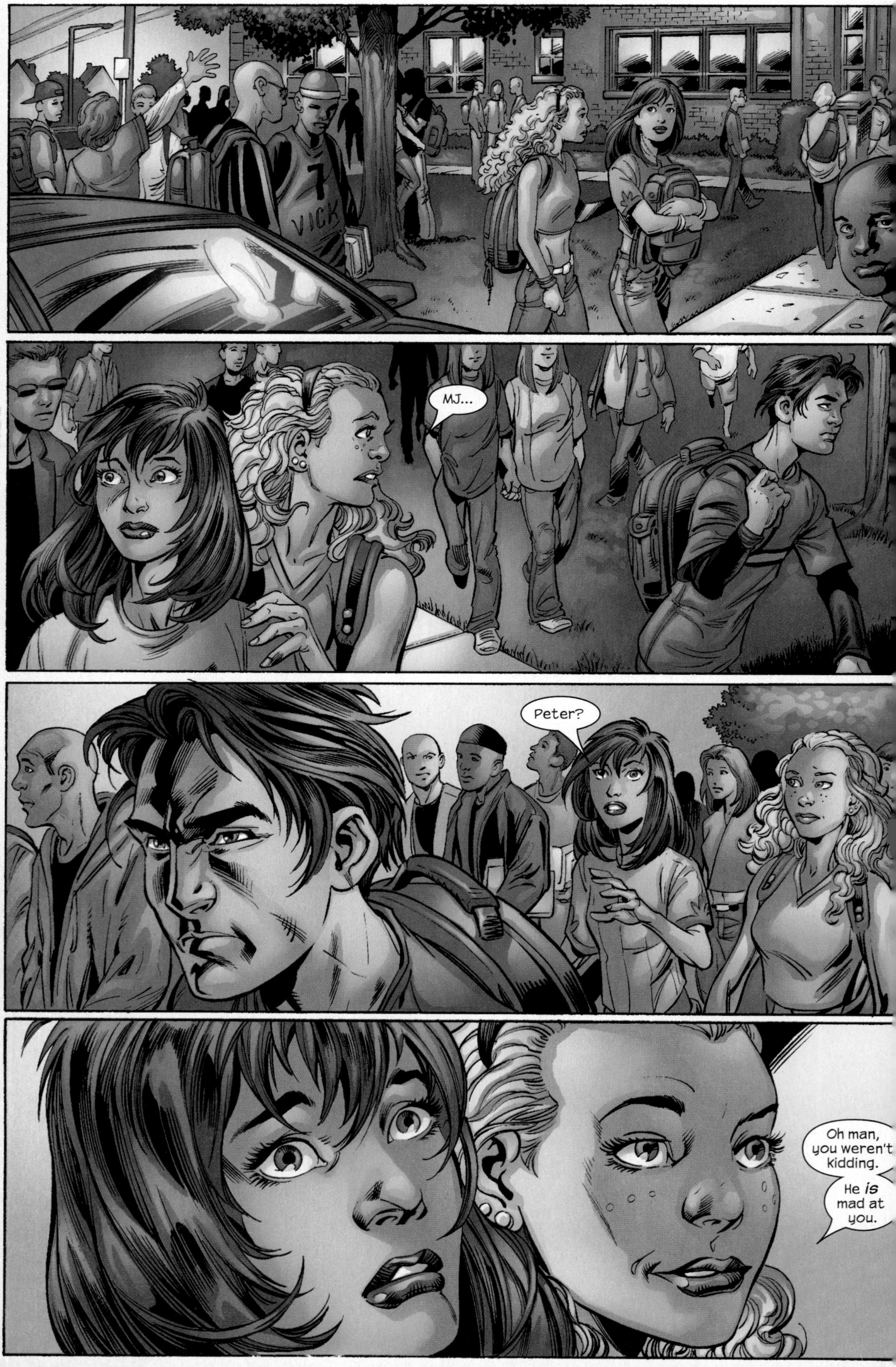

7
VICK
MJ...
Peter?
Oh man, you weren't kidding.
He *is* mad at you.

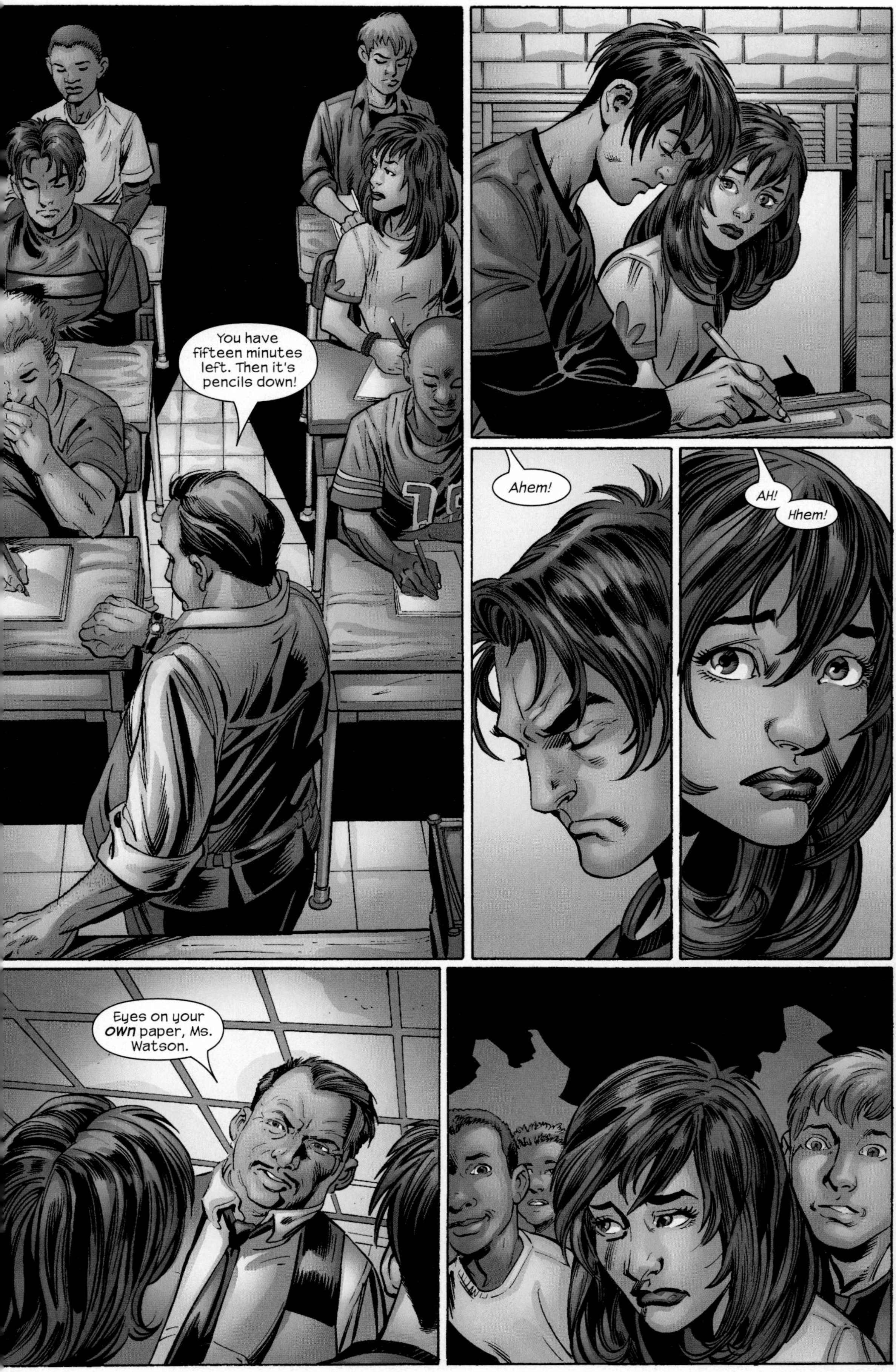
You have fifteen minutes left. Then it's pencils down!
Ahem!
AH!
Hhem!
Eyes on your OWN paper, Ms. Watson.

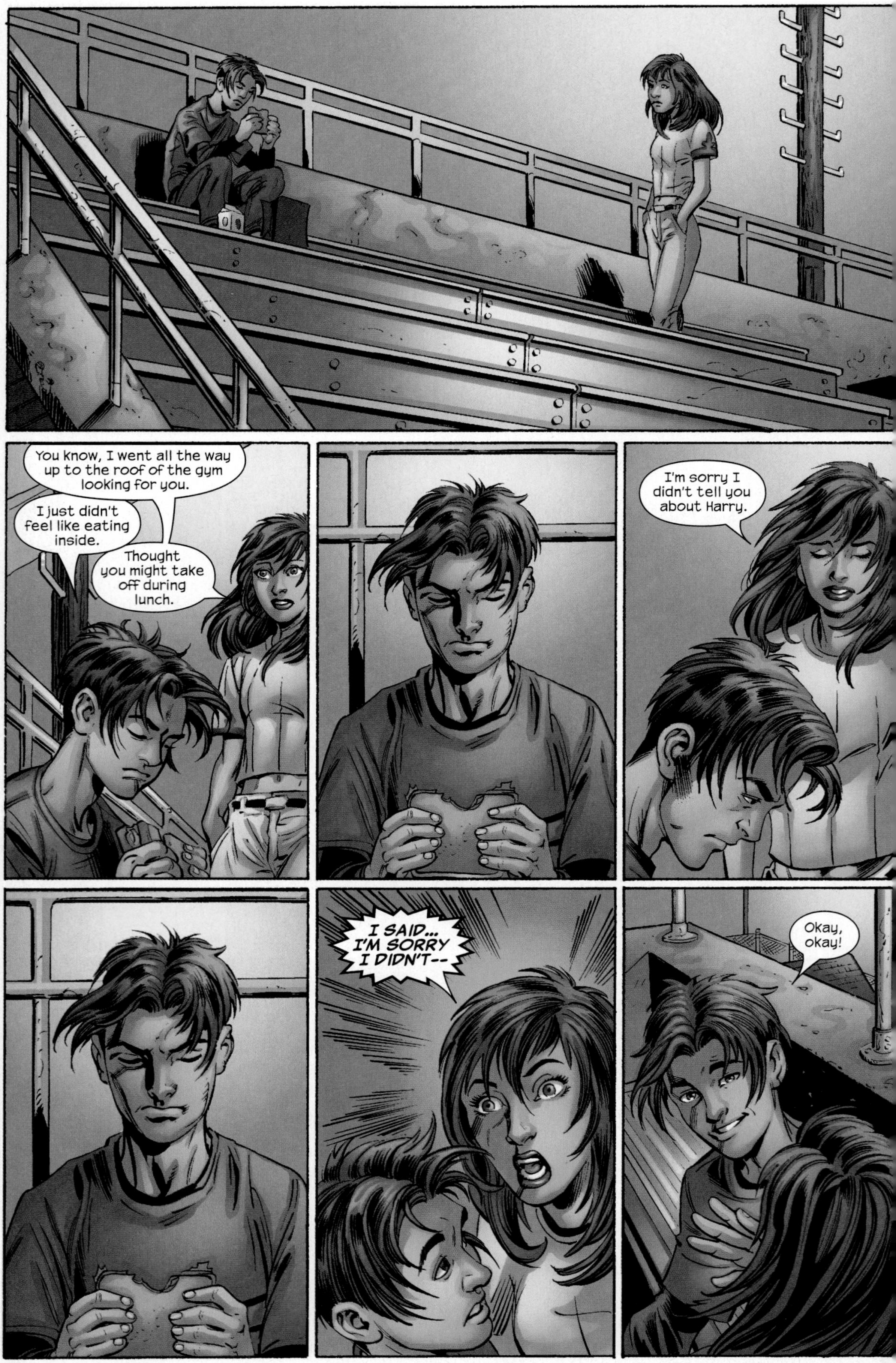
You know, I went all the way up to the roof of the gym looking for you.
I just didn't feel like eating inside.
Thought you might take off during lunch.
I'm sorry I didn't tell you about Harry.
I SAID... I'M SORRY I DIDN'T--
Okay, okay!

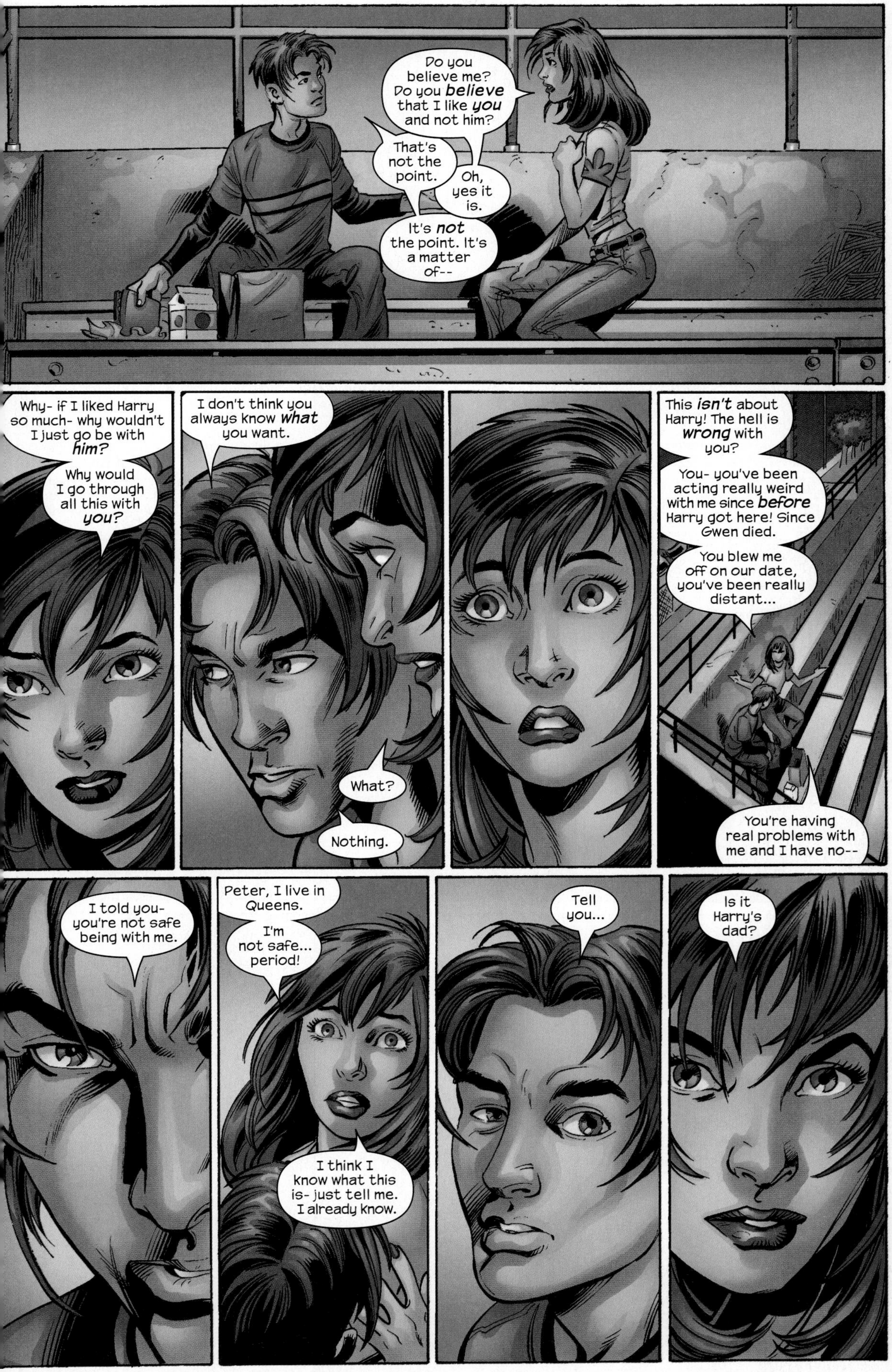

Do you believe me? Do you **believe** that I like ***you*** and not him?
That's not the point.
Oh, yes it is.
It's ***not*** the point. It's a matter of--
Why- if I liked Harry so much- why wouldn't I just go be with ***him?***
Why would I go through all this with ***you?***
I don't think you always know ***what*** you want.
What?
Nothing.
This ***isn't*** about Harry! The hell is ***wrong*** with you?
You- you've been acting really weird with me since ***before*** Harry got here! Since Gwen died.
You blew me off on our date, you've been really distant...
You're having real problems with me and I have no--
I told you- you're not safe being with me.
Peter, I live in Queens.
I'm not safe... period!
I think I know what this is- just tell me. I already know.
Tell you...
Is it Harry's dad?

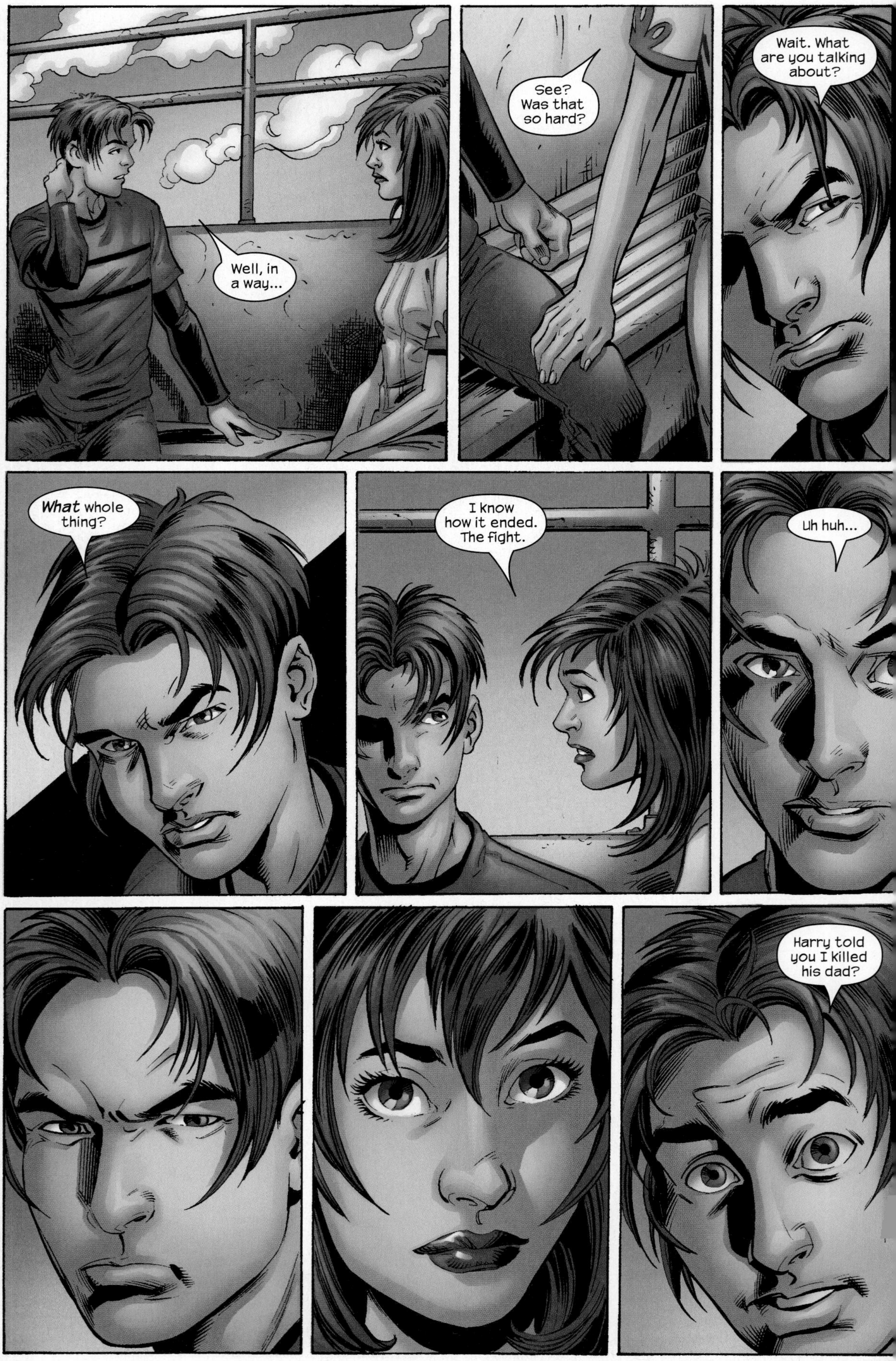
Well, in a way...
See? Was that so hard?
Wait. What are you talking about?
What whole thing?
I know how it ended. The fight.
Uh huh...
Harry told you I killed his dad?

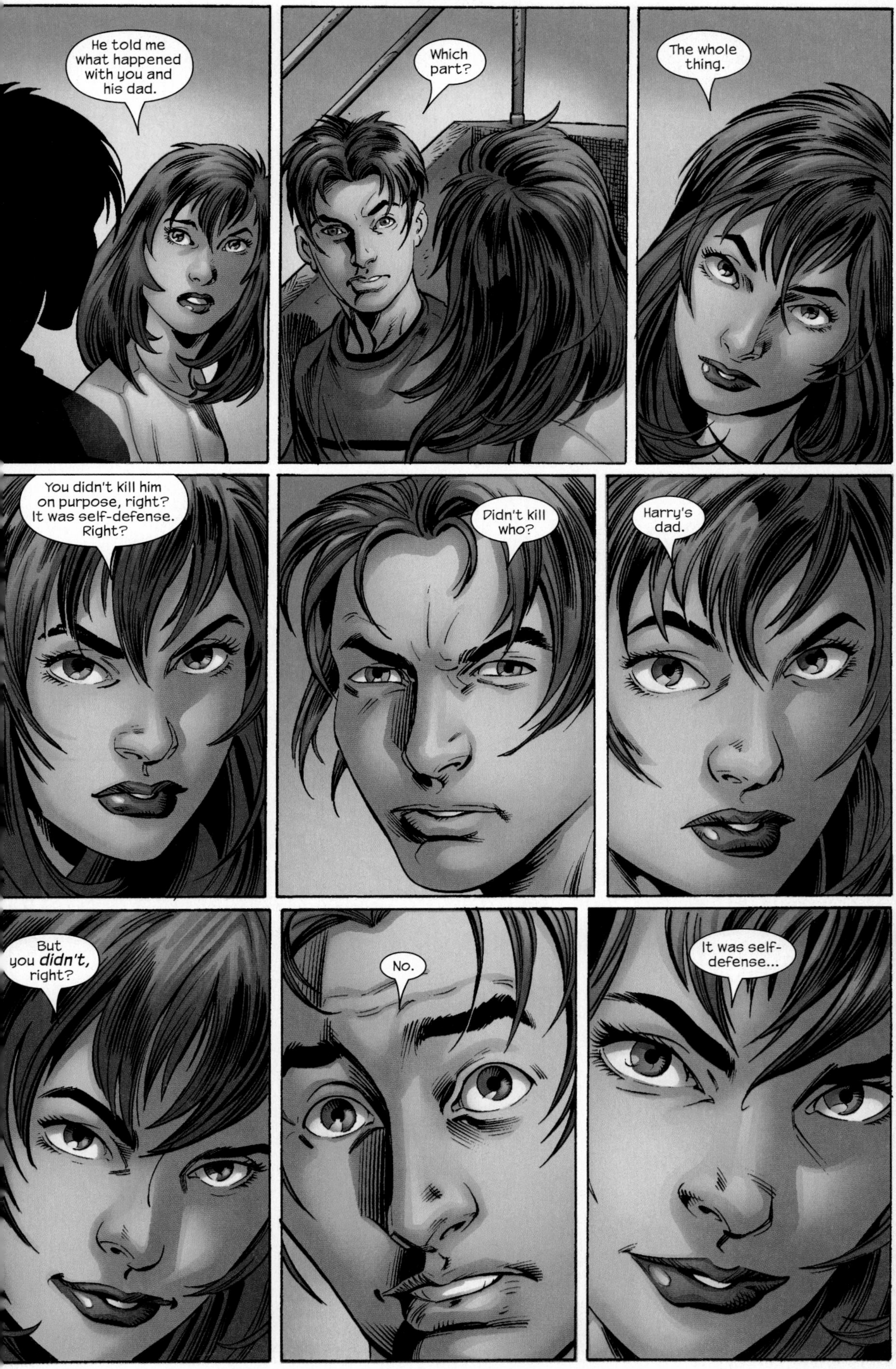
He told me what happened with you and his dad.
Which part?
The whole thing.
You didn't kill him on purpose, right? It was self-defense. Right?
Didn't kill who?
Harry's dad.
But you *didn't,* right?
No.
It was self-defense...

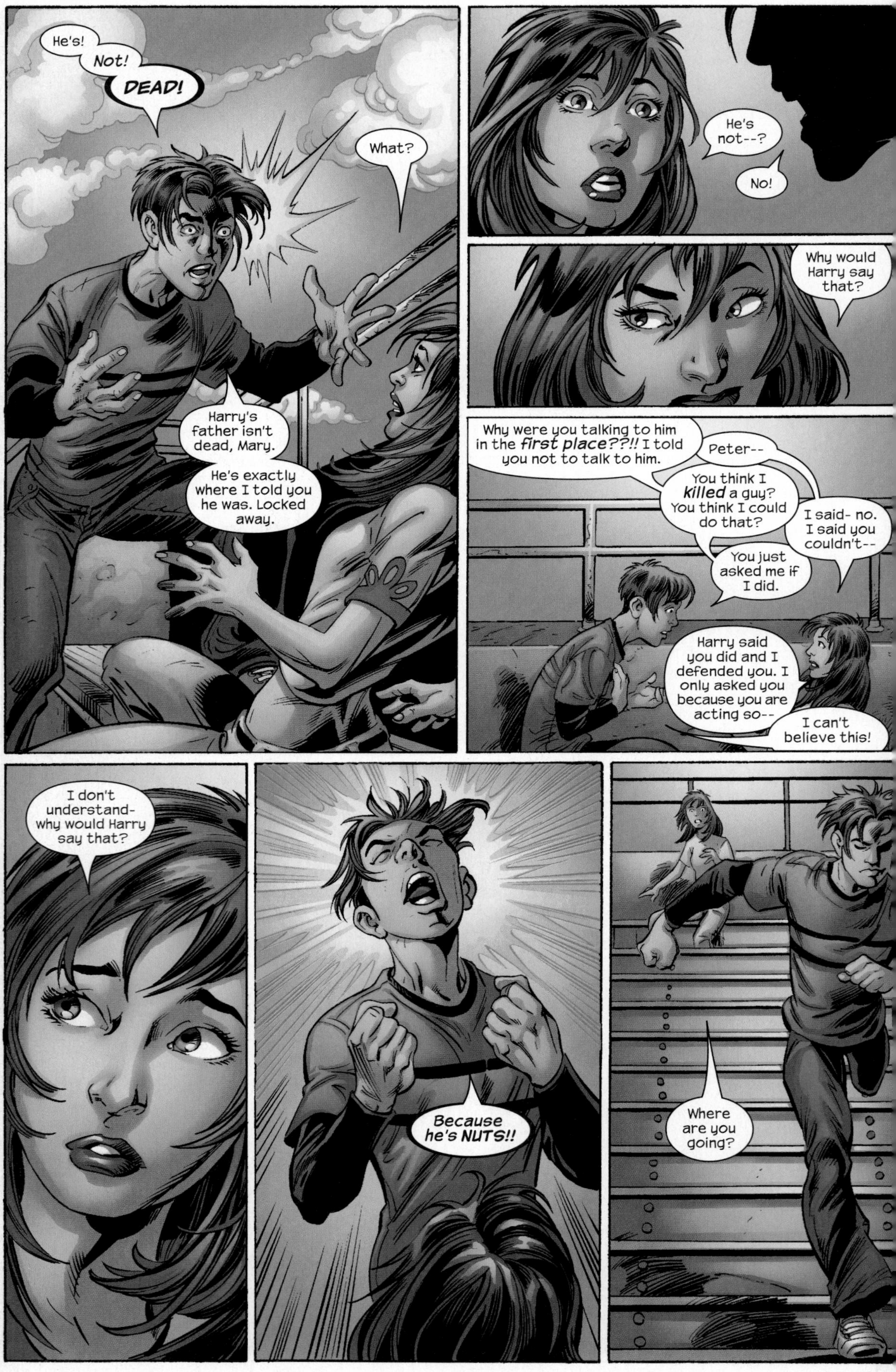
He's!
Not!
DEAD!
What?
Harry's father isn't dead, Mary.
He's exactly where I told you he was. Locked away.
He's not--?
No!
Why would Harry say that?
Why were you talking to him in the first place??!! I told you not to talk to him.
Peter--
You think I killed a guy? You think I could do that?
I said- no. I said you couldn't--
You just asked me if I did.
Harry said you did and I defended you. I only asked you because you are acting so--
I can't believe this!
I don't understand- why would Harry say that?
Because he's NUTS!!
Where are you going?

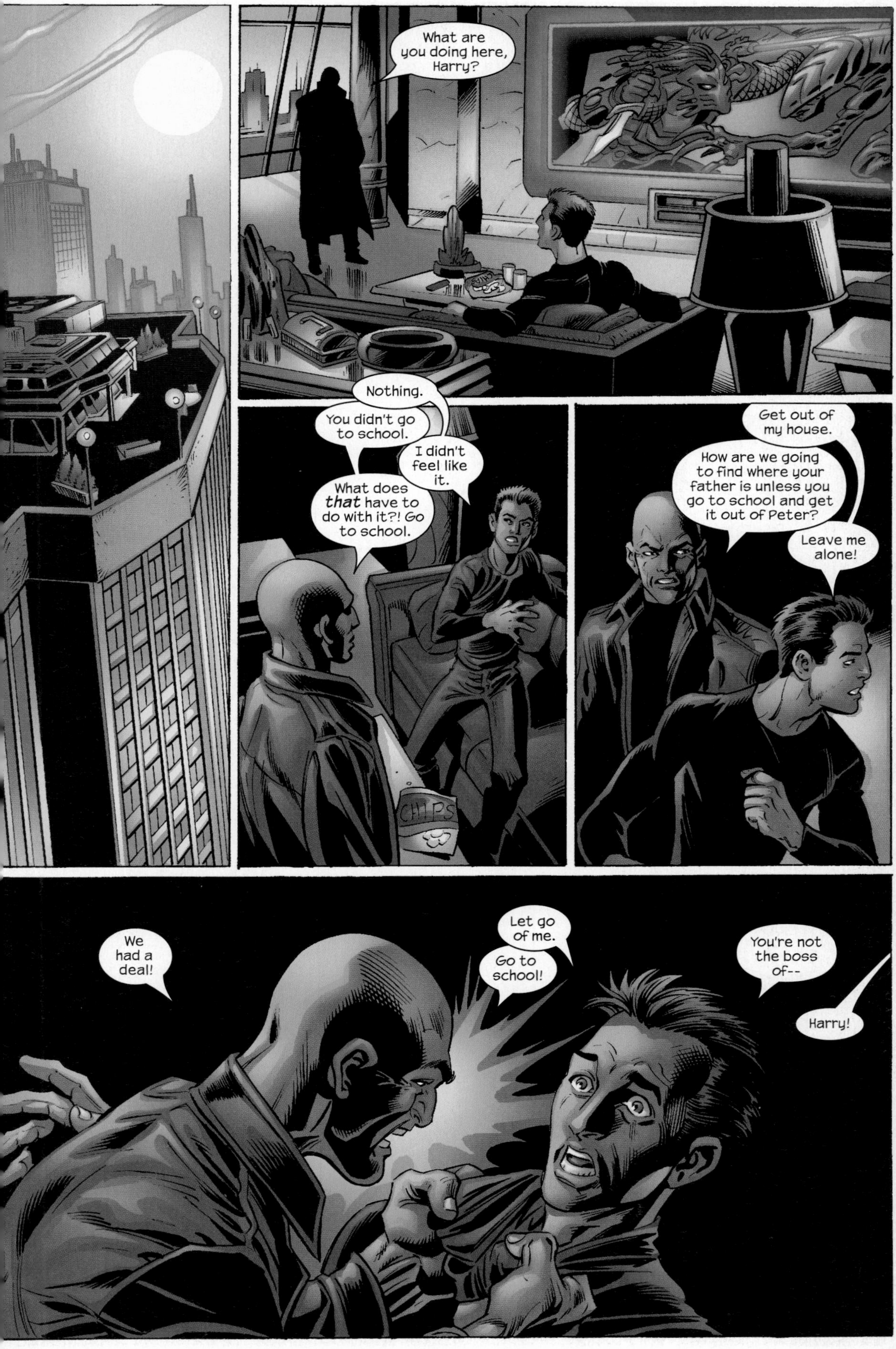
What are you doing here, Harry?
Nothing.
You didn't go to school.
I didn't feel like it.
What does *that* have to do with it?! Go to school.
CHIPS
Get out of my house.
How are we going to find where your father is unless you go to school and get it out of Peter?
Leave me alone!
We had a deal!
Let go of me.
Go to school!
You're not the boss of--
Harry!

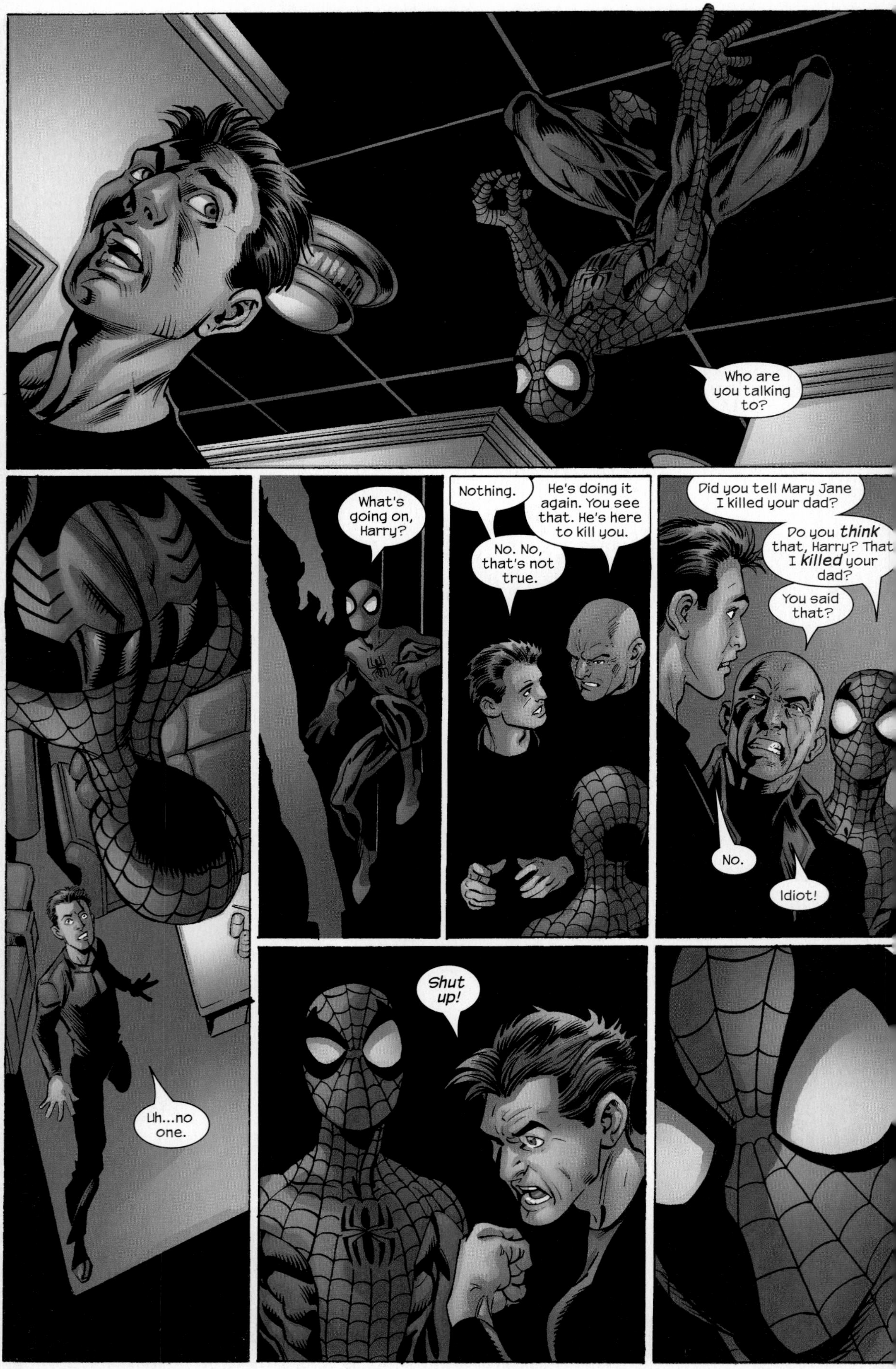
Who are you talking to?
Uh...no one.
What's going on, Harry?
Nothing.
He's doing it again. You see that. He's here to kill you.
No. No, that's not true.
Did you tell Mary Jane I killed your dad?
Do you think that, Harry? That I killed your dad?
You said that?
No.
Idiot!
Shut up!

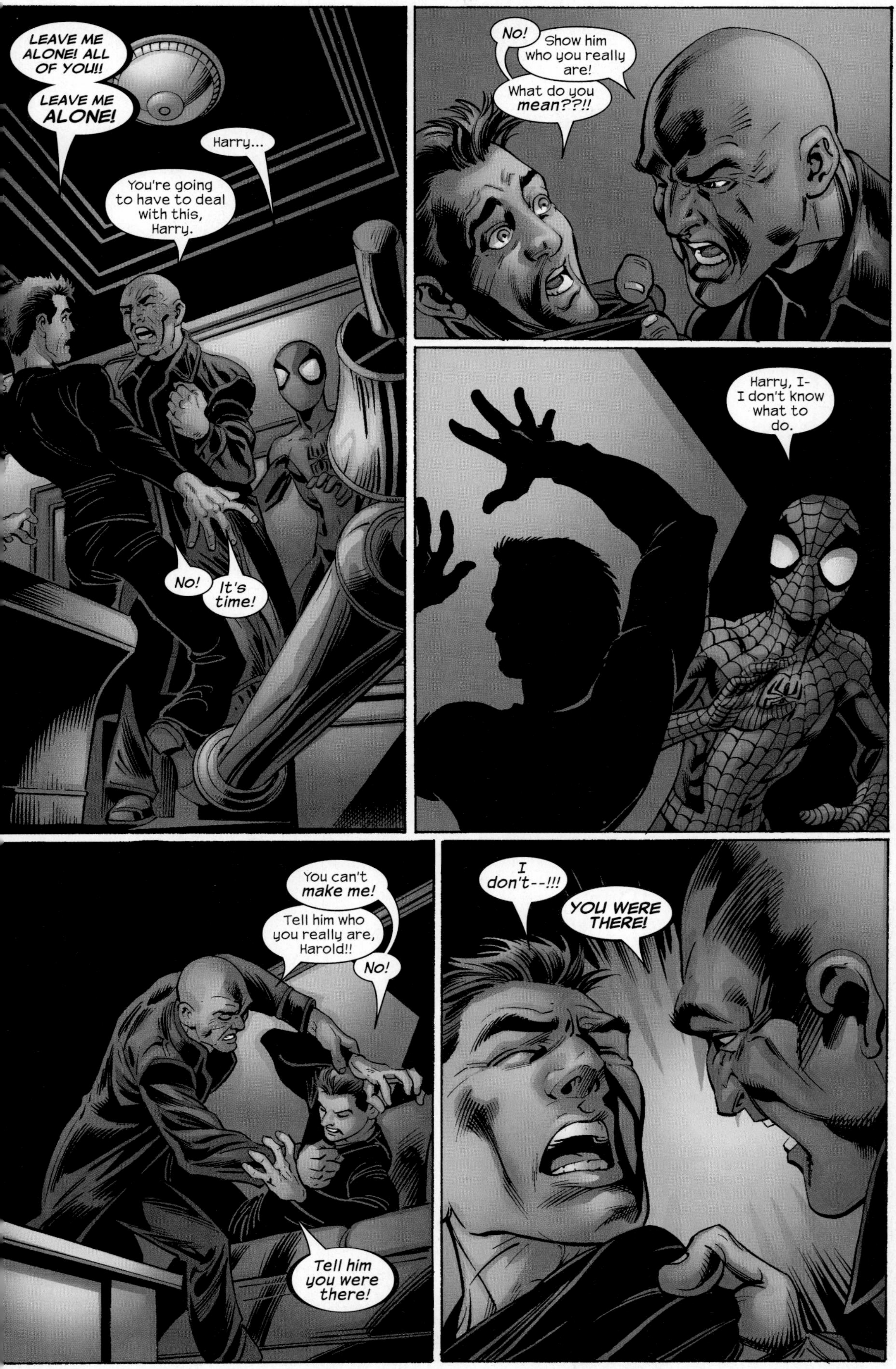
LEAVE ME ALONE! ALL OF YOU!!
LEAVE ME ALONE!
Harry...
You're going to have to deal with this, Harry.
No!
It's time!
No!
Show him who you really are!
What do you mean??!!
Harry, I- I don't know what to do.
You can't make me!
Tell him who you really are, Harold!!
No!
Tell him you were there!
I don't--!!!
YOU WERE THERE!

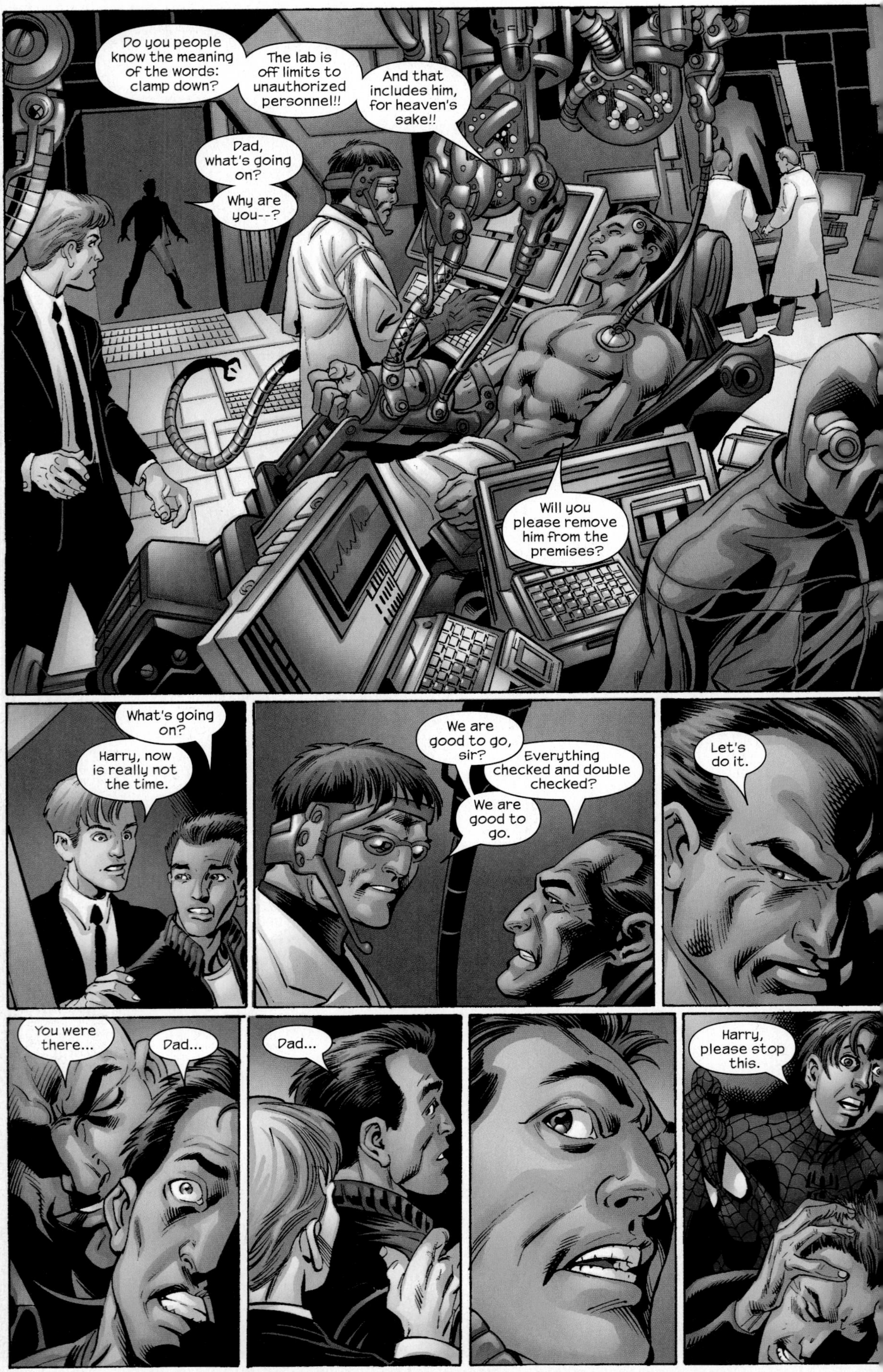
Do you people know the meaning of the words: clamp down?
The lab is off limits to unauthorized personnel!!
And that includes him, for heaven's sake!!
Dad, what's going on?
Why are you--?
Will you please remove him from the premises?
What's going on?
Harry, now is really not the time.
We are good to go, sir?
Everything checked and double checked?
We are good to go.
Let's do it.
You were there...
Dad...
Dad...
Harry, please stop this.

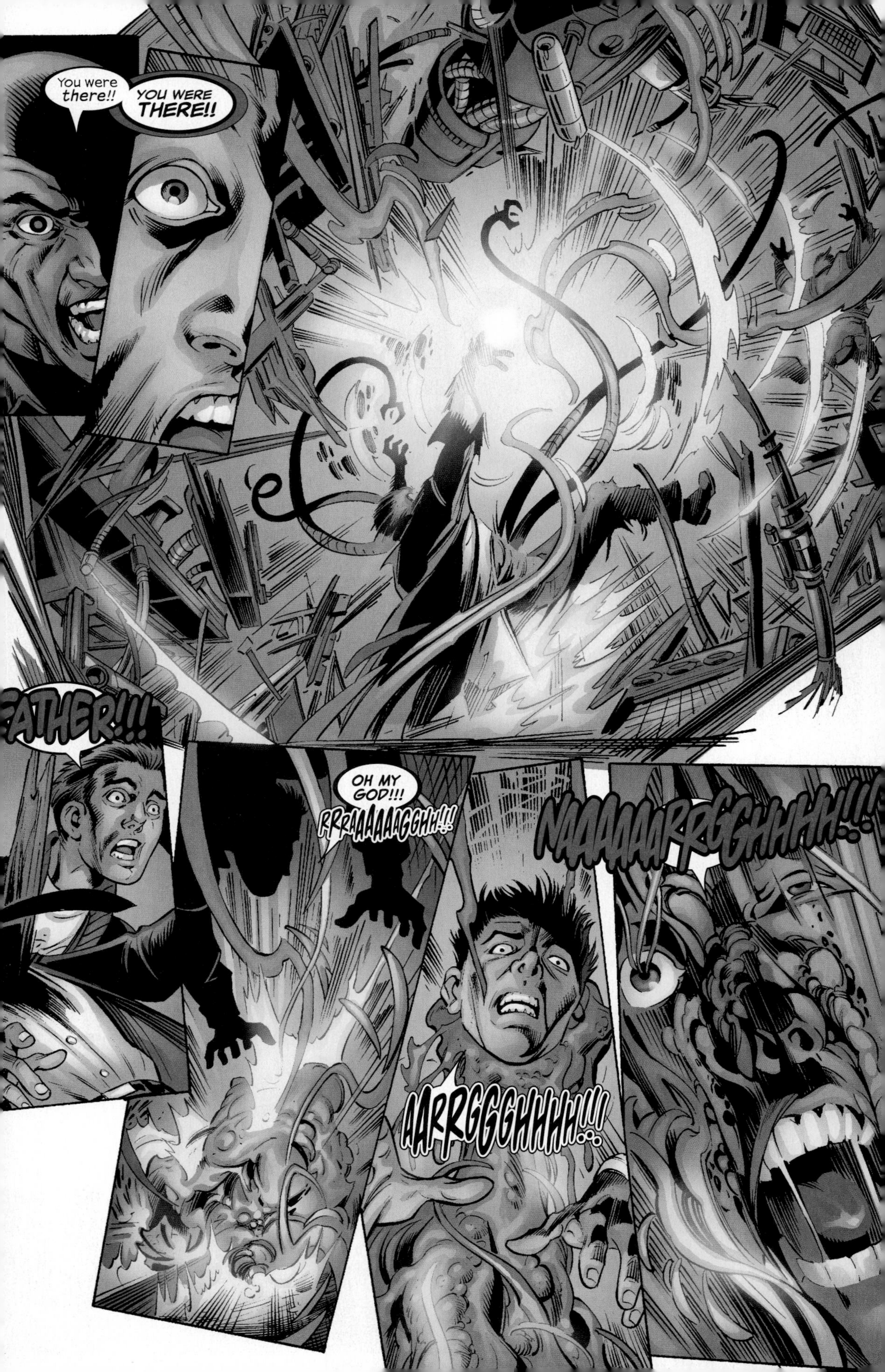
You were there!!
YOU WERE THERE!!
FATHER!!!
OH MY GOD!!!
RRRAAAAAAGGHH!!!
NAAAAAARRGGHHHH!!!
AARRGGGHHHH!!!

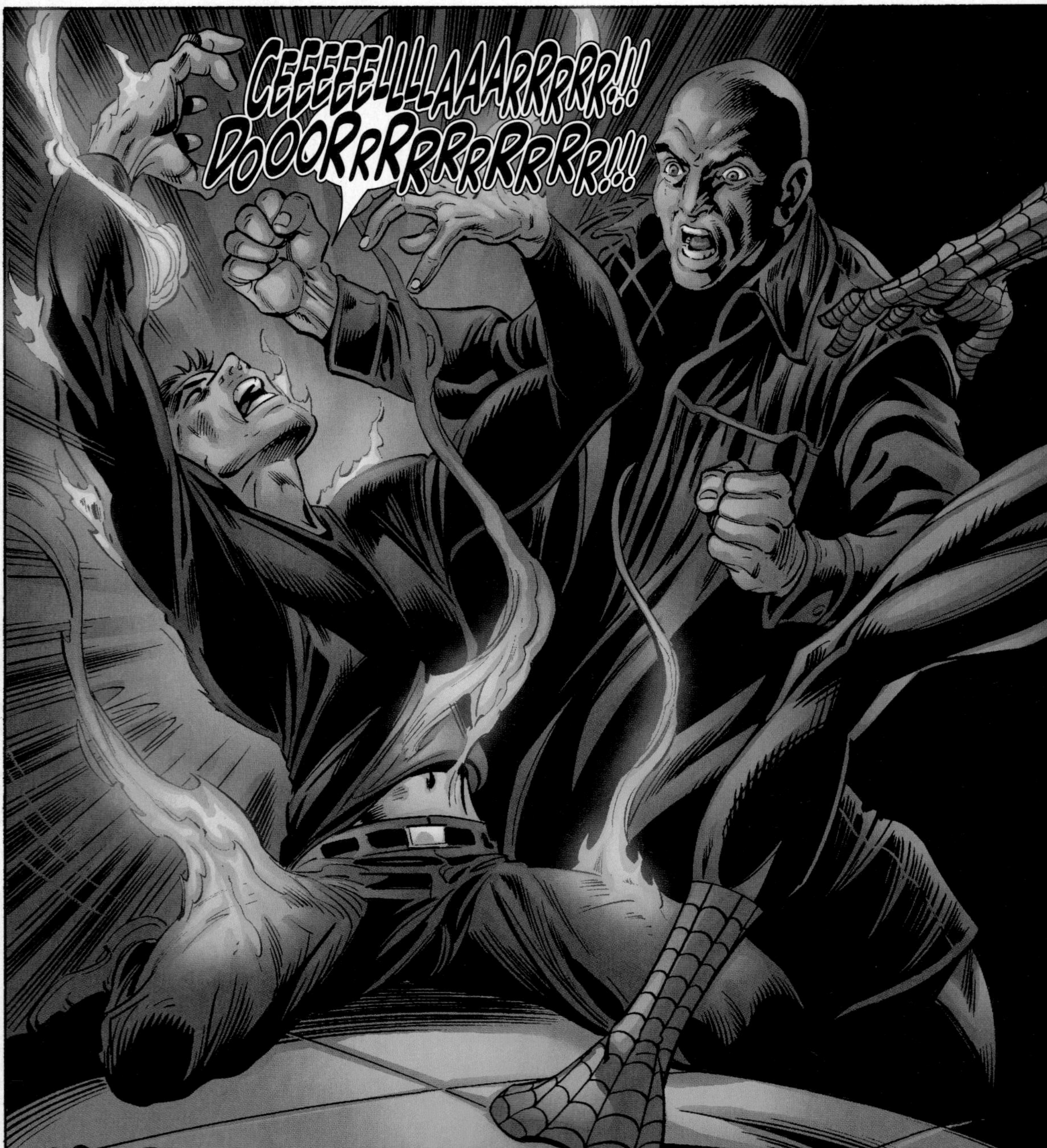
CEEEEELLLLAAARRRRR!!!
DOOORRRRRRRRRRR!!!

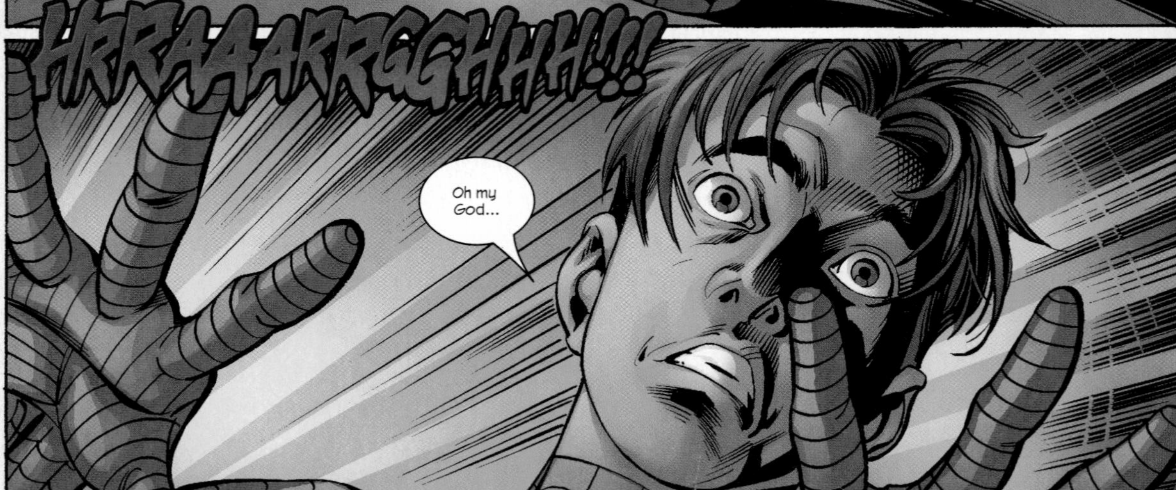
HRRAAARRGGHHH!!!
Oh my God...

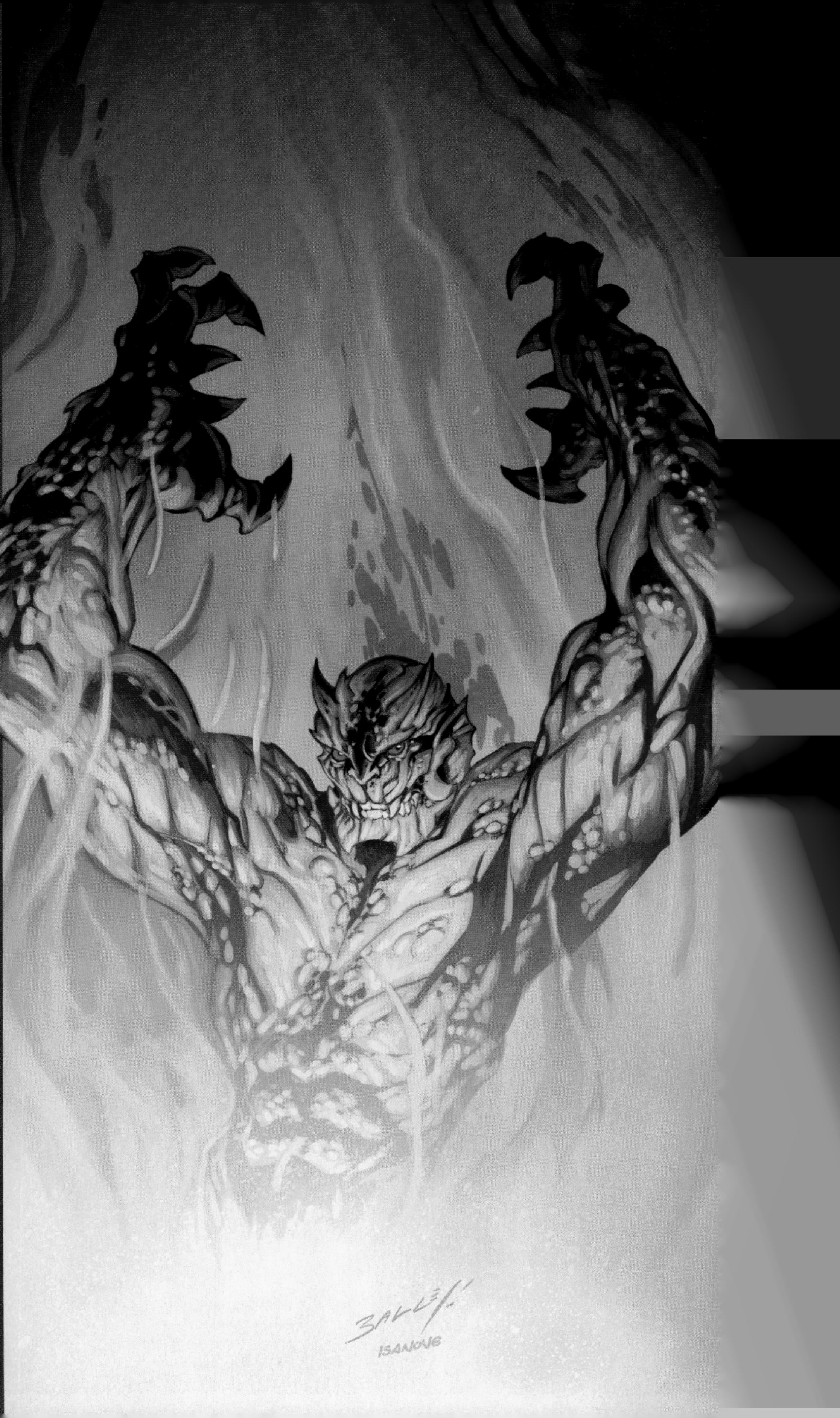
ISANOVE

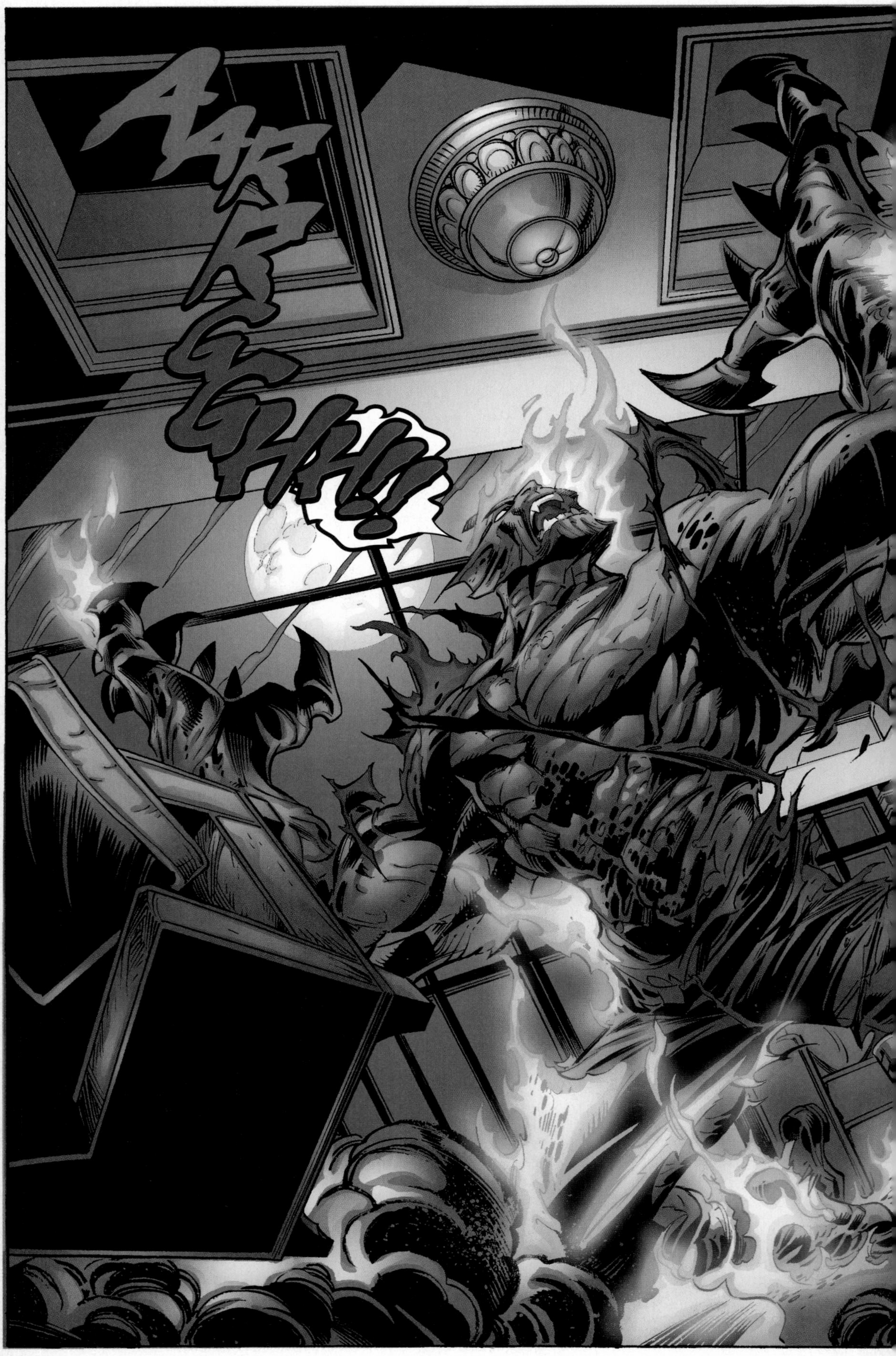
AARRGGHH!!

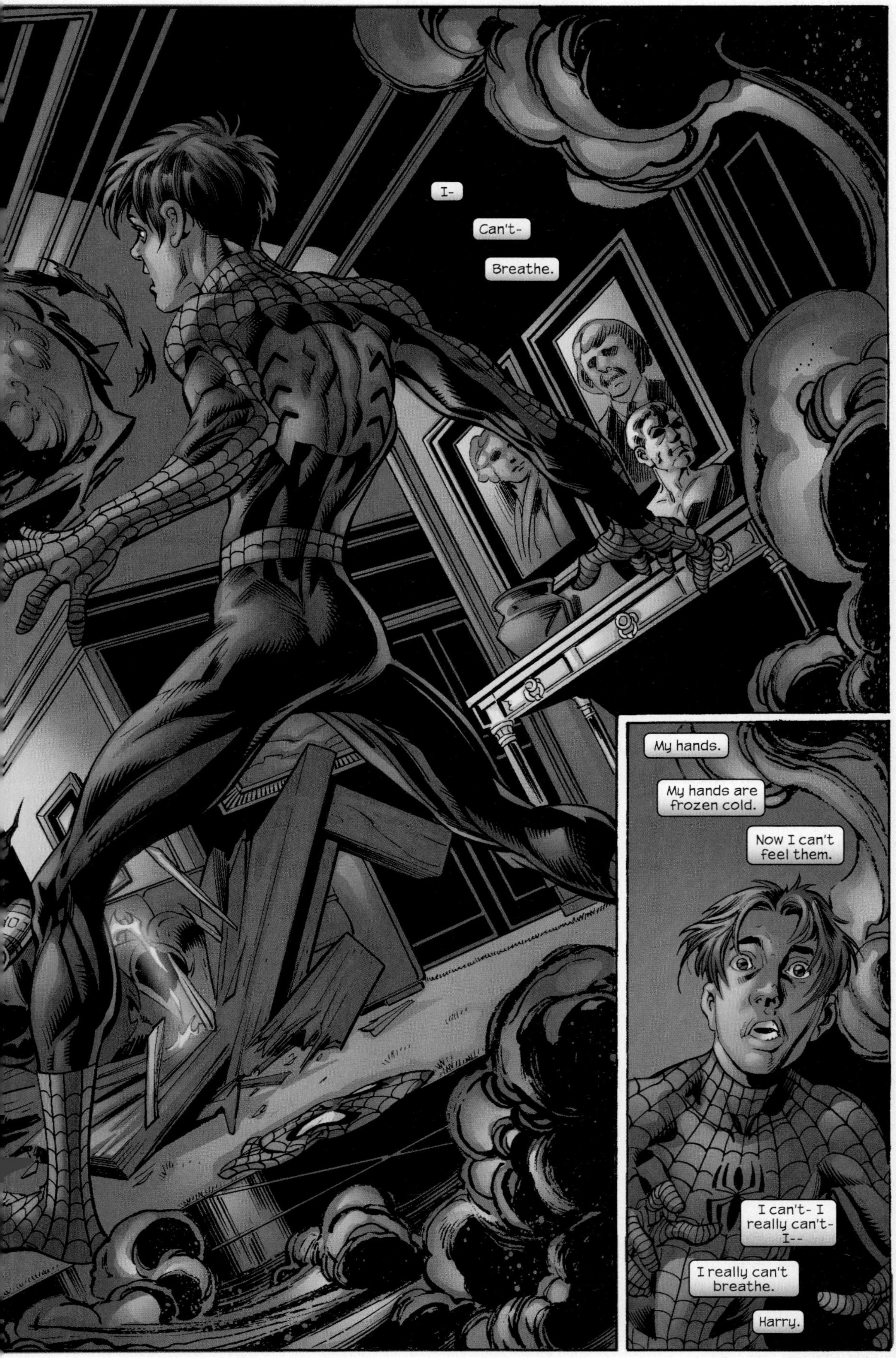
I-
Can't-
Breathe.
My hands.
My hands are frozen cold.
Now I can't feel them.
I can't- I really can't- I--
I really can't breathe.
Harry.

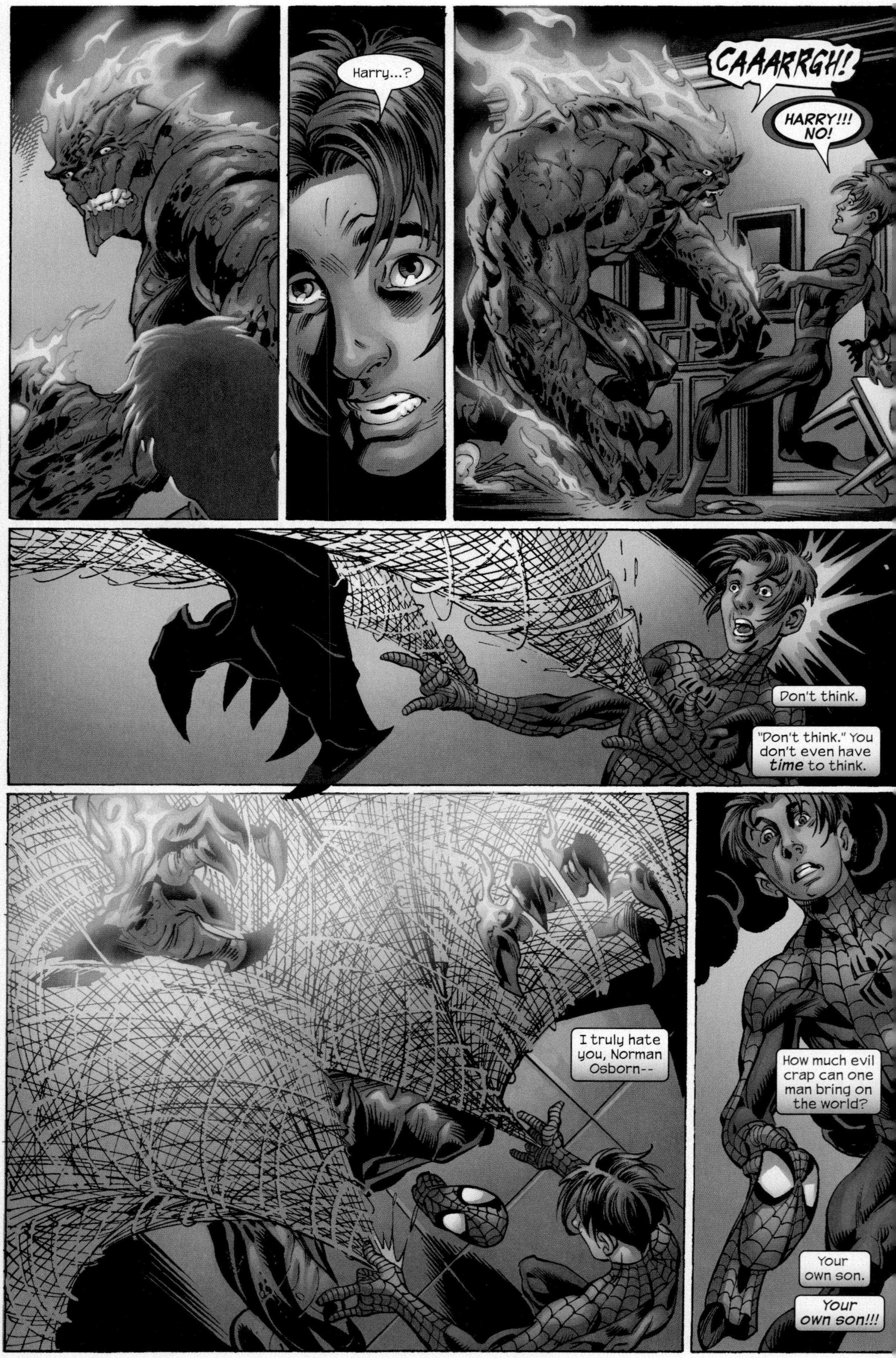
Harry...?
CAAARRGH!
HARRY!!! NO!
Don't think.
"Don't think." You don't even have *time* to think.
I truly hate you, Norman Osborn--
How much evil crap can one man bring on the world?
Your own son.
Your own son!!!

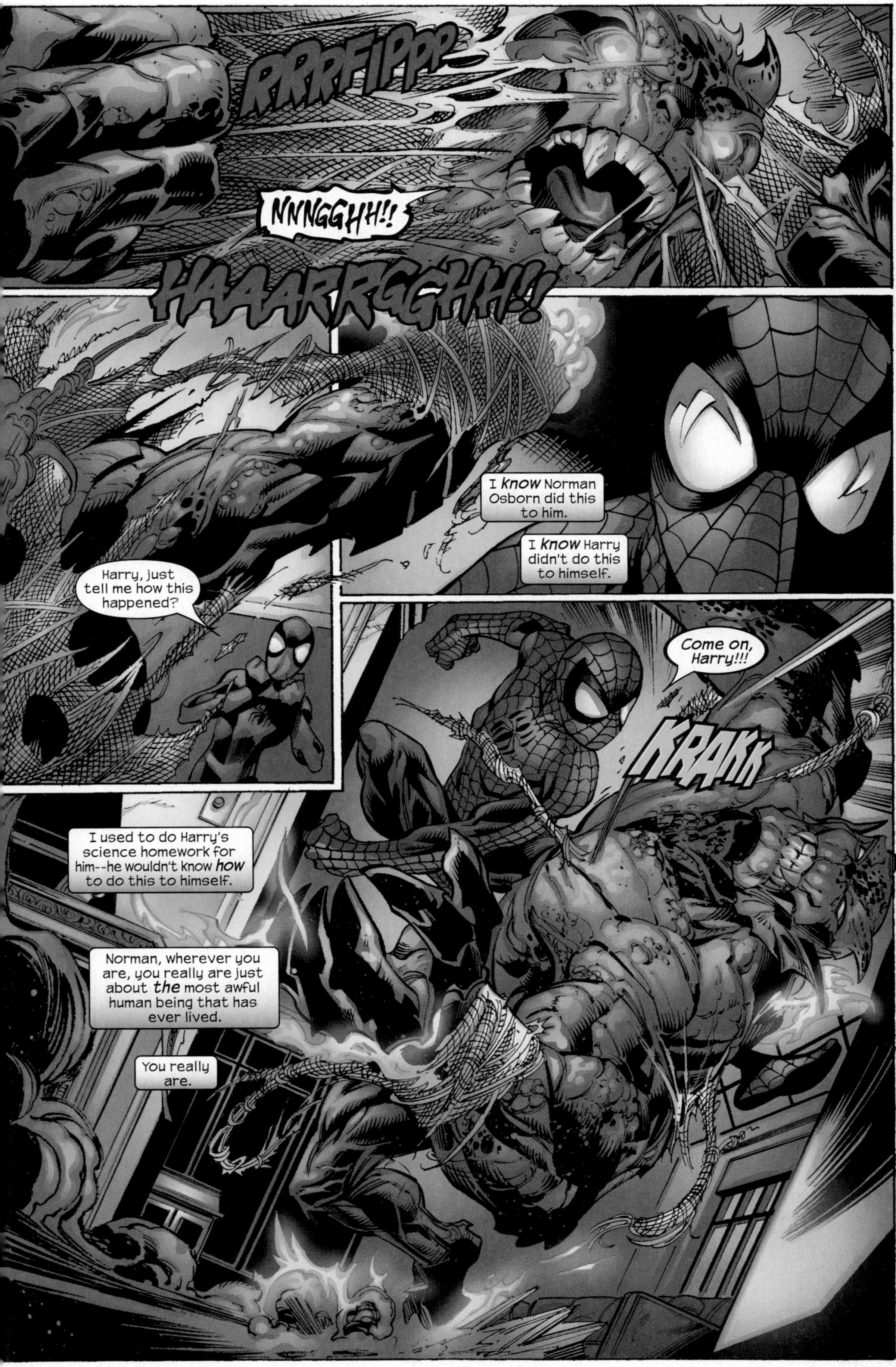
RRRFIPPP
NNNGGHH!!
HAAARRGGHH!!
I KNOW Norman Osborn did this to him.
I KNOW Harry didn't do this to himself.
Harry, just tell me how this happened?
Come on, Harry!!!
KRAKK
I used to do Harry's science homework for him--he wouldn't know HOW to do this to himself.
Norman, wherever you are, you really are just about THE most awful human being that has ever lived.
You really are.

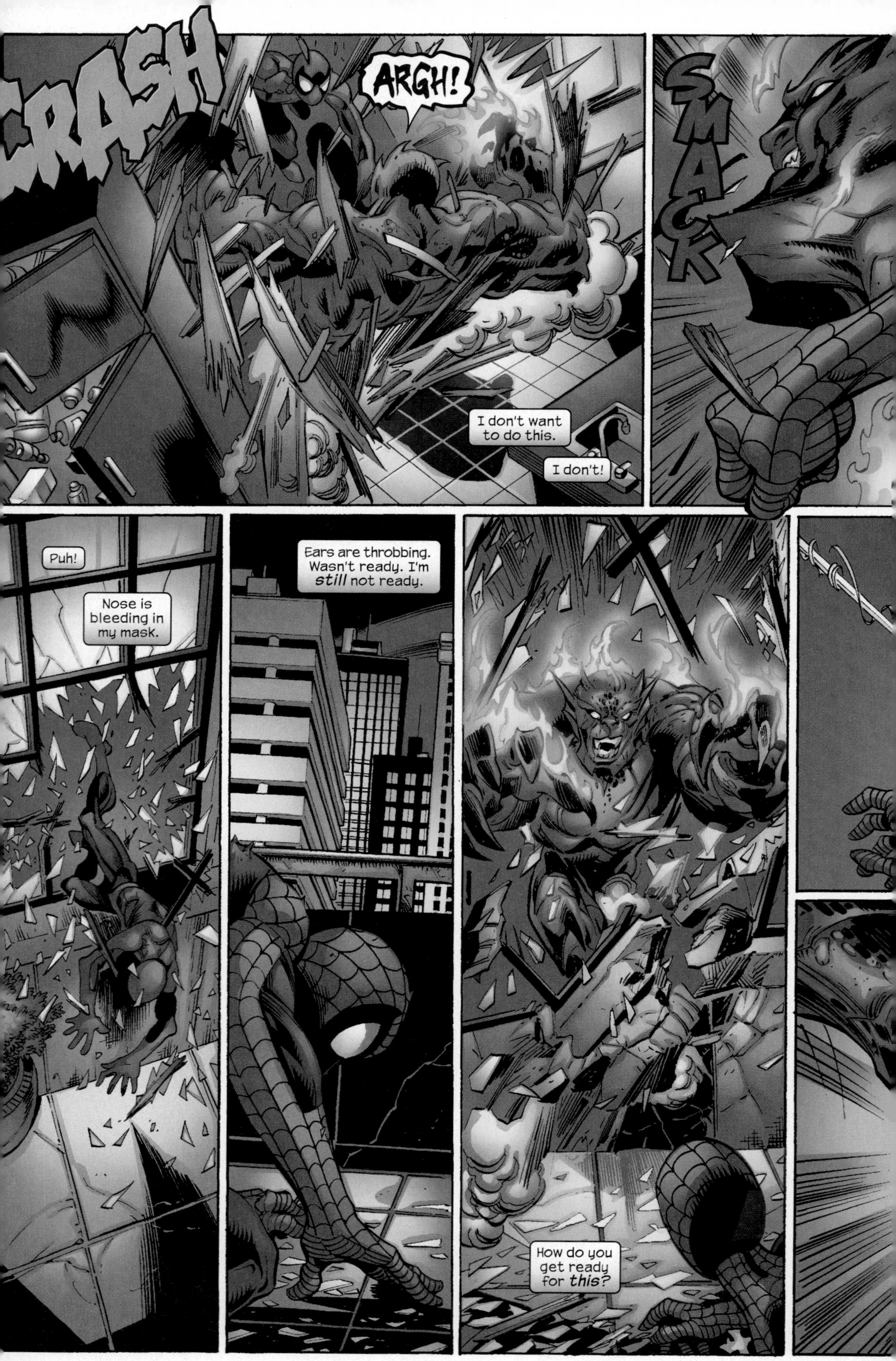
CRASH
ARGH!
I don't want to do this.
I don't!
SMACK
Puh!
Nose is bleeding in my mask.
Ears are throbbing. Wasn't ready. I'm *still* not ready.
How do you get ready for *this?*

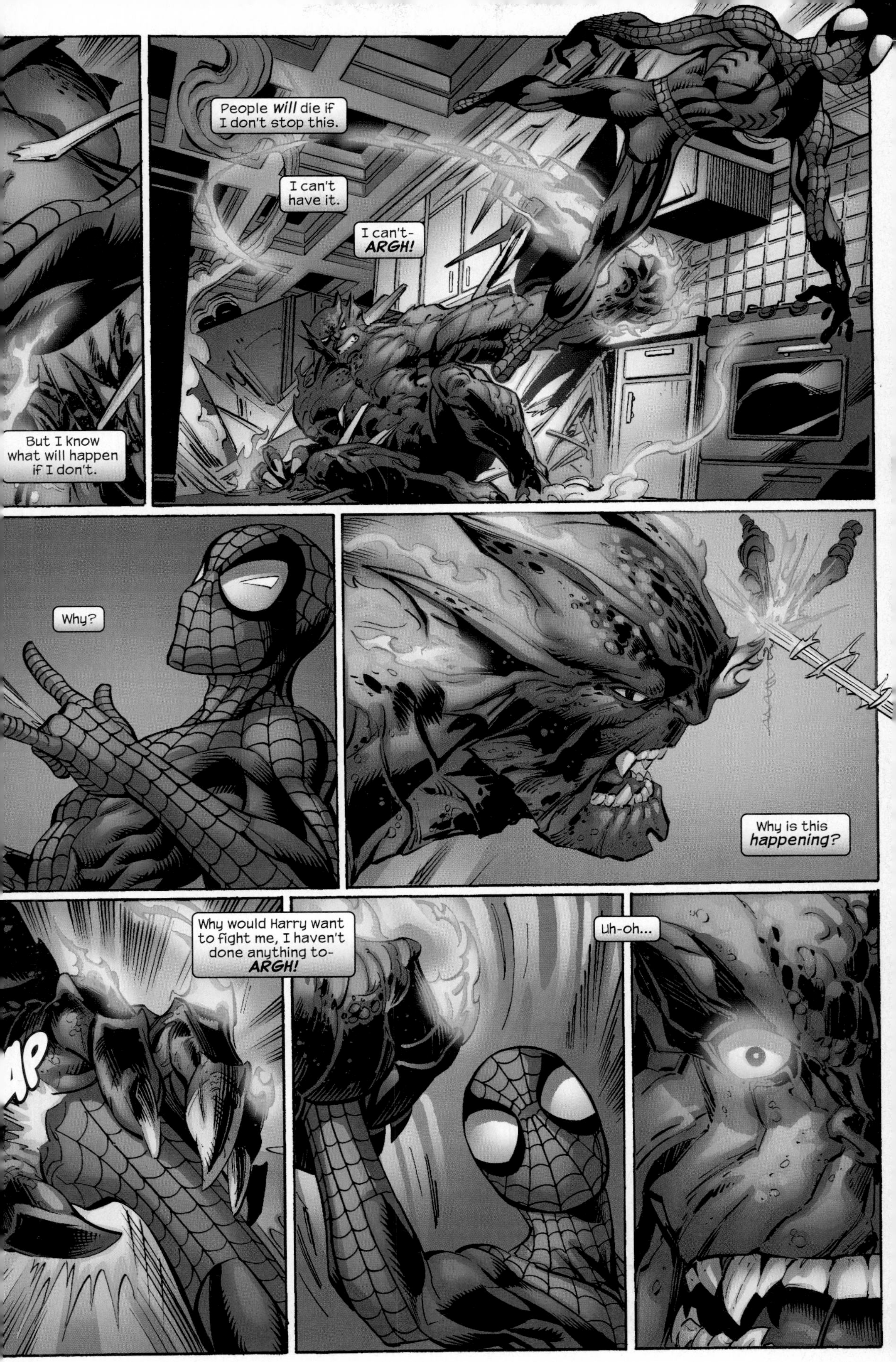

People *will* die if I don't stop this.
I can't have it.
I can't- **ARGH!**
But I know what will happen if I don't.
Why?
Why is this ***happening?***
Why would Harry want to fight me, I haven't done anything to- **ARGH!**
Uh-oh...

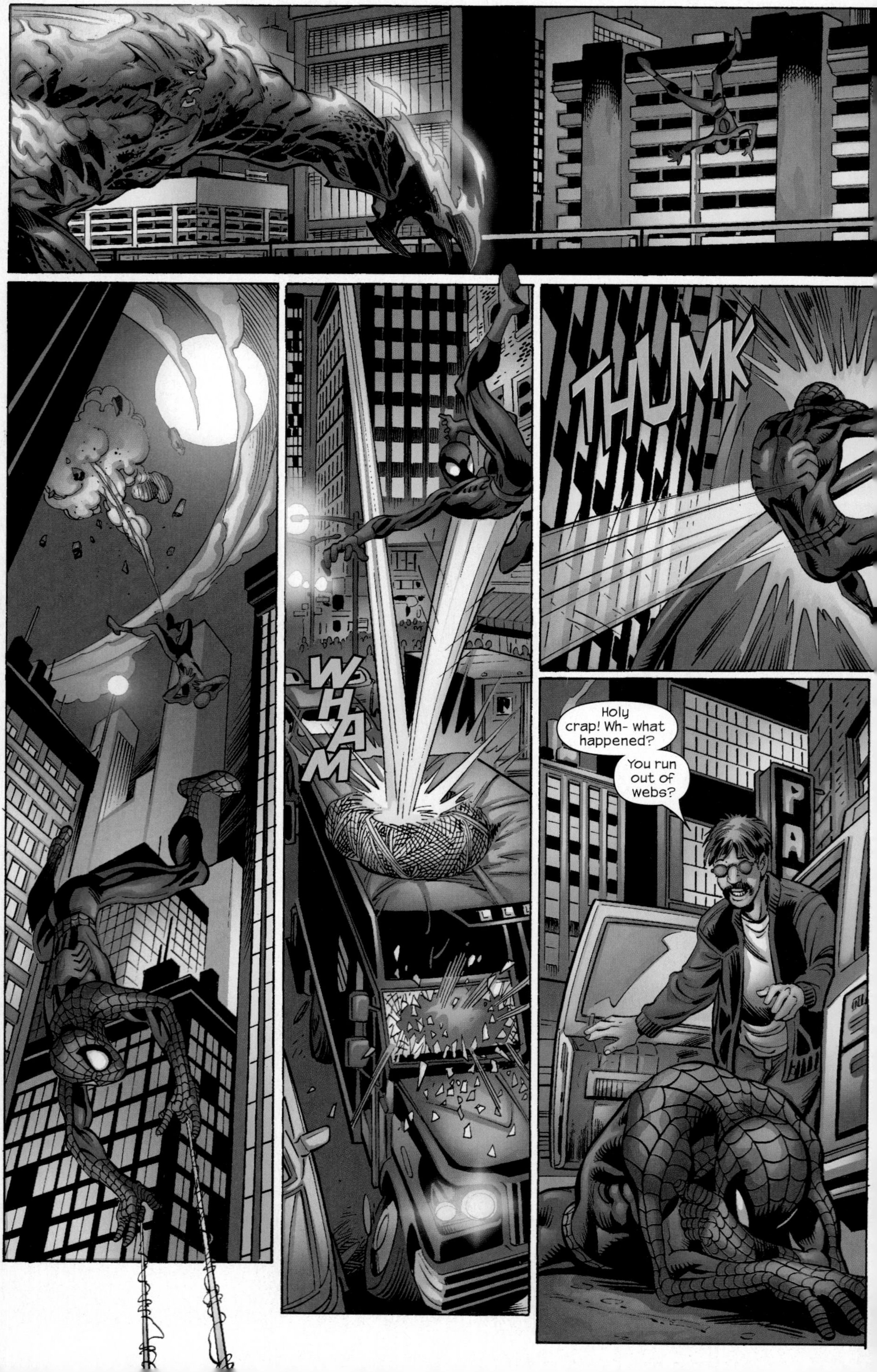
THUMK
WHAM
Holy crap! Wh- what happened?
You run out of webs?
PA

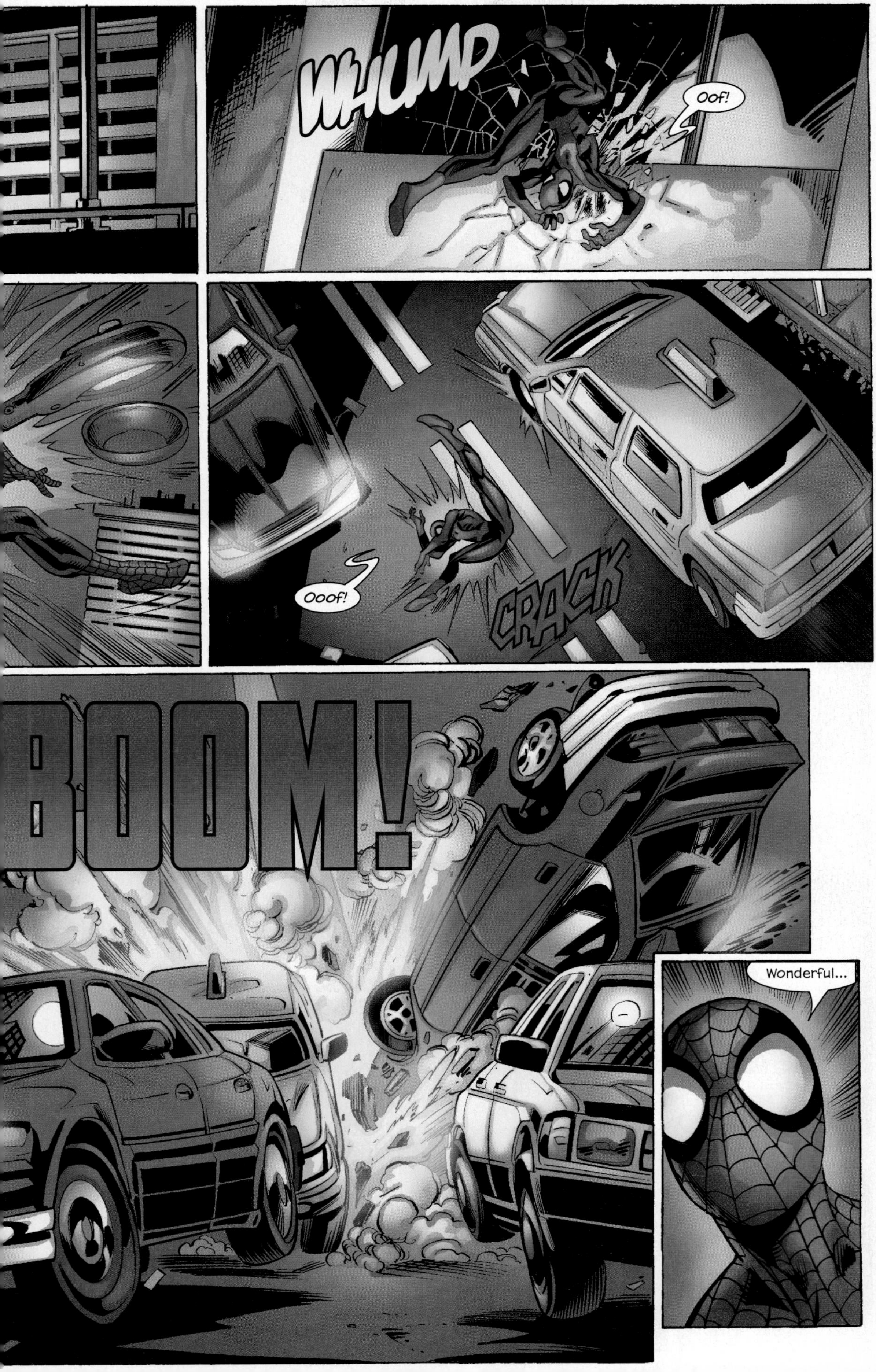
WHUMP
Oof!
Ooof!
CRACK
BOOM!
Wonderful...

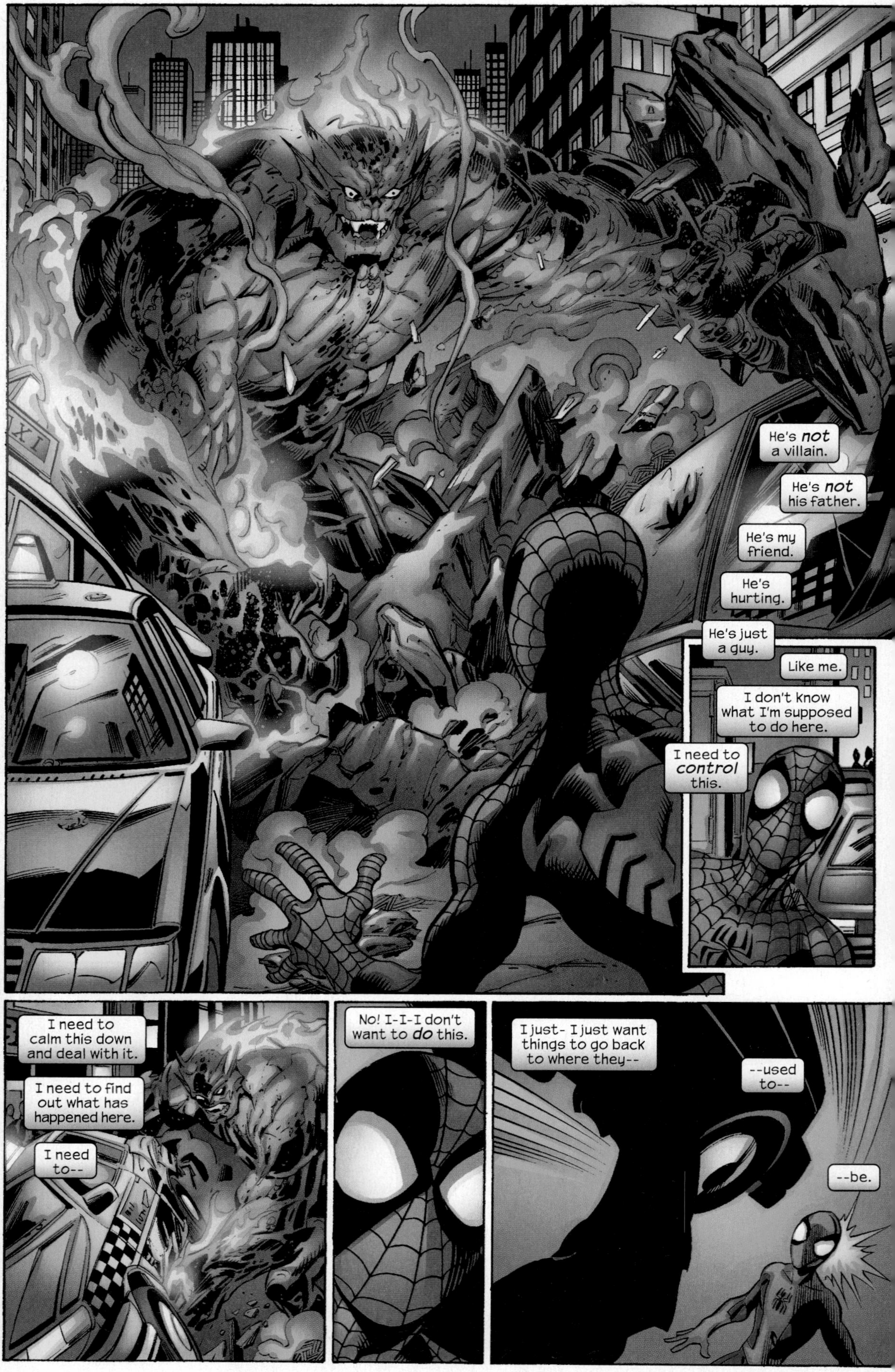
He's *not* a villain.
He's *not* his father.
He's my friend.
He's hurting.
He's just a guy.
Like me.
I don't know what I'm supposed to do here.
I need to *control* this.
I need to calm this down and deal with it.
I need to find out what has happened here.
I need to--
No! I-I-I don't want to *do* this.
I just- I just want things to go back to where they--
--used to--
--be.

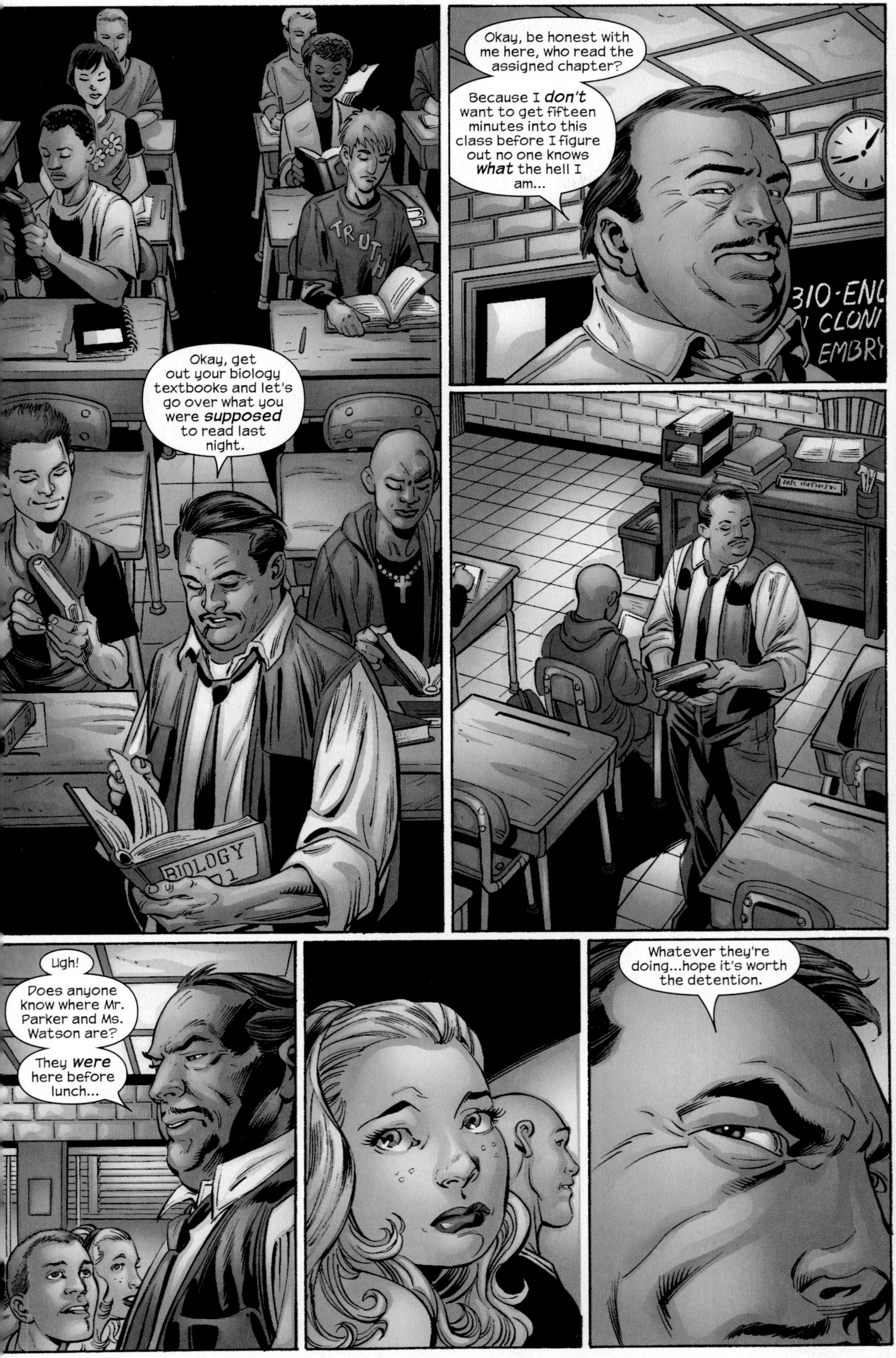

Okay, get out your biology textbooks and let's go over what you were *supposed* to read last night.
BIOLOGY
Okay, be honest with me here, who read the assigned chapter?
Because I *don't* want to get fifteen minutes into this class before I figure out no one knows *what* the hell I am...
Ugh!
Does anyone know where Mr. Parker and Ms. Watson are?
They *were* here before lunch...
Whatever they're doing...hope it's worth the detention.

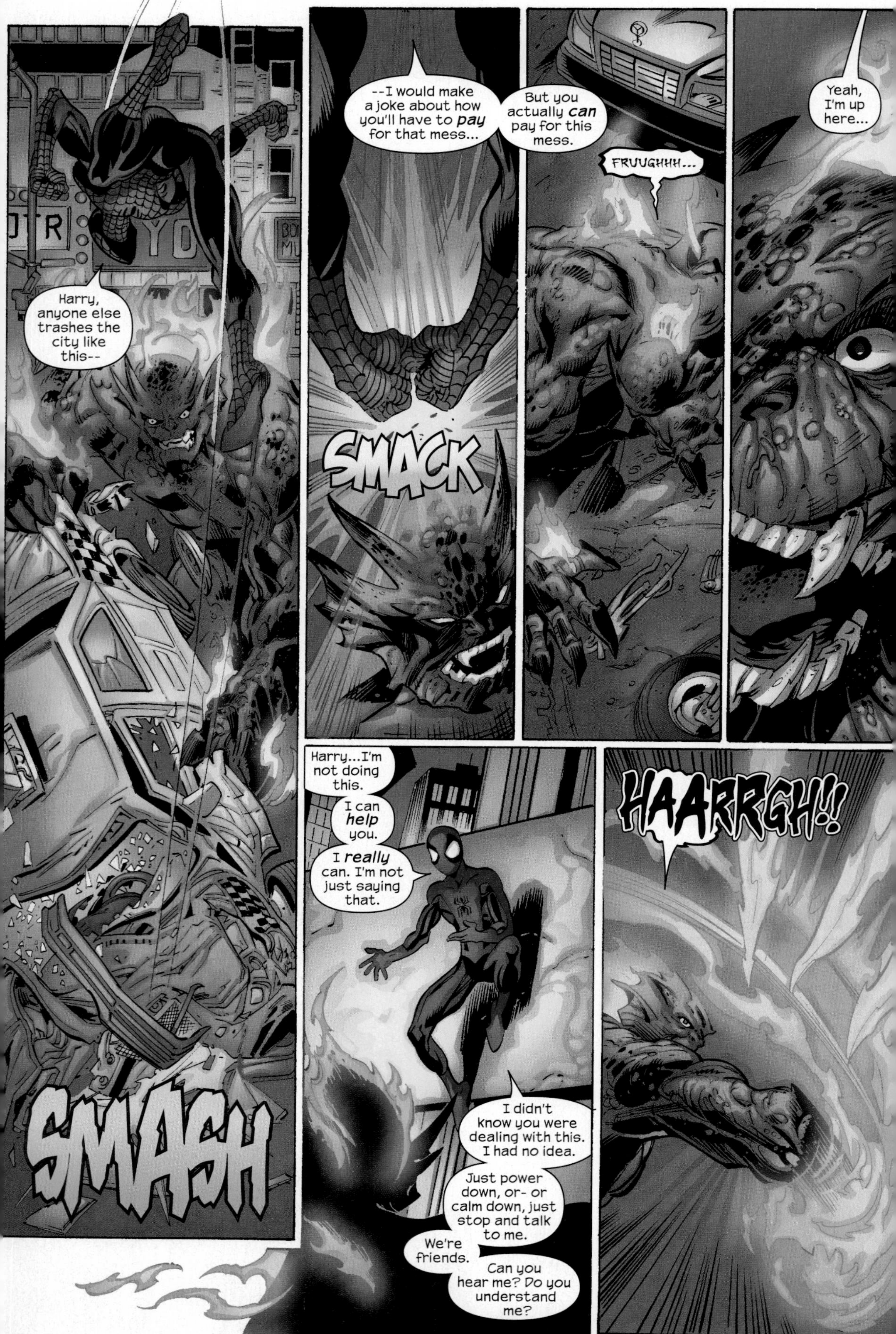

Harry, anyone else trashes the city like this--
--I would make a joke about how you'll have to pay for that mess...
But you actually can pay for this mess.
SMACK
FRUUGHHH...
Yeah, I'm up here...
SMASH
Harry...I'm not doing this.
I can help you.
I really can. I'm not just saying that.
I didn't know you were dealing with this. I had no idea.
Just power down, or- or calm down, just stop and talk to me.
We're friends.
Can you hear me? Do you understand me?
HAARRGH!!

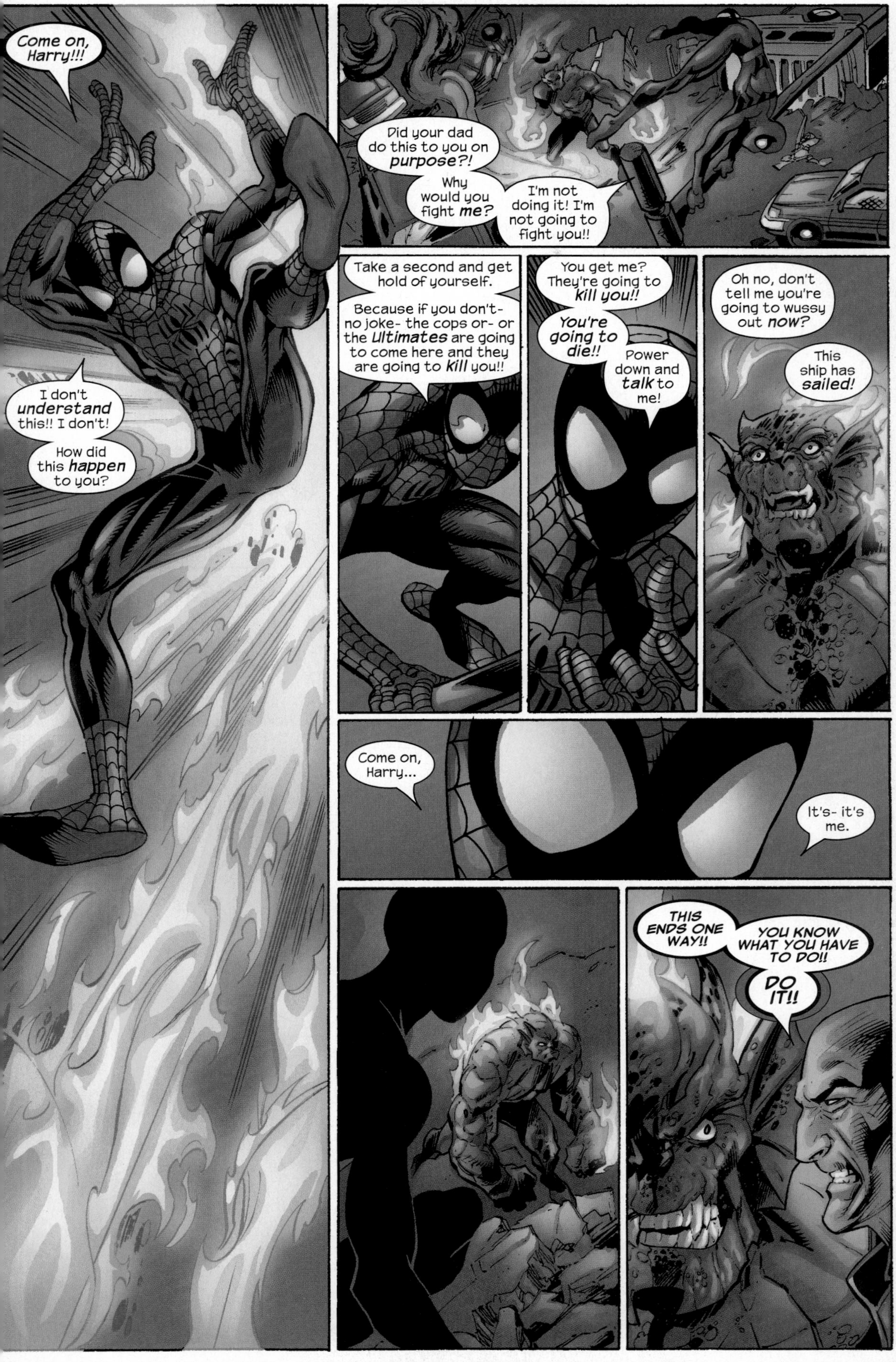

Come on, Harry!!!
I don't understand this!! I don't!
How did this happen to you?
Did your dad do this to you on purpose?!
Why would you fight me?
I'm not doing it! I'm not going to fight you!!
Take a second and get hold of yourself.
Because if you don't- no joke- the cops or- or the Ultimates are going to come here and they are going to kill you!!
You get me? They're going to kill you!!
You're going to die!!
Power down and talk to me!
Oh no, don't tell me you're going to wussy out now?
This ship has sailed!
Come on, Harry...
It's- it's me.
THIS ENDS ONE WAY!!
YOU KNOW WHAT YOU HAVE TO DO!!
DO IT!!

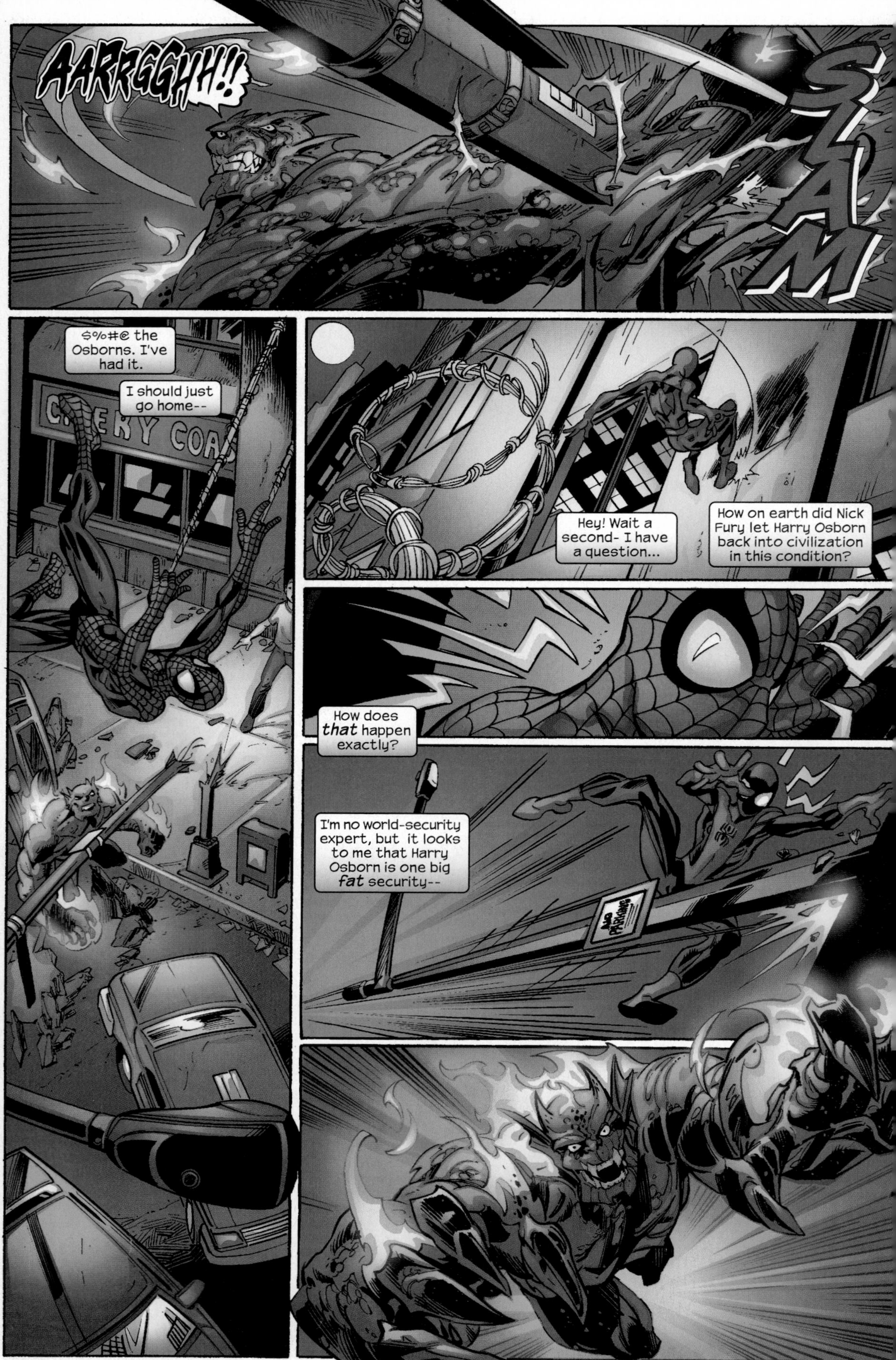
AARRGGHH!!
SLAM
$%#@ the Osborns. I've had it.
I should just go home--
Hey! Wait a second- I have a question...
How on earth did Nick Fury let Harry Osborn back into civilization in this condition?
How does *that* happen exactly?
I'm no world-security expert, but it looks to me that Harry Osborn is one big *fat* security--

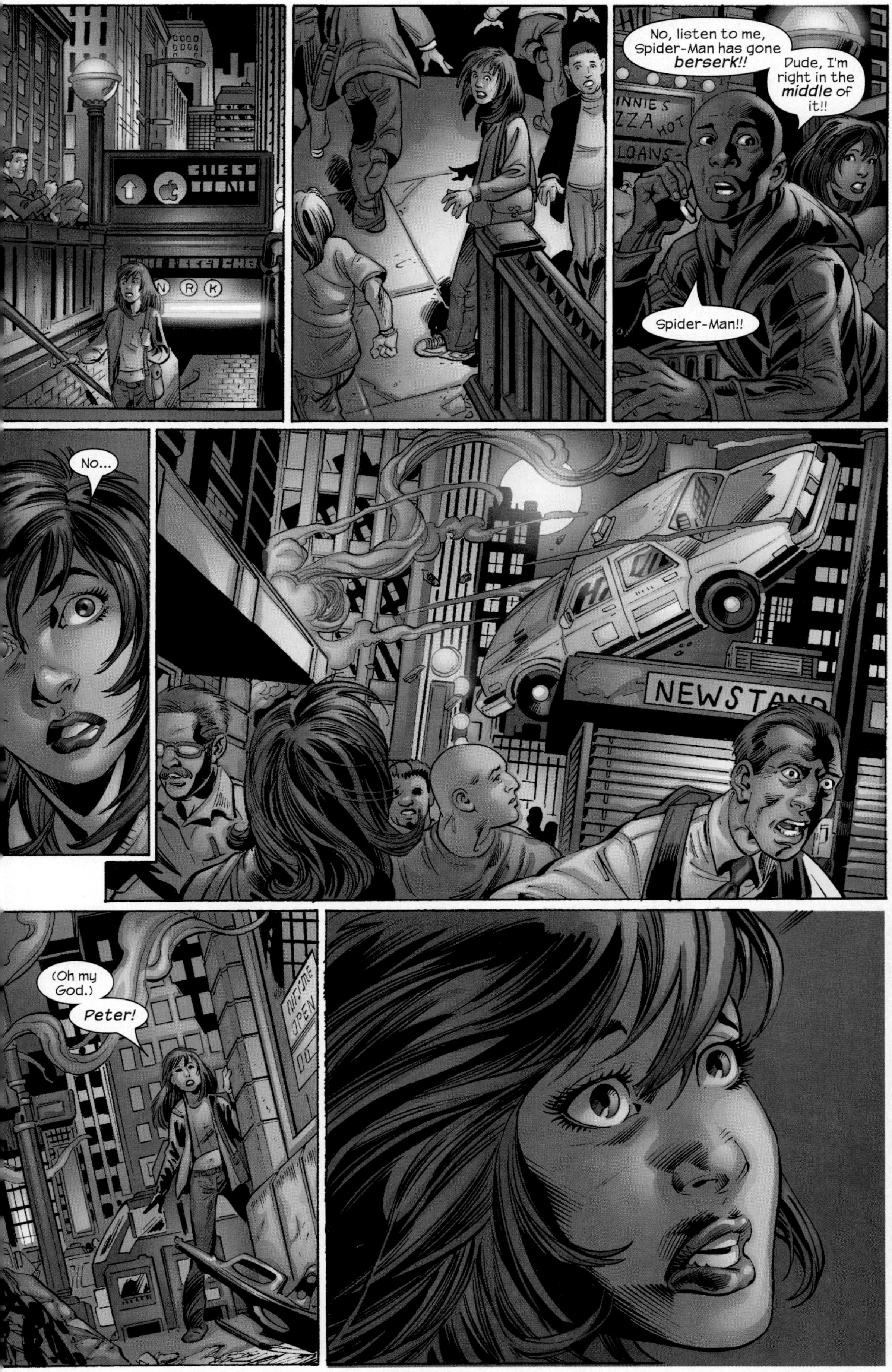

No, listen to me, Spider-Man has gone *berserk!!*
Dude, I'm right in the *middle* of it!!
Spider-Man!!
NEWSTAND
No...
(Oh my God.)
Peter!

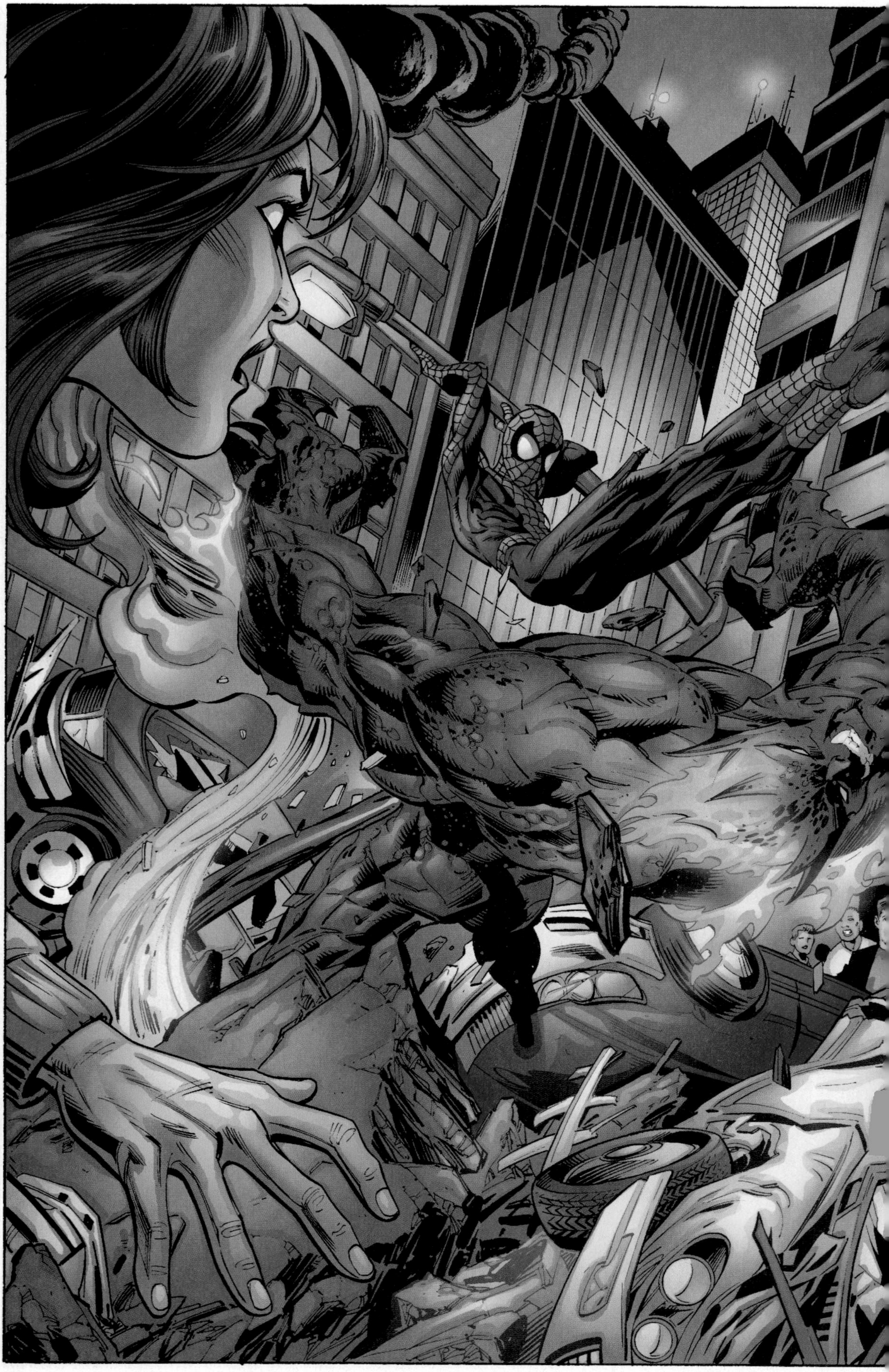

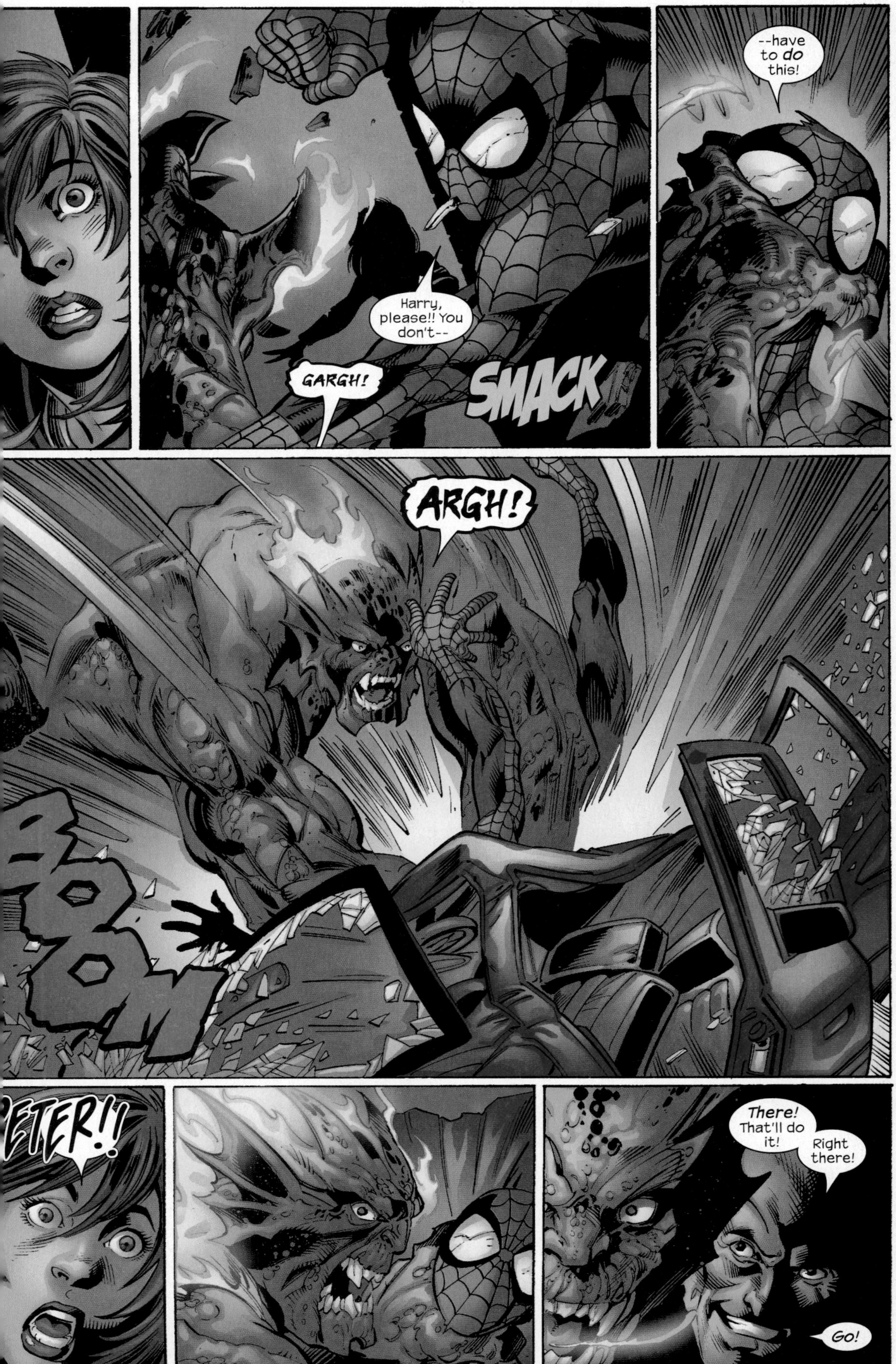

Harry, please!! You don't--
GARGH!
SMACK
--have to do this!
ARGH!
BOOM
PETER!!
There! That'll do it!
Right there!
Go!

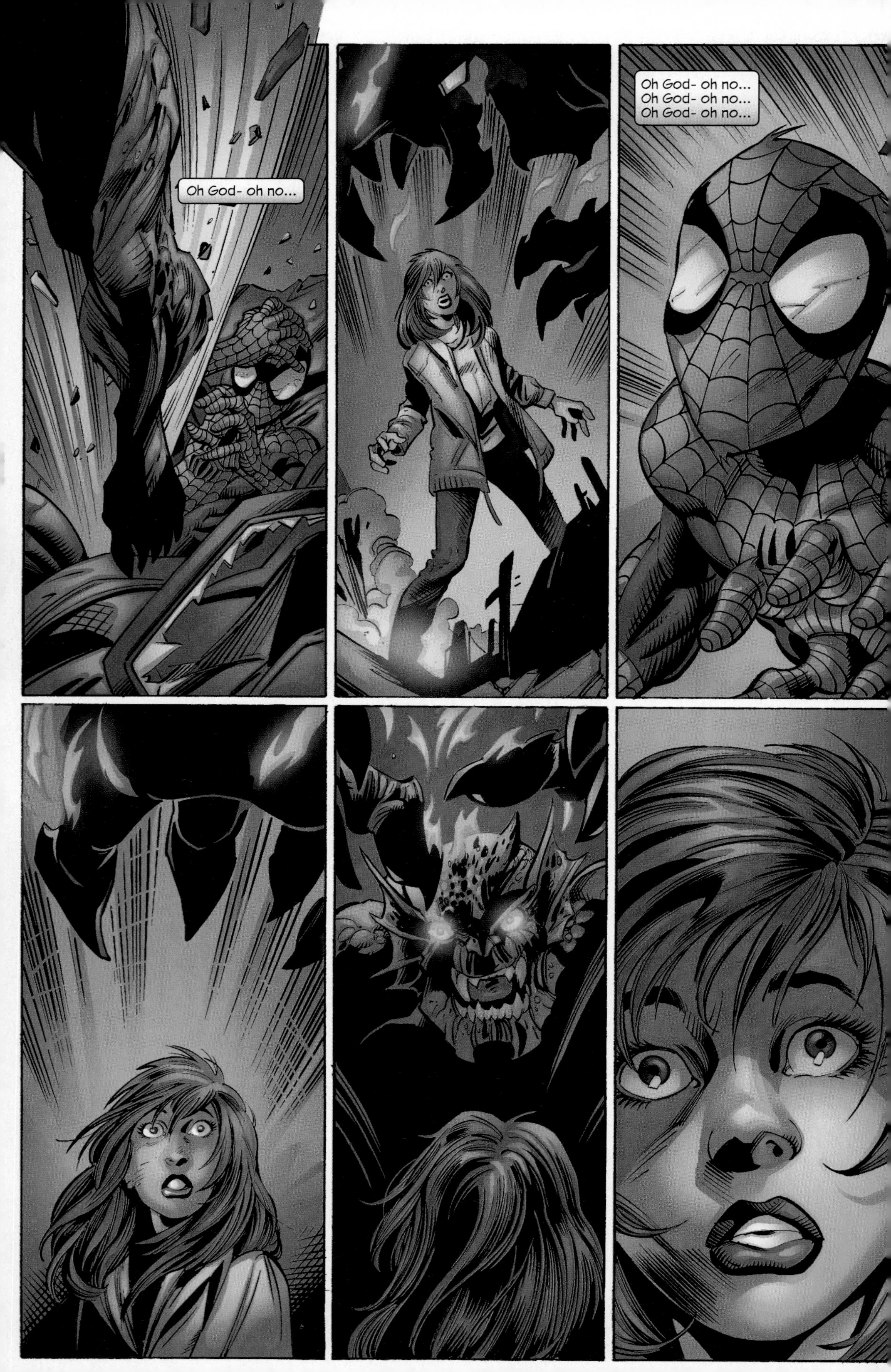
Oh God- oh no...
Oh God- oh no...
Oh God- oh no...
Oh God- oh no...

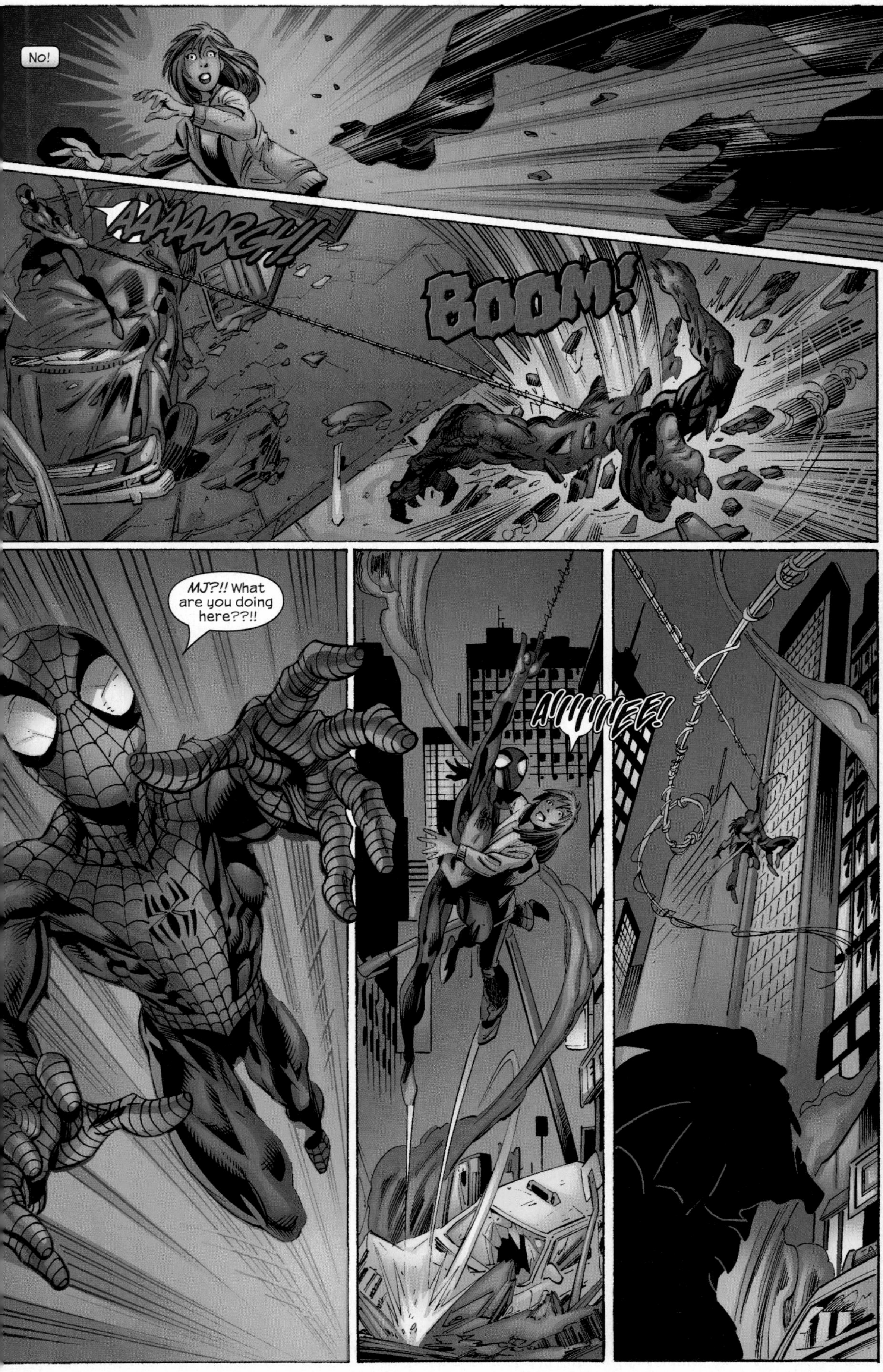
No!
AAAAARGH!!
BOOM!
MJ?!! What are you doing here??!!
AIIIIEEE!

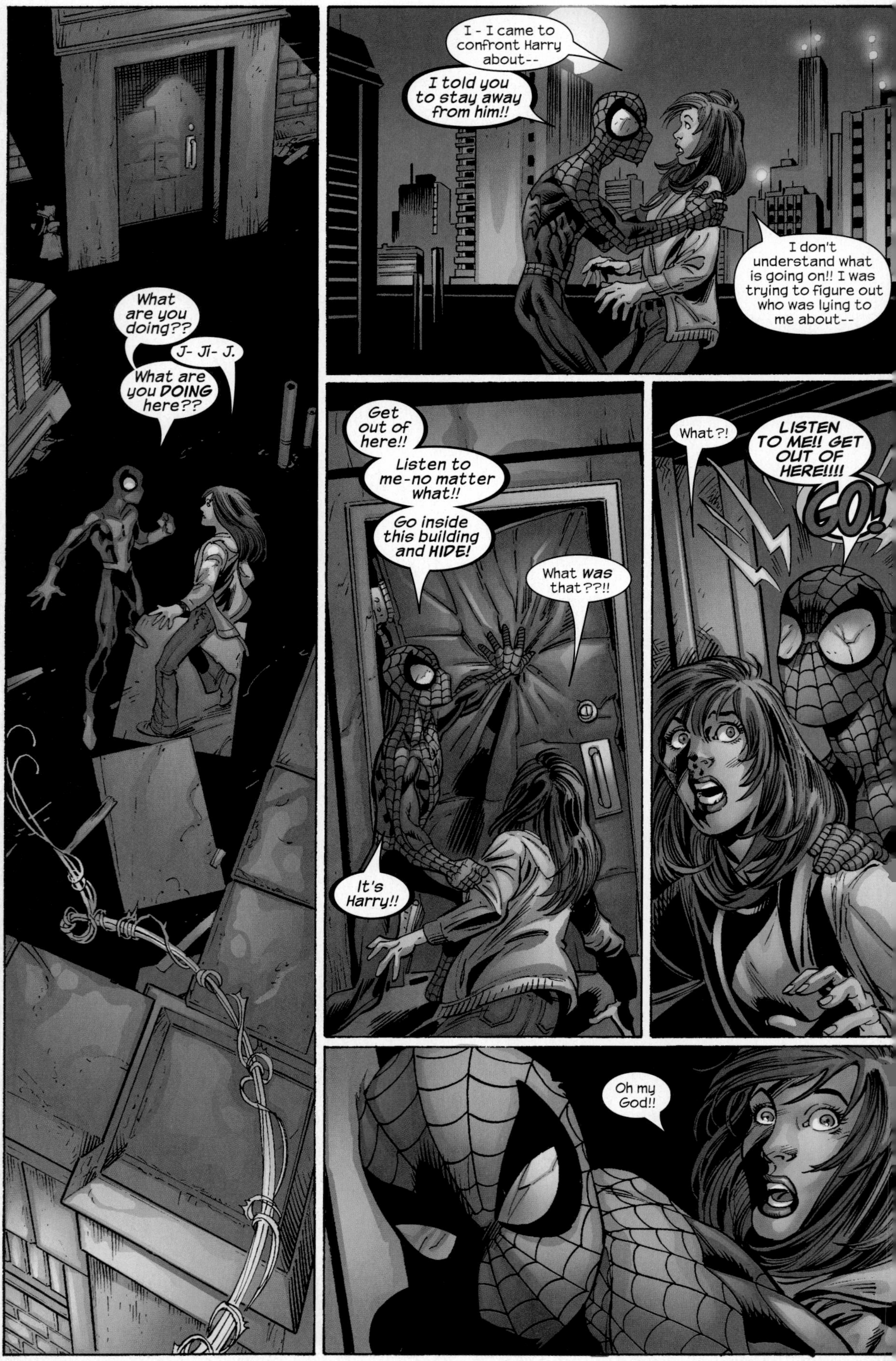

What are you doing??
J- Ji- J.
What are you DOING here??
I - I came to confront Harry about--
I told you to stay away from him!!
I don't understand what is going on!! I was trying to figure out who was lying to me about--
Get out of here!!
Listen to me-no matter what!!
Go inside this building and HIDE!
What was that??!!
It's Harry!!
What?!
LISTEN TO ME!! GET OUT OF HERE!!!!
GO!
Oh my God!!

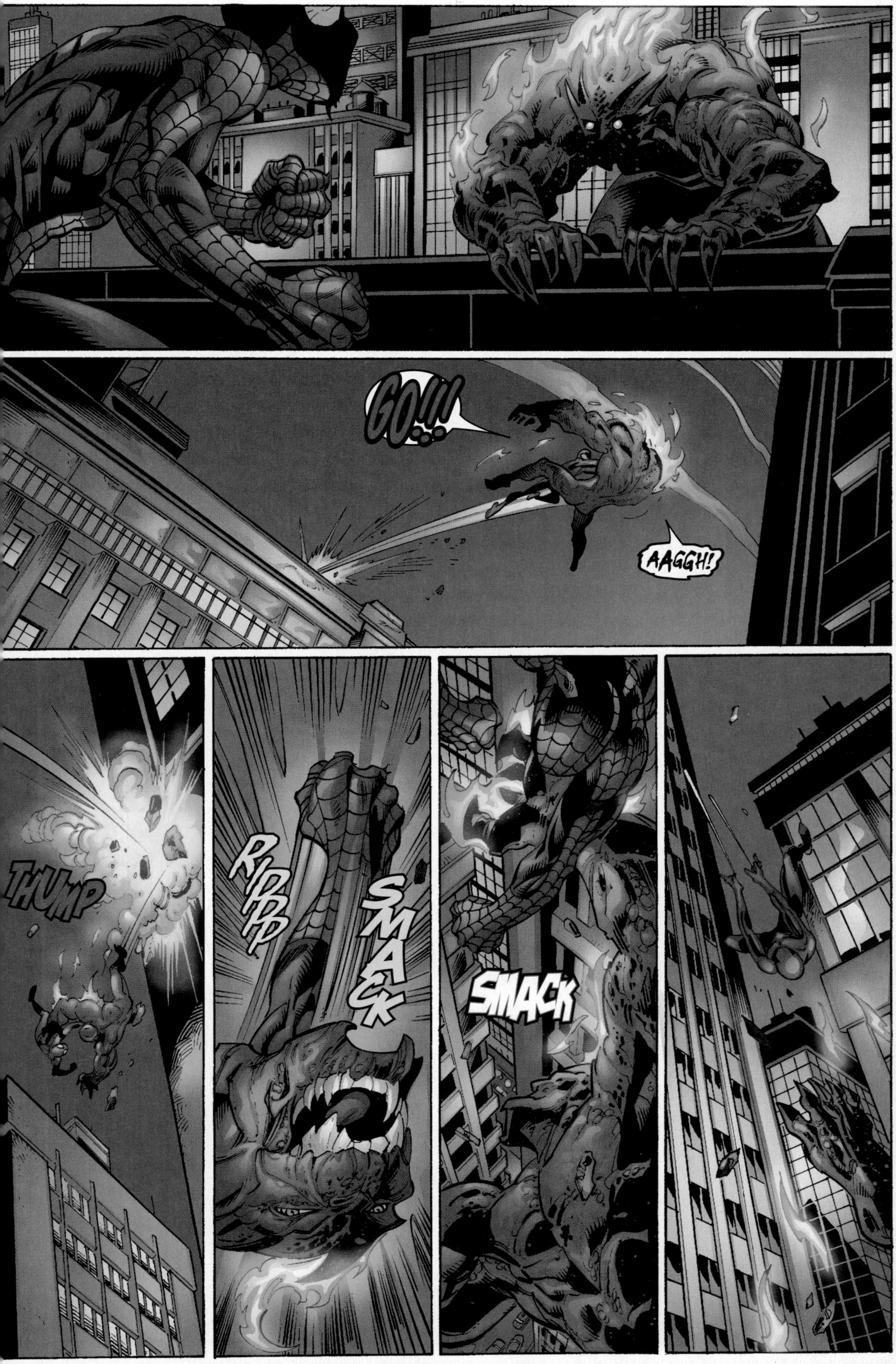
GO...!!!
AAGGH!
THUMP
RIPPP
SMACK
SMACK

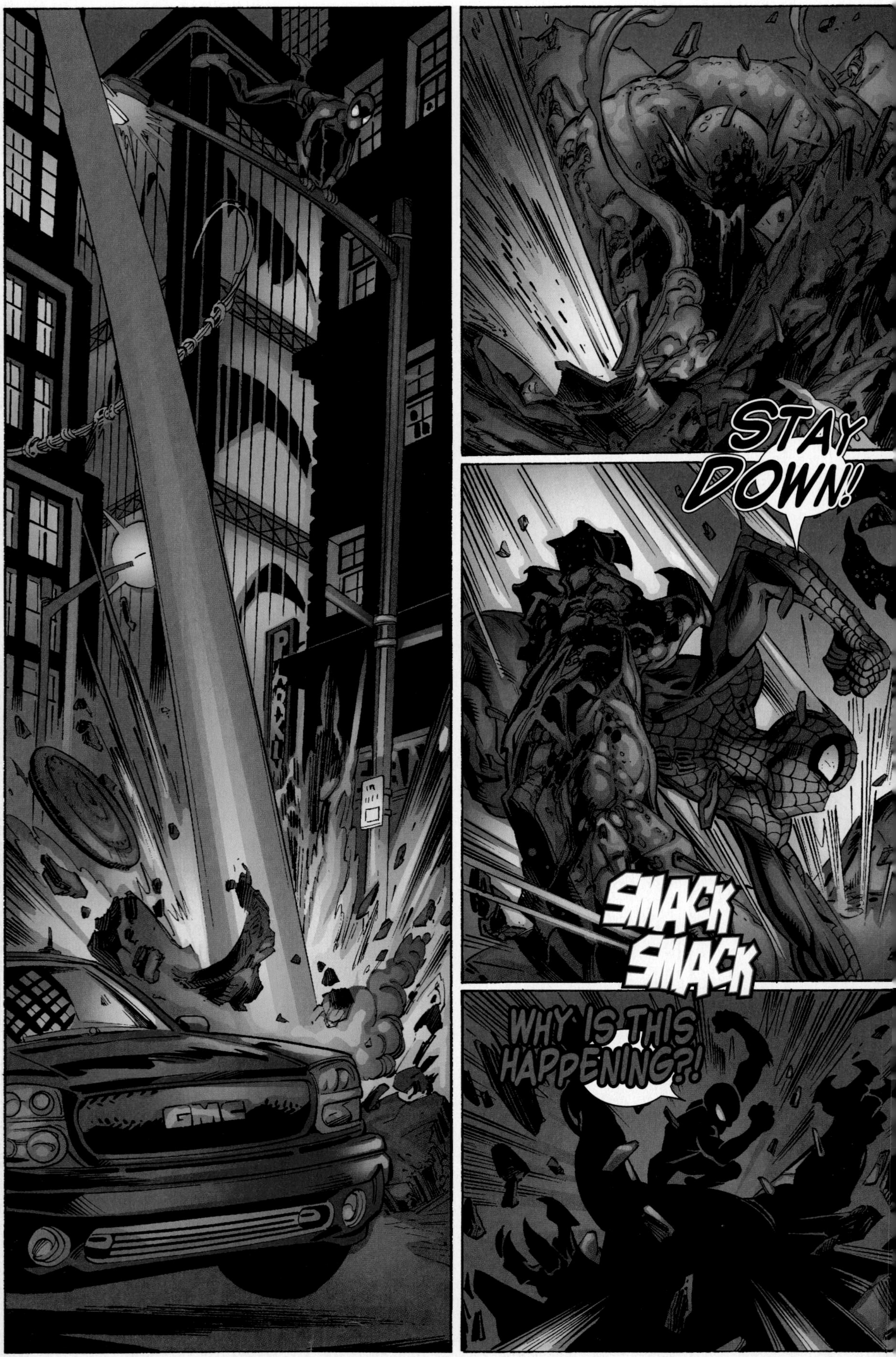
STAY DOWN!
SMACK SMACK
WHY IS THIS HAPPENING?!

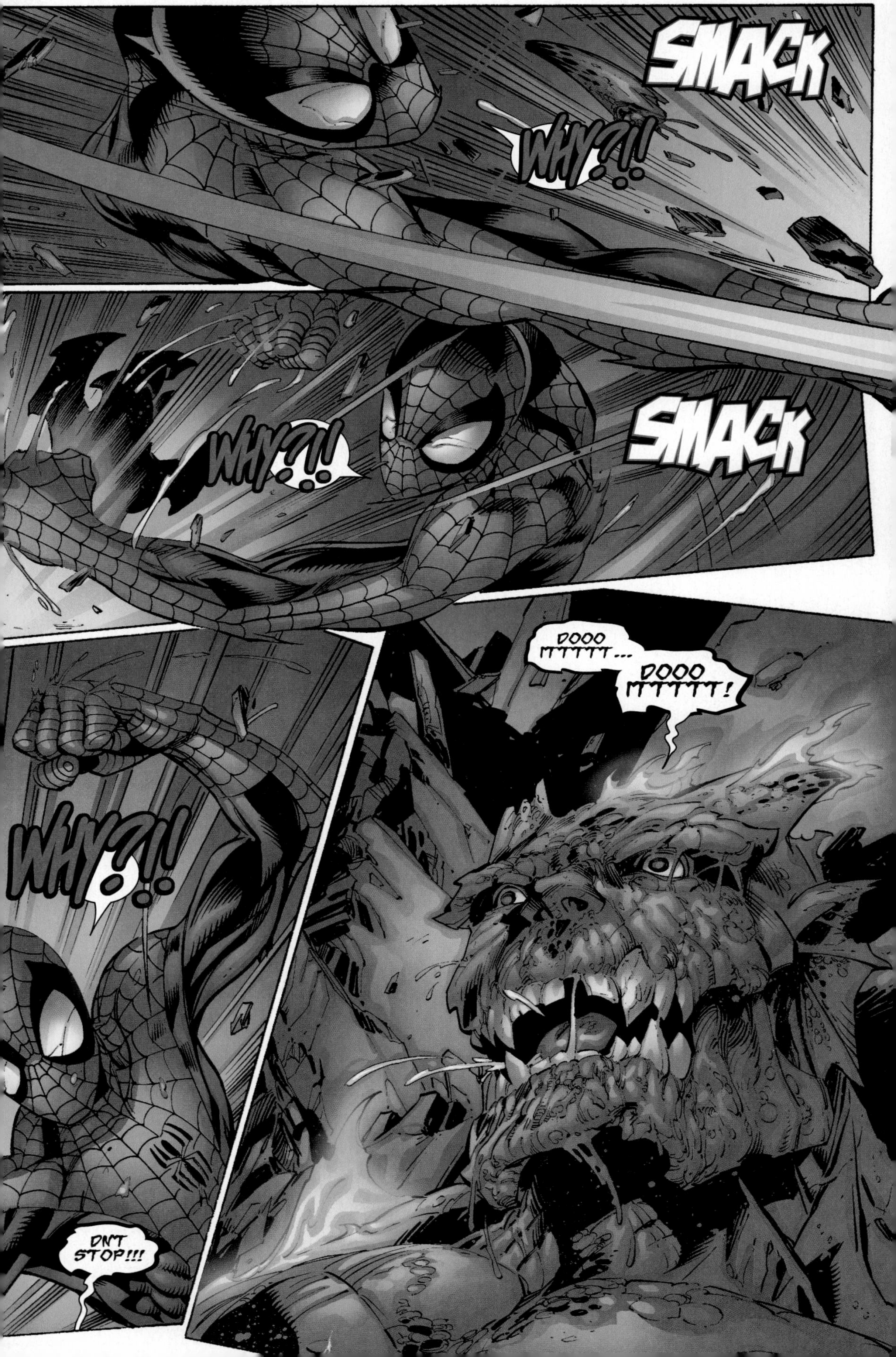
SMACK
WHY?!!
SMACK
WHY?!!
DOOO ITTTTT... DOOO ITTTTT!
WHY?!!
DN'T STOP!!!

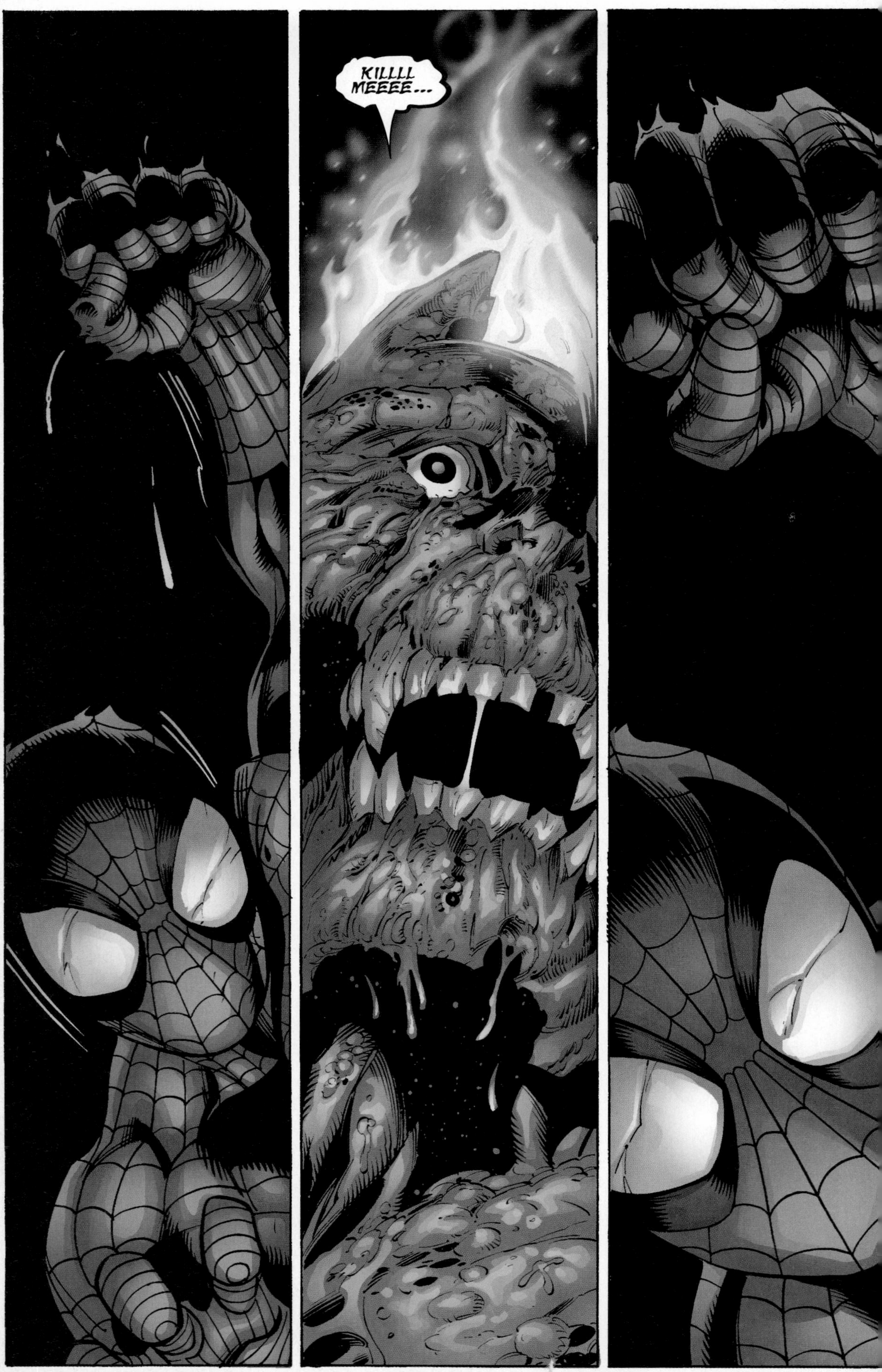
KILLLL MEEEE...

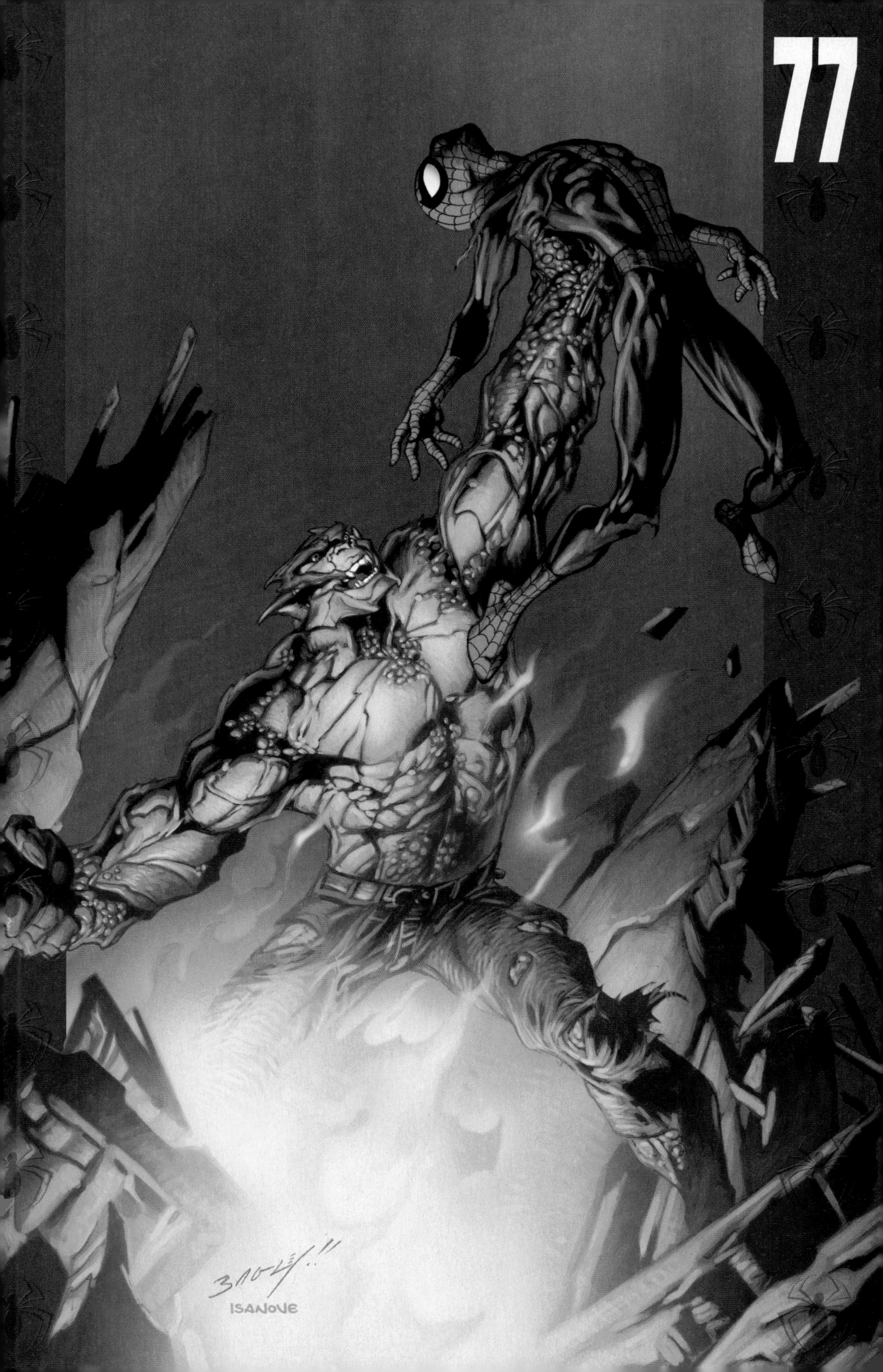
77

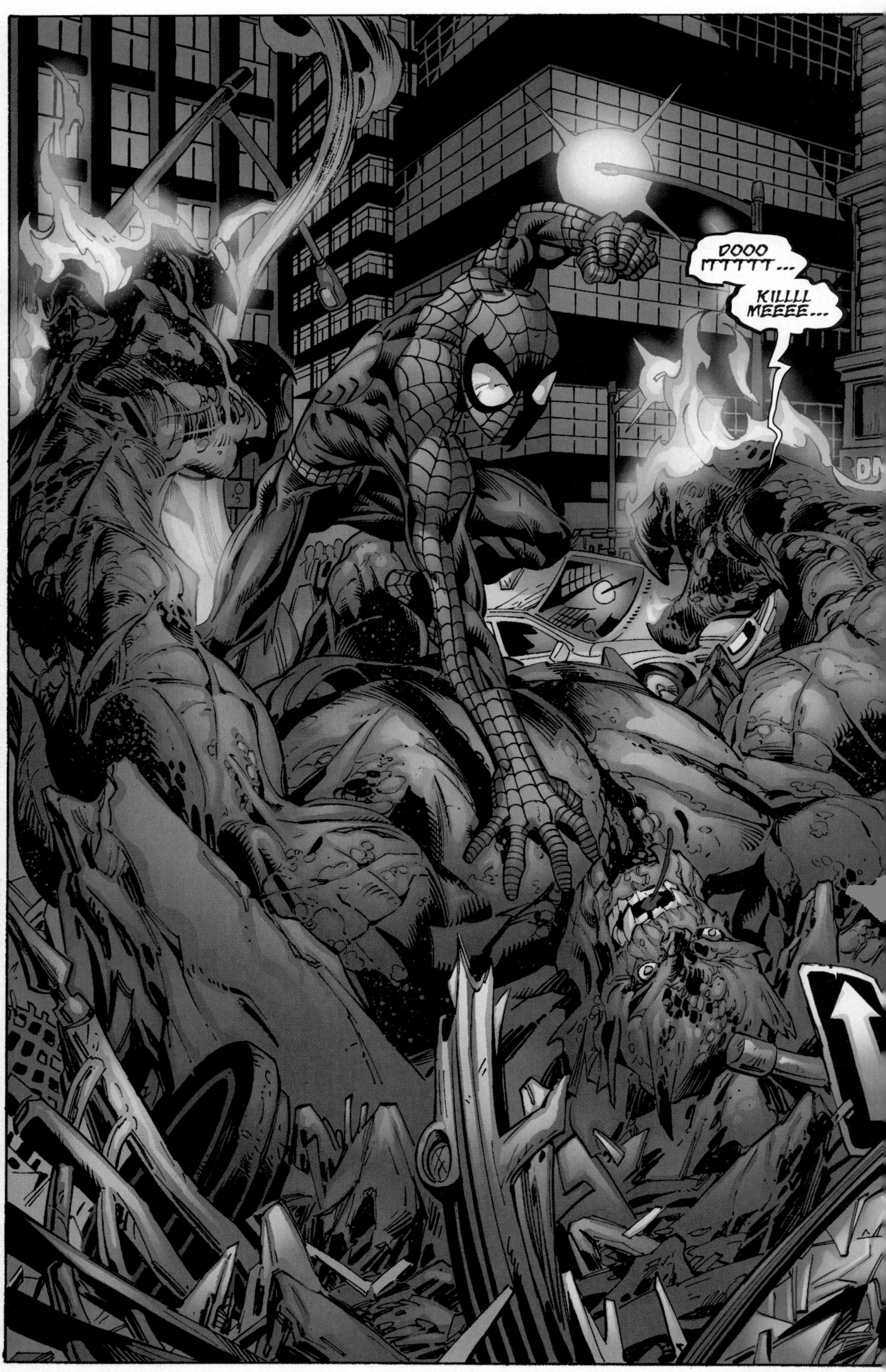
DOOO ITTTTT...
KILLLL MEEEE...

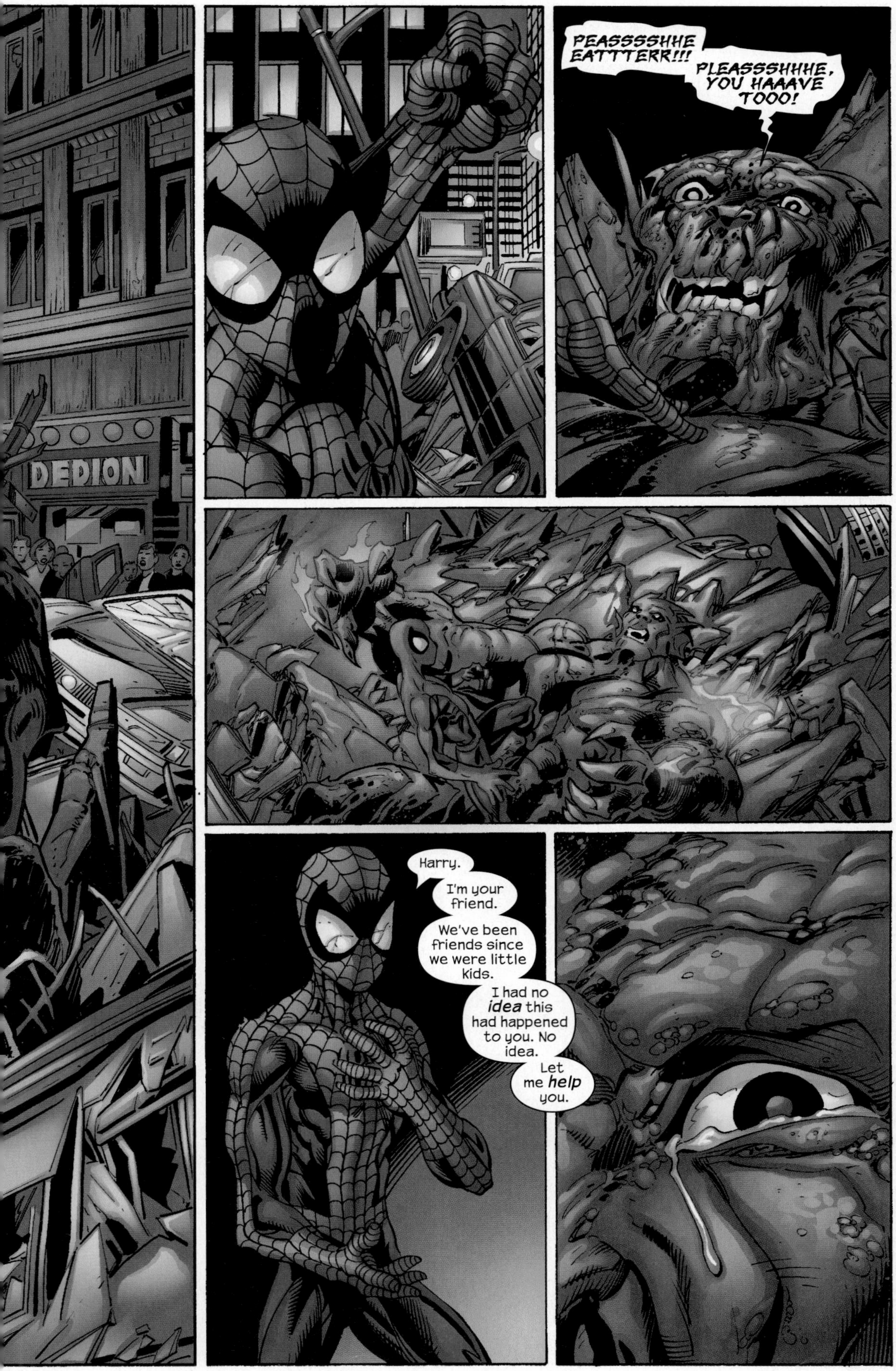
DEDION
PEASSSSHHE EATTTERR!!!
PLEASSSHHHE, YOU HAAAVE TOOO!
Harry.
I'm your friend.
We've been friends since we were little kids.
I had no *idea* this had happened to you. No idea.
Let me *help* you.

He's not going to do it! I told you, he's not a killer!!

OH GOOAAAD!!

I *told* you, only your father can end this!

Go get your father!!

AARRGHH!!

ROMOTA LMT

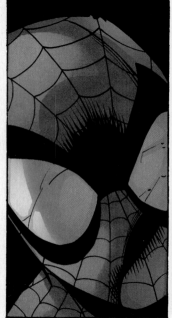

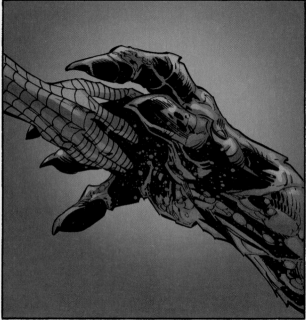

That's it.

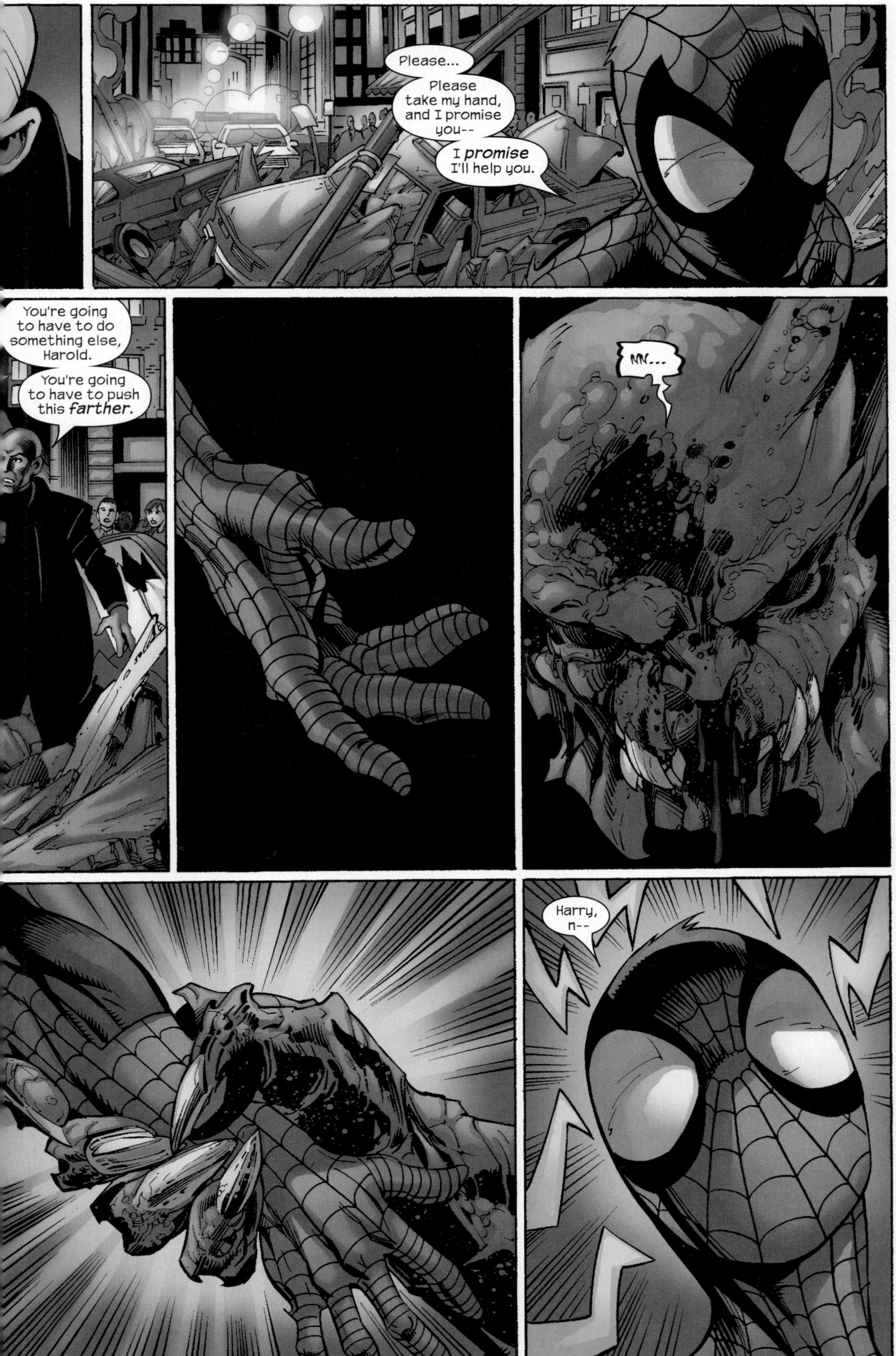
Please...
Please take my hand, and I promise you--
I *promise* I'll help you.
You're going to have to do something else, Harold.
You're going to have to push this *farther*.
NN...
Harry, n--

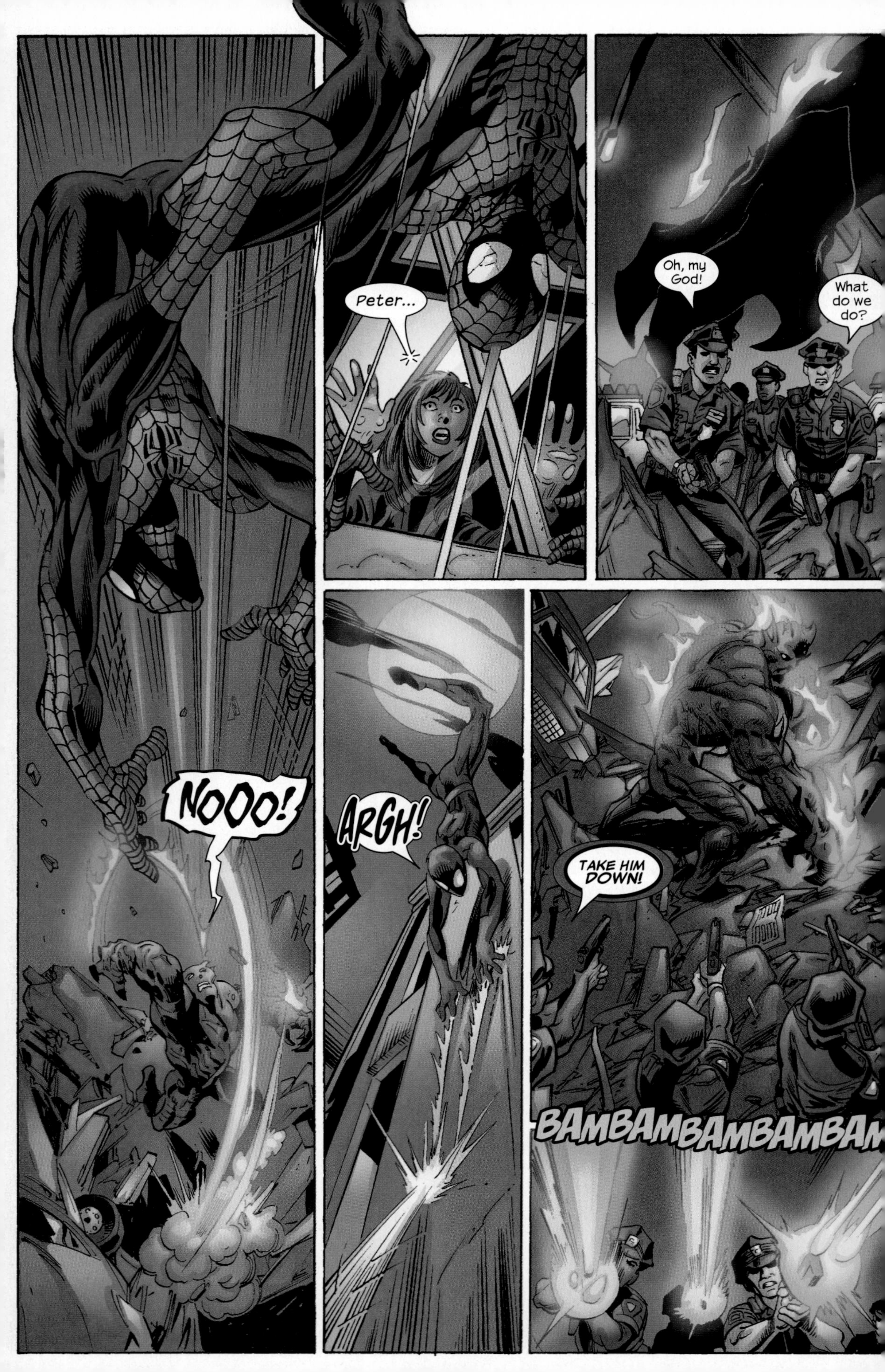

Peter...
Oh, my God!
What do we do?
NOOO!
ARGH!
TAKE HIM DOWN!
BAMBAMBAMBAMBAM

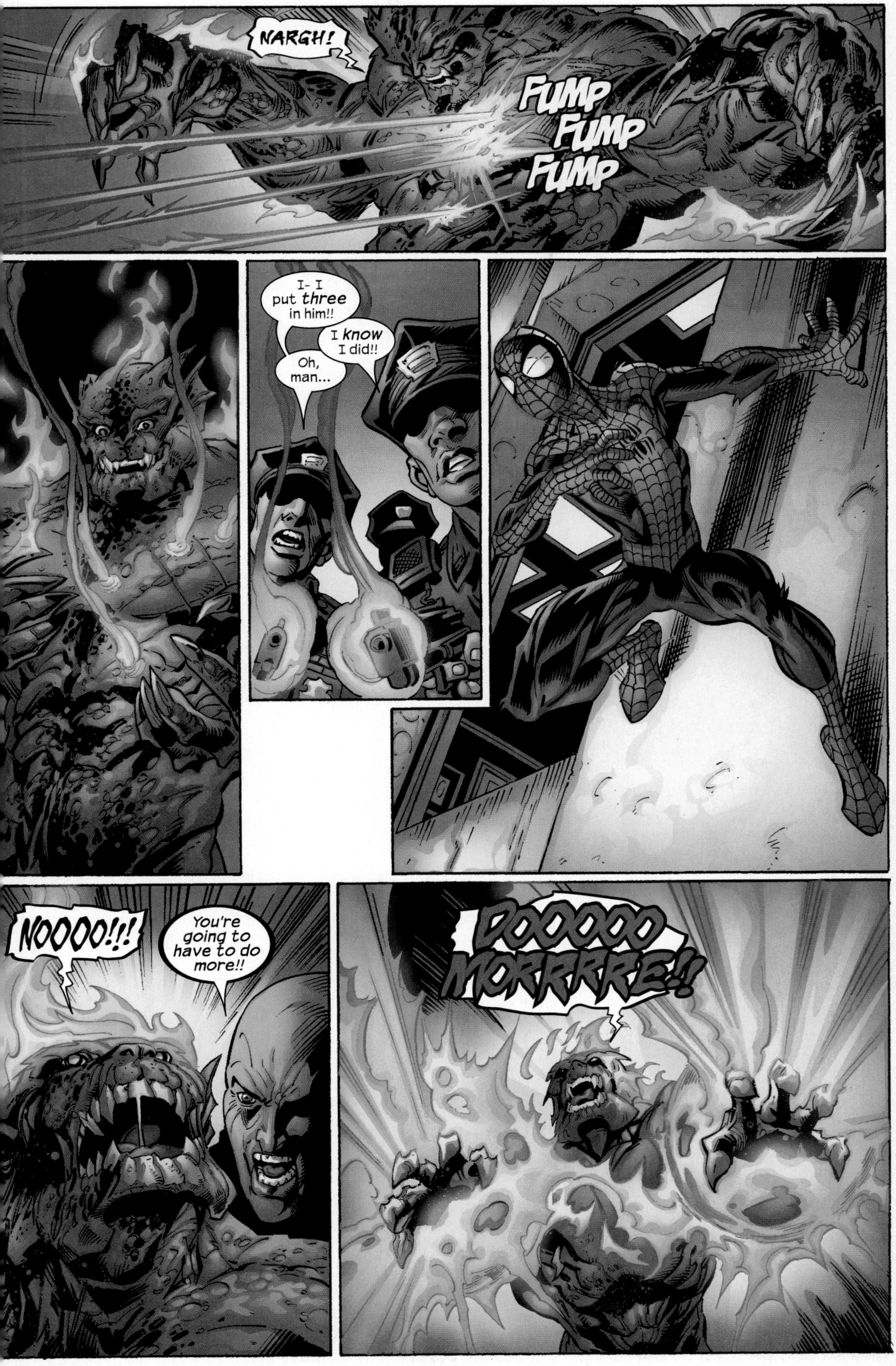
NARGH!
FUMP
FUMP
FUMP
I- I put three in him!!
I know I did!!
Oh, man...
NOOOO!!!
You're going to have to do more!!
DOOOOOO MORRRRE!!

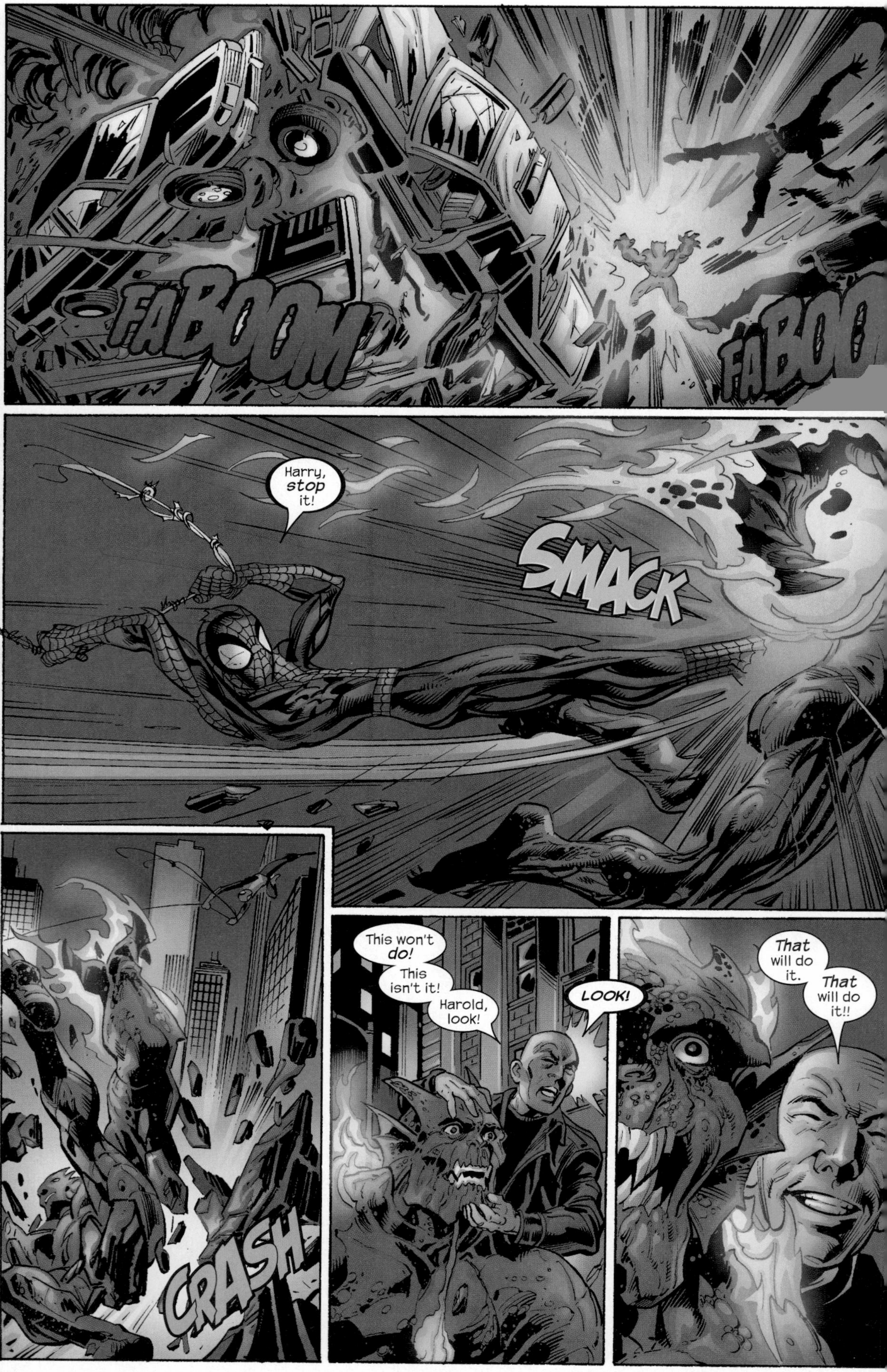
FABOOM
FABOOM
Harry, stop it!
SMACK
CRASH
This won't do!
This isn't it!
Harold, look!
LOOK!
That will do it.
That will do it!!

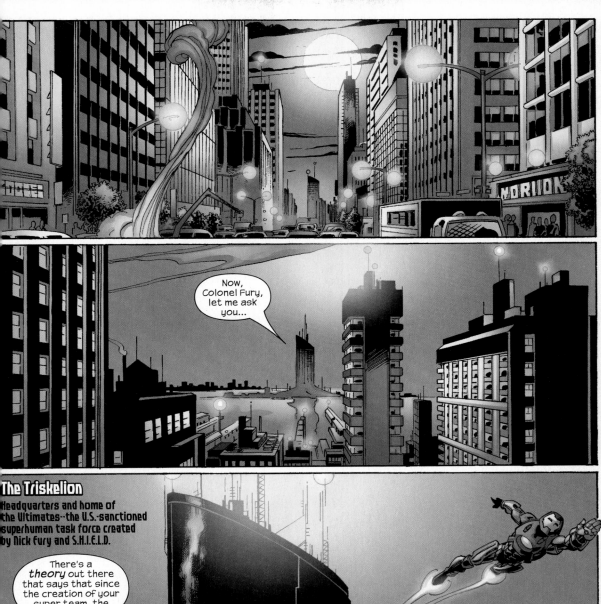

Now, Colonel Fury, let me ask you...

The Triskelion
Headquarters and home of the Ultimates--the U.S.-sanctioned superhuman task force created by Nick Fury and S.H.I.E.L.D.

There's a *theory* out there that says that since the creation of your super team, the Ultimates...

...the threats against our society have *escalated* in scope.

I'm not--

The idea being that the existence of the Ultimates has in *itself* brought on the very threats it has sworn to protect us from.

Wow. That- that is the dumbest bunch of--

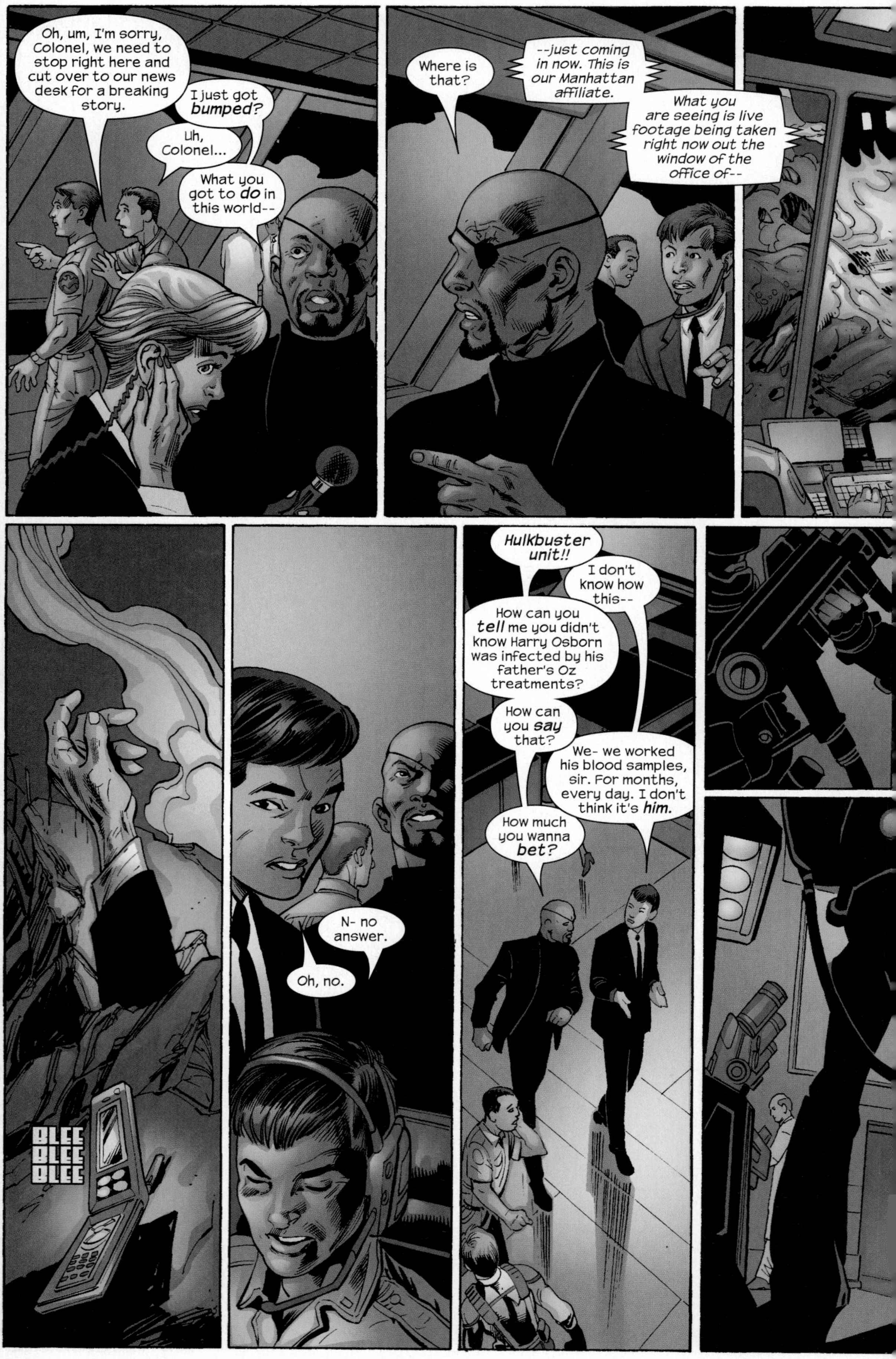
Oh, um, I'm sorry, Colonel, we need to stop right here and cut over to our news desk for a breaking story.
I just got bumped?
Uh, Colonel...
What you got to do in this world--
Where is that?
--just coming in now. This is our Manhattan affiliate.
What you are seeing is live footage being taken right now out the window of the office of--
BLEE BLEE BLEE
N- no answer.
Oh, no.
Hulkbuster unit!!
I don't know how this--
How can you tell me you didn't know Harry Osborn was infected by his father's Oz treatments?
How can you say that?
We- we worked his blood samples, sir. For months, every day. I don't think it's him.
How much you wanna bet?

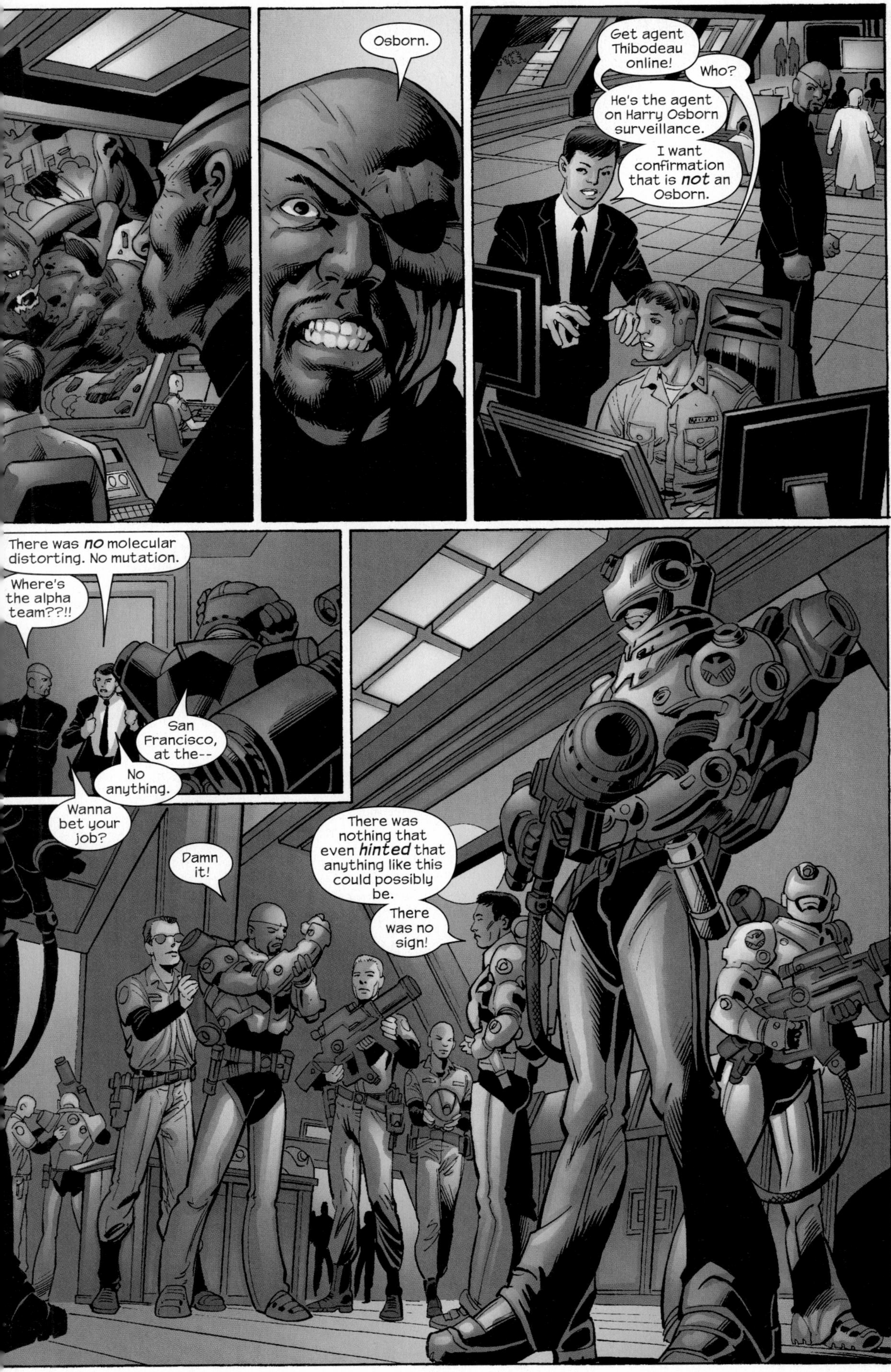

Osborn.
Get agent Thibodeau online!
Who?
He's the agent on Harry Osborn surveillance.
I want confirmation that is not an Osborn.
There was no molecular distorting. No mutation.
Where's the alpha team??!!
San Francisco, at the--
No anything.
Wanna bet your job?
Damn it!
There was nothing that even hinted that anything like this could possibly be.
There was no sign!

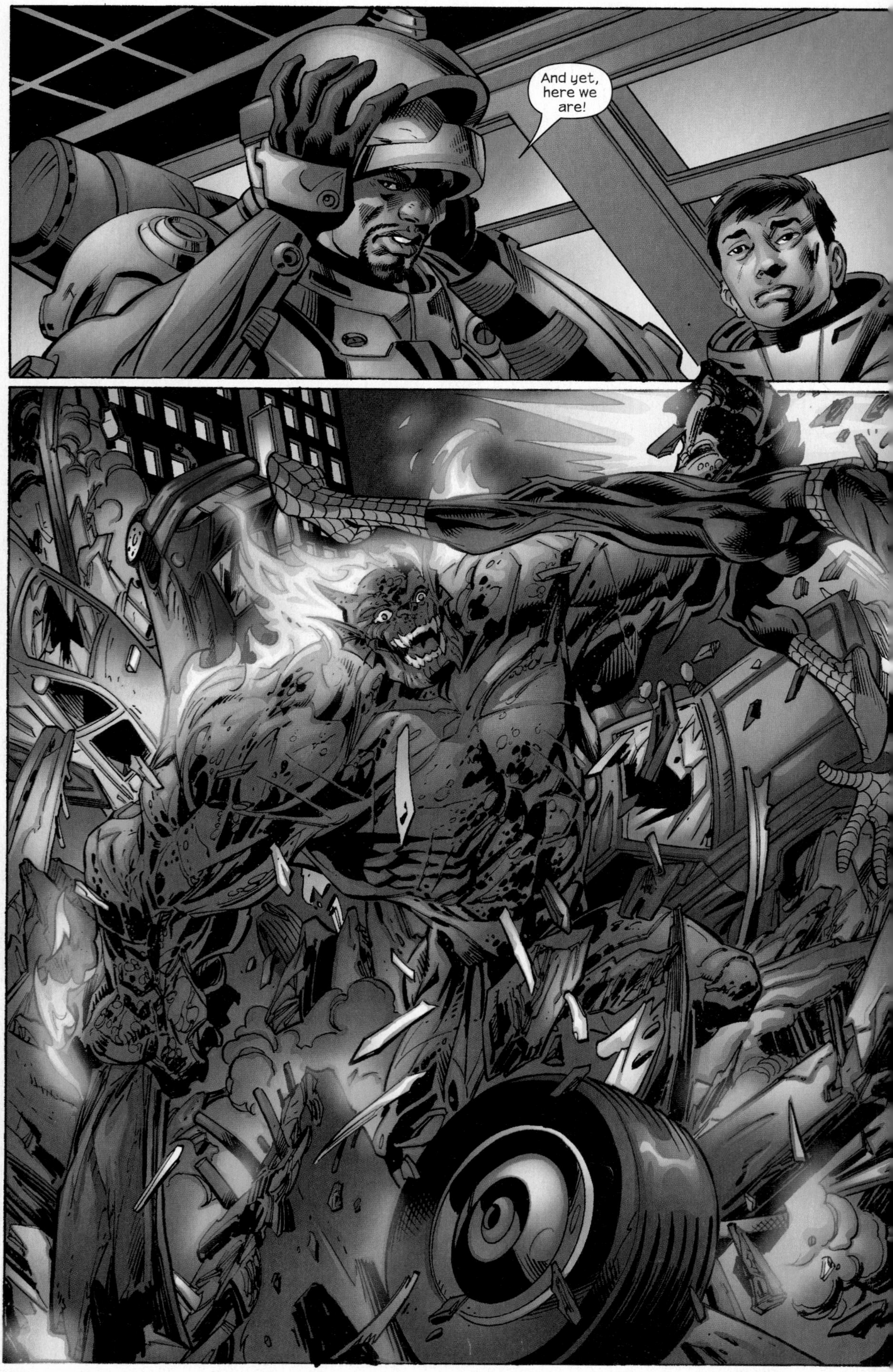
And yet, here we are!

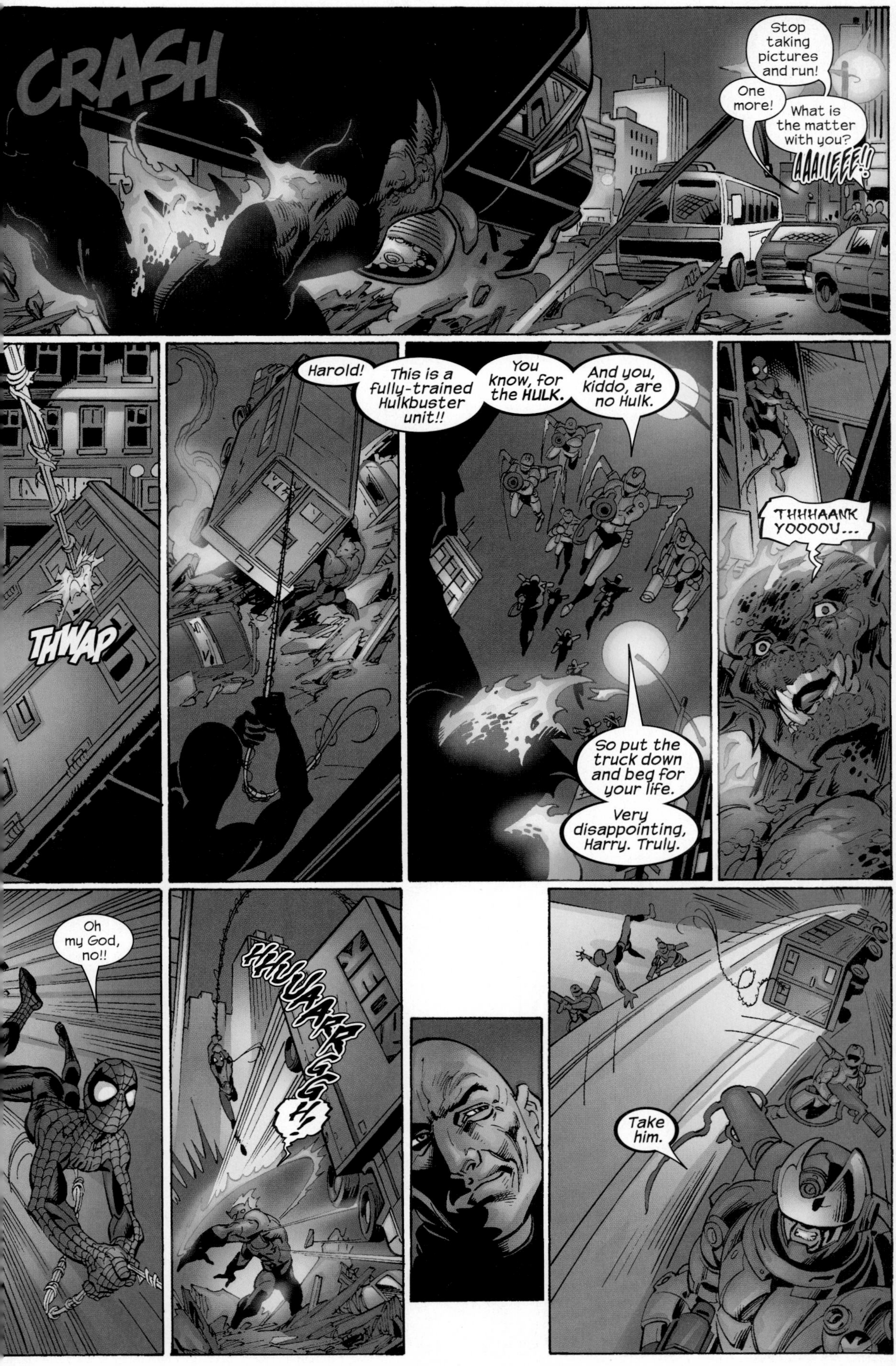
CRASH
Stop taking pictures and run!
One more!
What is the matter with you?
AAAIIEEE!!
THWAP
Harold!
This is a fully-trained Hulkbuster unit!!
You know, for the HULK.
And you, kiddo, are no Hulk.
So put the truck down and beg for your life.
Very disappointing, Harry. Truly.
THHHAANK YOOOOU...
Oh my God, no!!
HHUUAARRGGH!!
Take him.

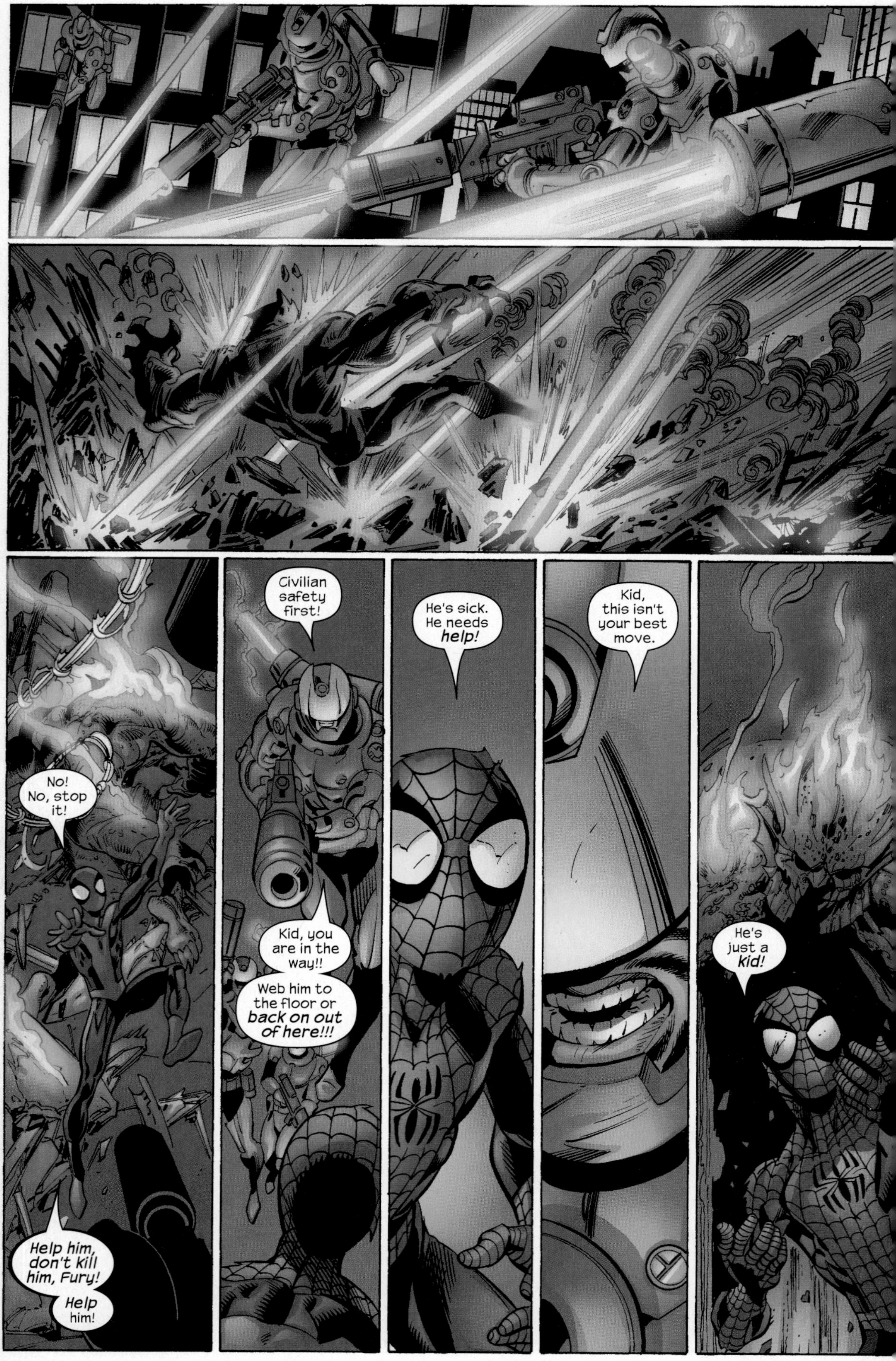
No! No, stop it!
Help him, don't kill him, Fury!
Help him!
Civilian safety first!
Kid, you are in the way!!
Web him to the floor or back on out of here!!!
He's sick. He needs help!
Kid, this isn't your best move.
He's just a kid!

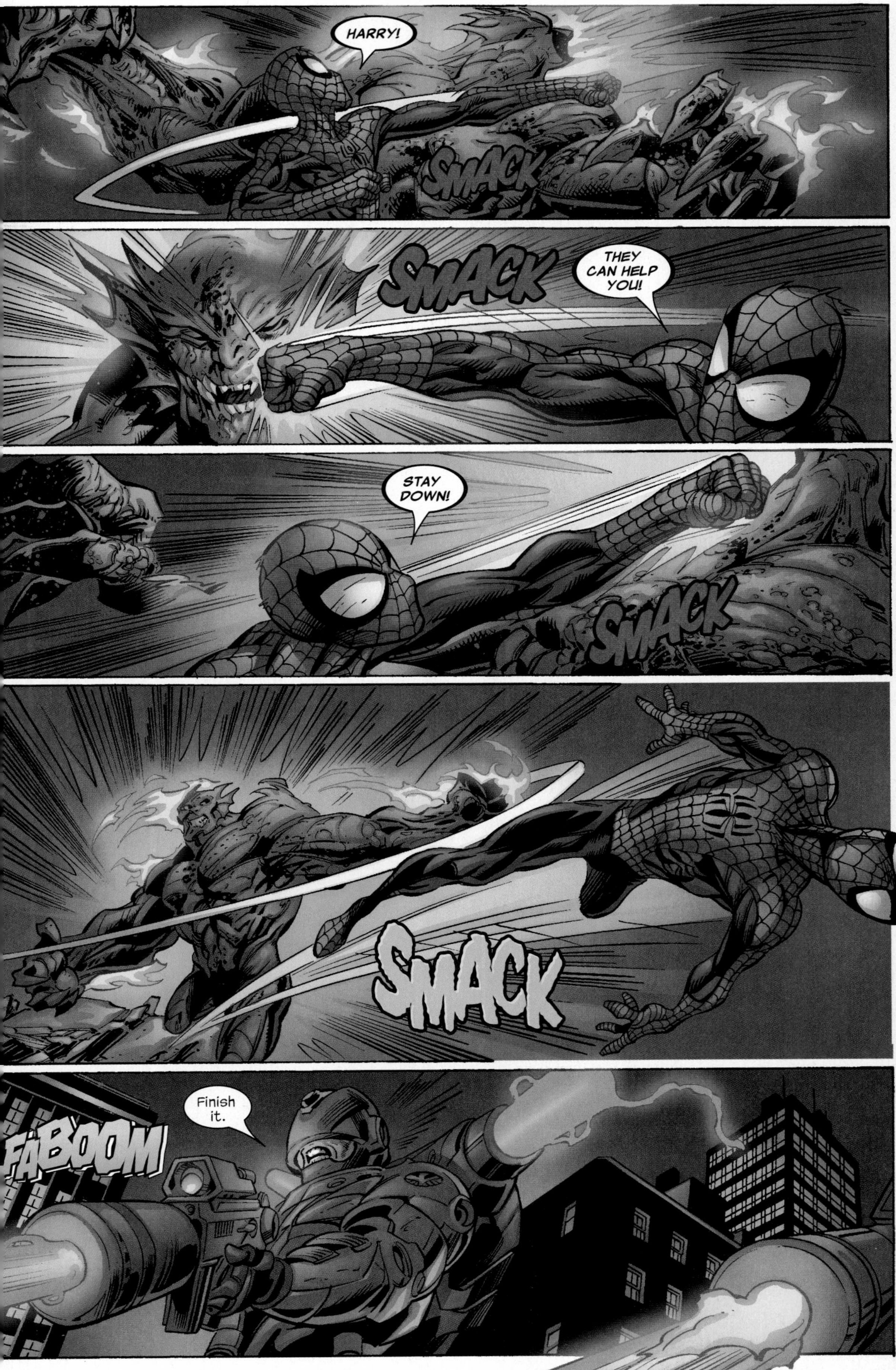
HARRY!
SMACK
SMACK
THEY CAN HELP YOU!
STAY DOWN!
SMACK
SMACK
FABOOM
Finish it.

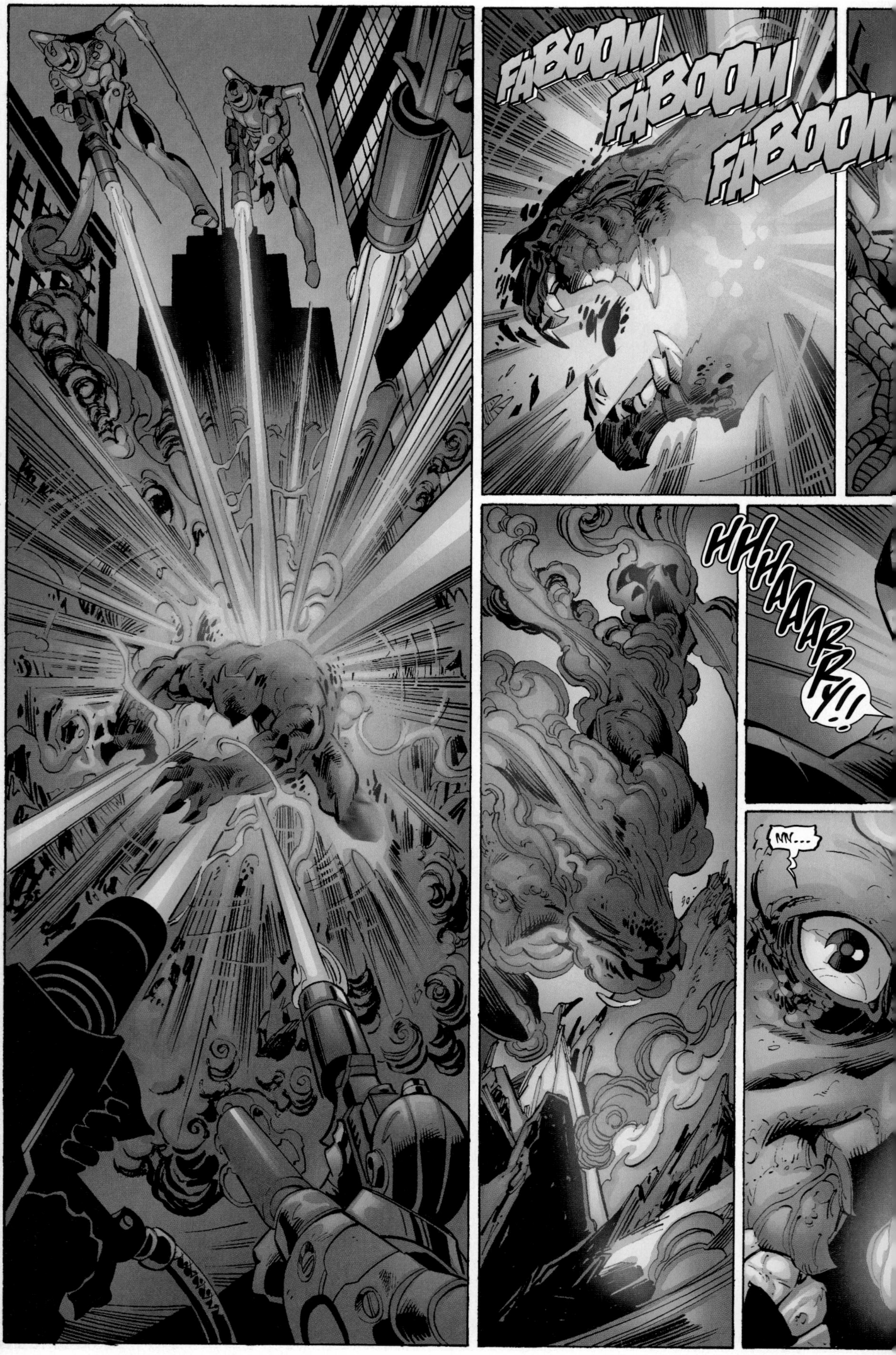
FaBOOM
FaBOOM
FaBOOM
HHHAAARRY!!
NN...

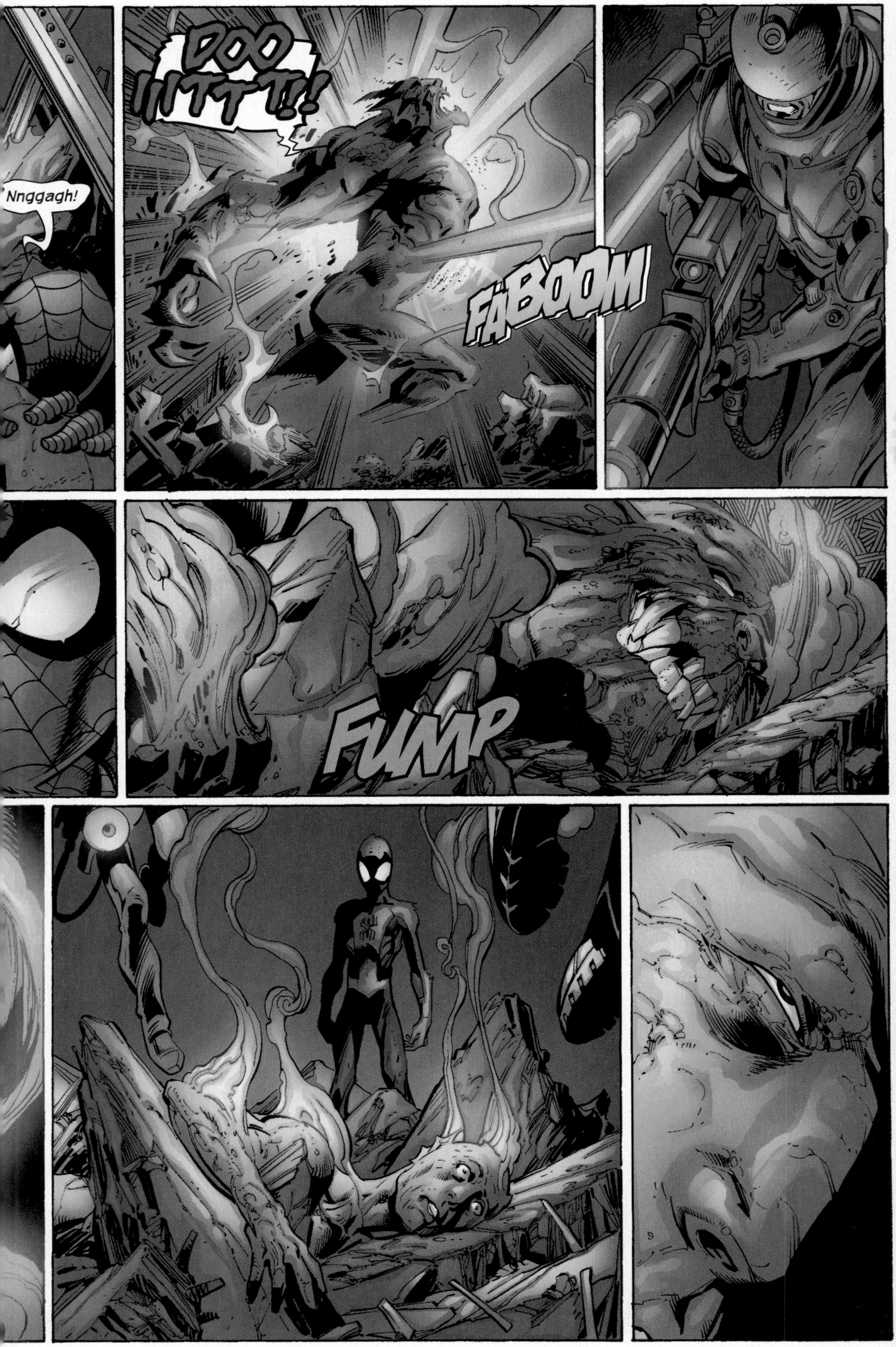
Nngggagh!
DOO IITTTT!!
FABOOM
FUMP

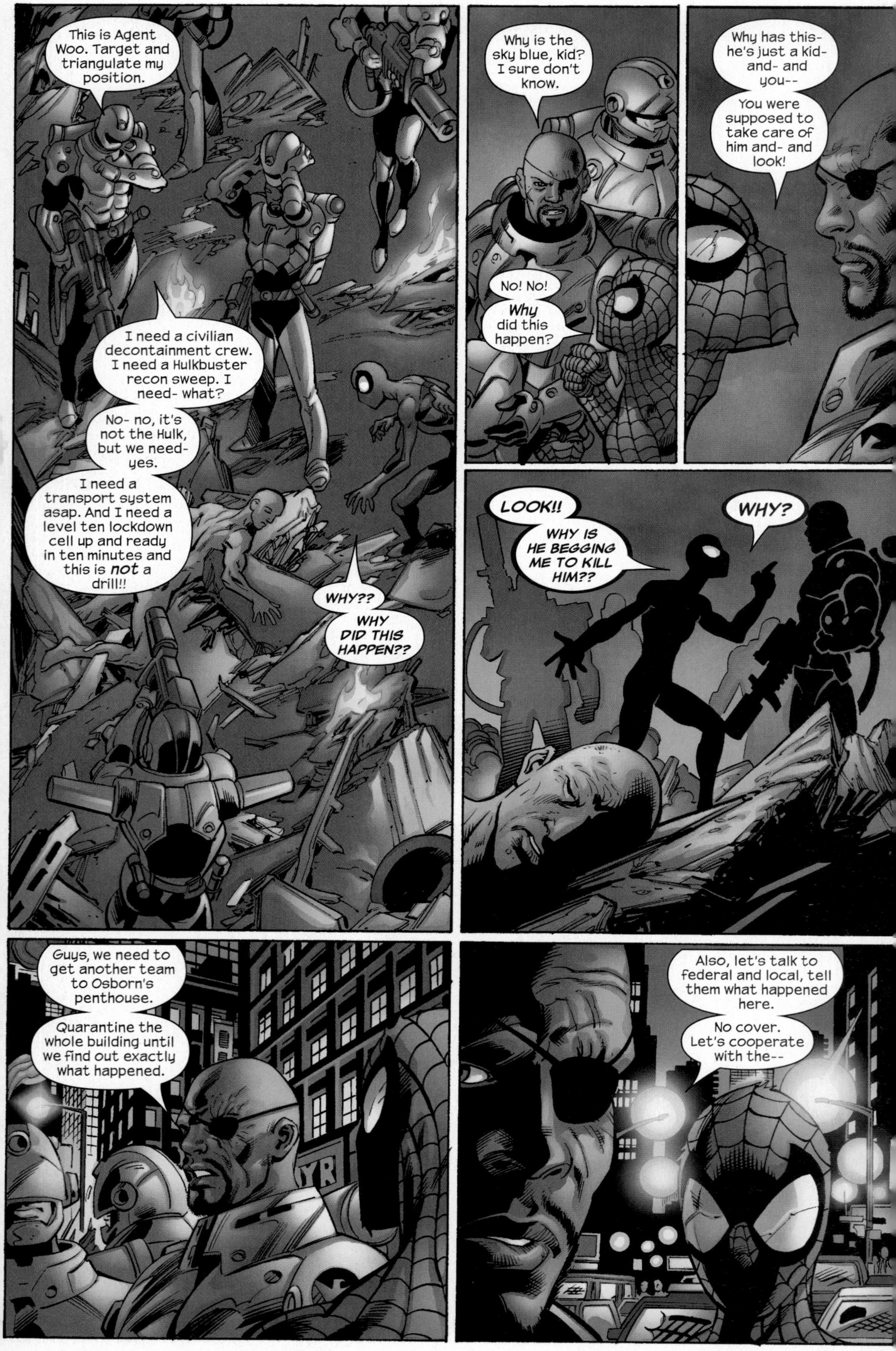
This is Agent Woo. Target and triangulate my position.
I need a civilian decontainment crew. I need a Hulkbuster recon sweep. I need- what?
No- no, it's not the Hulk, but we need- yes.
I need a transport system asap. And I need a level ten lockdown cell up and ready in ten minutes and this is *not* a drill!!
WHY??
WHY DID THIS HAPPEN??
Why is the sky blue, kid? I sure don't know.
No! No!
Why did this happen?
Why has this- he's just a kid- and- and you--
You were supposed to take care of him and- and look!
LOOK!!
WHY IS HE BEGGING ME TO KILL HIM??
WHY?
Guys, we need to get another team to Osborn's penthouse.
Quarantine the whole building until we find out exactly what happened.
Also, let's talk to federal and local, tell them what happened here.
No cover. Let's cooperate with the--

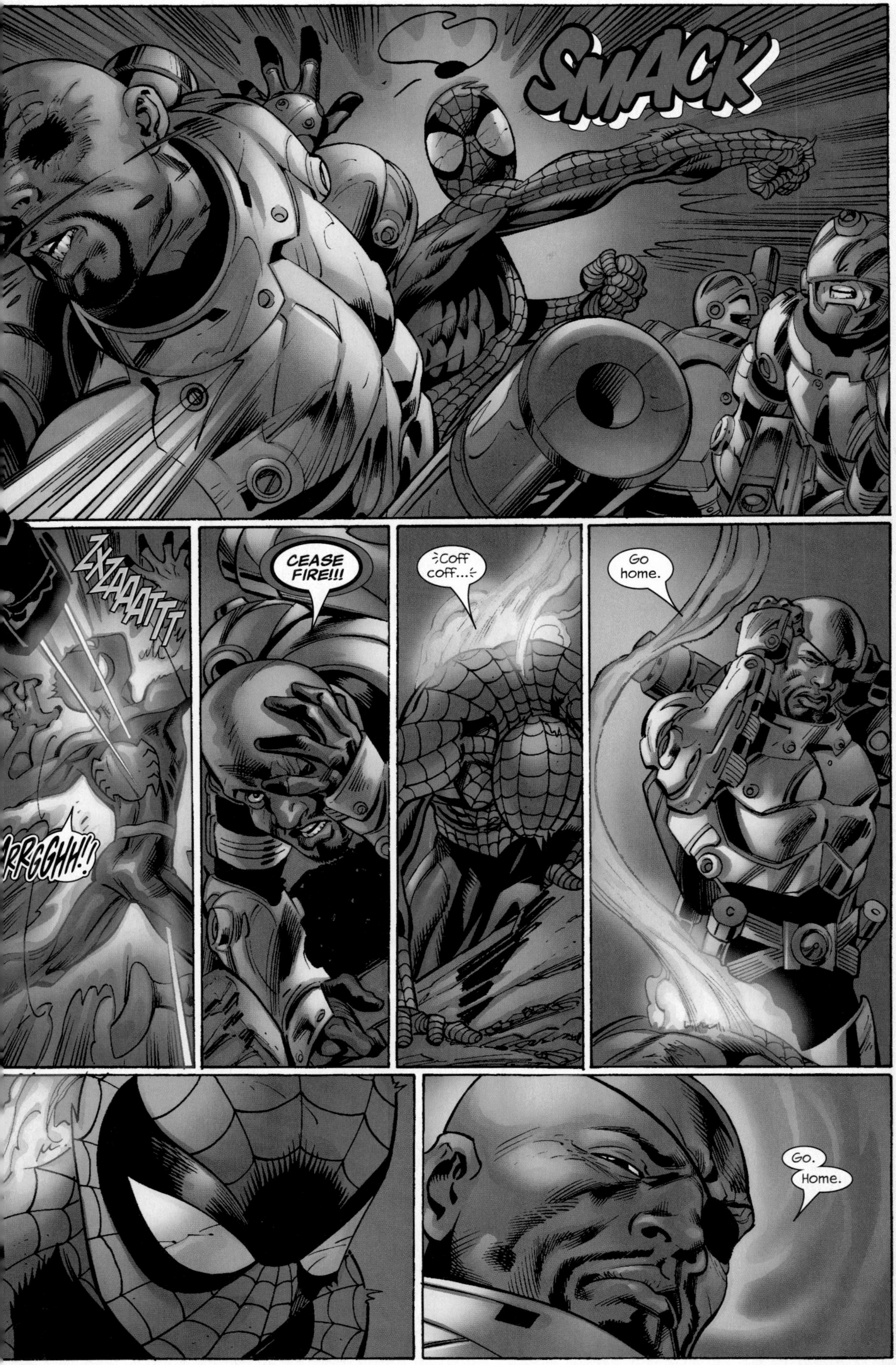
SMACK
ZXZAAATTTT
RRGGHH!!
CEASE FIRE!!!
Coff coff...
Go home.
Go.
Home.

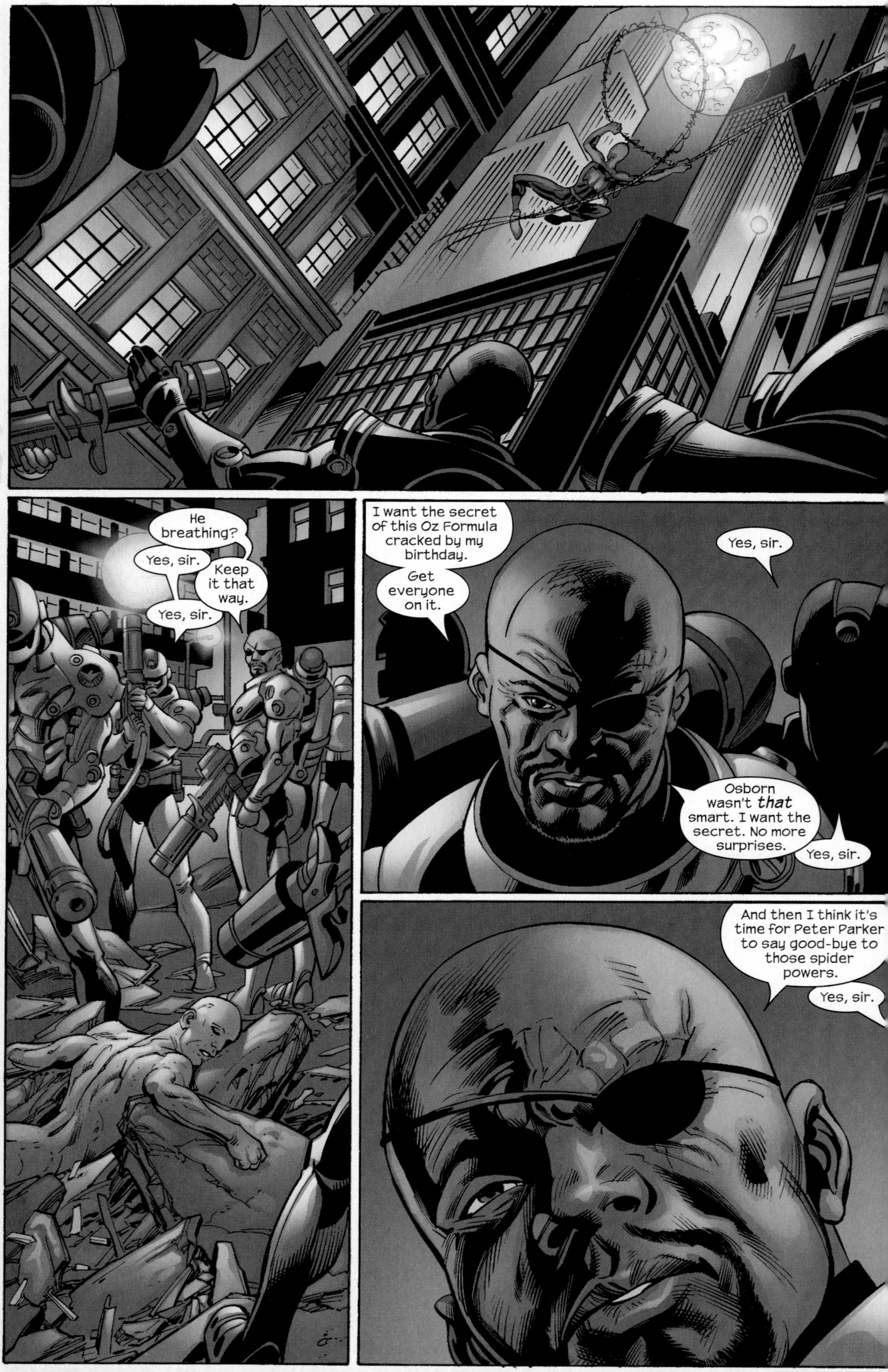
He breathing?
Yes, sir.
Keep it that way.
Yes, sir.
I want the secret of this Oz Formula cracked by my birthday.
Get everyone on it.
Yes, sir.
Osborn wasn't *that* smart. I want the secret. No more surprises.
Yes, sir.
And then I think it's time for Peter Parker to say good-bye to those spider powers.
Yes, sir.

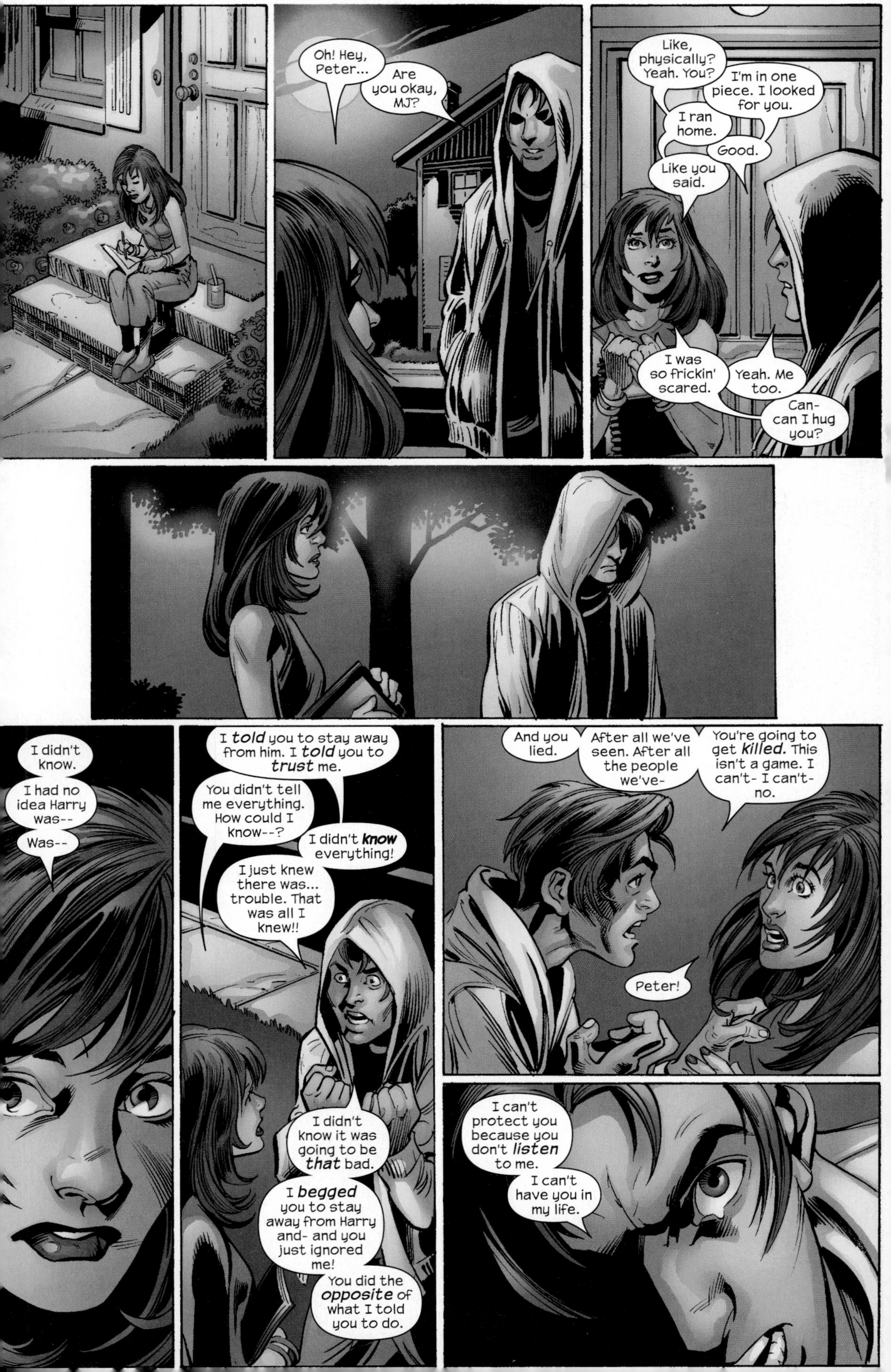
Oh! Hey, Peter...
Are you okay, MJ?
Like, physically? Yeah. You?
I'm in one piece. I looked for you.
I ran home.
Good.
Like you said.
I was so frickin' scared.
Yeah. Me too.
Can- can I hug you?
I didn't know.
I had no idea Harry was--
Was--
I told you to stay away from him. I told you to trust me.
You didn't tell me everything. How could I know--?
I didn't know everything!
I just knew there was... trouble. That was all I knew!!
I didn't know it was going to be that bad.
I begged you to stay away from Harry and- and you just ignored me!
You did the opposite of what I told you to do.
And you lied.
After all we've seen. After all the people we've-
You're going to get killed. This isn't a game. I can't- I can't- no.
Peter!
I can't protect you because you don't listen to me.
I can't have you in my life.

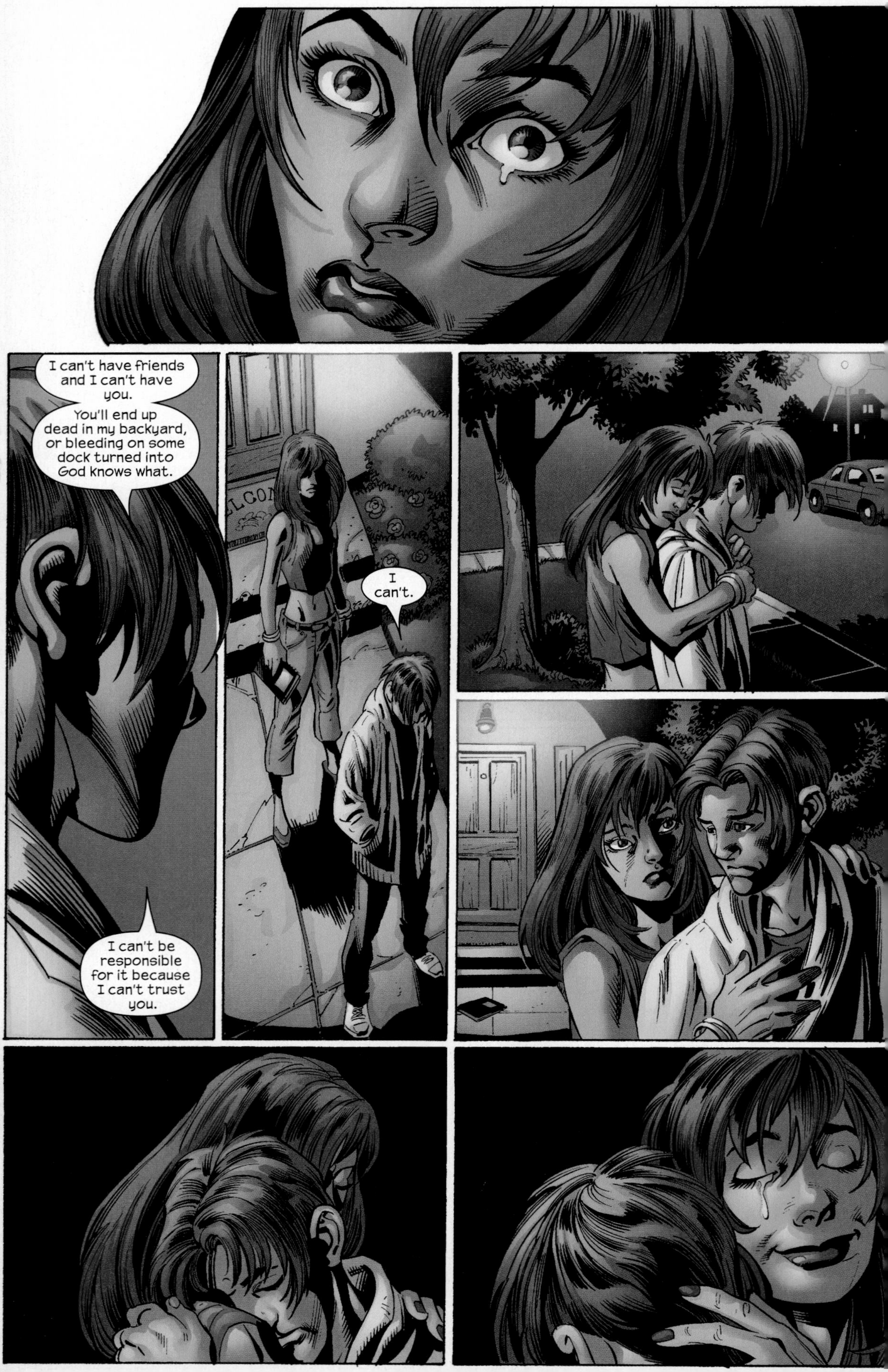
I can't have friends and I can't have you.
You'll end up dead in my backyard, or bleeding on some dock turned into God knows what.
I can't be responsible for it because I can't trust you.
I can't.

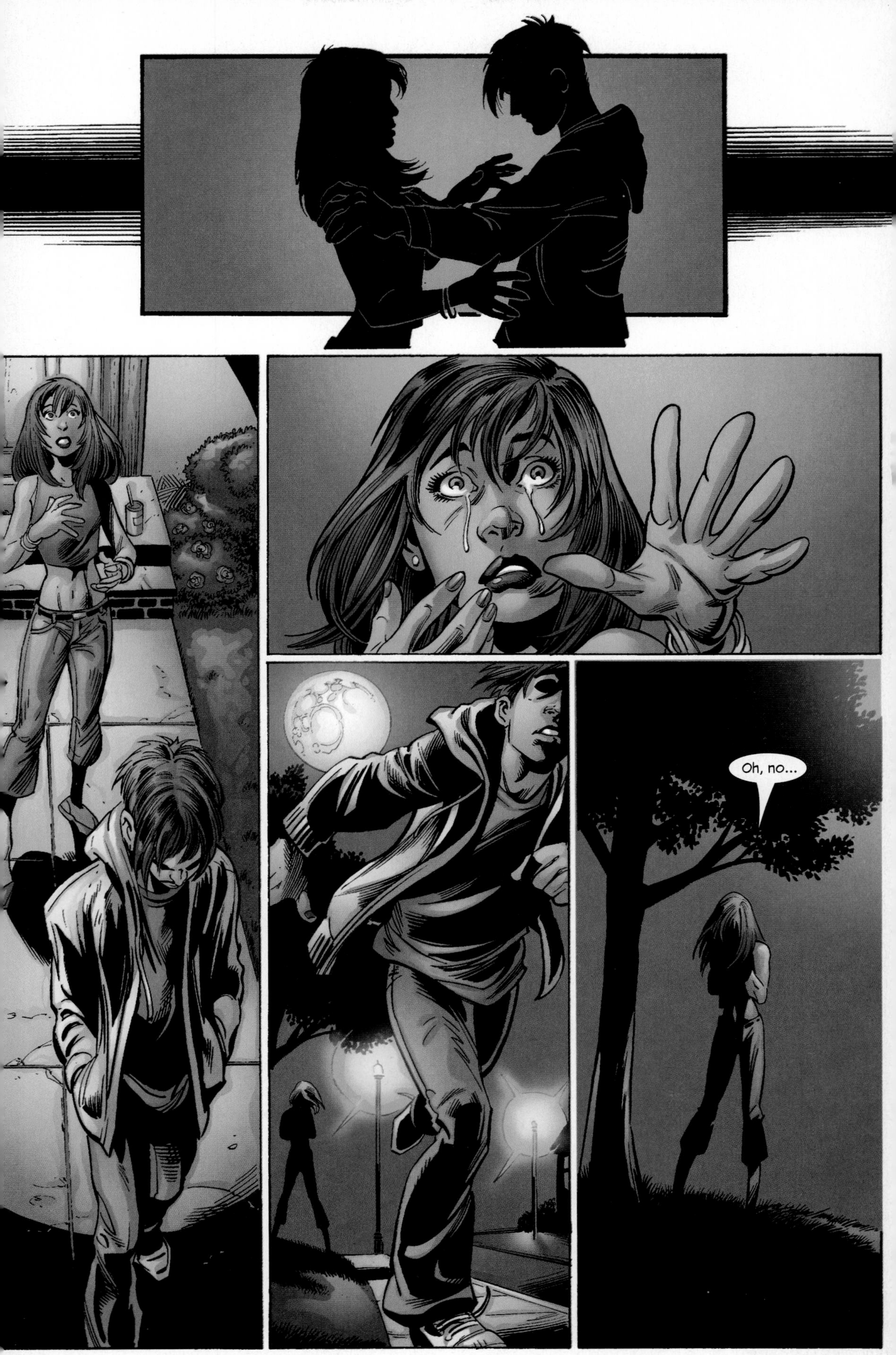
Oh, no...

78

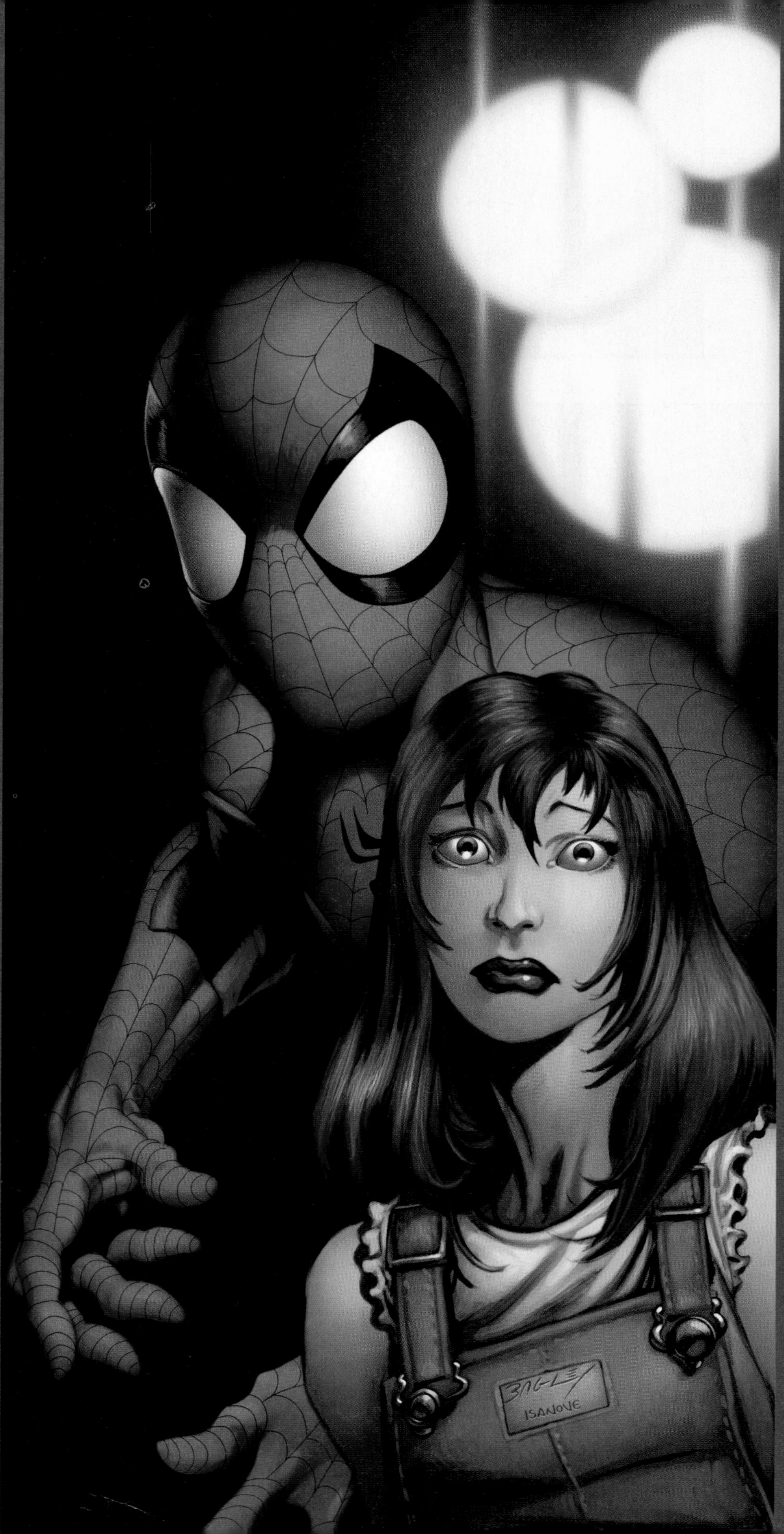
BAGLEY
ISANOVE

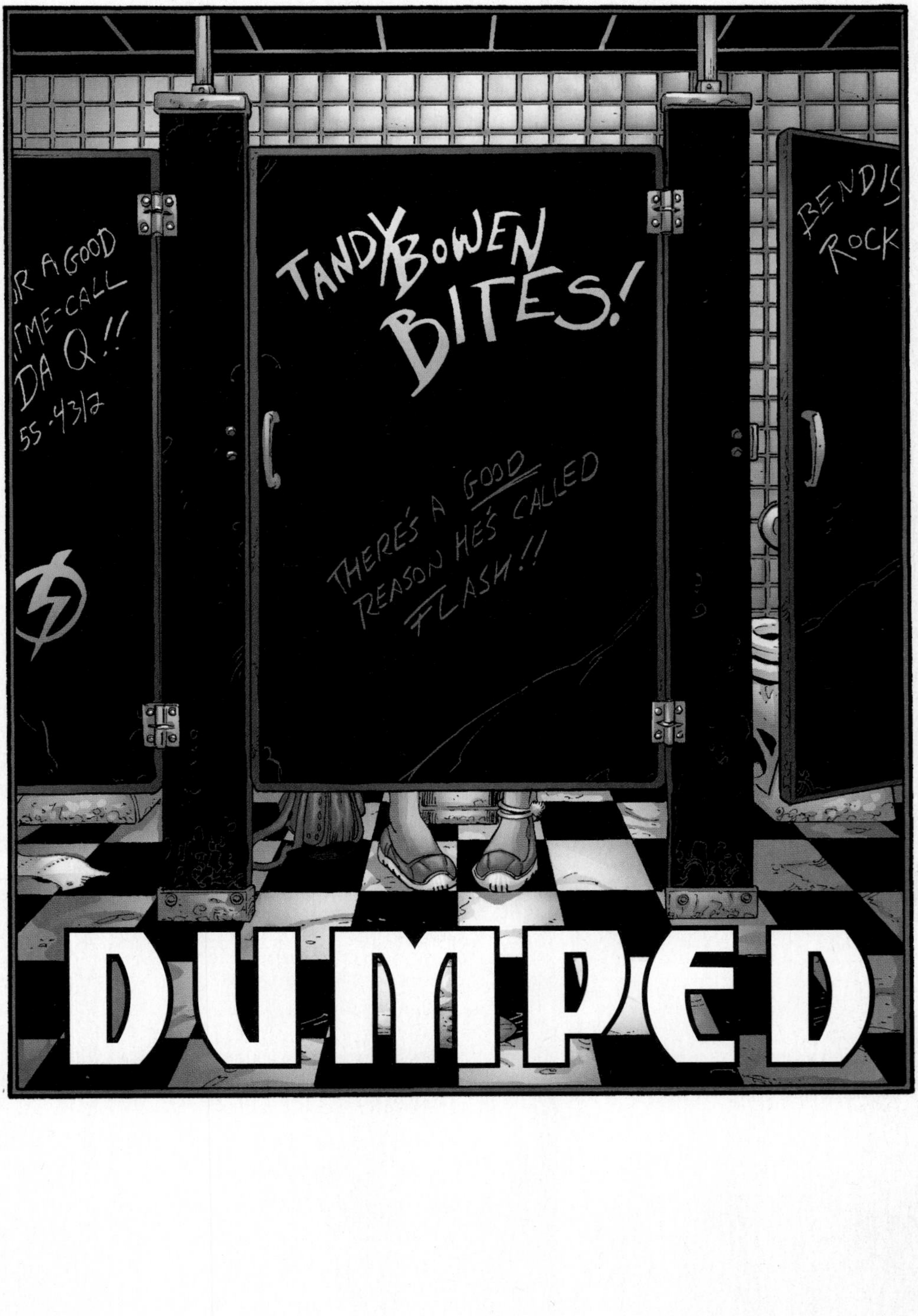

R A GOOD
TIME-CALL
DA Q!!
55-4312
TANDY BOWEN BITES!
THERE'S A GOOD REASON HE'S CALLED FLASH!!
BENDIS ROCK
DUMPED

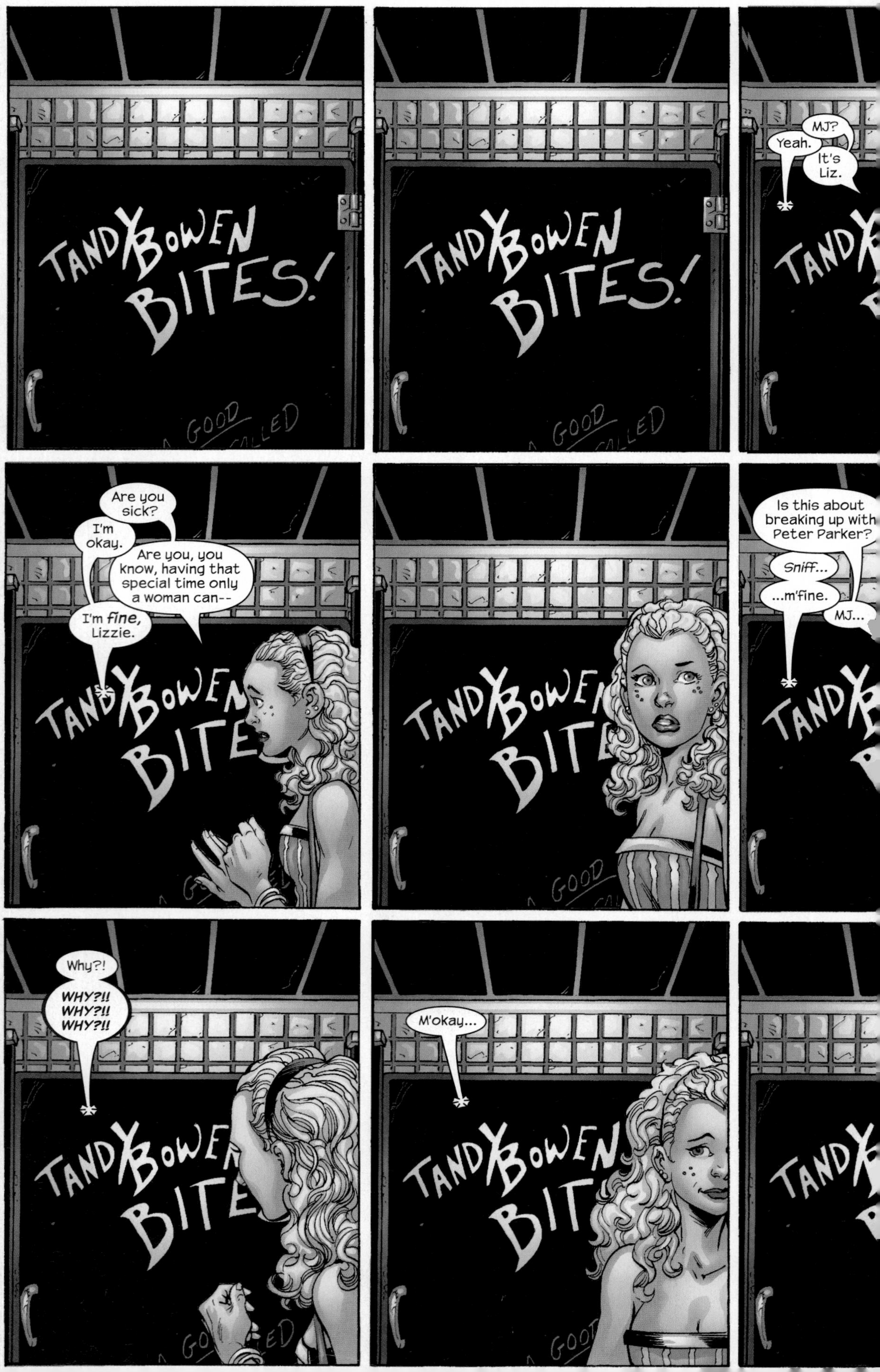

MJ?
Yeah.
It's Liz.
Are you sick?
I'm okay.
Are you, you know, having that special time only a woman can--
I'm *fine,* Lizzie.
Is this about breaking up with Peter Parker?
Sniff...
...m'fine.
MJ...
Why?!
WHY?!! WHY?!! WHY?!!
M'okay...

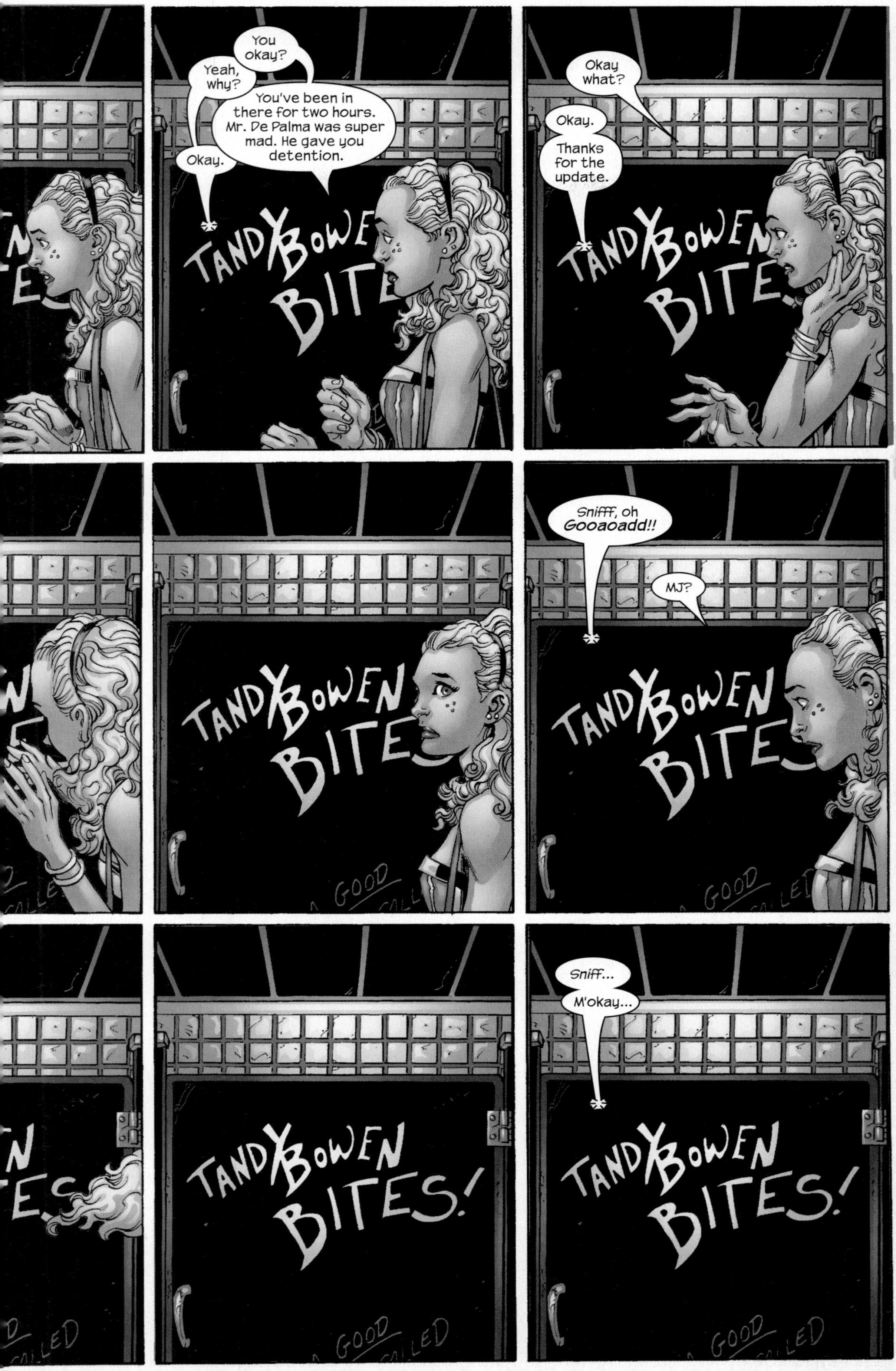

You okay?
Yeah, why?
You've been in there for two hours. Mr. De Palma was super mad. He gave you detention.
Okay.
TANDY BOWEN BITES
Okay what?
Okay.
Thanks for the update.
TANDY BOWEN BITES
TANDY BOWEN BITES
A GOOD
Sniff, oh Gooaoadd!!
MJ?
TANDY BOWEN BITES
A GOOD
TANDY BOWEN BITES!
A GOOD CALLED
Sniff...
M'okay...
TANDY BOWEN BITES!
A GOOD CALLED

You had to watch a DVD!

A DVD!!

Your homework was to watch a DVD and *still* you did not do it!!

I really want to know!

What is it going to *take* for you people to *do* your homework??

Because I am at my wit's end.

Is the invention of reality TV so astonishing that— Kenny!

Kenny, tell me what *you* did last night instead of your assigned homework?

Um...

Please, pleas[e] regale us all wi[th] stories of yo[ur] dazzling nightlife.

This life of yours that is so *full* that doing homework comes a distant third.

Why are you picking on *me*?

Oh, you think *this* is picking on you, young man? Wait until your parents get your midterm grade.

Well, what would you all like to discuss then?

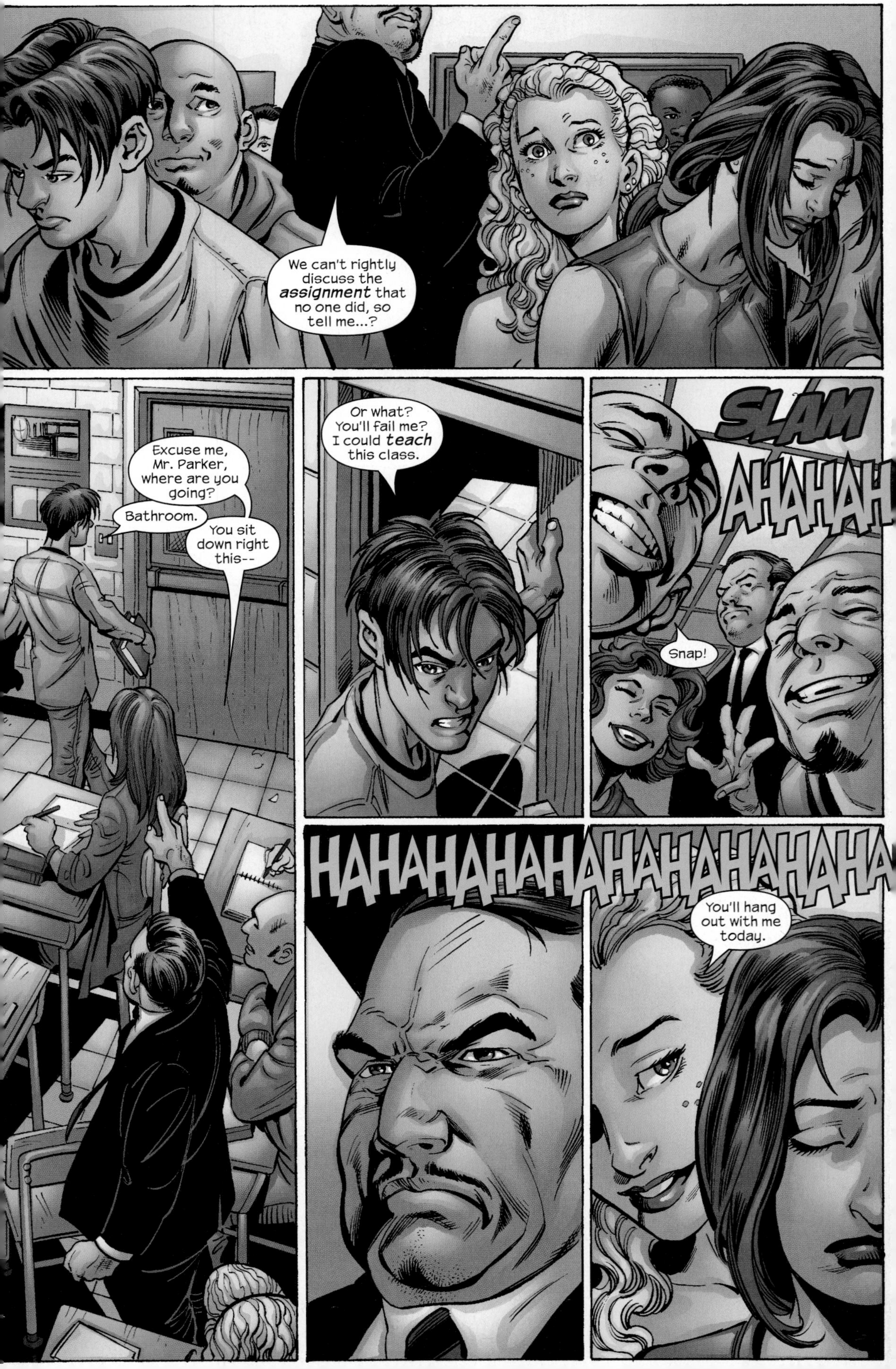
We can't rightly discuss the *assignment* that no one did, so tell me...?
Excuse me, Mr. Parker, where are you going?
Bathroom.
You sit down right this--
Or what? You'll fail me? I could *teach* this class.
SLAM
AHAHAH
Snap!
HAHAHAHAHAHAHAHAHAHAHA
You'll hang out with me today.

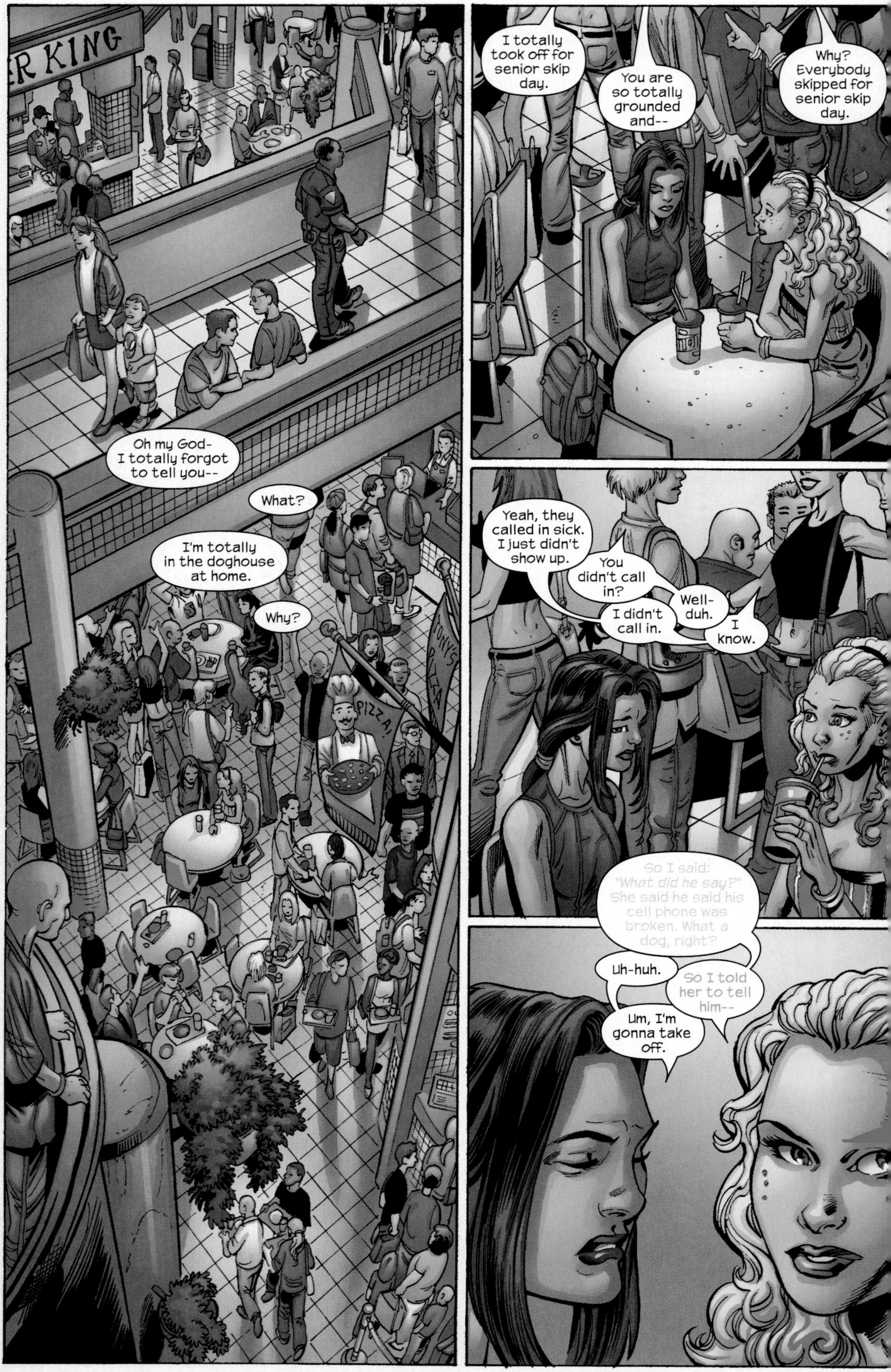
ER KING
Oh my God- I totally forgot to tell you--
What?
I'm totally in the doghouse at home.
Why?
PIZZA!
TONY'S PIZZA
I totally took off for senior skip day.
You are so totally grounded and--
Why? Everybody skipped for senior skip day.
Yeah, they called in sick. I just didn't show up.
You didn't call in?
I didn't call in.
Well- duh.
I know.
So I said: "What did he say?" She said he said his cell phone was broken. What a dog, right?
Uh-huh.
So I told her to tell him--
Um, I'm gonna take off.

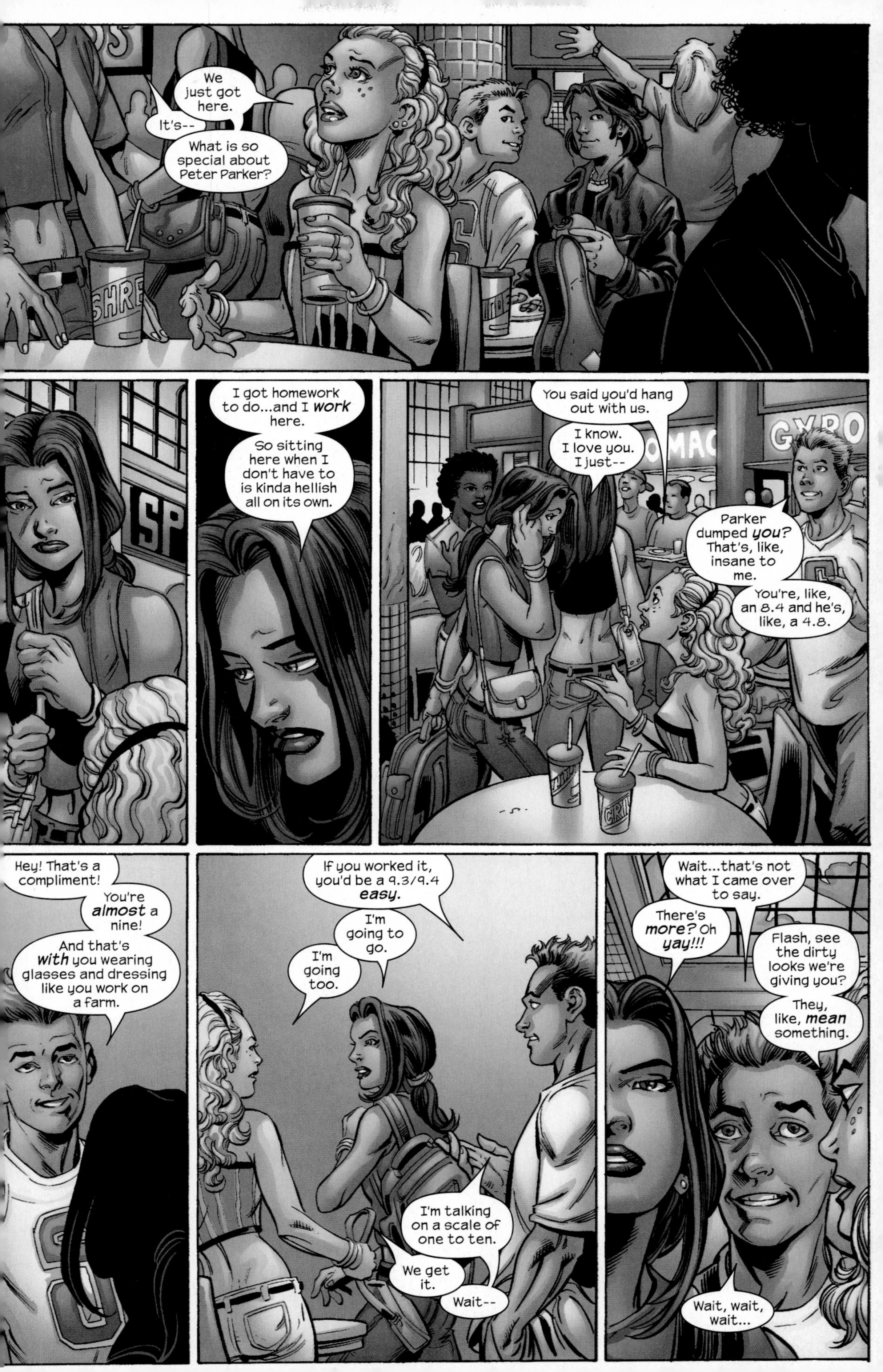

It's--
We just got here.
What is so special about Peter Parker?
I got homework to do...and I *work* here.
So sitting here when I don't have to is kinda hellish all on its own.
You said you'd hang out with us.
I know. I love you. I just--
Parker dumped *you?* That's, like, insane to me.
You're, like, an 8.4 and he's, like, a 4.8.
Hey! That's a compliment!
You're *almost* a nine!
And that's *with* you wearing glasses and dressing like you work on a farm.
If you worked it, you'd be a 9.3/9.4 *easy.*
I'm going to go.
I'm going too.
I'm talking on a scale of one to ten.
We get it.
Wait--
Wait...that's not what I came over to say.
There's *more?* Oh *yay!!!*
Flash, see the dirty looks we're giving you?
They, like, *mean* something.
Wait, wait, wait...

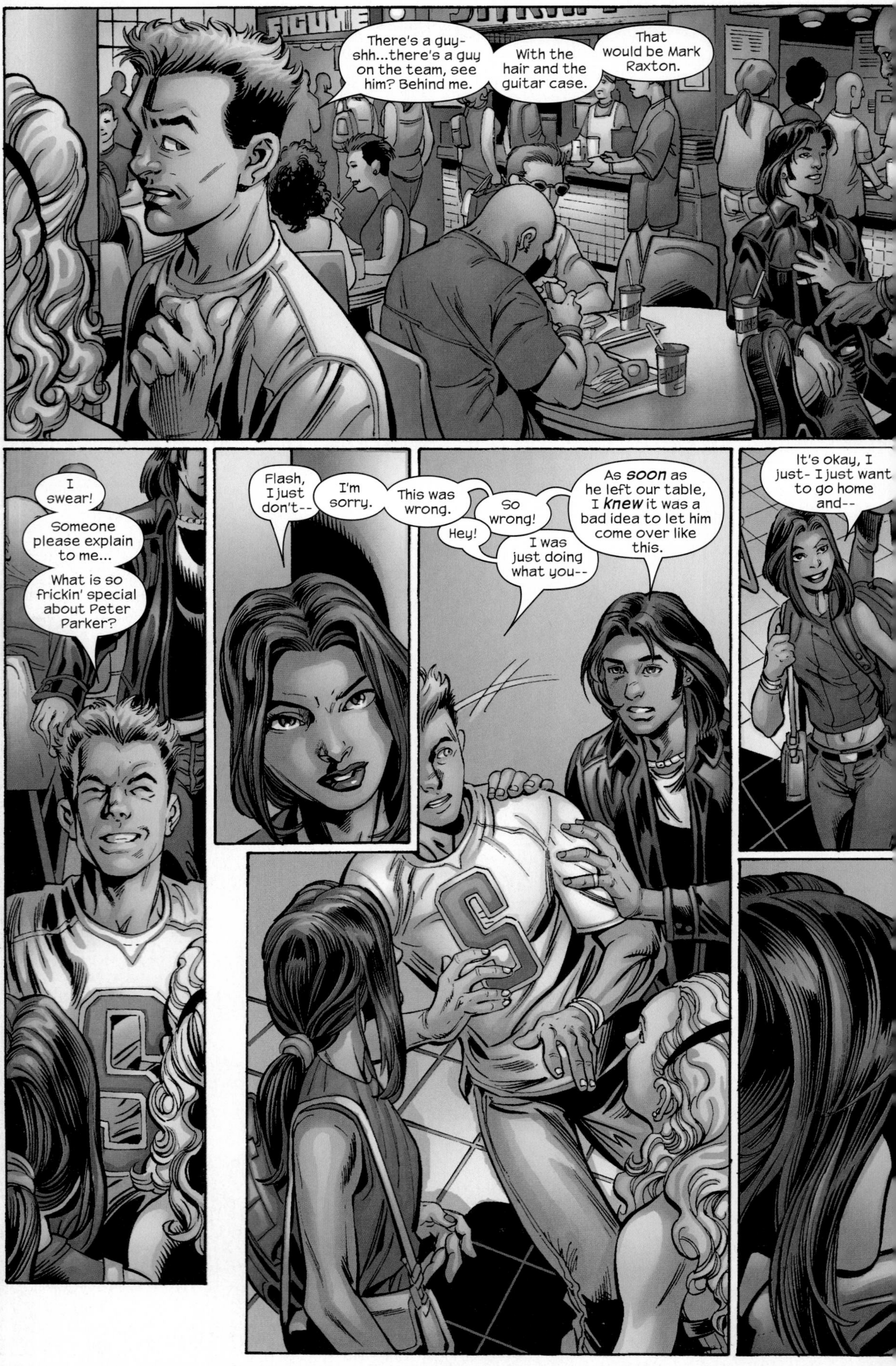
There's a guy-shh...there's a guy on the team, see him? Behind me.
With the hair and the guitar case.
That would be Mark Raxton.
I swear!
Someone please explain to me...
What is so frickin' special about Peter Parker?
Flash, I just don't--
I'm sorry.
This was wrong.
So wrong!
Hey!
I was just doing what you--
As *soon* as he left our table, I *knew* it was a bad idea to let him come over like this.
It's okay, I just- I just want to go home and--

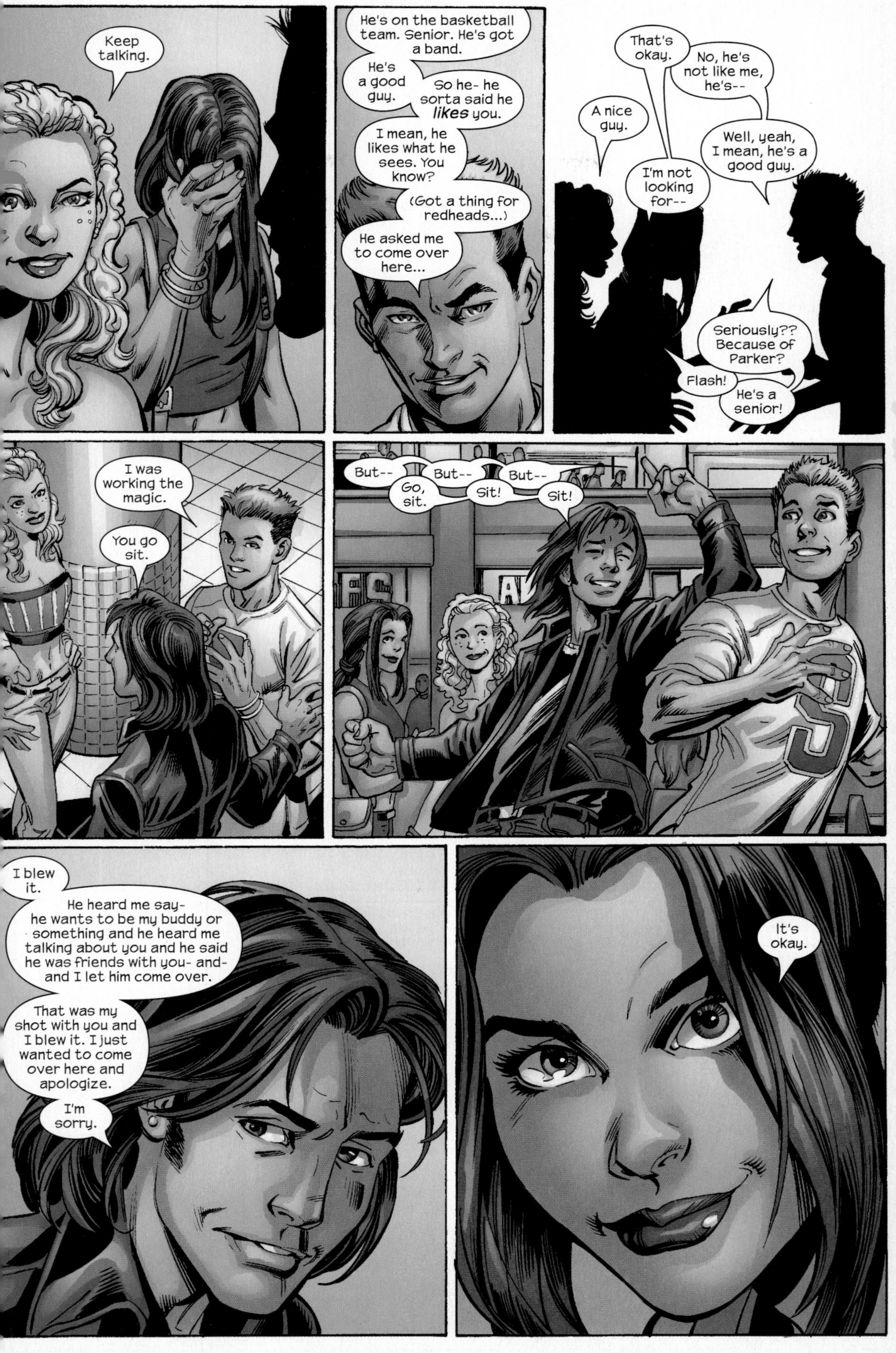

Keep talking.
He's on the basketball team. Senior. He's got a band.
He's a good guy.
So he- he sorta said he *likes* you.
I mean, he likes what he sees. You know?
(Got a thing for redheads...)
He asked me to come over here...
That's okay.
No, he's not like me, he's--
A nice guy.
I'm not looking for--
Well, yeah, I mean, he's a good guy.
Seriously?? Because of Parker?
Flash!
He's a senior!
I was working the magic.
You go sit.
But--
Go, sit.
But--
Sit!
But--
Sit!
I blew it.
He heard me say- he wants to be my buddy or something and he heard me talking about you and he said he was friends with you- and- and I let him come over.
That was my shot with you and I blew it. I just wanted to come over here and apologize.
I'm sorry.
It's okay.

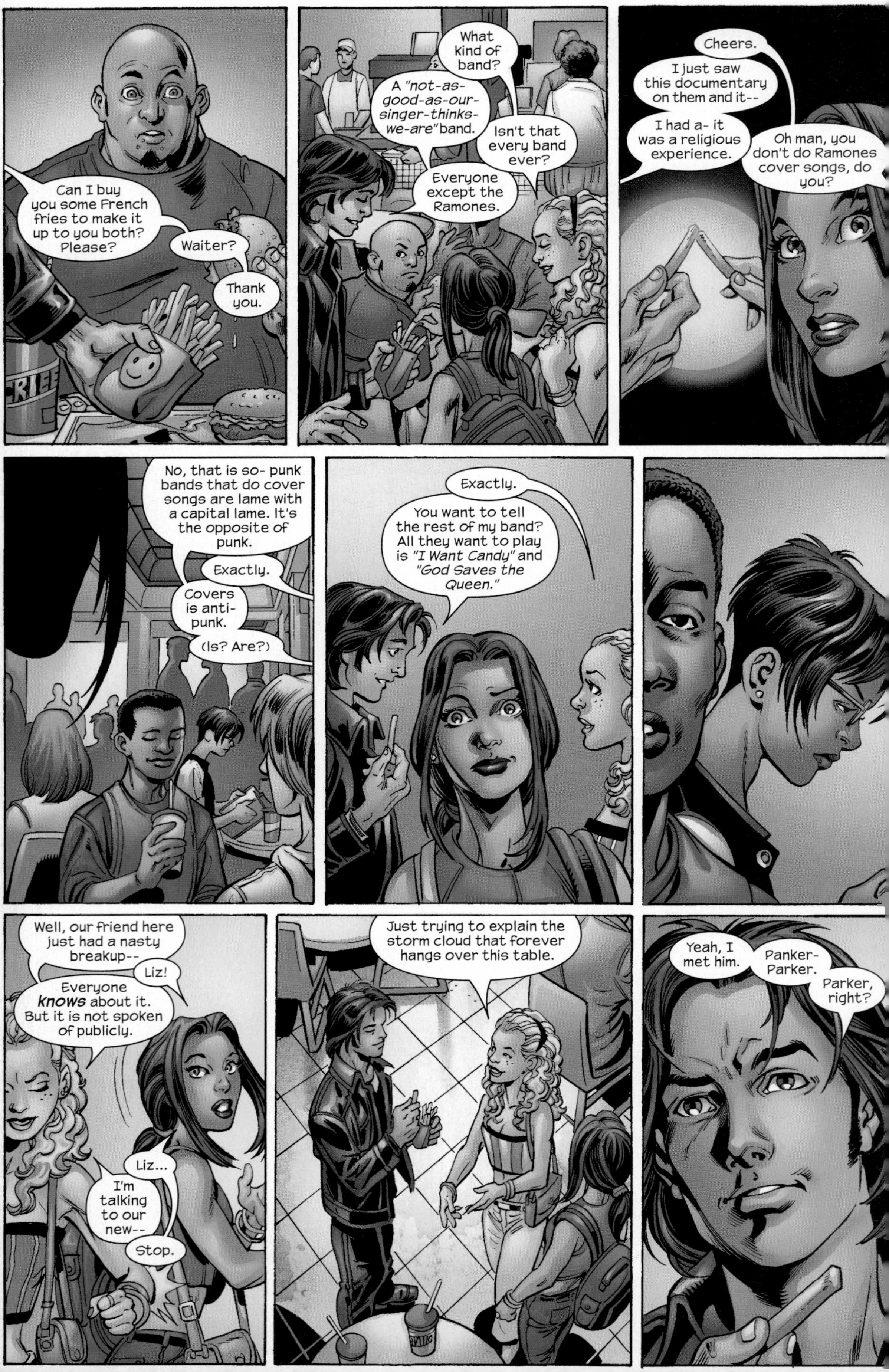
Can I buy you some French fries to make it up to you both? Please?
Waiter?
Thank you.
What kind of band?
A "not-as-good-as-our-singer-thinks-we-are" band.
Isn't that every band ever?
Everyone except the Ramones.
Cheers.
I just saw this documentary on them and it--
I had a- it was a religious experience.
Oh man, you don't do Ramones cover songs, do you?
No, that is so- punk bands that do cover songs are lame with a capital lame. It's the opposite of punk.
Exactly.
Covers is anti-punk.
(Is? Are?)
Exactly.
You want to tell the rest of my band? All they want to play is "I Want Candy" and "God Saves the Queen."
Well, our friend here just had a nasty breakup--
Liz!
Everyone **knows** about it. But it is not spoken of publicly.
Liz...
I'm talking to our new--
Stop.
Just trying to explain the storm cloud that forever hangs over this table.
Yeah, I met him.
Panker-Parker.
Parker, right?

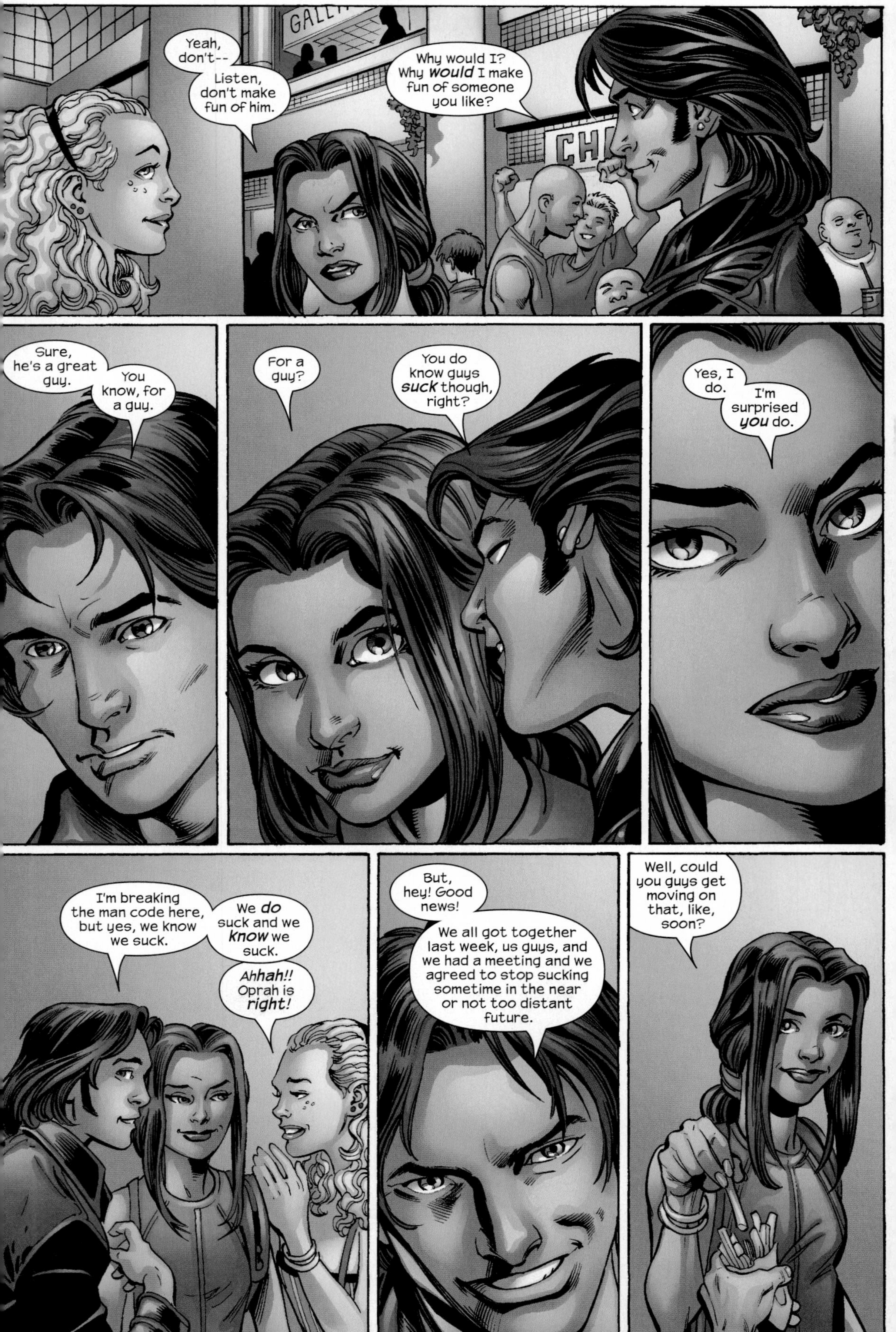
GALLE
Yeah, don't--
Listen, don't make fun of him.
Why would I? Why *would* I make fun of someone you like?
CH
Sure, he's a great guy.
You know, for a guy.
For a guy?
You do know guys *suck* though, right?
Yes, I do.
I'm surprised *you* do.
I'm breaking the man code here, but yes, we know we suck.
We *do* suck and we *know* we suck.
Ah*hah!!* Oprah is *right!*
But, hey! Good news!
We all got together last week, us guys, and we had a meeting and we agreed to stop sucking sometime in the near or not too distant future.
Well, could you guys get moving on that, like, soon?

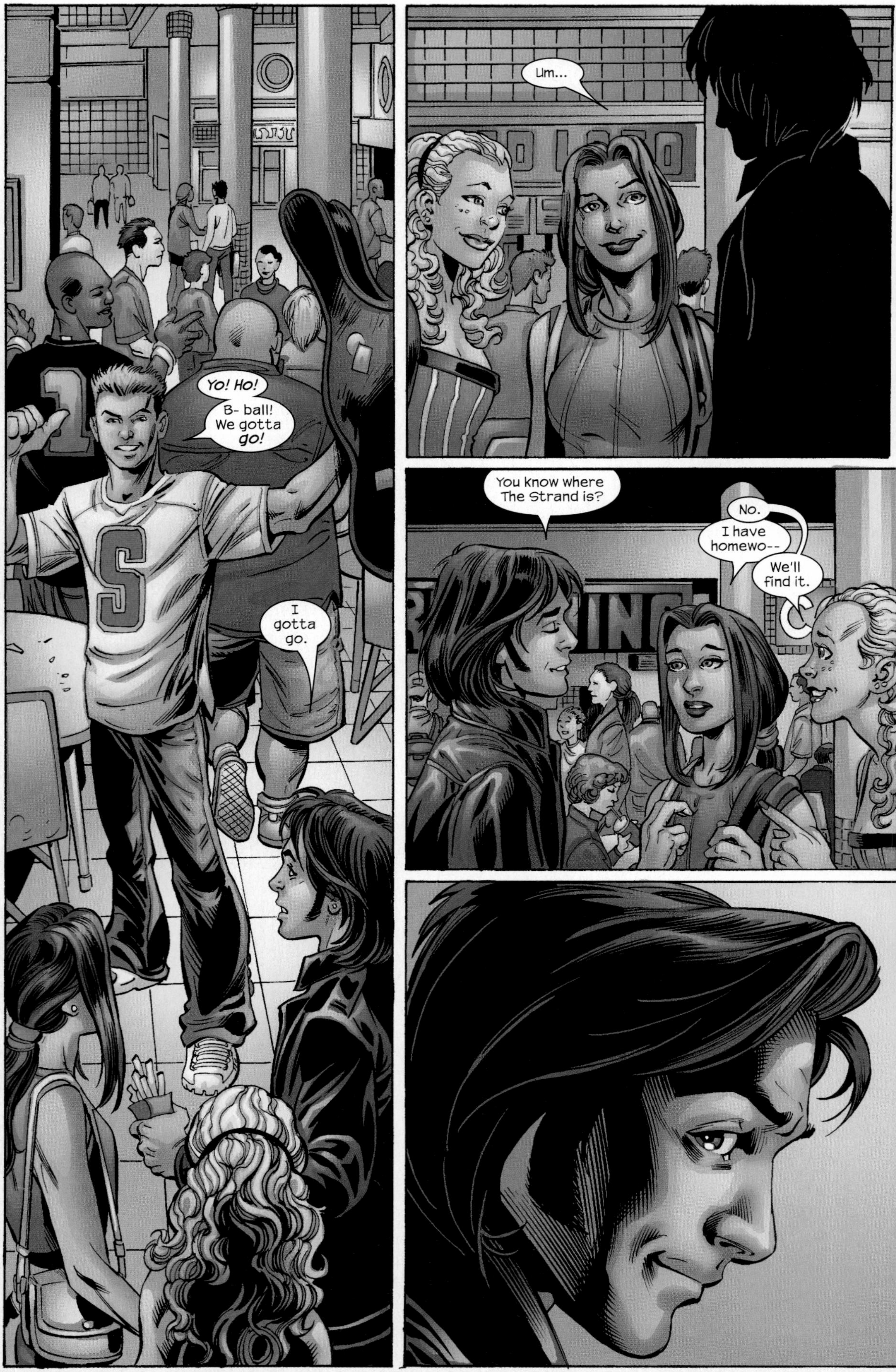

Yo! Ho!
B- ball! We gotta go!
I gotta go.
Um...
You know where The Strand is?
No.
I have homewo--
We'll find it.

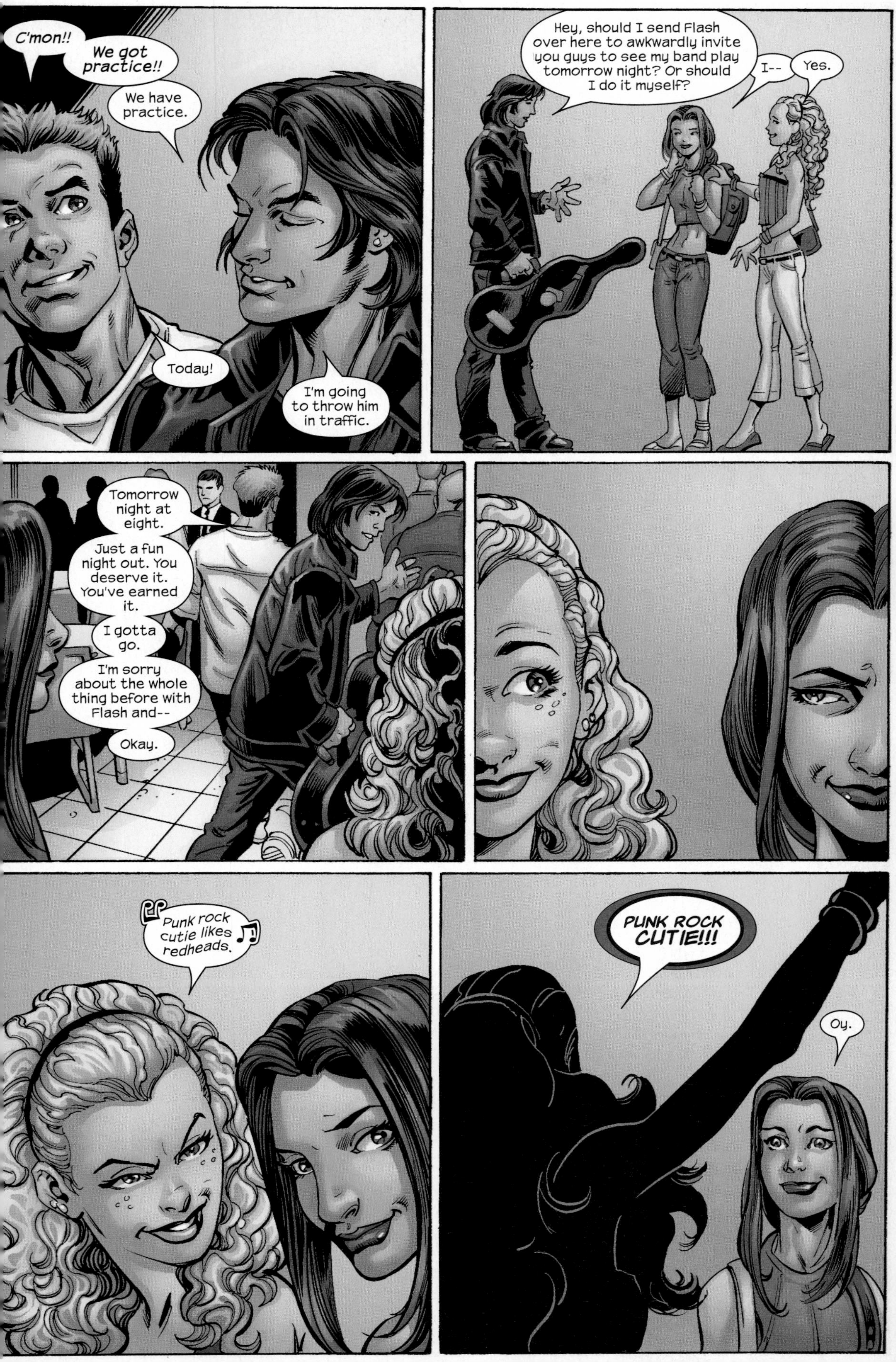
C'mon!!
We got practice!!
We have practice.
Today!
I'm going to throw him in traffic.
Hey, should I send Flash over here to awkwardly invite you guys to see my band play tomorrow night? Or should I do it myself?
I--
Yes.
Tomorrow night at eight.
Just a fun night out. You deserve it. You've earned it.
I gotta go.
I'm sorry about the whole thing before with Flash and--
Okay.
Punk rock cutie likes redheads.
PUNK ROCK CUTIE!!!
Oy.

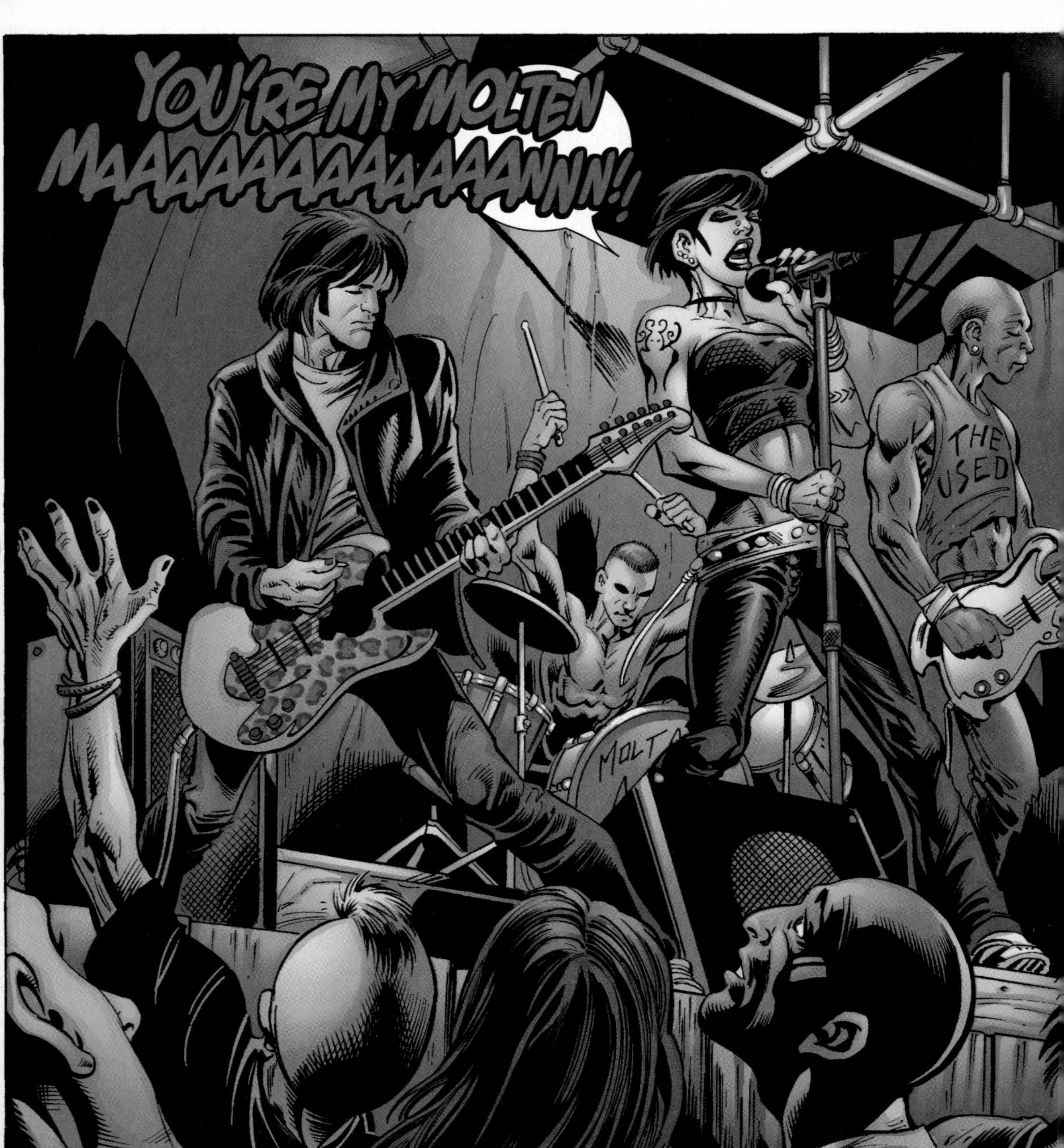
YOU'RE MY MOLTEN MAAAAAAAAAAAANNN!
THE USED
MOLT
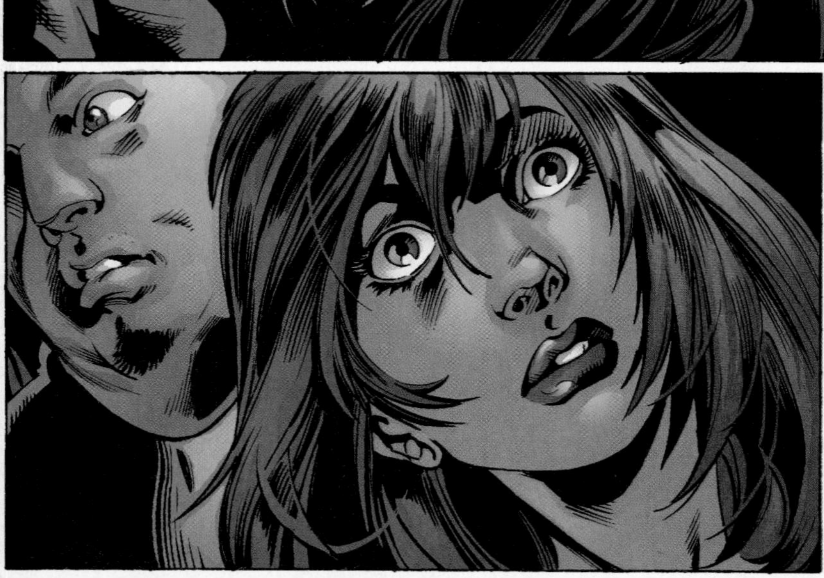
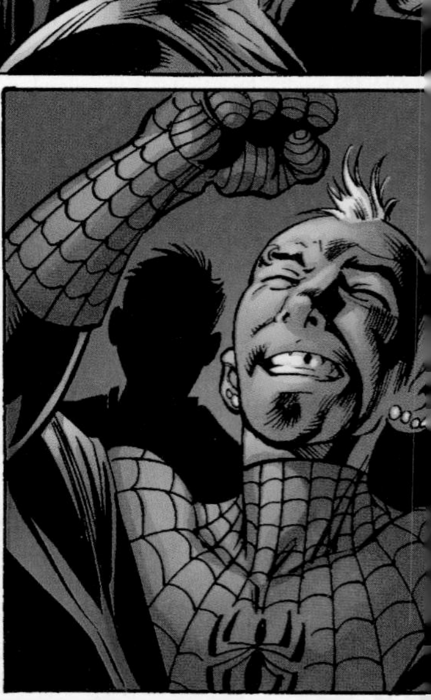

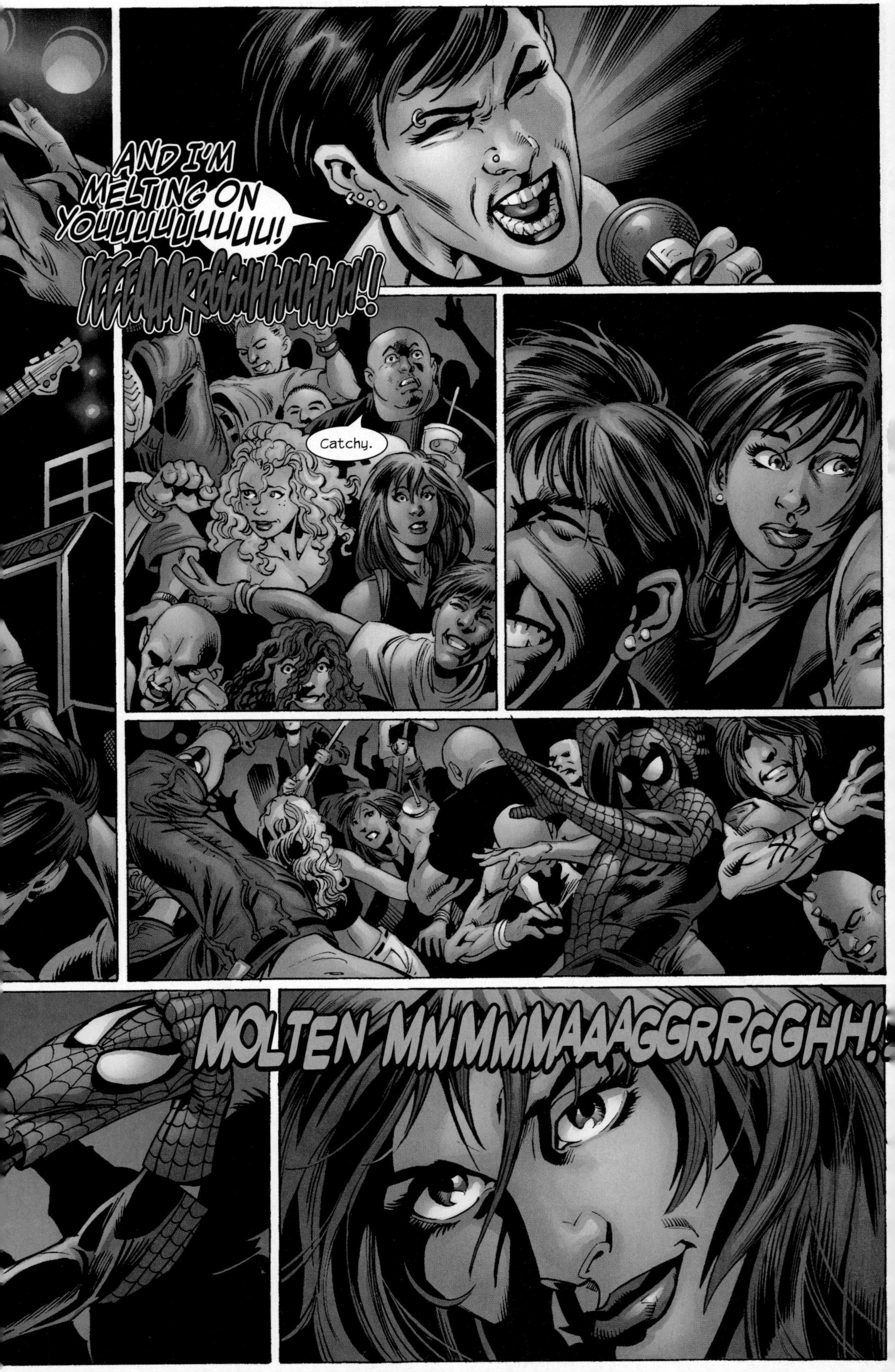
AND I'M MELTING ON YOUUUUUUUUUU!
YEEEAAARRGGHHHHHHH!!
Catchy.
MOLTEN MMMMMAAAGGRRGGHH!!

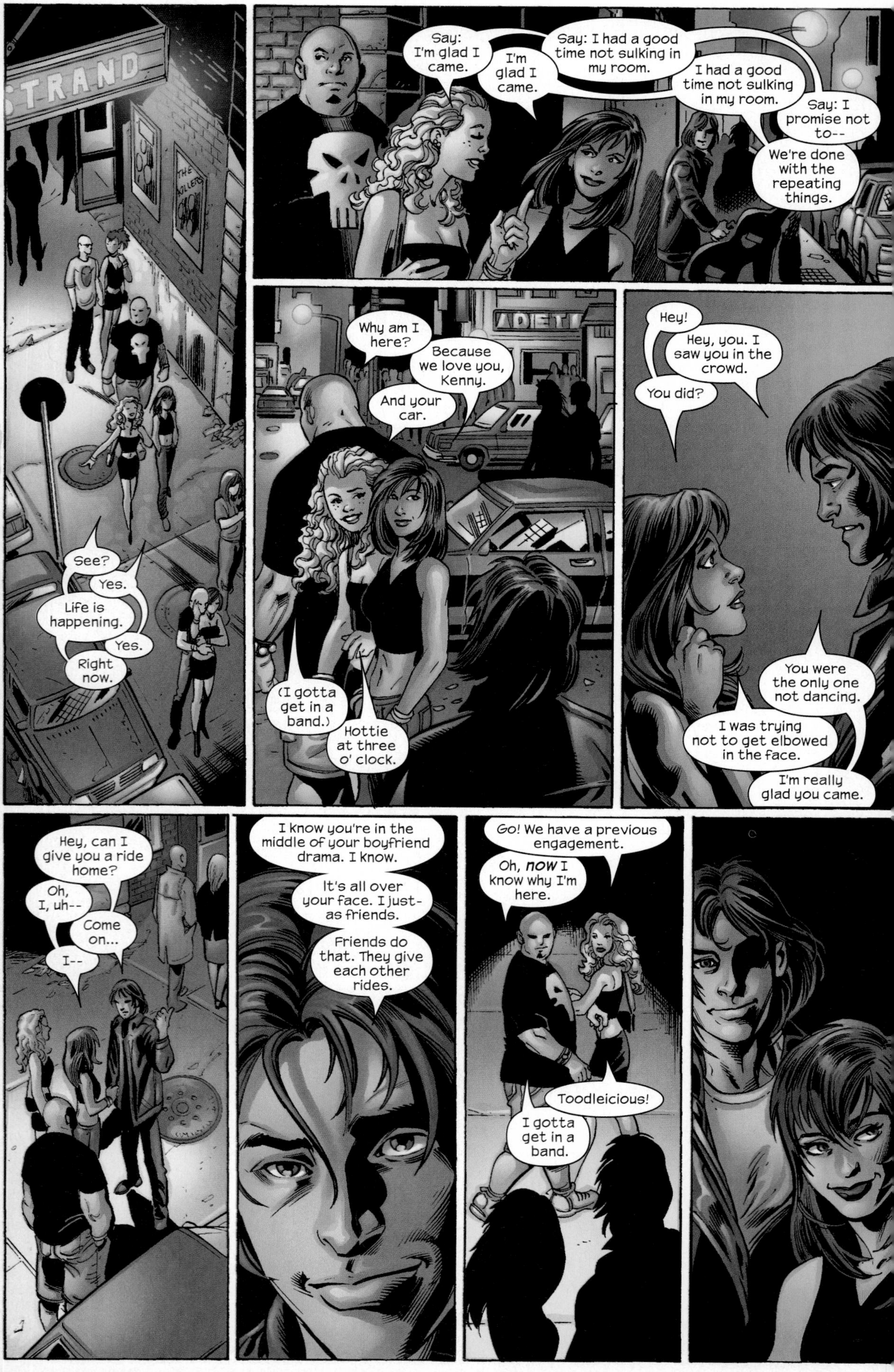
STRAND
THE KILLERS
See?
Yes.
Life is happening.
Yes.
Right now.
Say: I'm glad I came.
I'm glad I came.
Say: I had a good time not sulking in my room.
I had a good time not sulking in my room.
Say: I promise not to--
We're done with the repeating things.
Why am I here?
Because we love you, Kenny.
And your car.
(I gotta get in a band.)
Hottie at three o' clock.
Hey!
Hey, you. I saw you in the crowd.
You did?
You were the only one not dancing.
I was trying not to get elbowed in the face.
I'm really glad you came.
Hey, can I give you a ride home?
Oh, I, uh--
Come on...
I--
I know you're in the middle of your boyfriend drama. I know.
It's all over your face. I just-- as friends.
Friends do that. They give each other rides.
Go! We have a previous engagement.
Oh, *NOW* I know why I'm here.
Toodleicious!
I gotta get in a band.

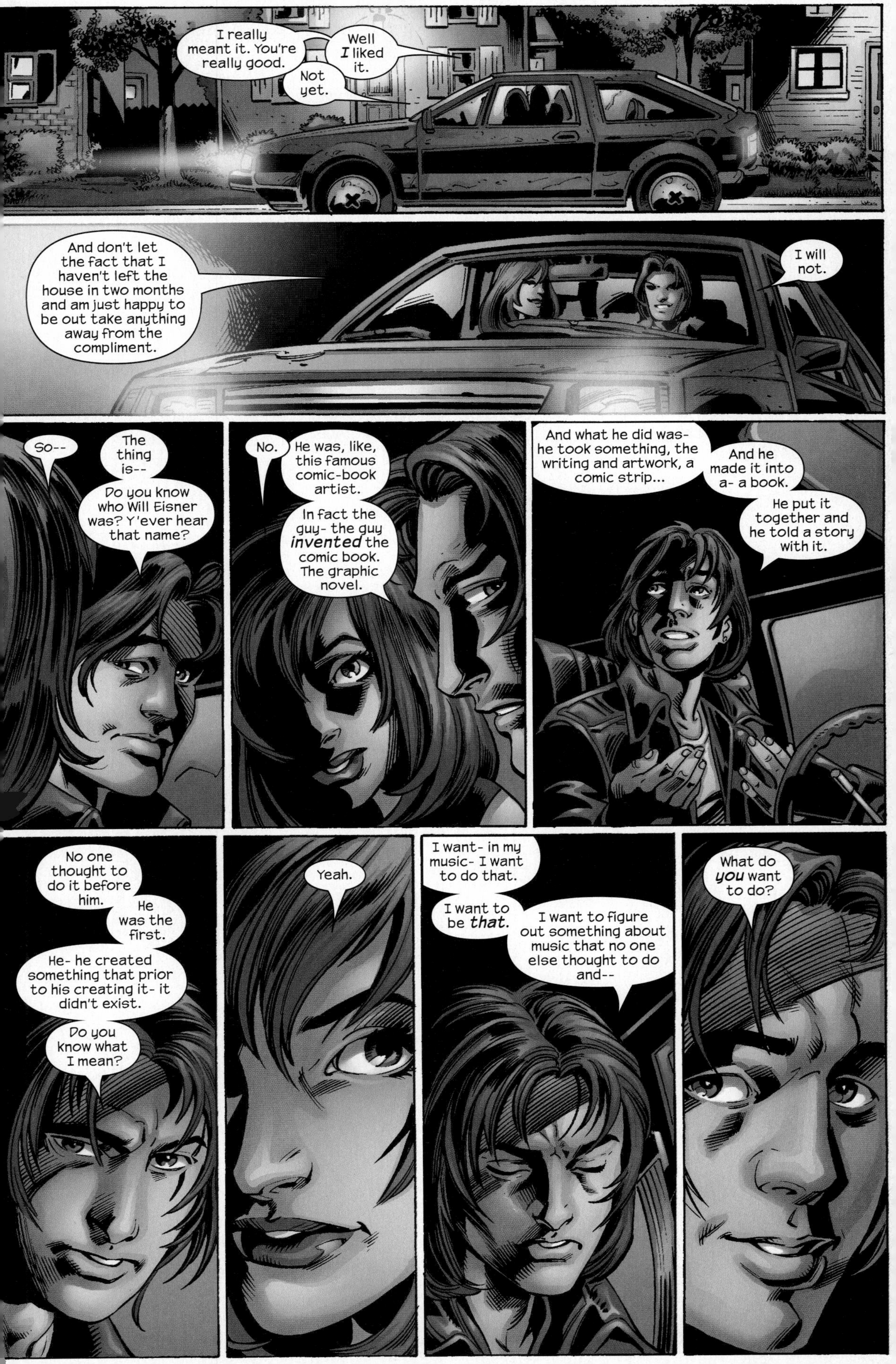

I really meant it. You're really good.
Well I liked it.
Not yet.
And don't let the fact that I haven't left the house in two months and am just happy to be out take anything away from the compliment.
I will not.
So--
The thing is--
Do you know who Will Eisner was? Y'ever hear that name?
No.
He was, like, this famous comic-book artist.
In fact the guy- the guy invented the comic book. The graphic novel.
And what he did was- he took something, the writing and artwork, a comic strip...
And he made it into a- a book.
He put it together and he told a story with it.
No one thought to do it before him.
He was the first.
He- he created something that prior to his creating it- it didn't exist.
Do you know what I mean?
Yeah.
I want- in my music- I want to do that.
I want to be that.
I want to figure out something about music that no one else thought to do and--
What do you want to do?

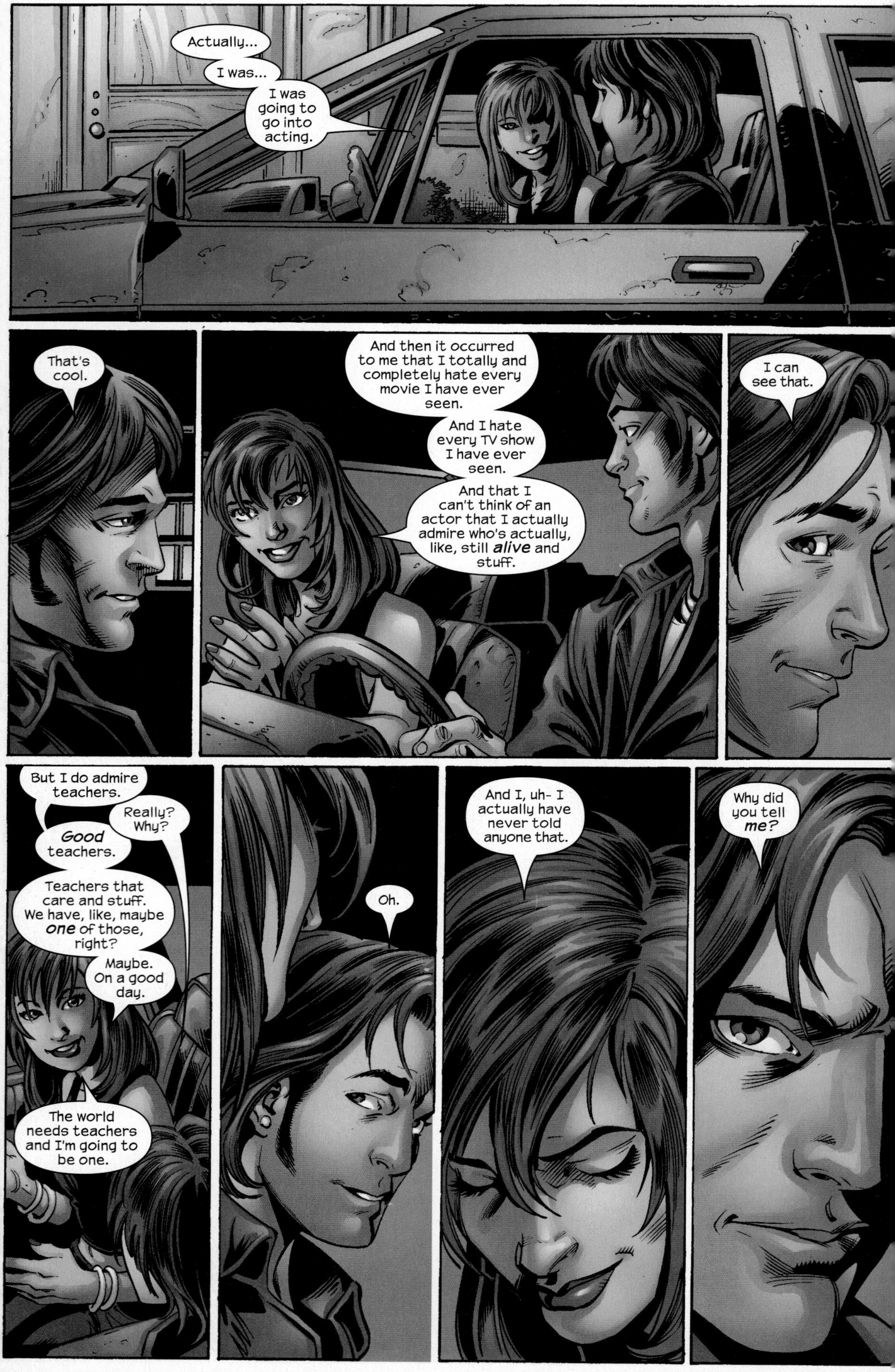

Actually...
I was...
I was going to go into acting.
That's cool.
And then it occurred to me that I totally and completely hate every movie I have ever seen.
And I hate every TV show I have ever seen.
And that I can't think of an actor that I actually admire who's actually, like, still *alive* and stuff.
I can see that.
But I do admire teachers.
Really? Why?
Good teachers.
Teachers that care and stuff. We have, like, maybe *one* of those, right?
Maybe. On a good day.
The world needs teachers and I'm going to be one.
Oh.
And I, uh- I actually have never told anyone that.
Why did you tell *me*?

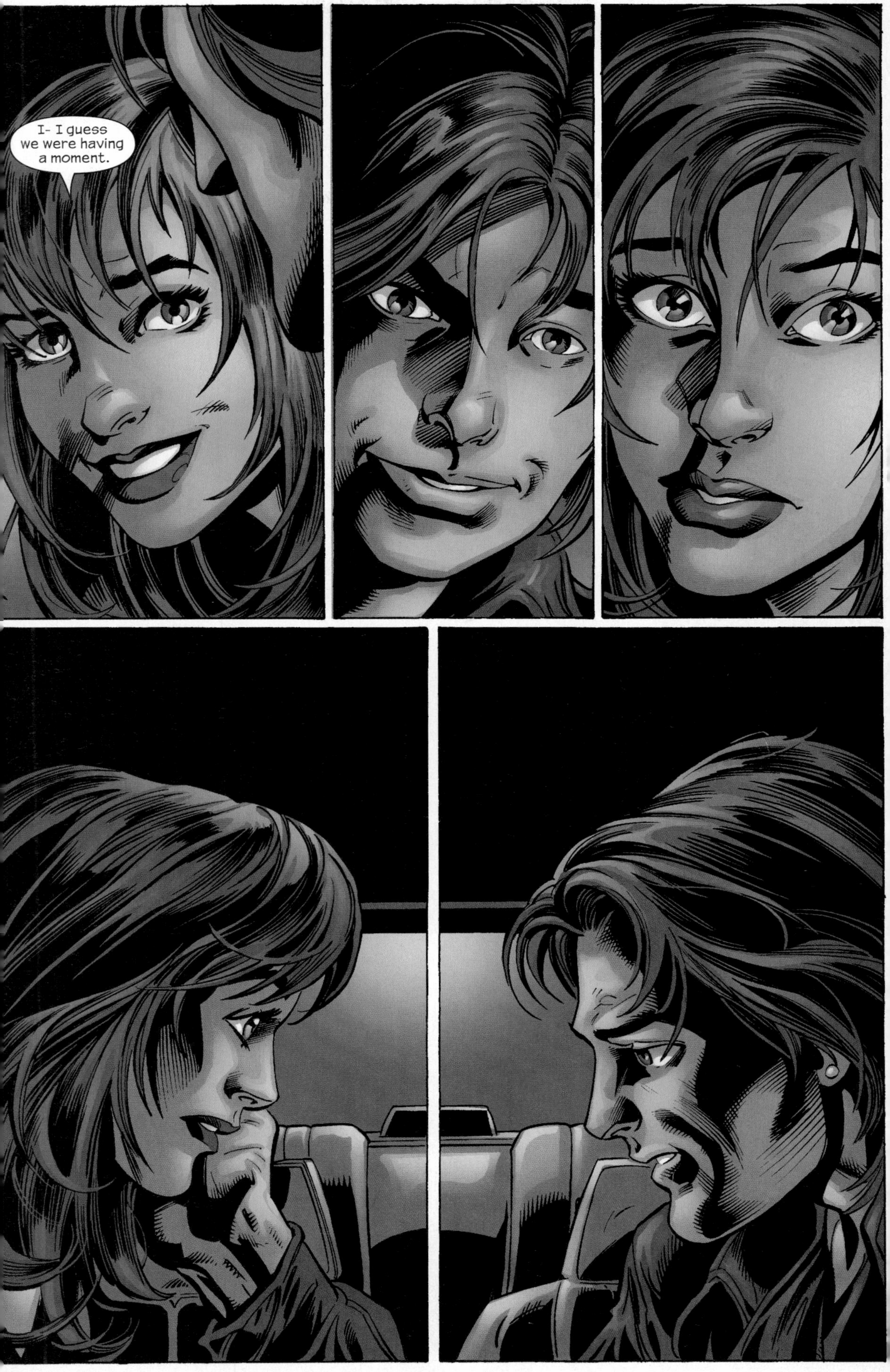
I- I guess
we were having
a moment.

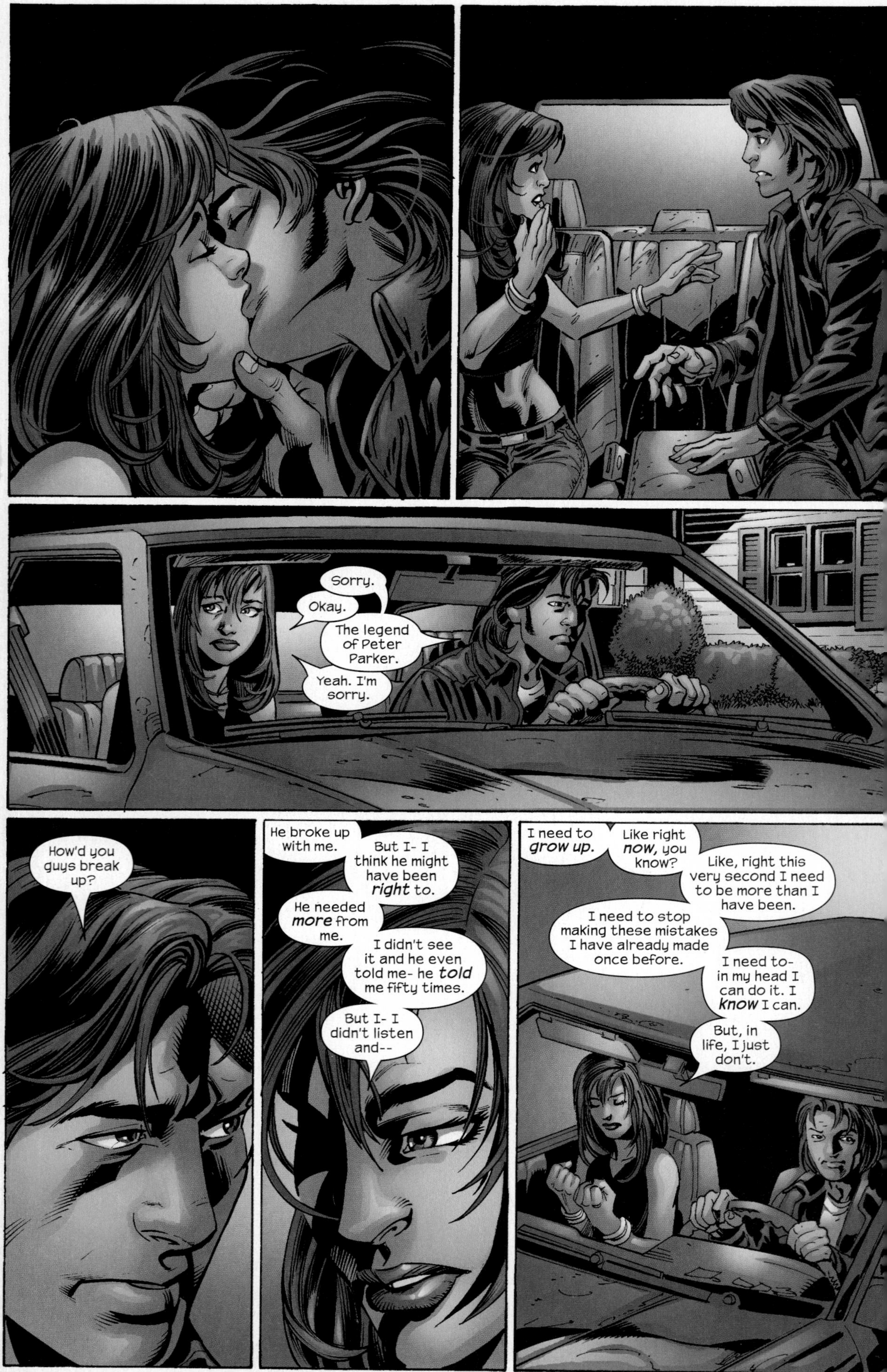

Sorry.
Okay.
The legend of Peter Parker.
Yeah. I'm sorry.
How'd you guys break up?
He broke up with me.
But I- I think he might have been *right* to.
He needed *more* from me.
I didn't see it and he even told me- he *told* me fifty times.
But I- I didn't listen and--
I need to *grow up.*
Like right *now,* you know?
Like, right this very second I need to be more than I have been.
I need to stop making these mistakes I have already made once before.
I need to- in my head I can do it. I *know* I can.
But, in life, I just don't.

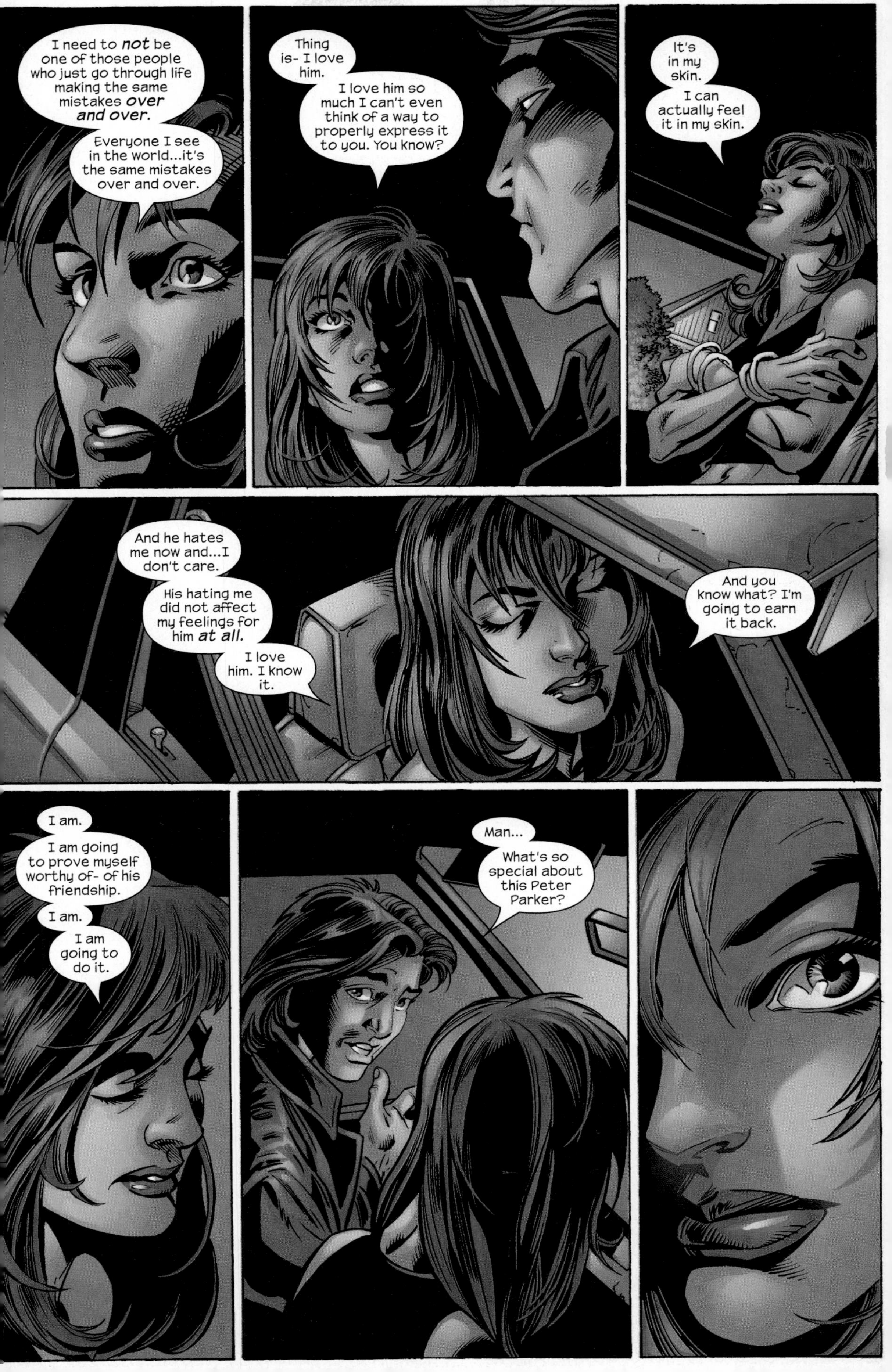

I need to *not* be one of those people who just go through life making the same mistakes *over and over.*
Everyone I see in the world...it's the same mistakes over and over.
Thing is- I love him.
I love him so much I can't even think of a way to properly express it to you. You know?
It's in my skin.
I can actually feel it in my skin.
And he hates me now and...I don't care.
His hating me did not affect my feelings for him *at all.*
I love him. I know it.
And you know what? I'm going to earn it back.
I am.
I am going to prove myself worthy of- of his friendship.
I am.
I am going to do it.
Man...
What's so special about this Peter Parker?

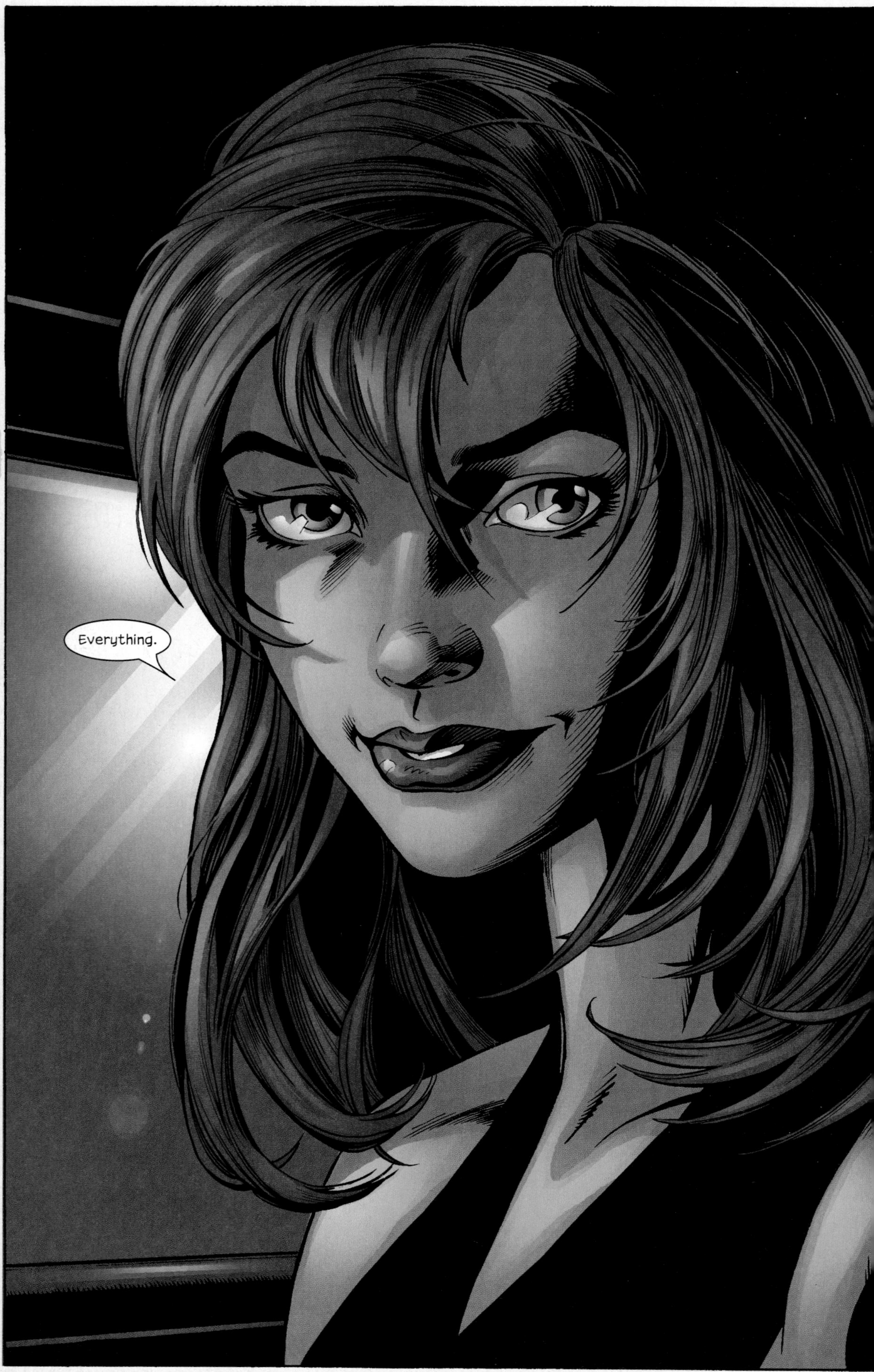
Everything.

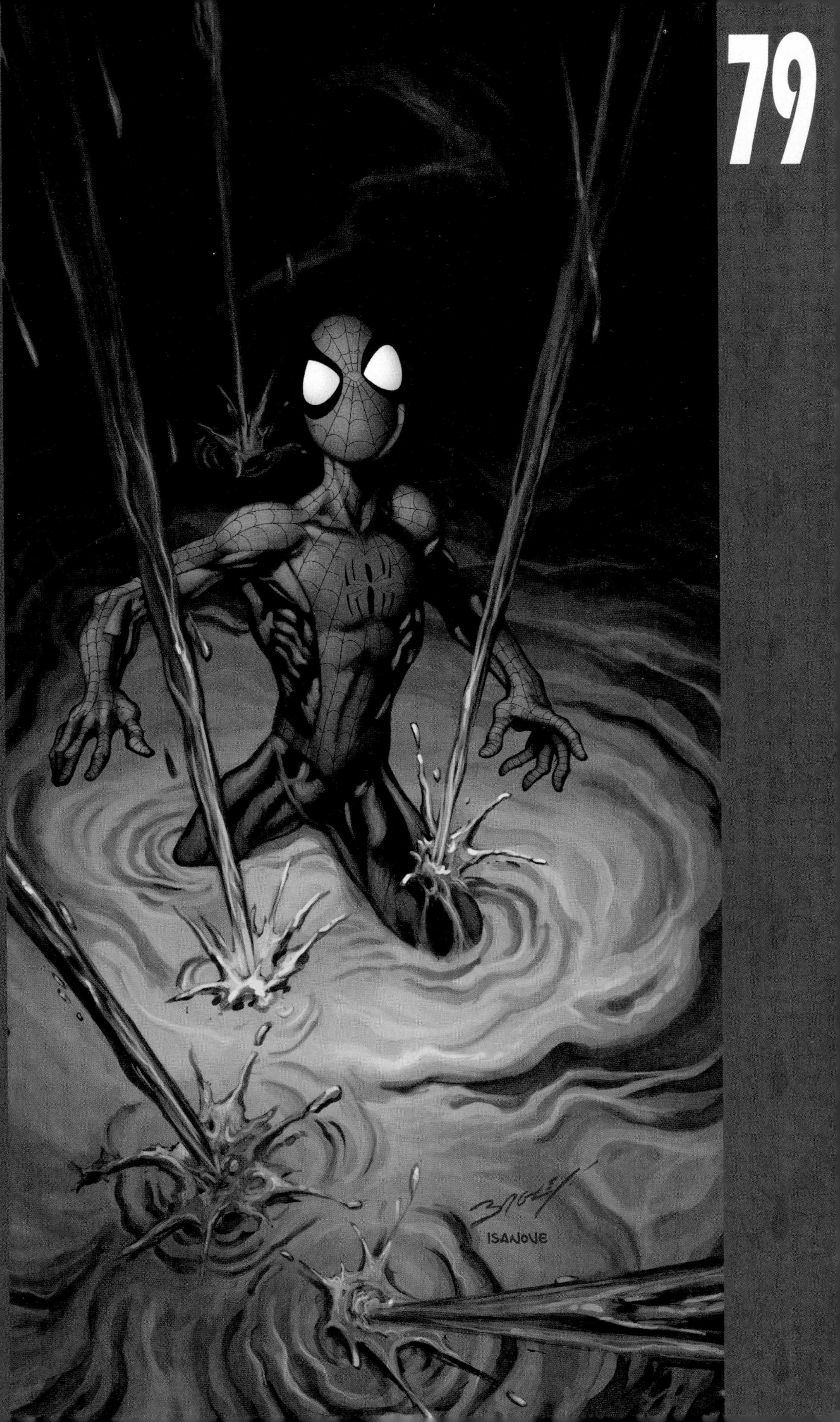
79
BAGLEY
ISANOVE

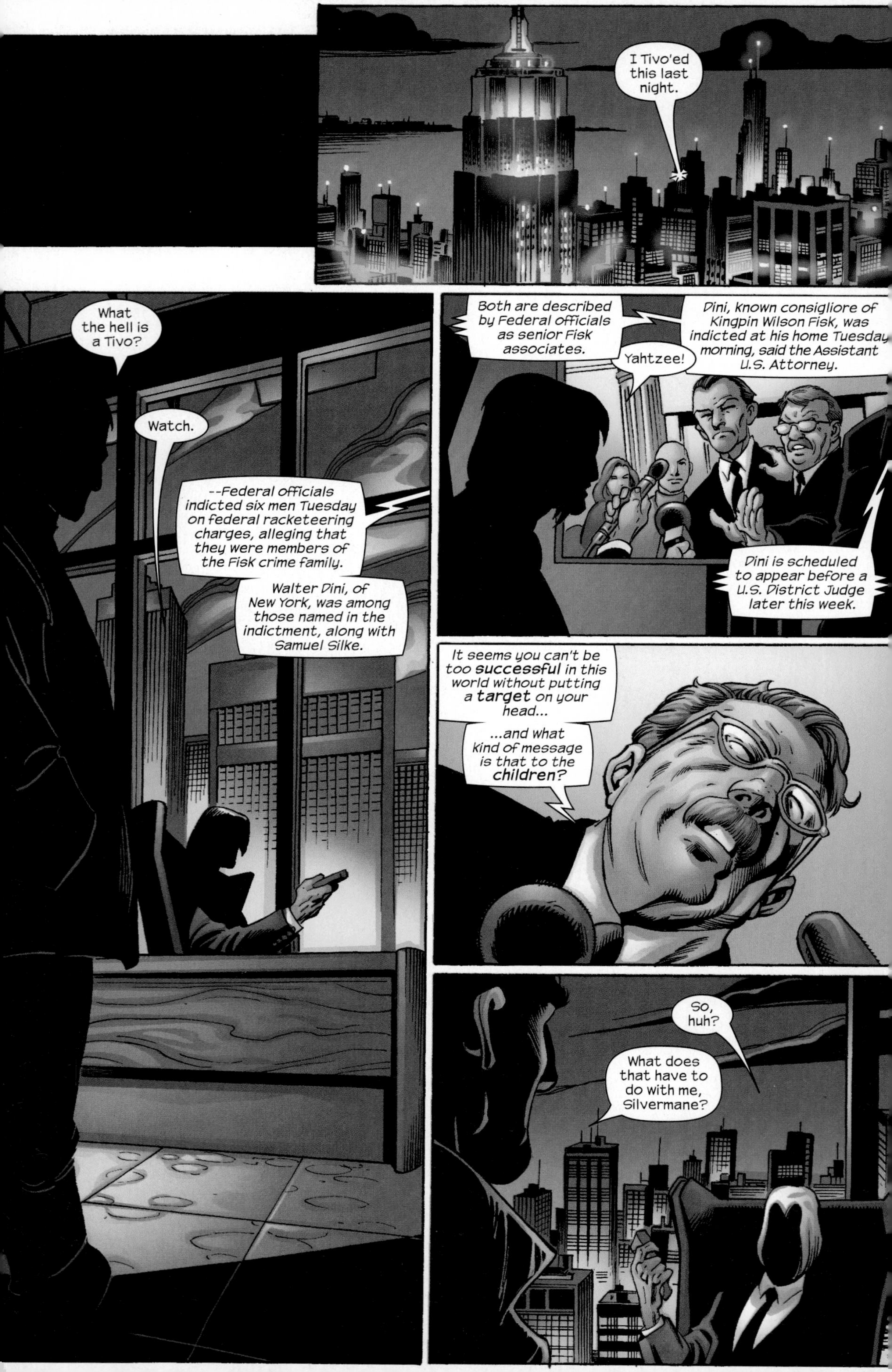
I Tivo'ed this last night.
What the hell is a Tivo?
Watch.
--Federal officials indicted six men Tuesday on federal racketeering charges, alleging that they were members of the Fisk crime family.
Walter Dini, of New York, was among those named in the indictment, along with Samuel Silke.
Both are described by Federal officials as senior Fisk associates.
Dini, known consigliore of Kingpin Wilson Fisk, was indicted at his home Tuesday morning, said the Assistant U.S. Attorney.
Yahtzee!
Dini is scheduled to appear before a U.S. District Judge later this week.
It seems you can't be too successful in this world without putting a target on your head...
...and what kind of message is that to the children?
So, huh?
What does that have to do with me, Silvermane?

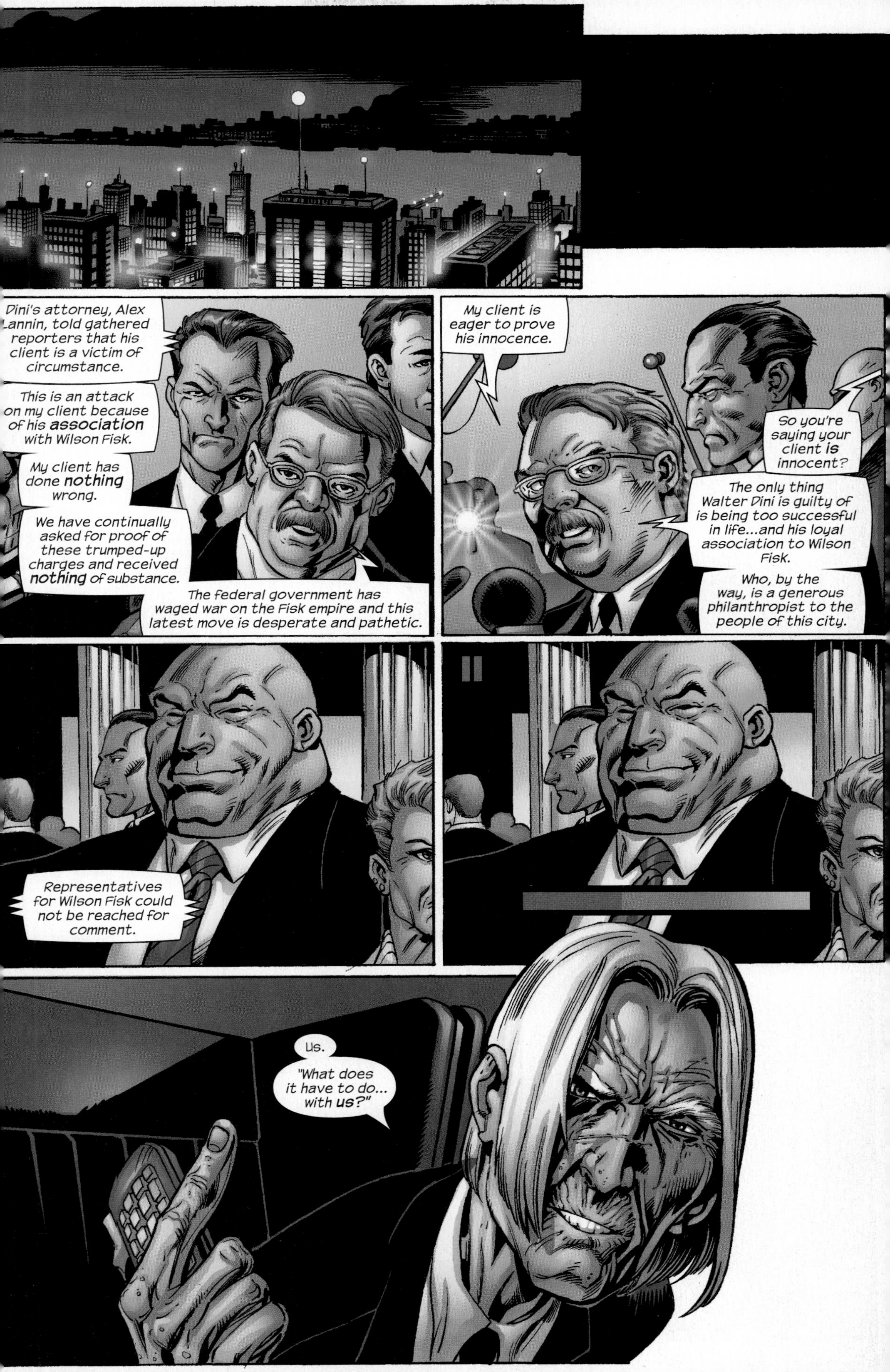
Dini's attorney, Alex Lannin, told gathered reporters that his client is a victim of circumstance.
This is an attack on my client because of his **association** with Wilson Fisk.
My client has done **nothing** wrong.
We have continually asked for proof of these trumped-up charges and received **nothing** of substance.
The federal government has waged war on the Fisk empire and this latest move is desperate and pathetic.
My client is eager to prove his innocence.
So you're saying your client **is** innocent?
The only thing Walter Dini is guilty of is being too successful in life...and his loyal association to Wilson Fisk.
Who, by the way, is a generous philanthropist to the people of this city.
Representatives for Wilson Fisk could not be reached for comment.
Us.
"What does it have to do... with **us?**"

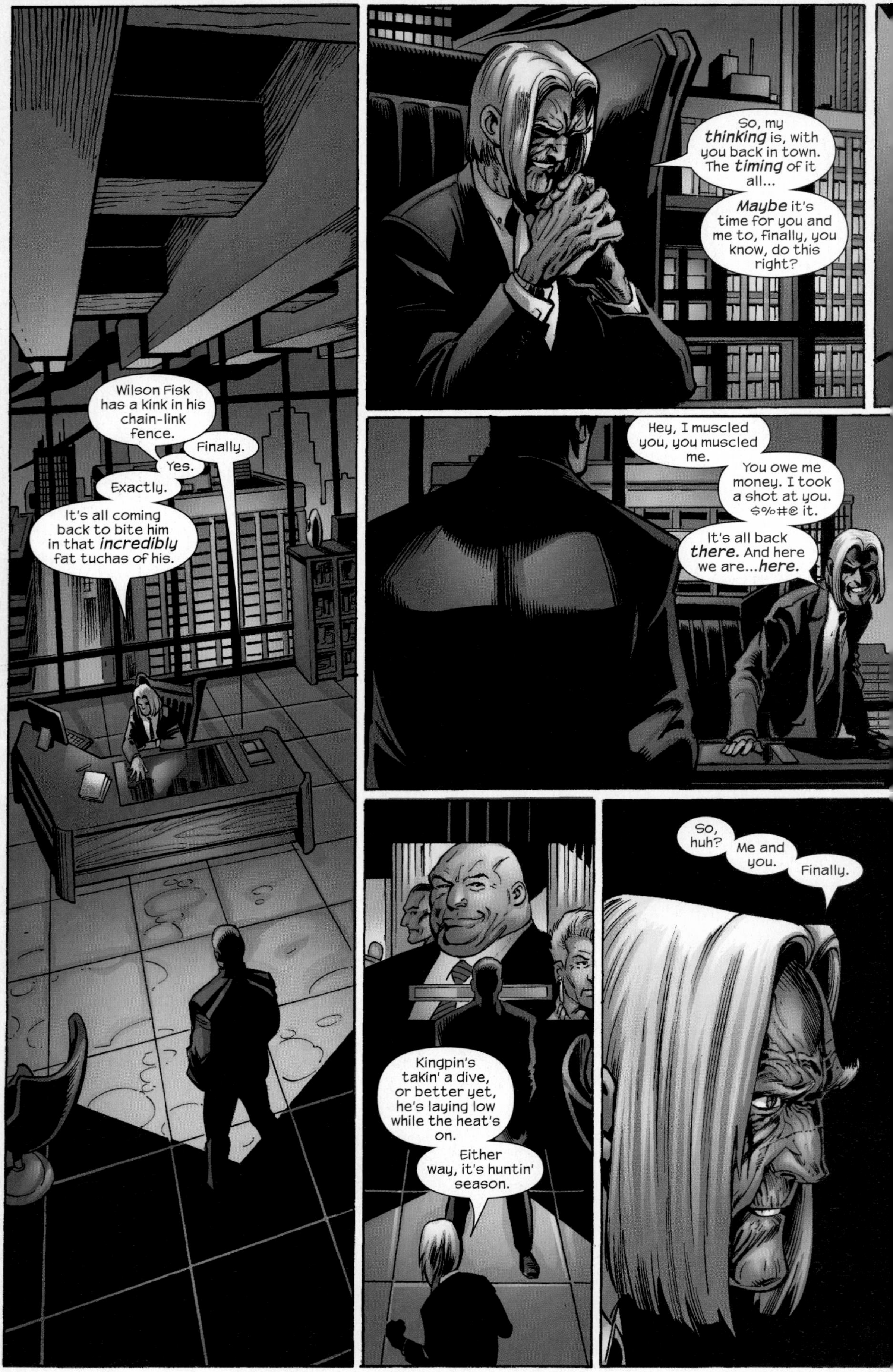

Wilson Fisk has a kink in his chain-link fence.
Finally.
Yes.
Exactly.
It's all coming back to bite him in that *incredibly* fat tuchas of his.
So, my *thinking* is, with you back in town. The *timing* of it all...
Maybe it's time for you and me to, finally, you know, do this right?
Hey, I muscled you, you muscled me.
You owe me money. I took a shot at you. $%#@ it.
It's all back *there.* And here we are...*here.*
Kingpin's takin' a dive, or better yet, he's laying low while the heat's on.
Either way, it's huntin' season.
So, huh?
Me and you.
Finally.

You want to work *together*.

It was going to happen eventually.

Really?

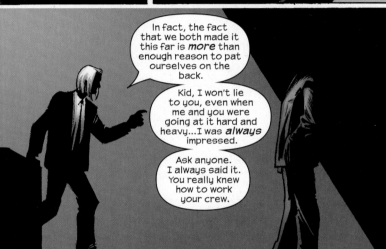

In fact, the fact that we both made it this far is *more* than enough reason to pat ourselves on the back.

Kid, I won't lie to you, even when me and you were going at it hard and heavy...I was *always* impressed.

Ask anyone. I always said it. You really knew how to work your crew.

What you *needed* was- and I say this in all due respect- you needed what I have up here.

A little bit more of this and *you* could'a been Kingpin.

See what I'm saying?

What do you think?

I like a lot of what you said.

A lot of it. Except the one part.

Okay...

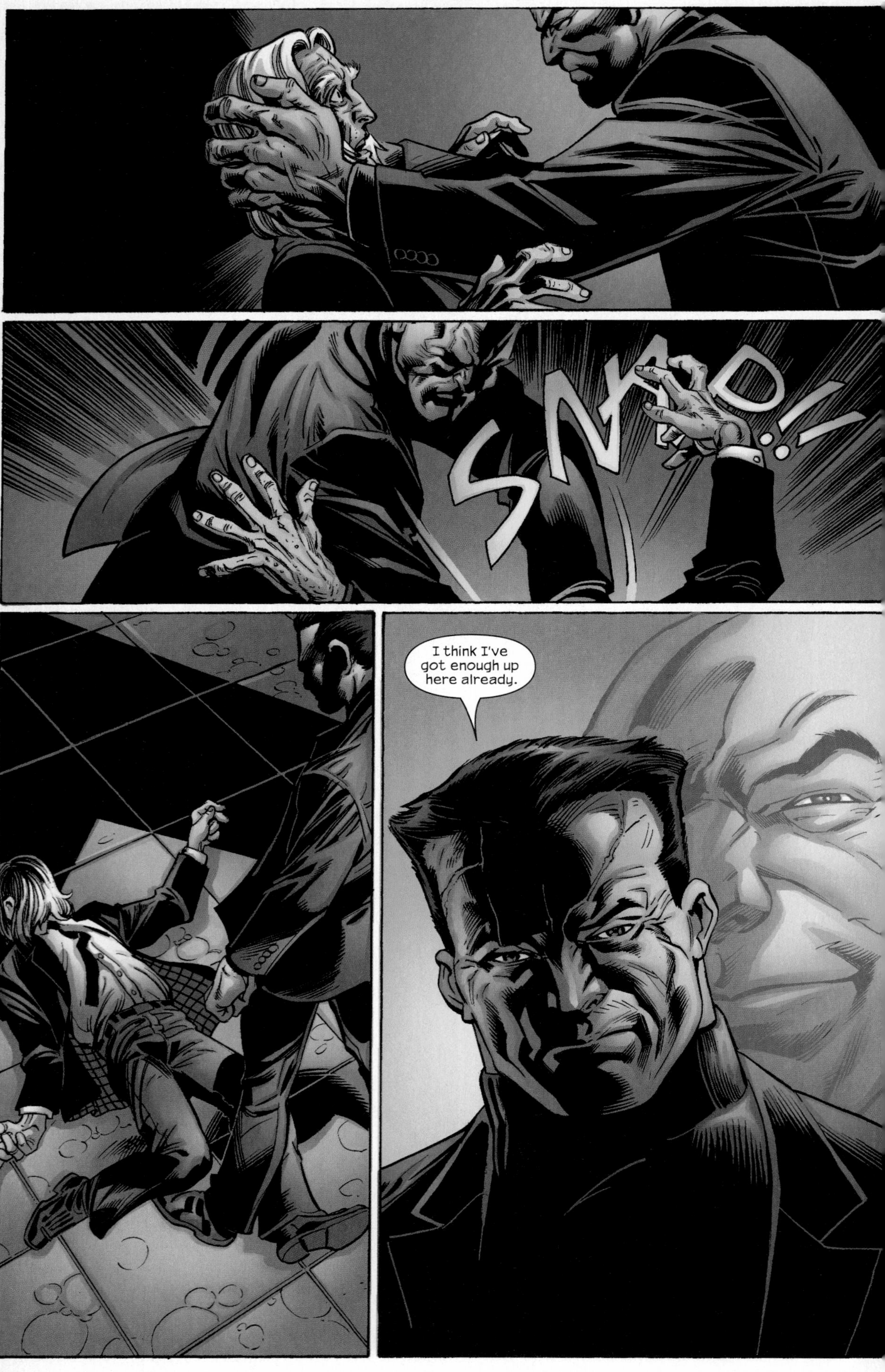
SNAP!!
I think I've got enough up here already.

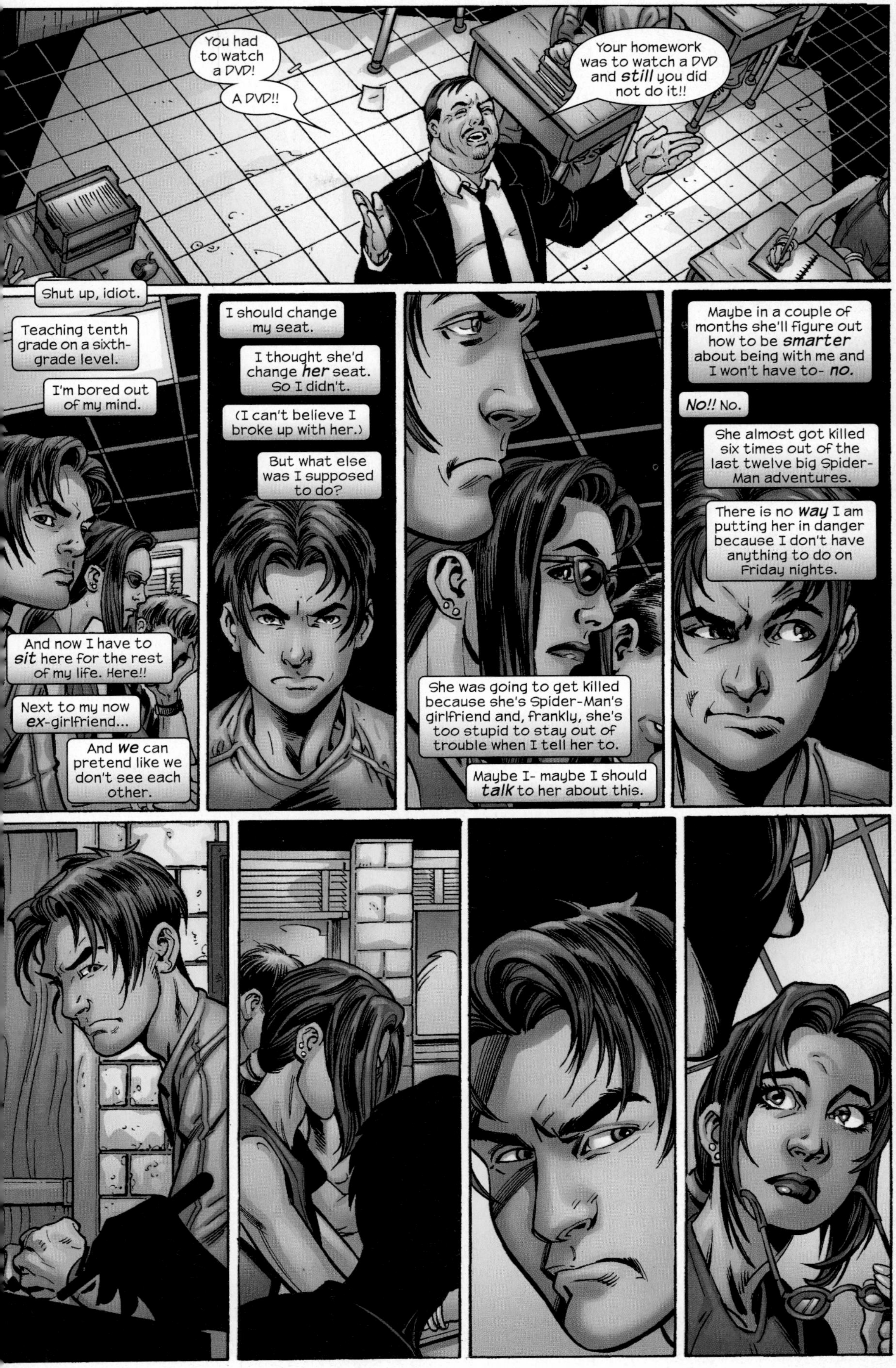

You had to watch a DVD!
A DVD!!
Your homework was to watch a DVD and still you did not do it!!
Shut up, idiot.
Teaching tenth grade on a sixth-grade level.
I'm bored out of my mind.
And now I have to sit here for the rest of my life. Here!!
Next to my now ex-girlfriend...
And we can pretend like we don't see each other.
I should change my seat.
I thought she'd change her seat. So I didn't.
(I can't believe I broke up with her.)
But what else was I supposed to do?
She was going to get killed because she's Spider-Man's girlfriend and, frankly, she's too stupid to stay out of trouble when I tell her to.
Maybe I- maybe I should talk to her about this.
Maybe in a couple of months she'll figure out how to be smarter about being with me and I won't have to- no.
No!! No.
She almost got killed six times out of the last twelve big Spider-Man adventures.
There is no way I am putting her in danger because I don't have anything to do on Friday nights.

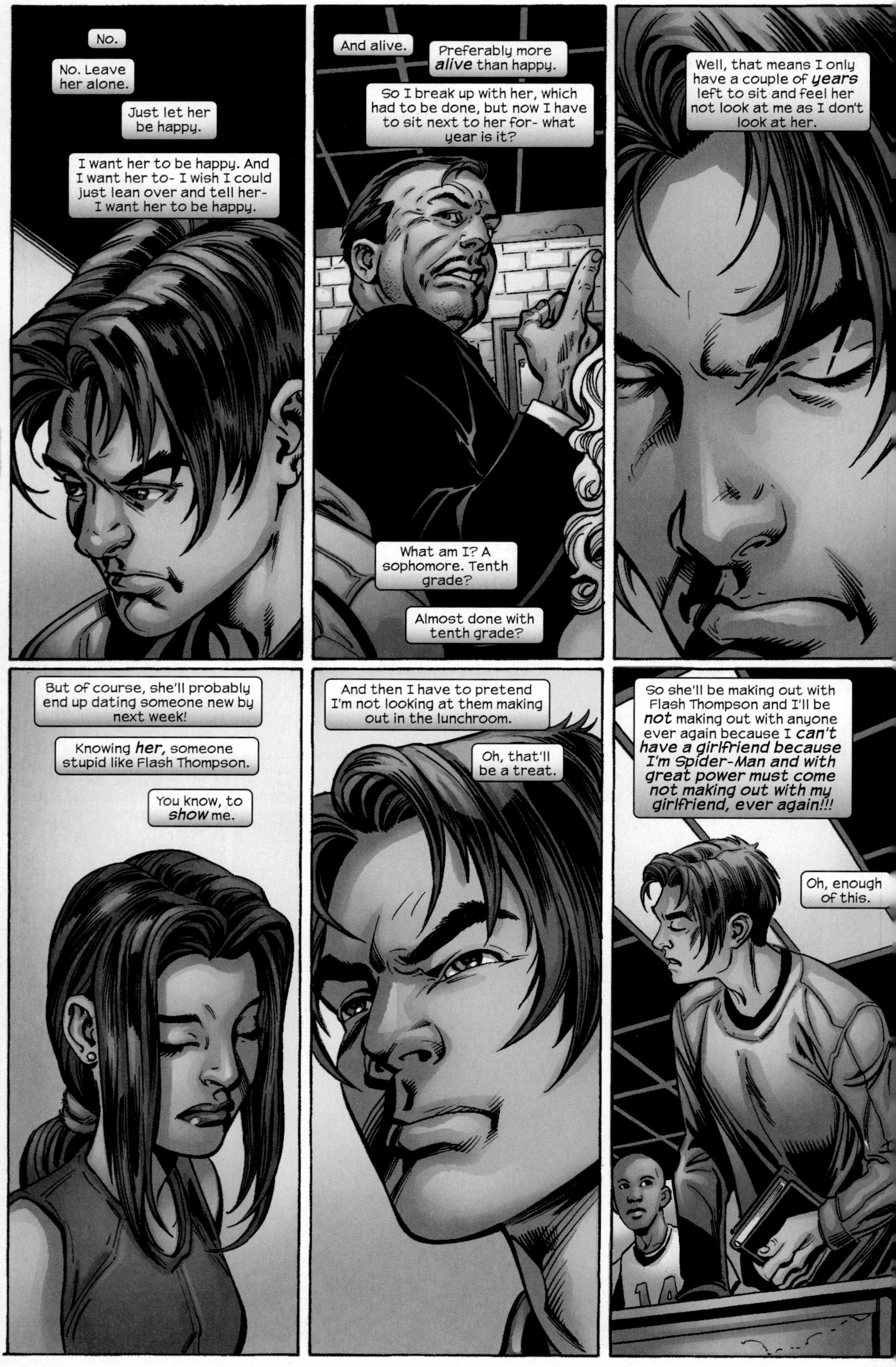
No.
No. Leave her alone.
Just let her be happy.
I want her to be happy. And I want her to- I wish I could just lean over and tell her- I want her to be happy.
And alive.
Preferably more *alive* than happy.
So I break up with her, which had to be done, but now I have to sit next to her for- what year is it?
What am I? A sophomore. Tenth grade?
Almost done with tenth grade?
Well, that means I only have a couple of *years* left to sit and feel her not look at me as I don't look at her.
But of course, she'll probably end up dating someone new by next week!
Knowing *her*, someone stupid like Flash Thompson.
You know, to *show* me.
And then I have to pretend I'm not looking at them making out in the lunchroom.
Oh, that'll be a treat.
So she'll be making out with Flash Thompson and I'll be *not* making out with anyone ever again because I *can't have a girlfriend because I'm Spider-Man and with great power must come not making out with my girlfriend, ever again!!!*
Oh, enough of this.

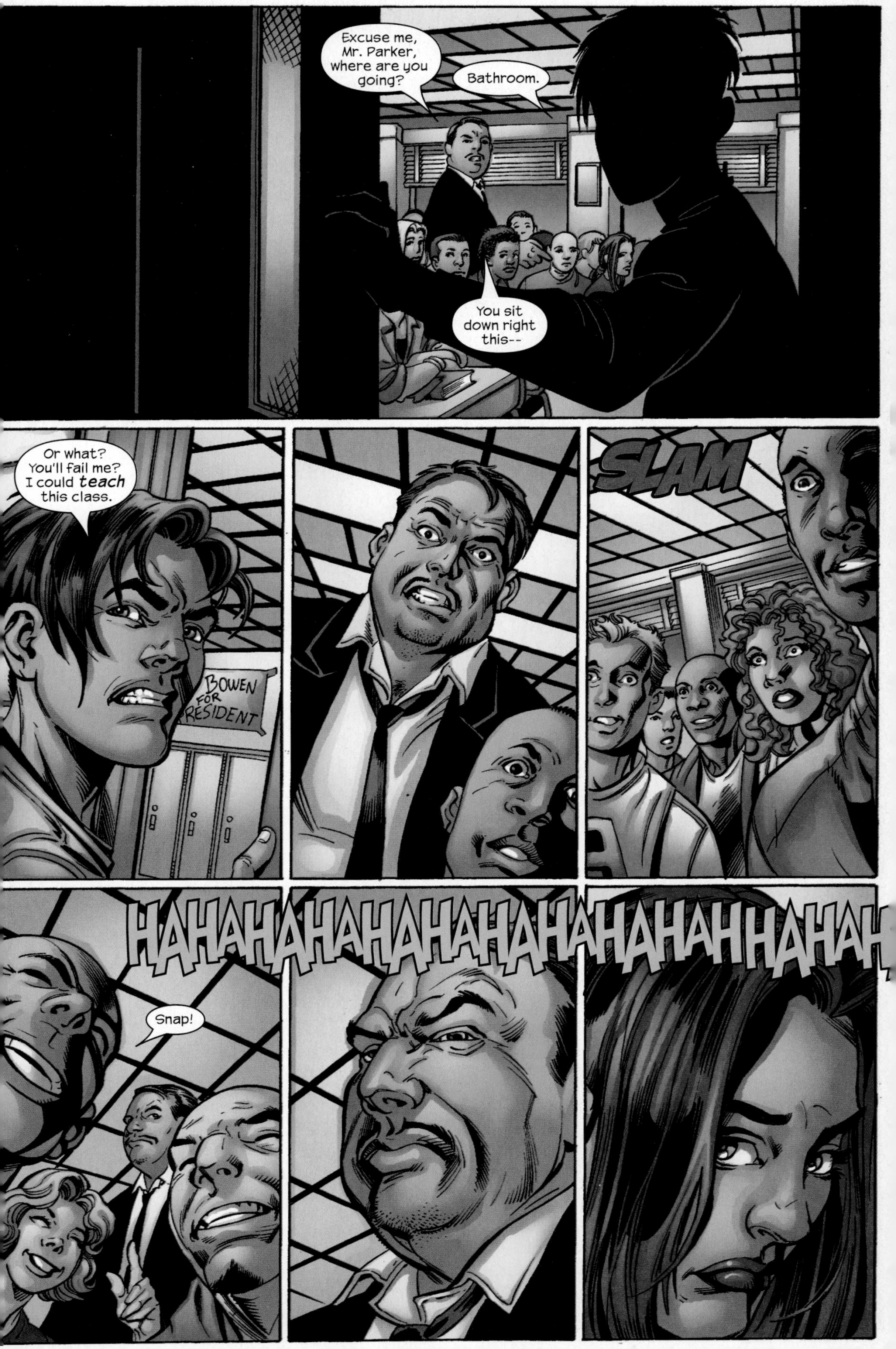
Excuse me, Mr. Parker, where are you going?
Bathroom.
You sit down right this--
Or what? You'll fail me? I could *teach* this class.
BOWEN FOR RESIDENT
SLAM
HAHAHAHAHAHAHAHAHAHAHAHHAHAH
Snap!

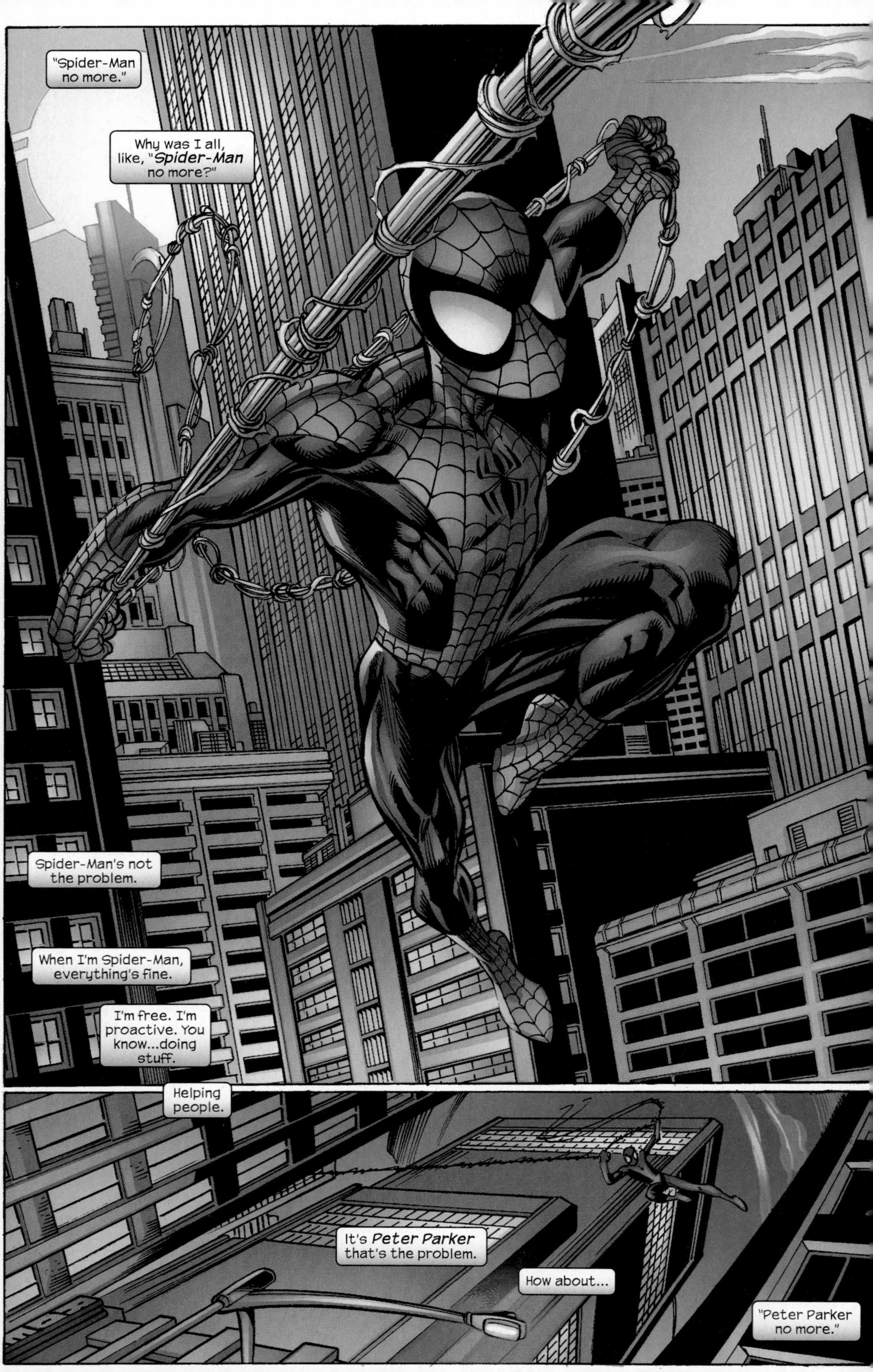
"Spider-Man no more."
Why was I all, like, "Spider-Man no more?"
Spider-Man's not the problem.
When I'm Spider-Man, everything's fine.
I'm free. I'm proactive. You know...doing stuff.
Helping people.
It's Peter Parker that's the problem.
How about...
"Peter Parker no more."

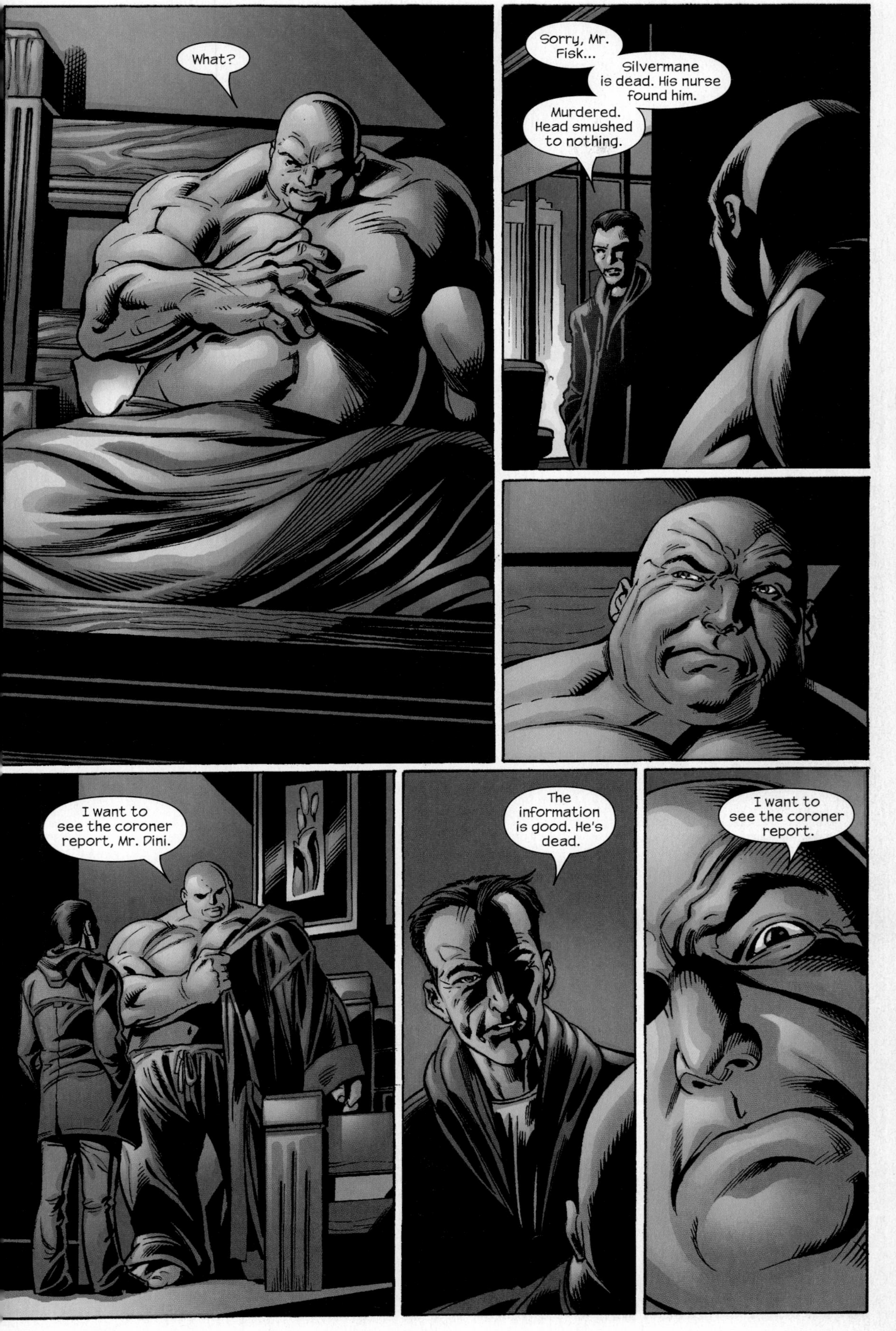

What?
Sorry, Mr. Fisk...
Silvermane is dead. His nurse found him.
Murdered. Head smushed to nothing.
I want to see the coroner report, Mr. Dini.
The information is good. He's dead.
I want to see the coroner report.

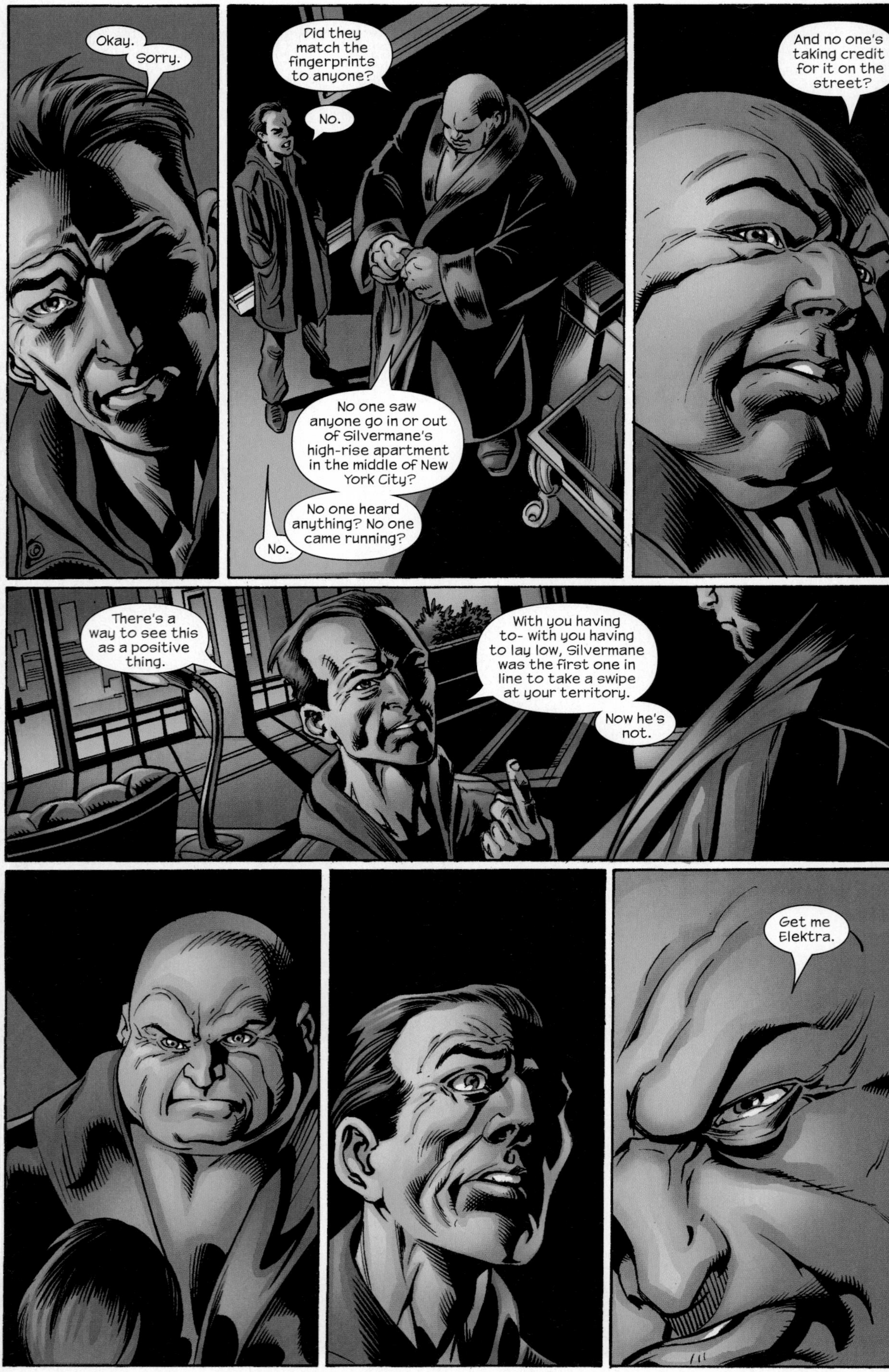
Okay.
Sorry.
Did they match the fingerprints to anyone?
No.
No one saw anyone go in or out of Silvermane's high-rise apartment in the middle of New York City?
No one heard anything? No one came running?
No.
And no one's taking credit for it on the street?
There's a way to see this as a positive thing.
With you having to- with you having to lay low, Silvermane was the first one in line to take a swipe at your territory.
Now he's not.
Get me Elektra.

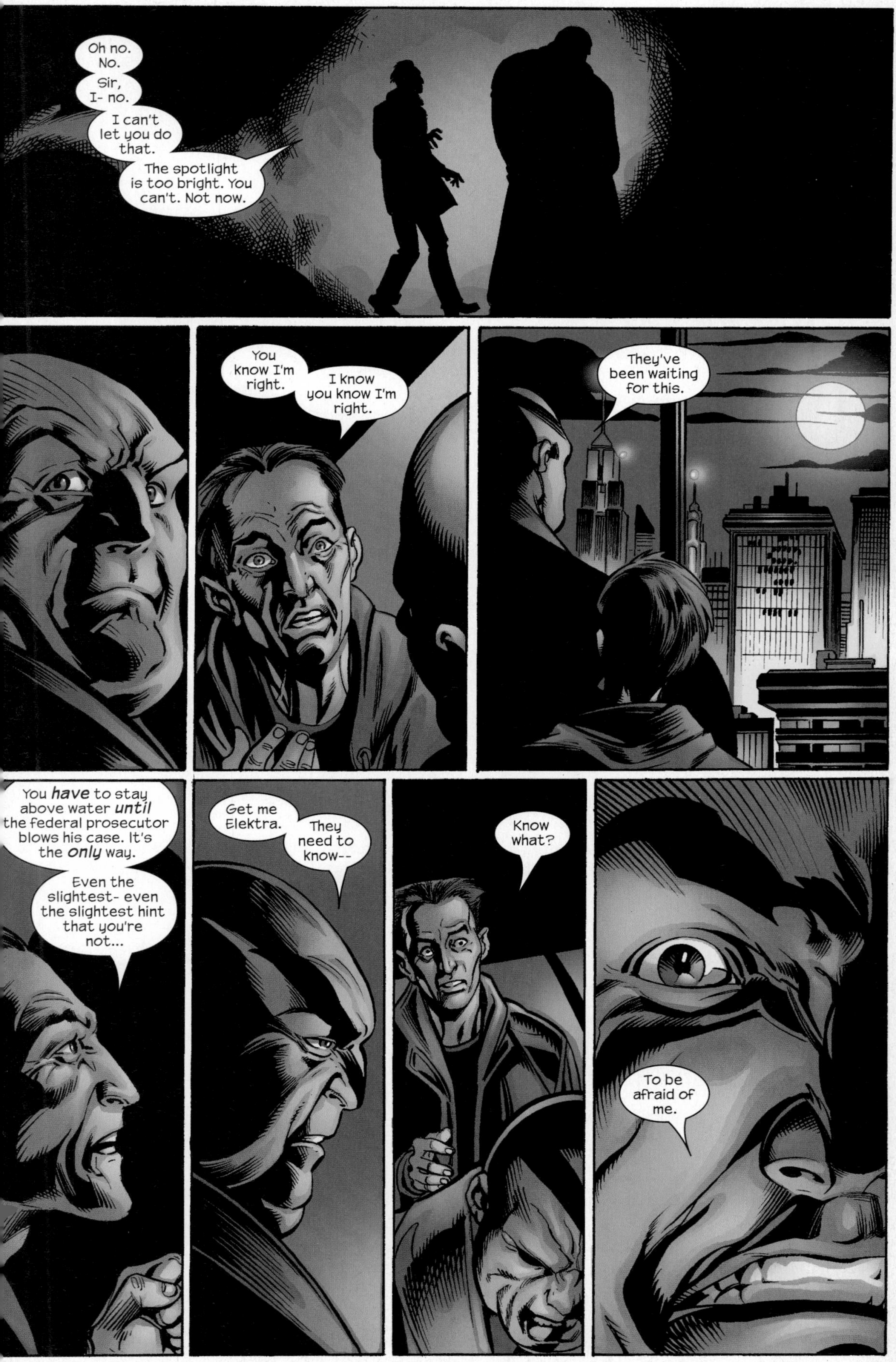
Oh no. No.
Sir, I- no.
I can't let you do that.
The spotlight is too bright. You can't. Not now.
You know I'm right.
I know you know I'm right.
They've been waiting for this.
You *have* to stay above water *until* the federal prosecutor blows his case. It's the *only* way.
Even the slightest- even the slightest hint that you're not...
Get me Elektra.
They need to know--
Know what?
To be afraid of me.

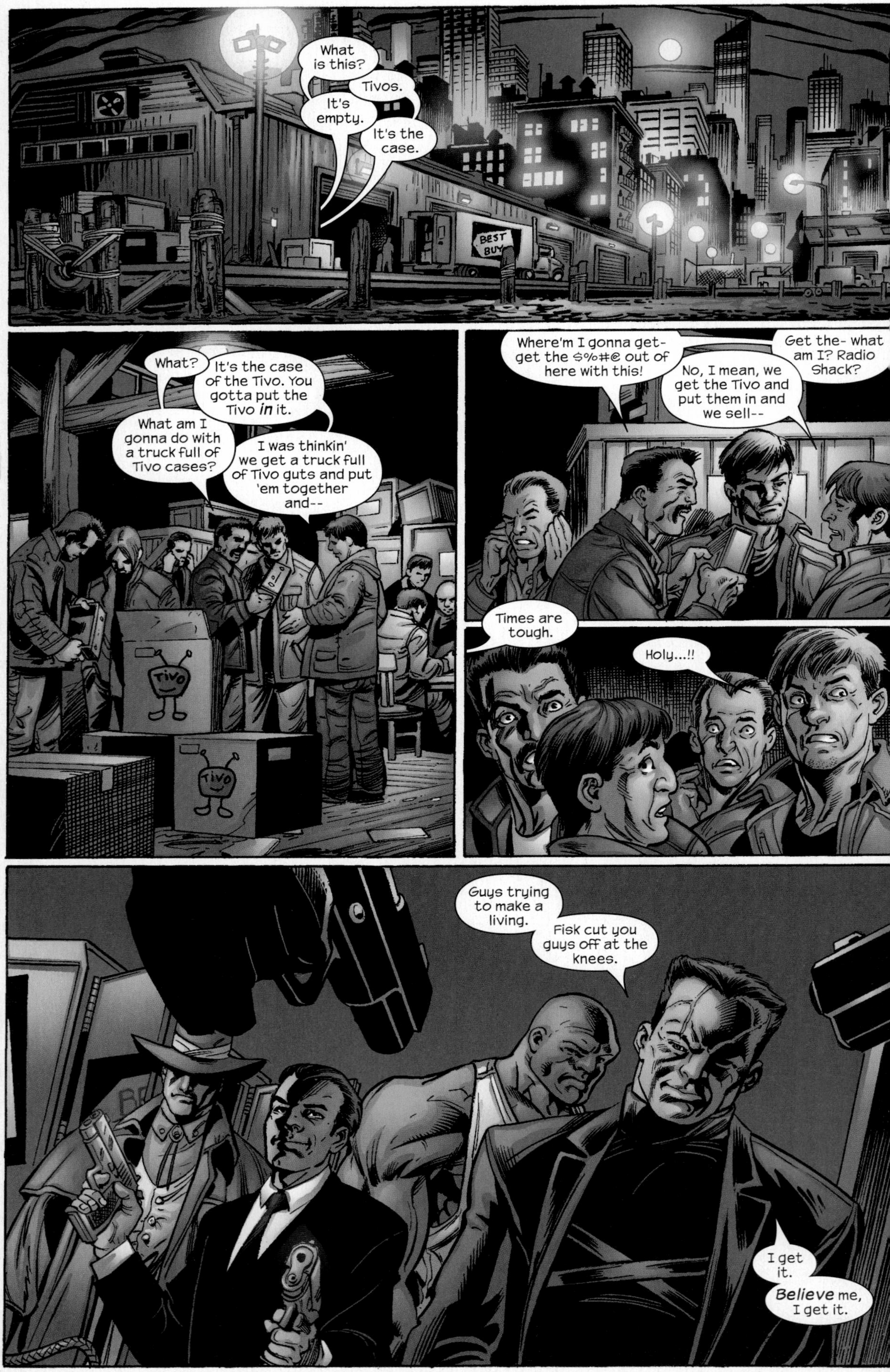
What is this?
Tivos.
It's empty.
It's the case.
What?
It's the case of the Tivo. You gotta put the Tivo *in* it.
What am I gonna do with a truck full of Tivo cases?
I was thinkin' we get a truck full of Tivo guts and put 'em together and--
Where'm I gonna get- get the $%#@ out of here with this!
No, I mean, we get the Tivo and put them in and we sell--
Get the- what am I? Radio Shack?
Times are tough.
Holy...!!
Guys trying to make a living.
Fisk cut you guys off at the knees.
I get it.
Believe me, I get it.

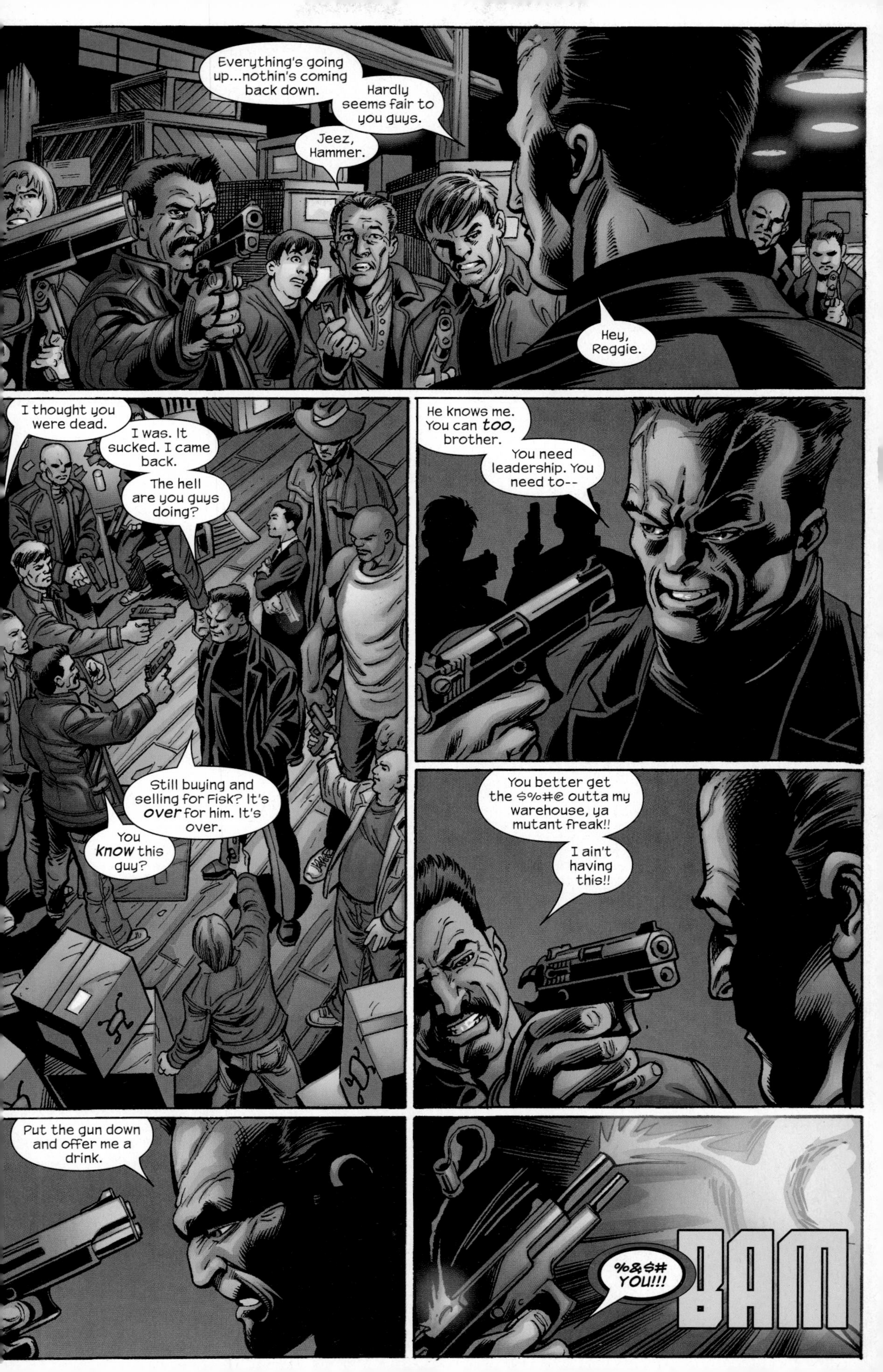
Everything's going up...nothin's coming back down.
Hardly seems fair to you guys.
Jeez, Hammer.
Hey, Reggie.
I thought you were dead.
I was. It sucked. I came back.
The hell are you guys doing?
Still buying and selling for Fisk? It's over for him. It's over.
You know this guy?
He knows me. You can too, brother.
You need leadership. You need to--
You better get the $%#@ outta my warehouse, ya mutant freak!!
I ain't having this!!
Put the gun down and offer me a drink.
%&$# YOU!!!
BAM

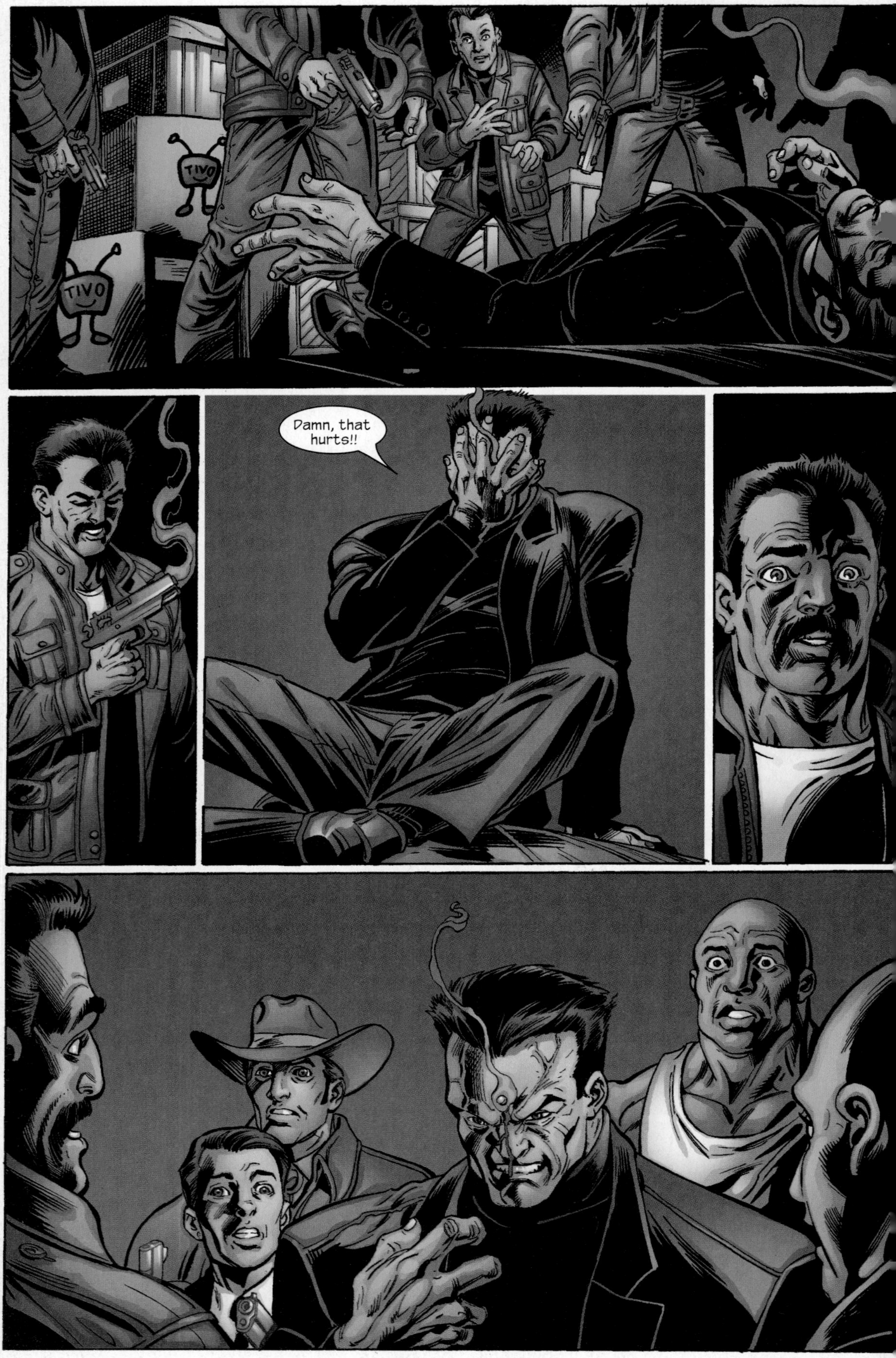
TIVO
TIVO
Damn, that hurts!!

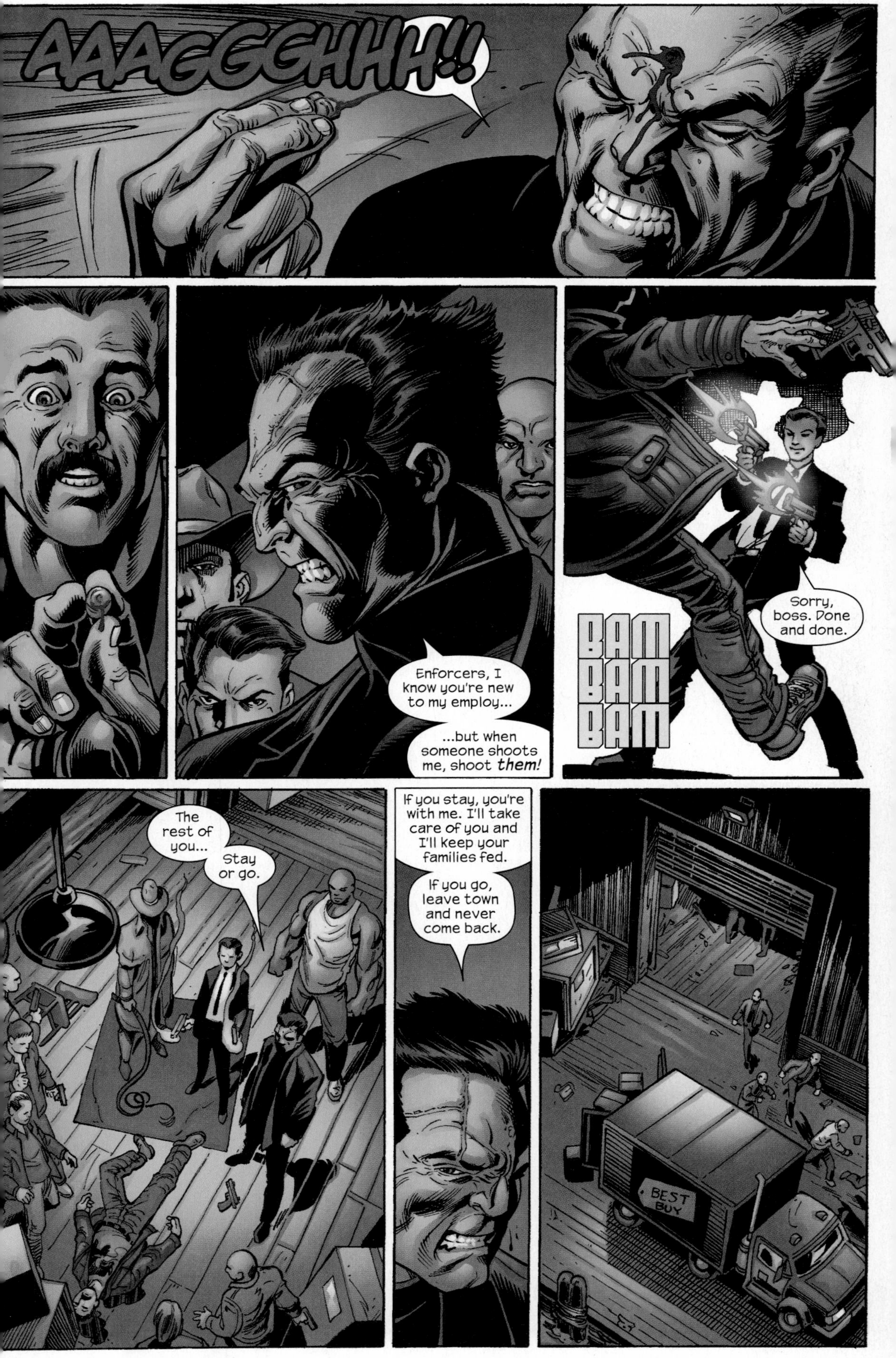
AAAGGGHHH!!
Enforcers, I know you're new to my employ...
...but when someone shoots me, shoot *them!*
BAM
BAM
BAM
Sorry, boss. Done and done.
The rest of you...
Stay or go.
If you stay, you're with me. I'll take care of you and I'll keep your families fed.
If you go, leave town and never come back.
BEST BUY

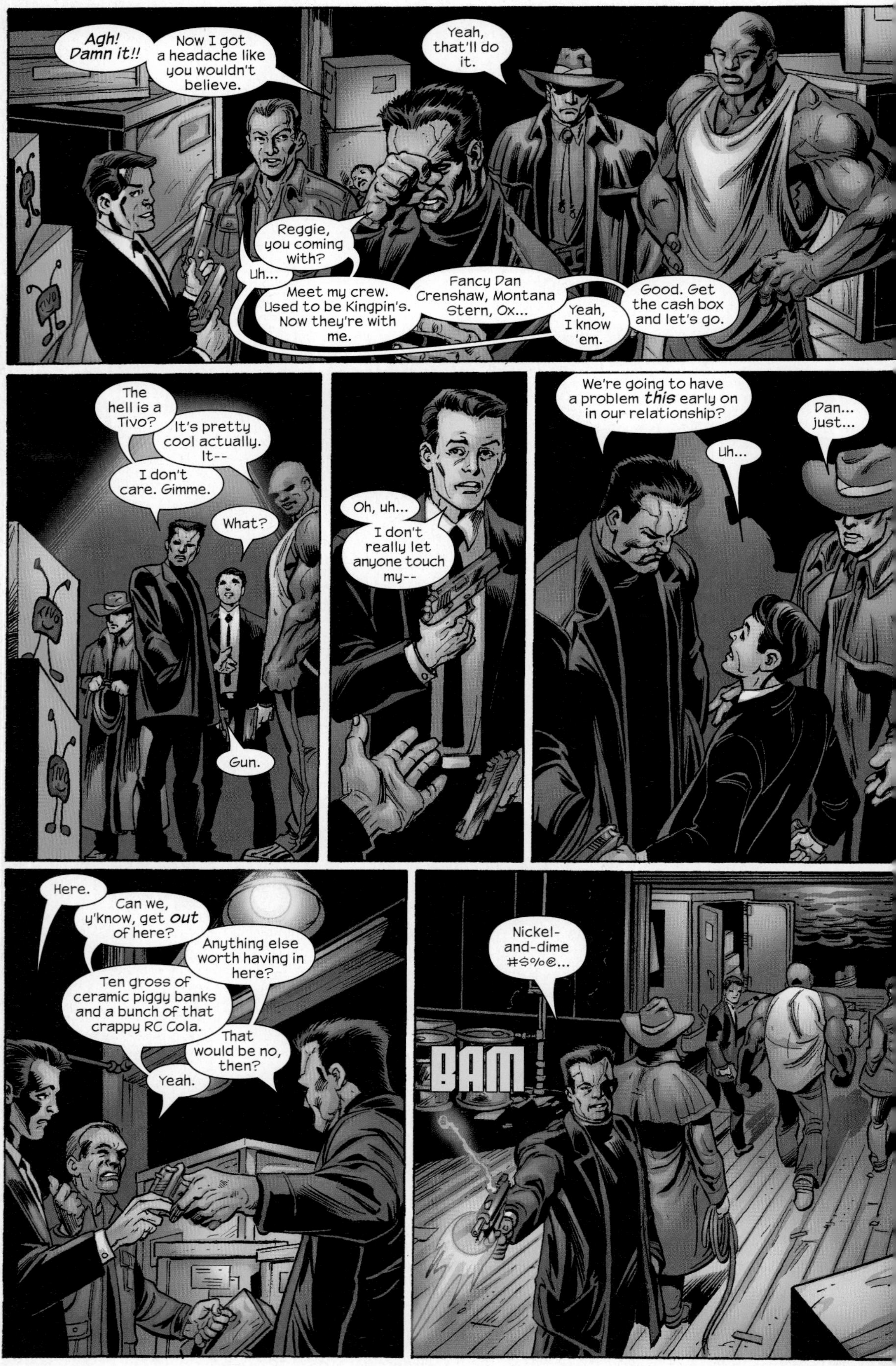

Agh! Damn it!!
Now I got a headache like you wouldn't believe.
Yeah, that'll do it.
Reggie, you coming with?
Uh...
Meet my crew. Used to be Kingpin's. Now they're with me.
Fancy Dan Crenshaw, Montana Stern, Ox...
Yeah, I know 'em.
Good. Get the cash box and let's go.
The hell is a Tivo?
It's pretty cool actually. It--
I don't care. Gimme.
What?
Gun.
Oh, uh...
I don't really let anyone touch my--
We're going to have a problem this early on in our relationship?
Uh...
Dan... just...
Here.
Can we, y'know, get out of here?
Anything else worth having in here?
Ten gross of ceramic piggy banks and a bunch of that crappy RC Cola.
That would be no, then?
Yeah.
Nickel-and-dime #$%@...
BAM

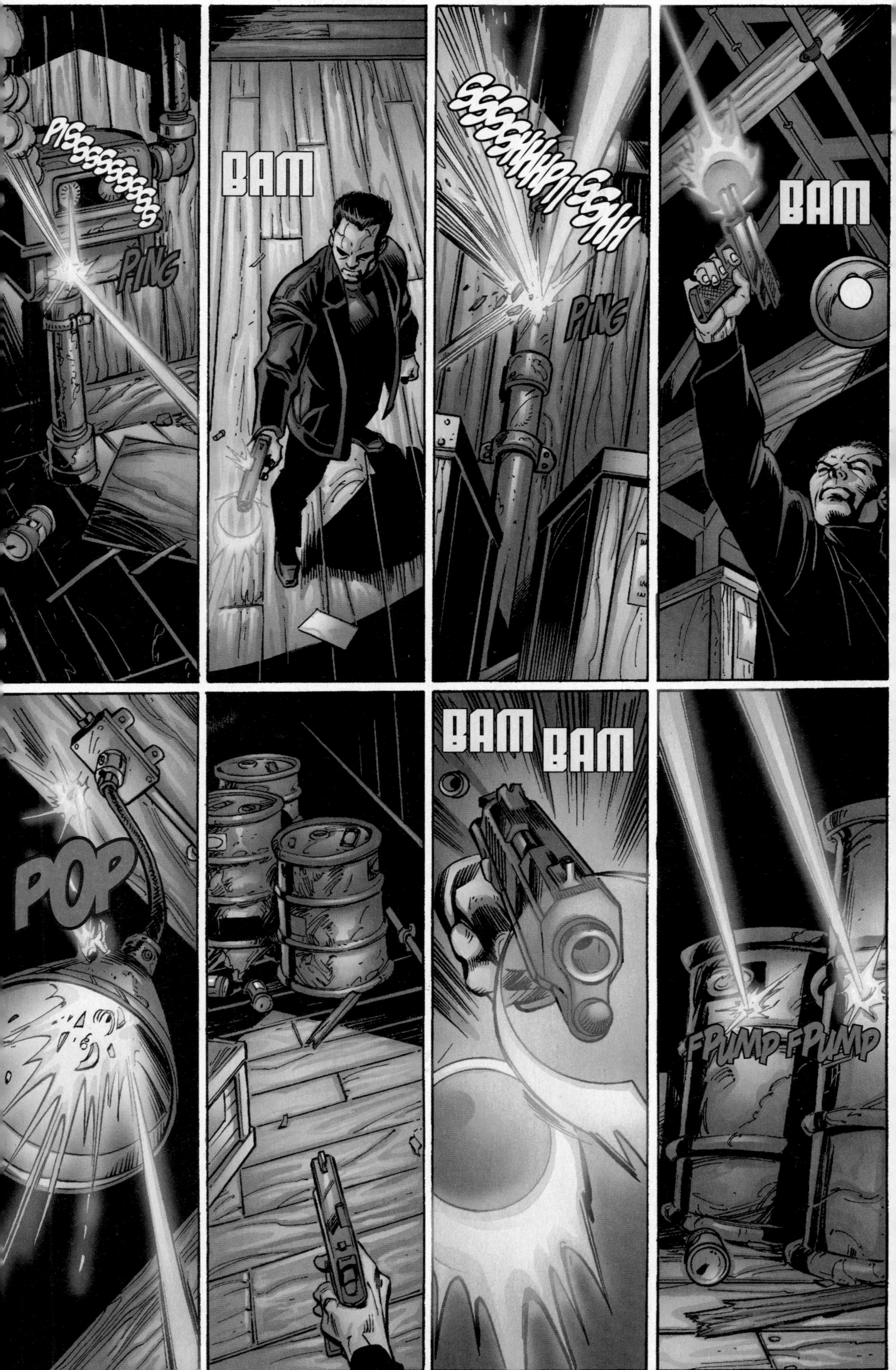
PISSSSSSSSS
PING
BAM
SSSSHHHPIISSHH
PING
BAM
POP
BAM
BAM
FPUMP FPUMP

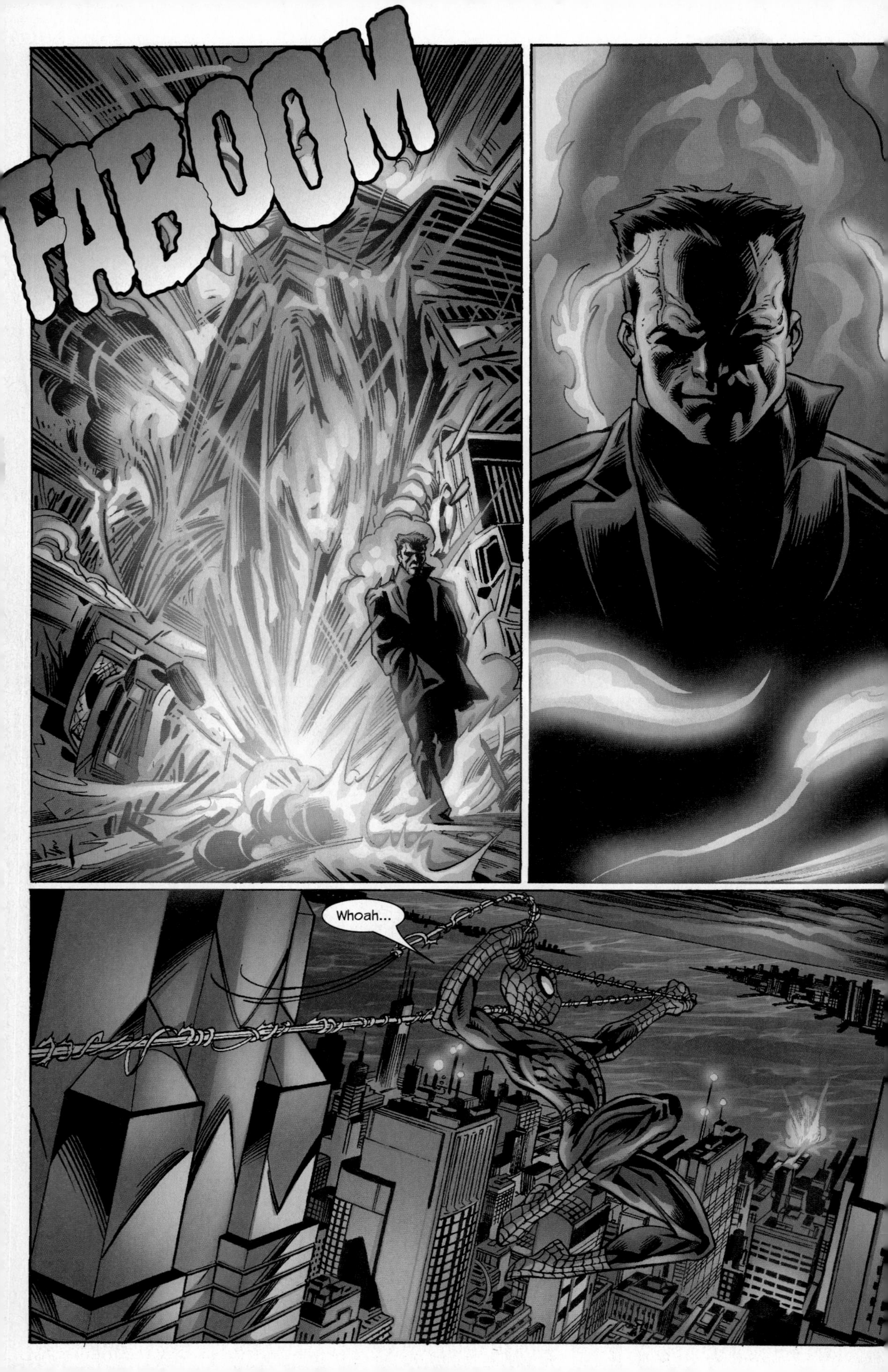
FABOOM
Whoah...

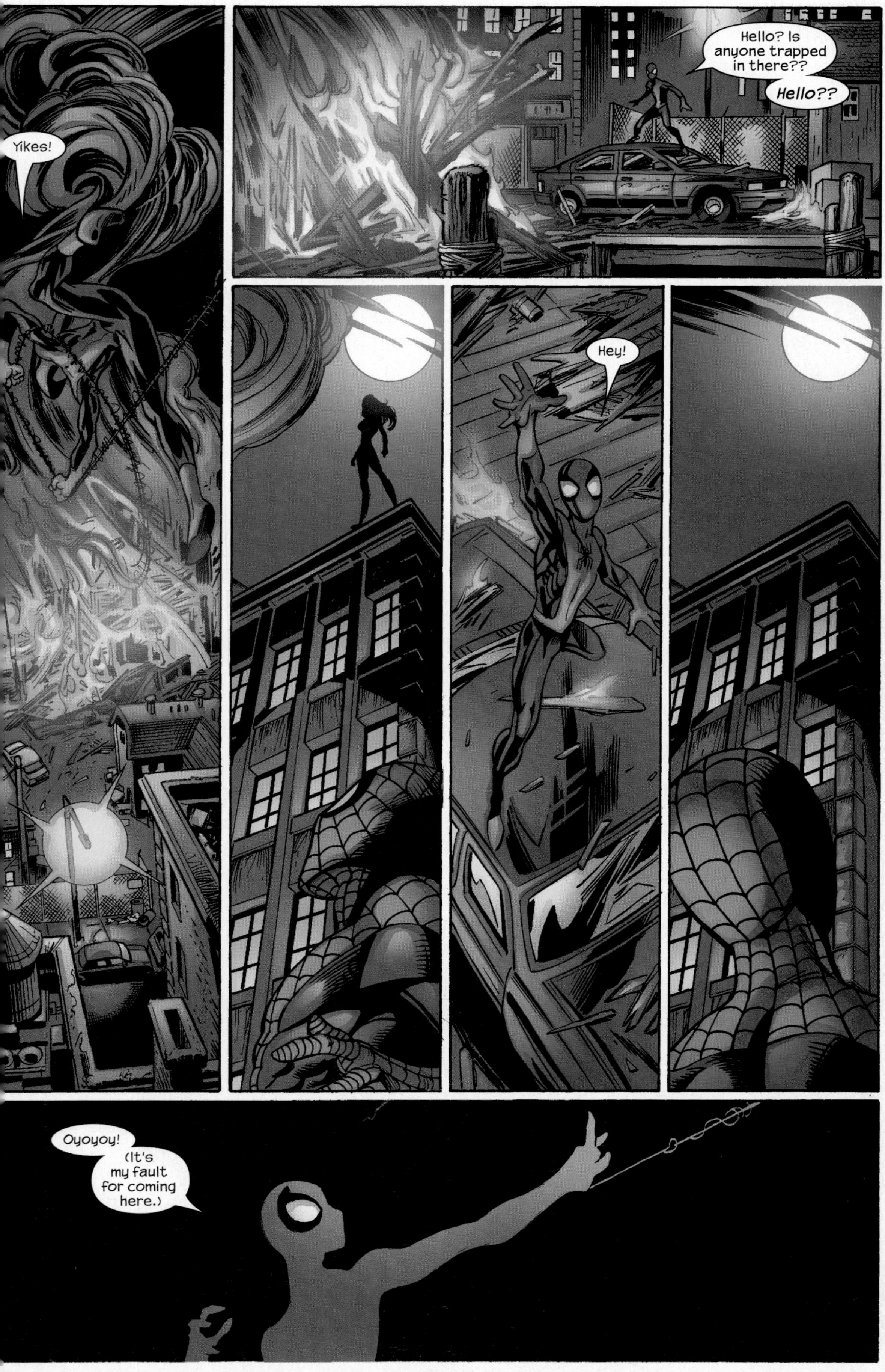
Yikes!
Hello? Is anyone trapped in there??
Hello??
Hey!
Oyoyoy!
(It's my fault for coming here.)

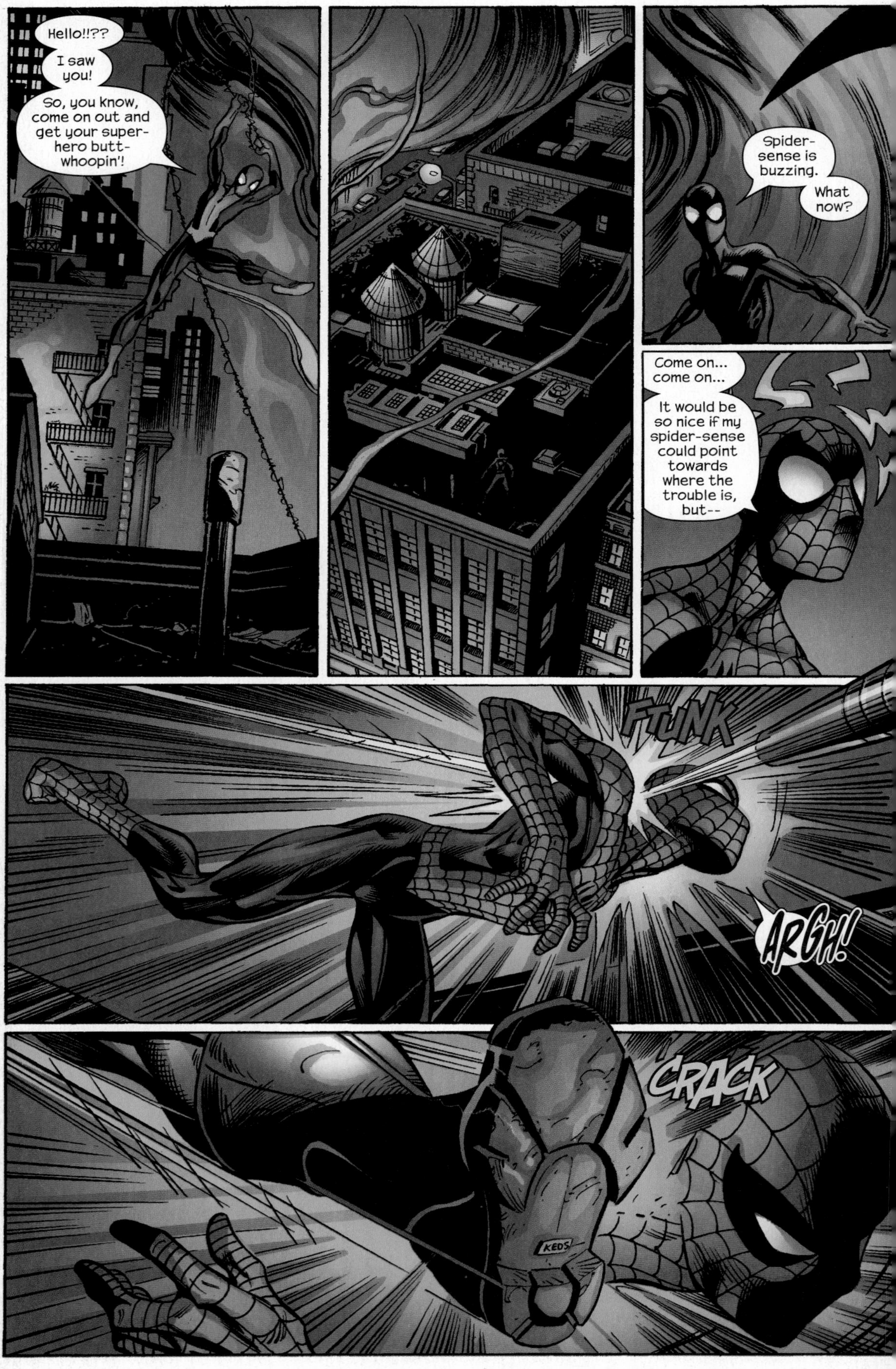
Hello!!??
I saw you!
So, you know, come on out and get your super-hero butt-whoopin'!
Spider-sense is buzzing.
What now?
Come on... come on...
It would be so nice if my spider-sense could point towards where the trouble is, but--
FTUNK
ARGH!
CRACK
KEDS

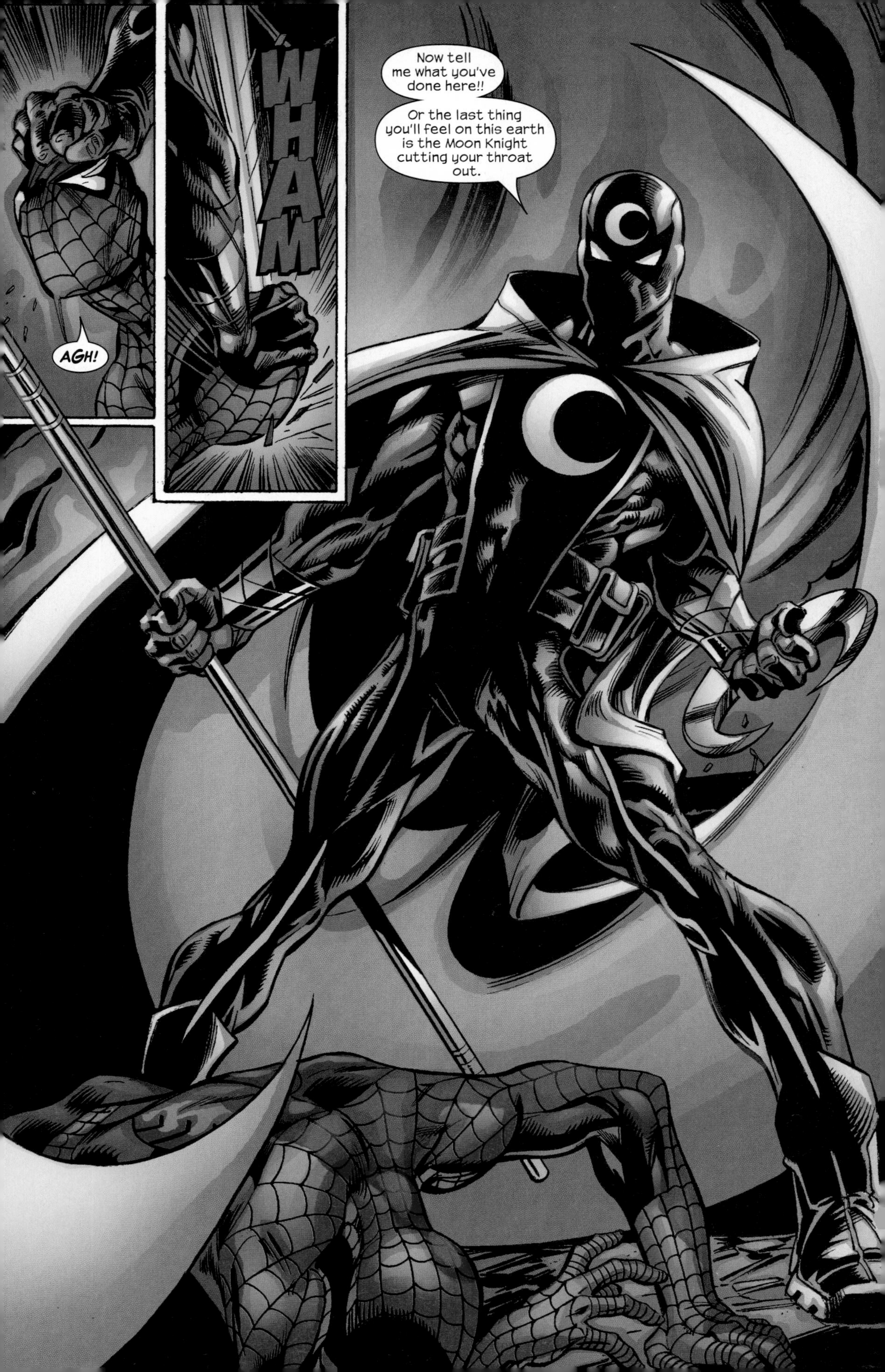

WHAM
AGH!
Now tell me what you've done here!!
Or the last thing you'll feel on this earth is the Moon Knight cutting your throat out.

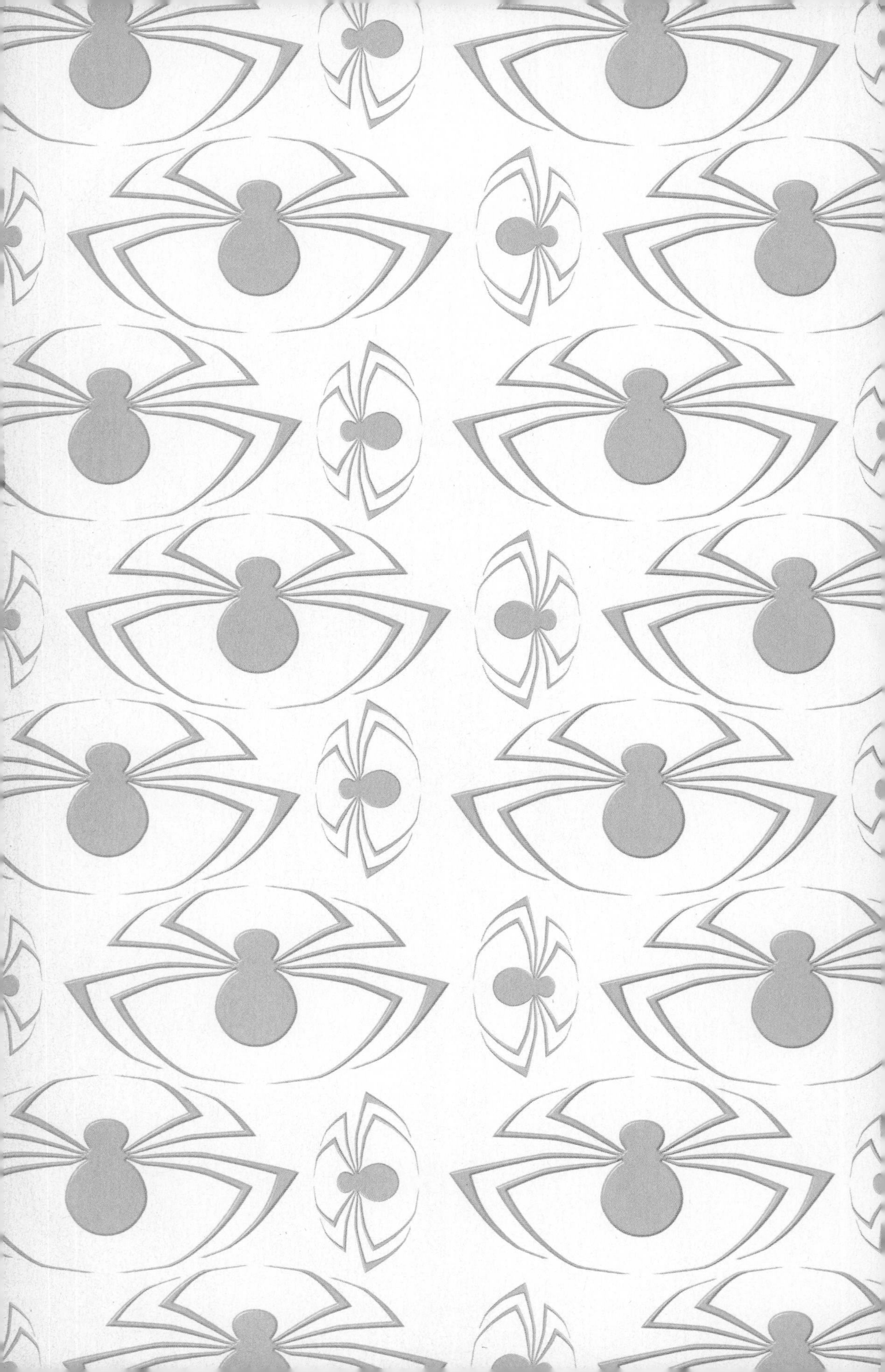

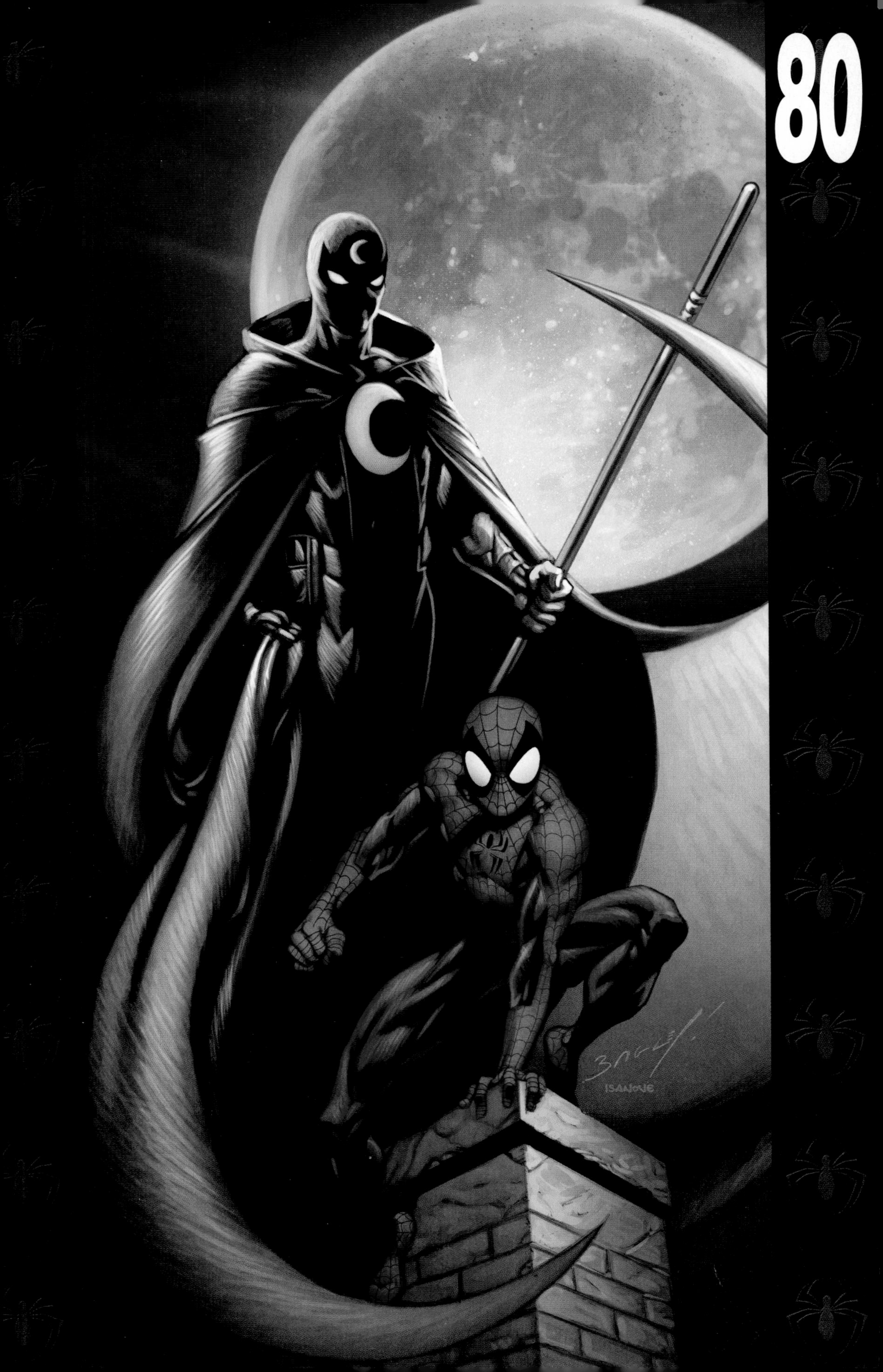
80

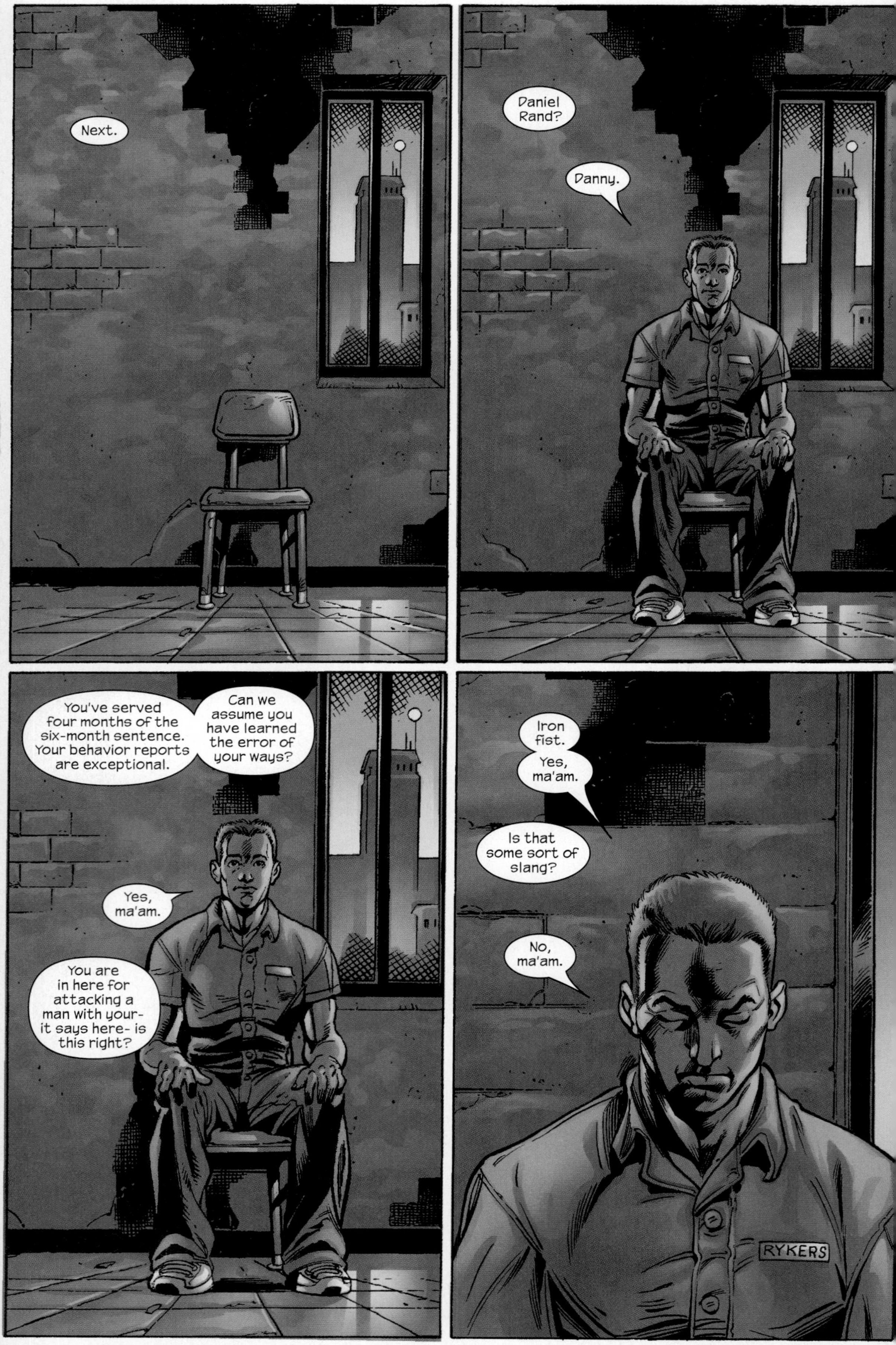
Next.
Daniel Rand?
Danny.
You've served four months of the six-month sentence. Your behavior reports are exceptional.
Can we assume you have learned the error of your ways?
Yes, ma'am.
You are in here for attacking a man with your- it says here- is this right?
Iron fist.
Yes, ma'am.
Is that some sort of slang?
No, ma'am.
RYKERS

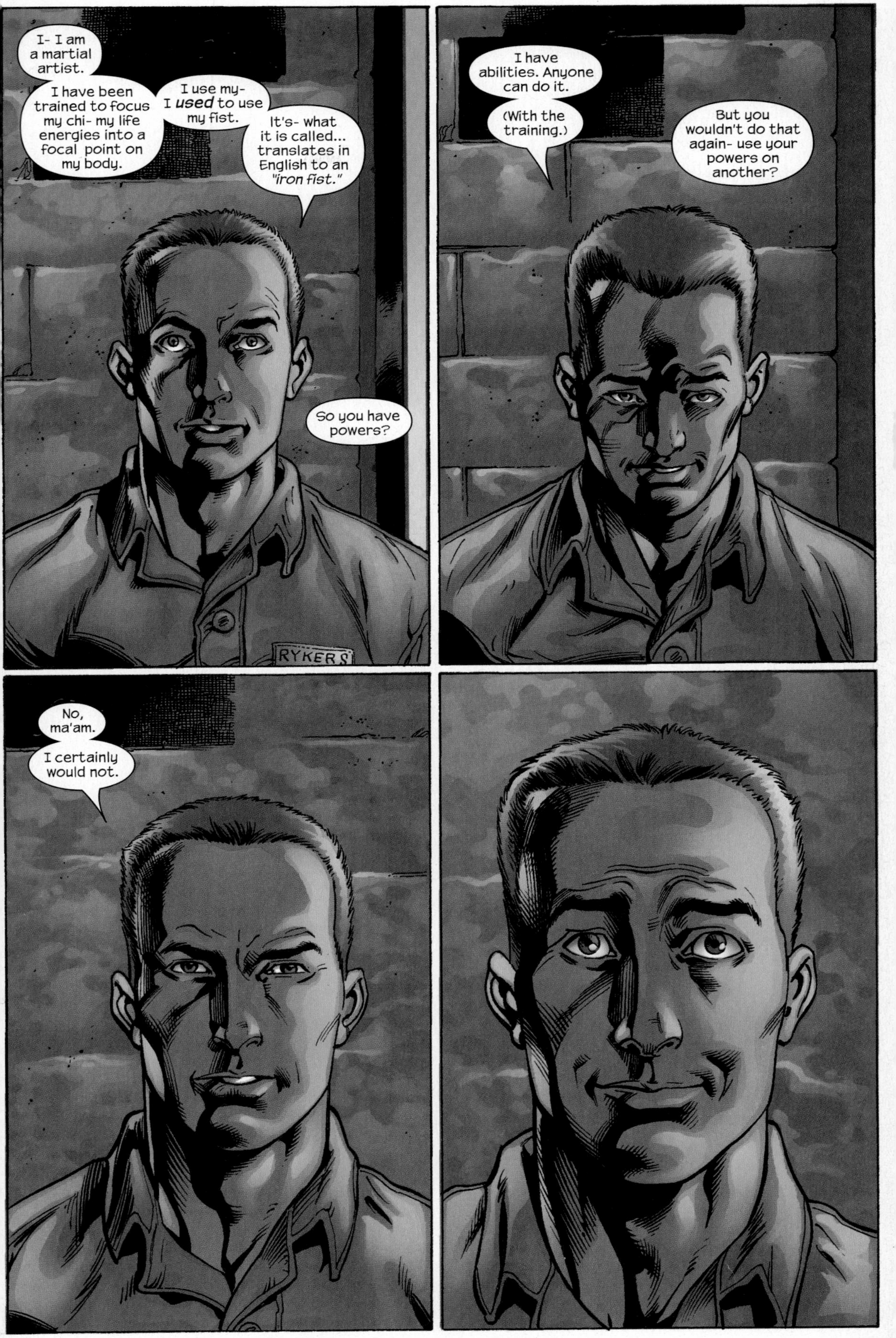

I- I am a martial artist.
I have been trained to focus my chi- my life energies into a focal point on my body.
I use my- I **used** to use my fist.
It's- what it is called... translates in English to an *"iron fist."*
So you have powers?
RYKERS
I have abilities. Anyone can do it.
(With the training.)
But you wouldn't do that again- use your powers on another?
No, ma'am.
I certainly would not.

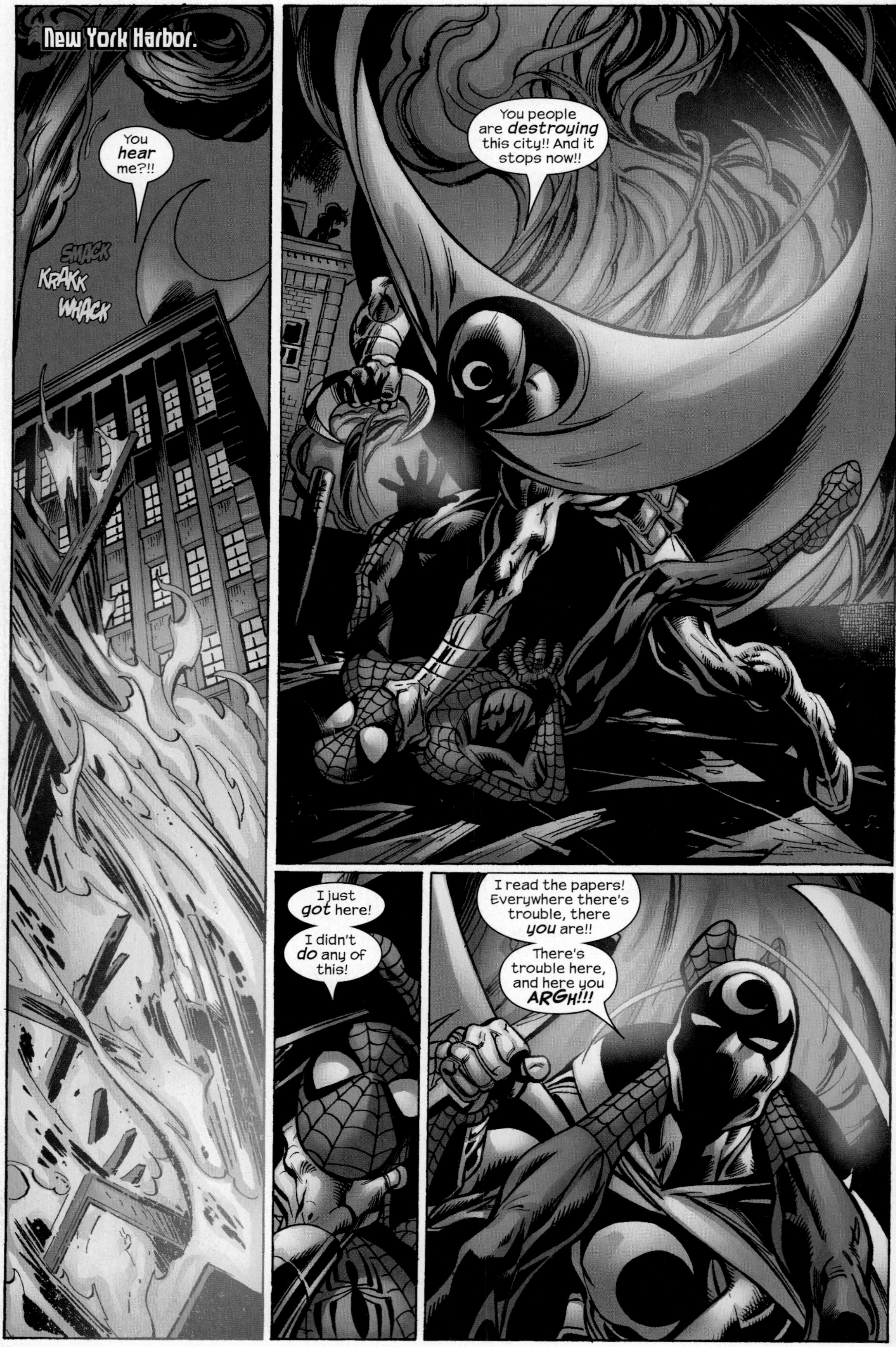
New York Harbor.
You hear me?!!
SMACK
KRAKK
WHACK
You people are destroying this city!! And it stops now!!
I just got here!
I didn't do any of this!
I read the papers! Everywhere there's trouble, there you are!!
There's trouble here, and here you ARGH!!!

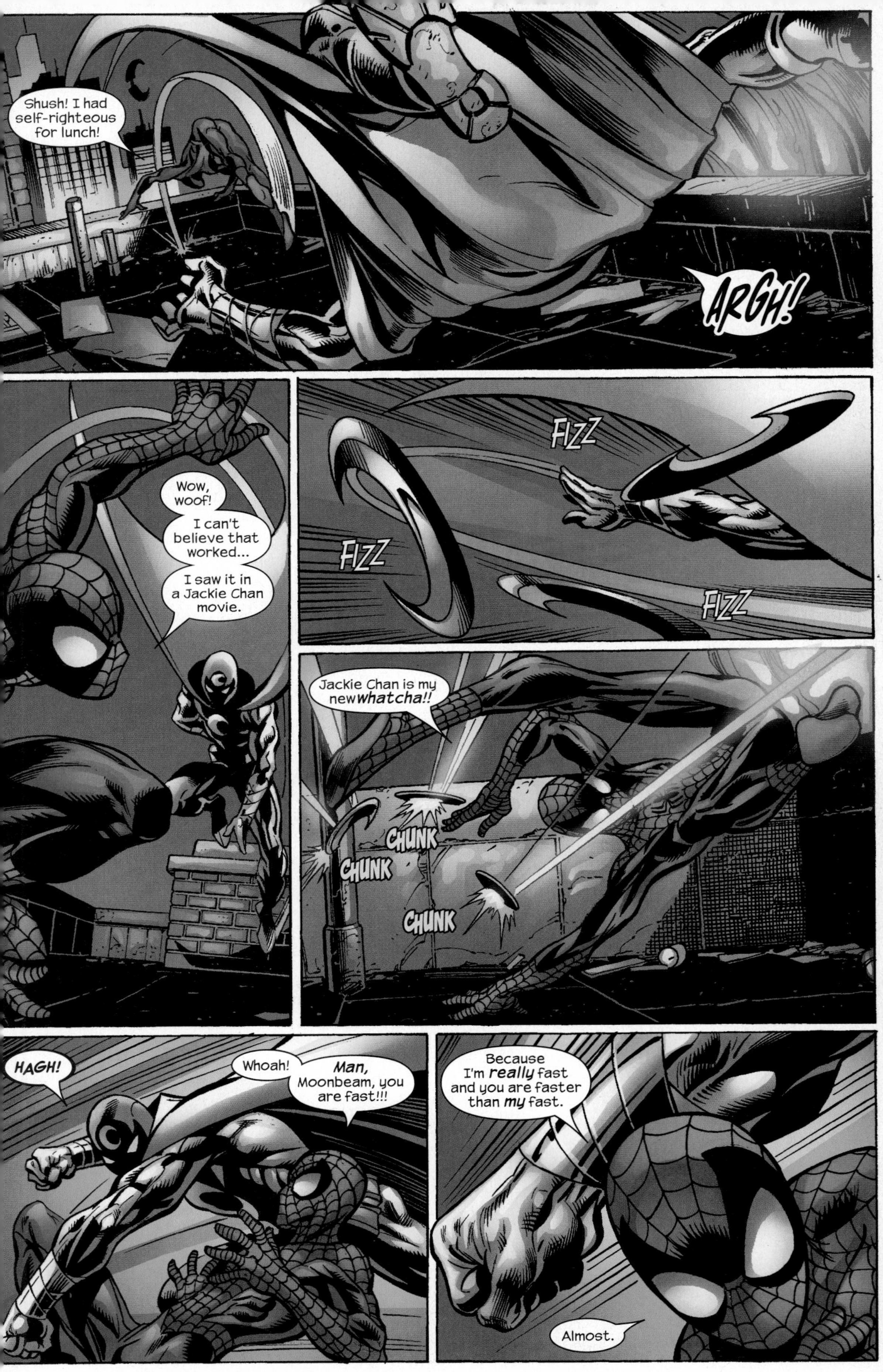
Shush! I had self-righteous for lunch!
ARGH!
Wow, woof!
I can't believe that worked...
I saw it in a Jackie Chan movie.
FIZZ
FIZZ
FIZZ
Jackie Chan is my new whatcha!!
CHUNK
CHUNK
CHUNK
HAGH!
Whoah!
Man, Moonbeam, you are fast!!!
Because I'm really fast and you are faster than my fast.
Almost.

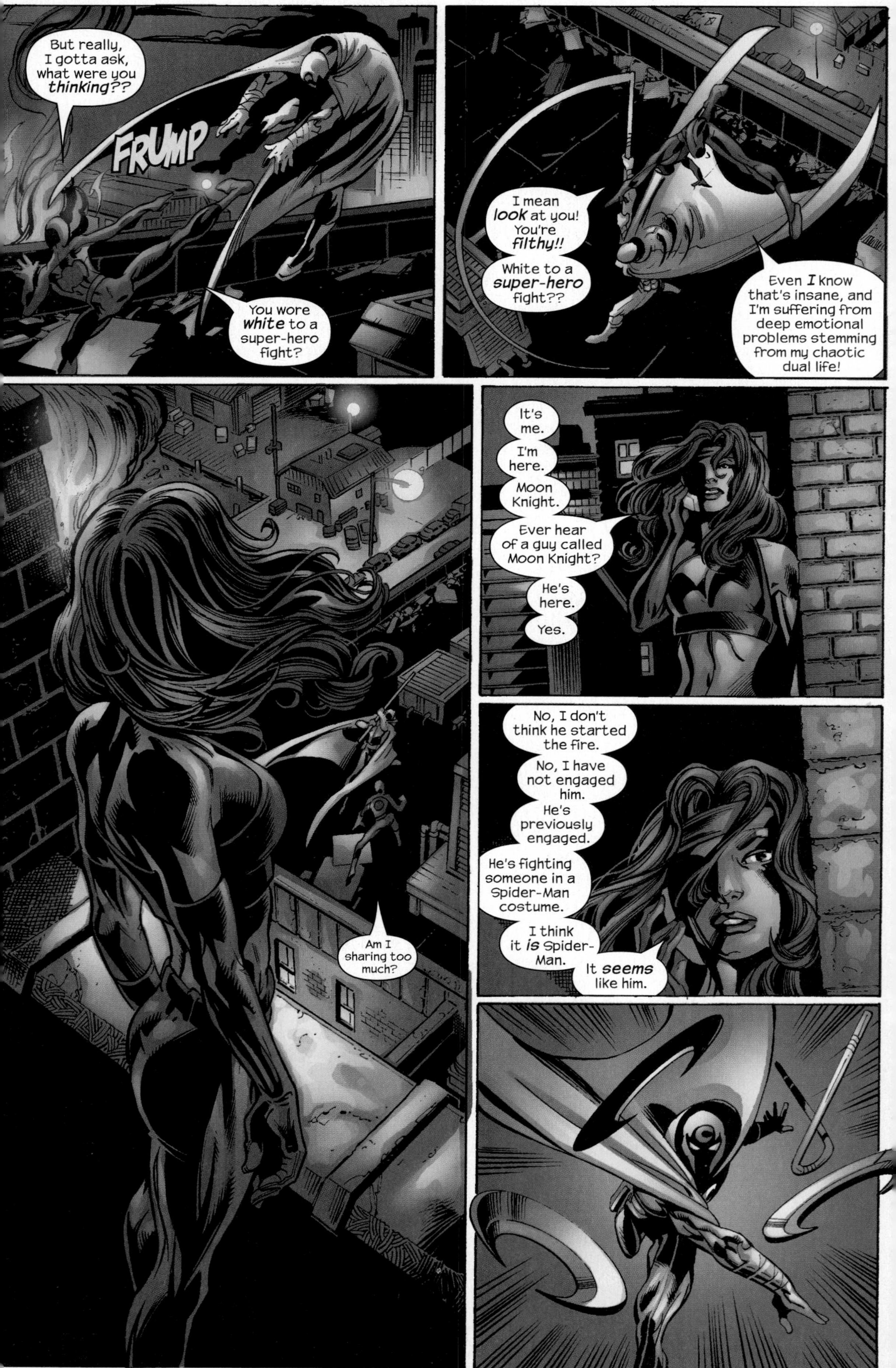

But really, I gotta ask, what were you thinking??
FRUMP
You wore white to a super-hero fight?
I mean look at you! You're filthy!!
White to a super-hero fight??
Even I know that's insane, and I'm suffering from deep emotional problems stemming from my chaotic dual life!
Am I sharing too much?
It's me.
I'm here.
Moon Knight.
Ever hear of a guy called Moon Knight?
He's here.
Yes.
No, I don't think he started the fire.
No, I have not engaged him.
He's previously engaged.
He's fighting someone in a Spider-Man costume.
I think it is Spider-Man.
It seems like him.

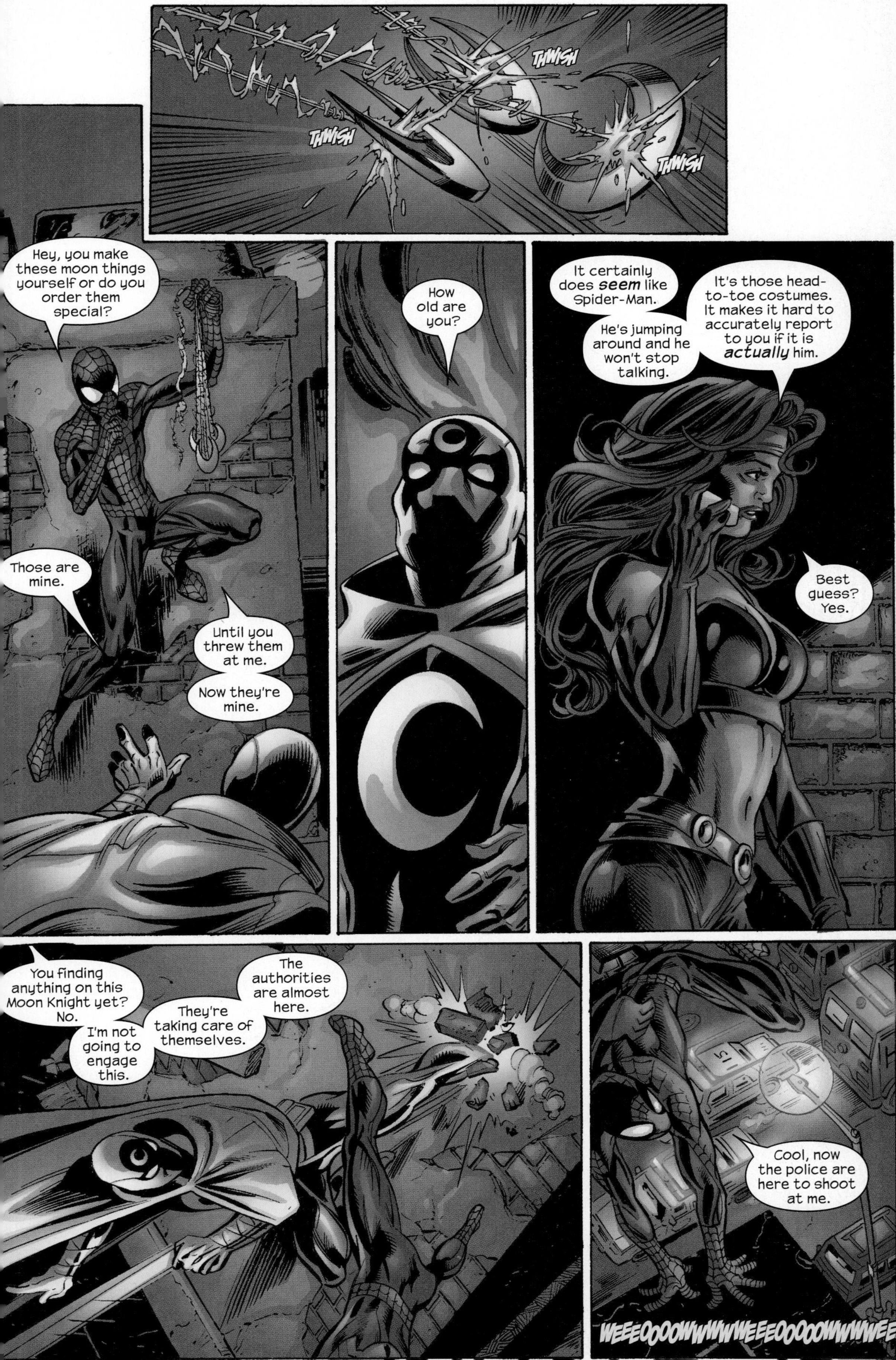
THWISH
THWISH
THWISH
Hey, you make these moon things yourself or do you order them special?
Those are mine.
Until you threw them at me.
Now they're mine.
How old are you?
It certainly does *seem* like Spider-Man.
He's jumping around and he won't stop talking.
It's those head-to-toe costumes. It makes it hard to accurately report to you if it is *actually* him.
Best guess? Yes.
You finding anything on this Moon Knight yet? No.
I'm not going to engage this.
They're taking care of themselves.
The authorities are almost here.
Cool, now the police are here to shoot at me.
WEEEOOOOWWWWWEEEOOOOOWWWWEE

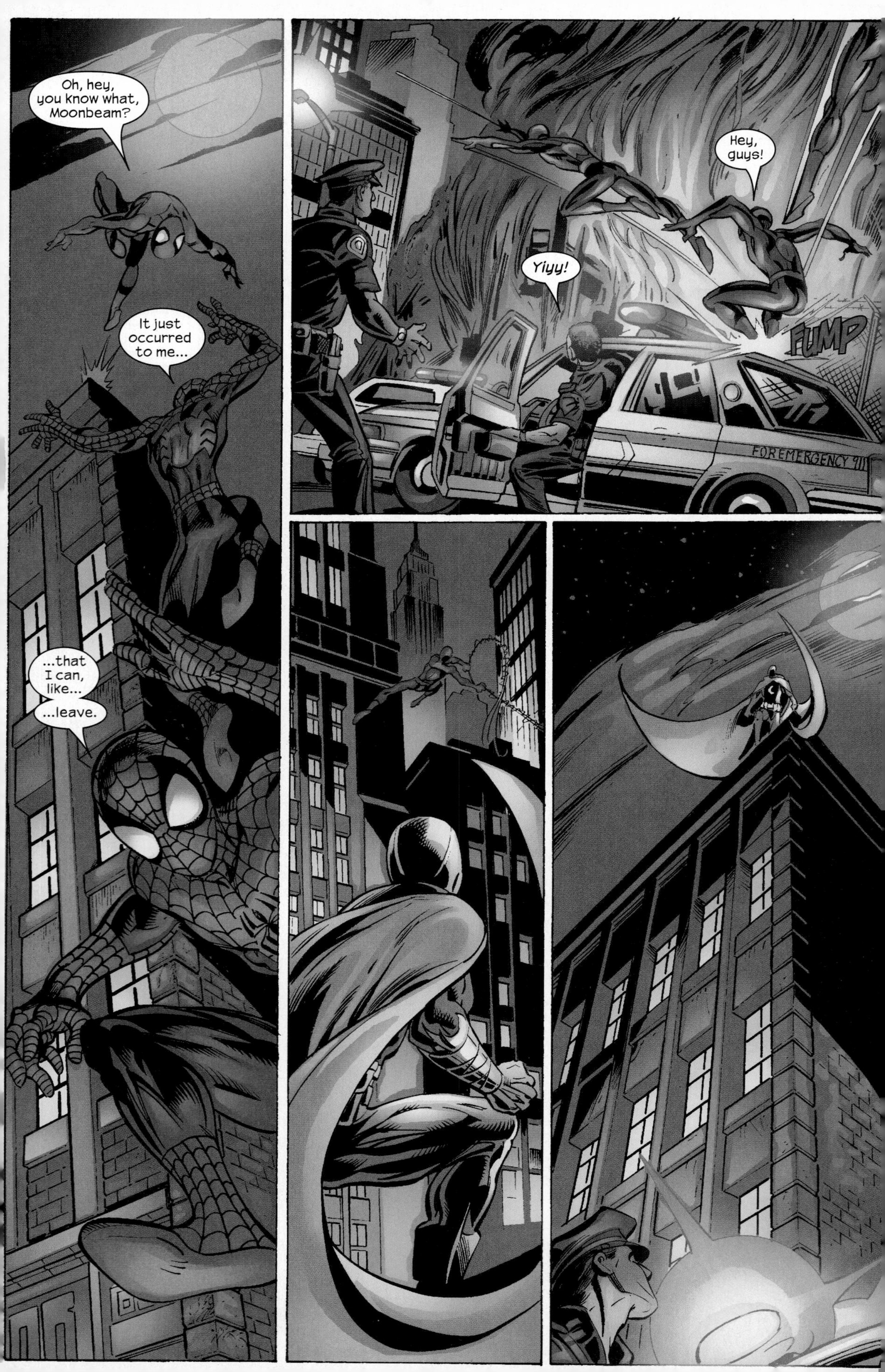
Oh, hey, you know what, Moonbeam?
It just occurred to me...
...that I can, like...
...leave.
Hey, guys!
Yiyy!
FUMP
FOR EMERGENCY 911

DAILY BUGLE

MOONMAN COMETH

SILVER DEAD

Allan Silverman

secteuer adipiscing elit, ncidunt ut laoreet dolore n wisi enim ad minim n ullamcorper suscipit modo consequat. Duis rerit in vulputate velit dolore eu feugiat nulla sto odio dignissim qui it augue duis dolore te

nostrud exerci tation quip ex ea commodo dolor in hendrerit in , vel illum dolore eu cumsan et iusto odio n zzril delenit augue rem ipsum dolor sit iam nonummy nibh agna aliquam erat

drerit in vulputate dolore eu feugiat an et iusto odio zril delenit augue n ipsum dolor sit n nonummy nibh na aliquam erat n, quis nostrud nisl ut aliquip ex

adipiscing elit, t laoreet dolore im ad minim orper suscipit nsequat. Duis vulputate velit feugiat nulla dignissim qui luis dolore te

exerci tation a commodo hendrerit in n dolore eu l iusto odio lenit augue n dolor sit mmy nibh quam erat

vulputate a feugiat sto odio it augue ny nibh um erat nostrud quip ex

g elit, lolore ninim scipit Duis velit nulla qui

Duis autem vel eum iriure velit esse molestie consequ nulla facilisis at vero ero dignissim qui blandit praes duis dolore te feugiat nulla amet, consectetuer adipiscin euismod tincidunt ut laoree volutpat. Ut wisi enim ad exerci tation ullamcorper sus ea commodo consequat.

Ut wisi enim ad minim veniam, quis ullamcorper suscipit lobortis nisl ut ali consequat. Duis autem vel eum iriure vulputate velit esse molestie consequat, feugiat nulla facilisis at vero eros et acc dignissim qui blandit praesent luptatum duis dolore te feugiat nulla facilisi. Lor amet, consectetuer adipiscing elit, sed dian euismod tincidunt ut laoreet dolore ma volutpat.

Duis autem vel eum iriure dolor in hend velit esse molestie consequat, vel illum nulla facilisis at vero eros et accumsa dignissim qui blandit praesent luptatum zz duis dolore te feugiat nulla facilisi. Lorem amet, consectetuer adipiscing elit, sed diam euismod tincidunt ut laoreet dolore magn volutpat. Ut wisi enim ad minim veniam exerci tation ullamcorper suscipit lobortis n ea commodo consequat.

Lorem ipsum dolor sit amet, consectetuer sed diam nonummy nibh euismod tincidunt ur magna aliquam erat volutpat. Ut wisi en veniam, quis nostrud exerci tation ullamc lobortis nisl ut aliquip ex ea commodo co autem vel eum iriure dolor in hendrerit in esse molestie consequat, vel illum dolore eu facilisis at vero eros et accumsan et iusto blandit praesent luptatum zzril delenit augu feugiat nulla facilisi.

Ut wisi enim ad minim veniam, quis nostrud exerci tation ullamcorper suscipit lobortis nisl ut aliquip ex ea commodo consequat. Duis autem vel eum iriure dolor in hendrerit in vulputate velit esse molestie consequat, vel illum dolore eu feugiat nulla facilisis at vero eros et accumsan et iusto odio dignissim qui blandit praesent luptatum zzril delenit augue amet, consectetuer adipiscing elit, sed diam nonummy nibh euismod tincidunt ut laoreet dolore magna aliquam erat volutpat.

Duis autem vel eum iriure dolor in hendrerit in velit esse molestie

Lorem ipsum dolor sit amet, consectetuer adipiscing elit, sed diam nonummy nibh euismod tincidunt ut laoreet dolore magna aliquam erat volutpat. Ut wisi enim ad minim veniam, quis nostrud exerci tation ullamcorper suscipit lobortis nisl ut aliquip ex ea commodo consequat. Duis autem vel eum iriure dolor in hendrerit in vulputate velit esse molestie consequat, vel illum dolore eu feugiat nulla facilisis at vero eros et accumsan et iusto odio dignissim qui blandit praesent luptatum zzril delenit augue duis dolore te feugiat nulla facilisi.

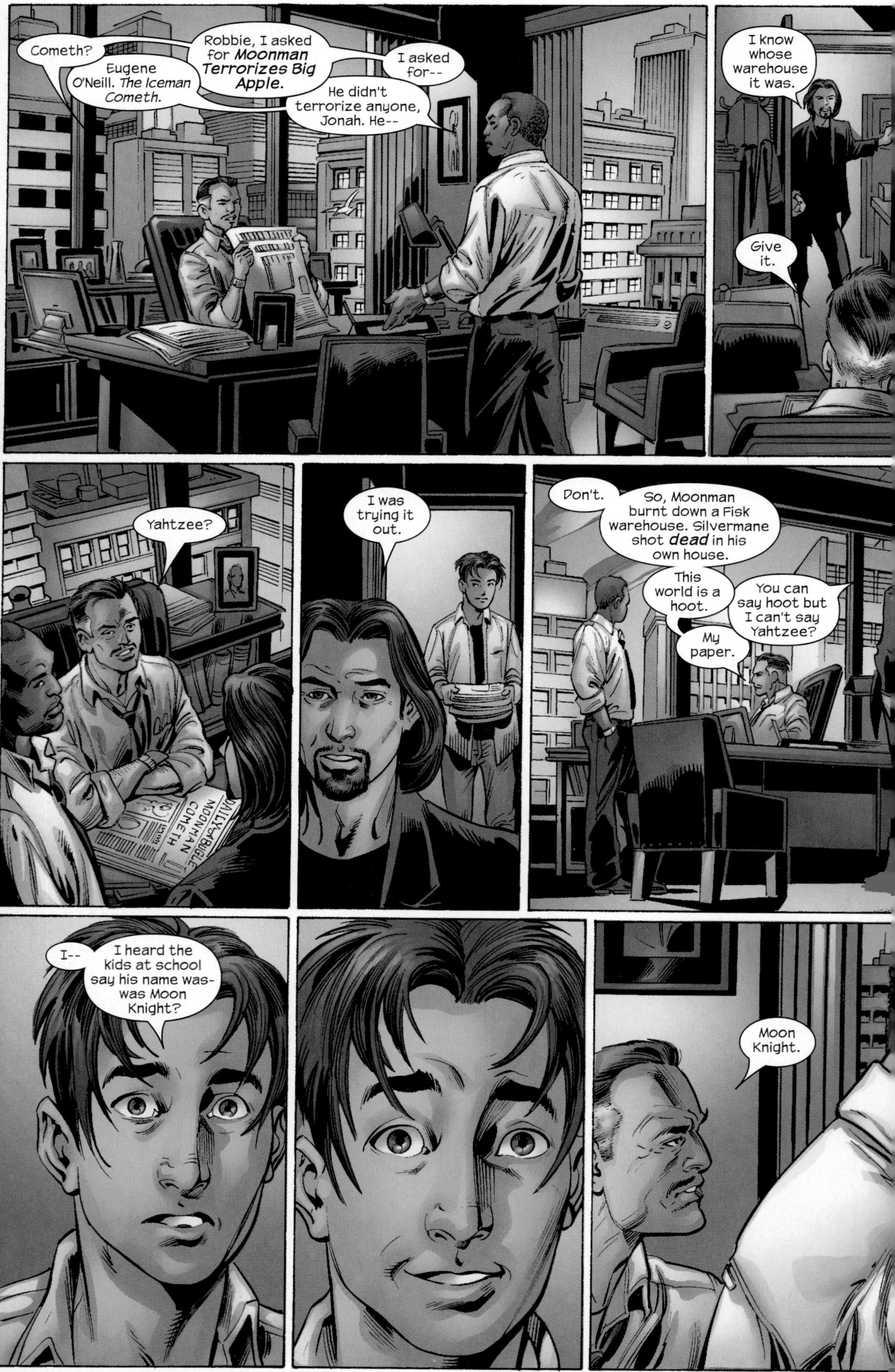
Robbie, I asked for *Moonman Terrorizes Big Apple.*
Cometh?
Eugene O'Neill. *The Iceman Cometh.*
I asked for--
He didn't terrorize anyone, Jonah. He--
I know whose warehouse it was.
Give it.
Yahtzee?
DAILY BUGLE
MOONMAN COMETH
I was trying it out.
Don't.
So, Moonman burnt down a Fisk warehouse. Silvermane shot *dead* in his own house.
This world is a hoot.
You can say hoot but I can't say Yahtzee?
My paper.
I--
I heard the kids at school say his name was-was Moon Knight?
Moon Knight.

Techster Incorporated- a division of Rolco which is a subsidiary of Sandler Electronics which is... drumroll...

Give it!

A division...

...of Fisk Enterprises.

Boom!

Yahtzee!!

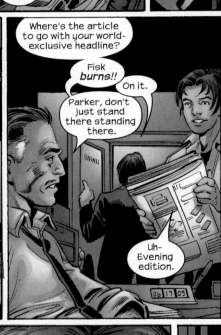

Where's the article to go with your world-exclusive headline?

Fisk *burns!!*

On it.

Parker, don't just stand there standing there.

Uh- Evening edition.

06 17 05

"Moonman."

Moon Knight.

What?

No. Moonman is funnier.

Go away.

PU
J.J.

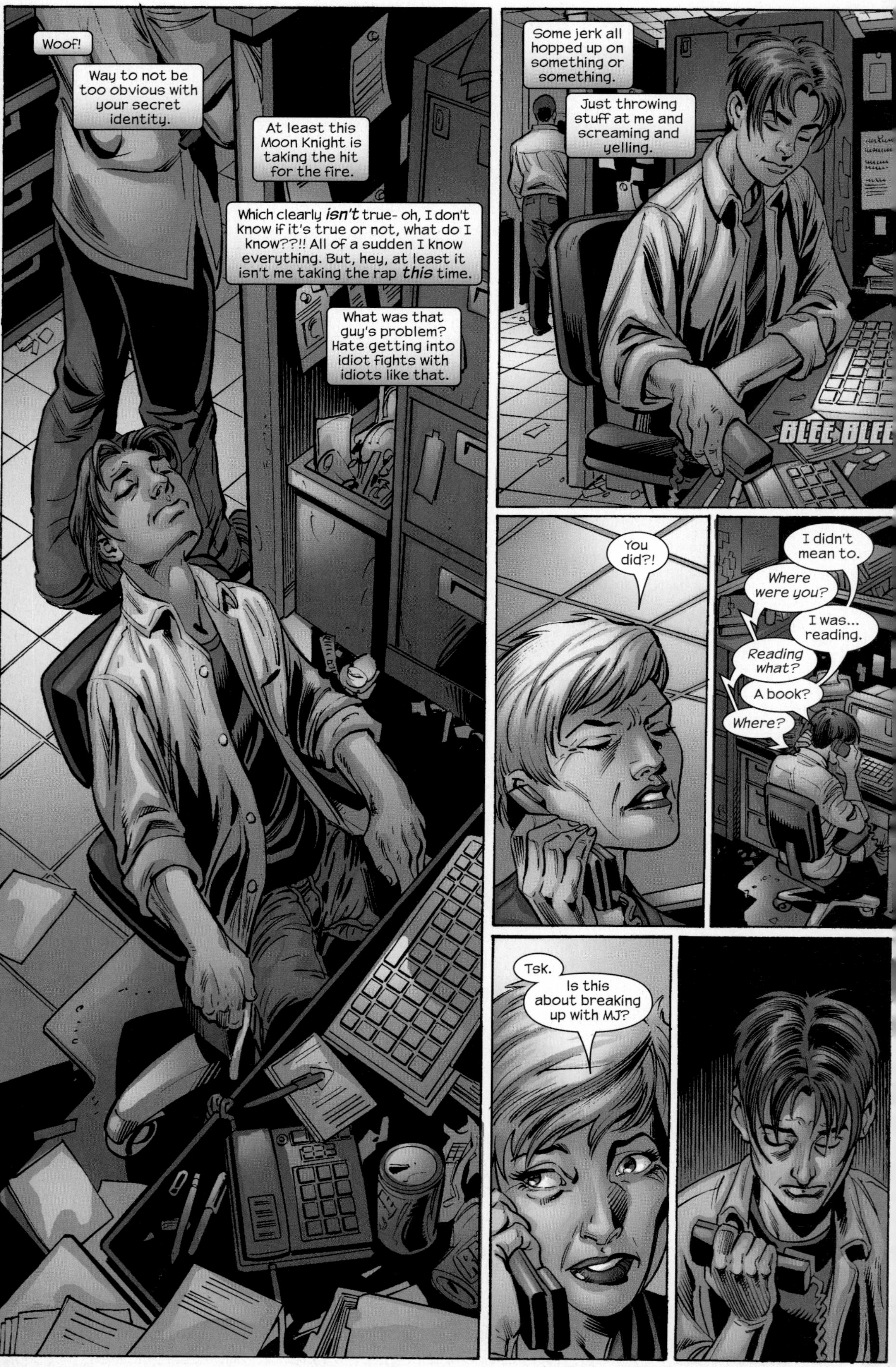
Woof!
Way to not be too obvious with your secret identity.
At least this Moon Knight is taking the hit for the fire.
Which clearly *isn't* true- oh, I don't know if it's true or not, what do I know??!! All of a sudden I know everything. But, hey, at least it isn't me taking the rap *this* time.
What was that guy's problem? Hate getting into idiot fights with idiots like that.
Some jerk all hopped up on something or something.
Just throwing stuff at me and screaming and yelling.
BLEE BLEE
You did?!
I didn't mean to.
Where were you?
I was... reading.
Reading what?
A book?
Where?
Tsk.
Is this about breaking up with MJ?

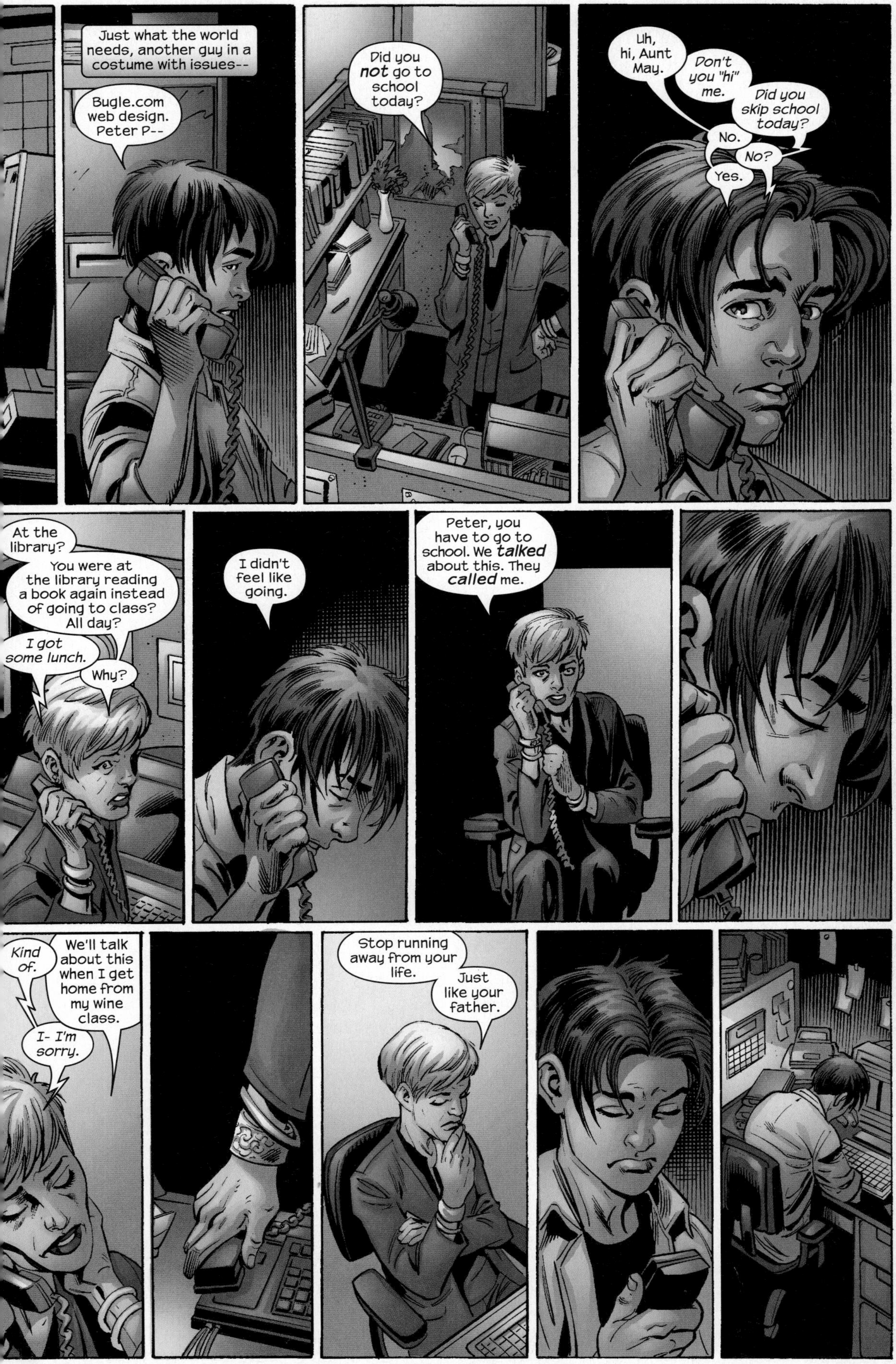
Just what the world needs, another guy in a costume with issues--
Bugle.com web design. Peter P--
Did you *not* go to school today?
Uh, hi, Aunt May.
Don't you "hi" me.
Did you skip school today?
No.
No?
Yes.
At the library?
You were at the library reading a book again instead of going to class? All day?
I got some lunch.
Why?
I didn't feel like going.
Peter, you have to go to school. We *talked* about this. They *called* me.
Kind of.
We'll talk about this when I get home from my wine class.
I- I'm sorry.
Stop running away from your life.
Just like your father.

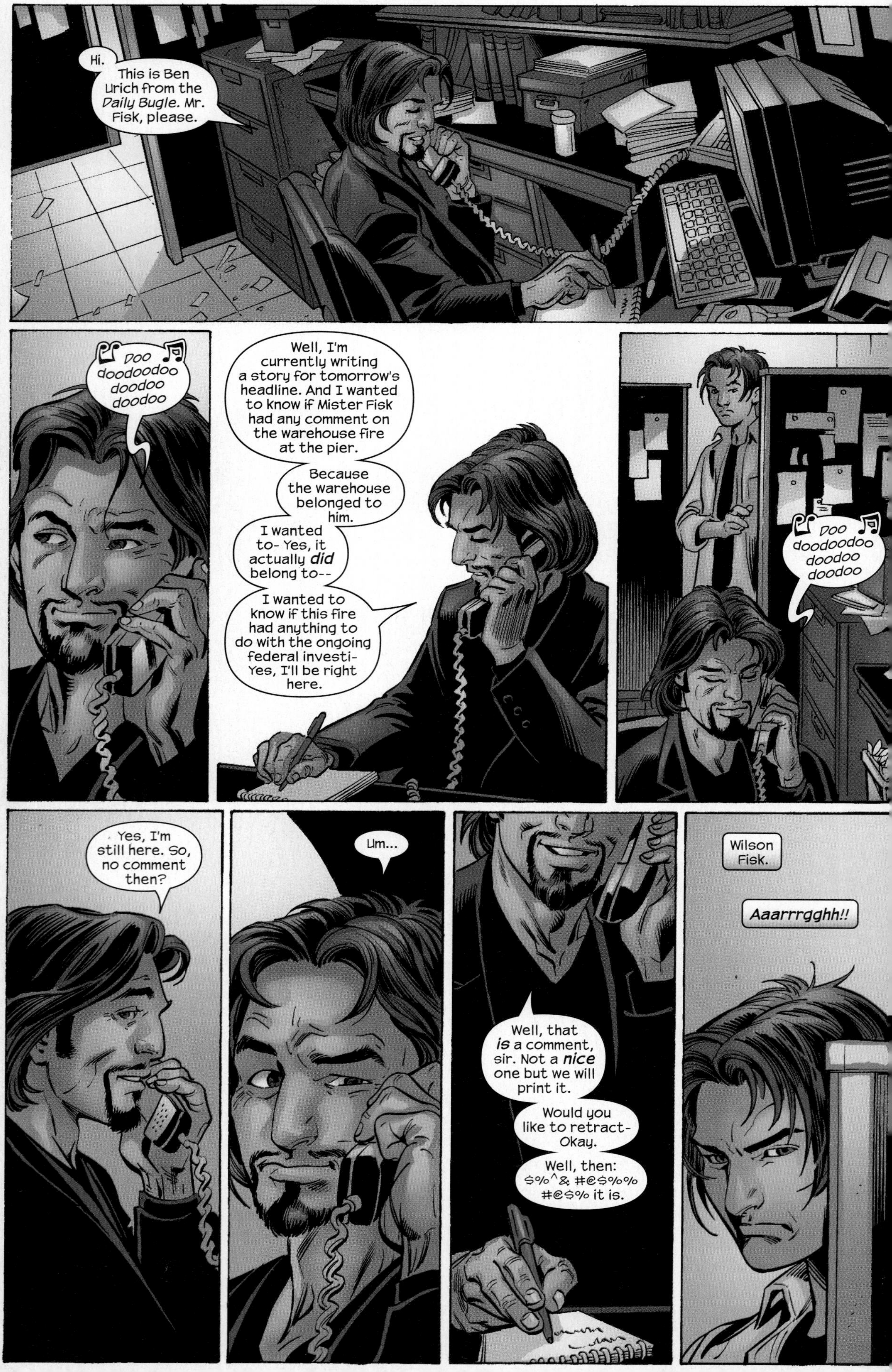

Hi.
This is Ben Urich from the *Daily Bugle*. Mr. Fisk, please.
Doo doodoodoo doodoo doodoo
Well, I'm currently writing a story for tomorrow's headline. And I wanted to know if Mister Fisk had any comment on the warehouse fire at the pier.
Because the warehouse belonged to him.
I wanted to- Yes, it actually ***did*** belong to--
I wanted to know if this fire had anything to do with the ongoing federal investi- Yes, I'll be right here.
Doo doodoodoo doodoo doodoo
Yes, I'm still here. So, no comment then?
Um...
Well, that ***is*** a comment, sir. Not a ***nice*** one but we will print it.
Would you like to retract- Okay.
Well, then: $%^& #@$%% #@$% it is.
Wilson Fisk.
Aaarrrgghh!!

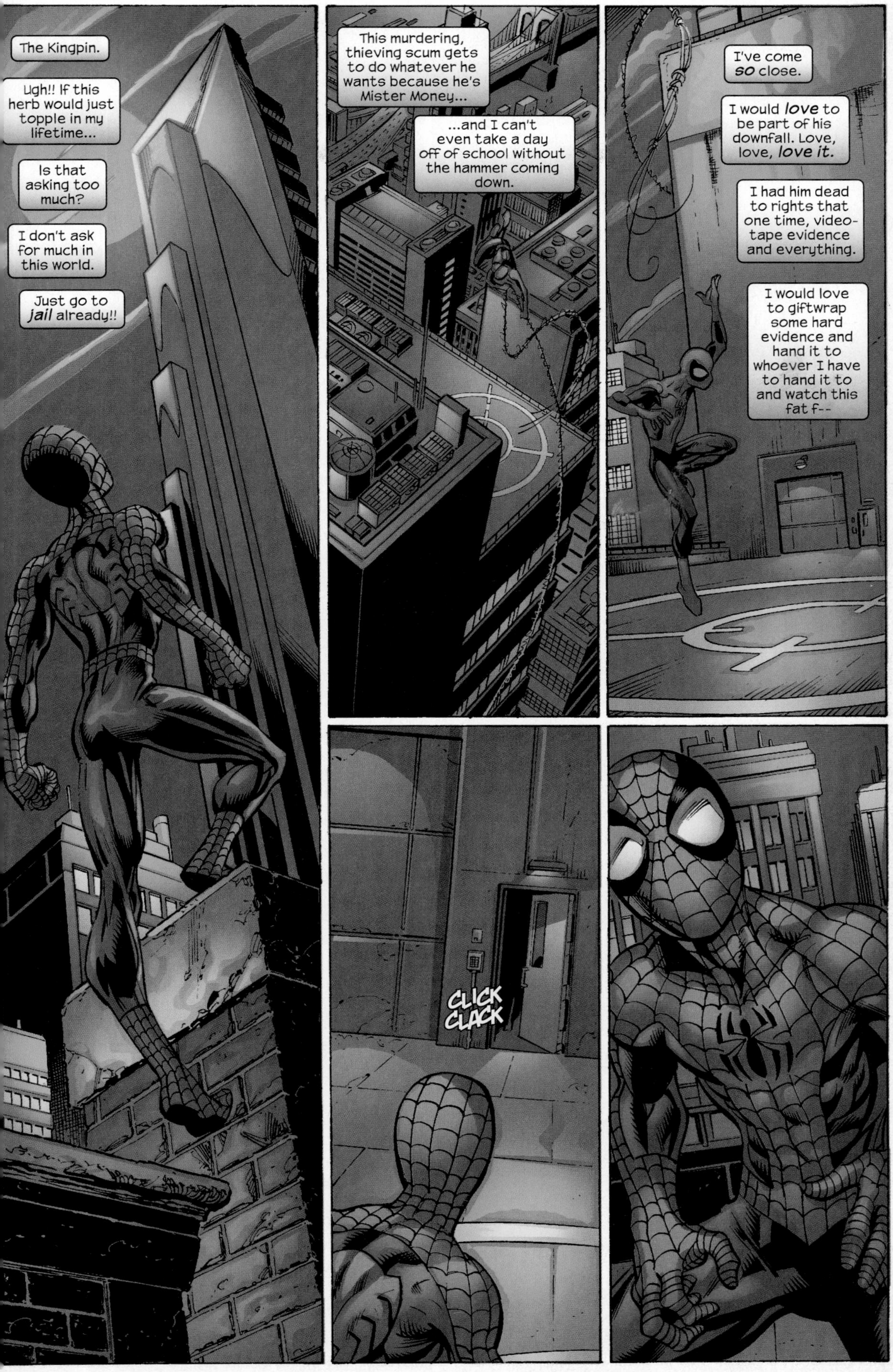
The Kingpin.
Ugh!! If this herb would just topple in my lifetime...
Is that asking too much?
I don't ask for much in this world.
Just go to *jail* already!!
This murdering, thieving scum gets to do whatever he wants because he's Mister Money...
...and I can't even take a day off of school without the hammer coming down.
I've come *so* close.
I would *love* to be part of his downfall. Love, love, *love it.*
I had him dead to rights that one time, video-tape evidence and everything.
I would love to giftwrap some hard evidence and hand it to whoever I have to hand it to and watch this fat f--
CLICK CLACK

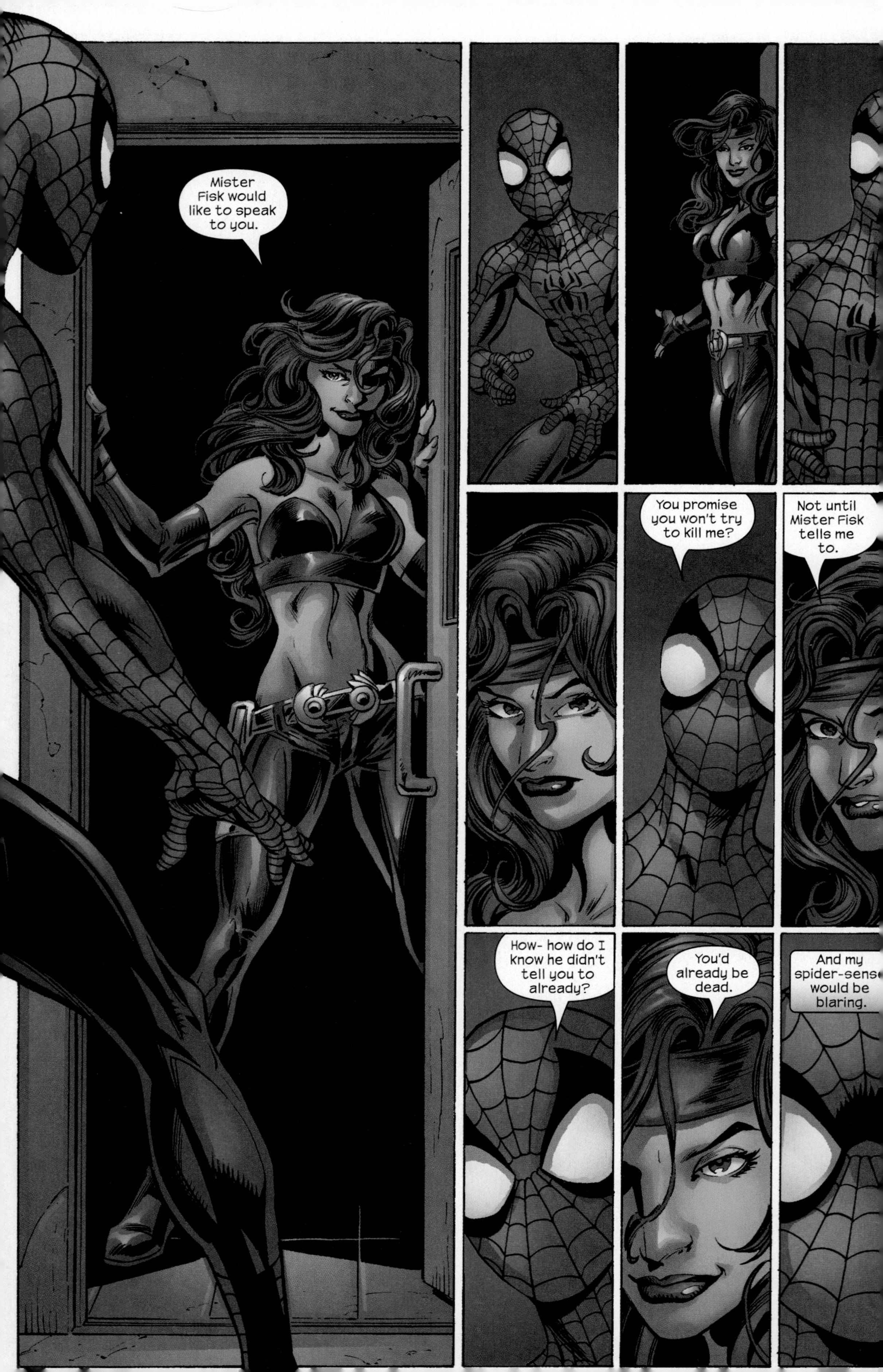
Mister Fisk would like to speak to you.
You promise you won't try to kill me?
Not until Mister Fisk tells me to.
How- how do I know he didn't tell you to already?
You'd already be dead.
And my spider-sens[e] would be blaring.

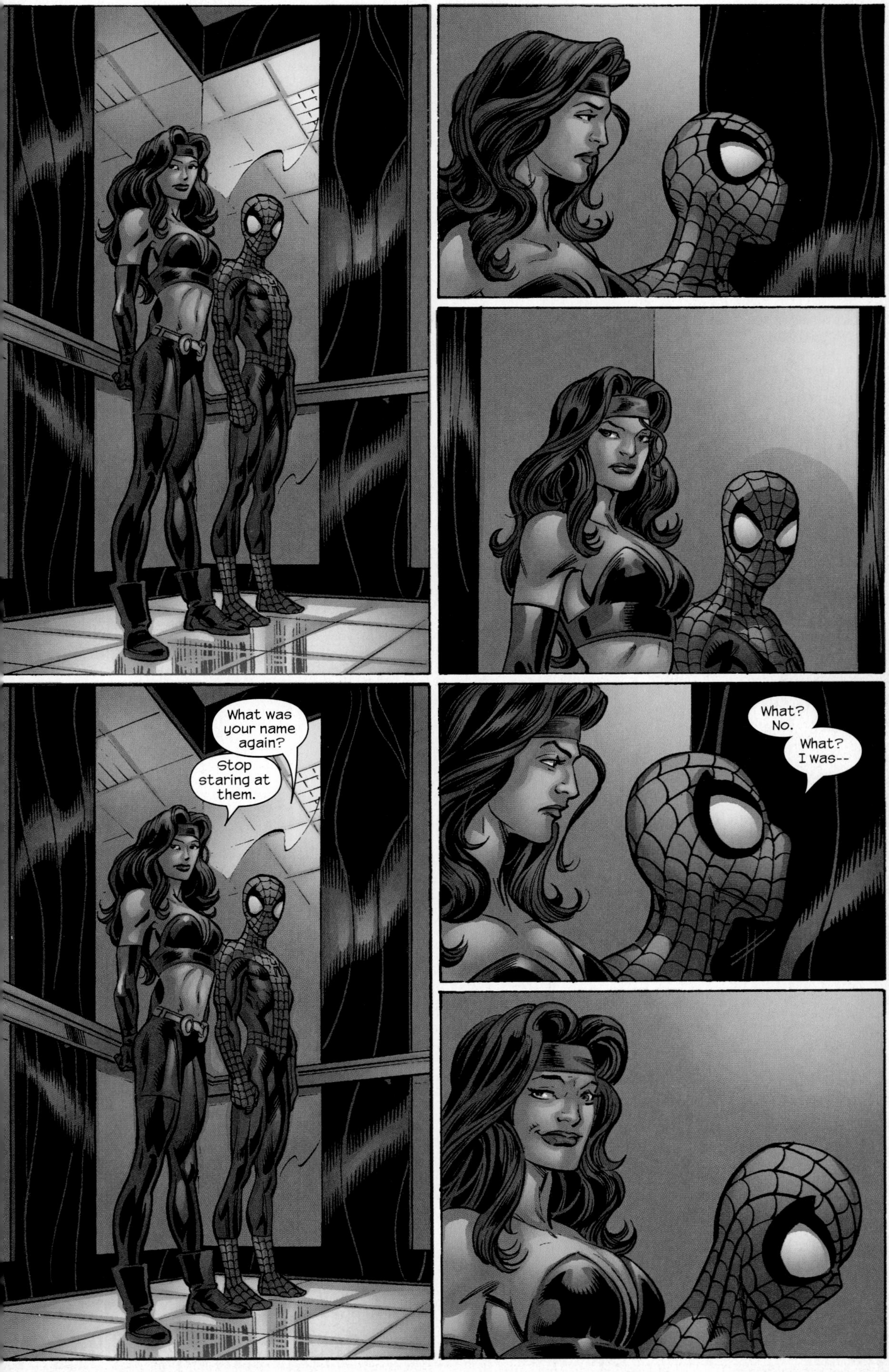
What was your name again?
Stop staring at them.
What? No.
What? I was--

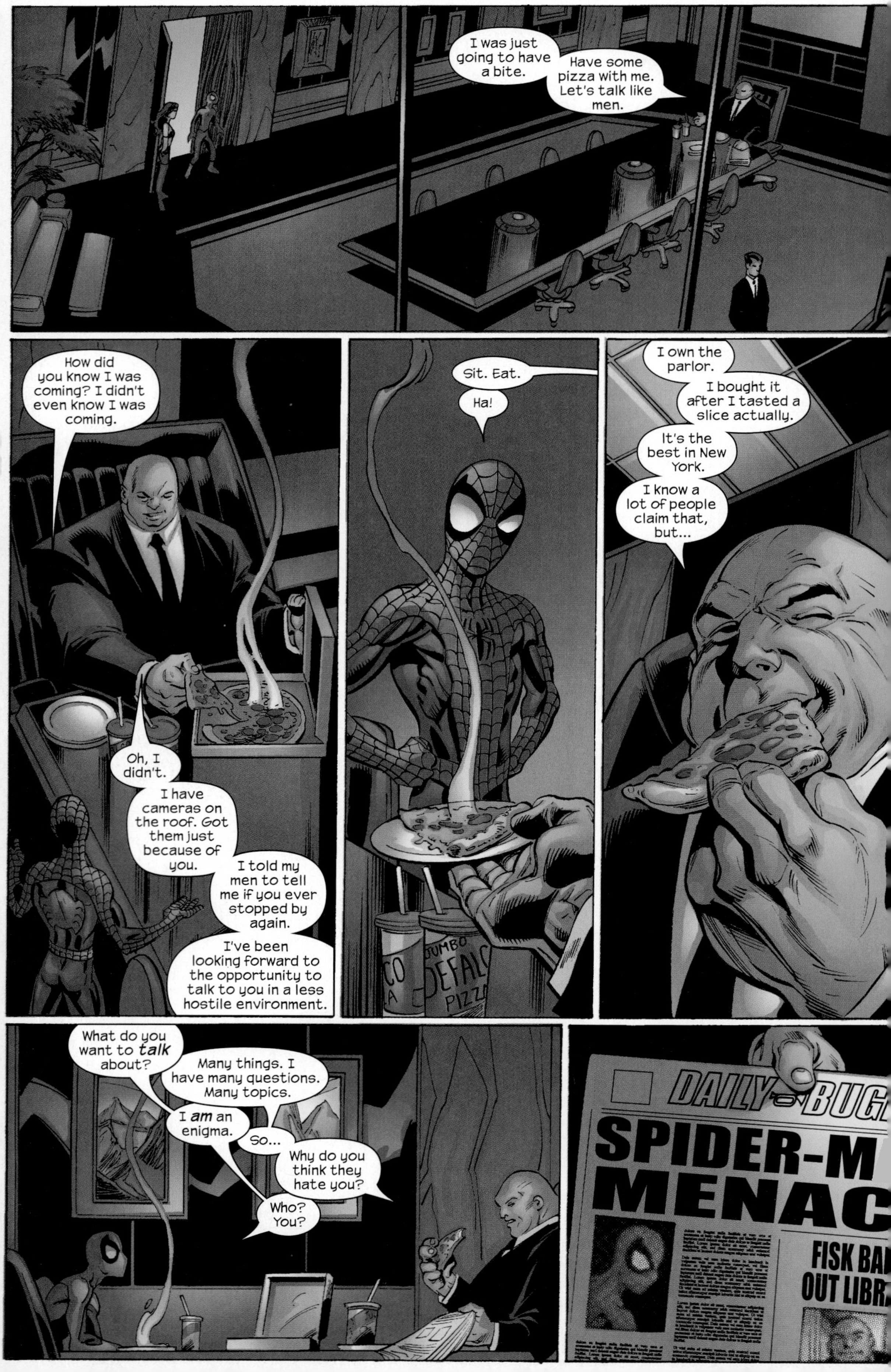
I was just going to have a bite.
Have some pizza with me. Let's talk like men.
How did you know I was coming? I didn't even know I was coming.
Oh, I didn't.
I have cameras on the roof. Got them just because of you.
I told my men to tell me if you ever stopped by again.
I've been looking forward to the opportunity to talk to you in a less hostile environment.
Sit. Eat.
Ha!
JUMBO
I own the parlor.
I bought it after I tasted a slice actually.
It's the best in New York.
I know a lot of people claim that, but...
What do you want to *talk* about?
Many things. I have many questions. Many topics.
I *am* an enigma.
So...
Why do you think they hate you?
Who? You?
DAILY BUG
SPIDER-M
MENAC
FISK BA
OUT LIBR

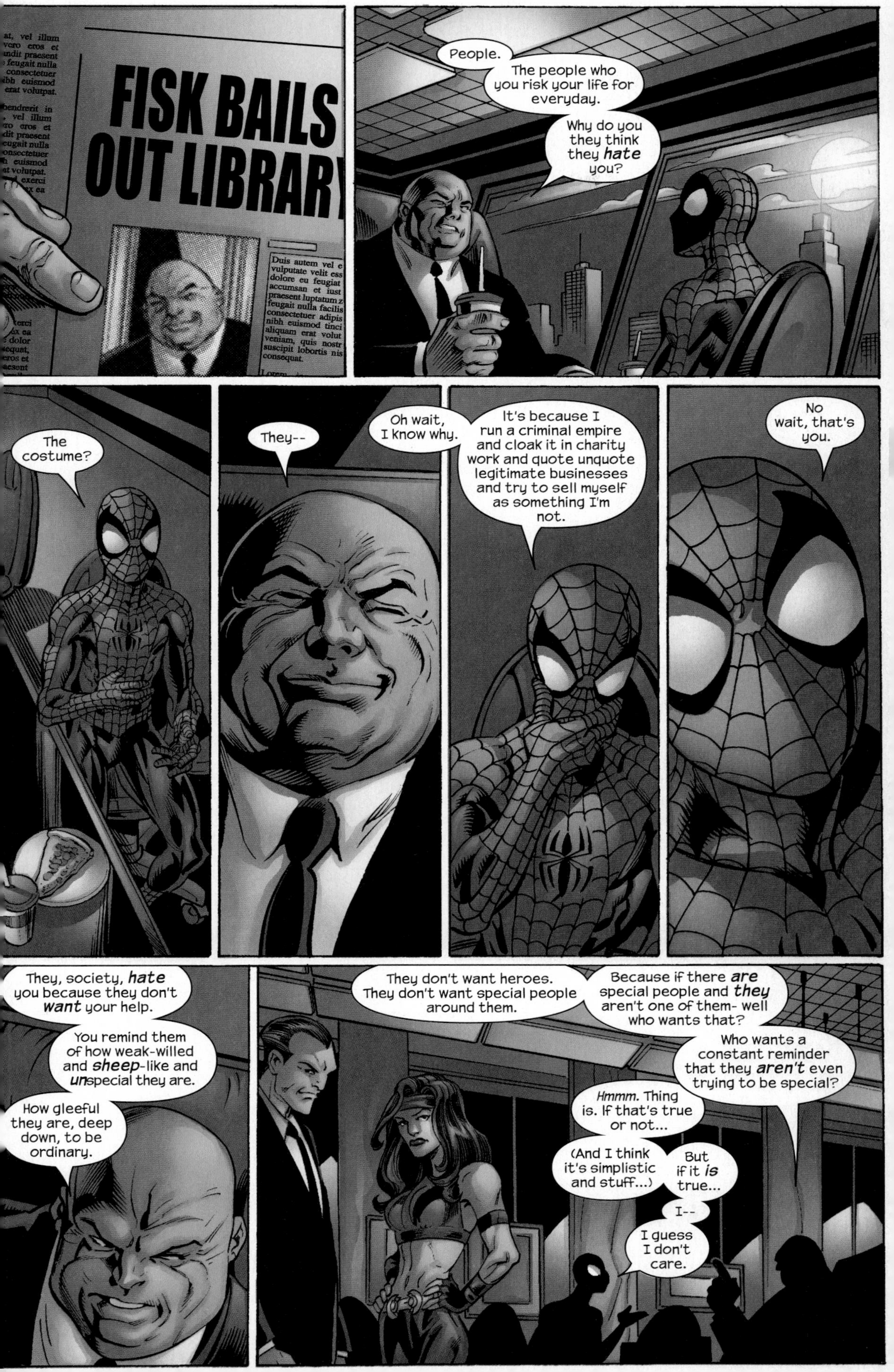
FISK BAILS OUT LIBRARY
People.
The people who you risk your life for everyday.
Why do you they think they *hate* you?
The costume?
They--
Oh wait, I know why.
It's because I run a criminal empire and cloak it in charity work and quote unquote legitimate businesses and try to sell myself as something I'm not.
No wait, that's you.
They, society, *hate* you because they don't *want* your help.
You remind them of how weak-willed and *sheep*-like and *un*special they are.
How gleeful they are, deep down, to be ordinary.
They don't want heroes. They don't want special people around them.
Because if there *are* special people and *they* aren't one of them- well who wants that?
Who wants a constant reminder that they *aren't* even trying to be special?
Hmmm. Thing is. If that's true or not...
(And I think it's simplistic and stuff...)
But if it *is* true...
I--
I guess I don't care.

That's sweet.

See, the difference between you and I is that you really are just a child.

You benefit from the wide-eyed optimism of youth. I do envy you that, somewhat.

But...like *many* of your decisions in life...it's just naïve.

And I *don't* envy that harsh cold slap of *reality* that will come your way soon enough.

But I guess it's inevitable.

Oh man, here it comes.

What's that?

You're about to tell me you have this- this amazing philosophy to justify your horrible life.

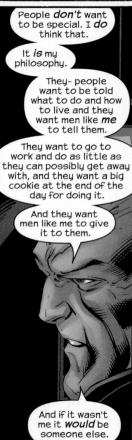

People *don't* want to be special. I *do* think that.

It *is* my philosophy.

They- people want to be told what to do and how to live and they want men like *me* to tell them.

They want to go to work and do as little as they can possibly get away with, and they want a big cookie at the end of the day for doing it.

And they want men like me to give it to them.

And if it wasn't me it *would* be someone else.

What do you want from me, Willie?

Here.

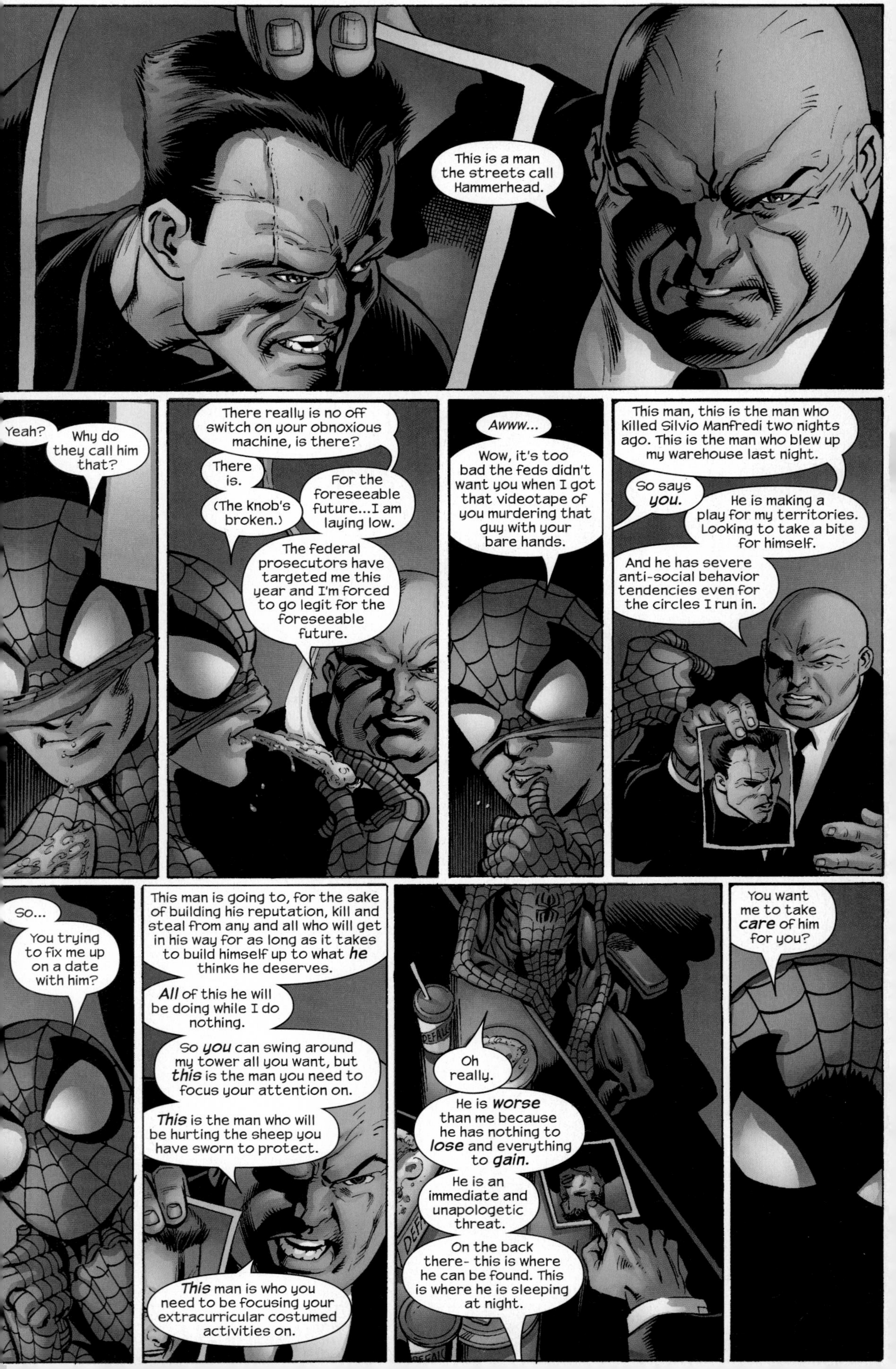

This is a man the streets call Hammerhead.
Yeah?
Why do they call him that?
There really is no off switch on your obnoxious machine, is there?
There is.
(The knob's broken.)
For the foreseeable future...I am laying low.
The federal prosecutors have targeted me this year and I'm forced to go legit for the foreseeable future.
Awww...
Wow, it's too bad the feds didn't want you when I got that videotape of you murdering that guy with your bare hands.
This man, this is the man who killed Silvio Manfredi two nights ago. This is the man who blew up my warehouse last night.
So says you.
He is making a play for my territories. Looking to take a bite for himself.
And he has severe anti-social behavior tendencies even for the circles I run in.
So...
You trying to fix me up on a date with him?
This man is going to, for the sake of building his reputation, kill and steal from any and all who will get in his way for as long as it takes to build himself up to what he thinks he deserves.
All of this he will be doing while I do nothing.
So you can swing around my tower all you want, but this is the man you need to focus your attention on.
This is the man who will be hurting the sheep you have sworn to protect.
This man is who you need to be focusing your extracurricular costumed activities on.
Oh really.
He is worse than me because he has nothing to lose and everything to gain.
He is an immediate and unapologetic threat.
On the back there- this is where he can be found. This is where he is sleeping at night.
You want me to take care of him for you?

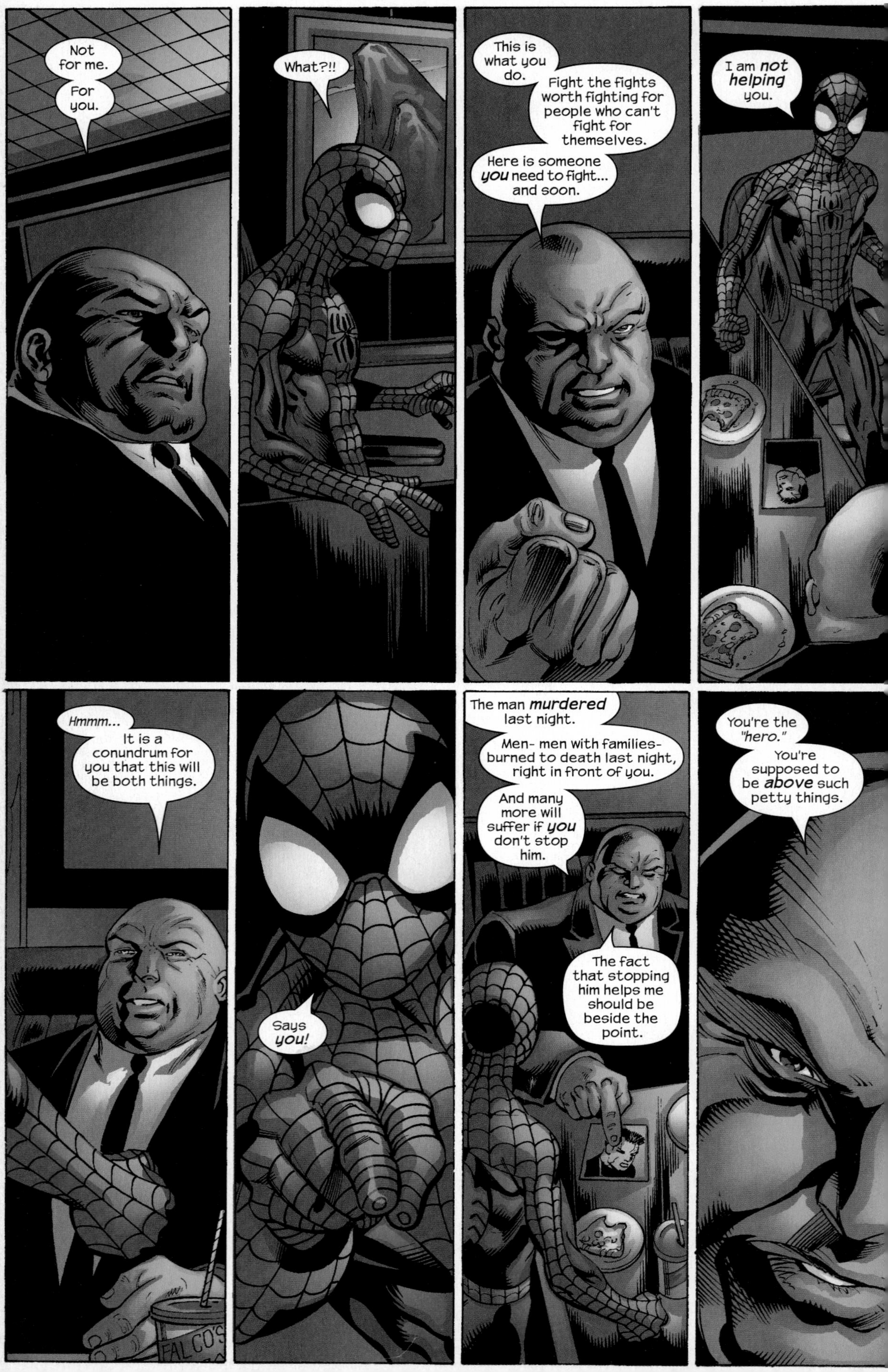
Not for me.
For you.
What?!!
This is what you do.
Fight the fights worth fighting for people who can't fight for themselves.
Here is someone *you* need to fight... and soon.
I am *not helping* you.
Hmmm...
It is a conundrum for you that this will be both things.
Says *you!*
The man *murdered* last night.
Men- men with families- burned to death last night, right in front of you.
And many more will suffer if *you* don't stop him.
The fact that stopping him helps me should be beside the point.
You're the *"hero."*
You're supposed to be *above* such petty things.
FALCO'S

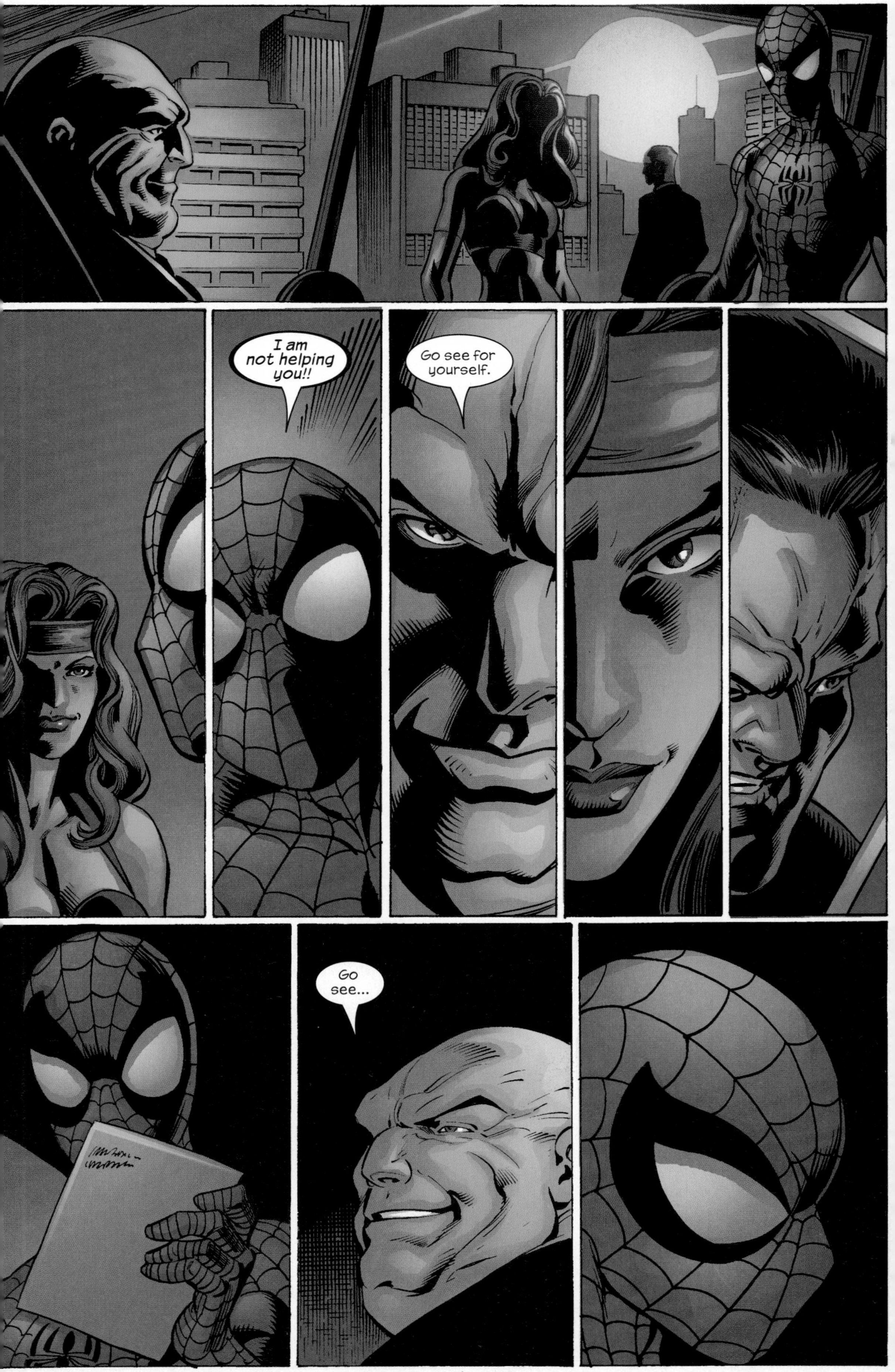
I am not helping you!!
Go see for yourself.
Go see...

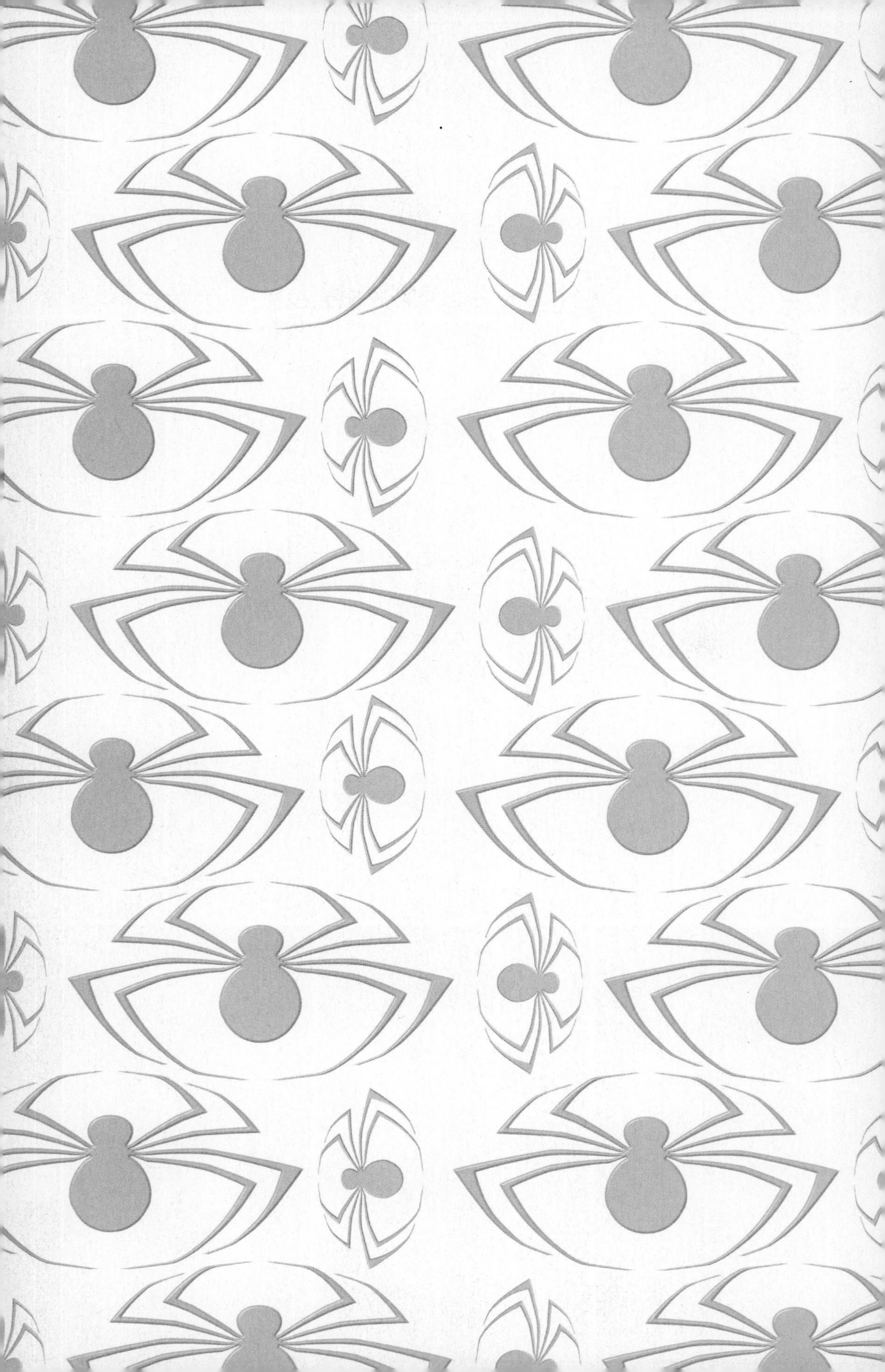

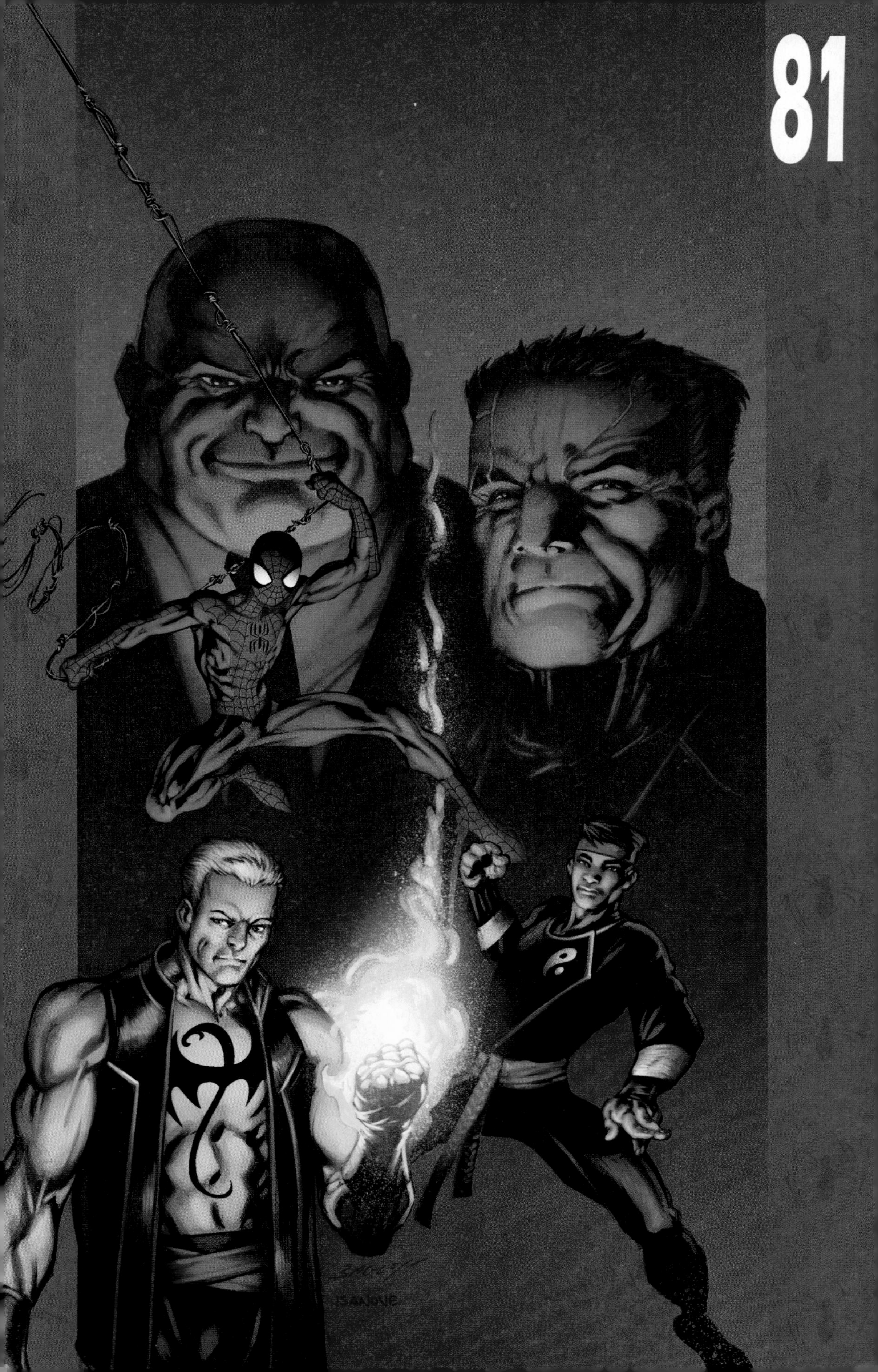
81

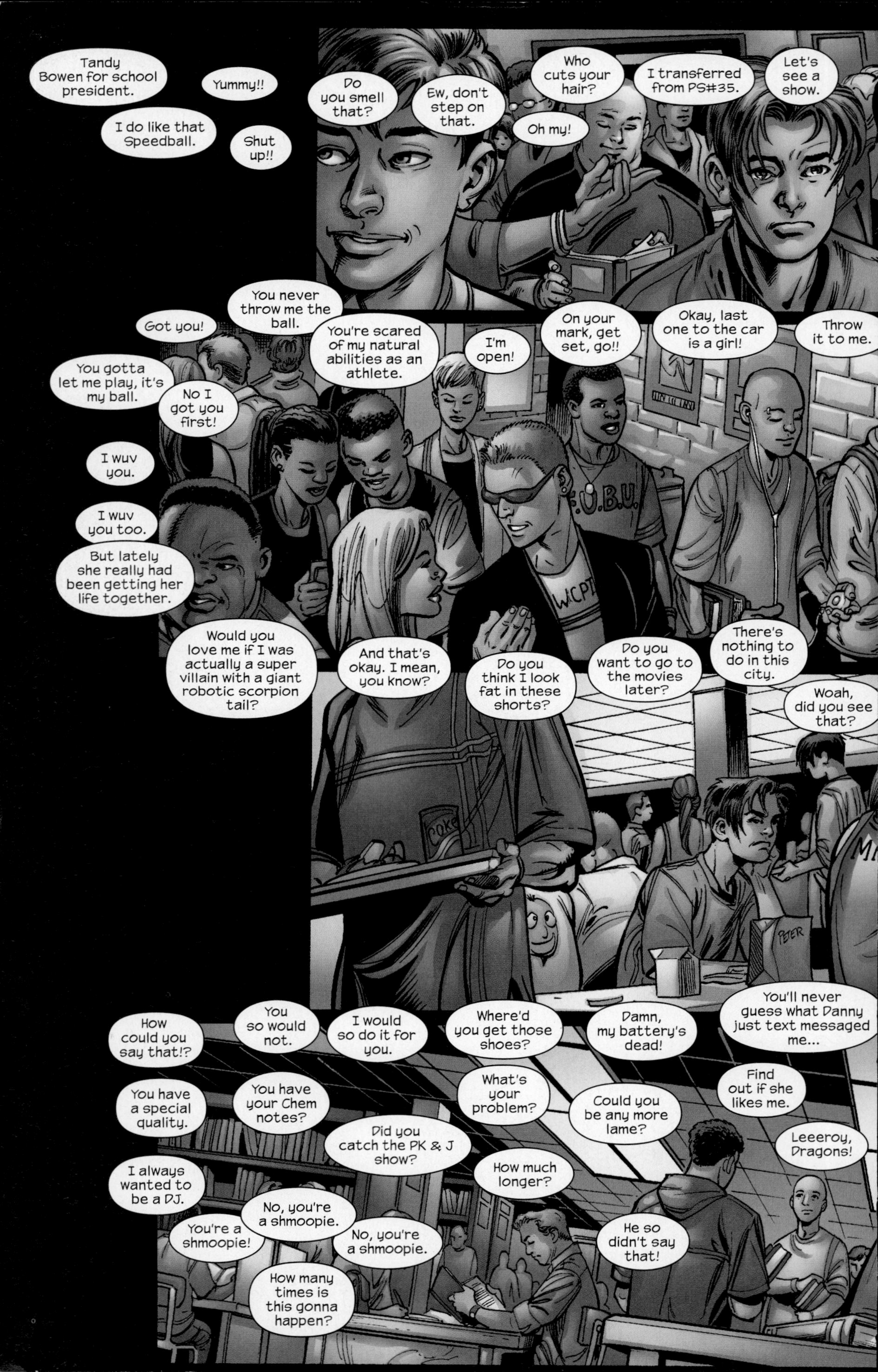

Tandy Bowen for school president.
Yummy!!
I do like that Speedball.
Shut up!!
Do you smell that?
Ew, don't step on that.
Who cuts your hair?
Oh my!
I transferred from PS#35.
Let's see a show.
Got you!
You never throw me the ball.
You gotta let me play, it's my ball.
No I got you first!
You're scared of my natural abilities as an athlete.
I'm open!
On your mark, get set, go!!
Okay, last one to the car is a girl!
Throw it to me.
I wuv you.
I wuv you too.
But lately she really had been getting her life together.
Would you love me if I was actually a super villain with a giant robotic scorpion tail?
And that's okay. I mean, you know?
Do you think I look fat in these shorts?
Do you want to go to the movies later?
There's nothing to do in this city.
Woah, did you see that?
How could you say that!?
You so would not.
I would so do it for you.
Where'd you get those shoes?
Damn, my battery's dead!
You'll never guess what Danny just text messaged me...
You have a special quality.
You have your Chem notes?
What's your problem?
Could you be any more lame?
Find out if she likes me.
Did you catch the PK & J show?
Leeeroy, Dragons!
I always wanted to be a DJ.
How much longer?
No, you're a shmoopie.
You're a shmoopie!
No, you're a shmoopie.
He so didn't say that!
How many times is this gonna happen?

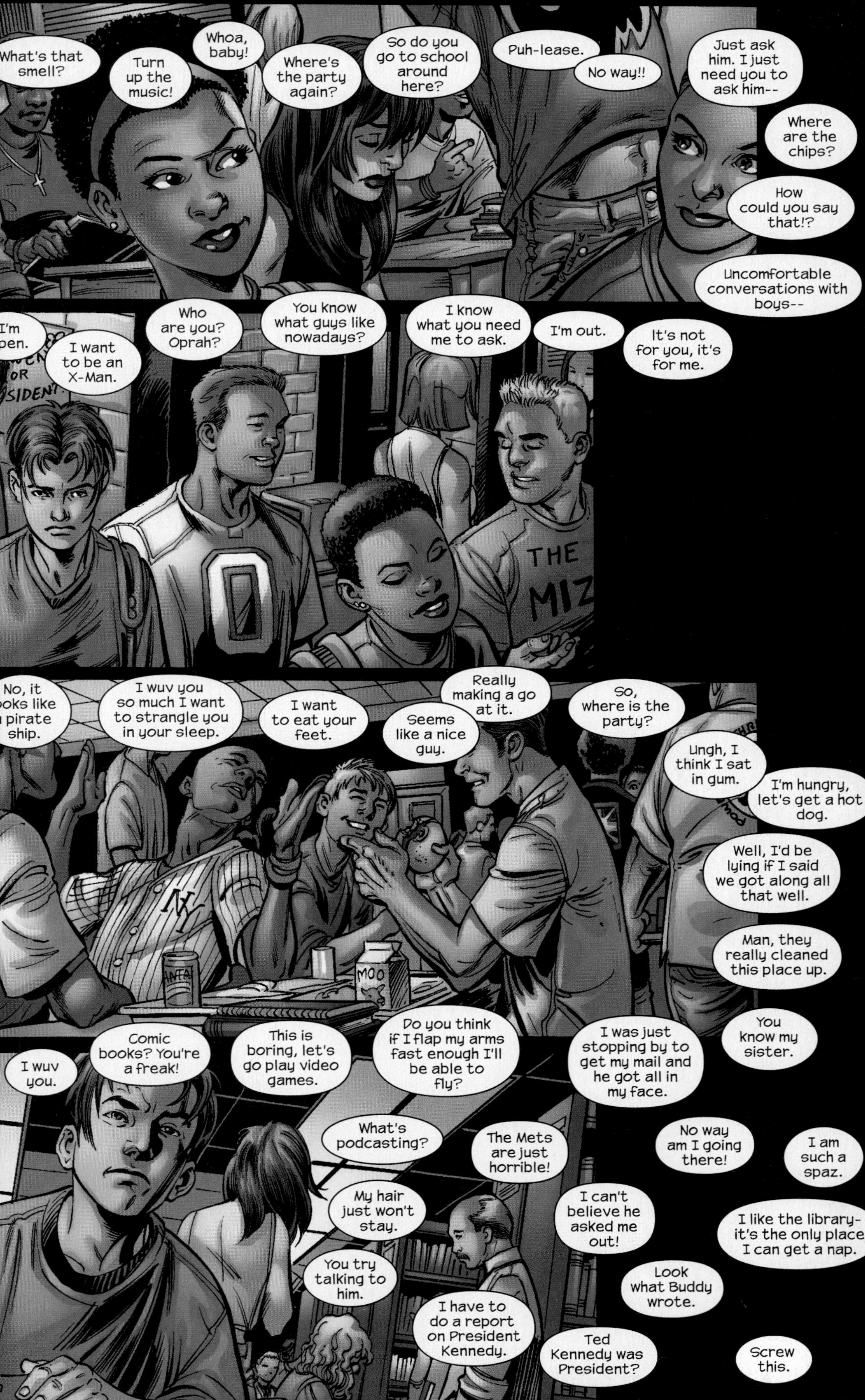
What's that smell?
Turn up the music!
Whoa, baby!
Where's the party again?
So do you go to school around here?
Puh-lease.
No way!!
Just ask him. I just need you to ask him--
Where are the chips?
How could you say that!?
Uncomfortable conversations with boys--
I'm pen.
I want to be an X-Man.
Who are you? Oprah?
You know what guys like nowadays?
I know what you need me to ask.
I'm out.
It's not for you, it's for me.
No, it ooks like pirate ship.
I wuv you so much I want to strangle you in your sleep.
I want to eat your feet.
Really making a go at it.
Seems like a nice guy.
So, where is the party?
Ungh, I think I sat in gum.
I'm hungry, let's get a hot dog.
Well, I'd be lying if I said we got along all that well.
Man, they really cleaned this place up.
I wuv you.
Comic books? You're a freak!
This is boring, let's go play video games.
Do you think if I flap my arms fast enough I'll be able to fly?
I was just stopping by to get my mail and he got all in my face.
You know my sister.
What's podcasting?
The Mets are just horrible!
No way am I going there!
I am such a spaz.
My hair just won't stay.
I can't believe he asked me out!
I like the library-it's the only place I can get a nap.
You try talking to him.
Look what Buddy wrote.
I have to do a report on President Kennedy.
Ted Kennedy was President?
Screw this.

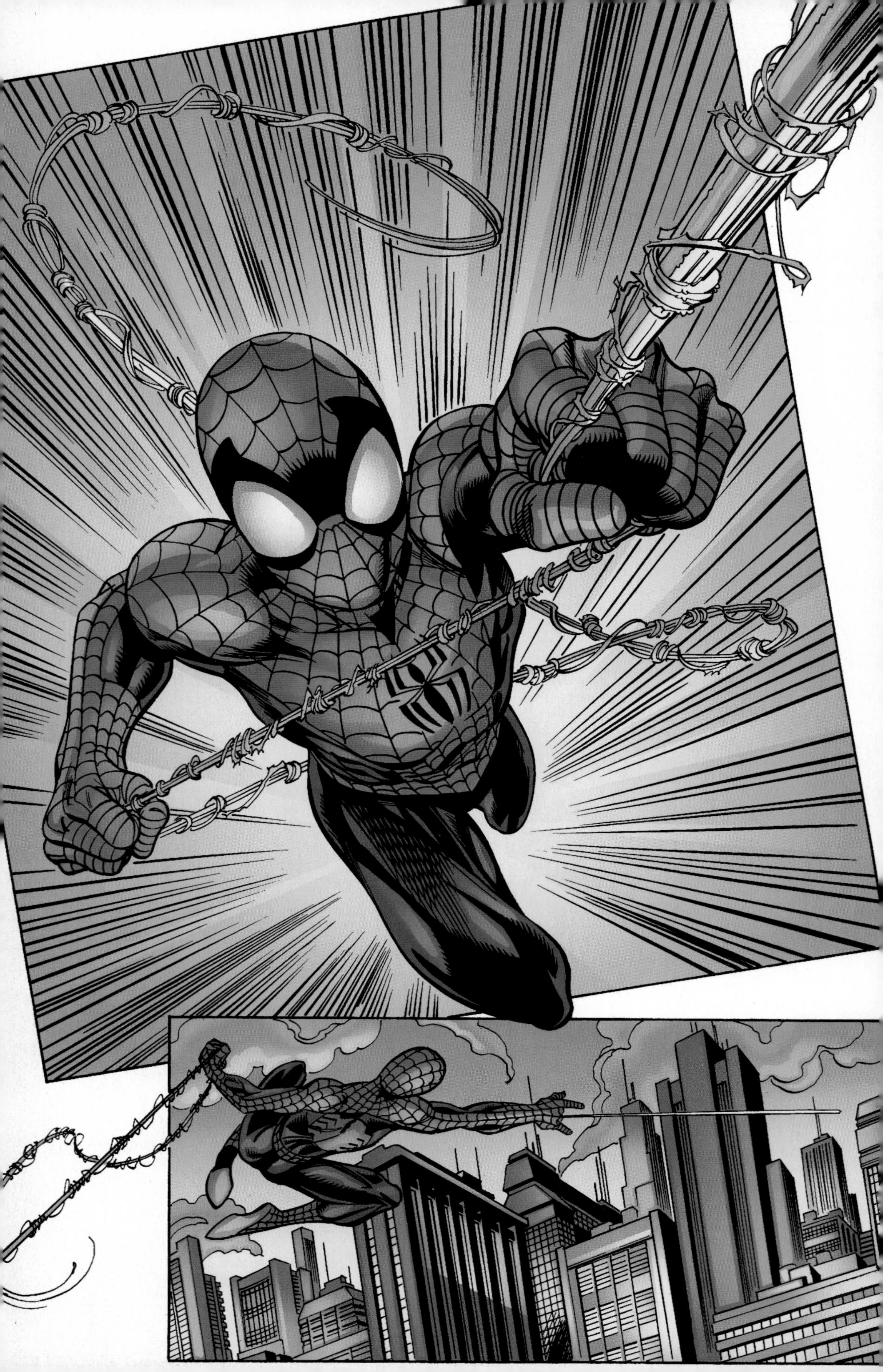

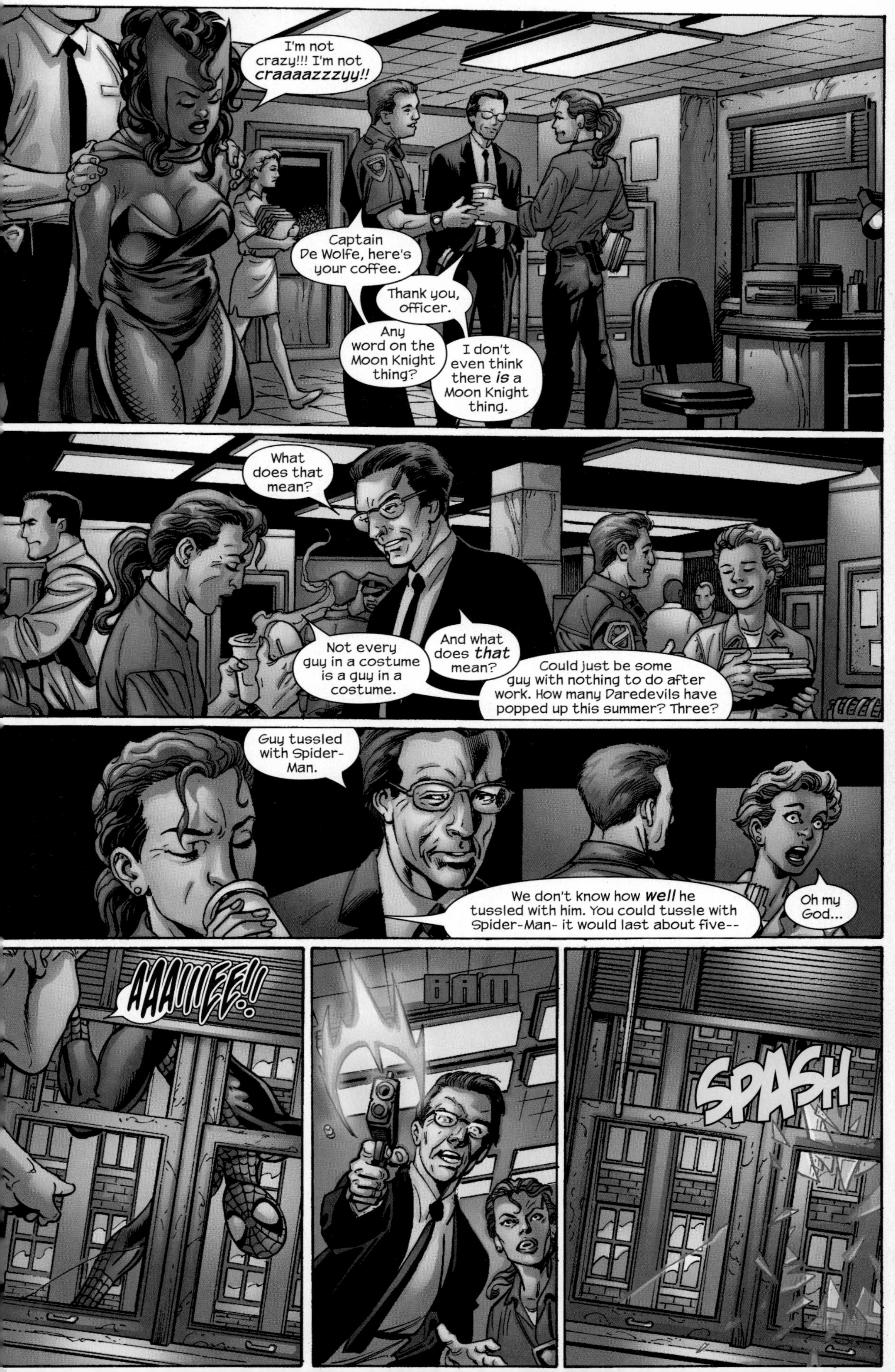
I'm not crazy!!! I'm not craaaazzzzyy!!
Captain De Wolfe, here's your coffee.
Thank you, officer.
Any word on the Moon Knight thing?
I don't even think there *is* a Moon Knight thing.
What does that mean?
Not every guy in a costume is a guy in a costume.
And what does *that* mean?
Could just be some guy with nothing to do after work. How many Daredevils have popped up this summer? Three?
Guy tussled with Spider-Man.
We don't know how *well* he tussled with him. You could tussle with Spider-Man- it would last about five--
Oh my God...
AAAIIIEE!!
BAM
SPASH

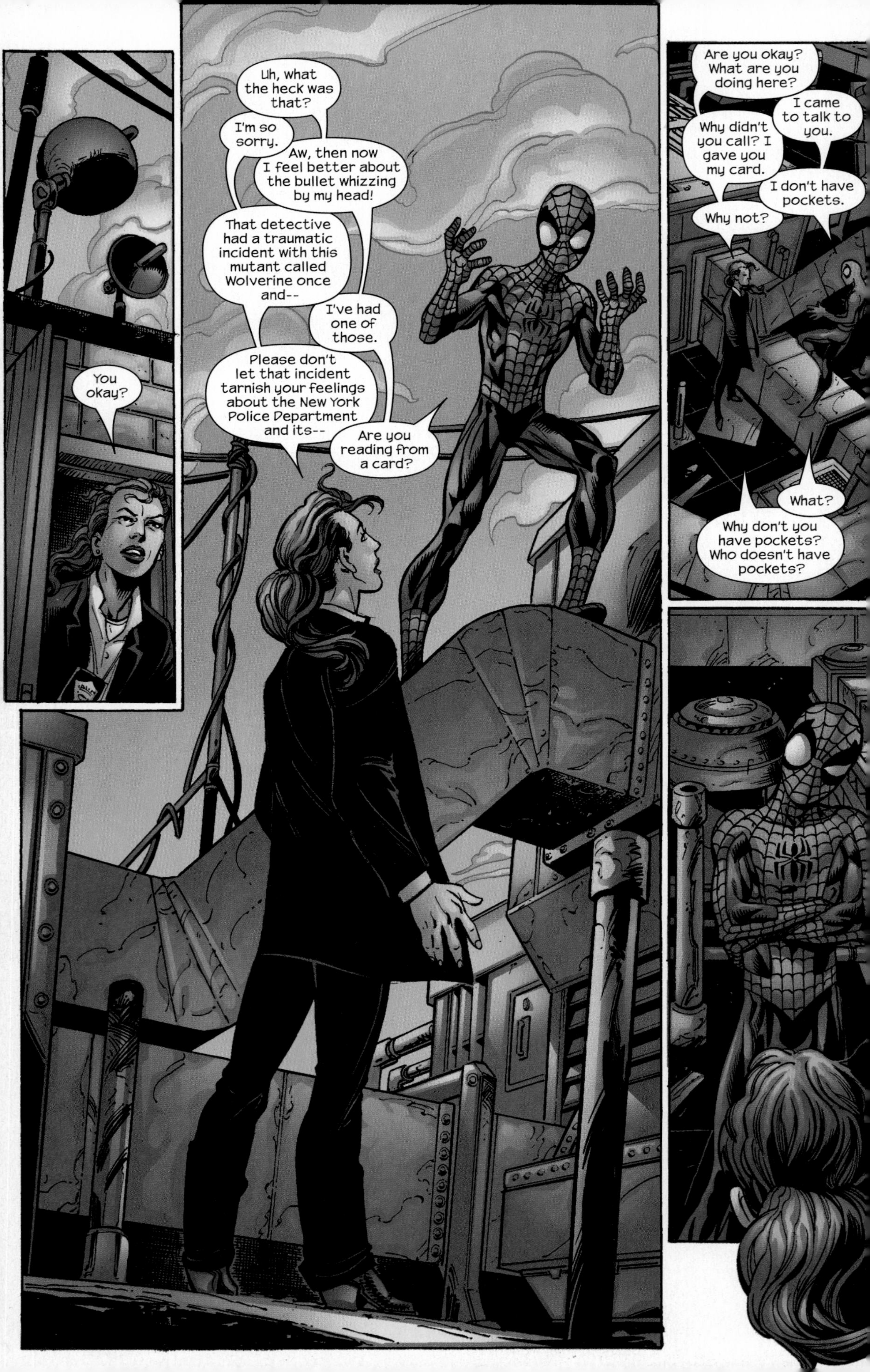
You okay?
Uh, what the heck was that?
I'm so sorry.
Aw, then now I feel better about the bullet whizzing by my head!
That detective had a traumatic incident with this mutant called Wolverine once and--
I've had one of those.
Please don't let that incident tarnish your feelings about the New York Police Department and its--
Are you reading from a card?
Are you okay? What are you doing here?
I came to talk to you.
Why didn't you call? I gave you my card.
I don't have pockets.
Why not?
What?
Why don't you have pockets? Who doesn't have pockets?

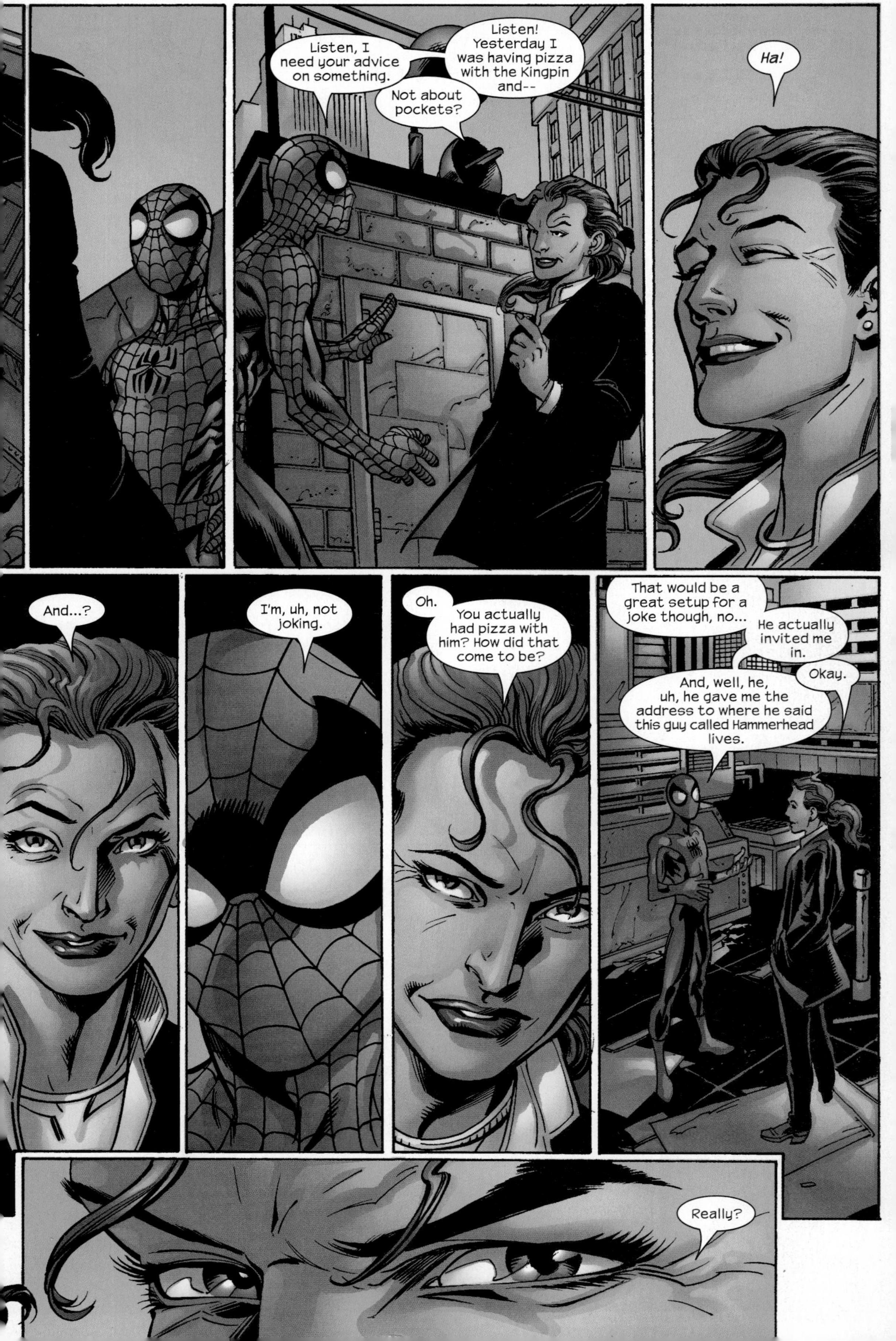
Listen, I need your advice on something.
Listen! Yesterday I was having pizza with the Kingpin and--
Not about pockets?
Ha!
And...?
I'm, uh, not joking.
Oh.
You actually had pizza with him? How did that come to be?
That would be a great setup for a joke though, no...
He actually invited me in.
Okay.
And, well, he, uh, he gave me the address to where he said this guy called Hammerhead lives.
Really?

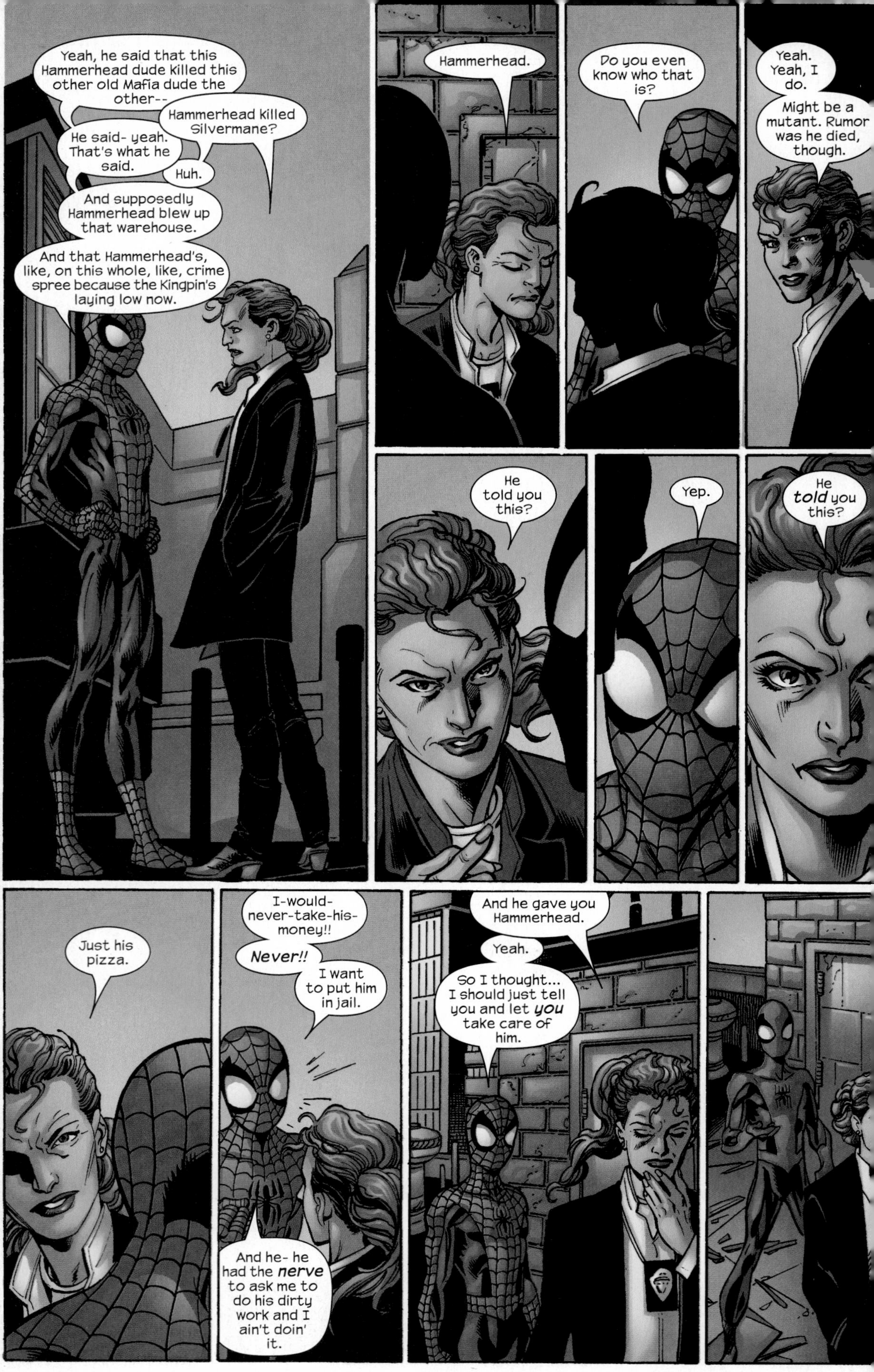
Yeah, he said that this Hammerhead dude killed this other old Mafia dude the other--
Hammerhead killed Silvermane?
He said- yeah. That's what he said.
Huh.
And supposedly Hammerhead blew up that warehouse.
And that Hammerhead's, like, on this whole, like, crime spree because the Kingpin's laying low now.
Hammerhead.
Do you even know who that is?
Yeah. Yeah, I do.
Might be a mutant. Rumor was he died, though.
He told you this?
Yep.
He *told* you this?
Just his pizza.
I-would-never-take-his-money!!
Never!!
I want to put him in jail.
And he- he had the *nerve* to ask me to do his dirty work and I ain't doin' it.
And he gave you Hammerhead.
Yeah.
So I thought... I should just tell you and let *you* take care of him.

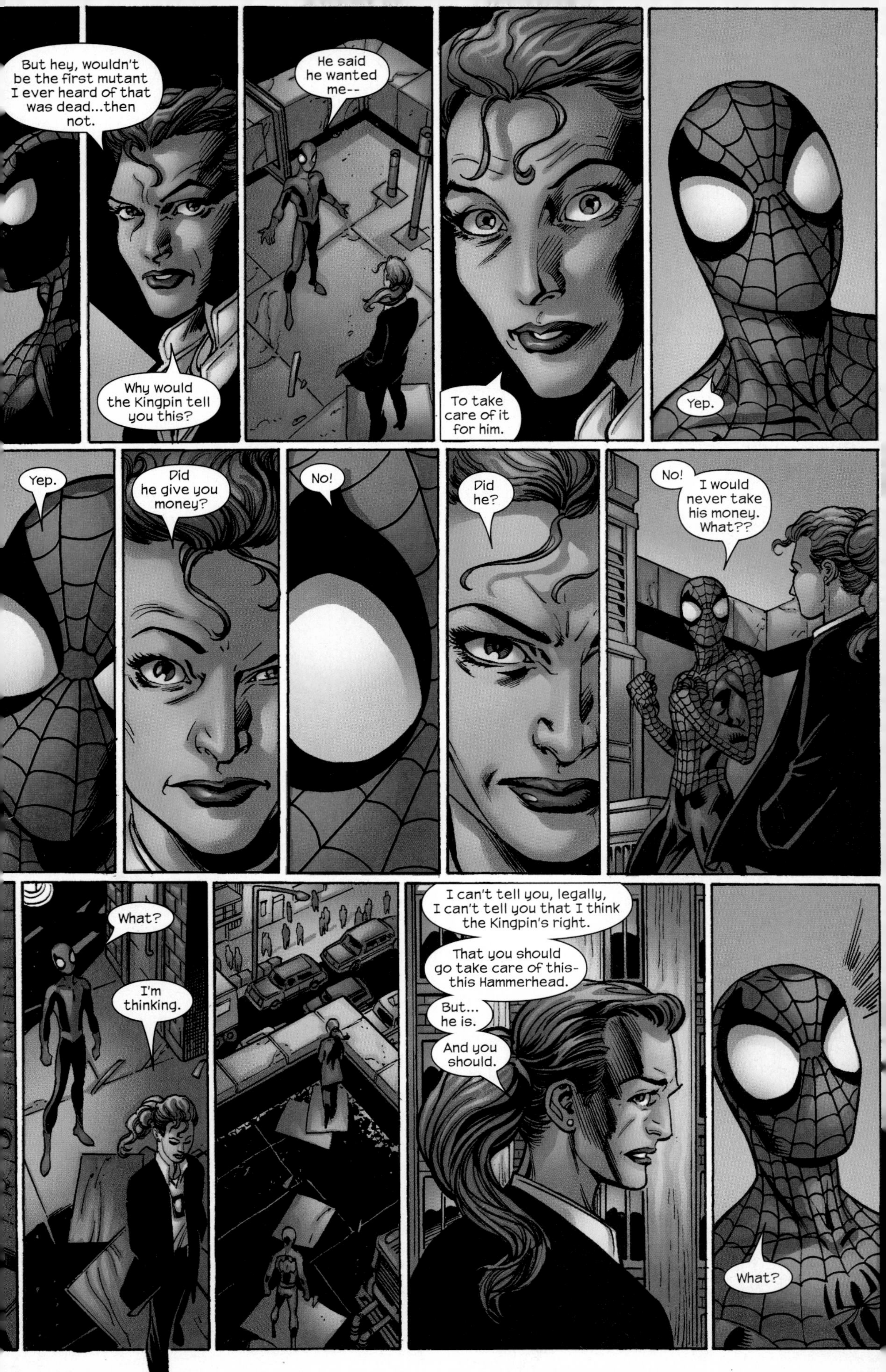
But hey, wouldn't be the first mutant I ever heard of that was dead...then not.
Why would the Kingpin tell you this?
He said he wanted me--
To take care of it for him.
Yep.
Yep.
Did he give you money?
No!
Did he?
No!
I would never take his money. What??
What?
I'm thinking.
I can't tell you, legally, I can't tell you that I think the Kingpin's right.
That you should go take care of this- this Hammerhead.
But... he is.
And you should.
What?

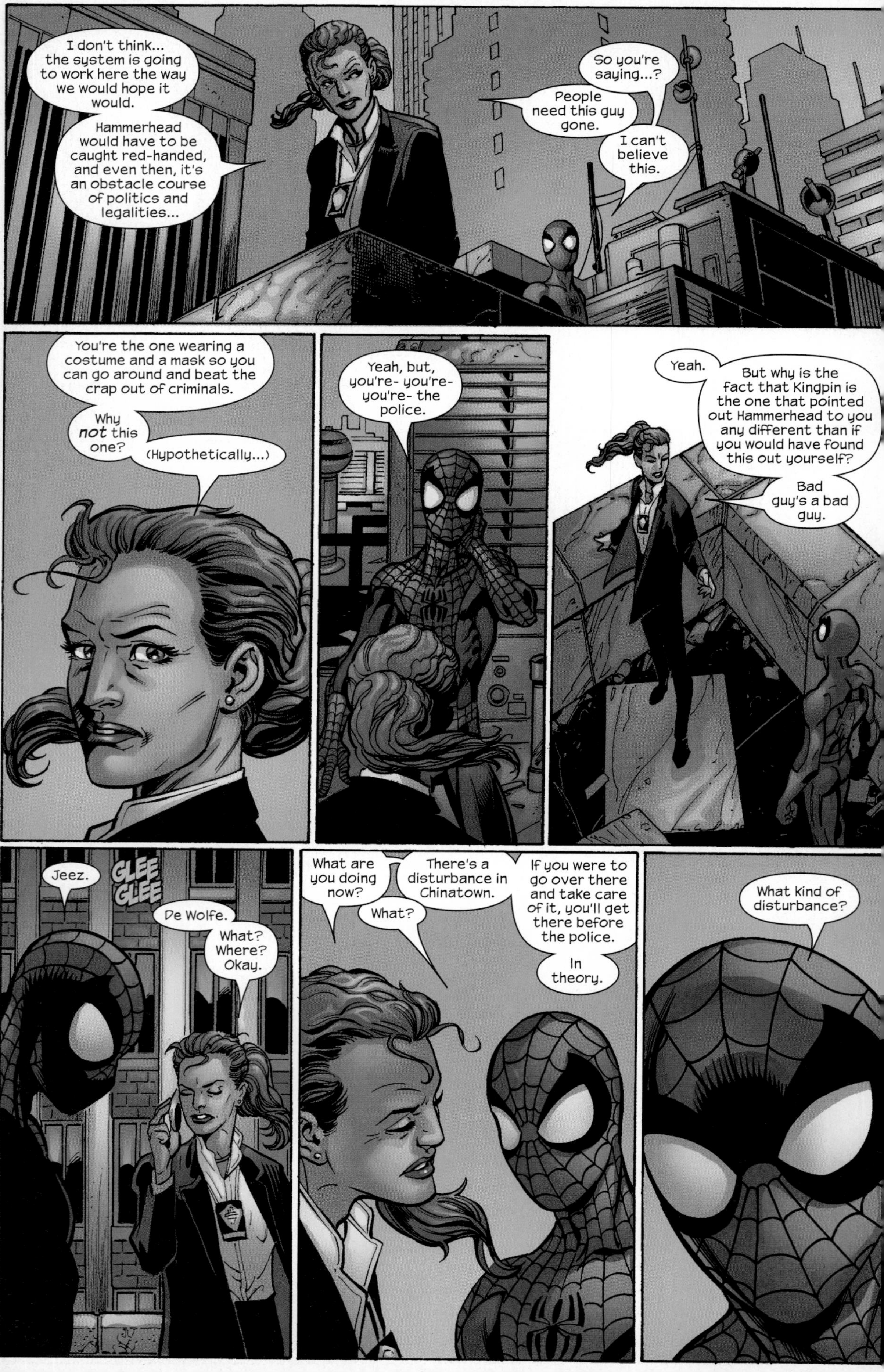
I don't think... the system is going to work here the way we would hope it would.
Hammerhead would have to be caught red-handed, and even then, it's an obstacle course of politics and legalities...
So you're saying...?
People need this guy gone.
I can't believe this.
You're the one wearing a costume and a mask so you can go around and beat the crap out of criminals.
Why *not* this one?
(Hypothetically...)
Yeah, but, you're- you're- you're- the police.
Yeah.
But why is the fact that Kingpin is the one that pointed out Hammerhead to you any different than if you would have found this out yourself?
Bad guy's a bad guy.
Jeez.
GLEE GLEE
De Wolfe.
What? Where? Okay.
What are you doing now?
There's a disturbance in Chinatown.
What?
If you were to go over there and take care of it, you'll get there before the police.
In theory.
What kind of disturbance?

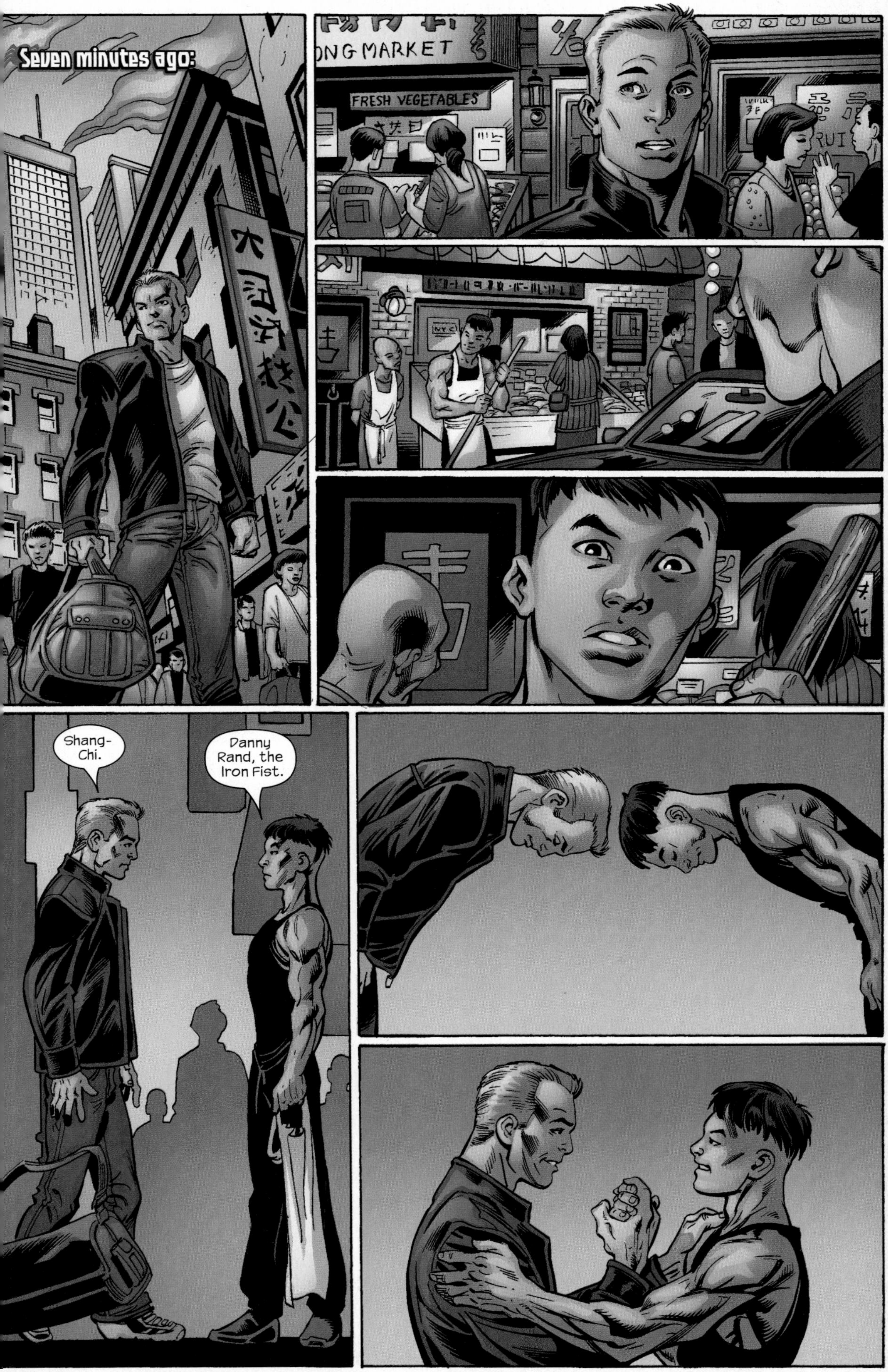

Seven minutes ago:
ONG MARKET
FRESH VEGETABLES
Shang-Chi.
Danny Rand, the Iron Fist.

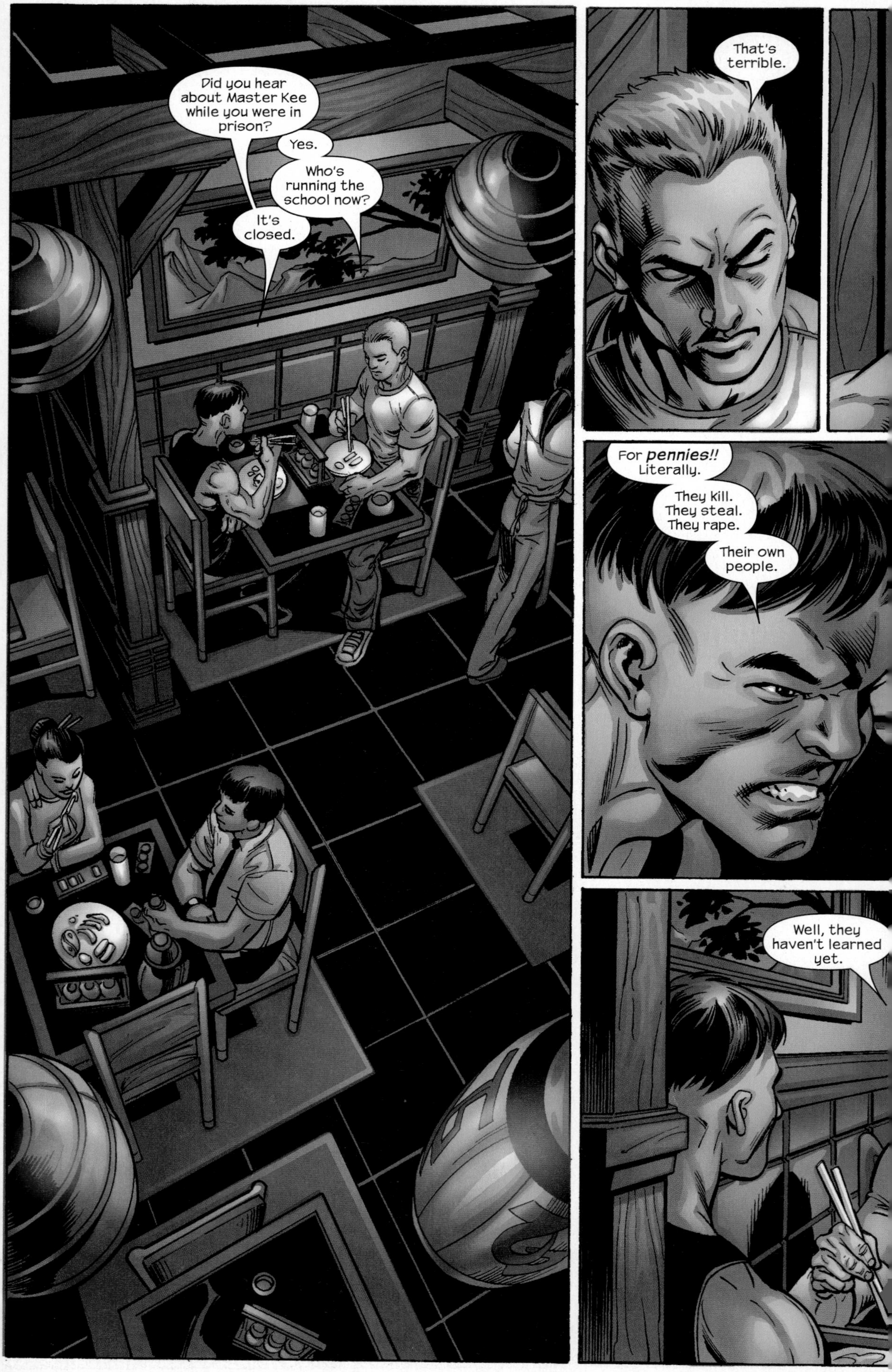
Did you hear about Master Kee while you were in prison?
Yes.
Who's running the school now?
It's closed.
That's terrible.
For *pennies!!* Literally.
They kill. They steal. They rape.
Their own people.
Well, they haven't learned yet.

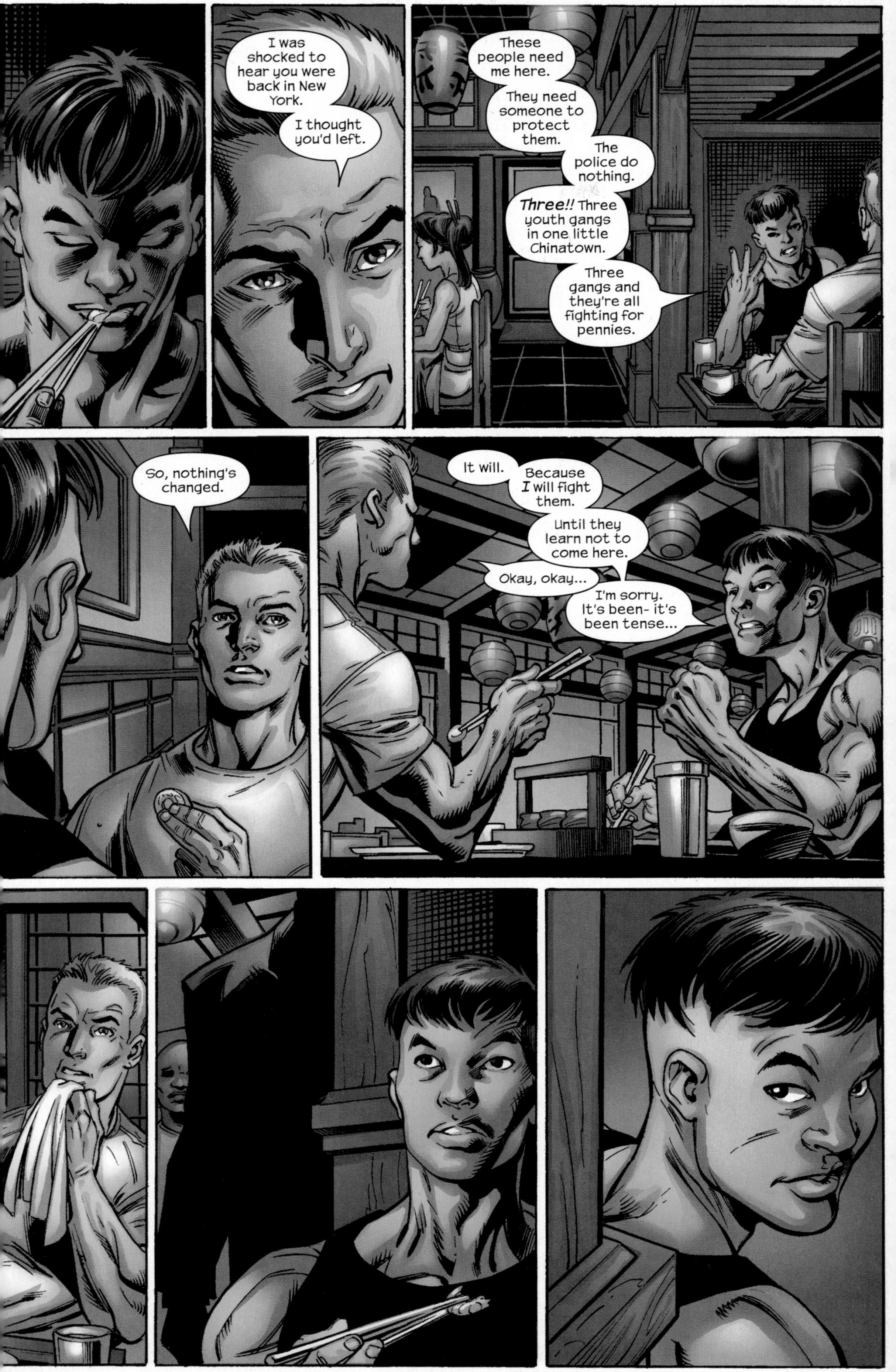
I was shocked to hear you were back in New York.
I thought you'd left.
These people need me here.
They need someone to protect them.
The police do nothing.
Three!! Three youth gangs in one little Chinatown.
Three gangs and they're all fighting for pennies.
So, nothing's changed.
It will.
Because I will fight them.
Until they learn not to come here.
Okay, okay...
I'm sorry. It's been- it's been tense...

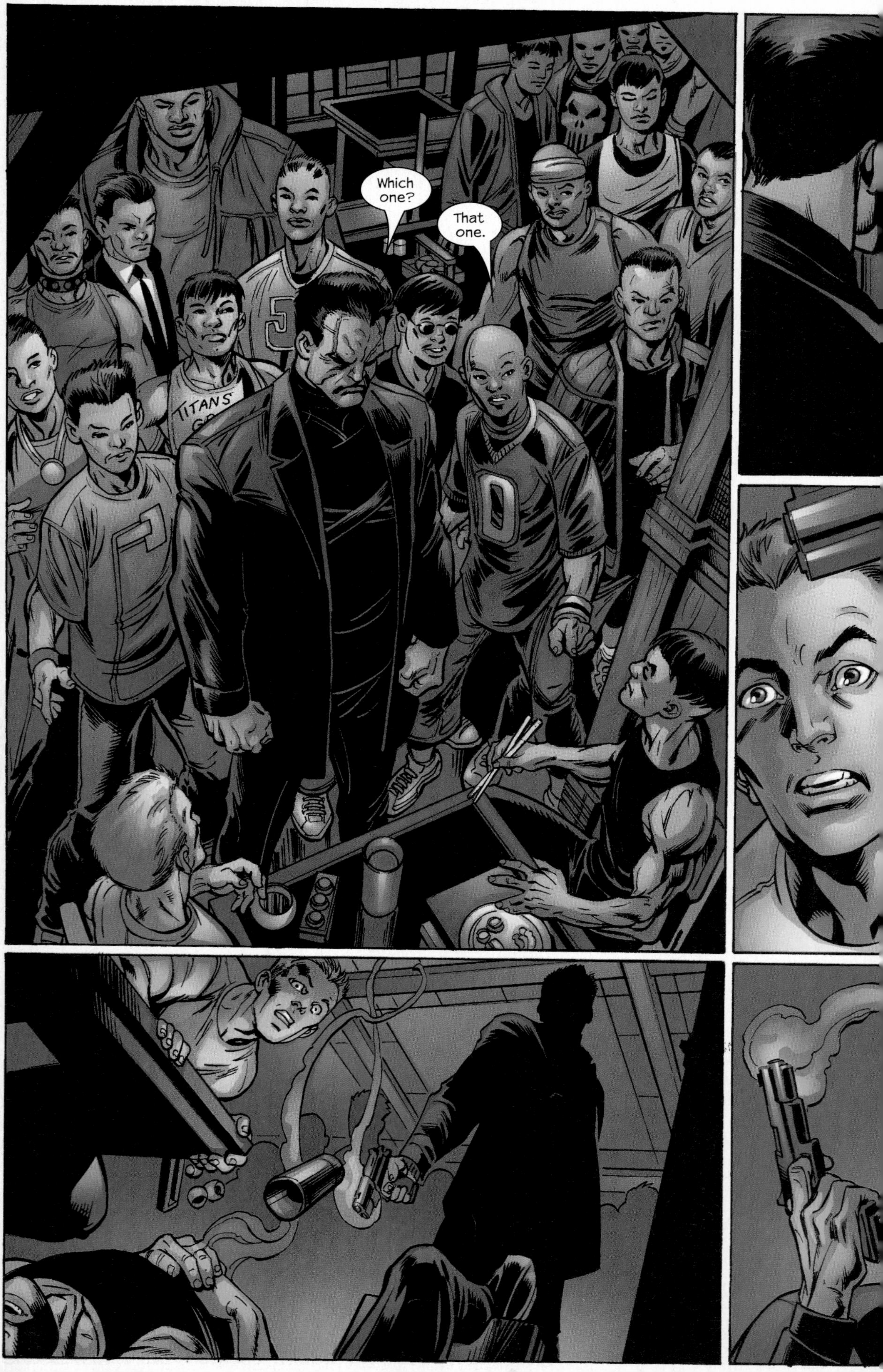
Which one?
That one.

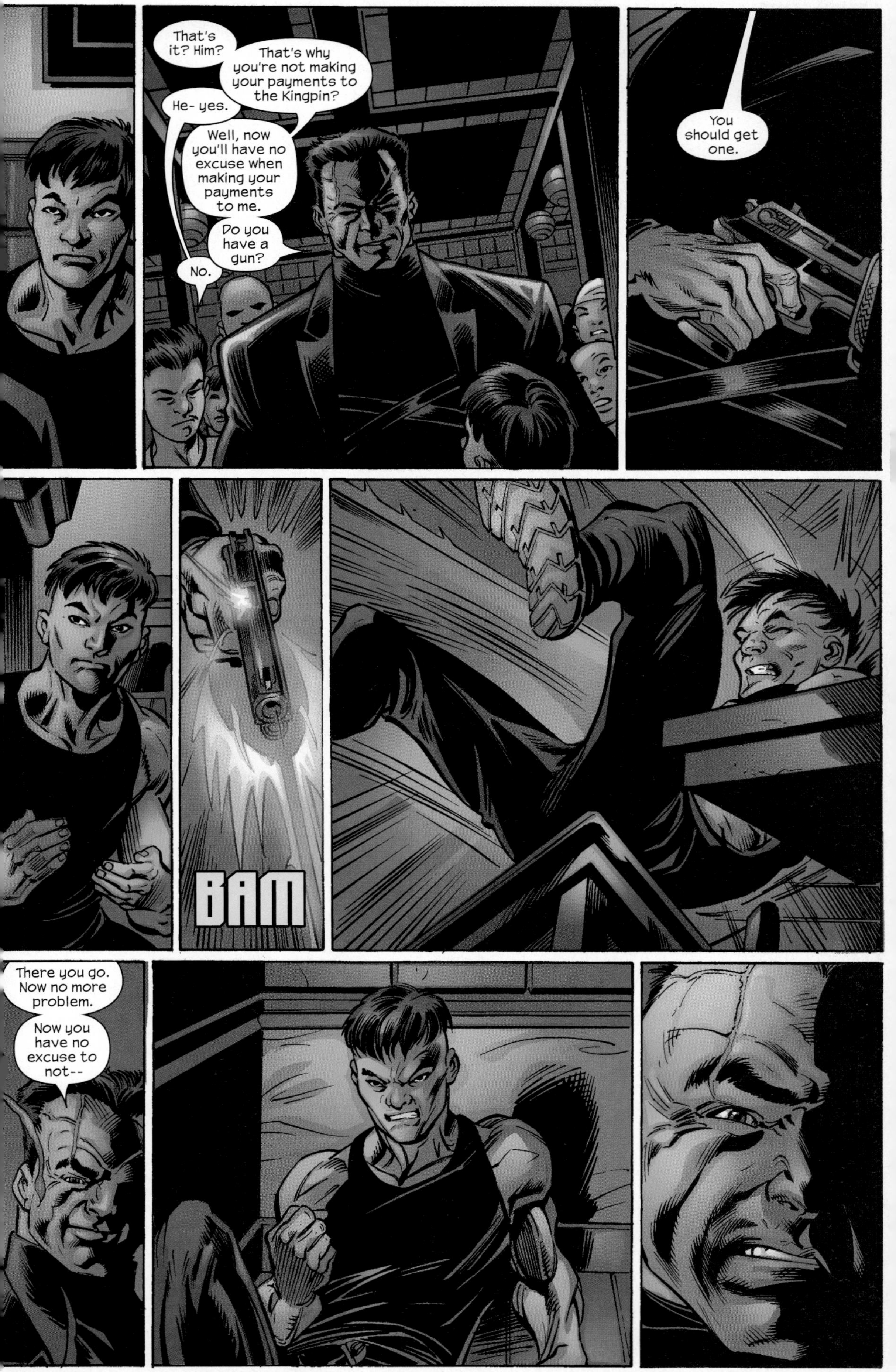
That's it? Him?
That's why you're not making your payments to the Kingpin?
He- yes.
Well, now you'll have no excuse when making your payments to me.
Do you have a gun?
No.
You should get one.
BAM
There you go. Now no more problem.
Now you have no excuse to not--

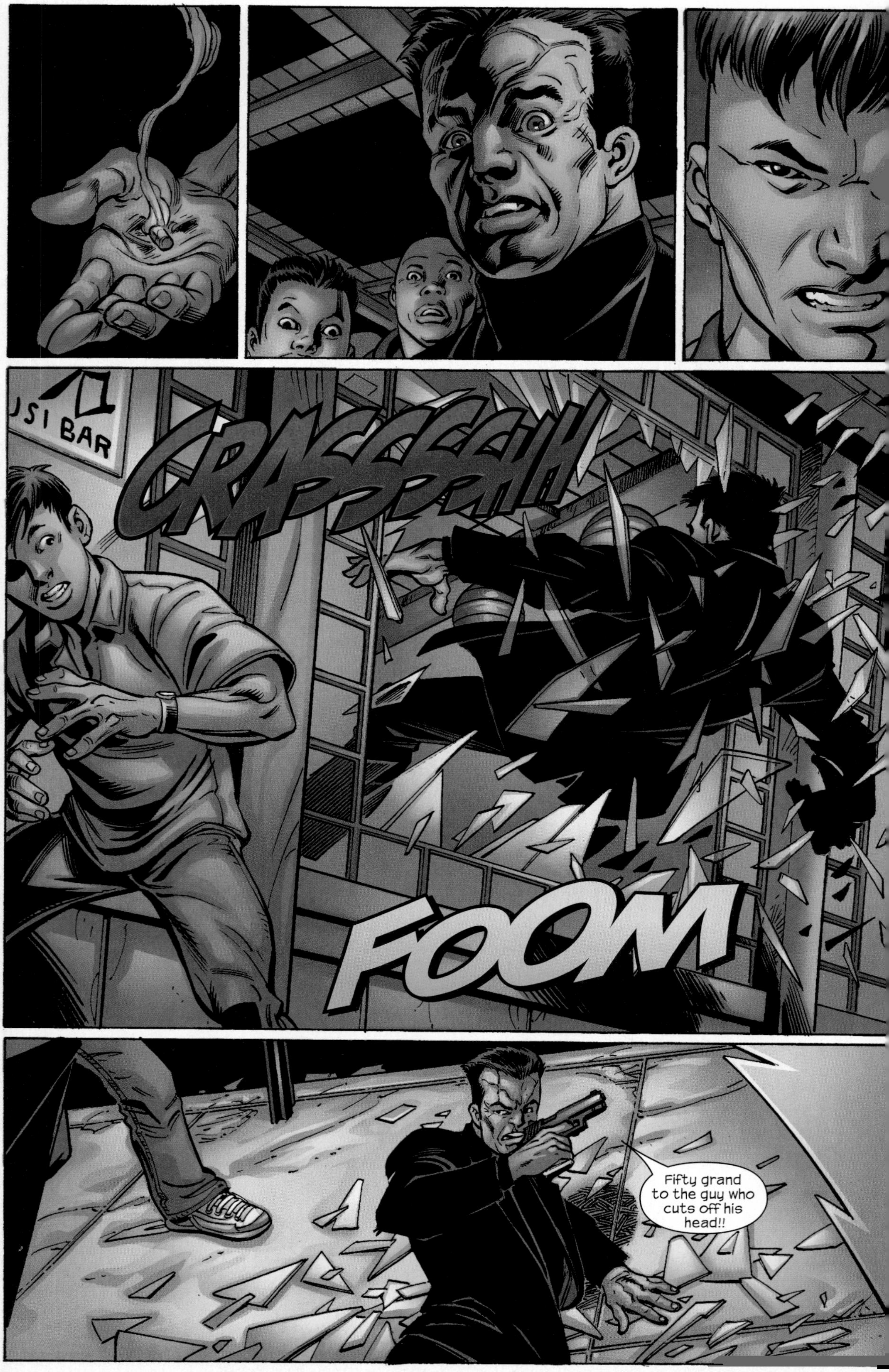
USI BAR
CRASSSHH
FOOM
Fifty grand to the guy who cuts off his head!!

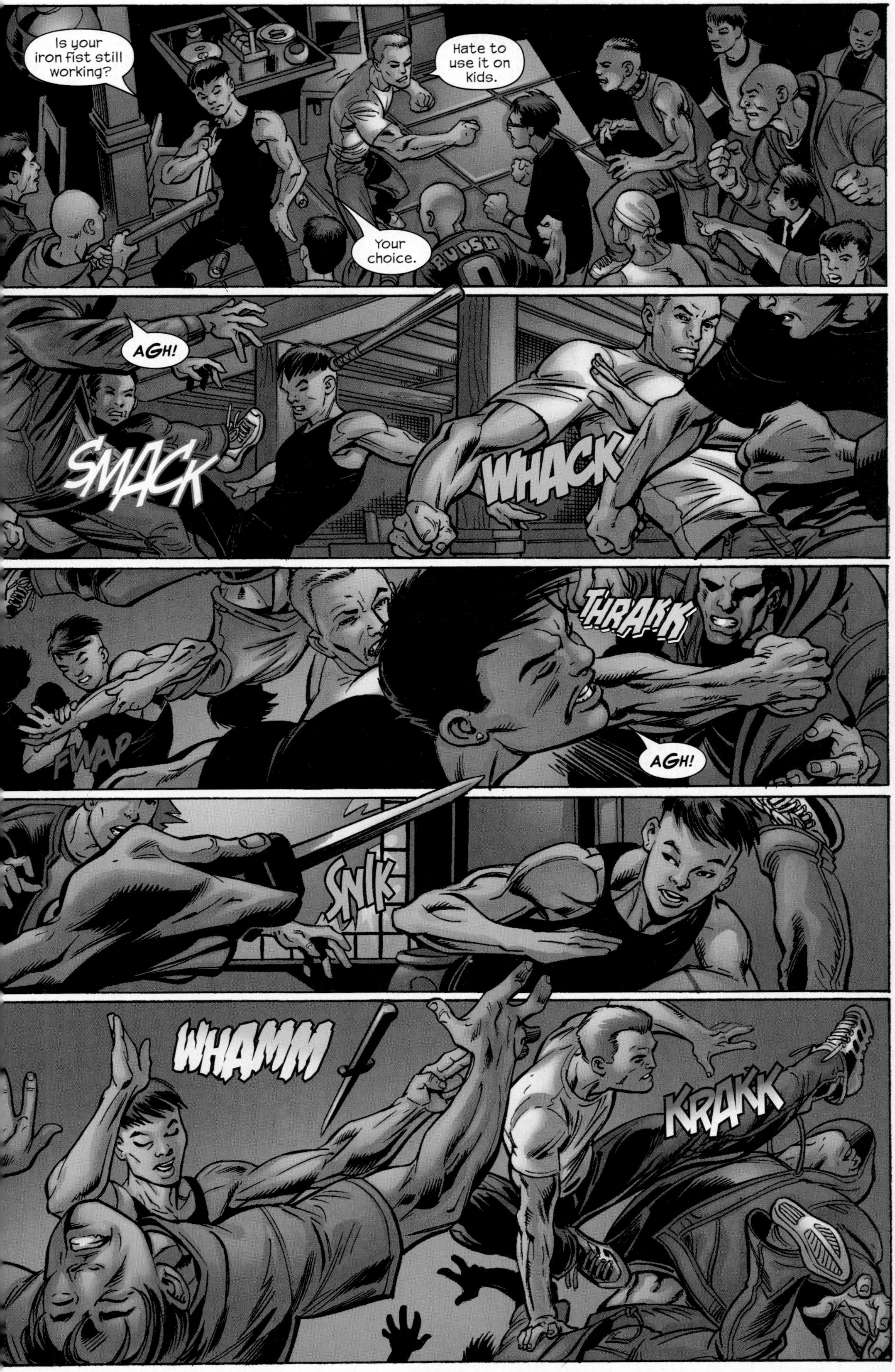
Is your iron fist still working?
Hate to use it on kids.
Your choice.
AGH!
SMACK
WHACK
THRAKK
FWAP
AGH!
SNIK
WHAMM
KRAKK

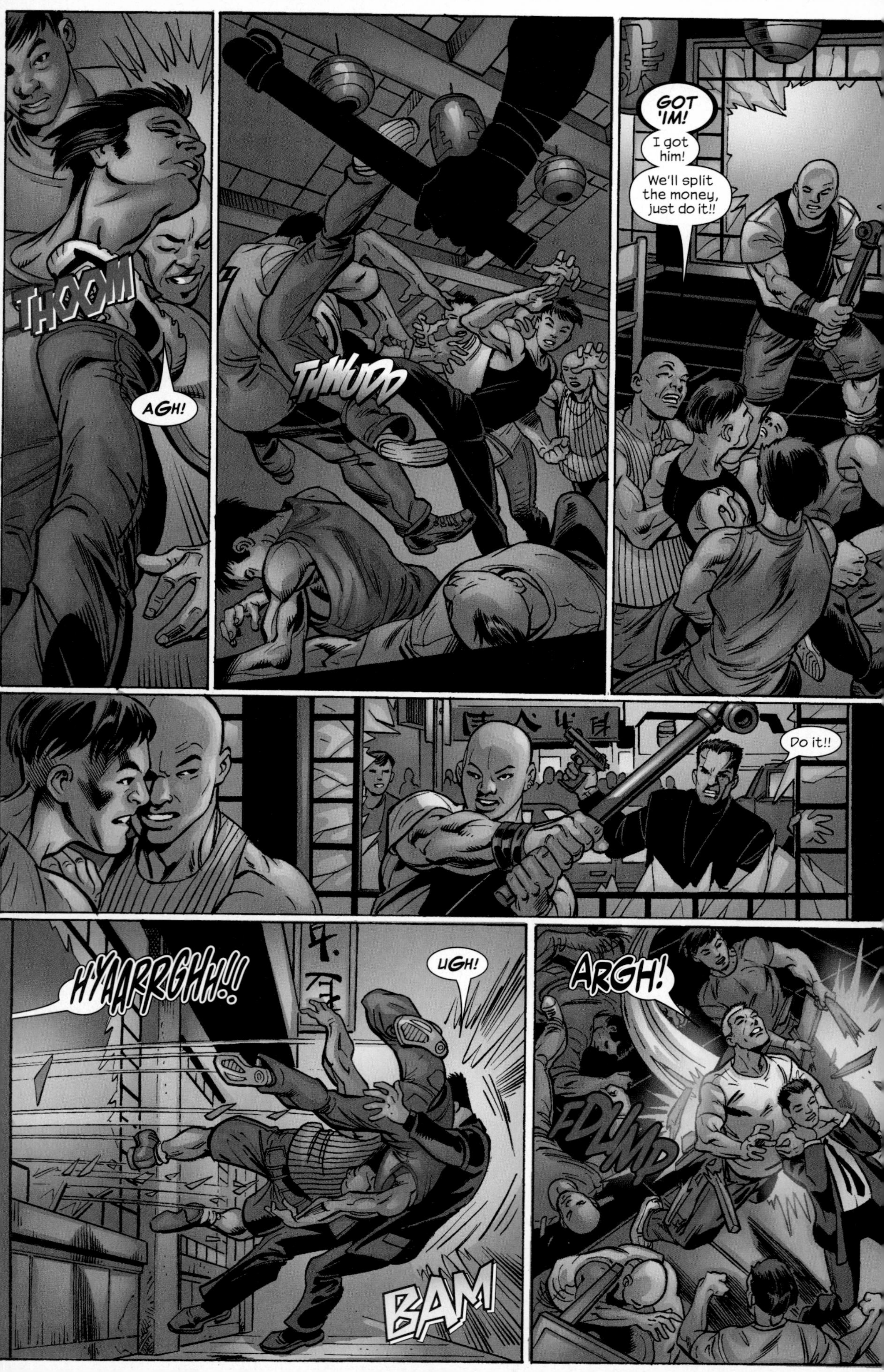
THOOM
AGH!
THWUDD
GOT 'IM!
I got him!
We'll split the money, just do it!!
Do it!!
HYAARRGHH!!
UGH!
BAM
ARGH!
FDUMP

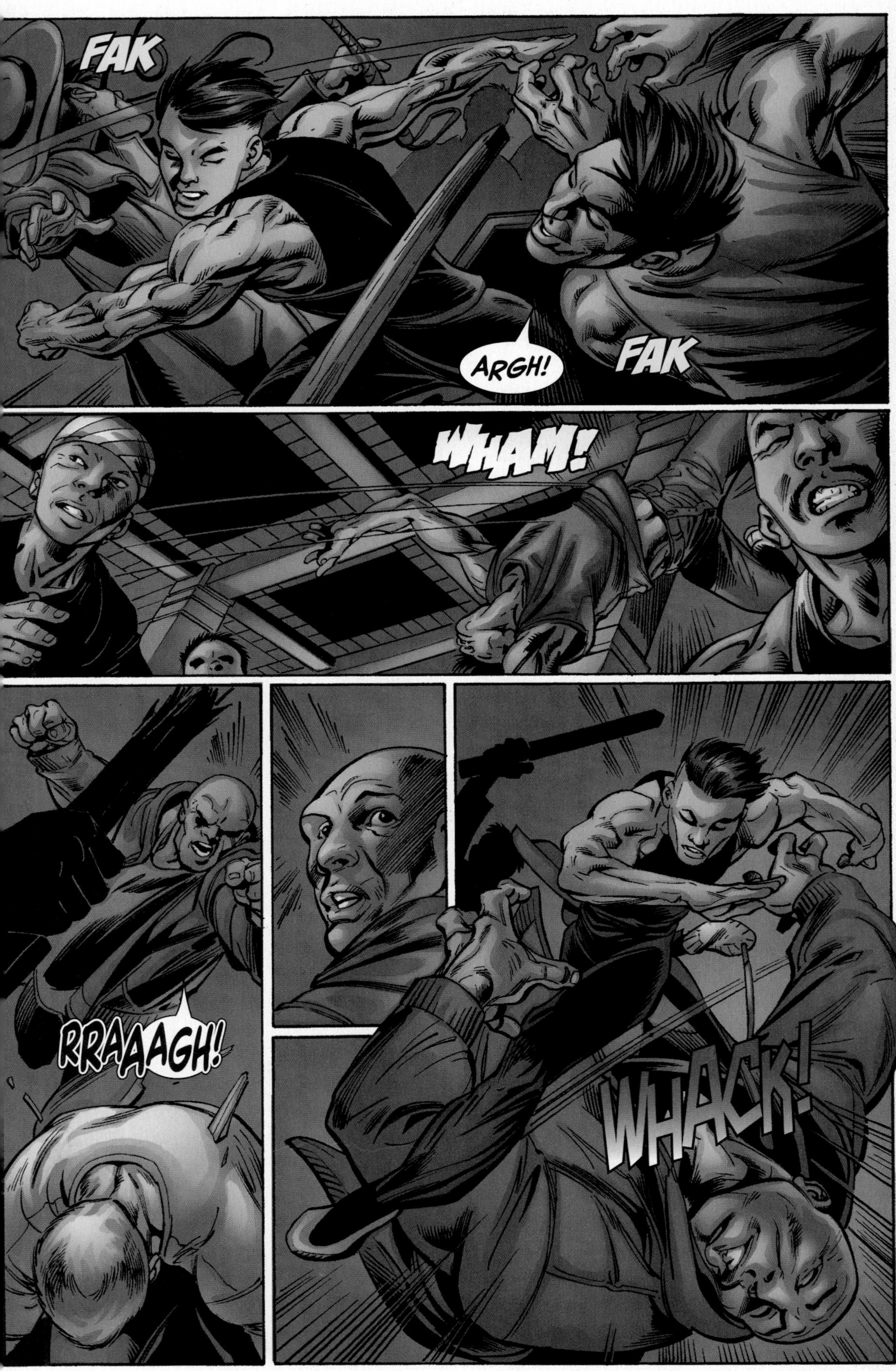
FAK
ARGH!
FAK
WHAM!
RRAAAGH!
WHACK!

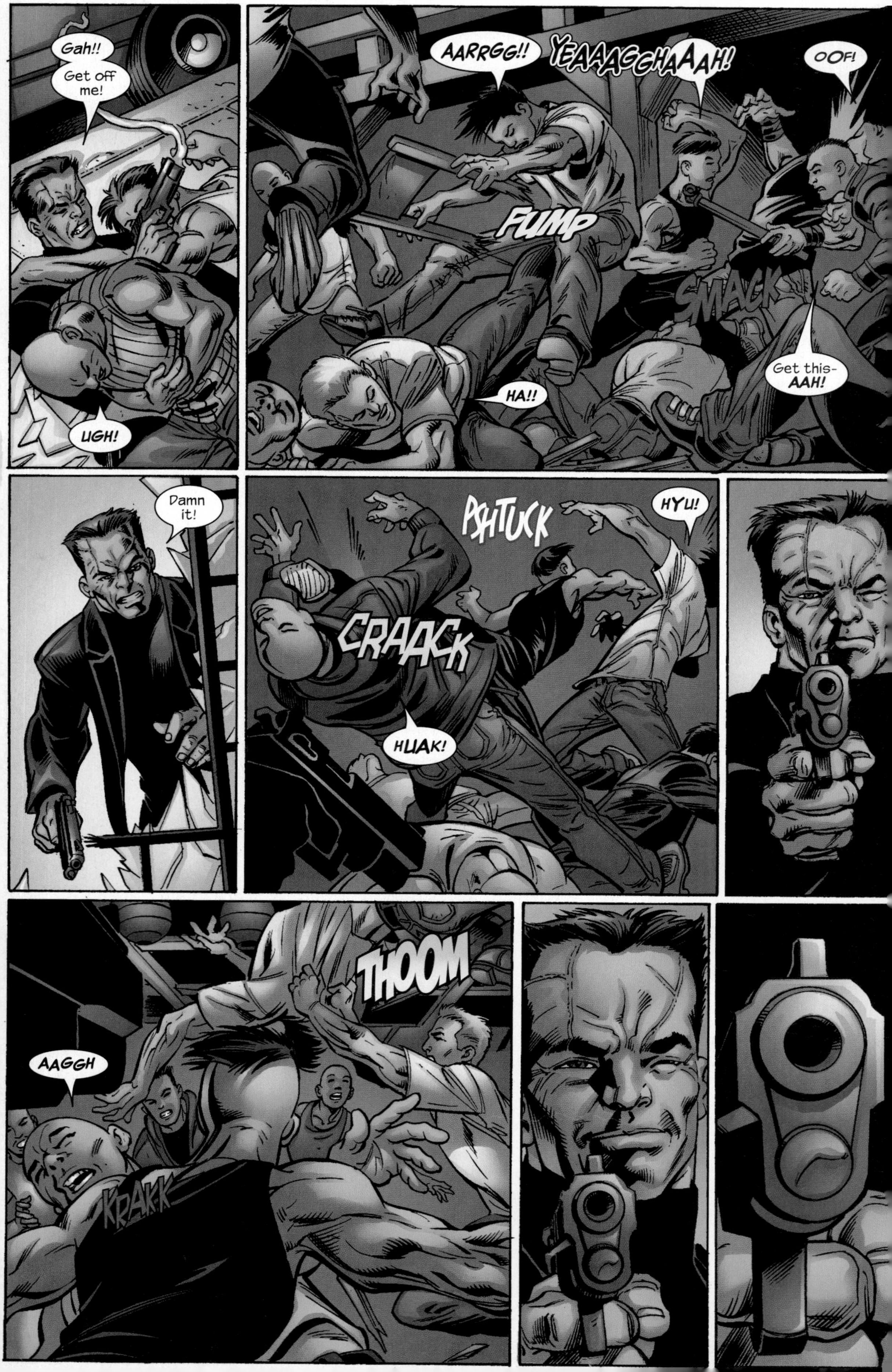

Gah!!
Get off me!
UGH!
AARRGG!!
YEAAAGGHAAAH!
OOF!
FUMP
SMACK
HA!!
Get this-
AAH!
Damn it!
PSHTUCK
HYU!
CRAAACK
HUAK!
THOOM
AAGGH
KRAKK

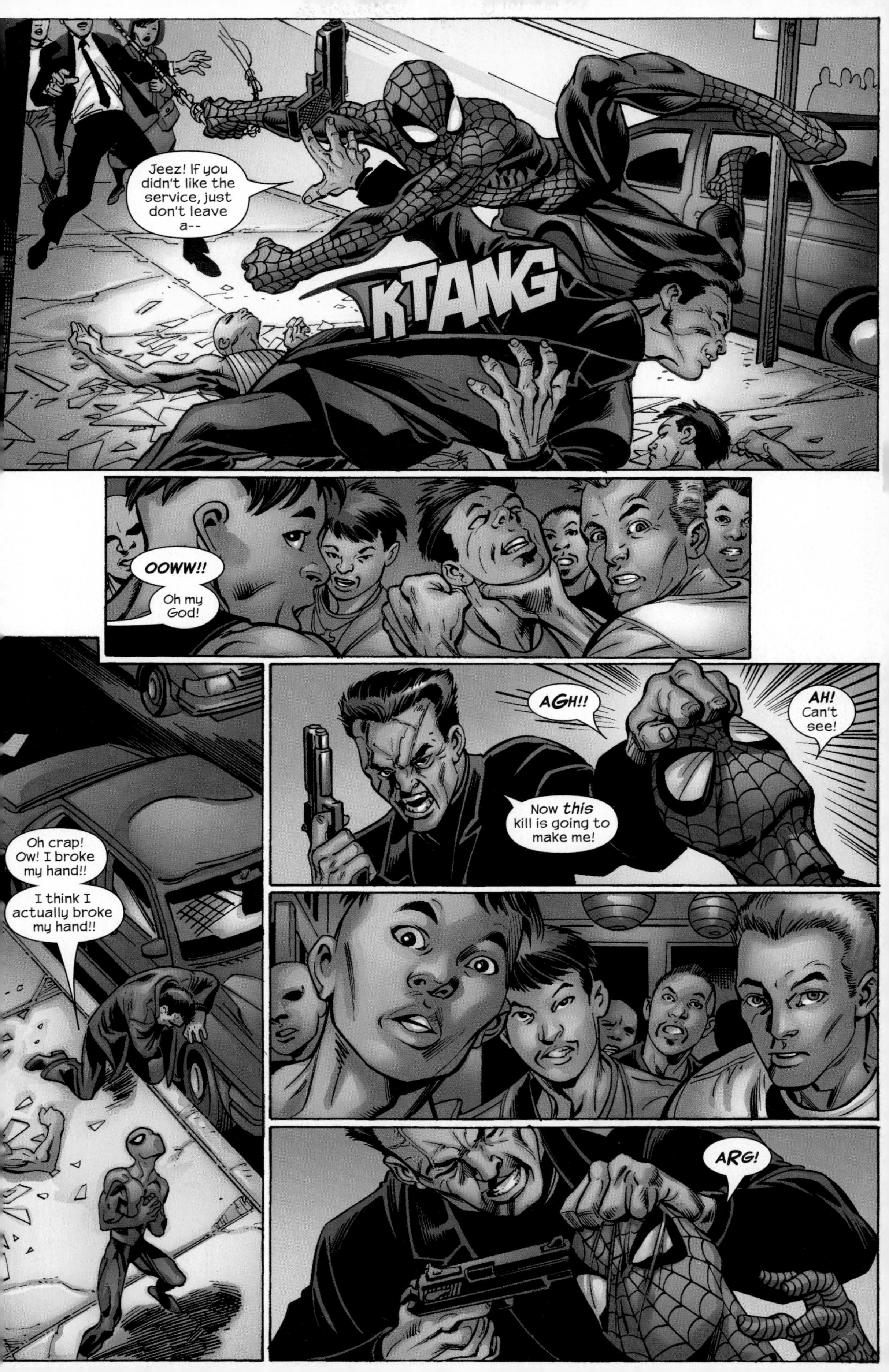
Jeez! If you didn't like the service, just don't leave a--
KTANG
OOWW!!
Oh my God!
AGH!!
AH! Can't see!
Now this kill is going to make me!
Oh crap! Ow! I broke my hand!!
I think I actually broke my hand!!
ARG!

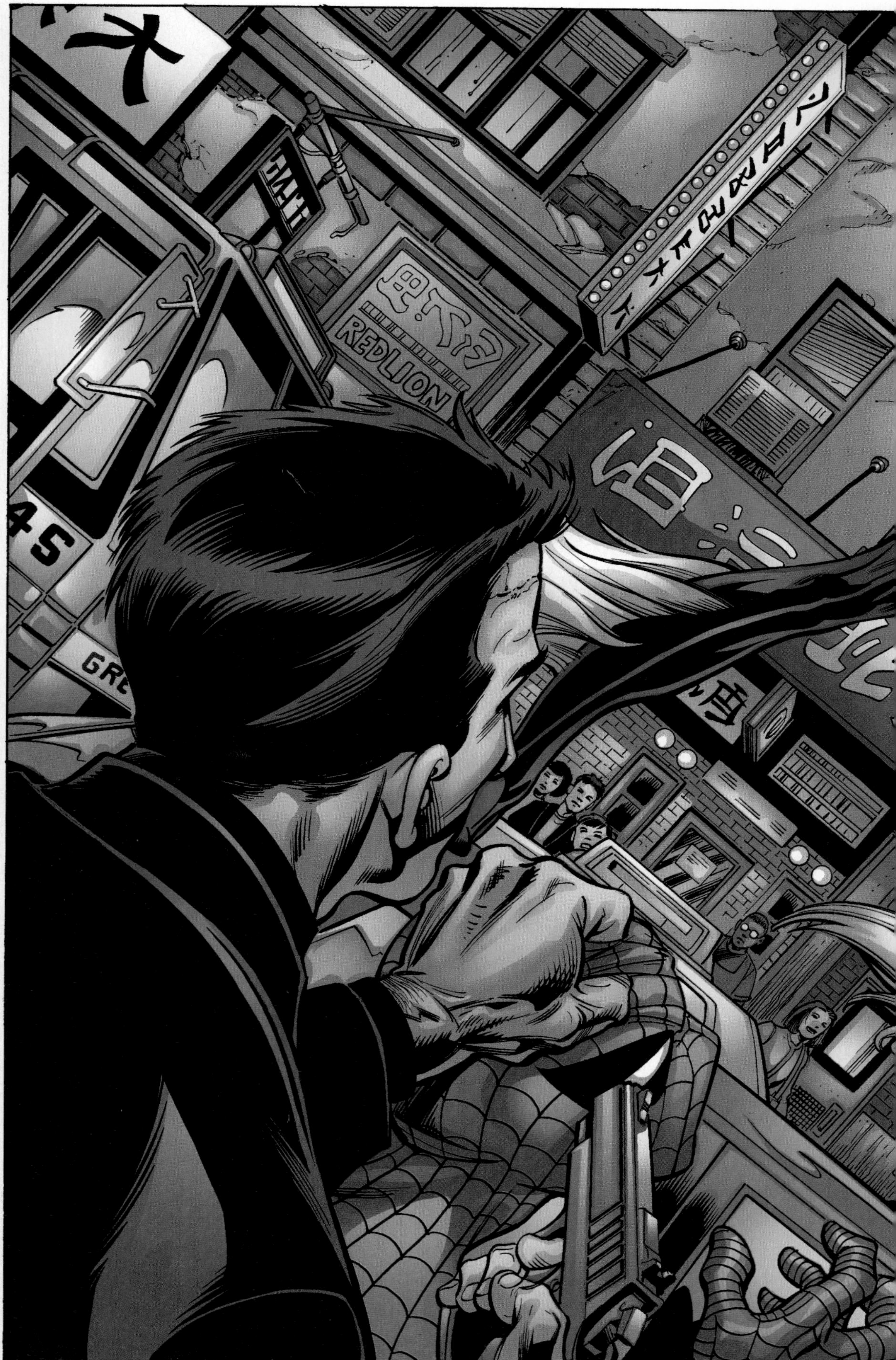
REDLION
45

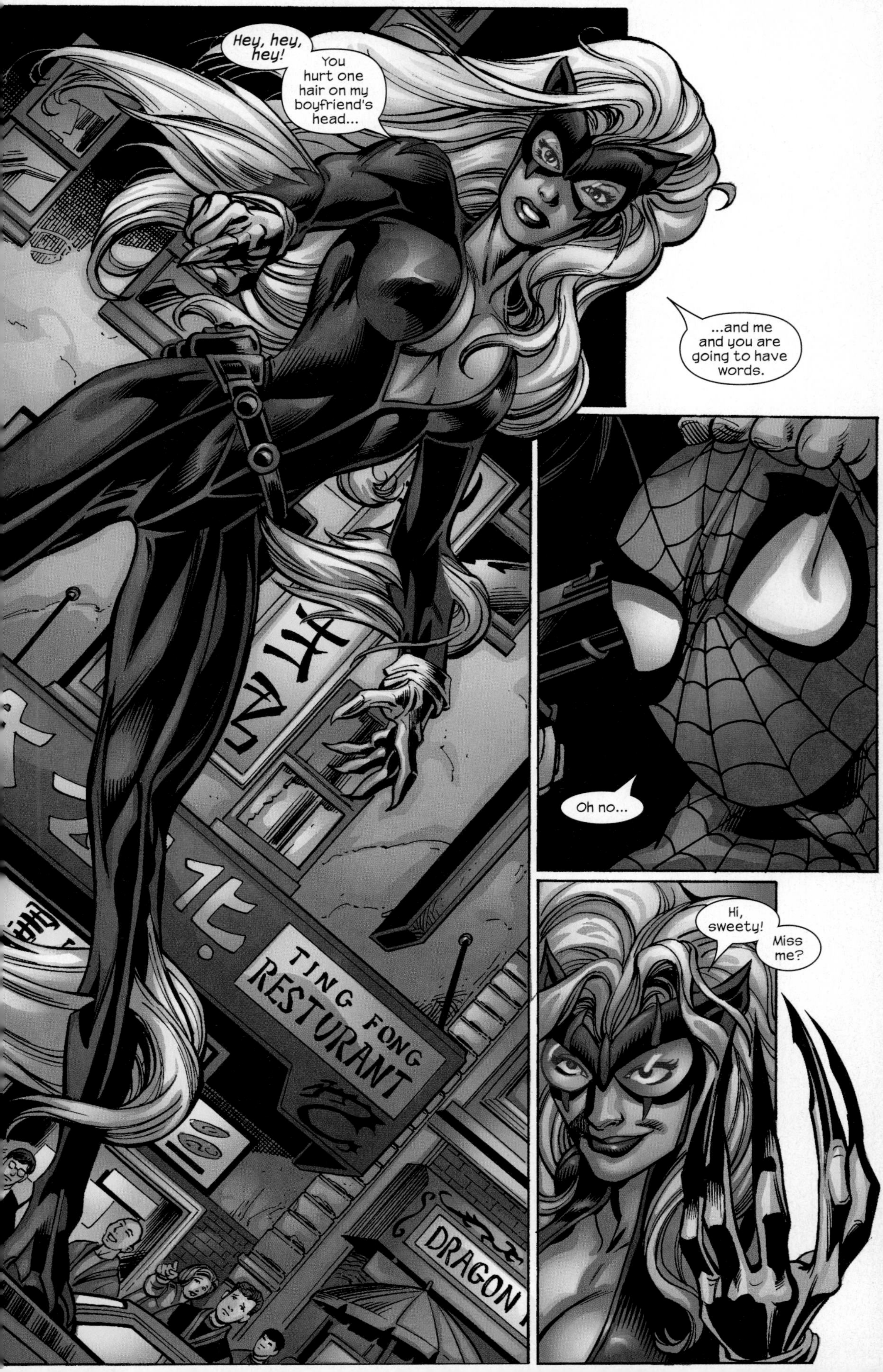
Hey, hey, hey!
You hurt one hair on my boyfriend's head...
...and me and you are going to have words.
TING FONG RESTURANT
DRAGON
Oh no...
Hi, sweety!
Miss me?

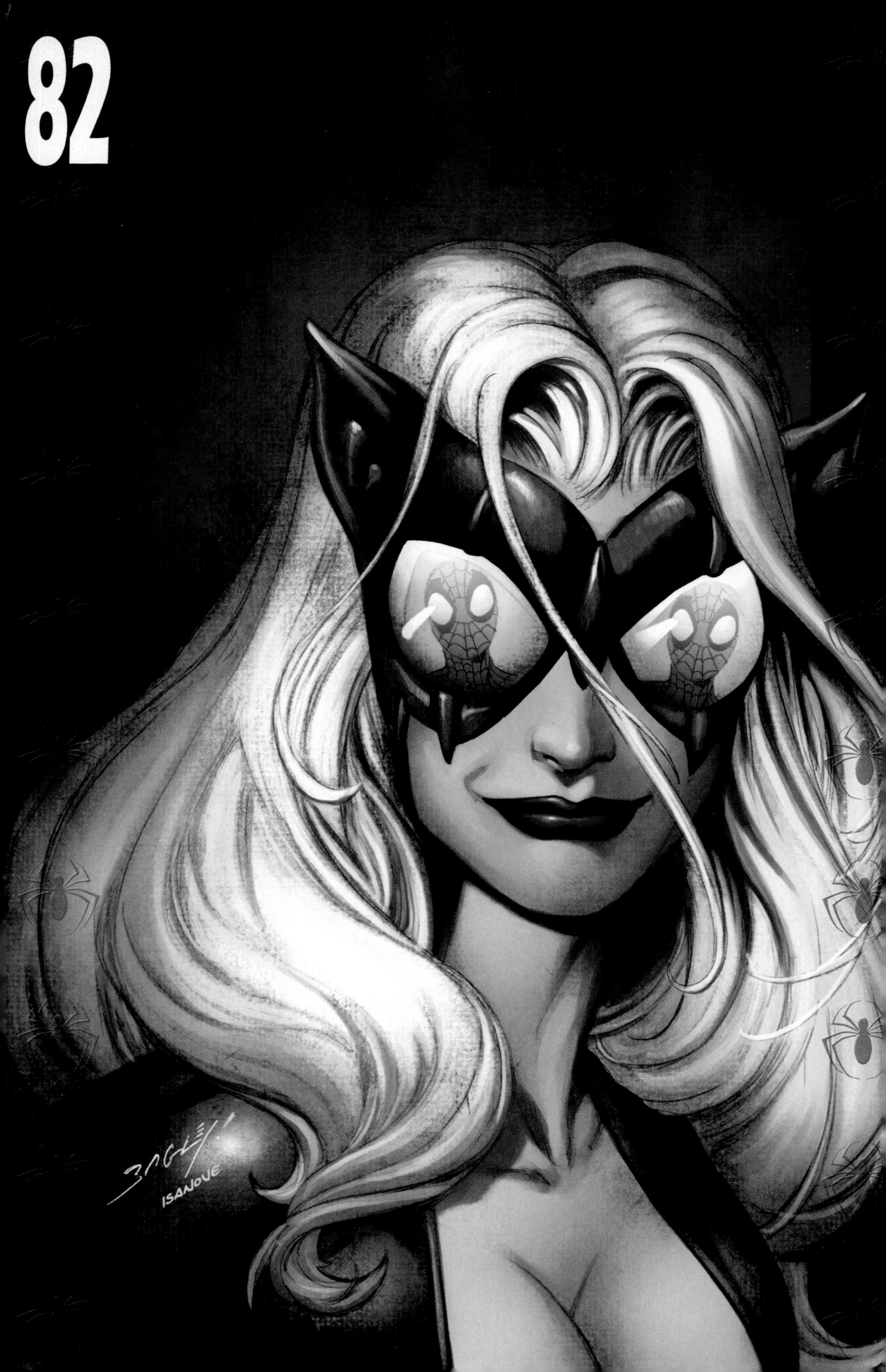
82
ISANOVE

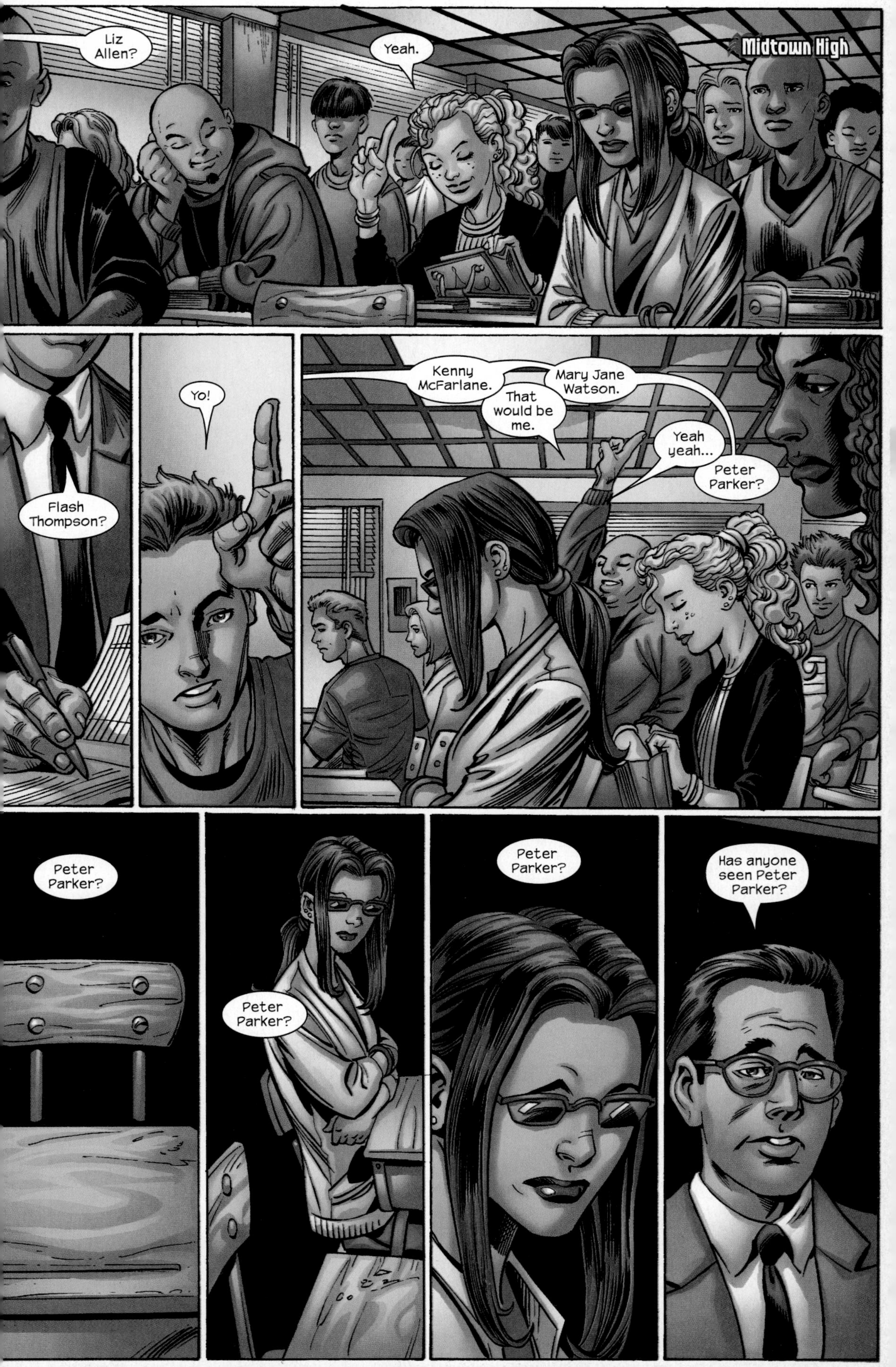

Midtown High
Liz Allen?
Yeah.
Flash Thompson?
Yo!
Kenny McFarlane.
That would be me.
Mary Jane Watson.
Yeah yeah...
Peter Parker?
Peter Parker?
Peter Parker?
Peter Parker?
Has anyone seen Peter Parker?

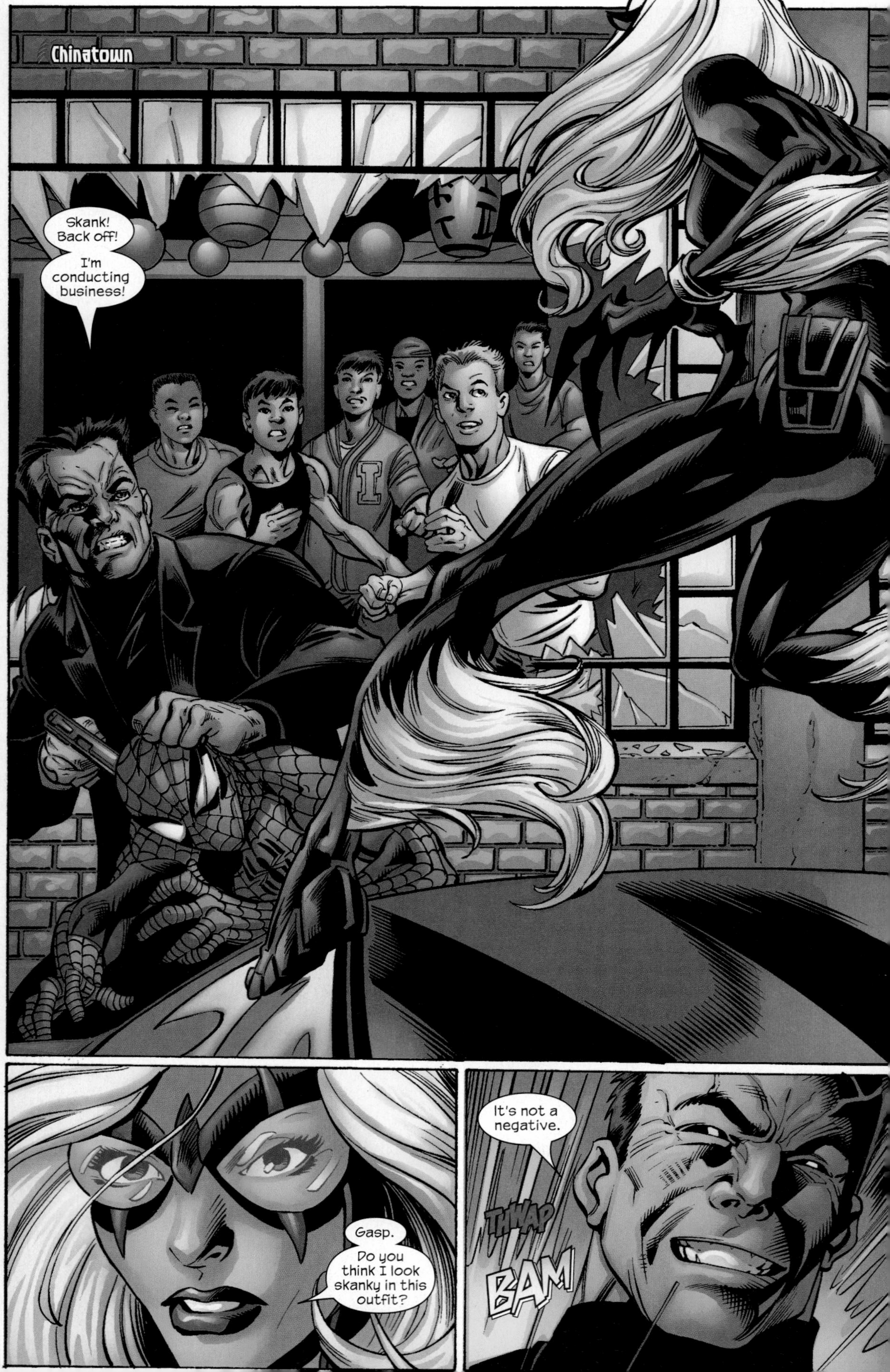
Chinatown
Skank! Back off!
I'm conducting business!
Gasp.
Do you think I look skanky in this outfit?
It's not a negative.
THWAP
BAM

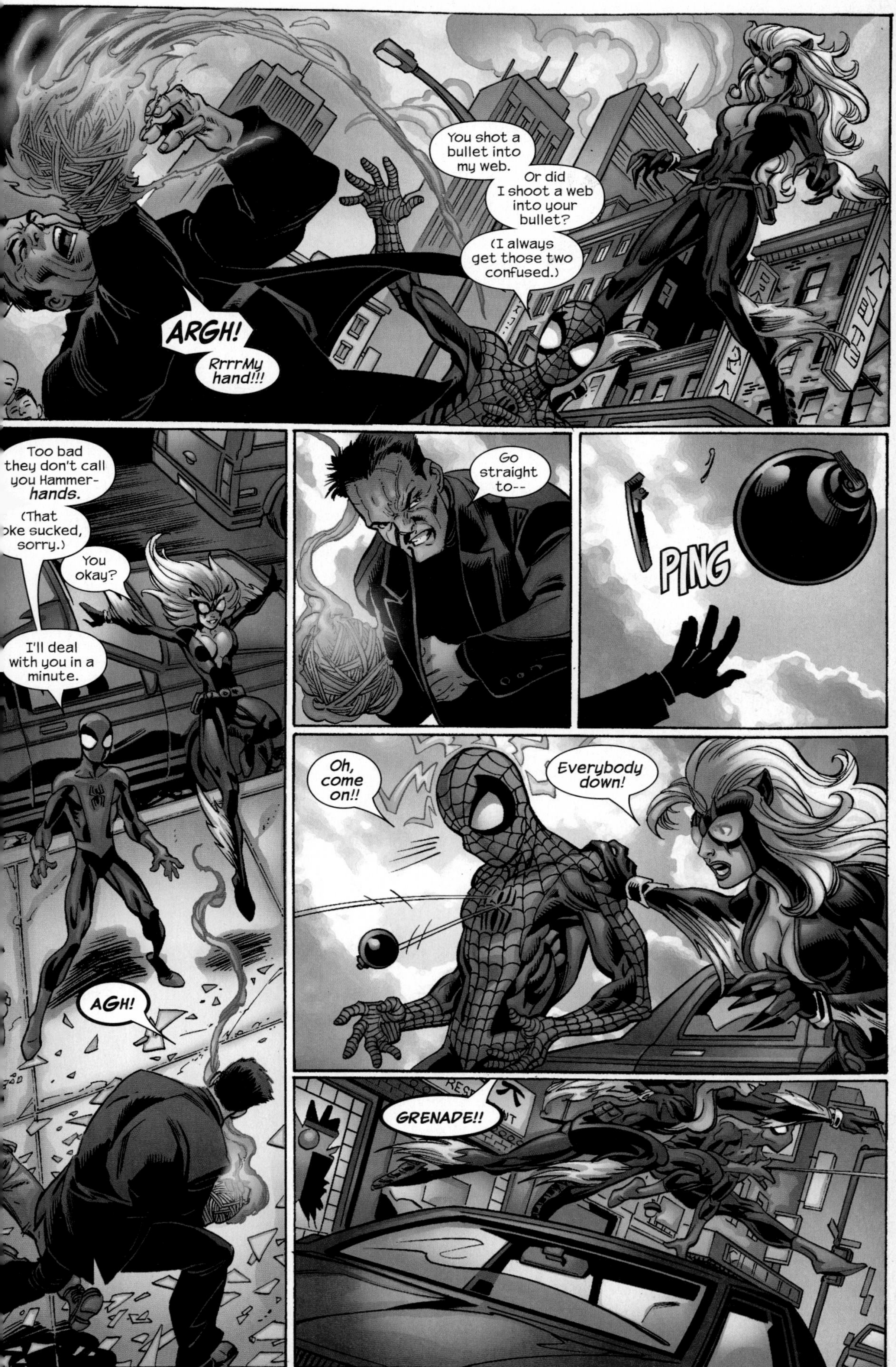
You shot a bullet into my web.
Or did I shoot a web into your bullet?
(I always get those two confused.)
ARGH!
RrrrMy hand!!!
Too bad they don't call you Hammer-hands.
(That joke sucked, sorry.)
You okay?
I'll deal with you in a minute.
AGH!
Go straight to--
PING
Oh, come on!!
Everybody down!
GRENADE!!

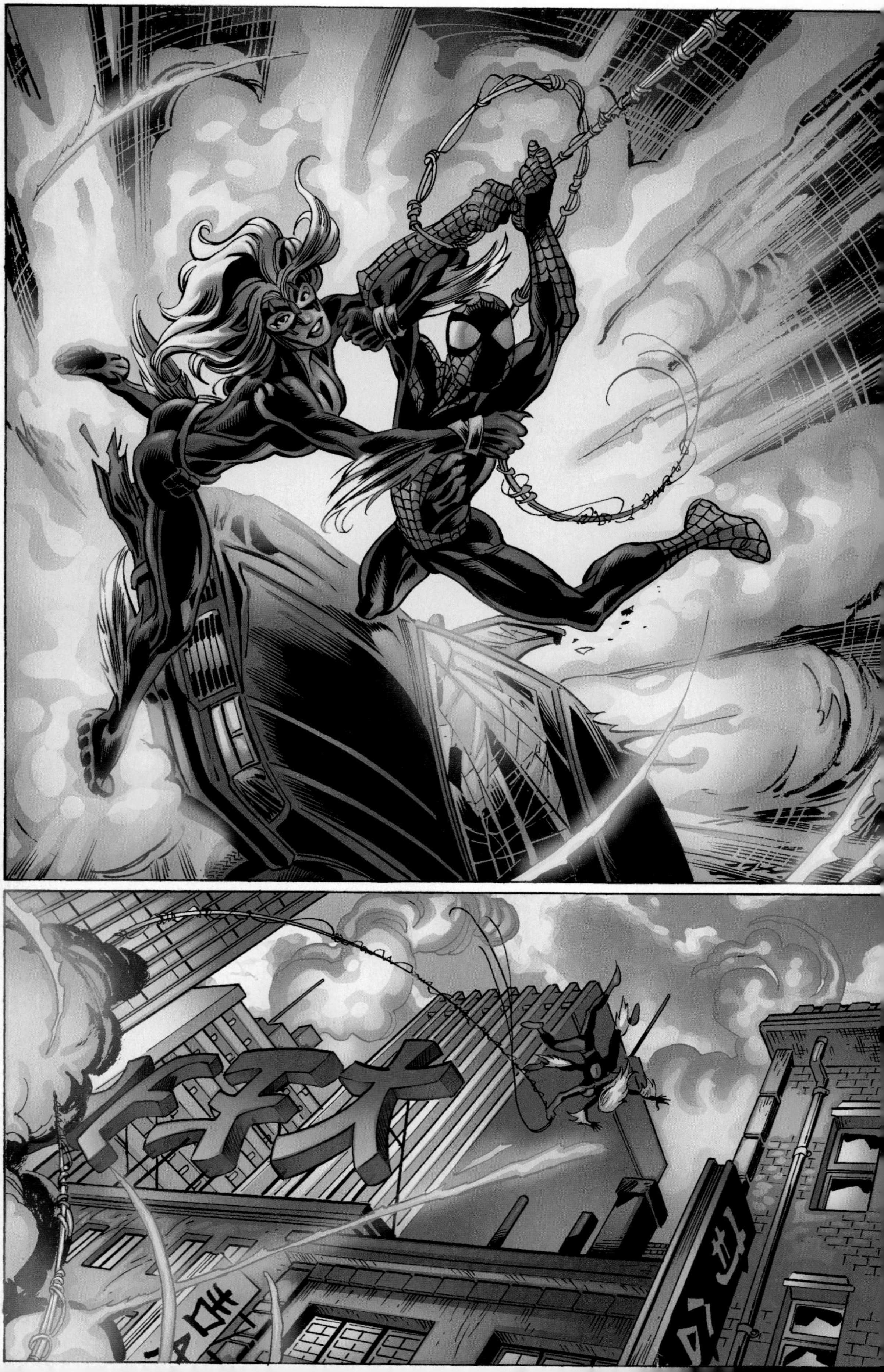

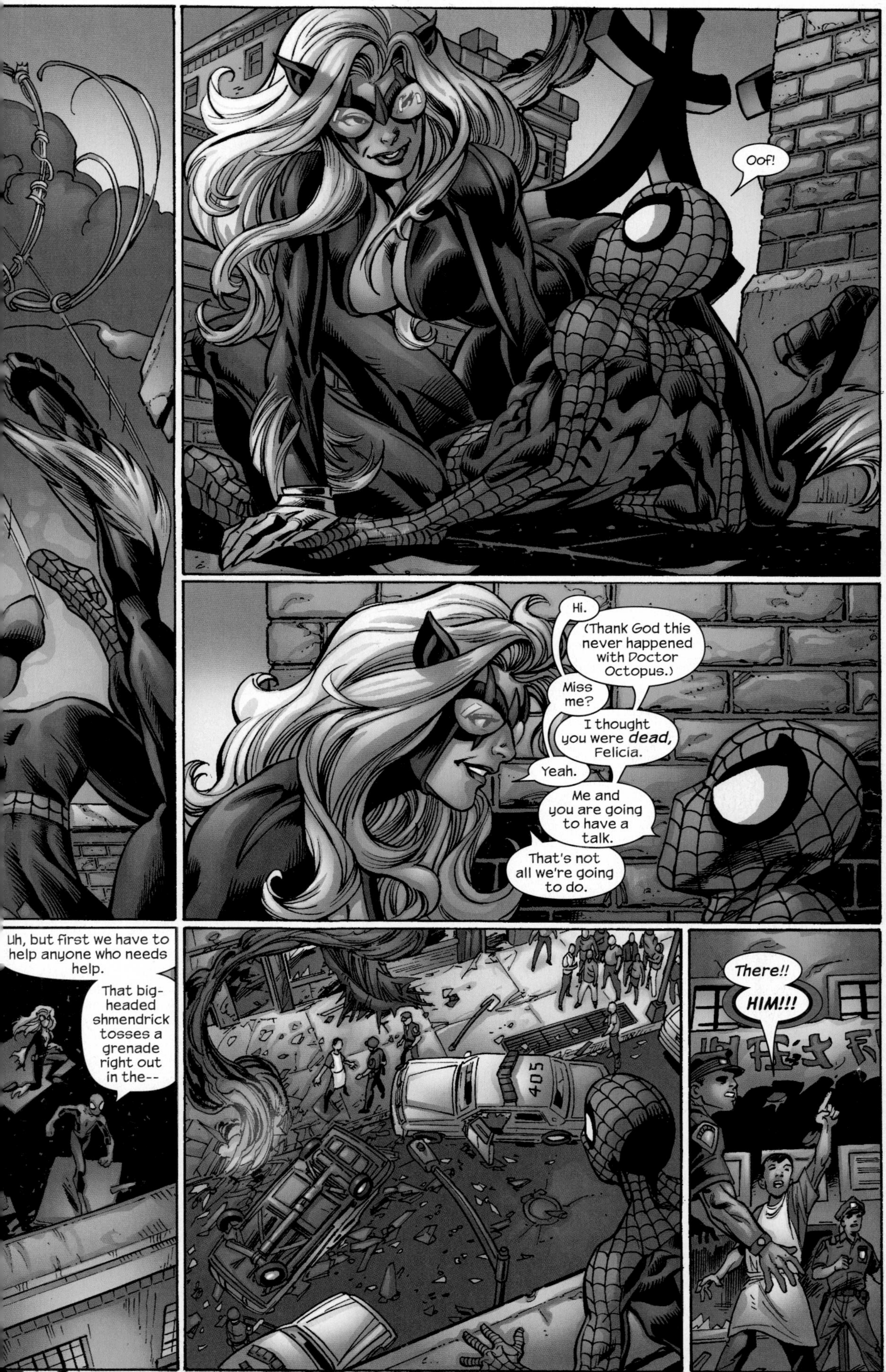

Oof!
Hi.
(Thank God this never happened with Doctor Octopus.)
Miss me?
I thought you were *dead,* Felicia.
Yeah.
Me and you are going to have a talk.
That's not all we're going to do.
Uh, but first we have to help anyone who needs help.
That big-headed shmendrick tosses a grenade right out in the--
There!!
HIM!!!

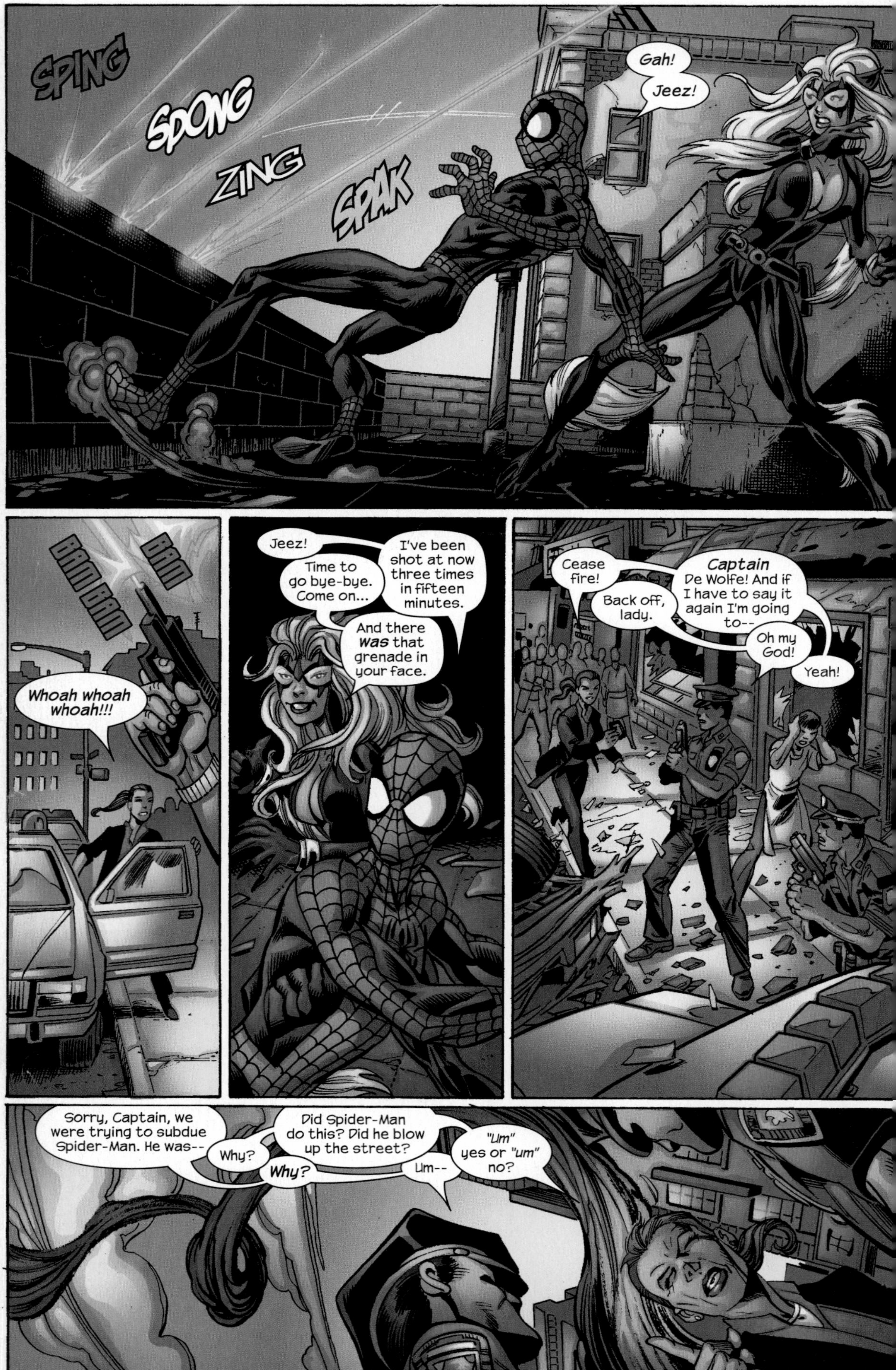

SPING
SPONG
ZING
SPAK
Gah!
Jeez!
BAM
BAM BAM
Whoah whoah whoah!!!
Jeez!
Time to go bye-bye. Come on...
I've been shot at now three times in fifteen minutes.
And there *was* that grenade in your face.
Cease fire!
Back off, lady.
Captain De Wolfe! And if I have to say it again I'm going to--
Oh my God!
Yeah!
Sorry, Captain, we were trying to subdue Spider-Man. He was--
Why?
Why?
Did Spider-Man do this? Did he blow up the street?
Um--
"Um" yes or "um" no?

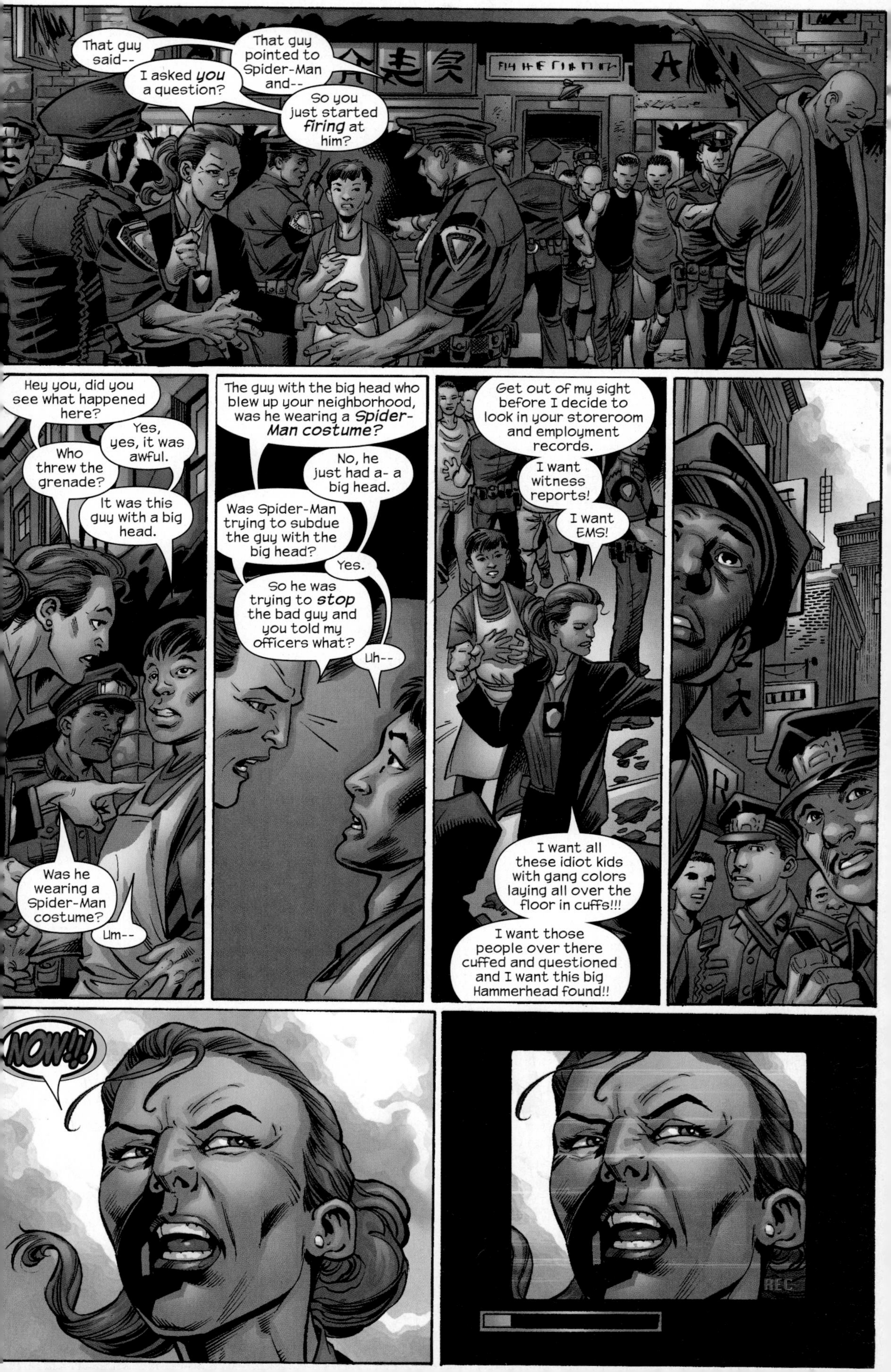

That guy said--
That guy pointed to Spider-Man and--
I asked *you* a question?
So you just started *firing* at him?
Hey you, did you see what happened here?
Yes, yes, it was awful.
Who threw the grenade?
It was this guy with a big head.
Was he wearing a Spider-Man costume?
Um--
The guy with the big head who blew up your neighborhood, was he wearing a *Spider-Man costume?*
No, he just had a- a big head.
Was Spider-Man trying to subdue the guy with the big head?
Yes.
So he was trying to *stop* the bad guy and you told my officers what?
Uh--
Get out of my sight before I decide to look in your storeroom and employment records.
I want witness reports!
I want EMS!
I want all these idiot kids with gang colors laying all over the floor in cuffs!!!
I want those people over there cuffed and questioned and I want this big Hammerhead found!!
NOW!!!
REC

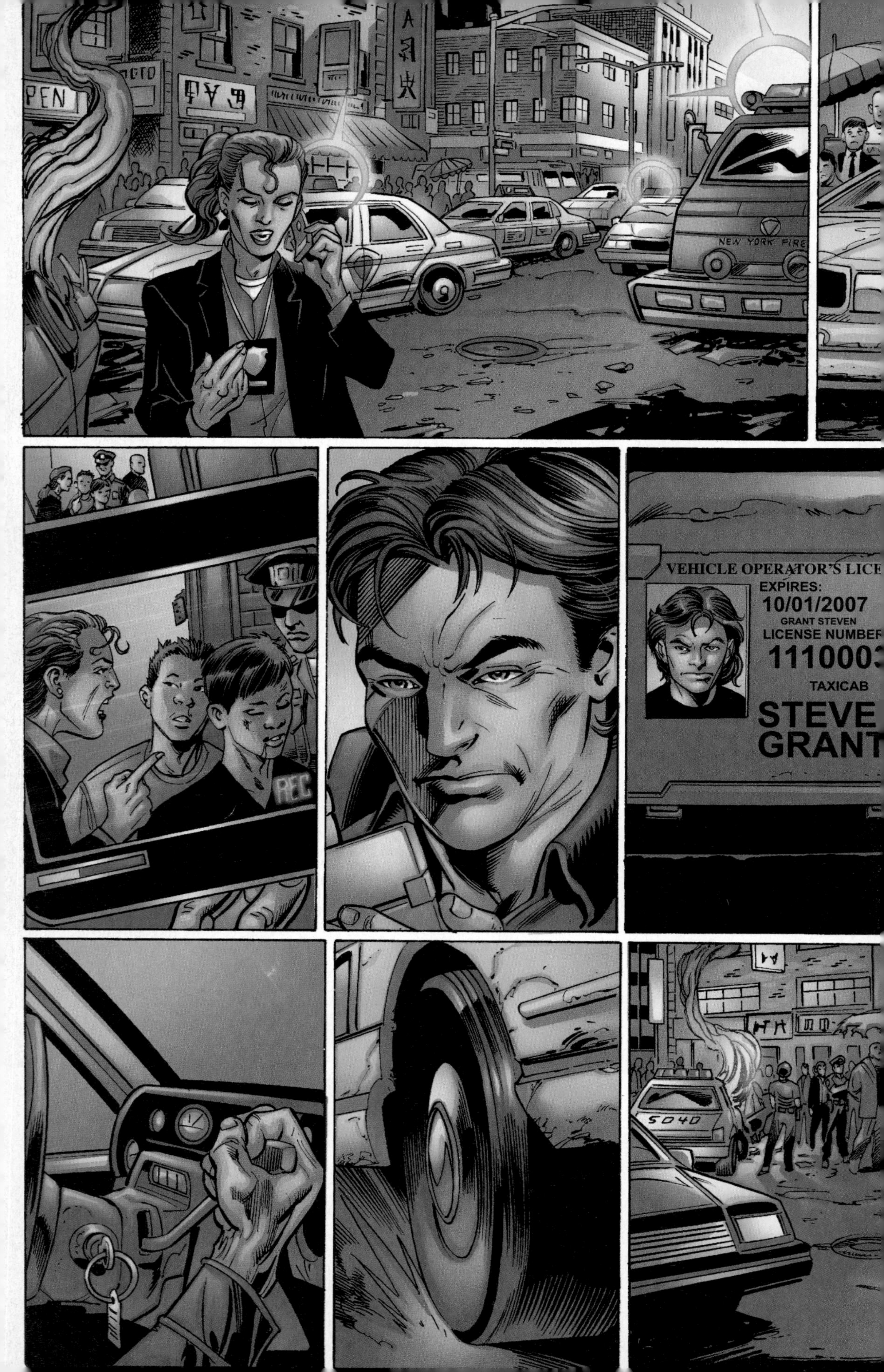

PEN
NEW YORK FIRE
REC
VEHICLE OPERATOR'S LICE
EXPIRES:
10/01/2007
GRANT STEVEN
LICENSE NUMBER
111000
TAXICAB
STEVE
GRANT
5040

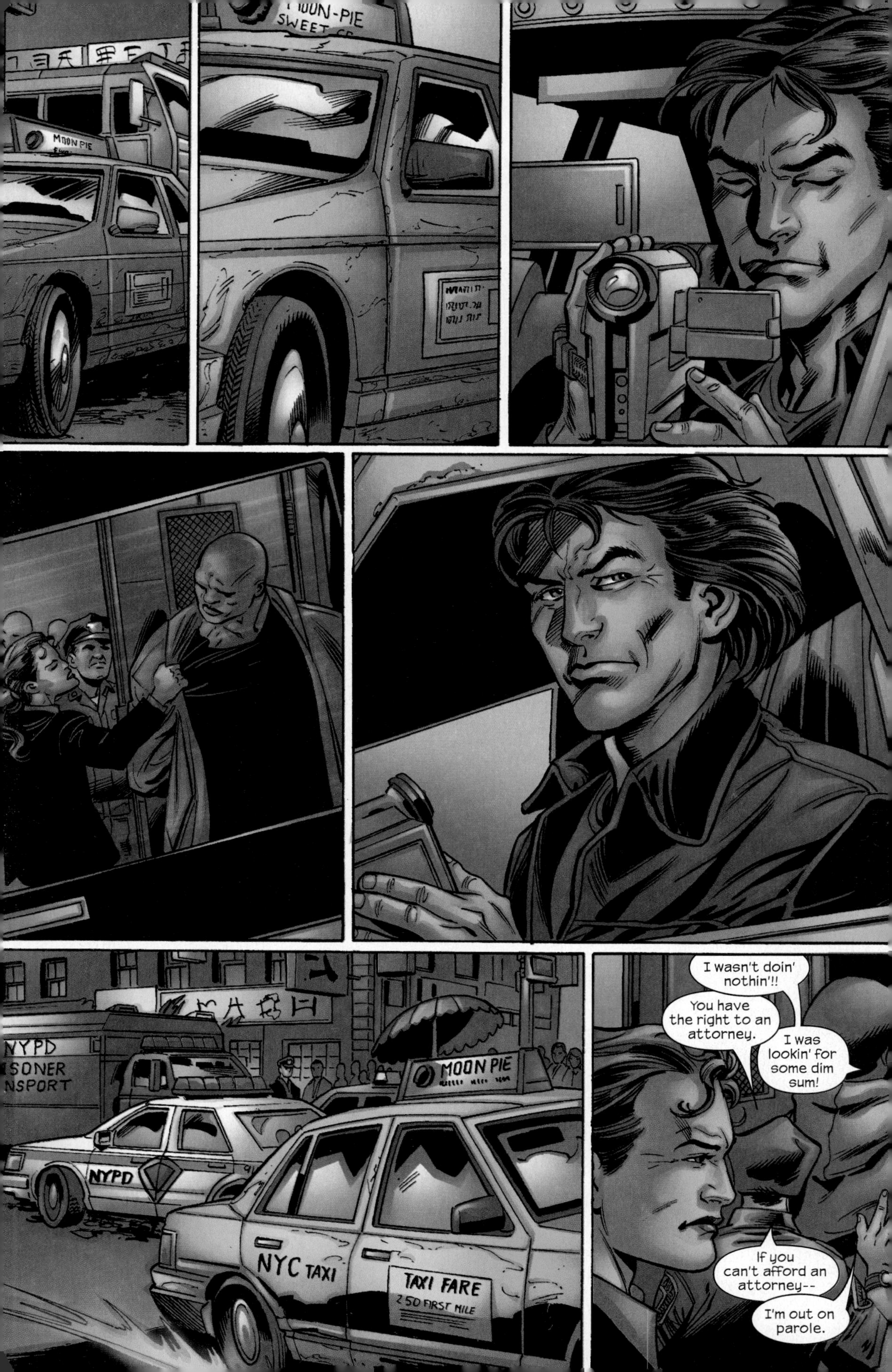

SWEET CO.
MOON PIE
NYPD
SONER
NSPORT
MOON PIE
NYPD
NYC TAXI
TAXI FARE
2.50 FIRST MILE
I wasn't doin' nothin'!!
You have the right to an attorney.
I was lookin' for some dim sum!
If you can't afford an attorney--
I'm out on parole.

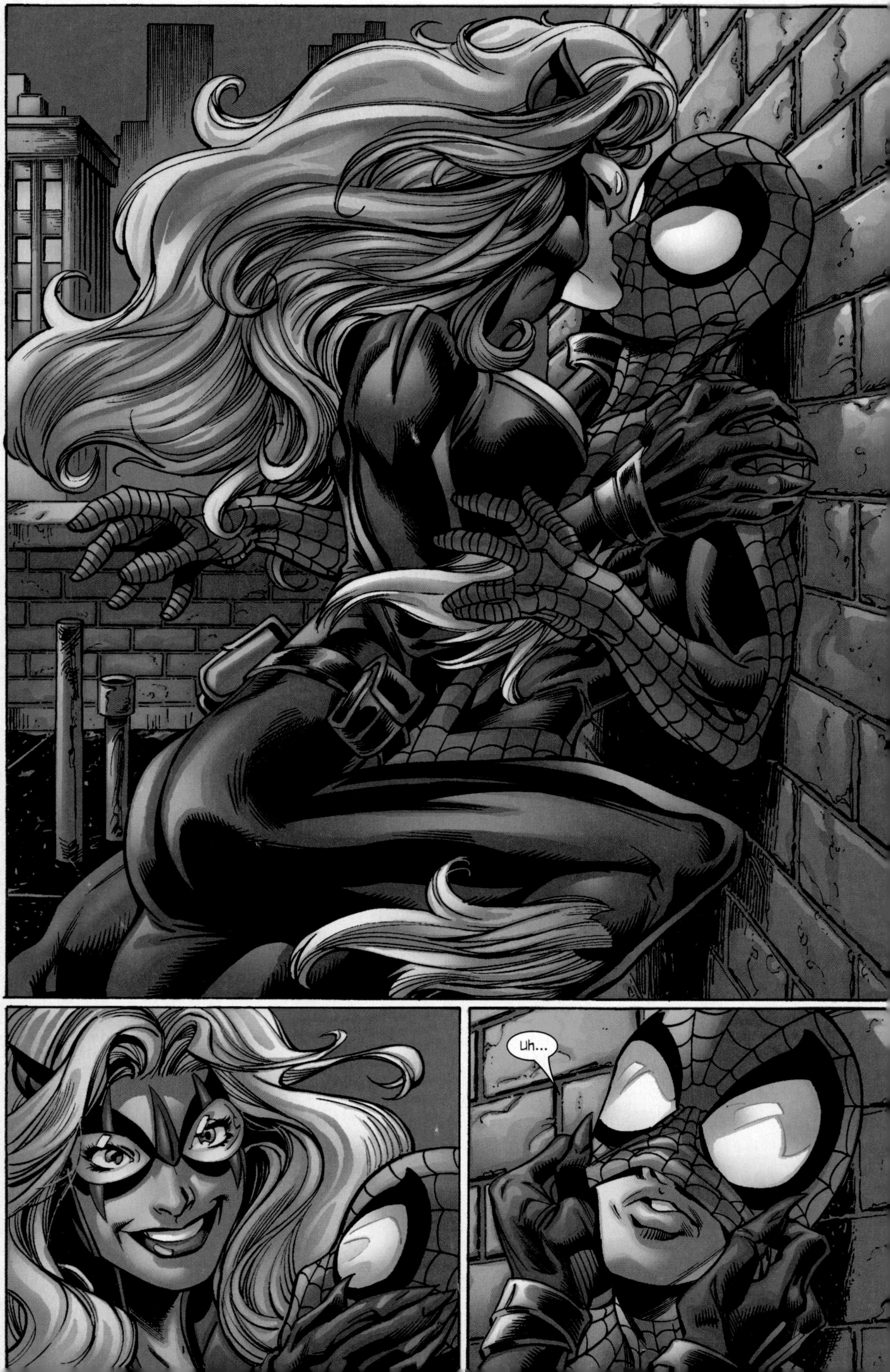
Uh...

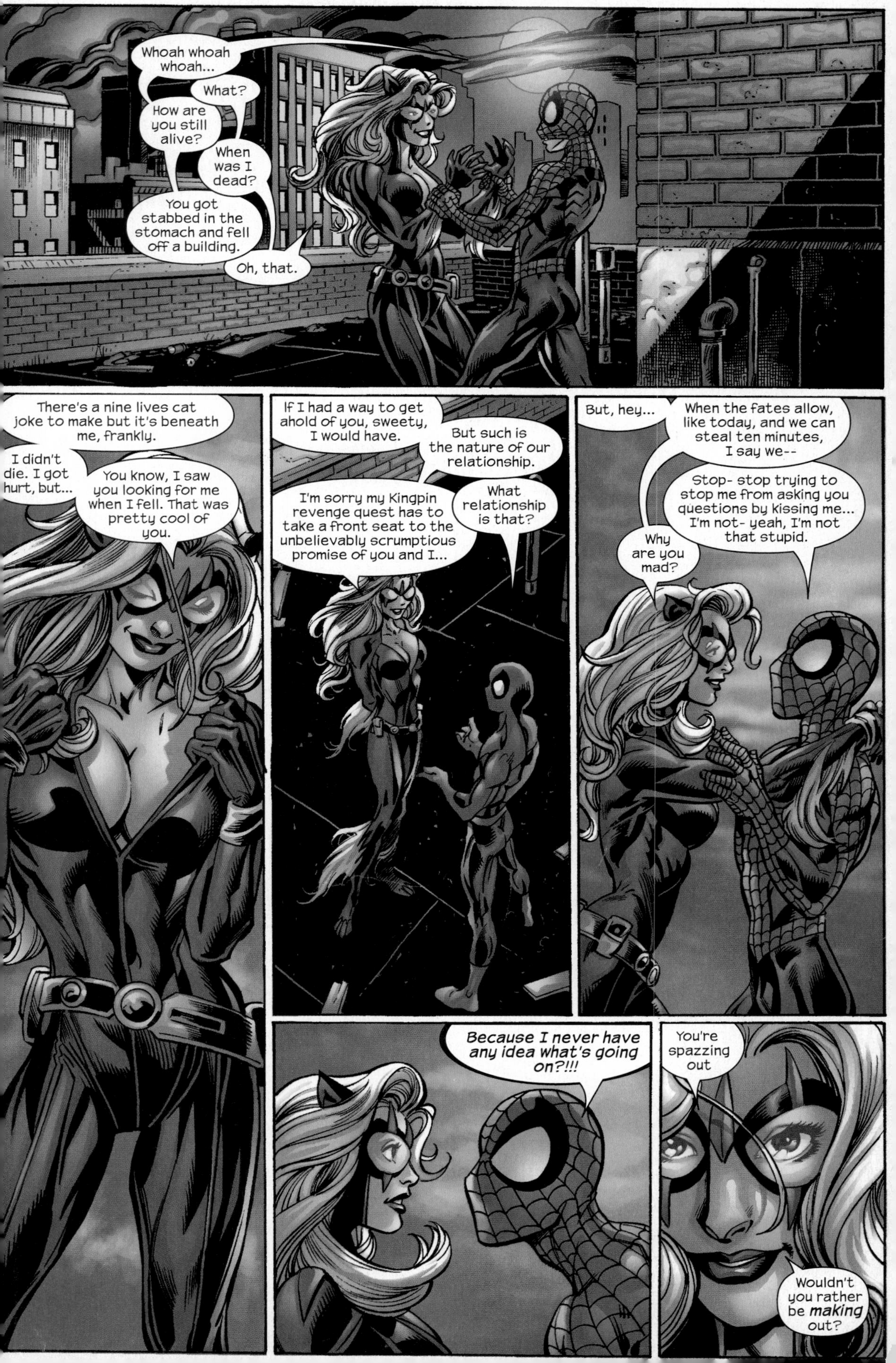
Whoah whoah whoah...
What?
How are you still alive?
When was I dead?
You got stabbed in the stomach and fell off a building.
Oh, that.
There's a nine lives cat joke to make but it's beneath me, frankly.
I didn't die. I got hurt, but...
You know, I saw you looking for me when I fell. That was pretty cool of you.
If I had a way to get ahold of you, sweety, I would have.
But such is the nature of our relationship.
I'm sorry my Kingpin revenge quest has to take a front seat to the unbelievably scrumptious promise of you and I...
What relationship is that?
But, hey...
When the fates allow, like today, and we can steal ten minutes, I say we--
Stop- stop trying to stop me from asking you questions by kissing me... I'm not- yeah, I'm not that stupid.
Why are you mad?
Because I never have any idea what's going on?!!!
You're spazzing out
Wouldn't you rather be making out?

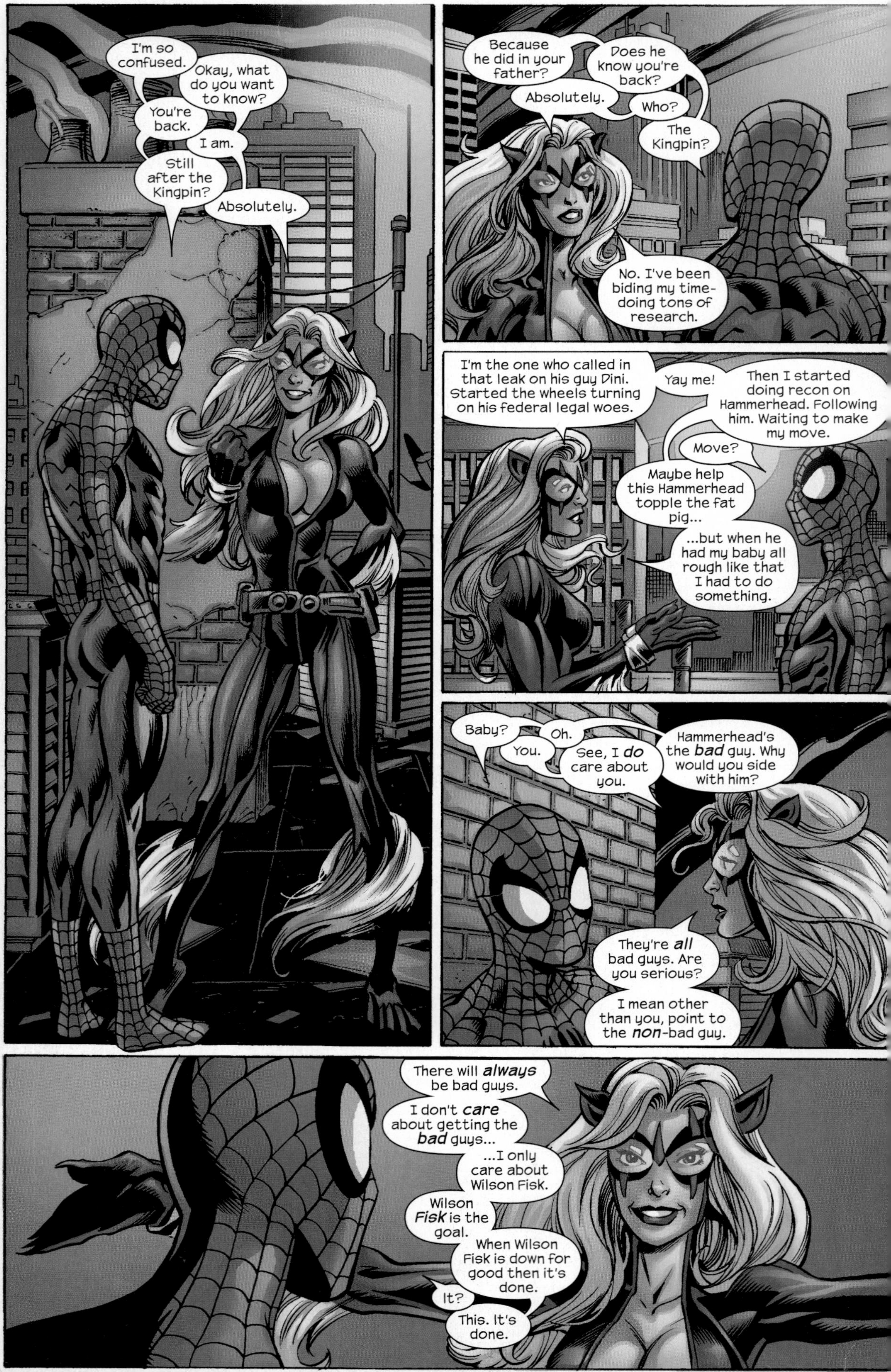

I'm so confused.
Okay, what do you want to know?
You're back.
I am.
Still after the Kingpin?
Absolutely.
Because he did in your father?
Absolutely.
Does he know you're back?
Who?
The Kingpin?
No. I've been biding my time-doing tons of research.
I'm the one who called in that leak on his guy Dini. Started the wheels turning on his federal legal woes.
Yay me!
Then I started doing recon on Hammerhead. Following him. Waiting to make my move.
Move?
Maybe help this Hammerhead topple the fat pig...
...but when he had my baby all rough like that I had to do something.
Baby?
Oh.
You.
See, I do care about you.
Hammerhead's the bad guy. Why would you side with him?
They're all bad guys. Are you serious?
I mean other than you, point to the non-bad guy.
There will always be bad guys.
I don't care about getting the bad guys...
...I only care about Wilson Fisk.
Wilson Fisk is the goal.
When Wilson Fisk is down for good then it's done.
It?
This. It's done.

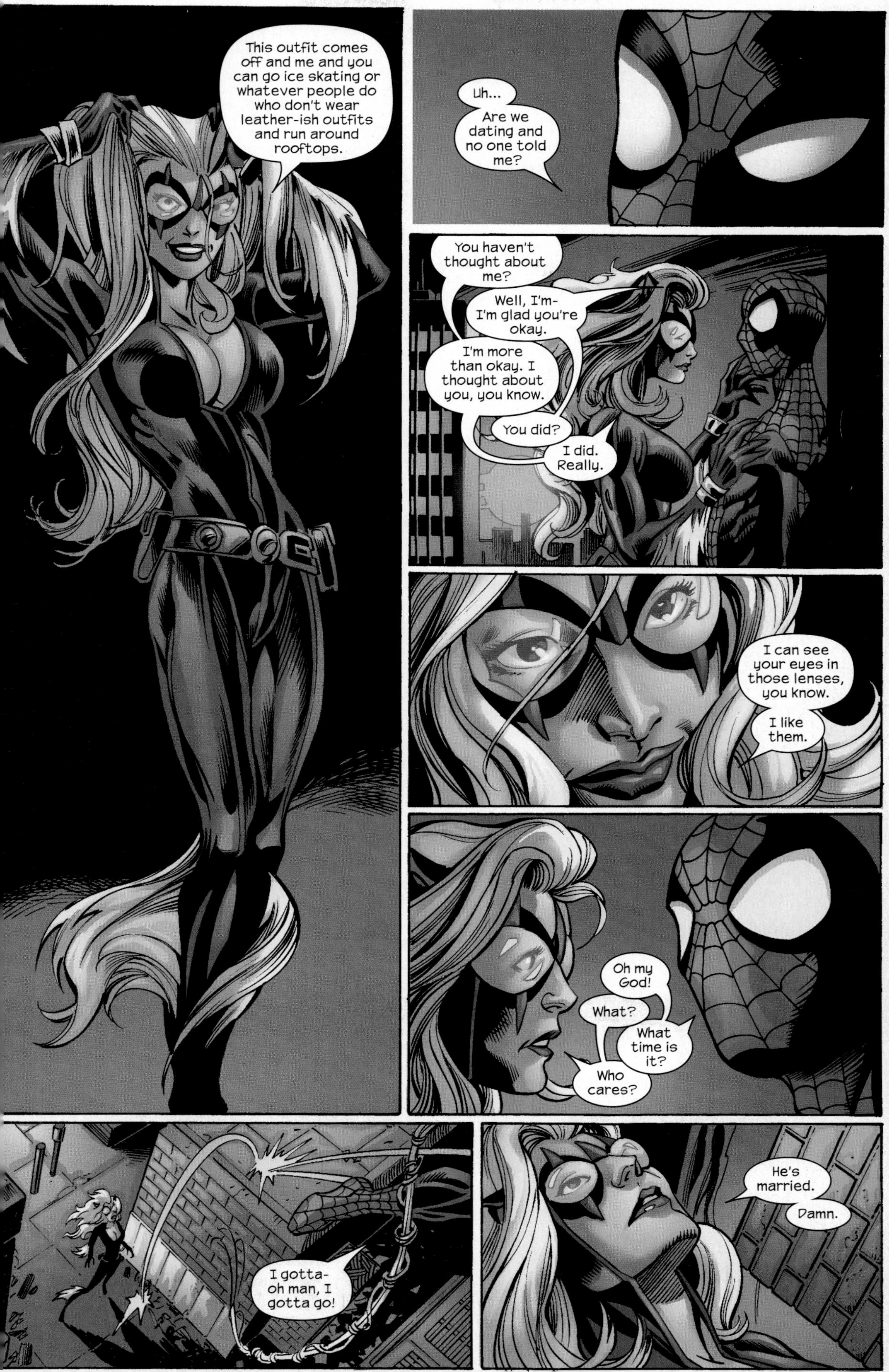
This outfit comes off and me and you can go ice skating or whatever people do who don't wear leather-ish outfits and run around rooftops.
Uh...
Are we dating and no one told me?
You haven't thought about me?
Well, I'm- I'm glad you're okay.
I'm more than okay. I thought about you, you know.
You did?
I did. Really.
I can see your eyes in those lenses, you know.
I like them.
Oh my God!
What?
What time is it?
Who cares?
I gotta- oh man, I gotta go!
He's married.
Damn.

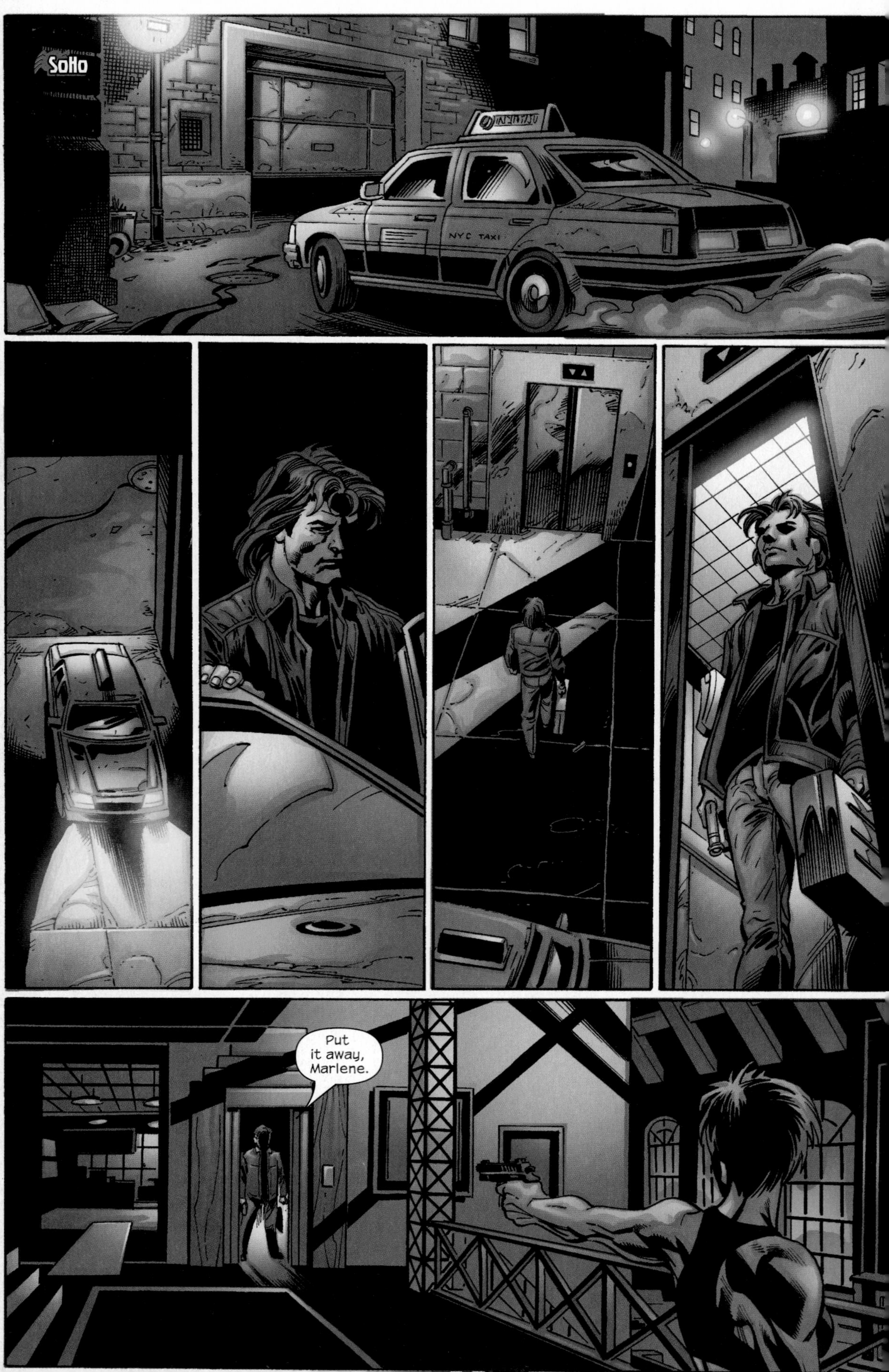
SoHo
NYC TAXI
Put it away, Marlene.

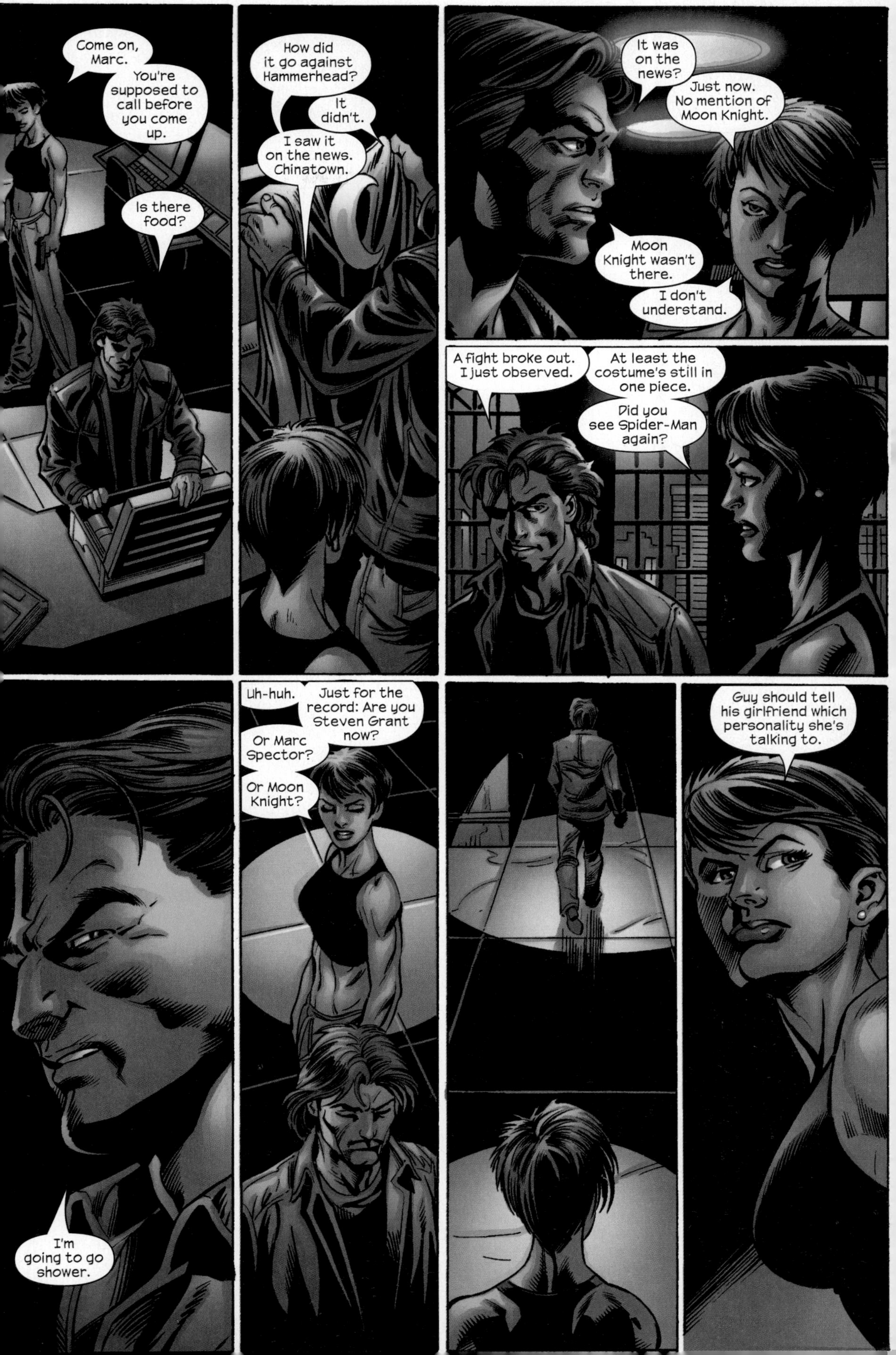
Come on, Marc.
You're supposed to call before you come up.
Is there food?
How did it go against Hammerhead?
It didn't.
I saw it on the news. Chinatown.
It was on the news?
Just now. No mention of Moon Knight.
Moon Knight wasn't there.
I don't understand.
A fight broke out. I just observed.
At least the costume's still in one piece.
Did you see Spider-Man again?
I'm going to go shower.
Uh-huh.
Just for the record: Are you Steven Grant now?
Or Marc Spector?
Or Moon Knight?
Guy should tell his girlfriend which personality she's talking to.

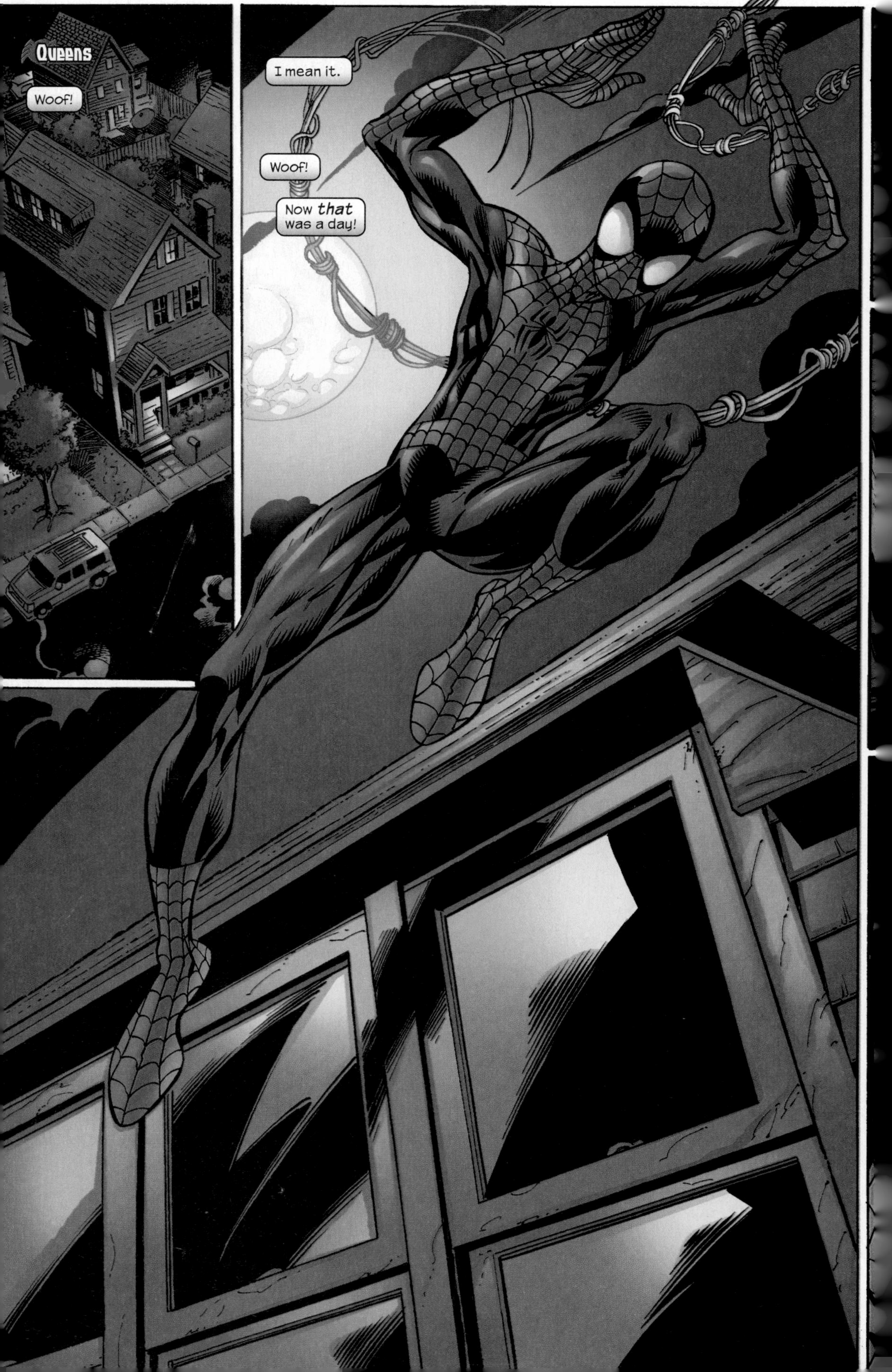
Queens
Woof!
I mean it.
Woof!
Now *that* was a day!

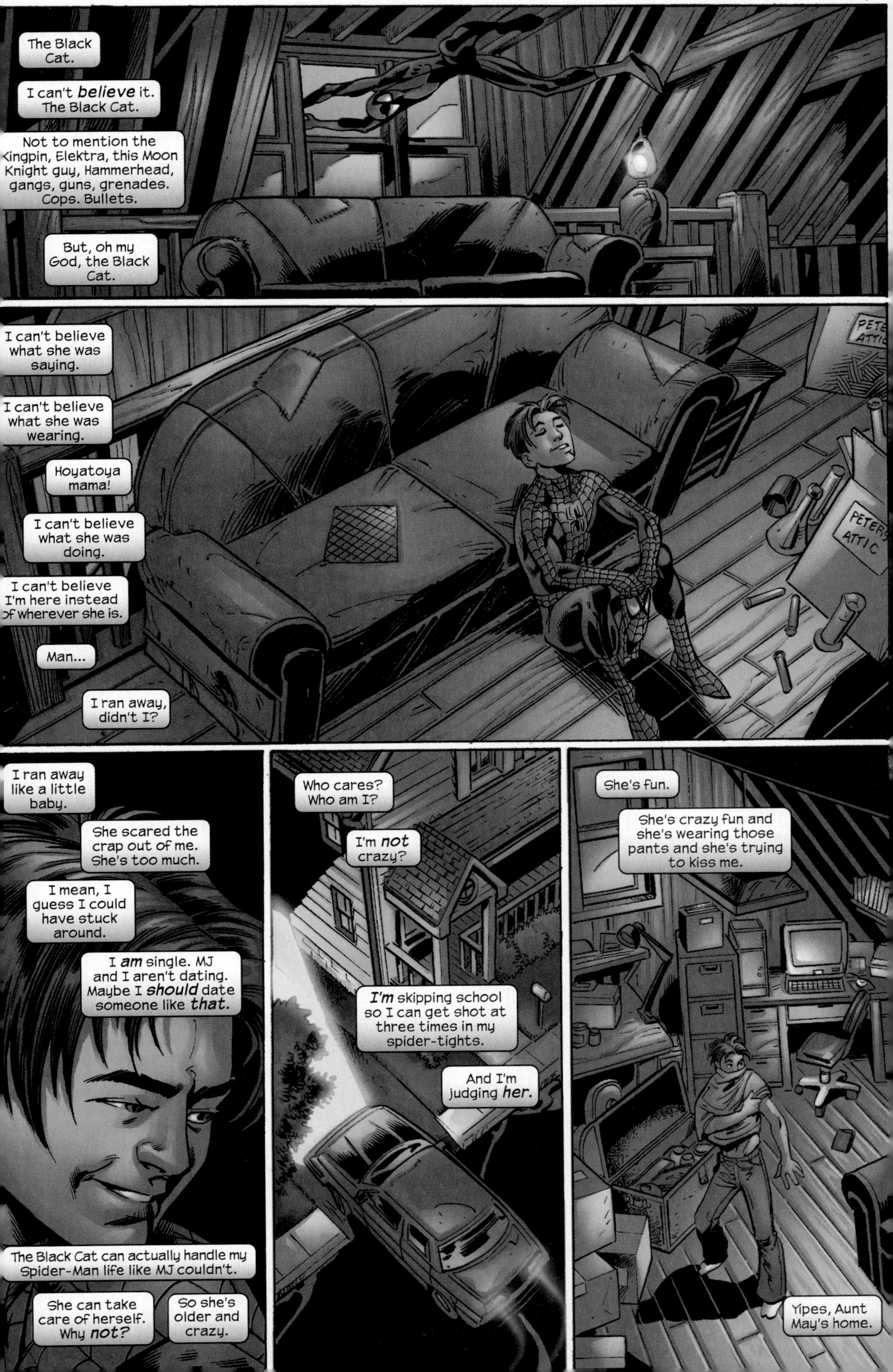
The Black Cat.
I can't *believe* it. The Black Cat.
Not to mention the Kingpin, Elektra, this Moon Knight guy, Hammerhead, gangs, guns, grenades. Cops. Bullets.
But, oh my God, the Black Cat.
I can't believe what she was saying.
I can't believe what she was wearing.
Hoyatoya mama!
I can't believe what she was doing.
I can't believe I'm here instead of wherever she is.
Man...
I ran away, didn't I?
I ran away like a little baby.
She scared the crap out of me. She's too much.
I mean, I guess I could have stuck around.
I *am* single. MJ and I aren't dating. Maybe I *should* date someone like *that.*
The Black Cat can actually handle my Spider-Man life like MJ couldn't.
She can take care of herself. Why *not?*
So she's older and crazy.
Who cares? Who am I?
I'm *not* crazy?
I'm skipping school so I can get shot at three times in my spider-tights.
And I'm judging *her.*
She's fun.
She's crazy fun and she's wearing those pants and she's trying to kiss me.
Yipes, Aunt May's home.

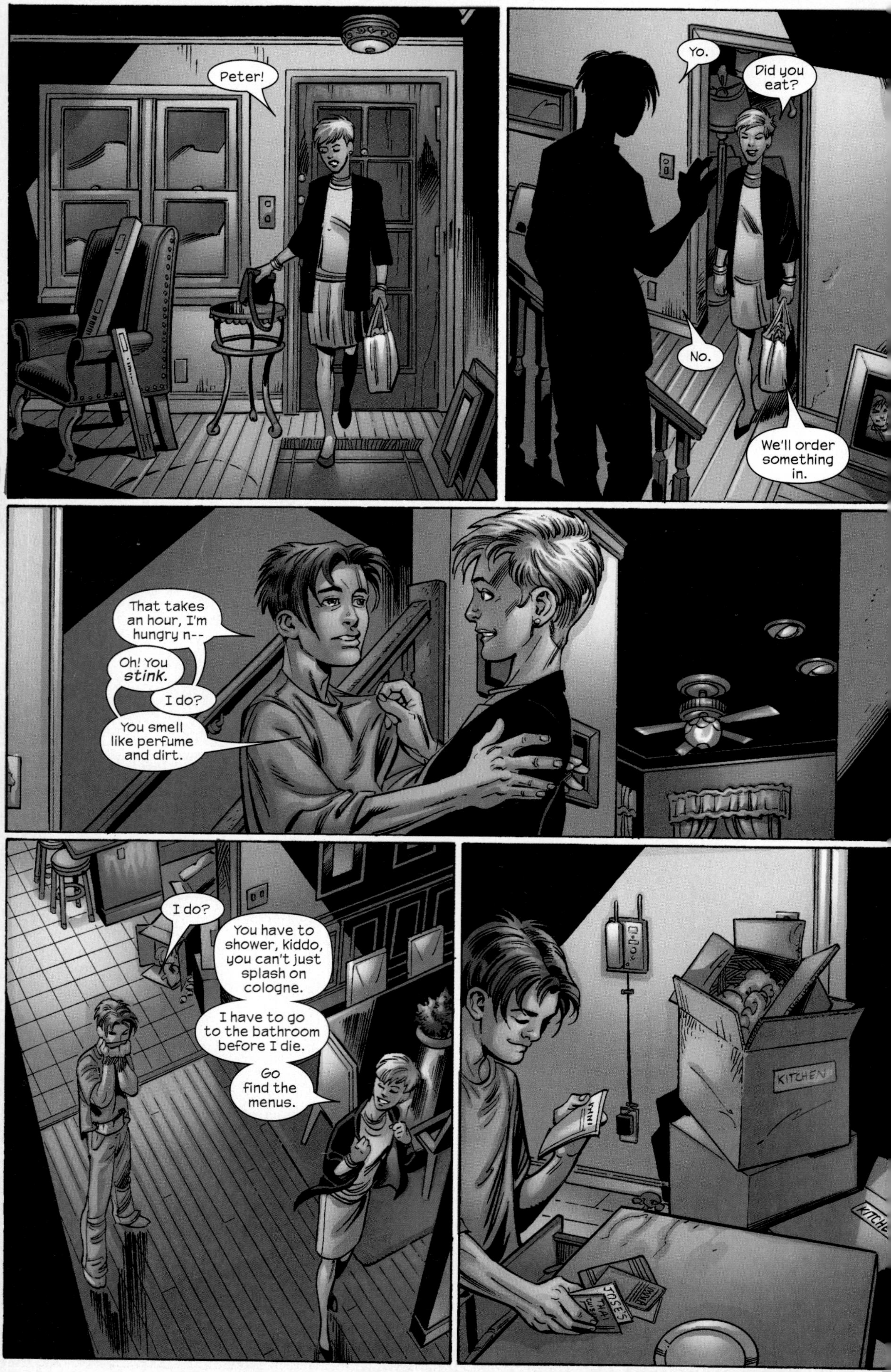
Peter!
Yo.
Did you eat?
No.
We'll order something in.
That takes an hour, I'm hungry n--
Oh! You *stink.*
I do?
You smell like perfume and dirt.
I do?
You have to shower, kiddo, you can't just splash on cologne.
I have to go to the bathroom before I die.
Go find the menus.
KITCHEN
JOSE'S

You have one message.

Ms Parker, this is Peter's principal. Um, Peter up and left class in the middle of the day. Could you call me so we can--

BEEP

Message deleted.

You want Chinese or pizza?

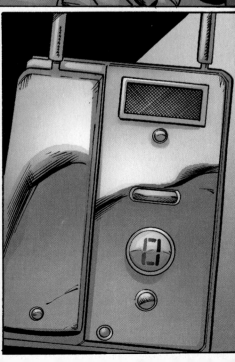

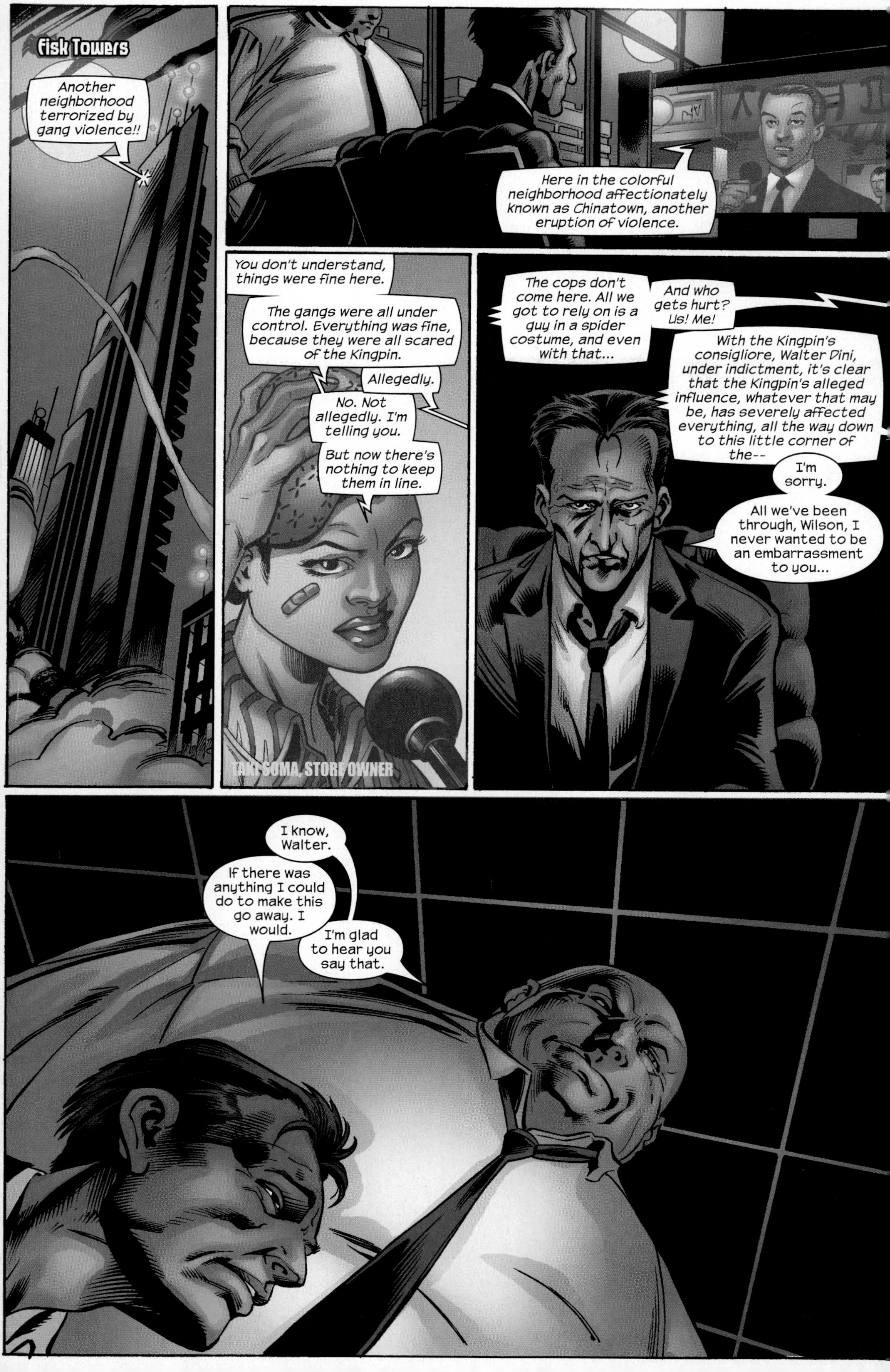
Fisk Towers
Another neighborhood terrorized by gang violence!!
Here in the colorful neighborhood affectionately known as Chinatown, another eruption of violence.
You don't understand, things were fine here.
The gangs were all under control. Everything was fine, because they were all scared of the Kingpin.
Allegedly.
No. Not allegedly. I'm telling you.
But now there's nothing to keep them in line.
TAKI SOMA, STORE OWNER
The cops don't come here. All we got to rely on is a guy in a spider costume, and even with that...
And who gets hurt? Us! Me!
With the Kingpin's consigliore, Walter Dini, under indictment, it's clear that the Kingpin's alleged influence, whatever that may be, has severely affected everything, all the way down to this little corner of the--
I'm sorry.
All we've been through, Wilson, I never wanted to be an embarrassment to you...
I know, Walter.
If there was anything I could do to make this go away. I would.
I'm glad to hear you say that.

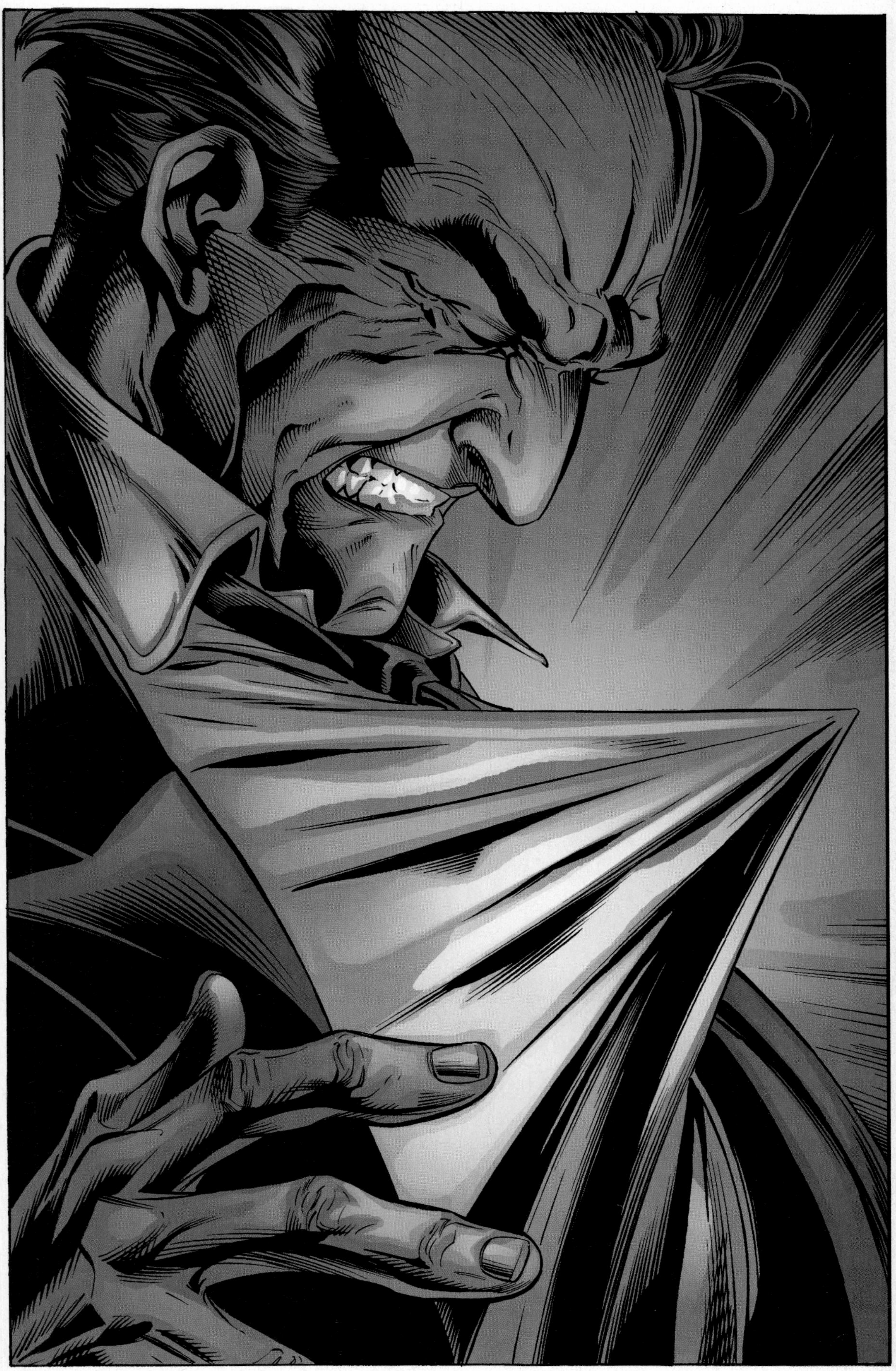

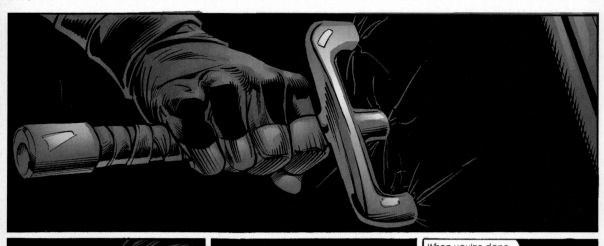

Elektra, Make it disappear. The chair as well.

Yes, sir.

When you're done, report back to me.

The gloves are off.

Hammerhead, Moon Knight, Spider-Man...

It's time to clean this up.

Hope you're ready for the task.

I am.

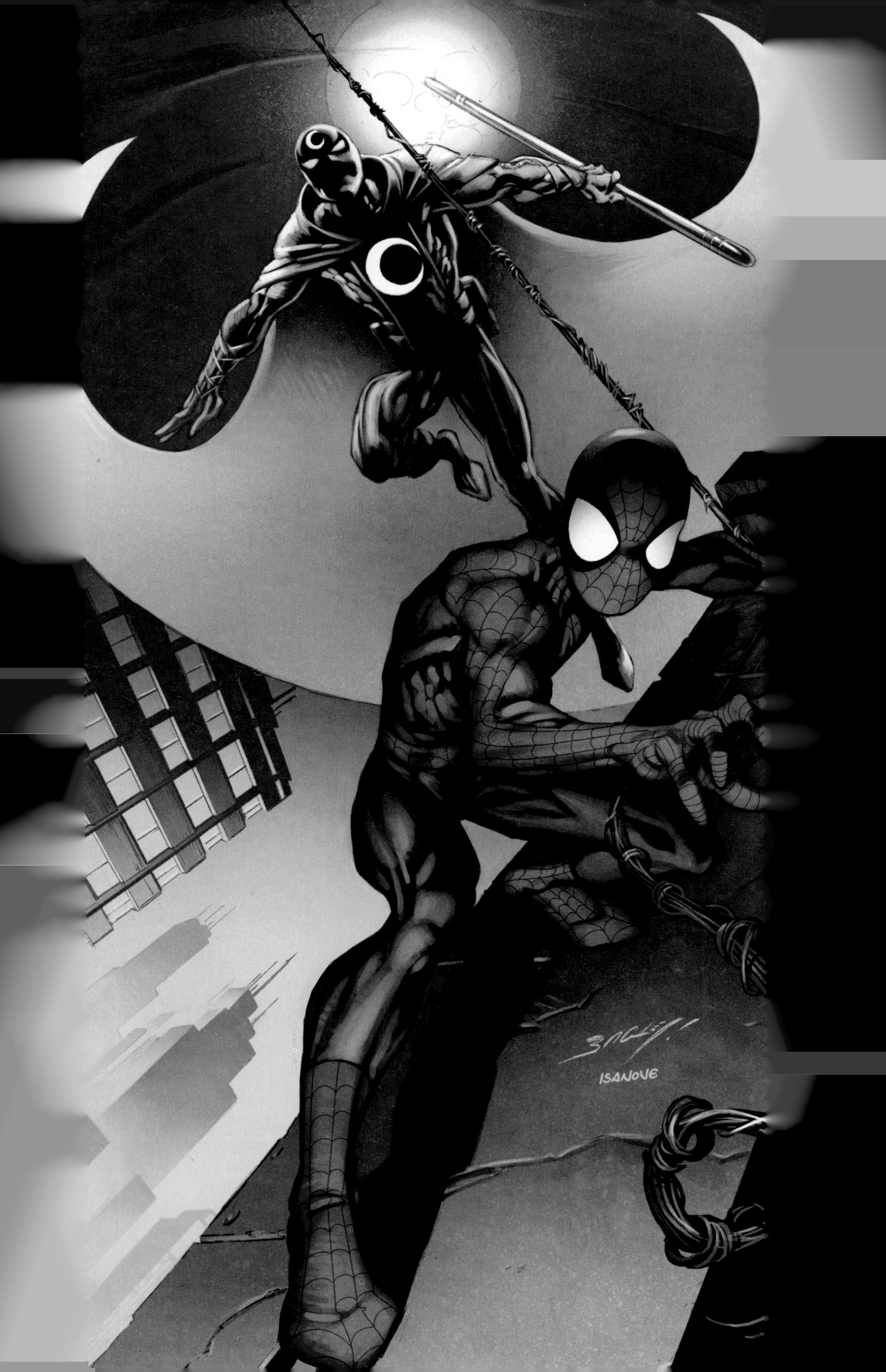
ISANOVE

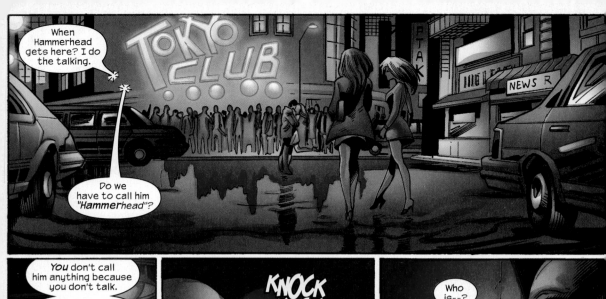

When Hammerhead gets here? I do the talking.

Do we have to call him "Hammerhead"?

You don't call him anything because you don't talk.

If he's the new Kingpin, we need to set the tone for our relationship early.

I'm not giving in to this nickname crap.

You don't talk.

"Hammerhead."

You're still talking. *Stop.*

KNOCK
KNOCK

Okay, okay. This is it.

Who is--?

SHUCK

CHANG

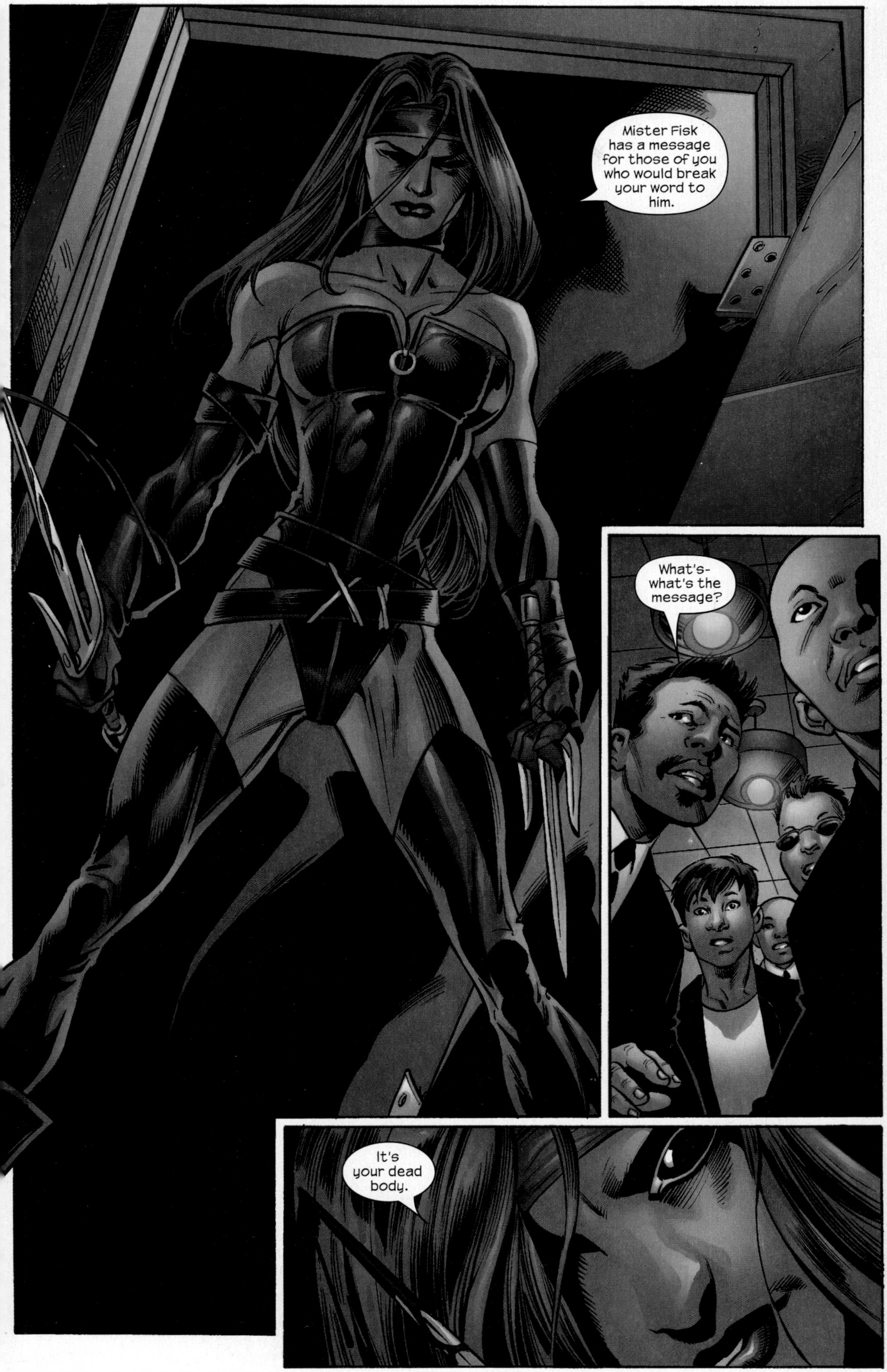
Mister Fisk has a message for those of you who would break your word to him.
What's- what's the message?
It's your dead body.

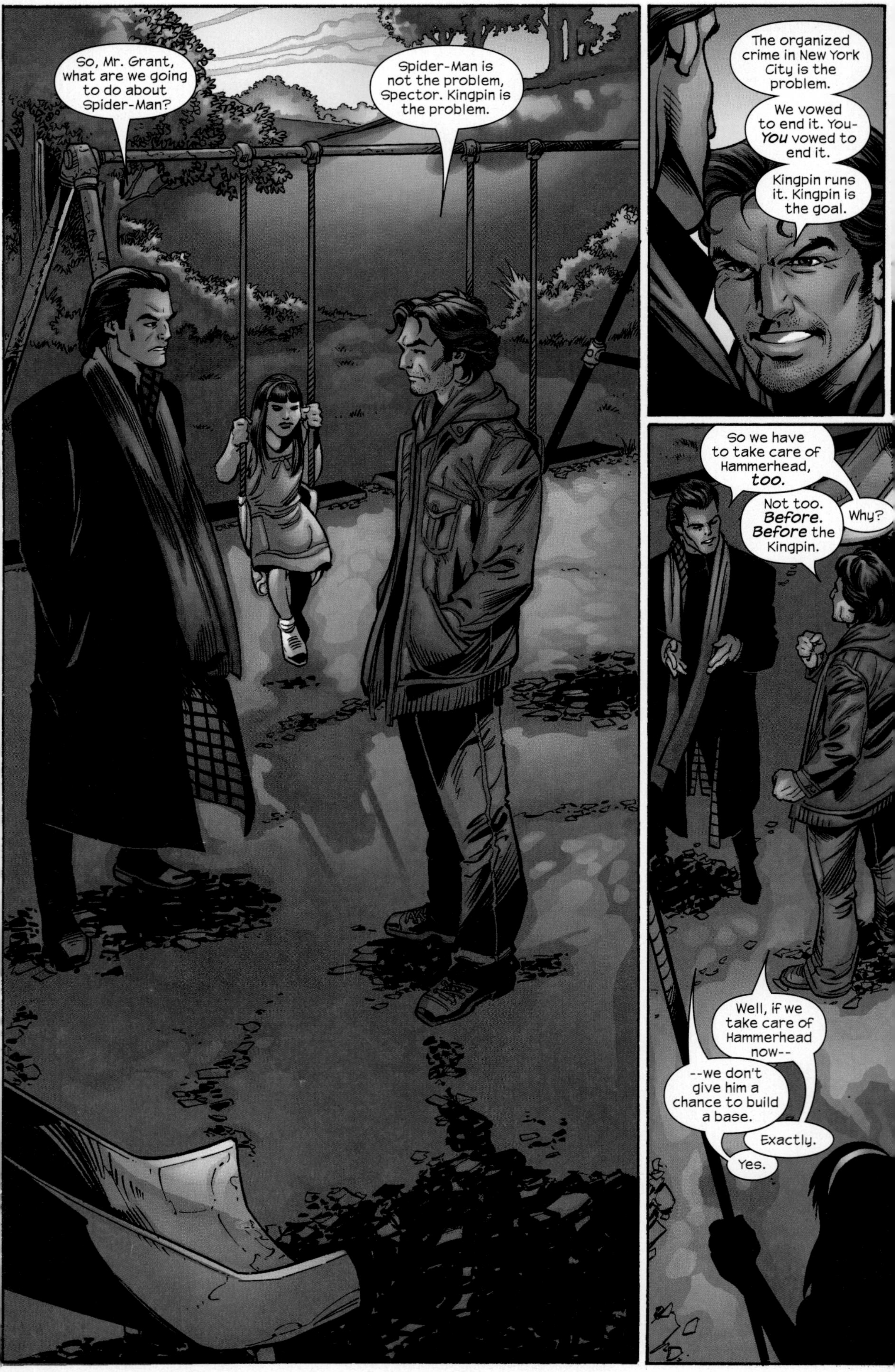

So, Mr. Grant, what are we going to do about Spider-Man?
Spider-Man is not the problem, Spector. Kingpin is the problem.
The organized crime in New York City is the problem.
We vowed to end it. You- *You* vowed to end it.
Kingpin runs it. Kingpin is the goal.
So we have to take care of Hammerhead, ***too.***
Not too. ***Before. Before*** the Kingpin.
Why?
Well, if we take care of Hammerhead now--
--we don't give him a chance to build a base.
Exactly.
Yes.

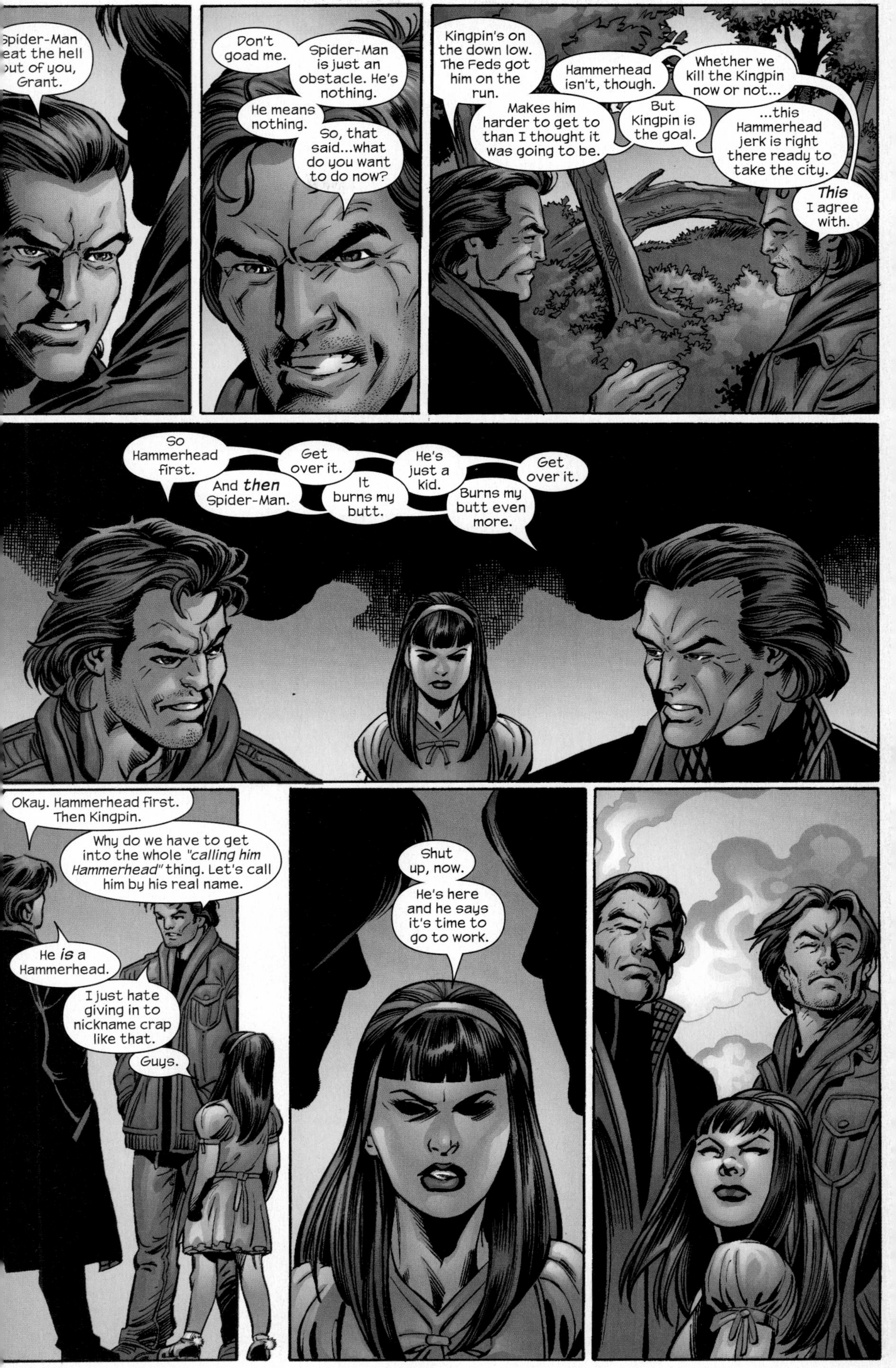
Spider-Man beat the hell out of you, Grant.
Don't goad me.
Spider-Man is just an obstacle. He's nothing.
He means nothing.
So, that said...what do you want to do now?
Kingpin's on the down low. The Feds got him on the run.
Makes him harder to get to than I thought it was going to be.
Hammerhead isn't, though.
But Kingpin is the goal.
Whether we kill the Kingpin now or not...
...this Hammerhead jerk is right there ready to take the city.
This I agree with.
So Hammerhead first.
And *then* Spider-Man.
Get over it.
It burns my butt.
He's just a kid.
Burns my butt even more.
Get over it.
Okay. Hammerhead first. Then Kingpin.
Why do we have to get into the whole *"calling him Hammerhead"* thing. Let's call him by his real name.
He *is* a Hammerhead.
I just hate giving in to nickname crap like that.
Guys.
Shut up, now.
He's here and he says it's time to go to work.

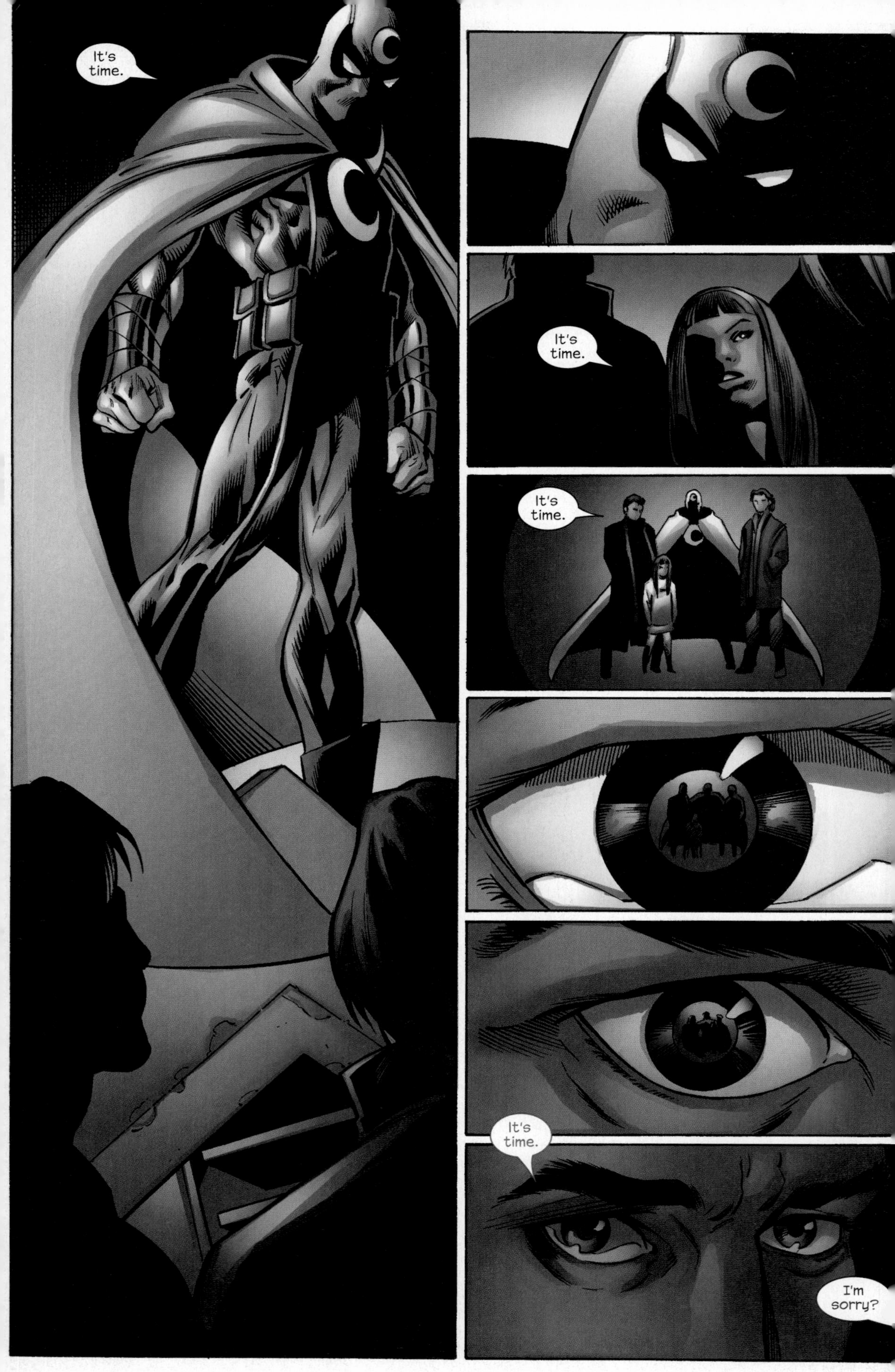
It's time.
It's time.
It's time.
It's time.
I'm sorry?

Mr. Spector, did you say something?

Hmmm?

You whispered something, sir. *"It's time"*?

Let's break for lunch. I have a meeting downtown.

You do? But your schedule--

Thanks, everyone.

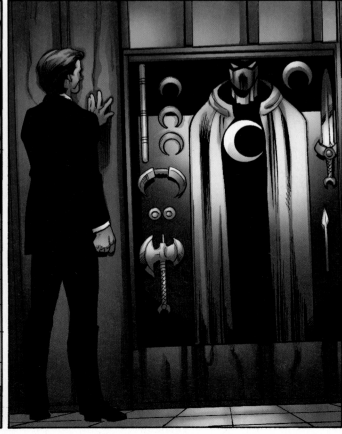

It's time.

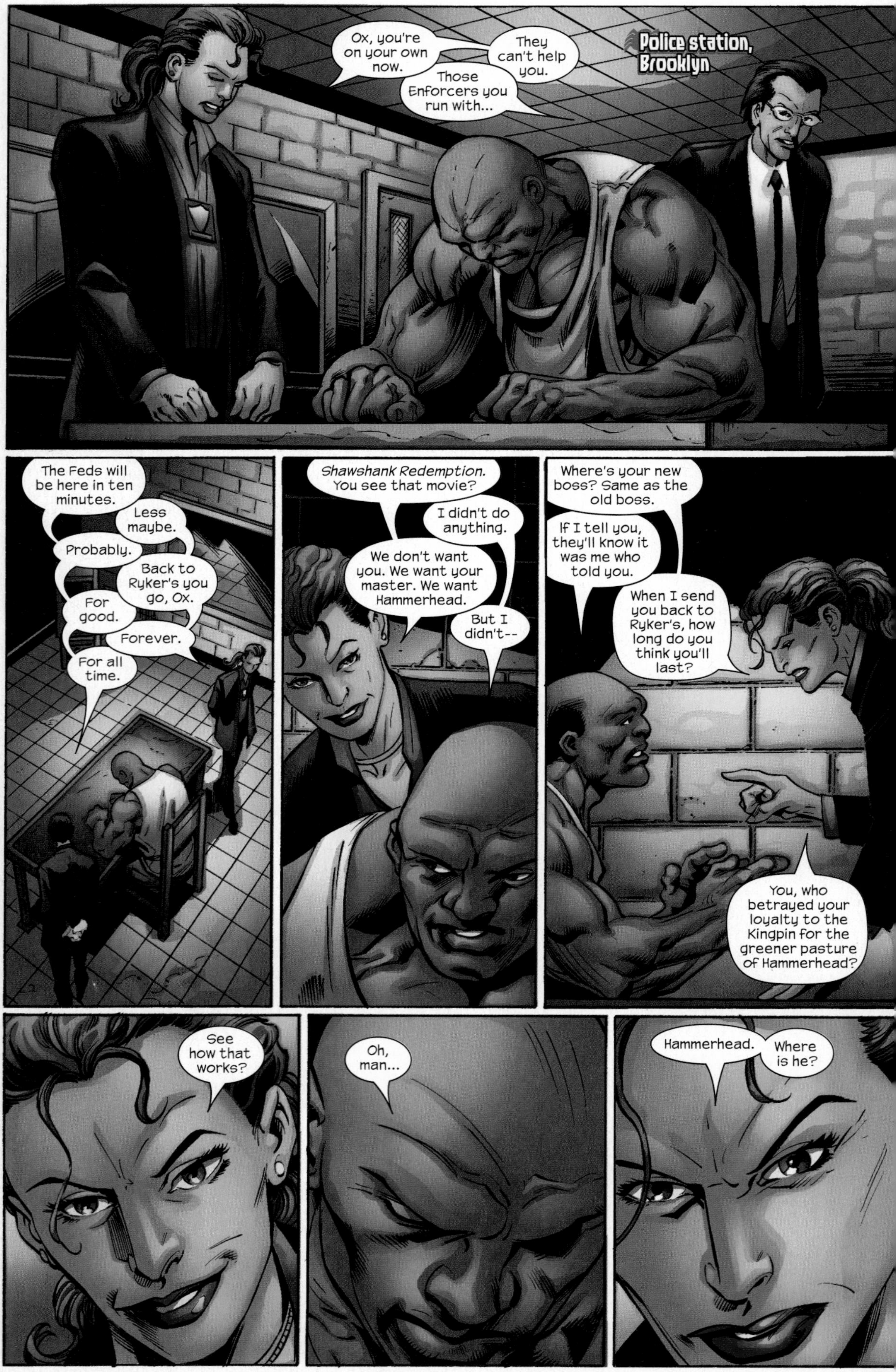
Police station, Brooklyn
Ox, you're on your own now.
They can't help you.
Those Enforcers you run with...
The Feds will be here in ten minutes.
Less maybe.
Probably.
Back to Ryker's you go, Ox.
For good.
Forever.
For all time.
Shawshank Redemption. You see that movie?
I didn't do anything.
We don't want you. We want your master. We want Hammerhead.
But I didn't--
Where's your new boss? Same as the old boss.
If I tell you, they'll know it was me who told you.
When I send you back to Ryker's, how long do you think you'll last?
You, who betrayed your loyalty to the Kingpin for the greener pasture of Hammerhead?
See how that works?
Oh, man...
Hammerhead.
Where is he?

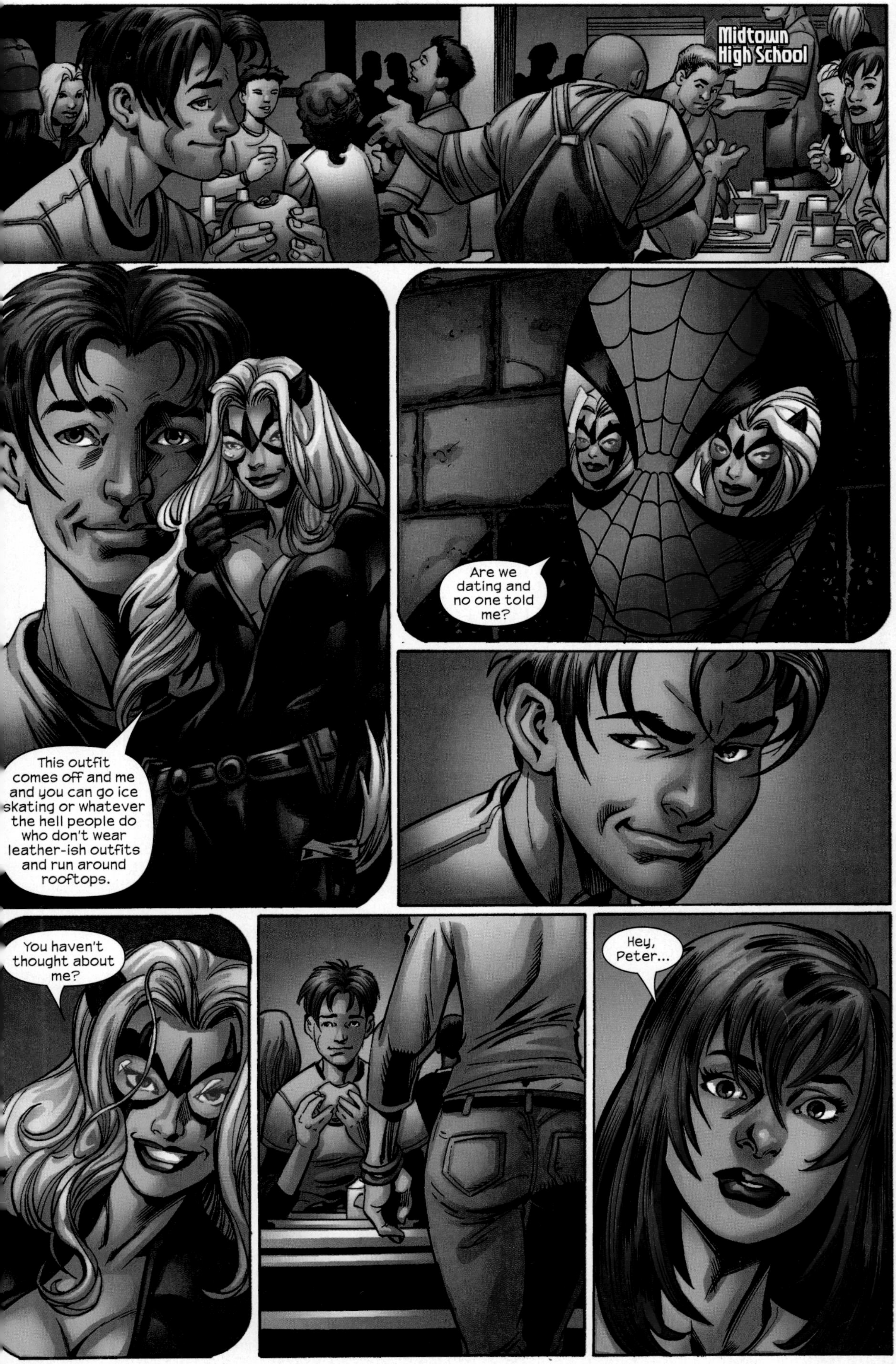

Midtown High School
Are we dating and no one told me?
This outfit comes off and me and you can go ice skating or whatever the hell people do who don't wear leather-ish outfits and run around rooftops.
You haven't thought about me?
Hey, Peter...

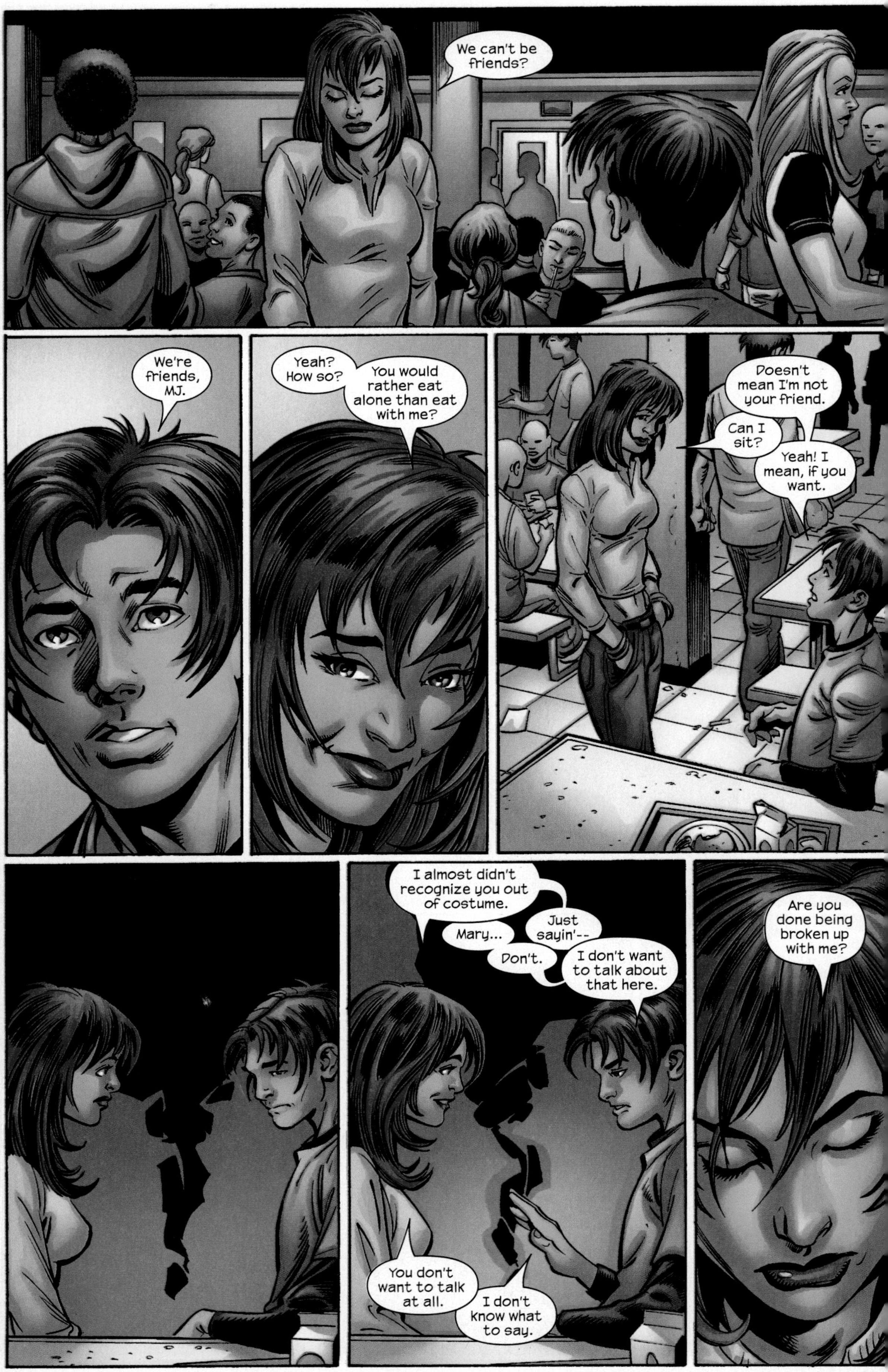
We can't be friends?
We're friends, MJ.
Yeah? How so?
You would rather eat alone than eat with me?
Doesn't mean I'm not your friend.
Can I sit?
Yeah! I mean, if you want.
I almost didn't recognize you out of costume.
Just sayin'--
Mary...
Don't.
I don't want to talk about that here.
You don't want to talk at all.
I don't know what to say.
Are you done being broken up with me?

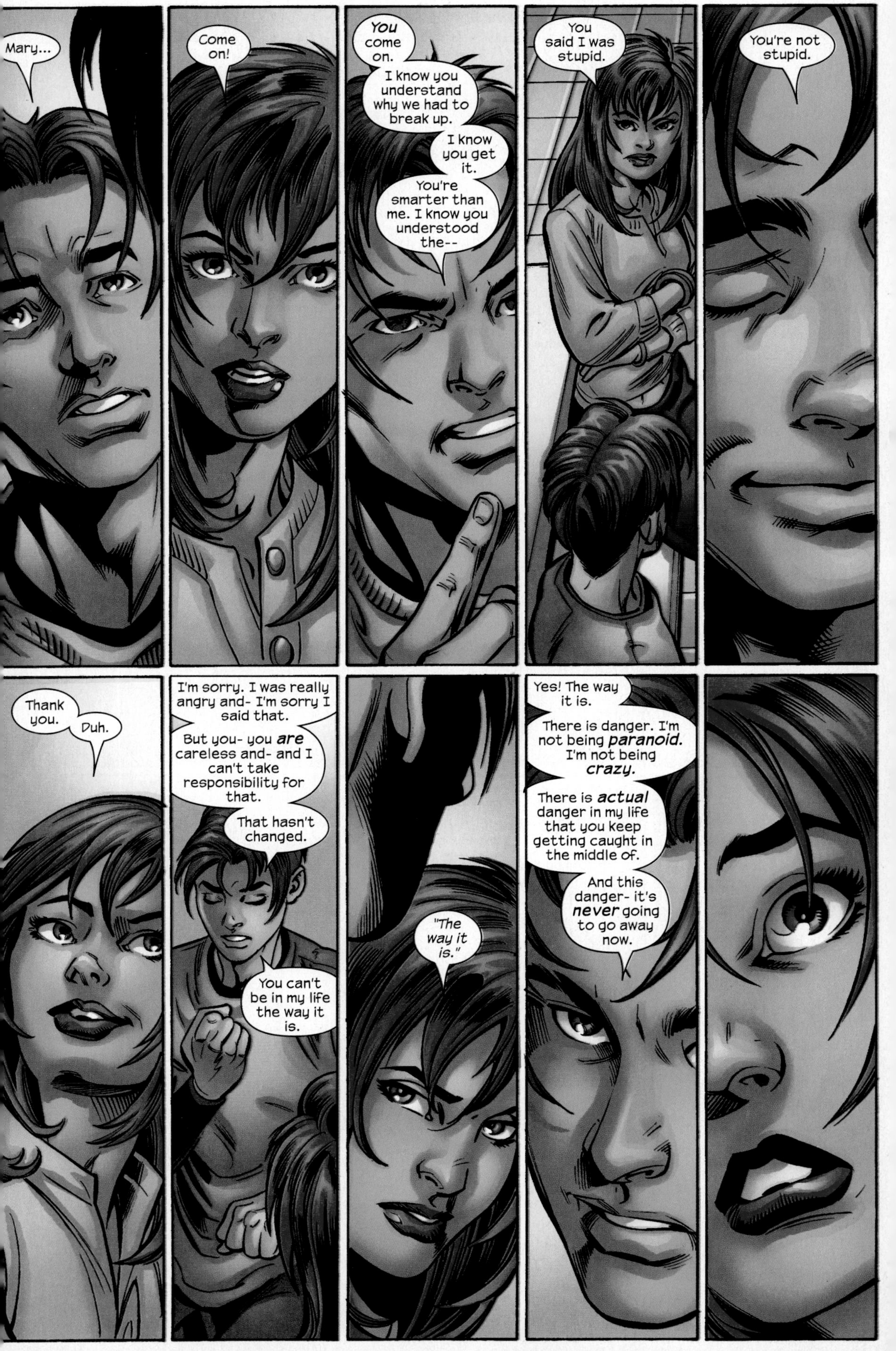
Mary...
Come on!
You come on.
I know you understand why we had to break up.
I know you get it.
You're smarter than me. I know you understood the--
You said I was stupid.
You're not stupid.
Thank you.
Duh.
I'm sorry. I was really angry and- I'm sorry I said that.
But you- you are careless and- and I can't take responsibility for that.
That hasn't changed.
You can't be in my life the way it is.
"The way it is."
Yes! The way it is.
There is danger. I'm not being paranoid. I'm not being crazy.
There is actual danger in my life that you keep getting caught in the middle of.
And this danger- it's never going to go away now.

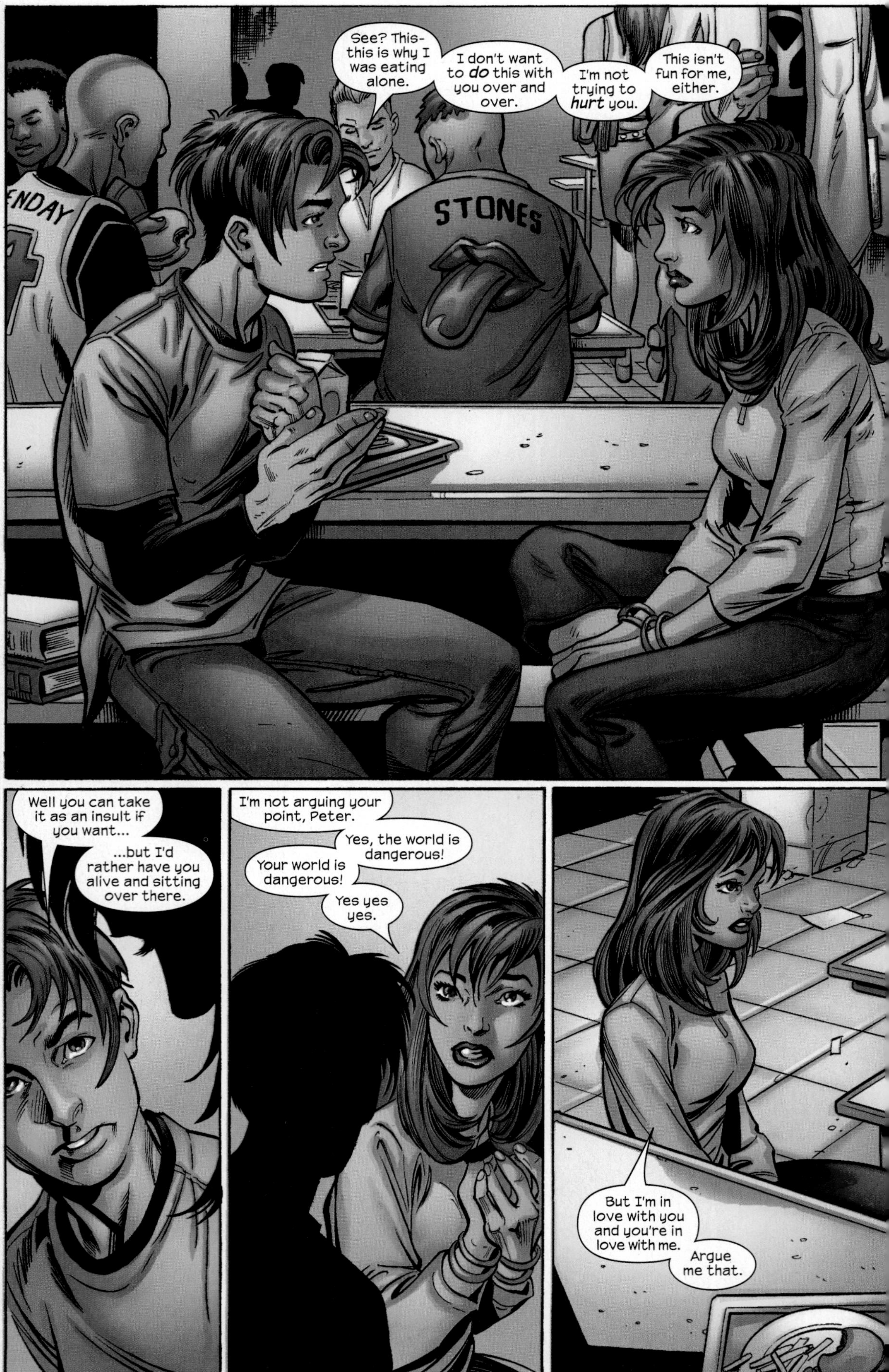

ENDAY
STONES
See? This- this is why I was eating alone.
I don't want to *do* this with you over and over.
I'm not trying to *hurt* you.
This isn't fun for me, either.
Well you can take it as an insult if you want...
...but I'd rather have you alive and sitting over there.
I'm not arguing your point, Peter.
Yes, the world is dangerous!
Your world is dangerous!
Yes yes yes.
But I'm in love with you and you're in love with me.
Argue me that.

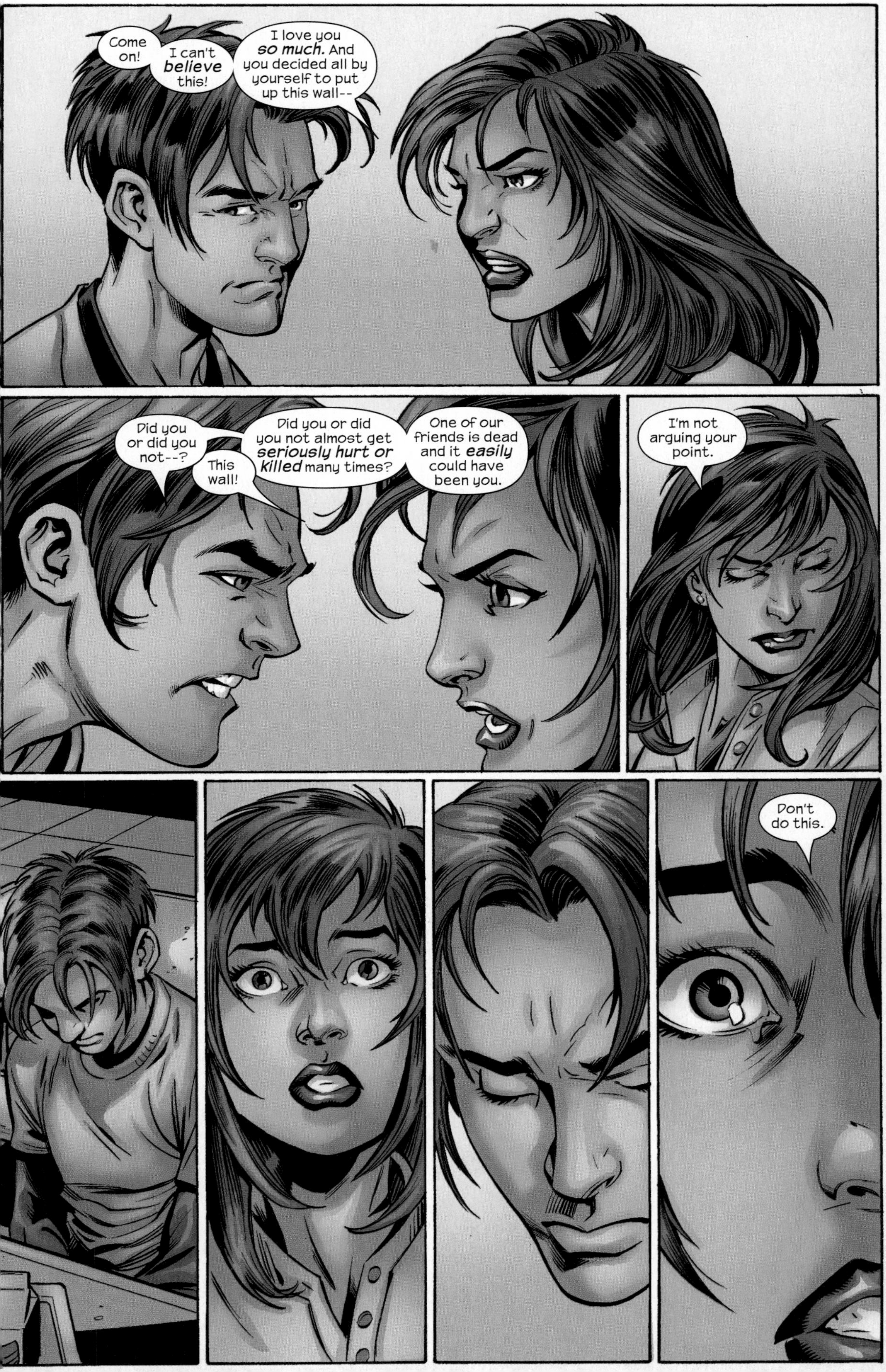
Come on!
I can't *believe* this!
I love you *so much.* And you decided all by yourself to put up this wall--
Did you or did you not--?
This wall!
Did you or did you not almost get *seriously hurt or killed* many times?
One of our friends is dead and it *easily* could have been you.
I'm not arguing your point.
Don't do this.

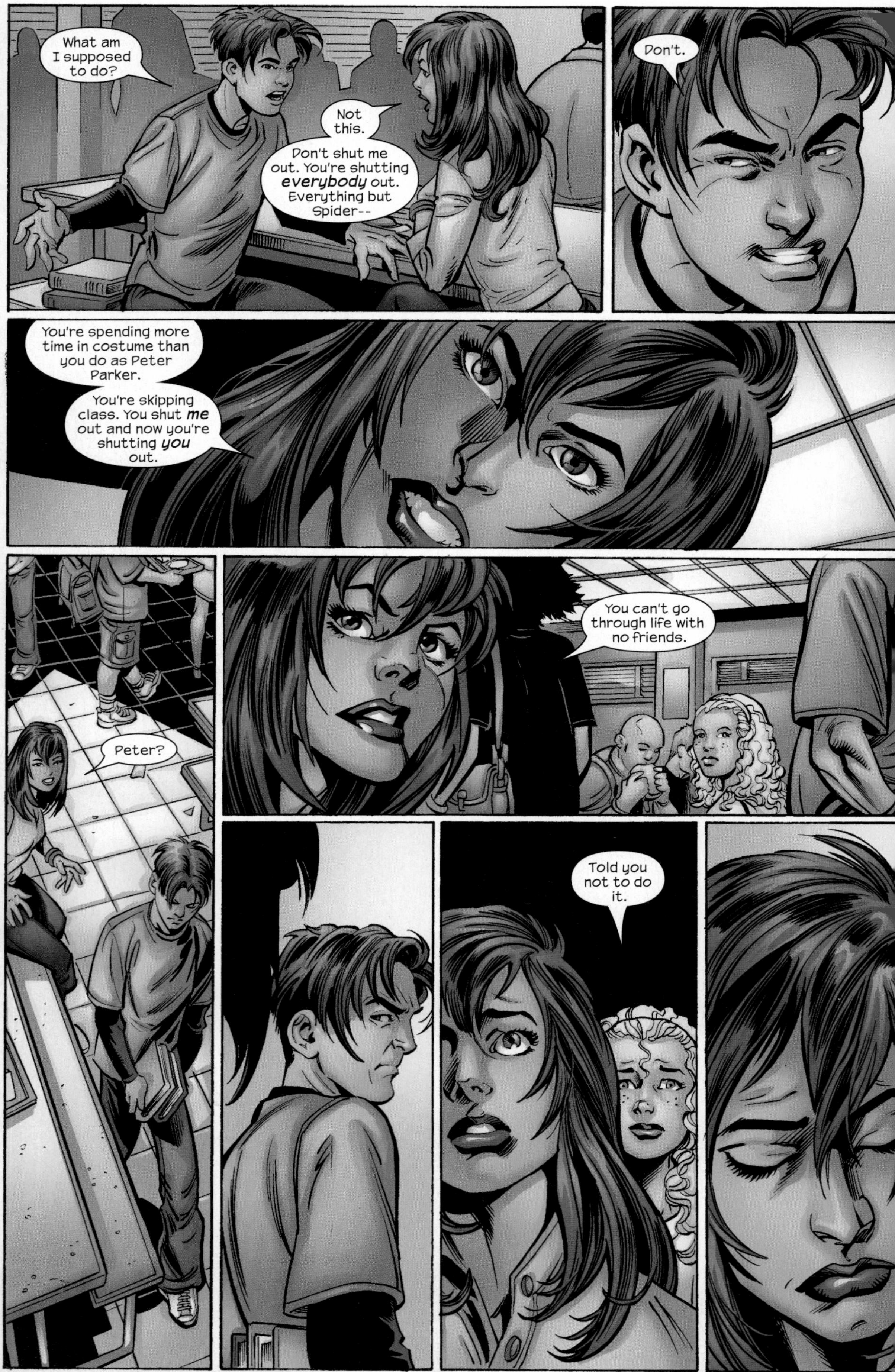
What am I supposed to do?
Not this.
Don't shut me out. You're shutting *everybody* out. Everything but Spider--
Don't.
You're spending more time in costume than you do as Peter Parker.
You're skipping class. You shut *me* out and now you're shutting *you* out.
Peter?
You can't go through life with no friends.
Told you not to do it.

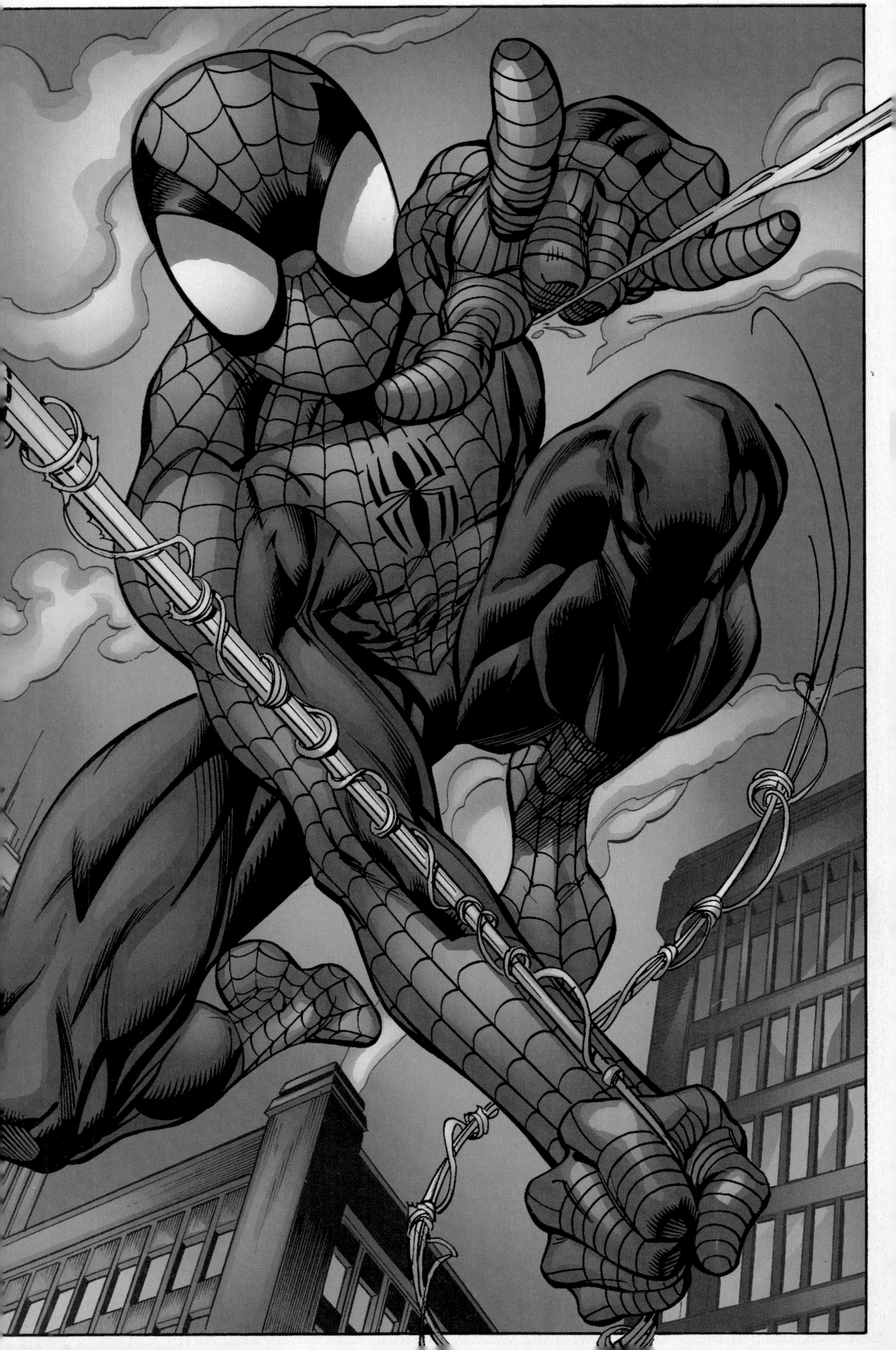

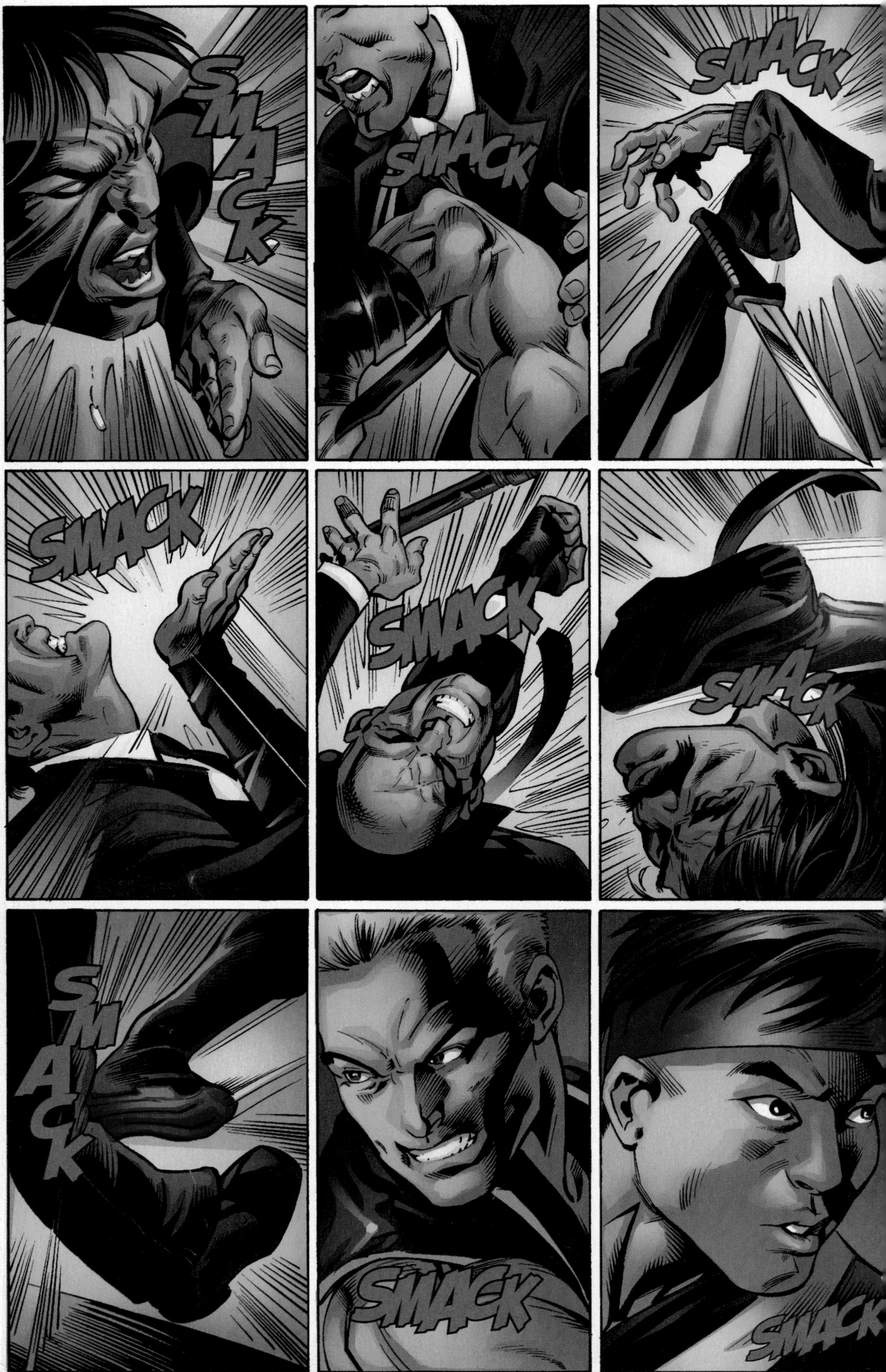
SMACK
SMACK
SMACK
SMACK
SMACK
SMACK
SMACK
SMACK
SMACK

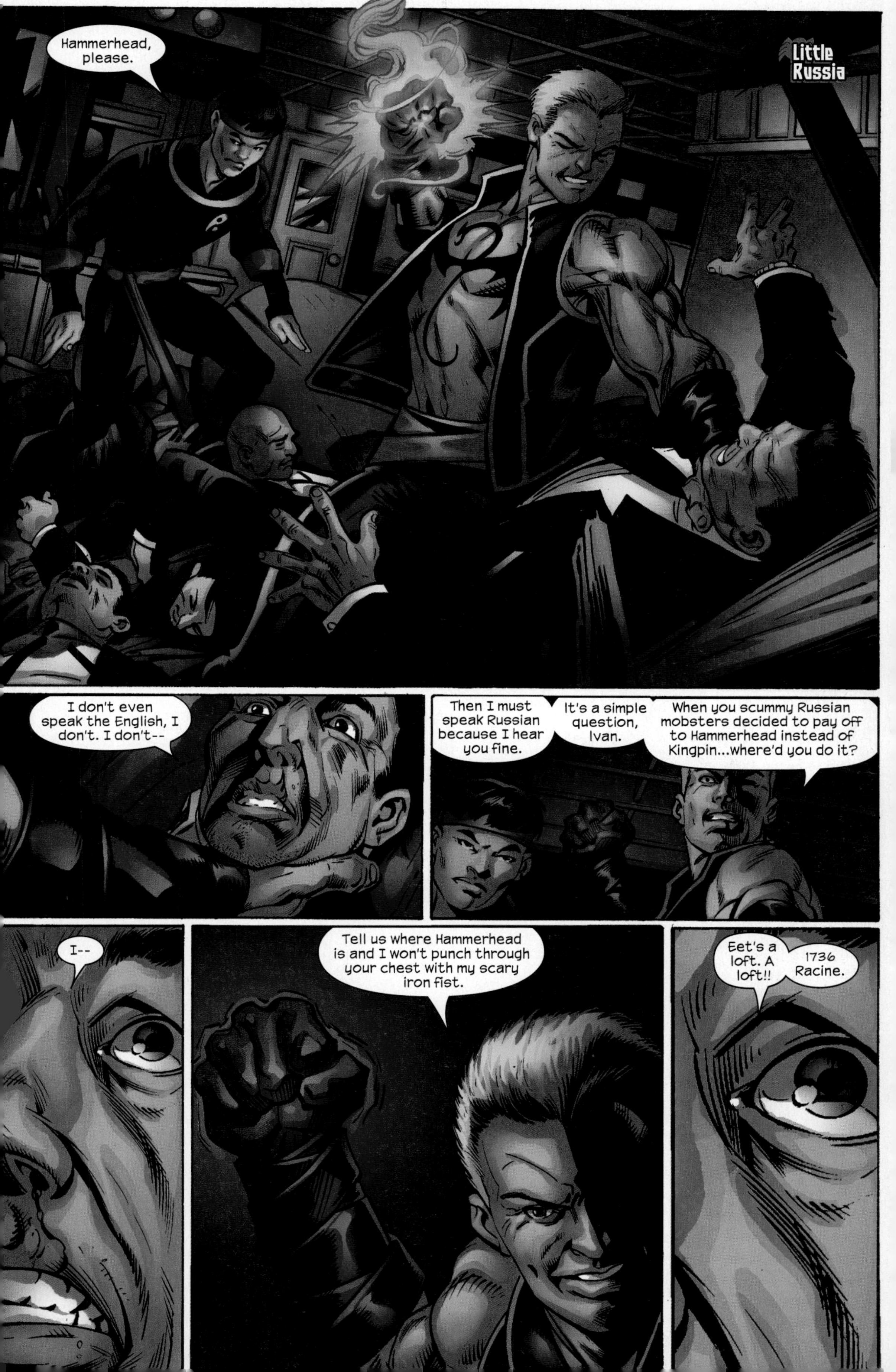
Hammerhead, please.
Little Russia
I don't even speak the English, I don't. I don't--
Then I must speak Russian because I hear you fine.
It's a simple question, Ivan.
When you scummy Russian mobsters decided to pay off to Hammerhead instead of Kingpin...where'd you do it?
I--
Tell us where Hammerhead is and I won't punch through your chest with my scary iron fist.
Eet's a loft. A loft!!
1736 Racine.

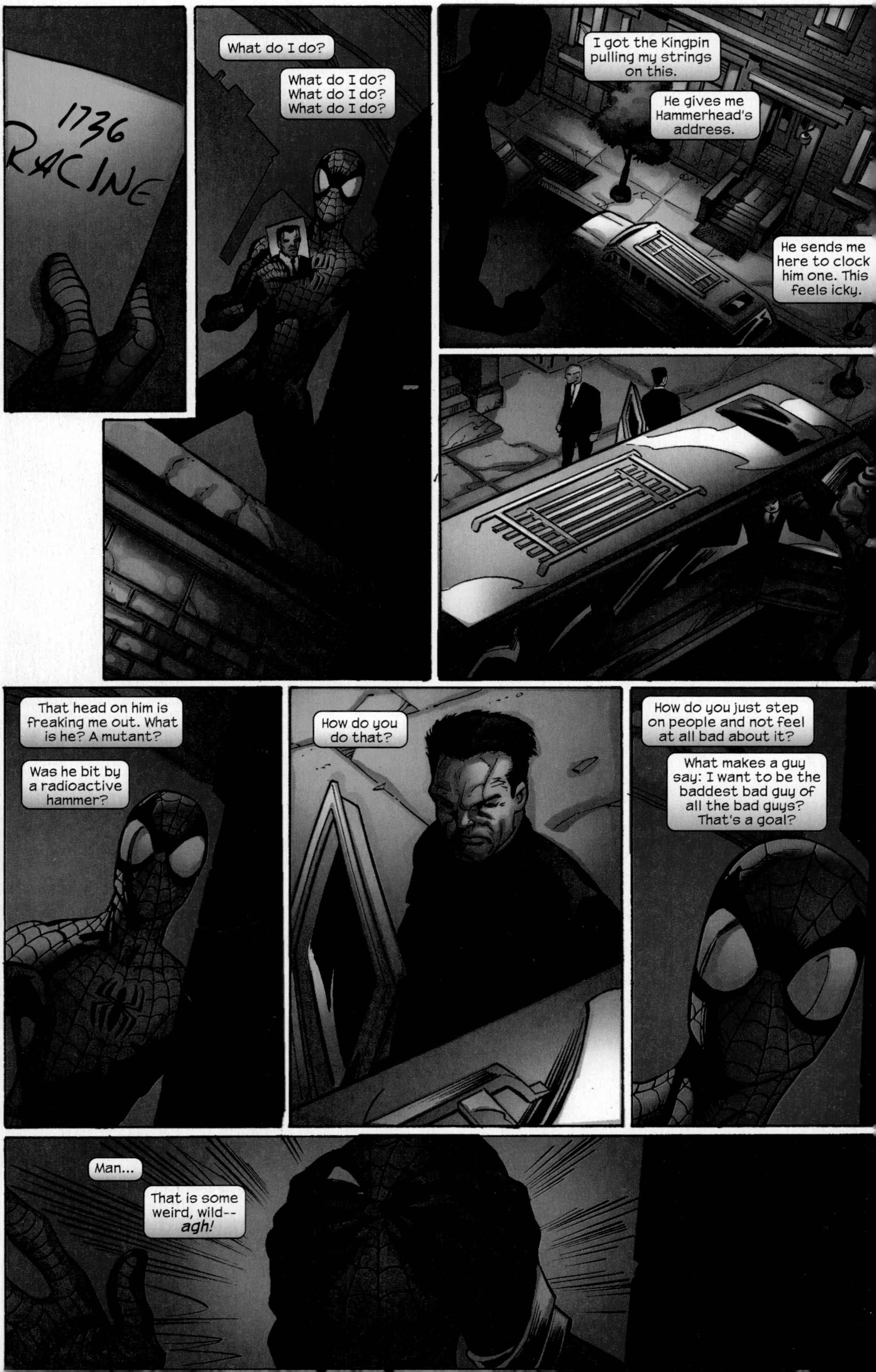
1736
RACINE
What do I do?
What do I do? What do I do? What do I do?
I got the Kingpin pulling my strings on this.
He gives me Hammerhead's address.
He sends me here to clock him one. This feels icky.
That head on him is freaking me out. What is he? A mutant?
Was he bit by a radioactive hammer?
How do you do that?
How do you just step on people and not feel at all bad about it?
What makes a guy say: I want to be the baddest bad guy of all the bad guys? That's a goal?
Man...
That is some weird, wild-- *agh!*

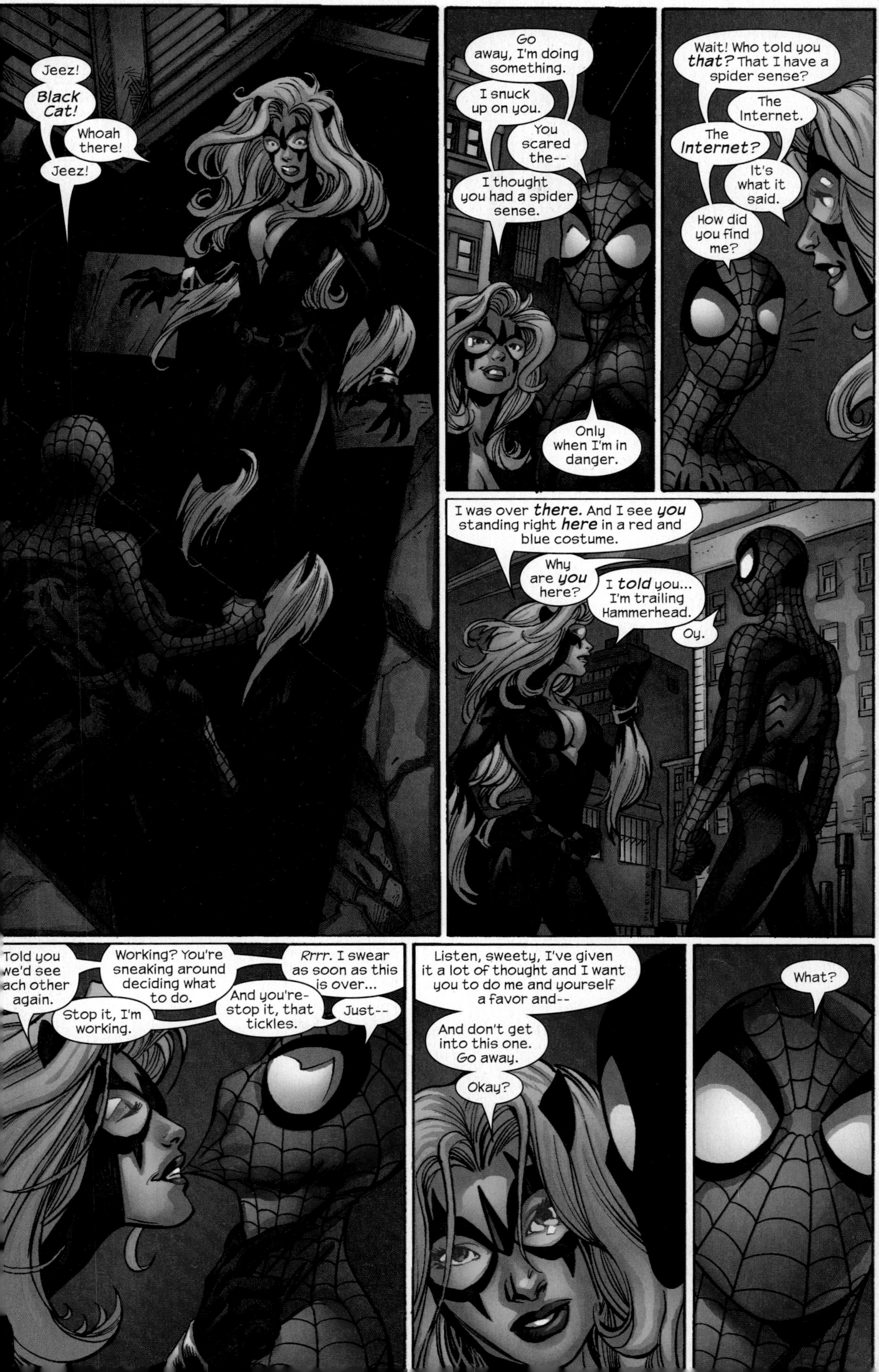
Jeez!
Black Cat!
Whoah there!
Jeez!
Go away, I'm doing something.
I snuck up on you.
You scared the--
I thought you had a spider sense.
Only when I'm in danger.
Wait! Who told you that? That I have a spider sense?
The Internet.
The Internet?
It's what it said.
How did you find me?
I was over there. And I see you standing right here in a red and blue costume.
Why are you here?
I told you... I'm trailing Hammerhead.
Oy.
Told you we'd see ach other again.
Working? You're sneaking around deciding what to do.
Stop it, I'm working.
And you're- stop it, that tickles.
Rrrr. I swear as soon as this is over...
Just--
Listen, sweety, I've given it a lot of thought and I want you to do me and yourself a favor and--
And don't get into this one. Go away.
Okay?
What?

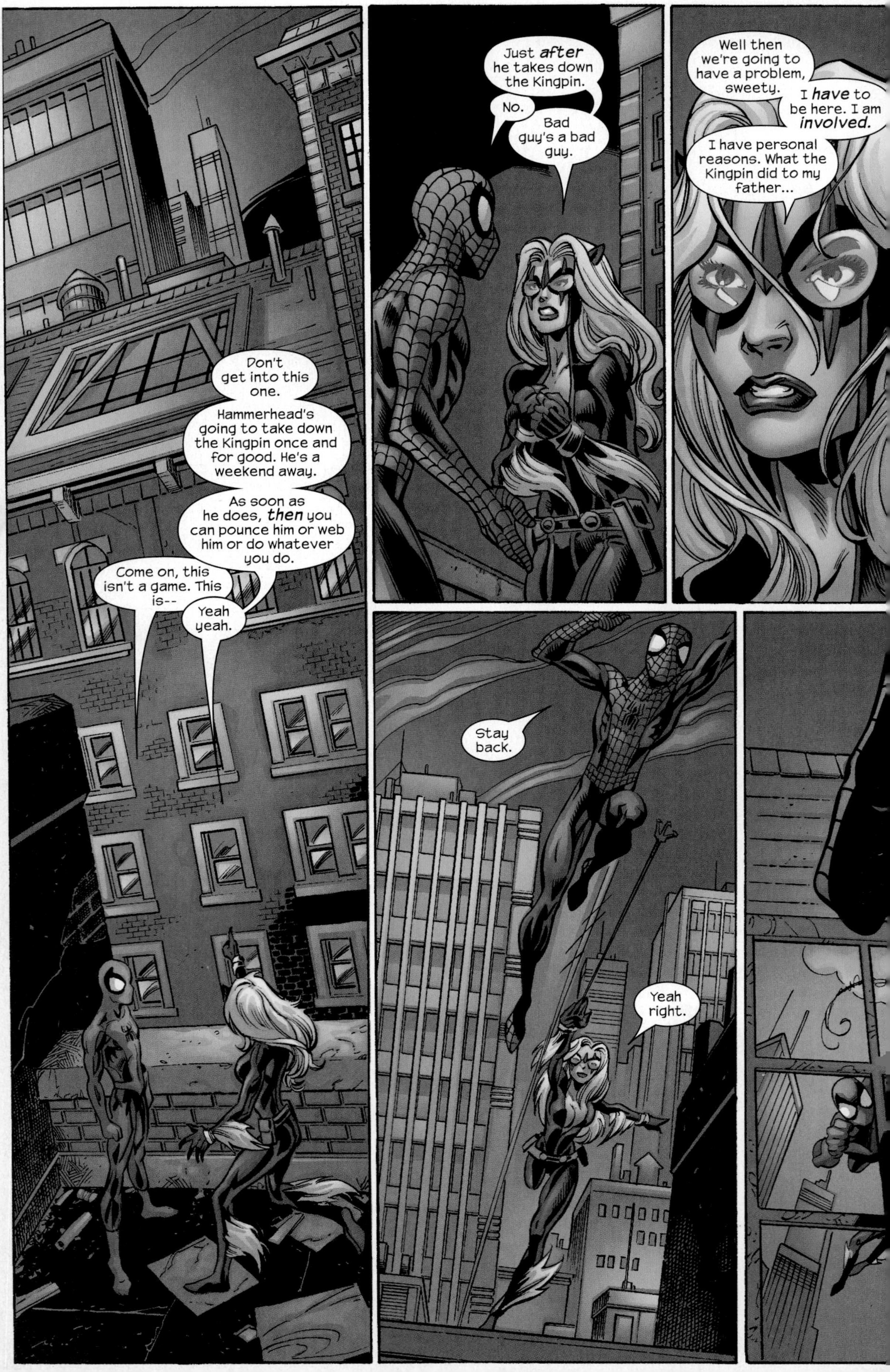
Don't get into this one.
Hammerhead's going to take down the Kingpin once and for good. He's a weekend away.
As soon as he does, *then* you can pounce him or web him or do whatever you do.
Come on, this isn't a game. This is--
Yeah yeah.
Just *after* he takes down the Kingpin.
No.
Bad guy's a bad guy.
Well then we're going to have a problem, sweety.
I *have* to be here. I am *involved.*
I have personal reasons. What the Kingpin did to my father...
Stay back.
Yeah right.

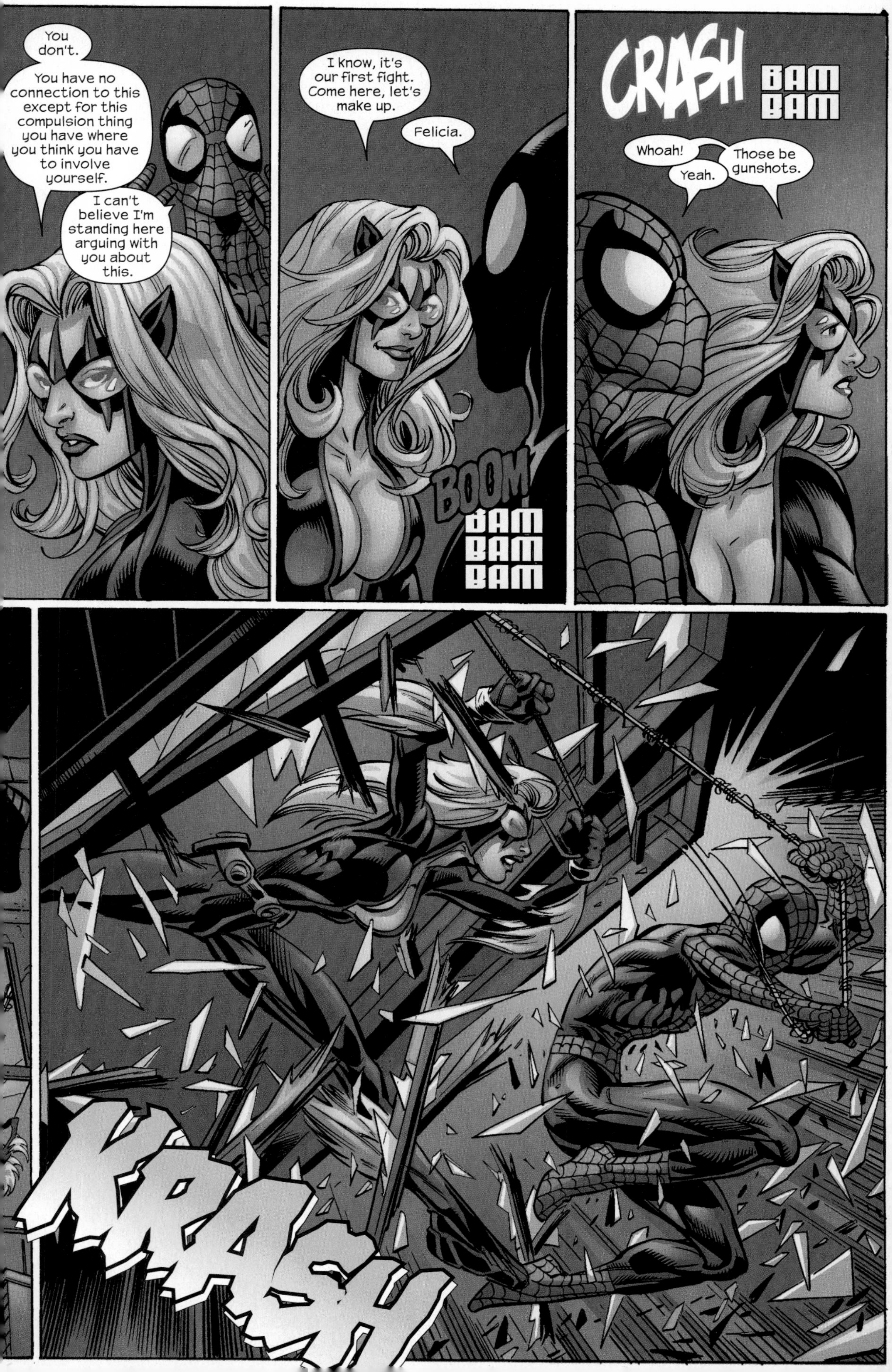

You don't.
You have no connection to this except for this compulsion thing you have where you think you have to involve yourself.
I can't believe I'm standing here arguing with you about this.
I know, it's our first fight. Come here, let's make up.
Felicia.
BOOM
BAM BAM BAM
CRASH
BAM BAM
Whoah!
Yeah.
Those be gunshots.
KRASH

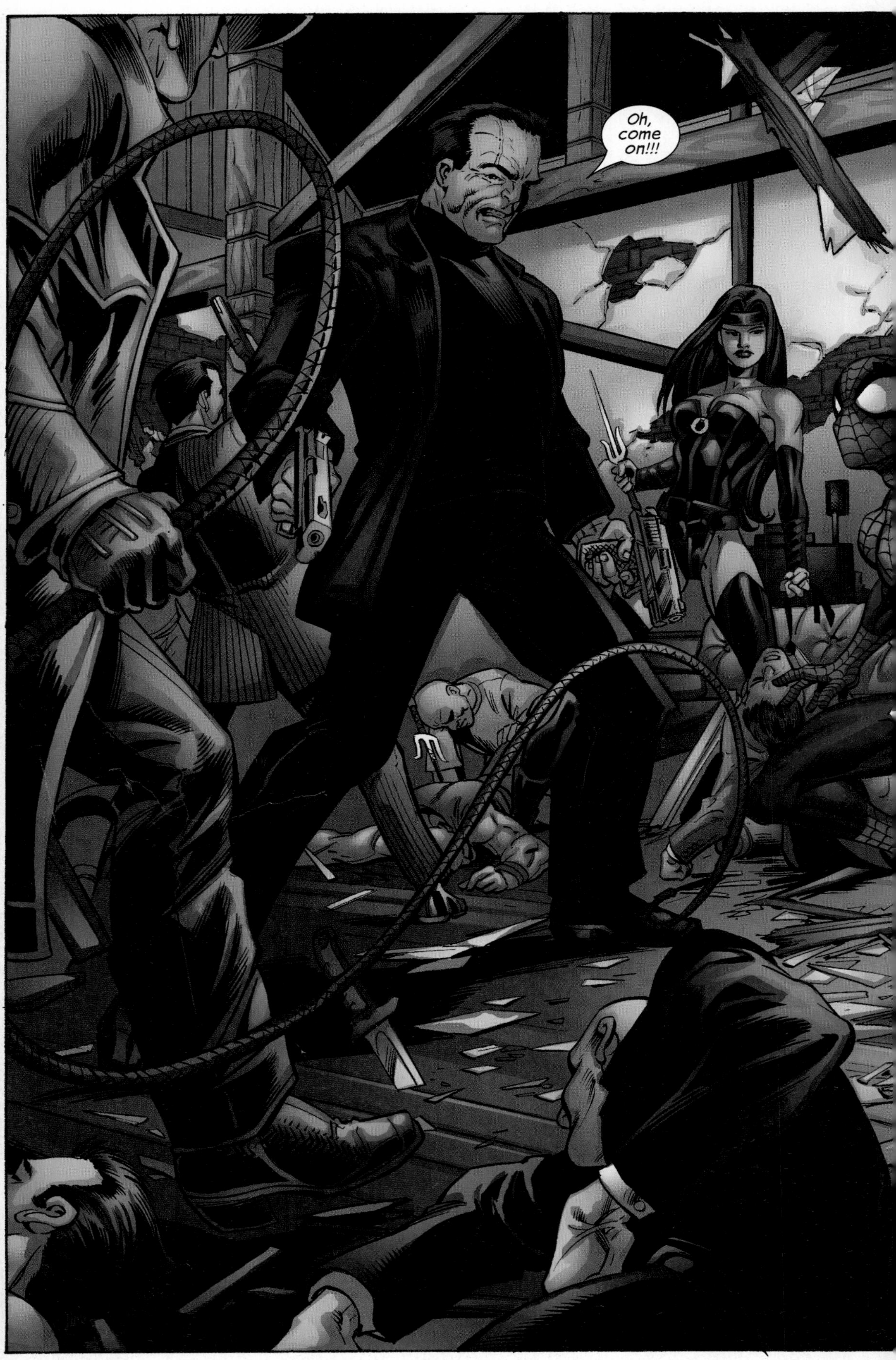
Oh, come on!!!

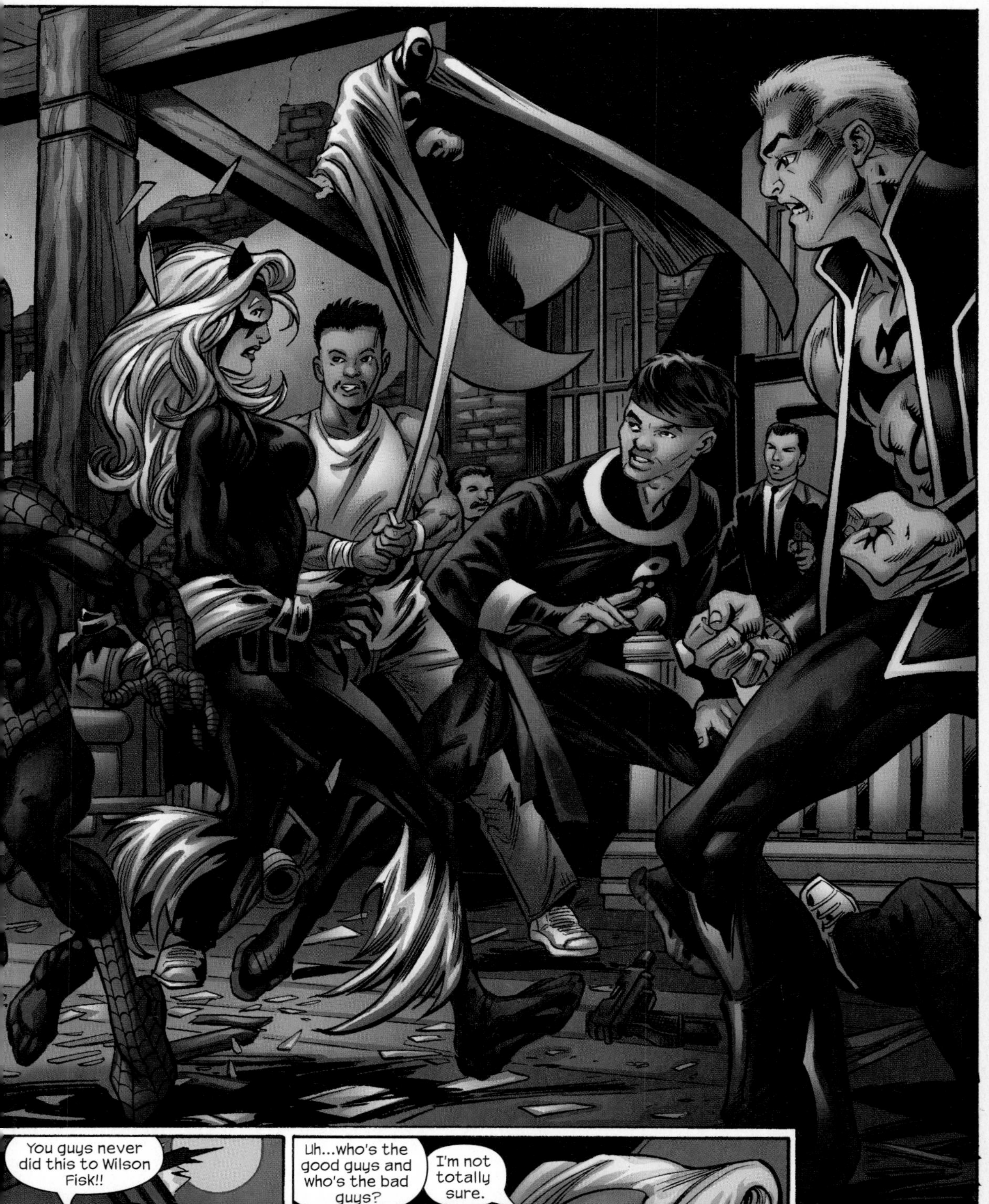

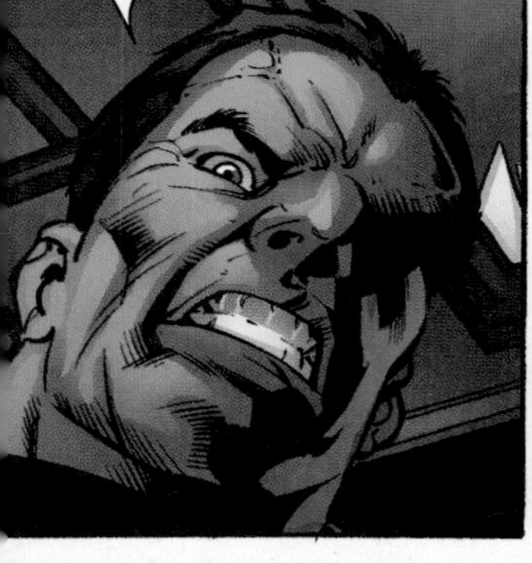
You guys never did this to Wilson Fisk!!

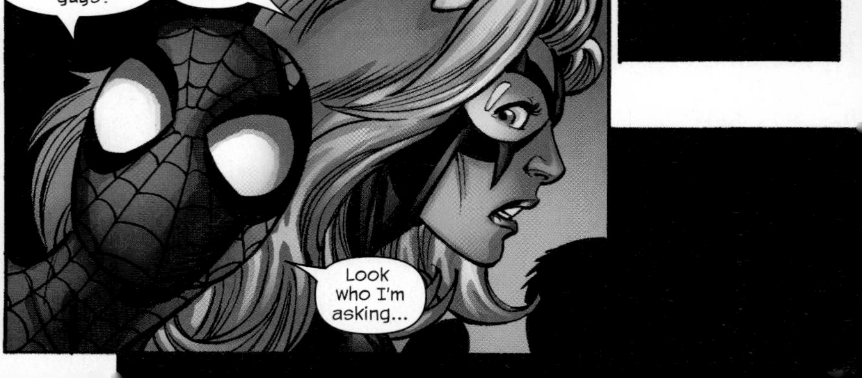
Uh...who's the good guys and who's the bad guys?
I'm not totally sure.
Look who I'm asking...

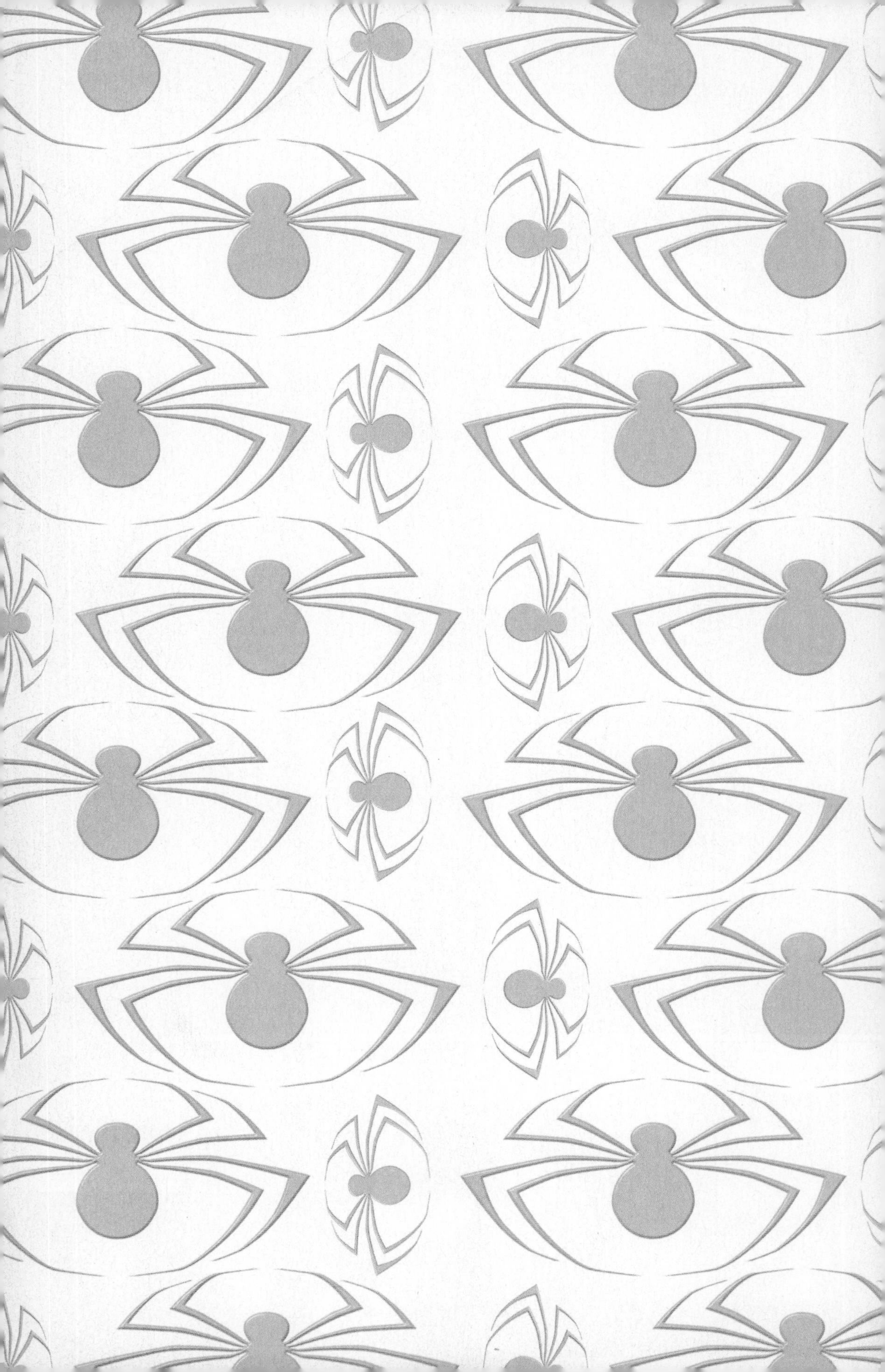

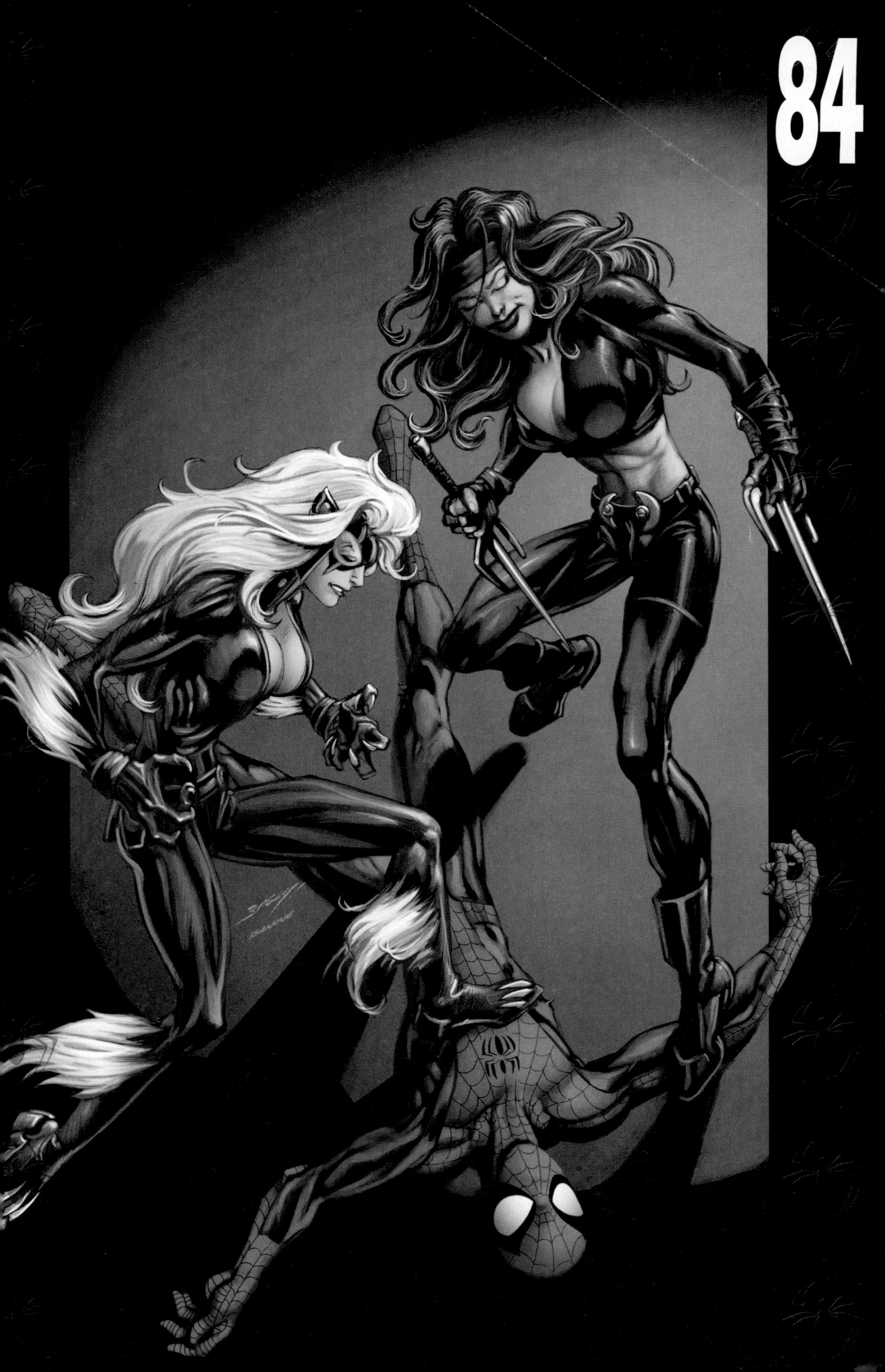
84

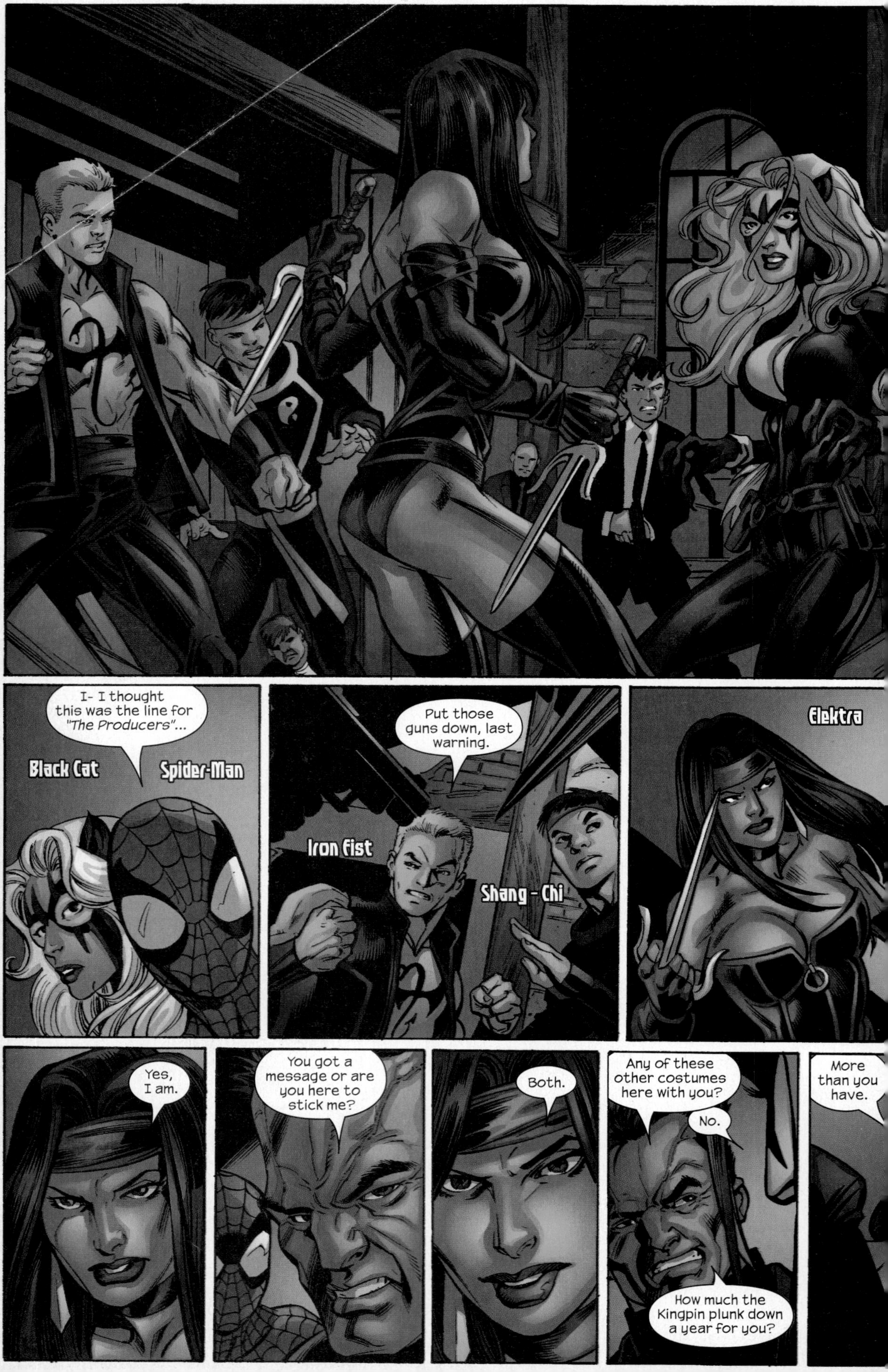
I- I thought this was the line for "The Producers"...
Black Cat
Spider-Man
Put those guns down, last warning.
Iron Fist
Shang - Chi
Elektra
Yes, I am.
You got a message or are you here to stick me?
Both.
Any of these other costumes here with you?
No.
More than you have.
How much the Kingpin plunk down a year for you?

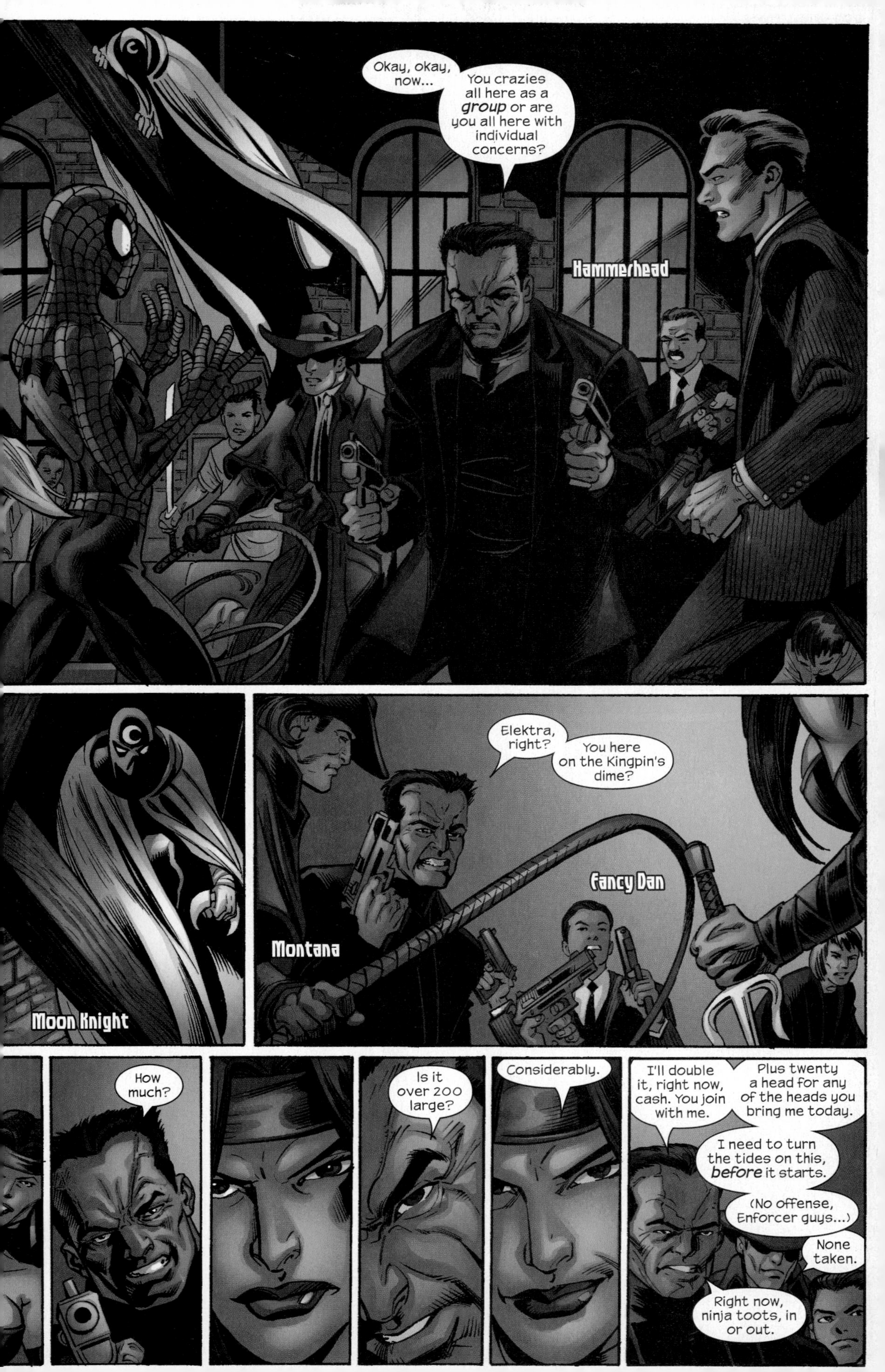
Okay, okay, now...
You crazies all here as a group or are you all here with individual concerns?
Hammerhead
Elektra, right?
You here on the Kingpin's dime?
Fancy Dan
Montana
Moon Knight
How much?
Is it over 200 large?
Considerably.
I'll double it, right now, cash. You join with me.
Plus twenty a head for any of the heads you bring me today.
I need to turn the tides on this, before it starts.
(No offense, Enforcer guys...)
None taken.
Right now, ninja toots, in or out.

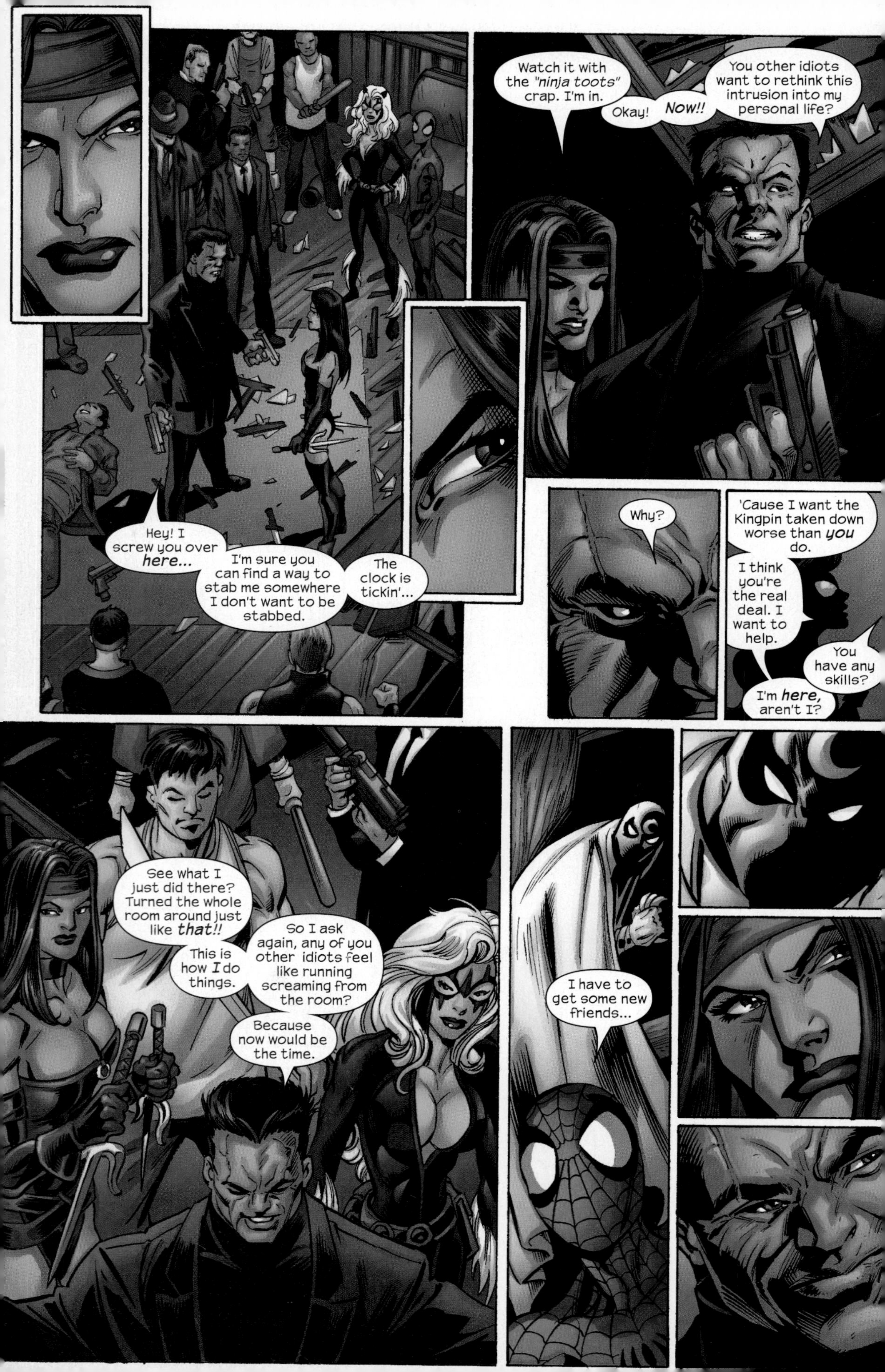
Watch it with the "ninja toots" crap. I'm in.
Okay!
NOW!!
You other idiots want to rethink this intrusion into my personal life?
Hey! I screw you over here...
I'm sure you can find a way to stab me somewhere I don't want to be stabbed.
The clock is tickin'...
Why?
'Cause I want the Kingpin taken down worse than you do.
I think you're the real deal. I want to help.
You have any skills?
I'm here, aren't I?
See what I just did there? Turned the whole room around just like that!!
This is how I do things.
So I ask again, any of you other idiots feel like running screaming from the room?
Because now would be the time.
I have to get some new friends...

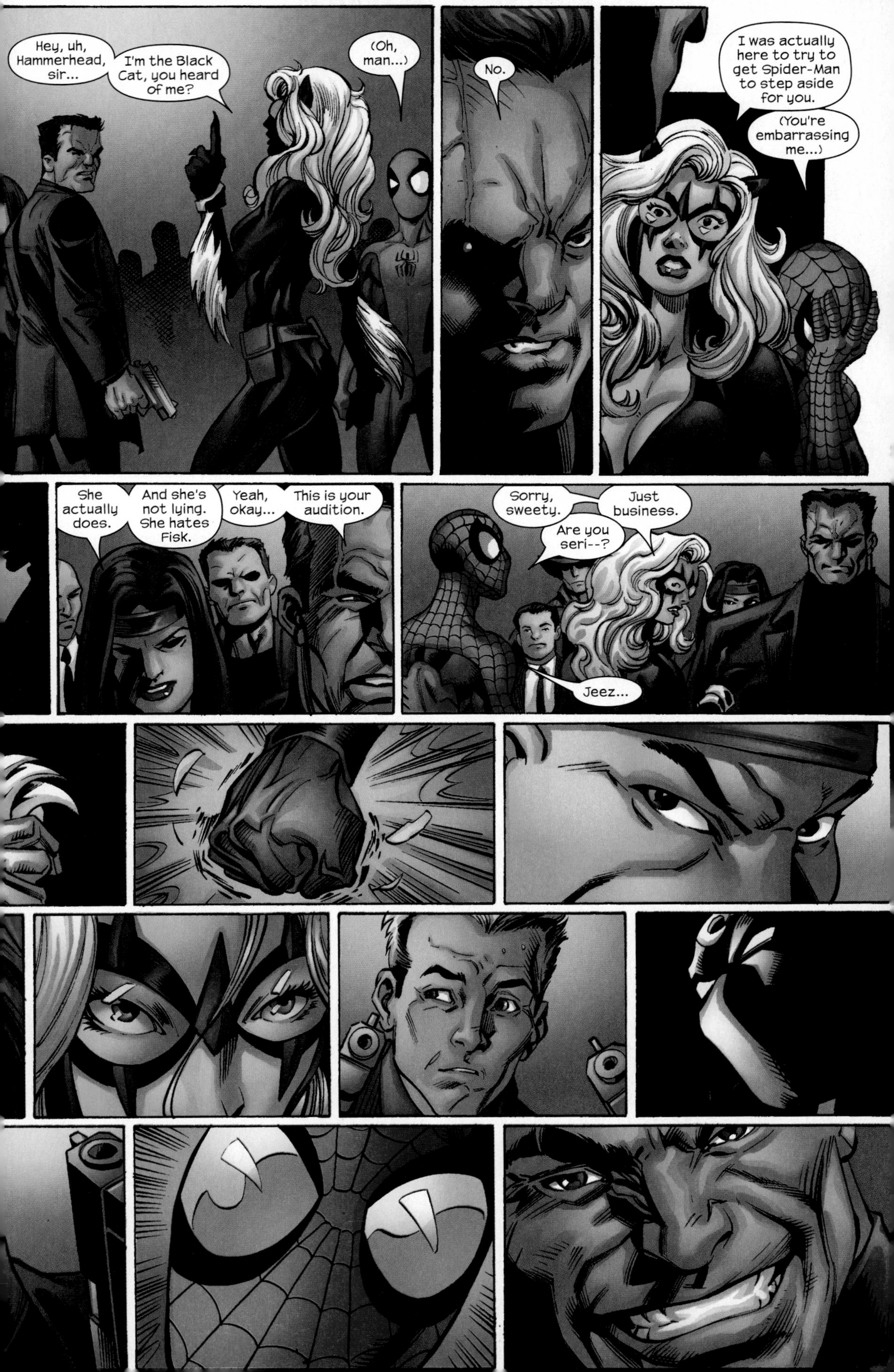
Hey, uh, Hammerhead, sir...
I'm the Black Cat, you heard of me?
(Oh, man...)
No.
I was actually here to try to get Spider-Man to step aside for you.
(You're embarrassing me...)
She actually does.
And she's not lying. She hates Fisk.
Yeah, okay...
This is your audition.
Sorry, sweety.
Just business.
Are you seri--?
Jeez...

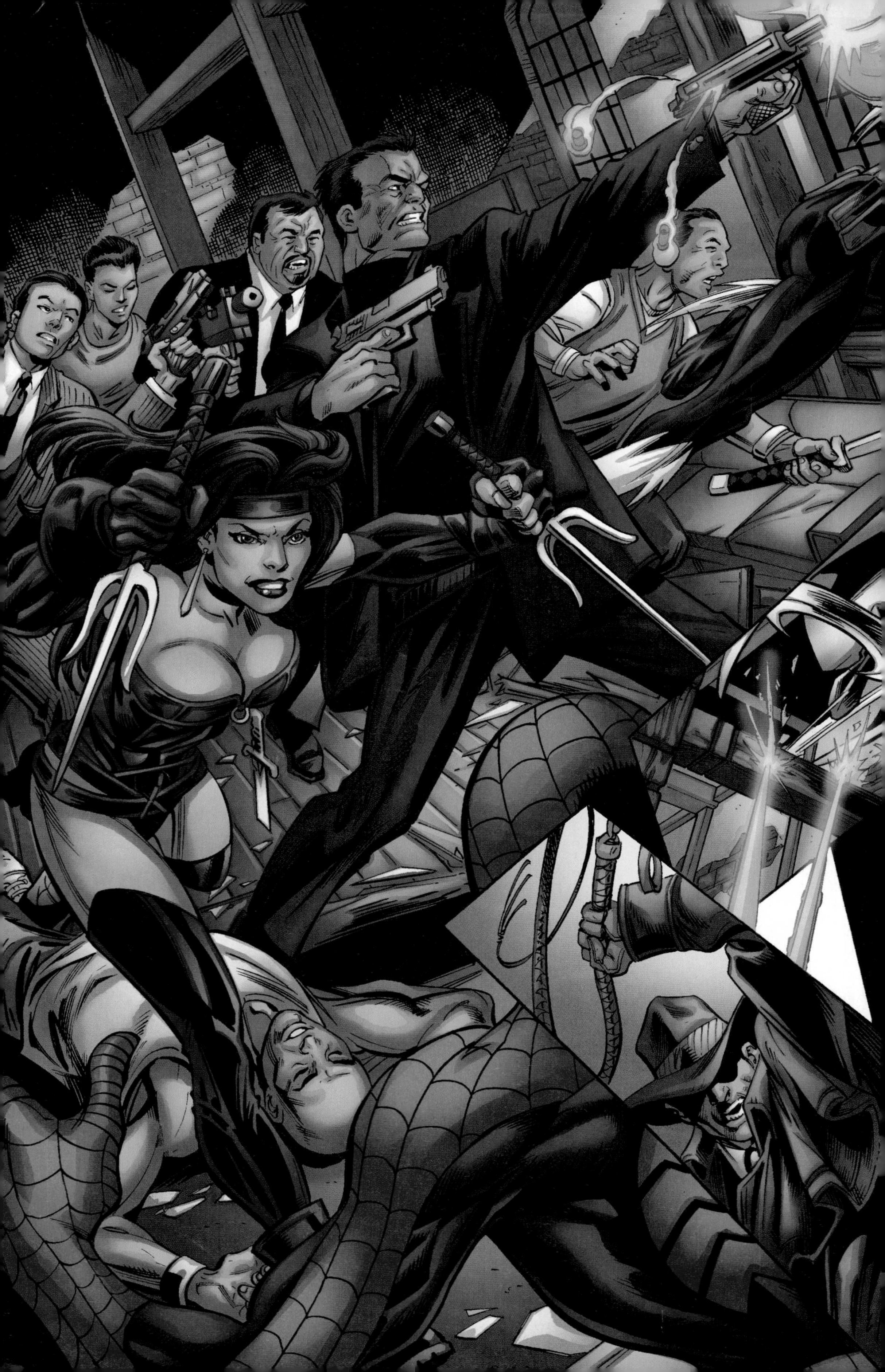

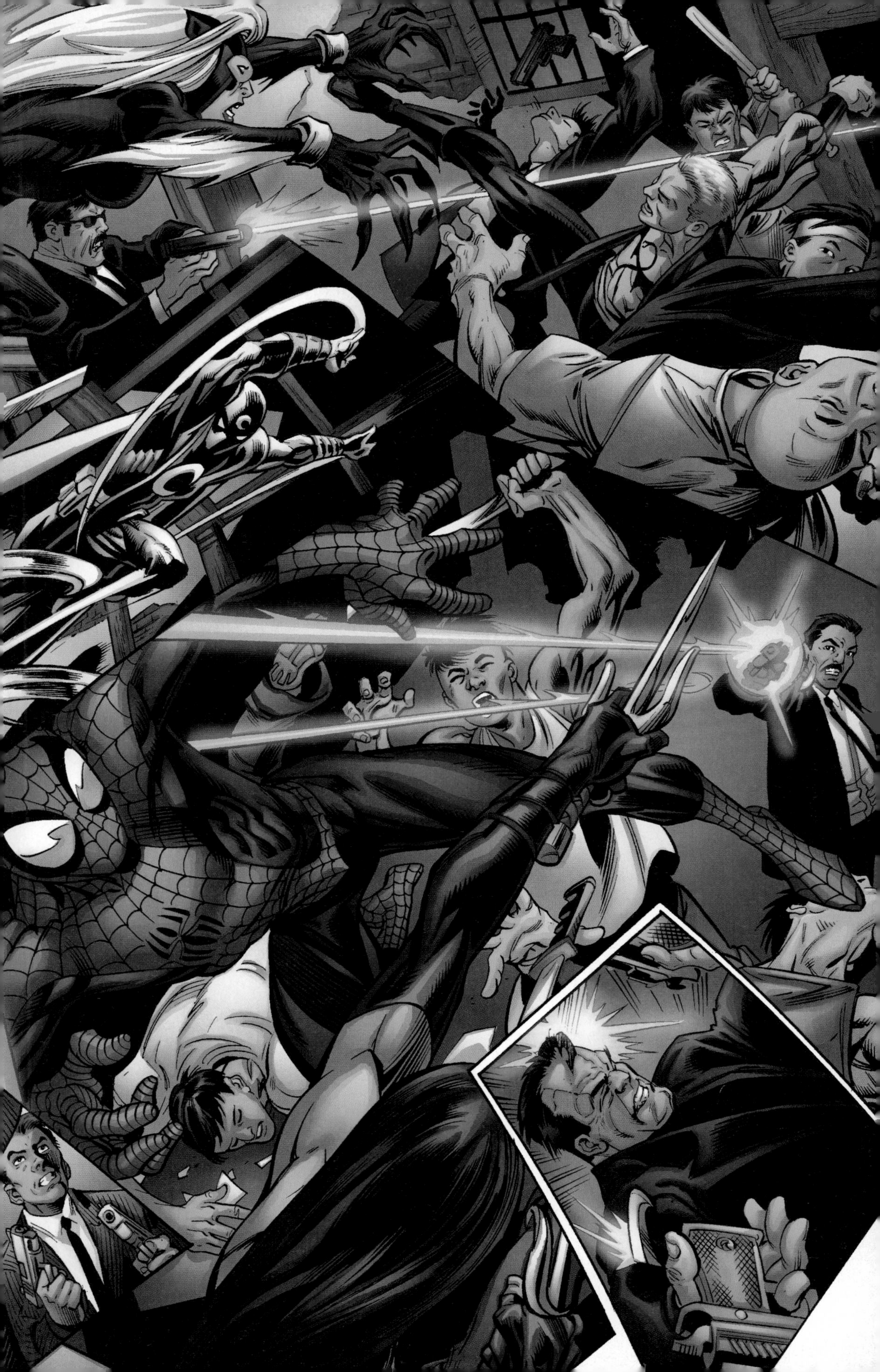

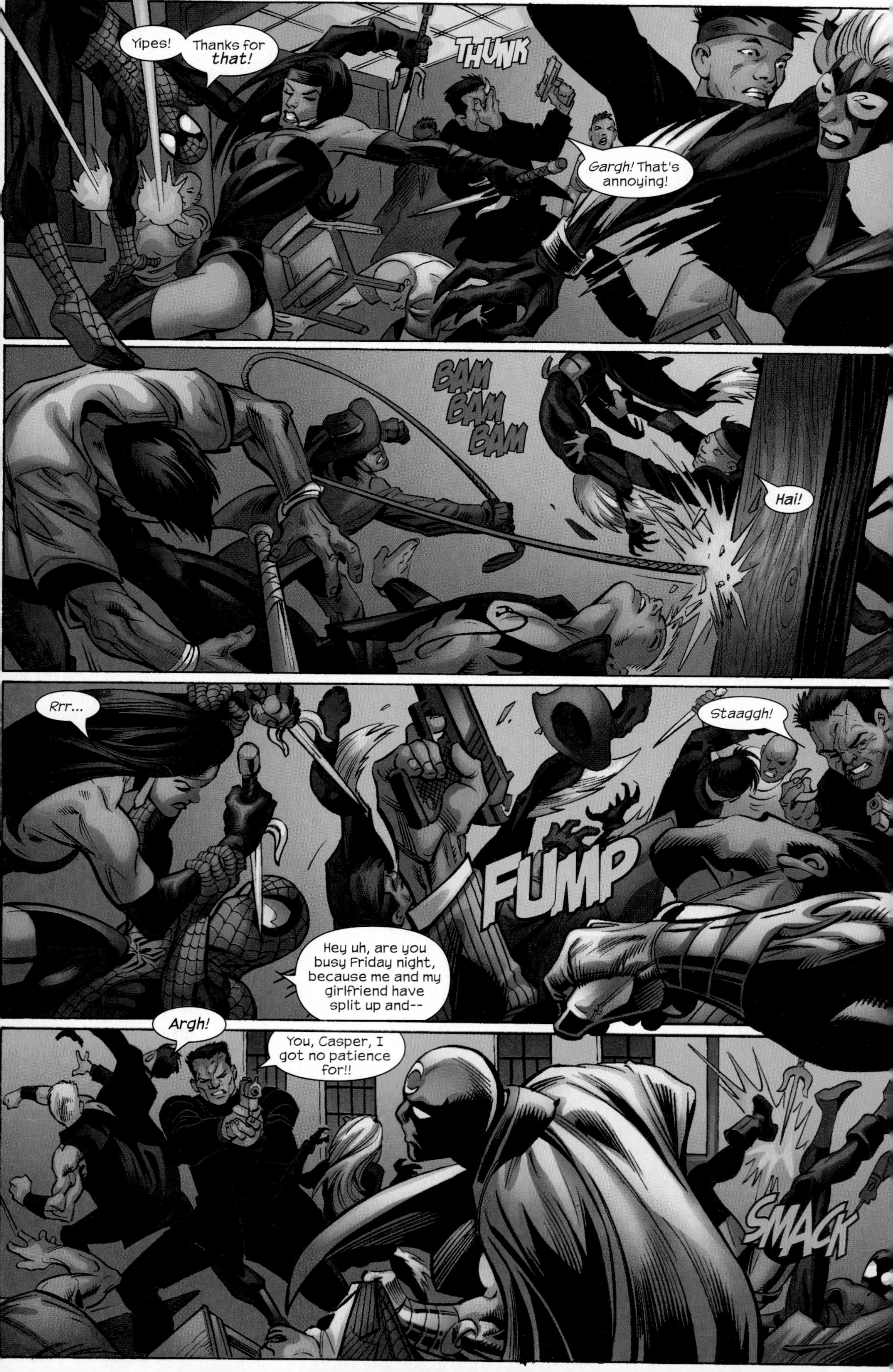
Yipes!
Thanks for that!
THUNK
Gargh! That's annoying!
BAM BAM BAM
Hai!
Rrr...
Staaggh!
FUMP
Hey uh, are you busy Friday night, because me and my girlfriend have split up and--
Argh!
You, Casper, I got no patience for!!
SMACK

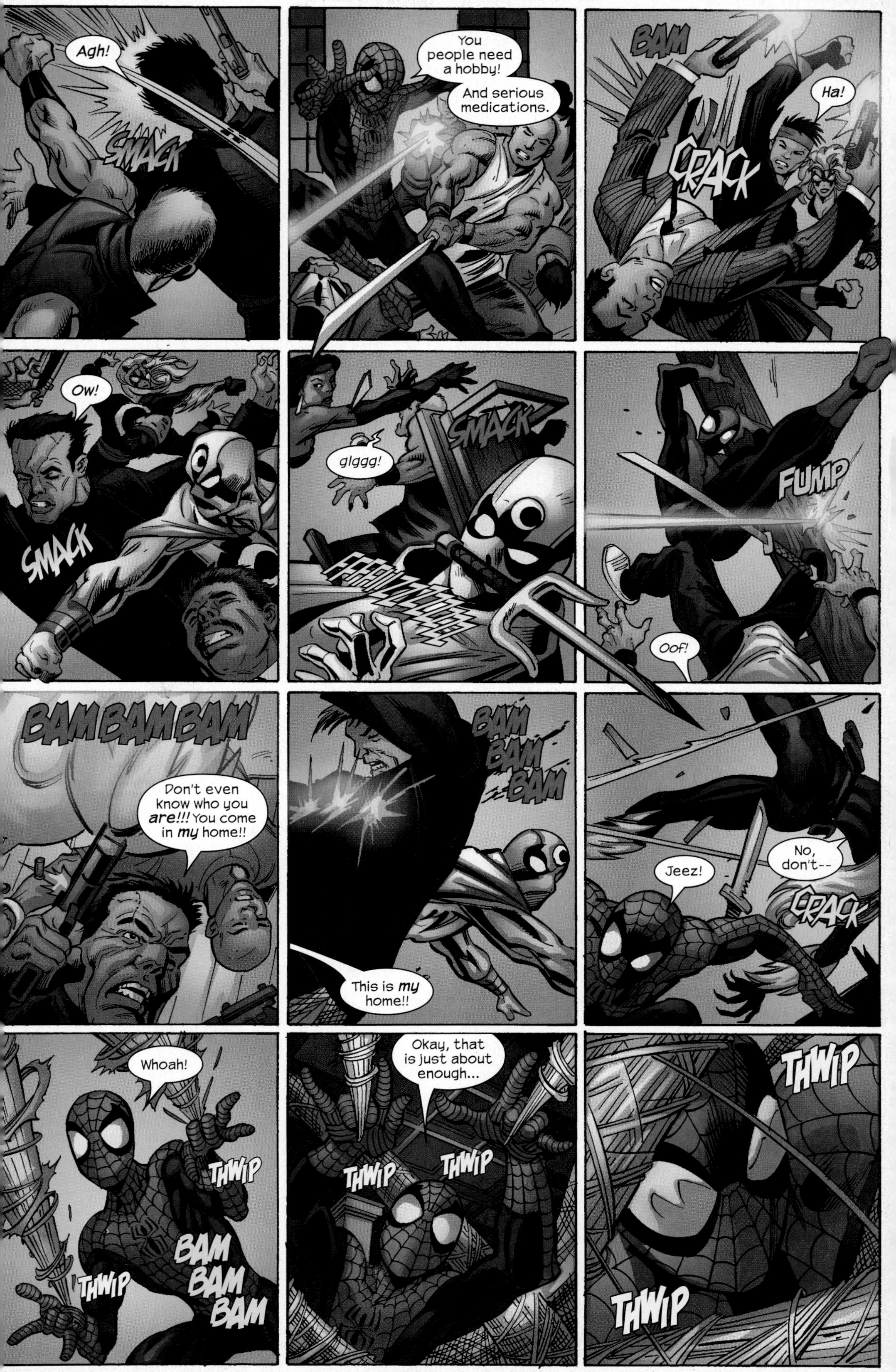
Agh!
SMACK
You people need a hobby!
And serious medications.
BAM
Ha!
CRACK
Ow!
SMACK
glggg!
SMACK
FUMP
Oof!
BAM BAM BAM
Don't even know who you are!!! You come in my home!!
BAM BAM BAM
This is my home!!
Jeez!
No, don't--
CRACK
Whoah!
THWIP
BAM BAM BAM
THWIP
Okay, that is just about enough...
THWIP
THWIP
THWIP
THWIP

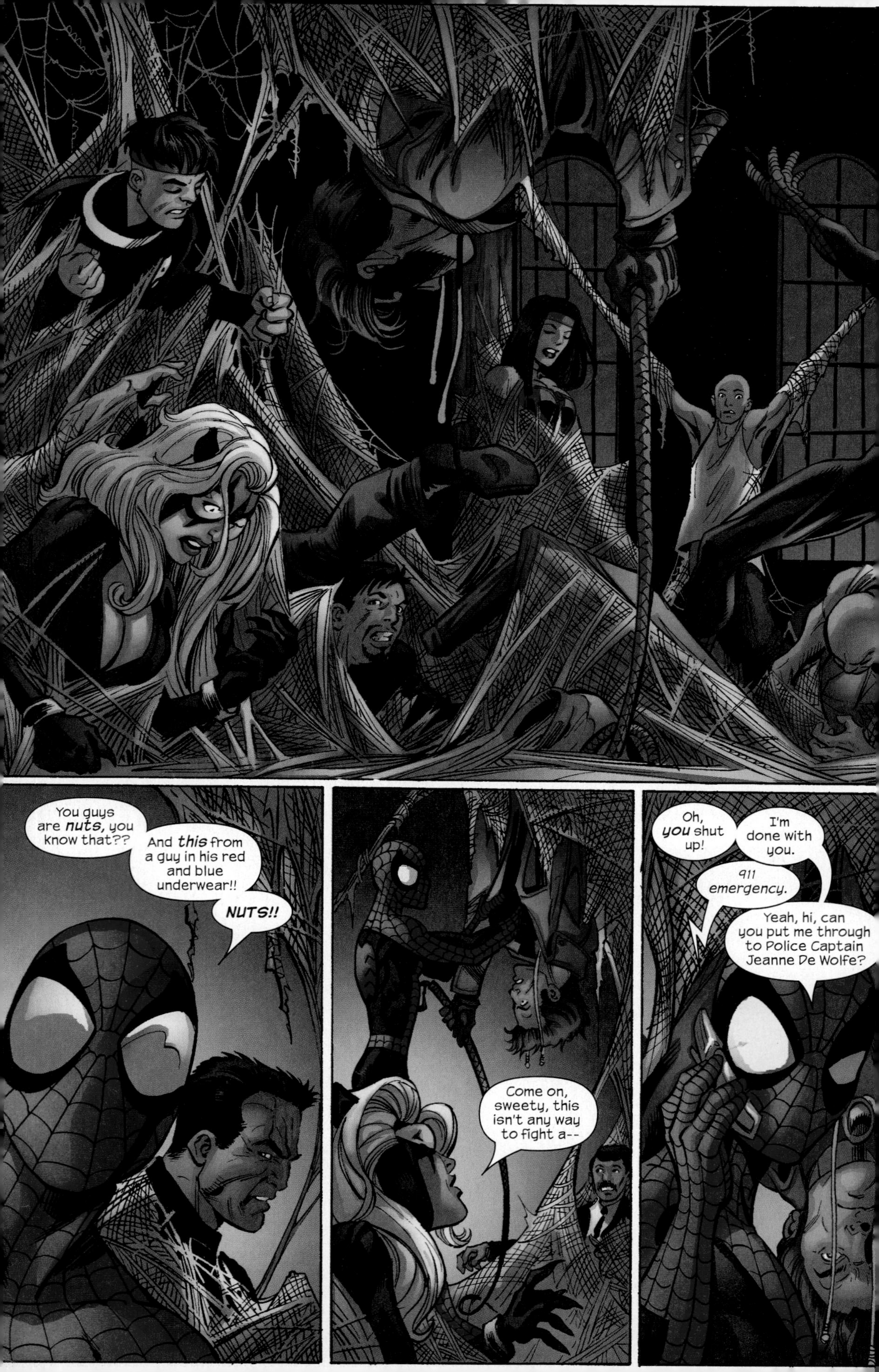
You guys are *nuts,* you know that??
And *this* from a guy in his red and blue underwear!!
NUTS!!
Come on, sweety, this isn't any way to fight a--
Oh, *you* shut up!
I'm done with you.
911 emergency.
Yeah, hi, can you put me through to Police Captain Jeanne De Wolfe?

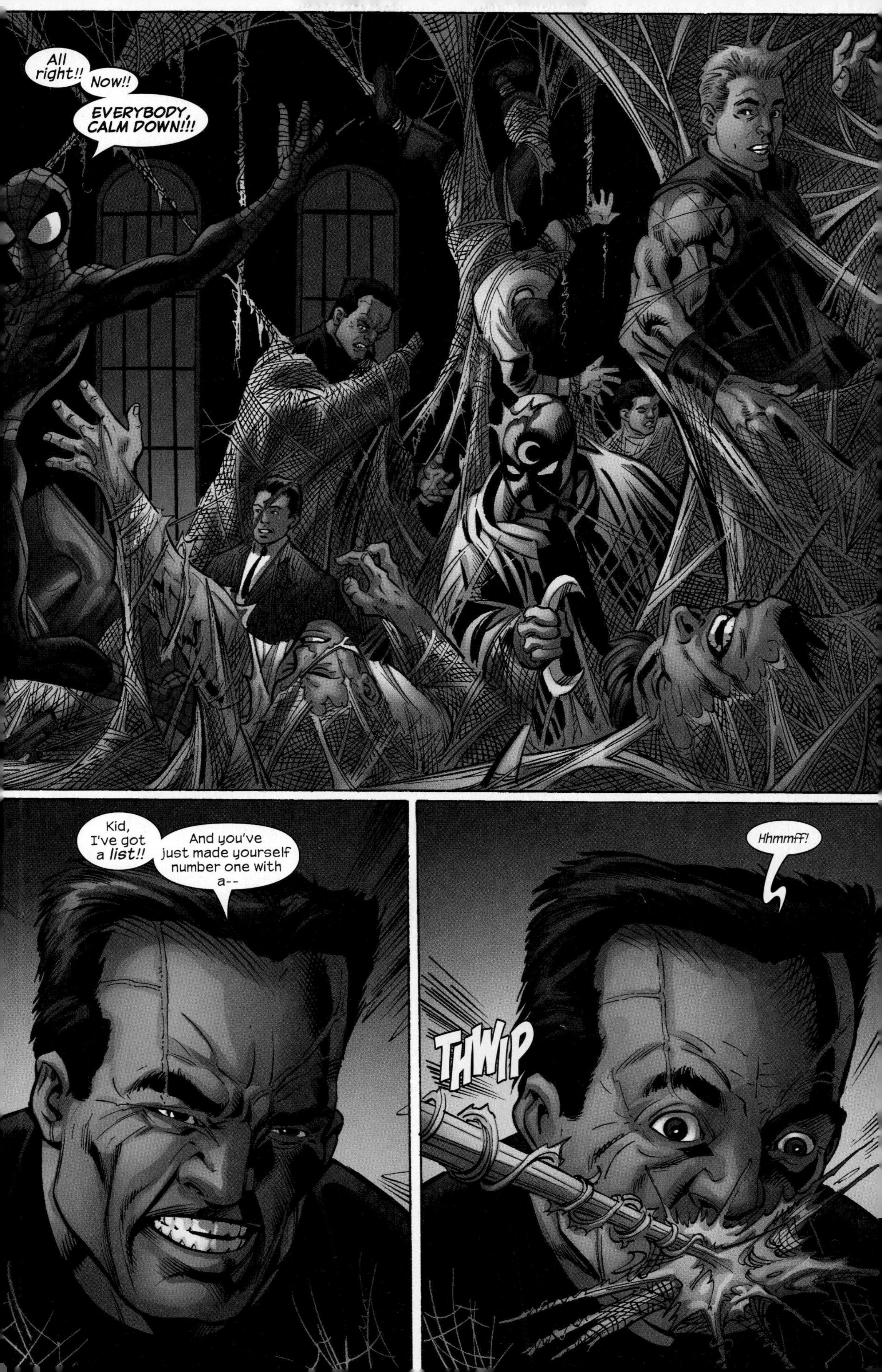
All right!!
Now!!
EVERYBODY, CALM DOWN!!!
Kid, I've got a list!!
And you've just made yourself number one with a--
THWIP
Hhmmff!

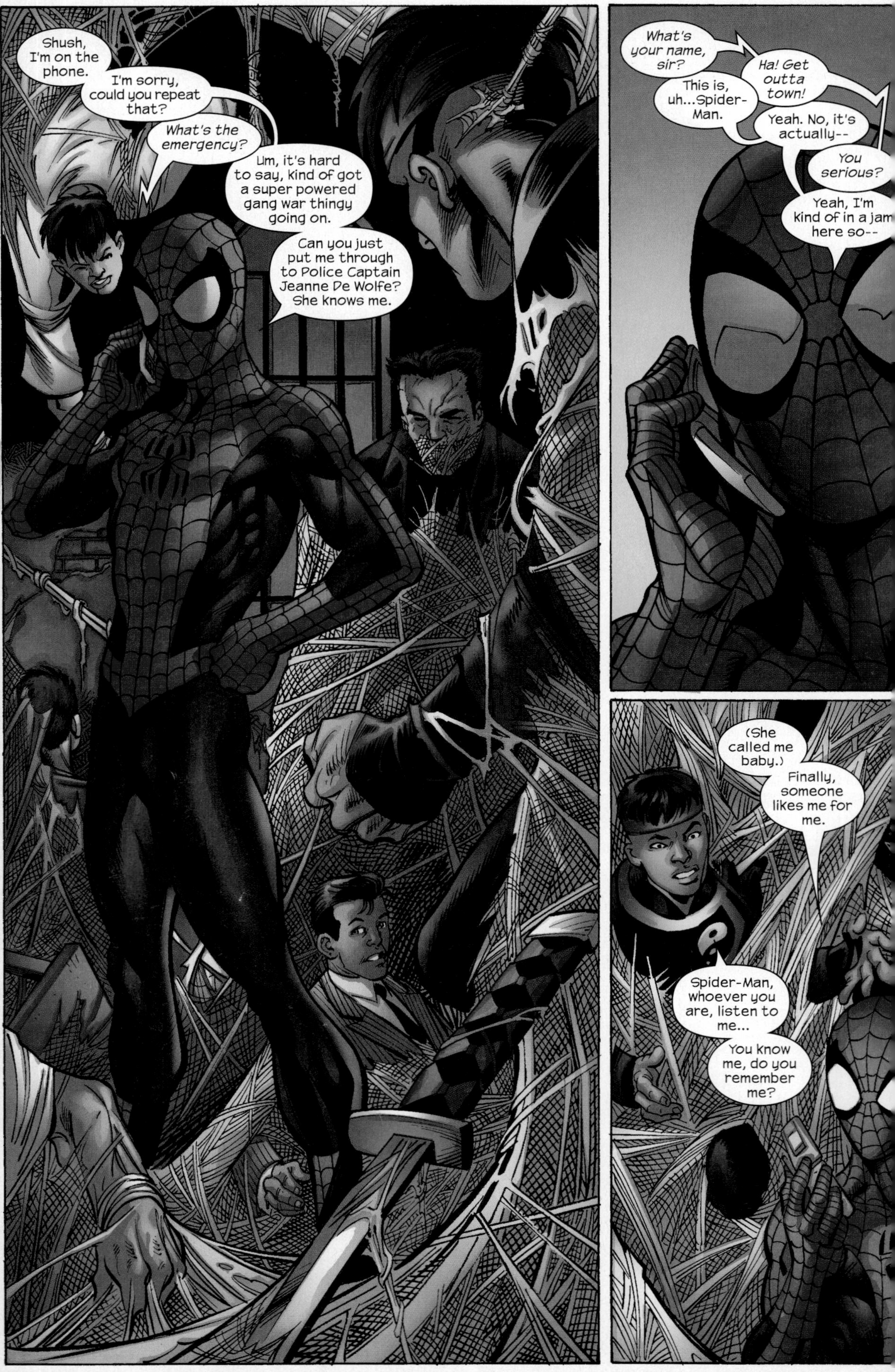
Shush, I'm on the phone.
I'm sorry, could you repeat that?
What's the emergency?
Um, it's hard to say, kind of got a super powered gang war thingy going on.
Can you just put me through to Police Captain Jeanne De Wolfe? She knows me.
What's your name, sir?
This is, uh...Spider-Man.
Ha! Get outta town!
Yeah. No, it's actually--
You serious?
Yeah, I'm kind of in a jam here so--
(She called me baby.)
Finally, someone likes me for me.
Spider-Man, whoever you are, listen to me...
You know me, do you remember me?

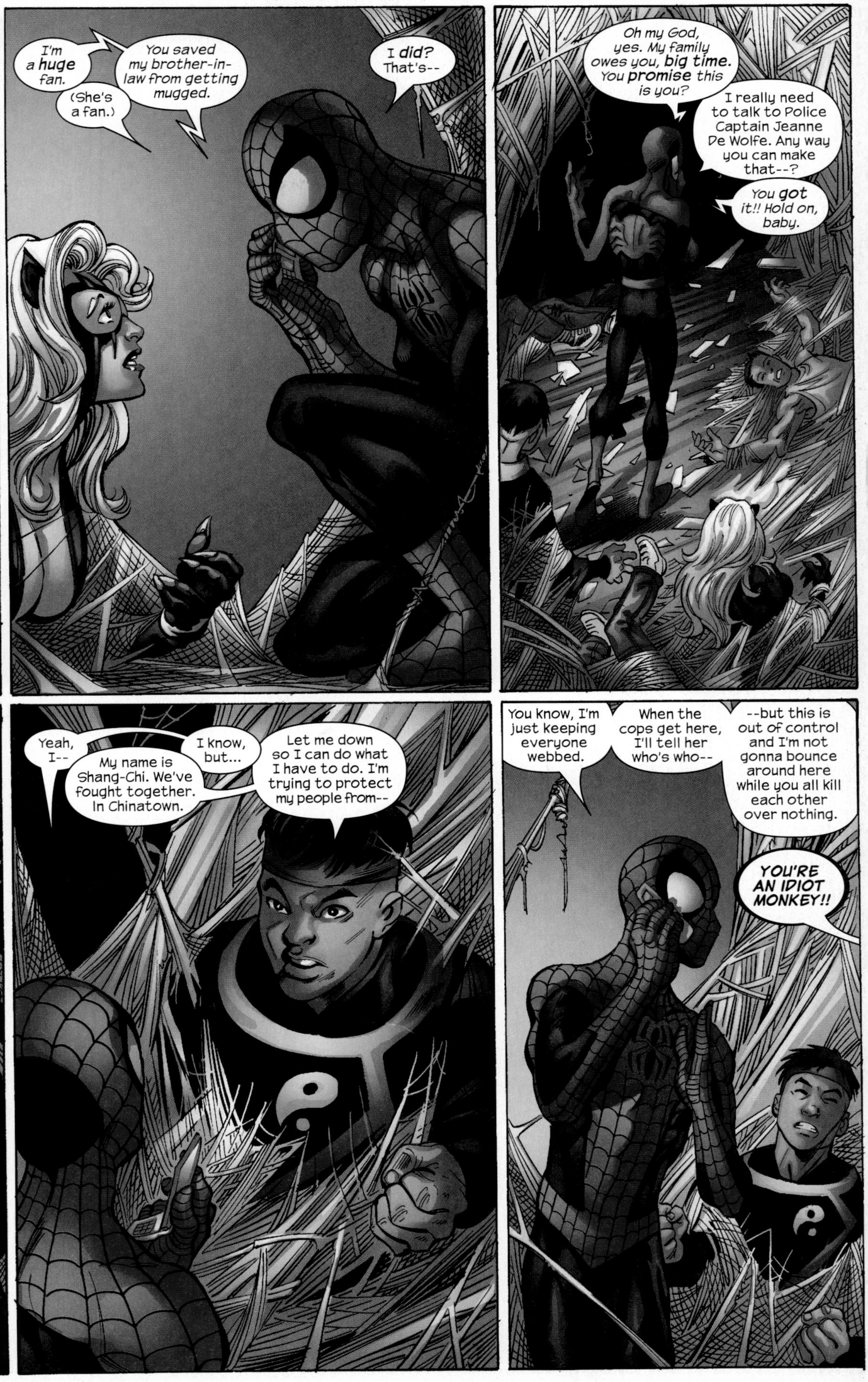
I'm a huge fan.
You saved my brother-in-law from getting mugged.
(She's a fan.)
I did? That's--
Oh my God, yes. My family owes you, big time. You promise this is you?
I really need to talk to Police Captain Jeanne De Wolfe. Any way you can make that--?
You got it!! Hold on, baby.
Yeah, I--
My name is Shang-Chi. We've fought together. In Chinatown.
I know, but...
Let me down so I can do what I have to do. I'm trying to protect my people from--
You know, I'm just keeping everyone webbed.
When the cops get here, I'll tell her who's who--
--but this is out of control and I'm not gonna bounce around here while you all kill each other over nothing.
YOU'RE AN IDIOT MONKEY!!

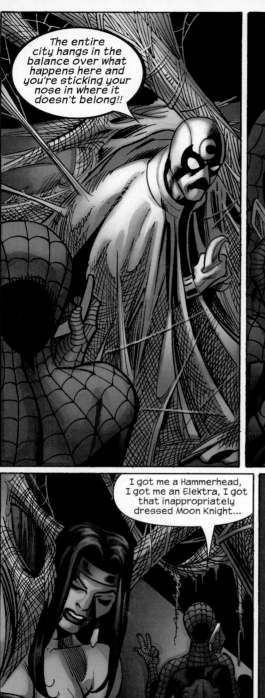

The entire city hangs in the balance over what happens here and you're sticking your nose in where it doesn't belong!!

The entire city?

The entire city.

Can you believe he wears white to a super hero fight?

Just leave me alone...

I got me a Hammerhead, I got me an Elektra, I got that inappropriately dressed Moon Knight...

Kingpin's Elektra?

Oy, please tell me there's not more than one.

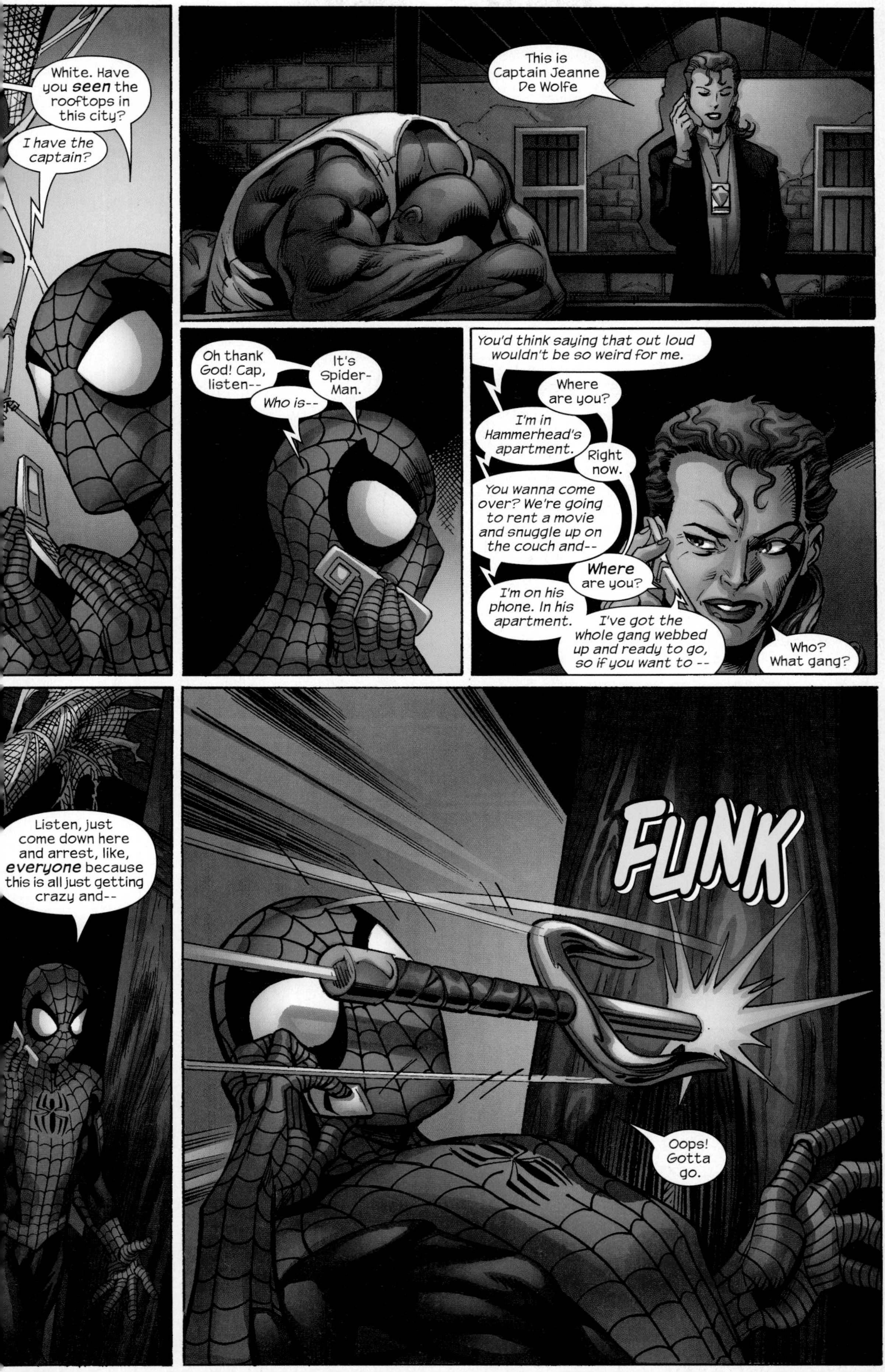
White. Have you **seen** the rooftops in this city?
I have the captain?
This is Captain Jeanne De Wolfe
Oh thank God! Cap, listen--
Who is--
It's Spider-Man.
You'd think saying that out loud wouldn't be so weird for me.
Where are you?
I'm in Hammerhead's apartment.
Right now.
You wanna come over? We're going to rent a movie and snuggle up on the couch and--
Where are you?
I'm on his phone. In his apartment.
I've got the whole gang webbed up and ready to go, so if you want to --
Who? What gang?
Listen, just come down here and arrest, like, ***everyone*** because this is all just getting crazy and--
FUNK
Oops! Gotta go.

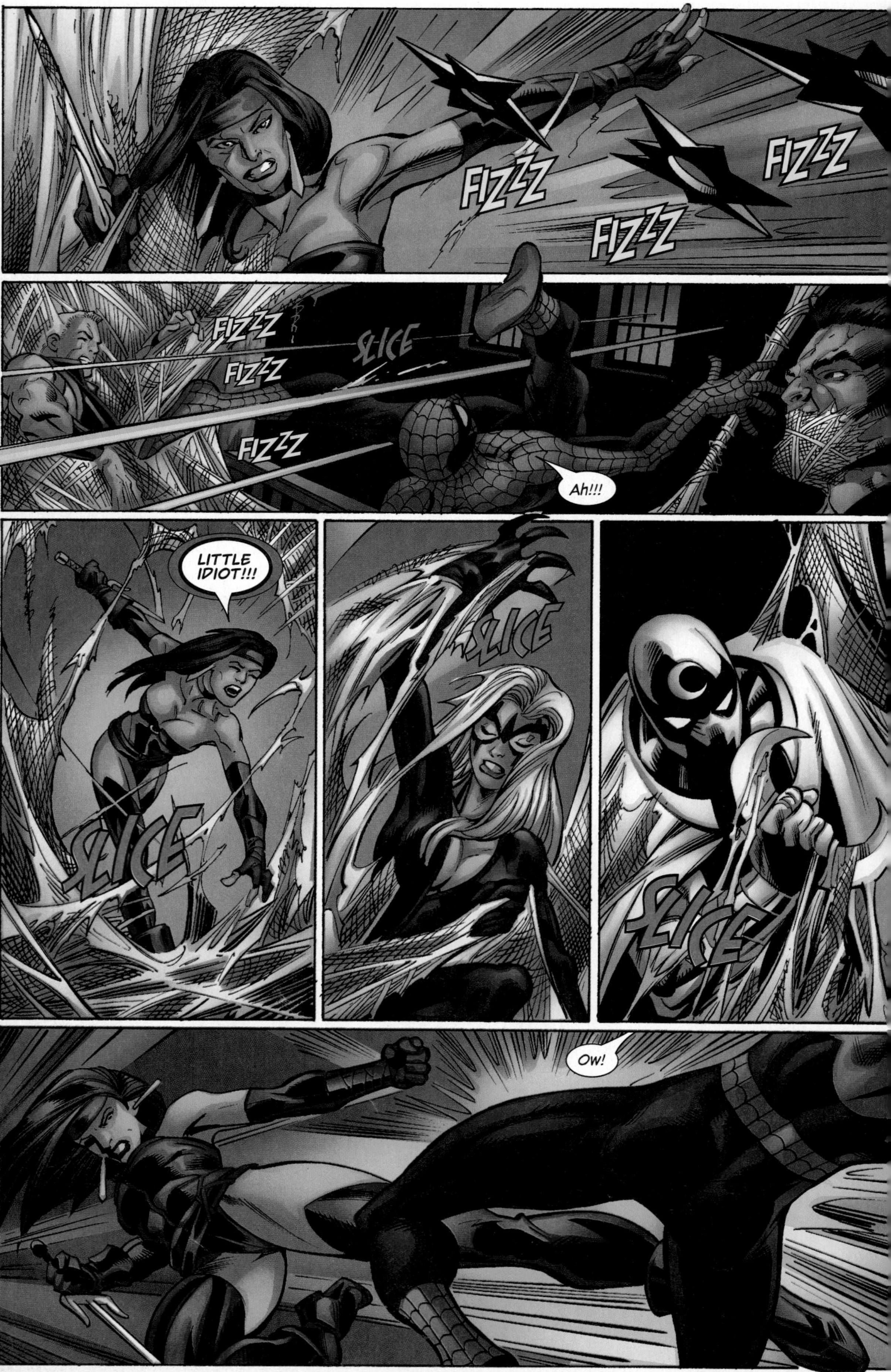
FIZZZ
FIZZZ
FIZZZ
FIZZZ
FIZZZ
SLICE
FIZZZ
Ah!!!
LITTLE IDIOT!!!
SLICE
SLICE
SLICE
OW!

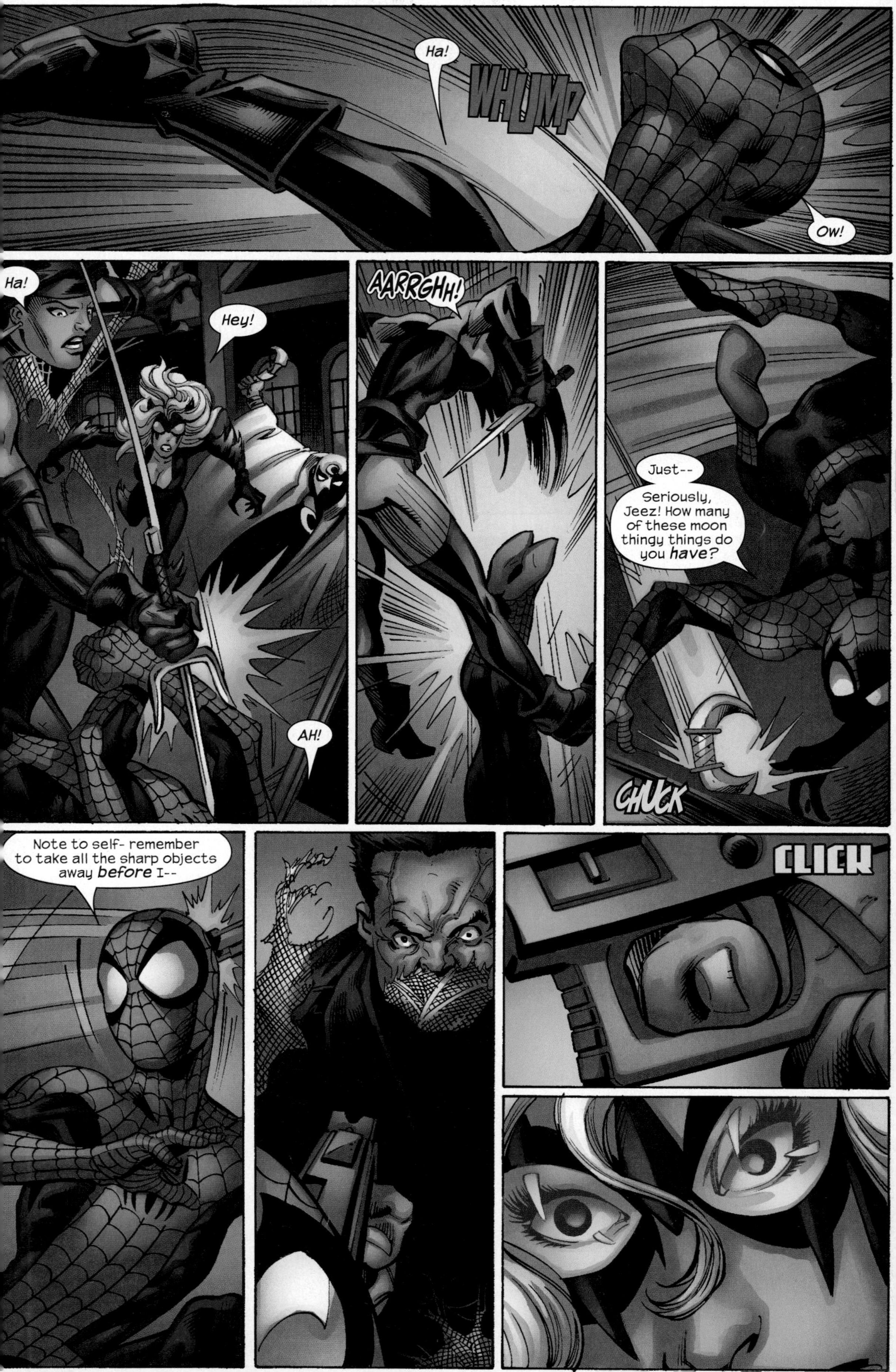
Ha!
WHUMP
Ow!
Ha!
Hey!
AH!
AARRGHH!
Just--
Seriously, Jeez! How many of these moon thingy things do you *have*?
CHUCK
Note to self- remember to take all the sharp objects away *before* I--
CLICK

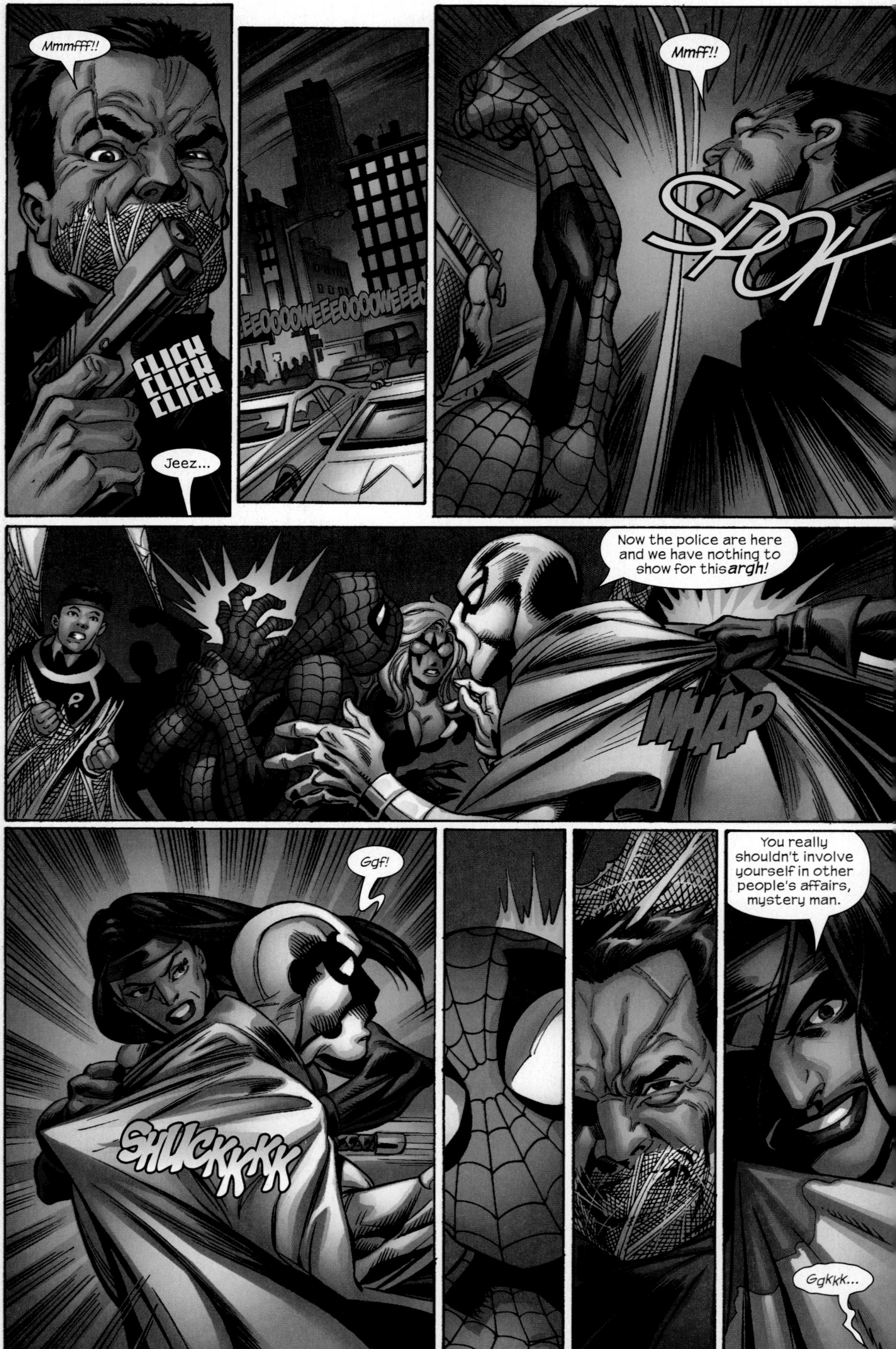

Mmmfff!!
CLICK CLICK CLICK
Jeez...
EEOOOOWEEEOOOOWEEEO
Mmff!!
SPOK
Now the police are here and we have nothing to show for this*argh!*
WHAP
Ggf!
SHUCKKKK
You really shouldn't involve yourself in other people's affairs, mystery man.
Ggkkk...

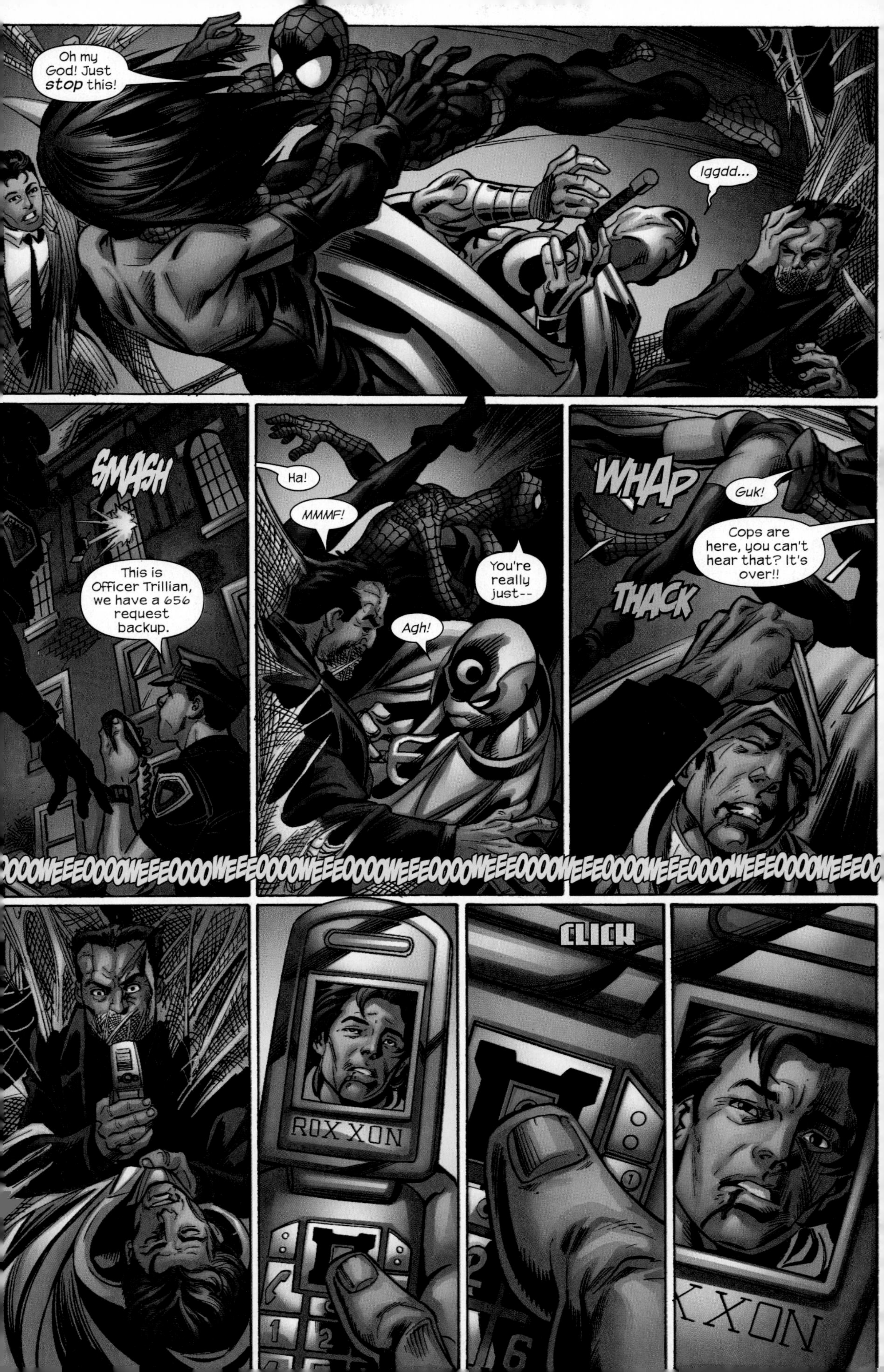
Oh my God! Just stop this!
Iggdd...
SMASH
This is Officer Trillian, we have a 656 request backup.
Ha!
MMMF!
You're really just--
Agh!
WHAP
Guk!
Cops are here, you can't hear that? It's over!!
THACK
OOOWEEEOOOOWEEEOOOOWEEEOOOOWEEEOOOOWEEEOOOOWEEEOOOOWEEEOOOOWEEEOOOOWEEEOO
ROXXON
CLICK
XXON

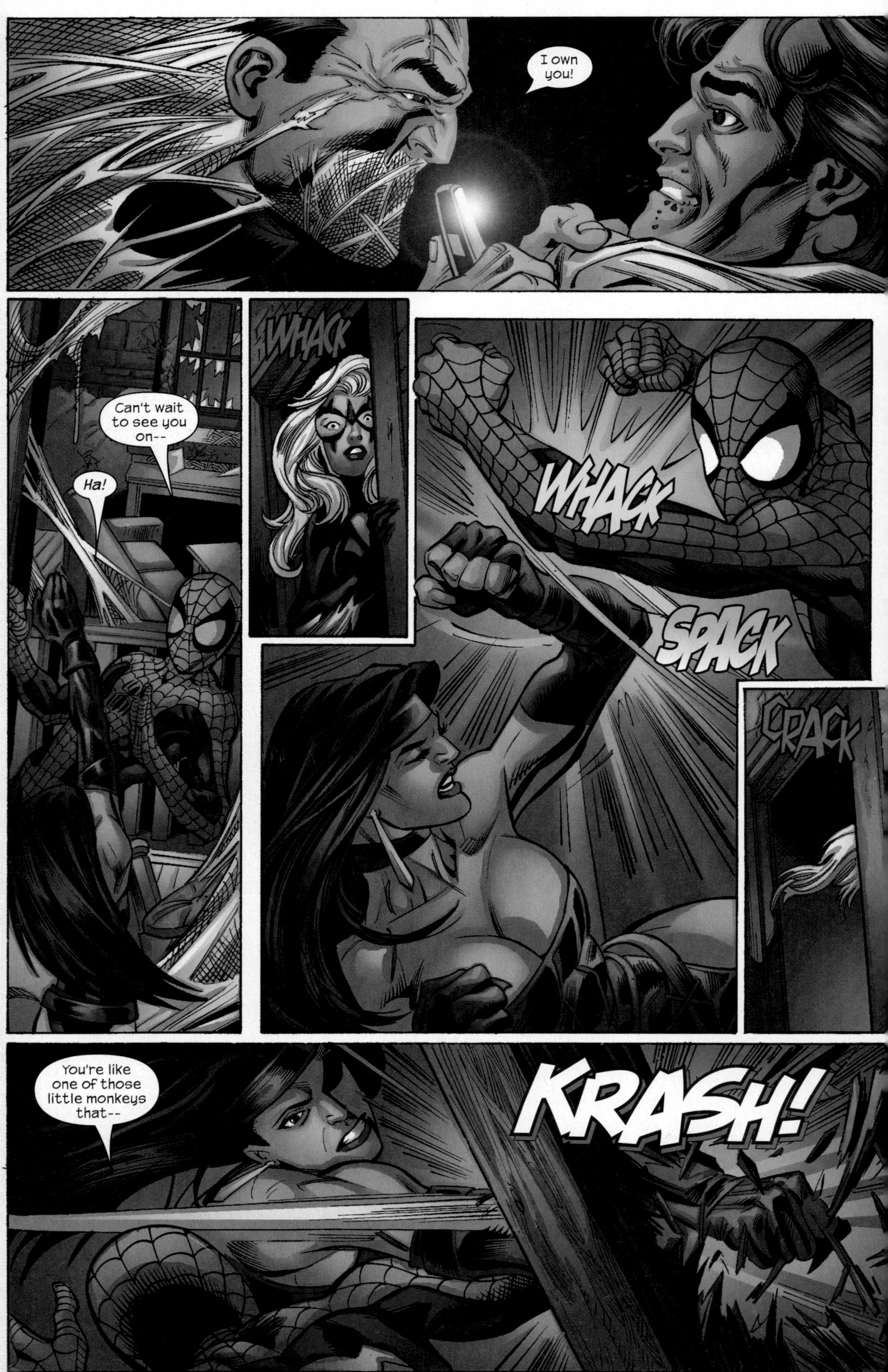
I own you!
Can't wait to see you on--
Ha!
WHACK
WHACK
SPACK
CRACK
You're like one of those little monkeys that--
KRASH!

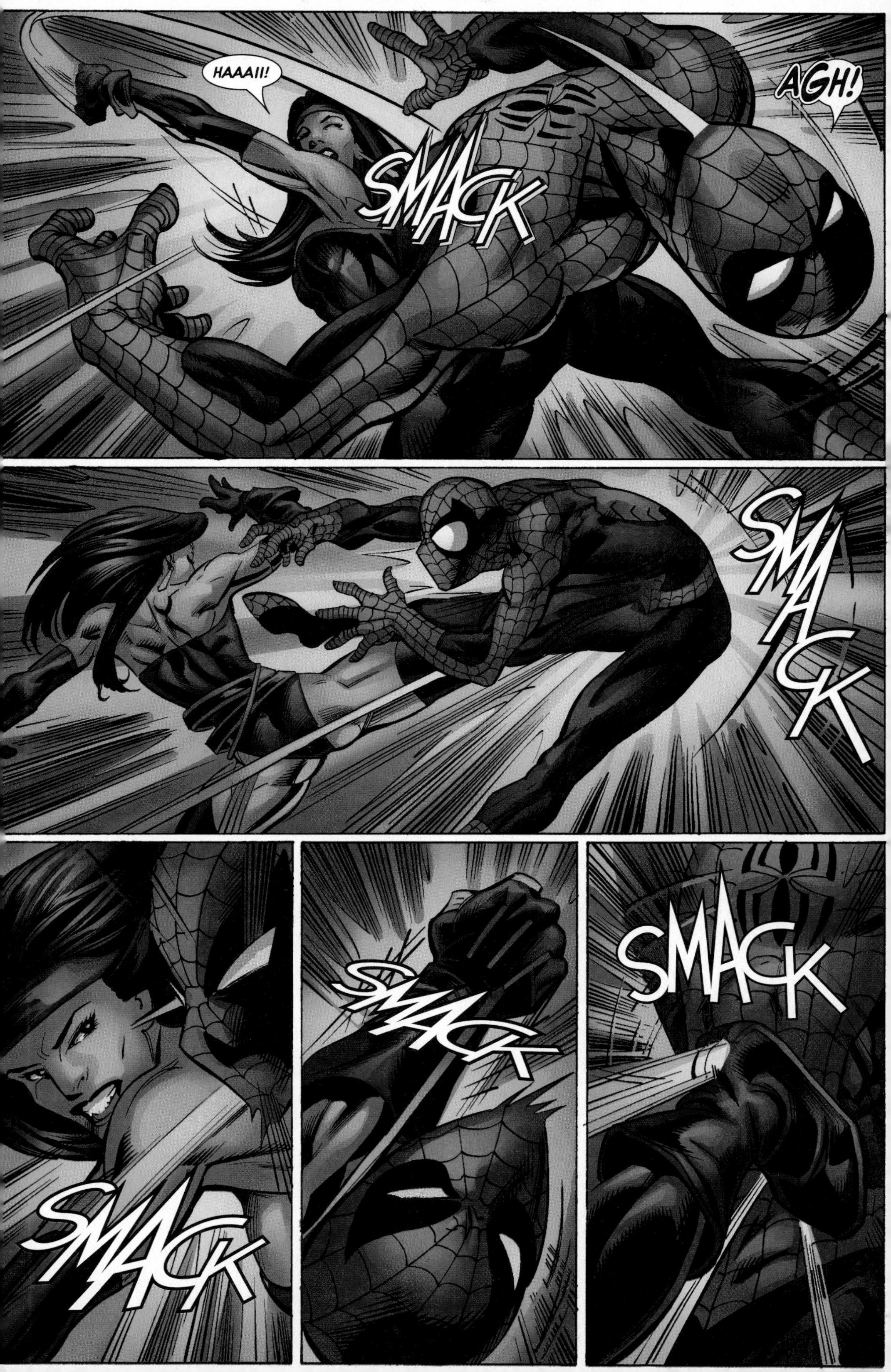
HAAAII!
SMACK
AGH!
SMACK
SMACK
SMACK
SMACK

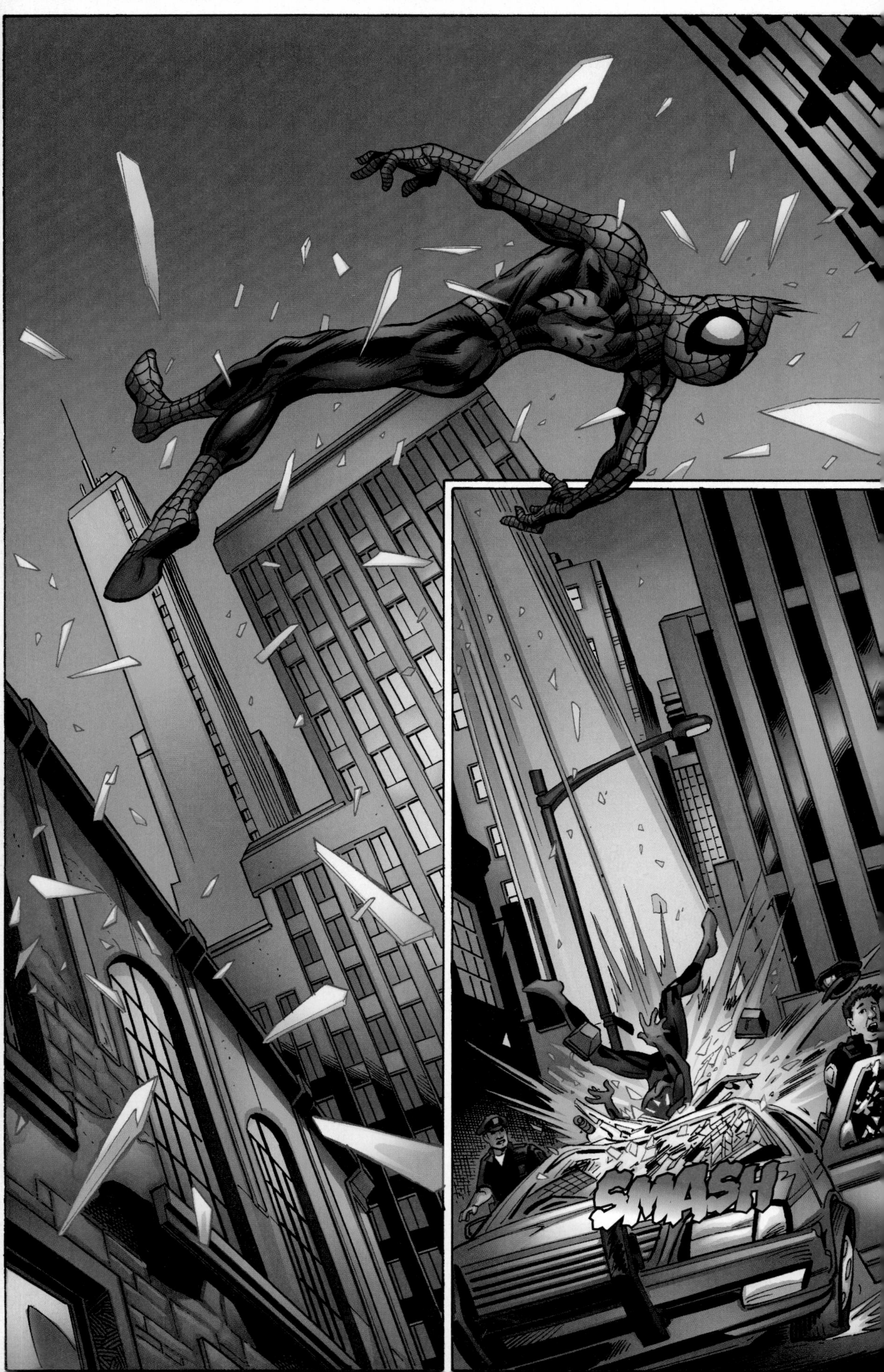
SMASH!

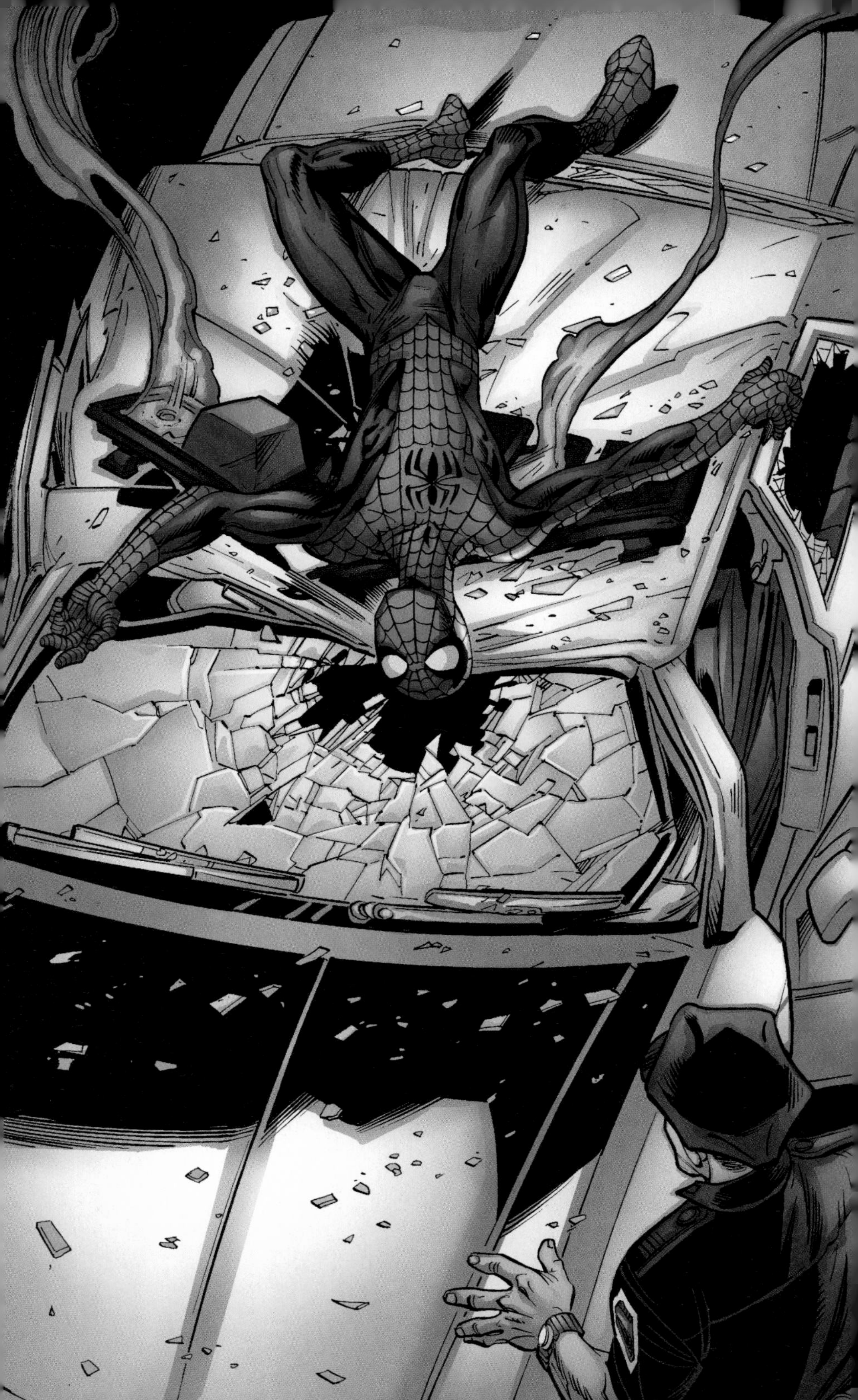

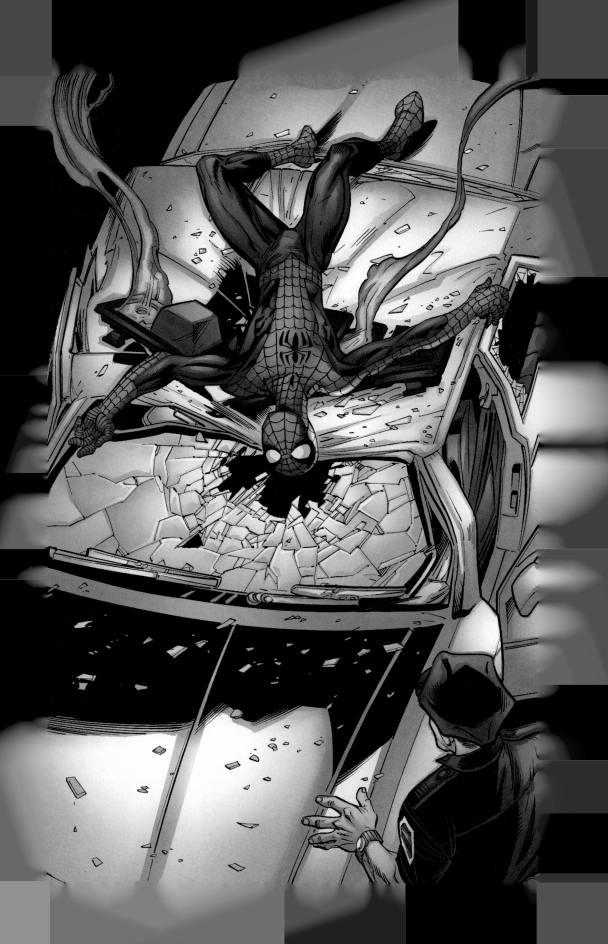

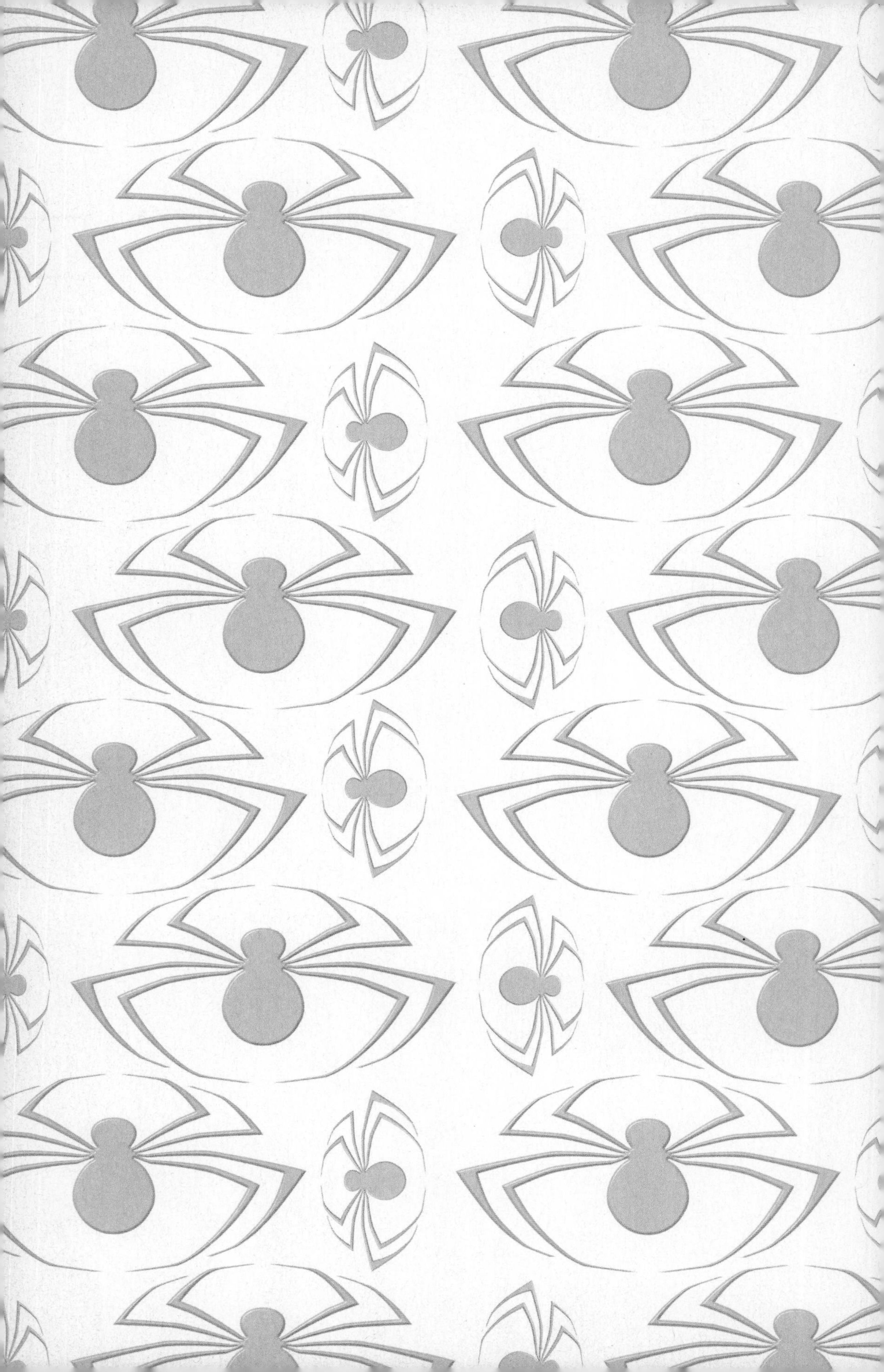

85

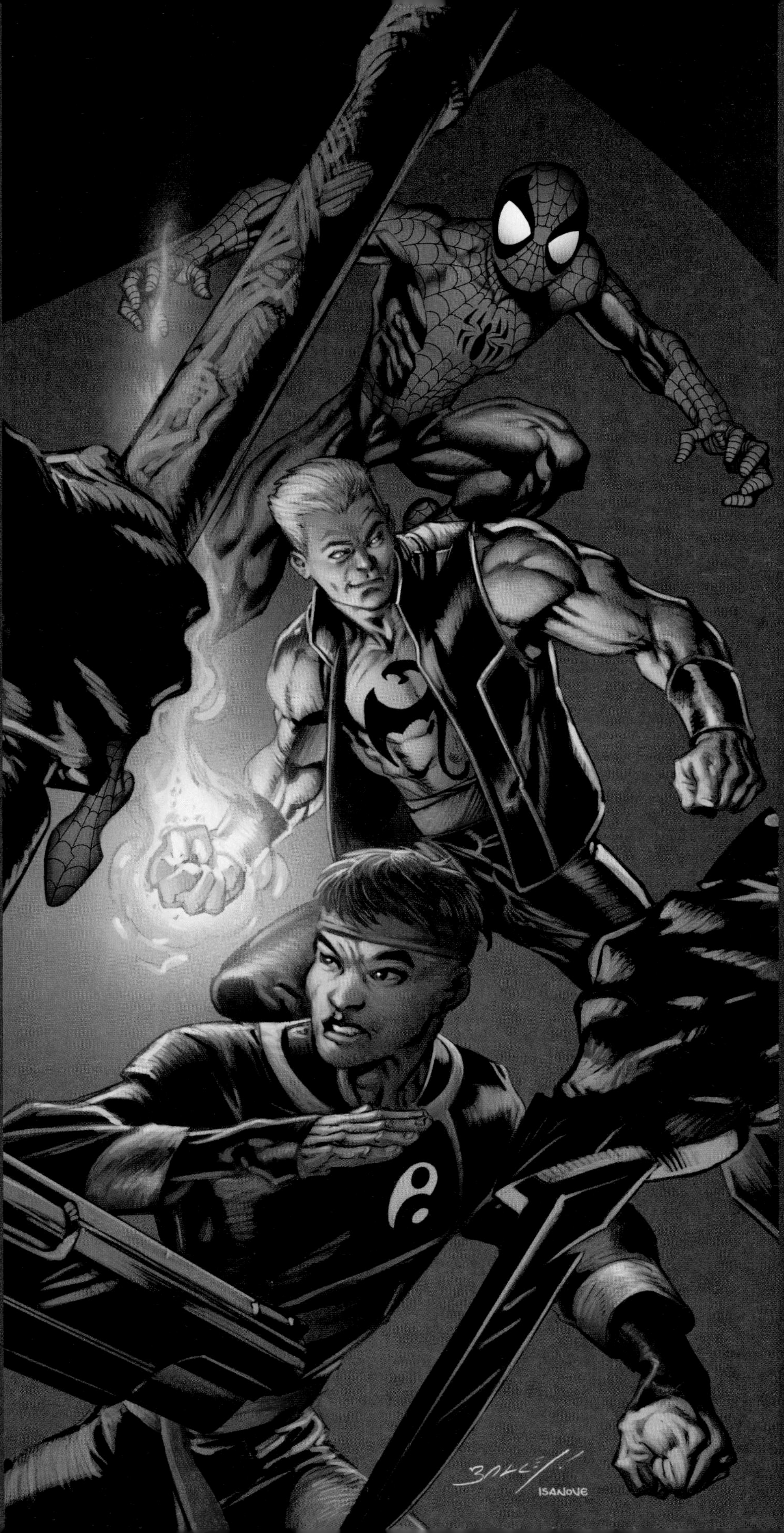

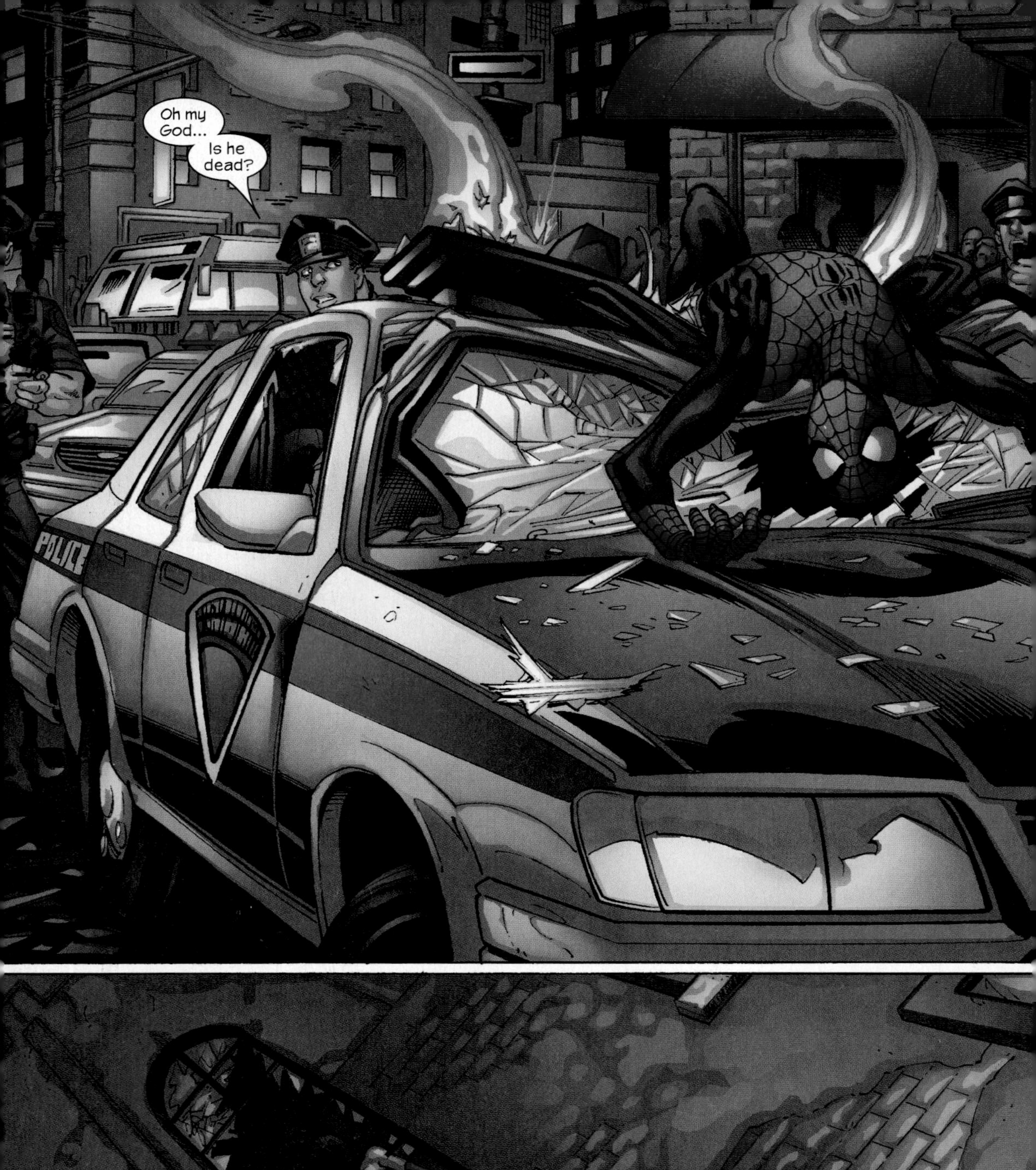
Oh my God...
Is he dead?
POLICE

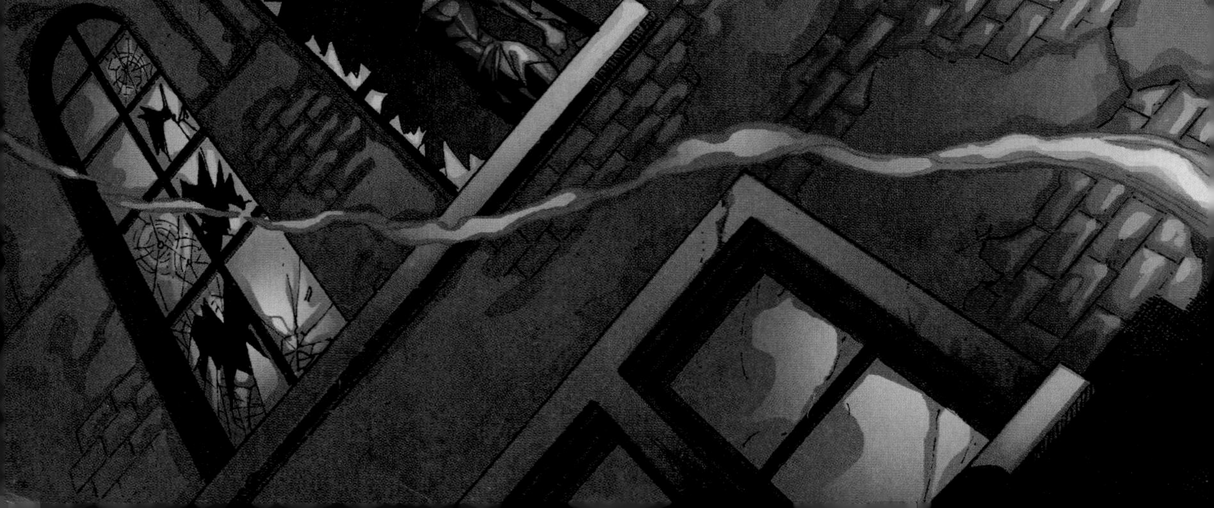

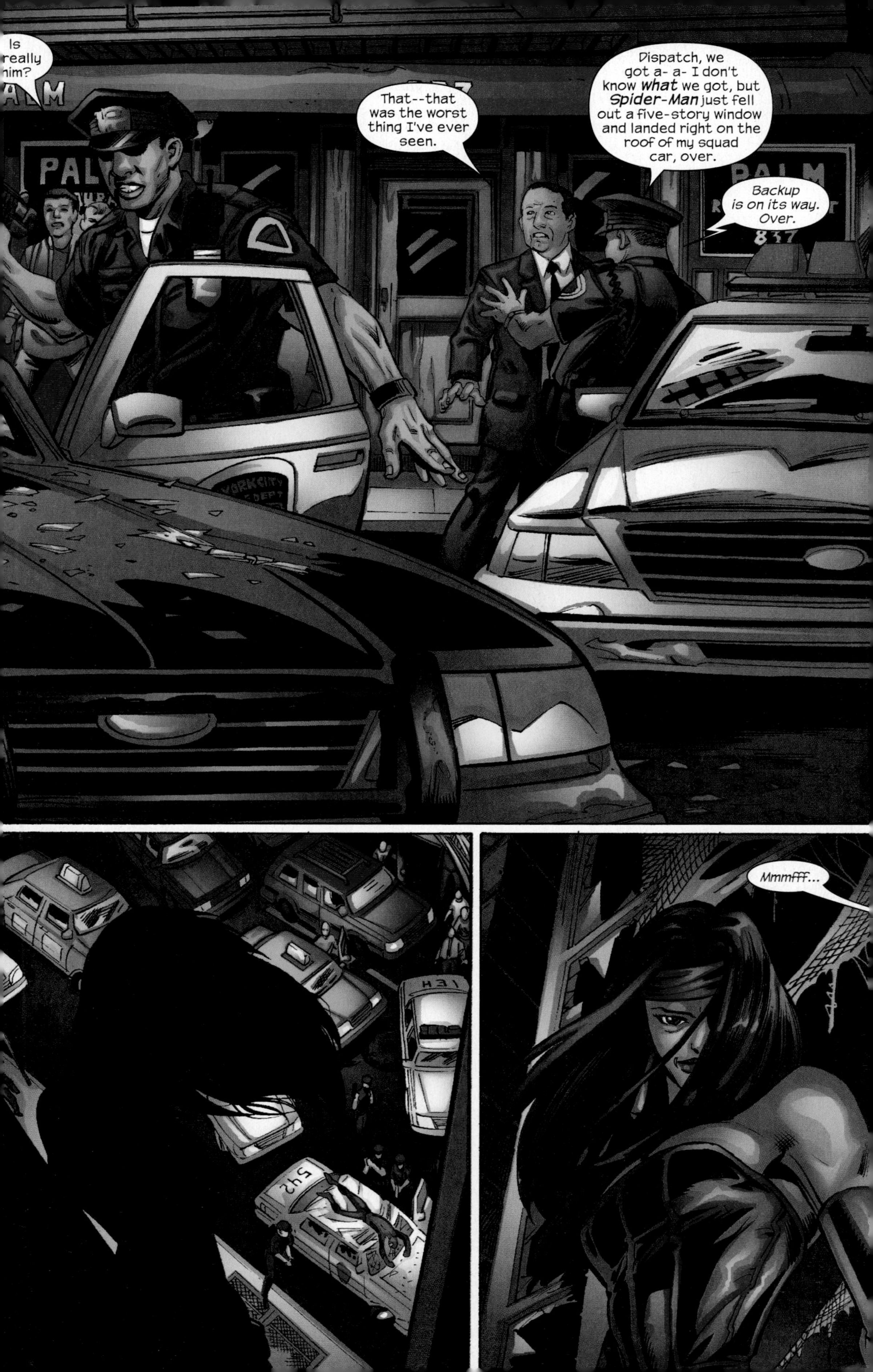
Is
really
him?
That--that was the worst thing I've ever seen.
Dispatch, we got a- a- I don't know *what* we got, but *Spider-Man* just fell out a five-story window and landed right on the roof of my squad car, over.
Backup is on its way. Over.
PALM
PALM
837
Mmmfff...

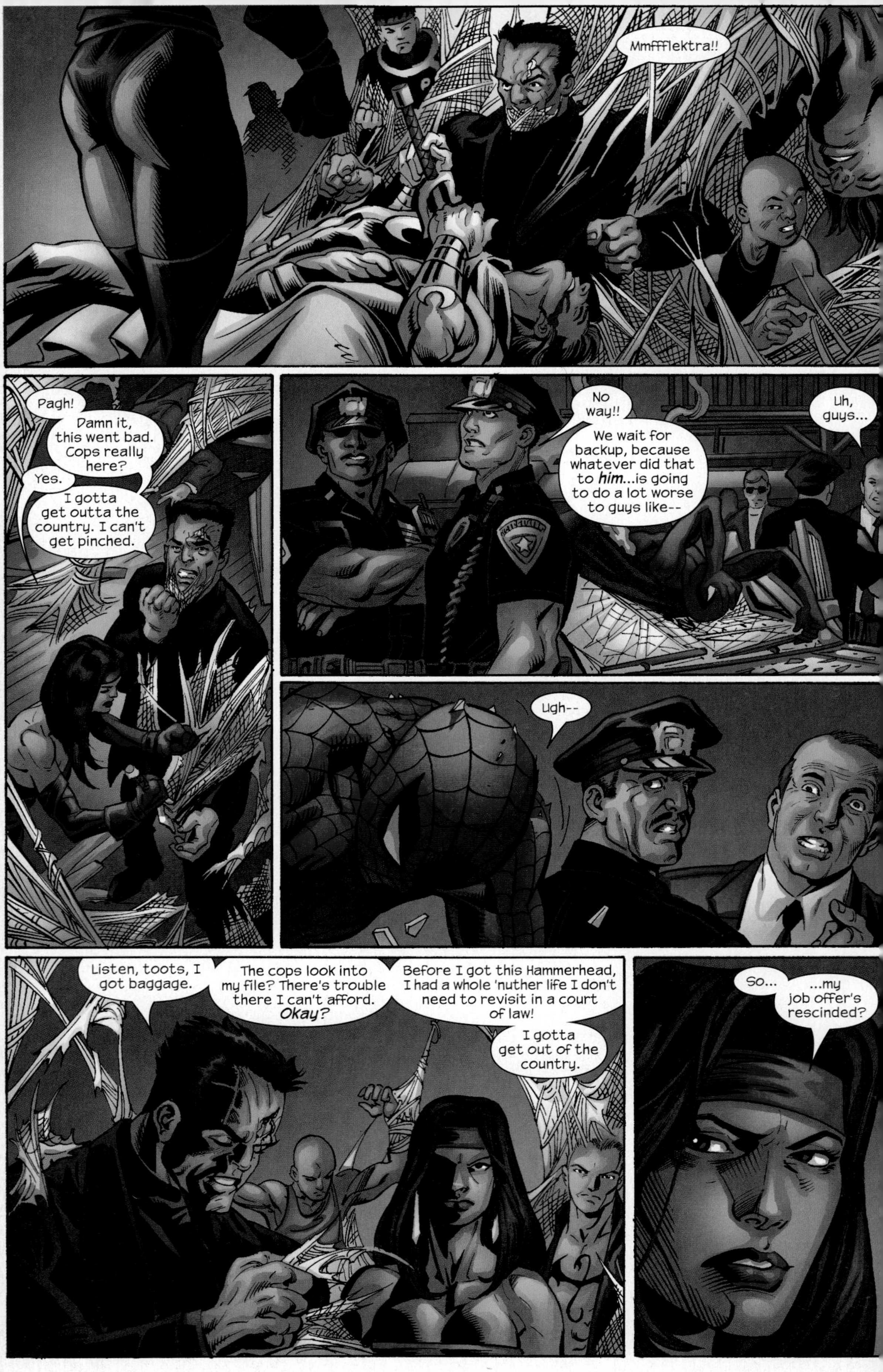
Mmfffflektra!!
Pagh!
Damn it, this went bad. Cops really here?
Yes.
I gotta get outta the country. I can't get pinched.
No way!!
We wait for backup, because whatever did that to *him*...is going to do a lot worse to guys like--
Uh, guys...
Ugh--
Listen, toots, I got baggage.
The cops look into my file? There's trouble there I can't afford. *Okay?*
Before I got this Hammerhead, I had a whole 'nuther life I don't need to revisit in a court of law!
I gotta get out of the country.
So...
...my job offer's rescinded?

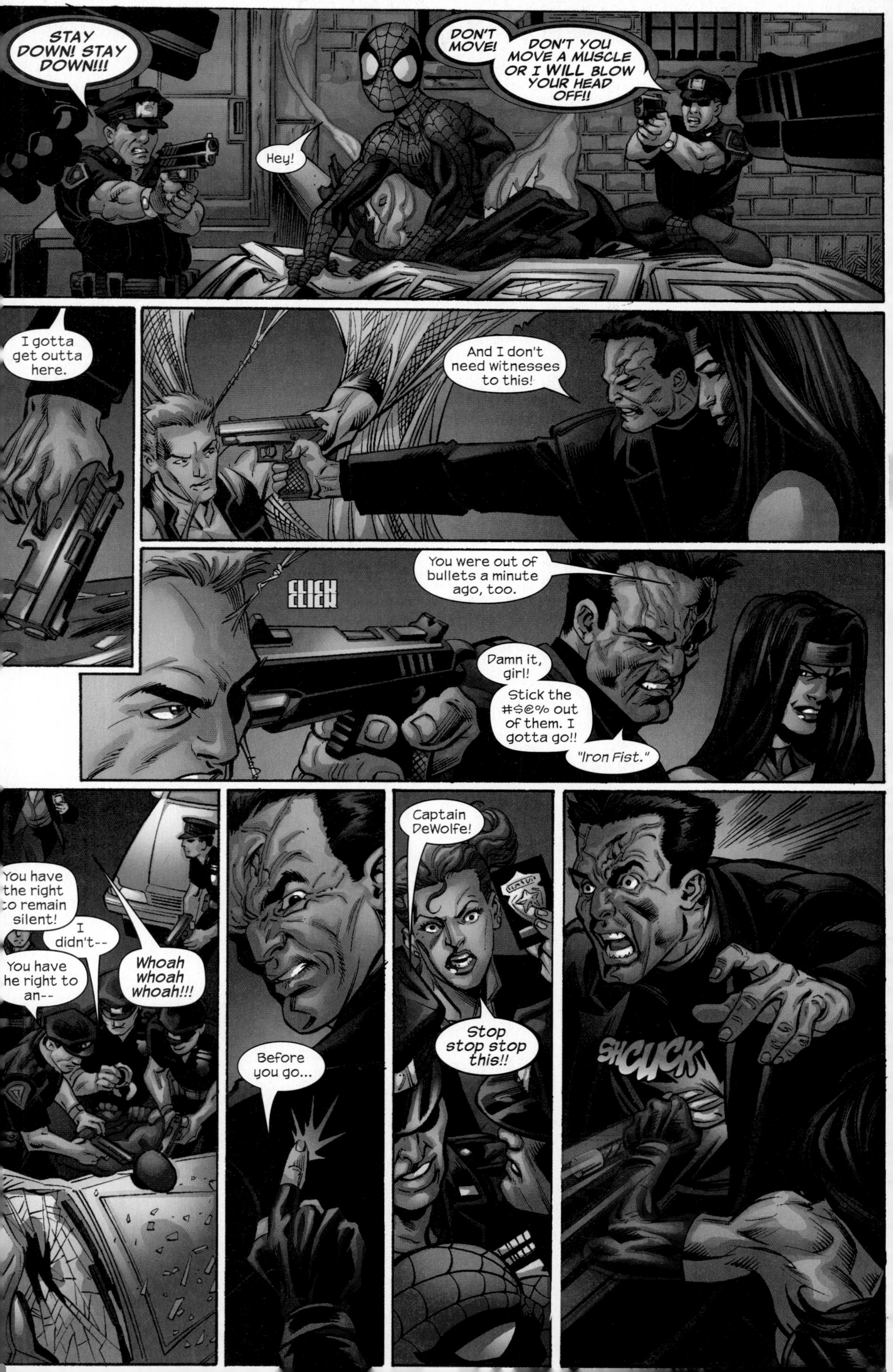
STAY DOWN! STAY DOWN!!!
Hey!
DON'T MOVE!
DON'T YOU MOVE A MUSCLE OR I WILL BLOW YOUR HEAD OFF!!
I gotta get outta here.
And I don't need witnesses to this!
CLICK CLICK
You were out of bullets a minute ago, too.
Damn it, girl!
Stick the #$@% out of them. I gotta go!!
"Iron Fist."
You have the right to remain silent!
I didn't--
You have he right to an--
Whoah whoah whoah!!!
Before you go...
Captain DeWolfe!
Stop stop stop this!!
SHCUCK

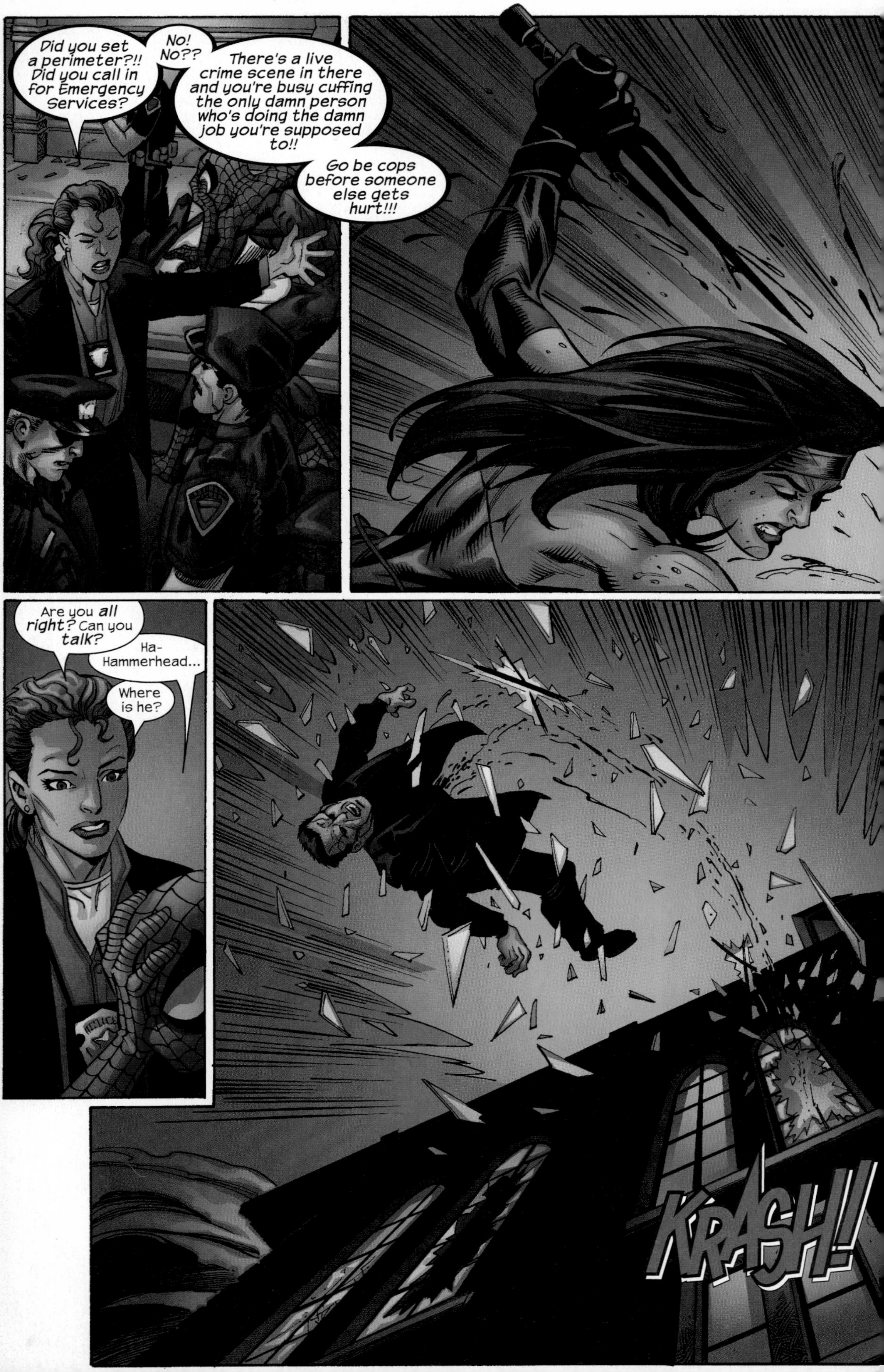
Did you set a perimeter?!! Did you call in for Emergency Services?
No! No??
There's a live crime scene in there and you're busy cuffing the only damn person who's doing the damn job you're supposed to!!
Go be cops before someone else gets hurt!!!
Are you all right? Can you talk?
Ha- Hammerhead...
Where is he?
KRASH!!

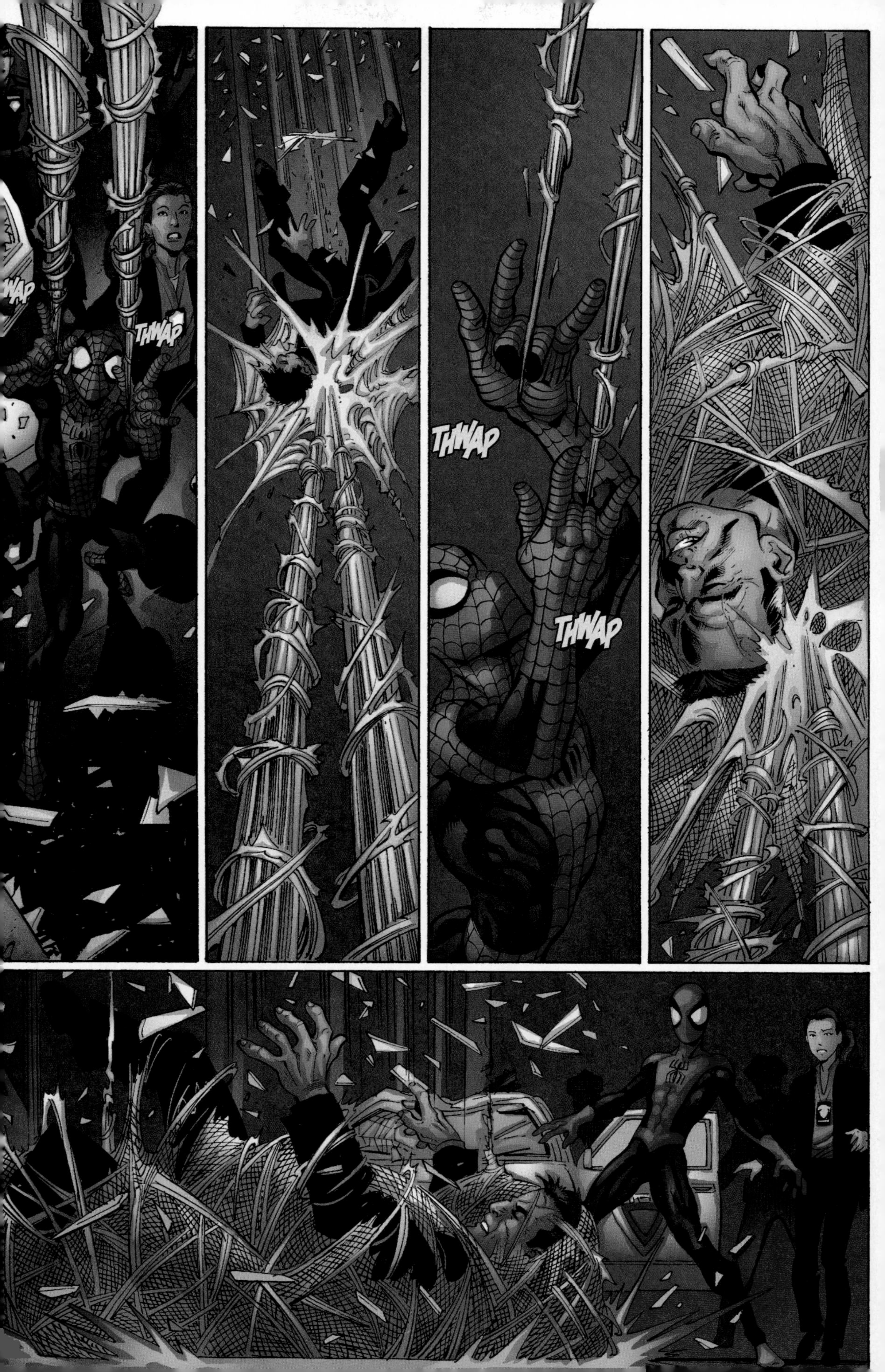
THWAP
THWAP
THWAP

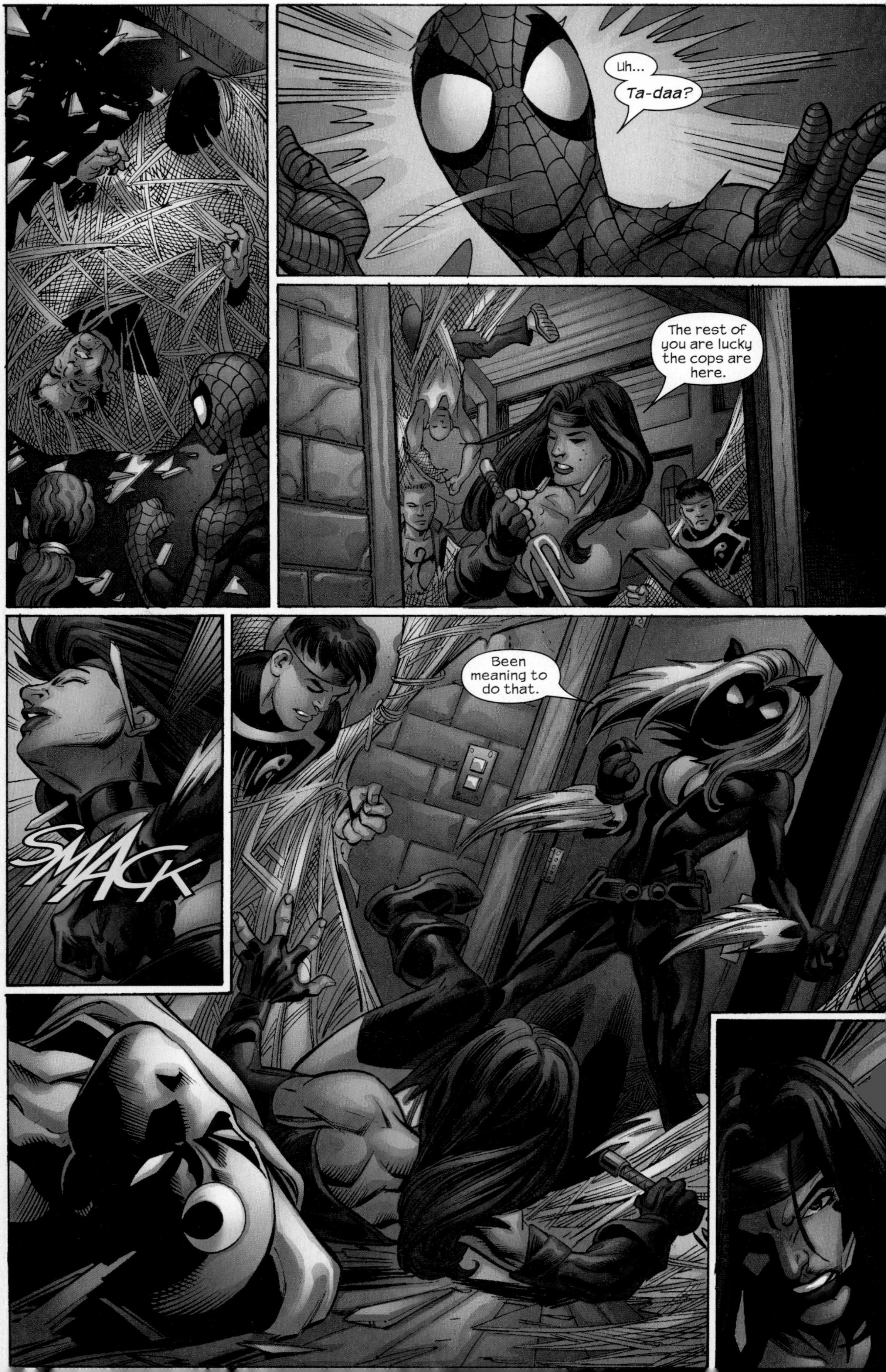
Uh...
Ta-daa?
The rest of you are lucky the cops are here.
SMACK
Been meaning to do that.

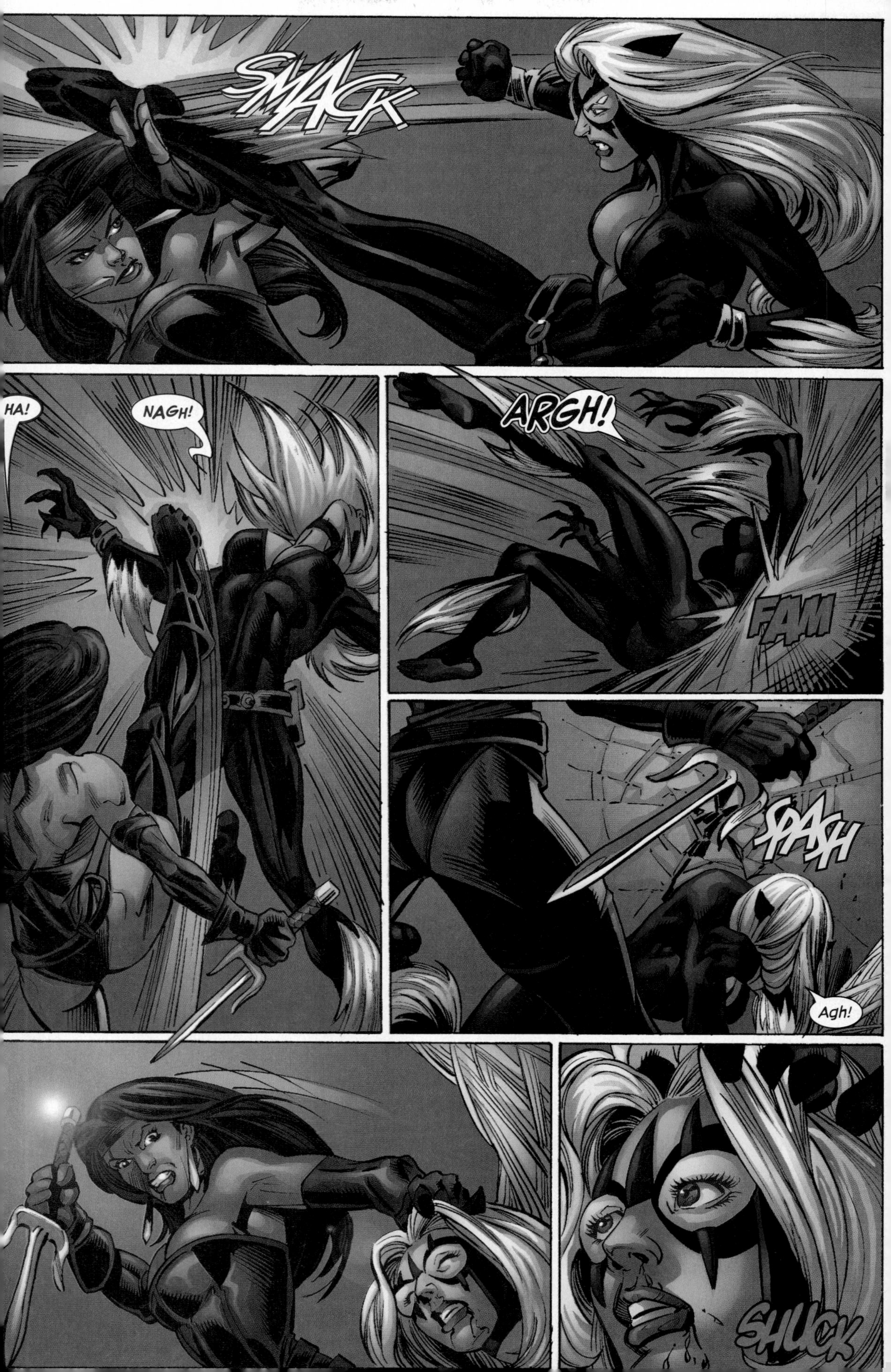
SMACK
HA!
NAGH!
ARGH!
FAM
SPASH
Agh!
SHUCK

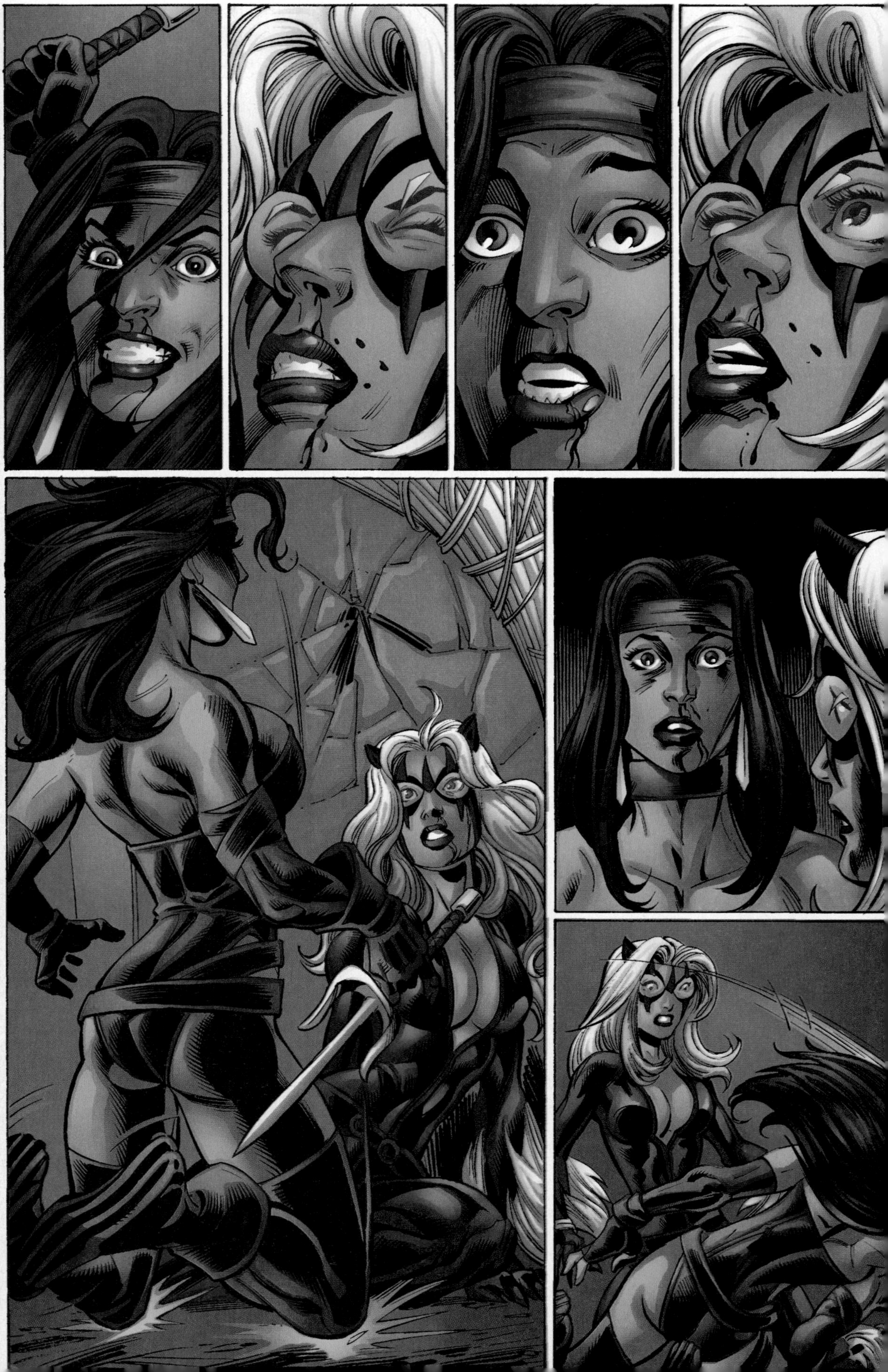

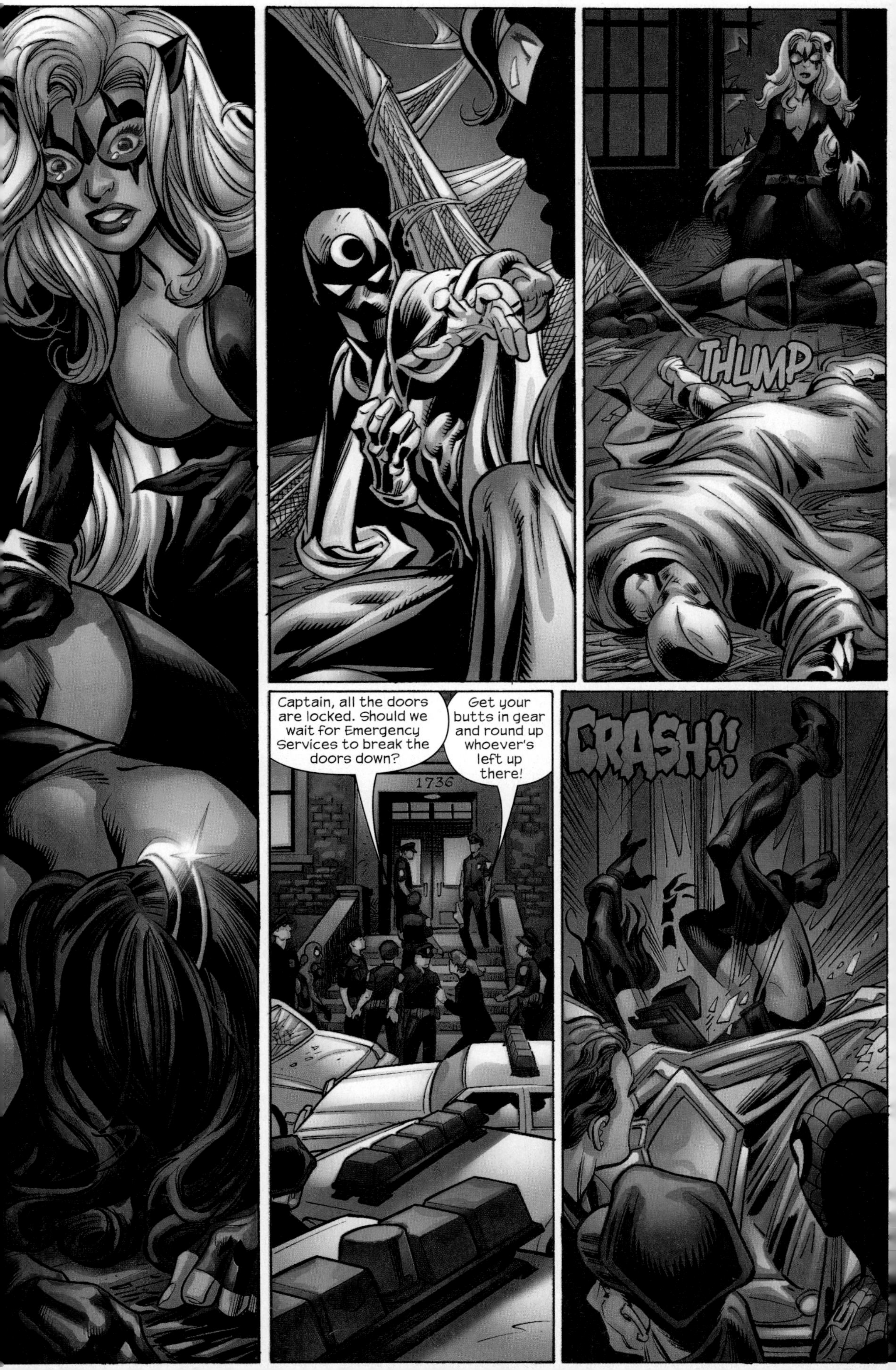
THUMP
Captain, all the doors are locked. Should we wait for Emergency Services to break the doors down?
Get your butts in gear and round up whoever's left up there!
1736
CRASH!!

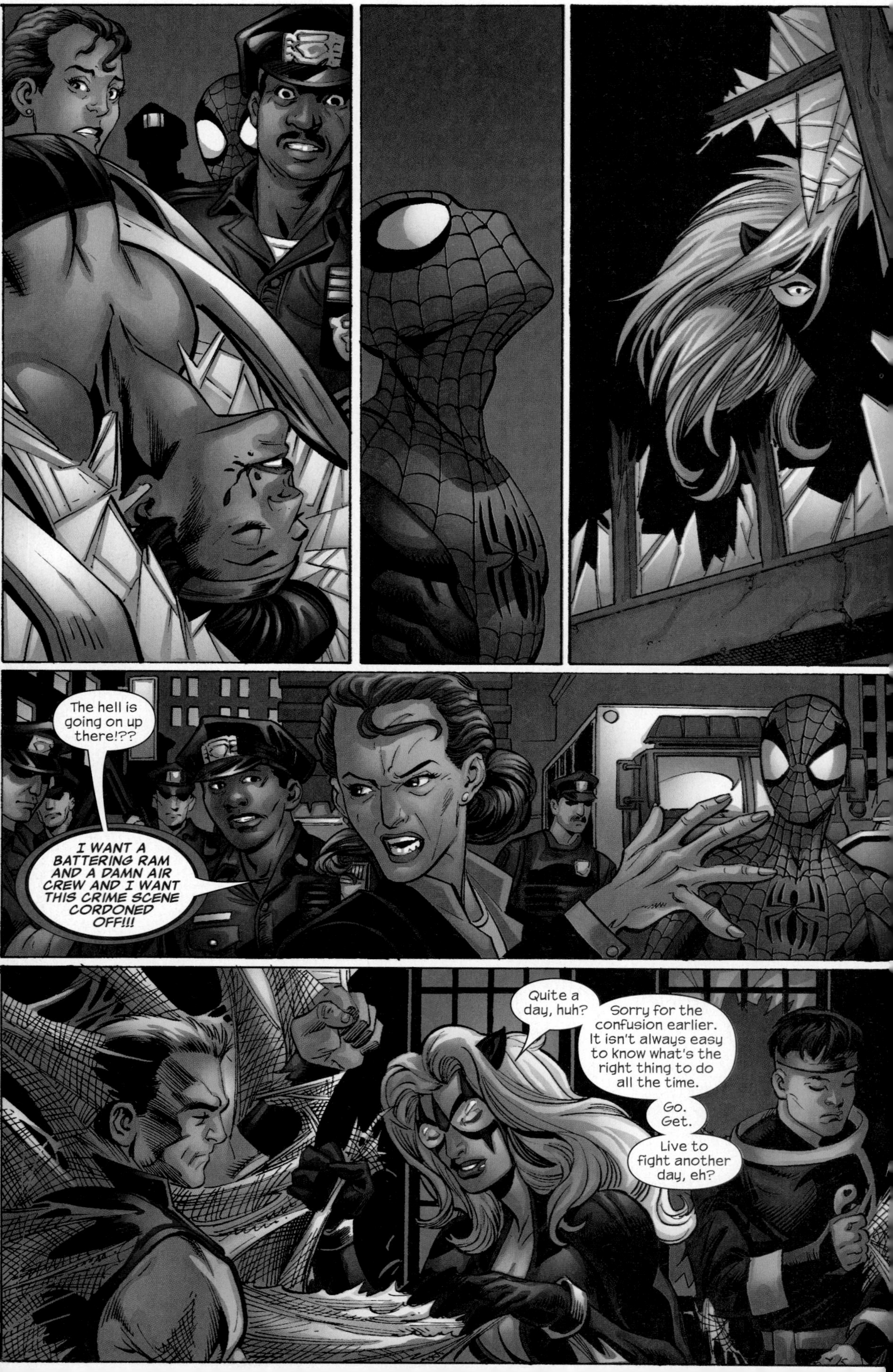

The hell is going on up there!??
I WANT A BATTERING RAM AND A DAMN AIR CREW AND I WANT THIS CRIME SCENE CORDONED OFF!!!
Quite a day, huh?
Sorry for the confusion earlier. It isn't always easy to know what's the right thing to do all the time.
Go. Get.
Live to fight another day, eh?

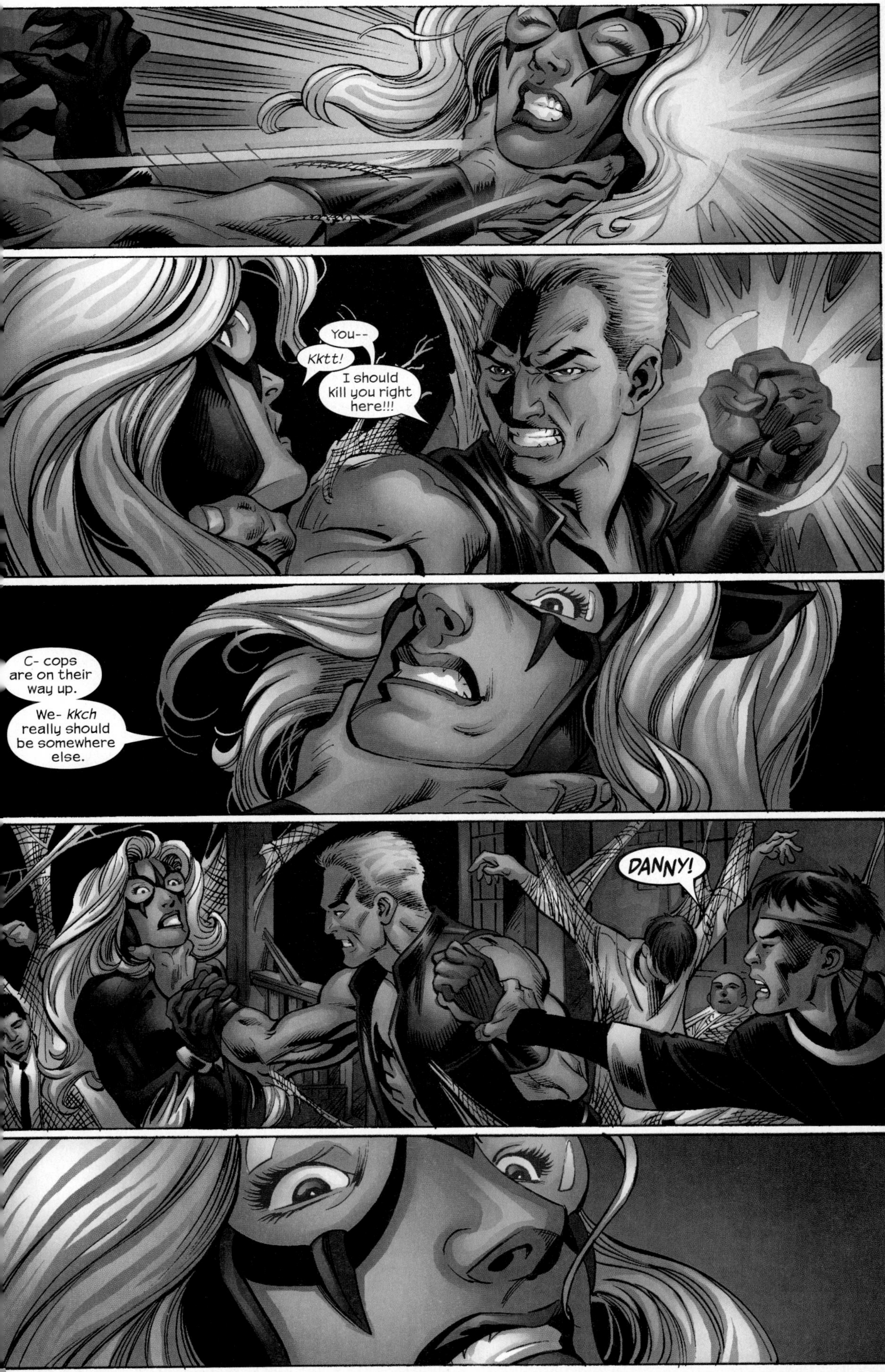
You--
Kktt!
I should kill you right here!!!
C- cops are on their way up.
We- kkch really should be somewhere else.
DANNY!

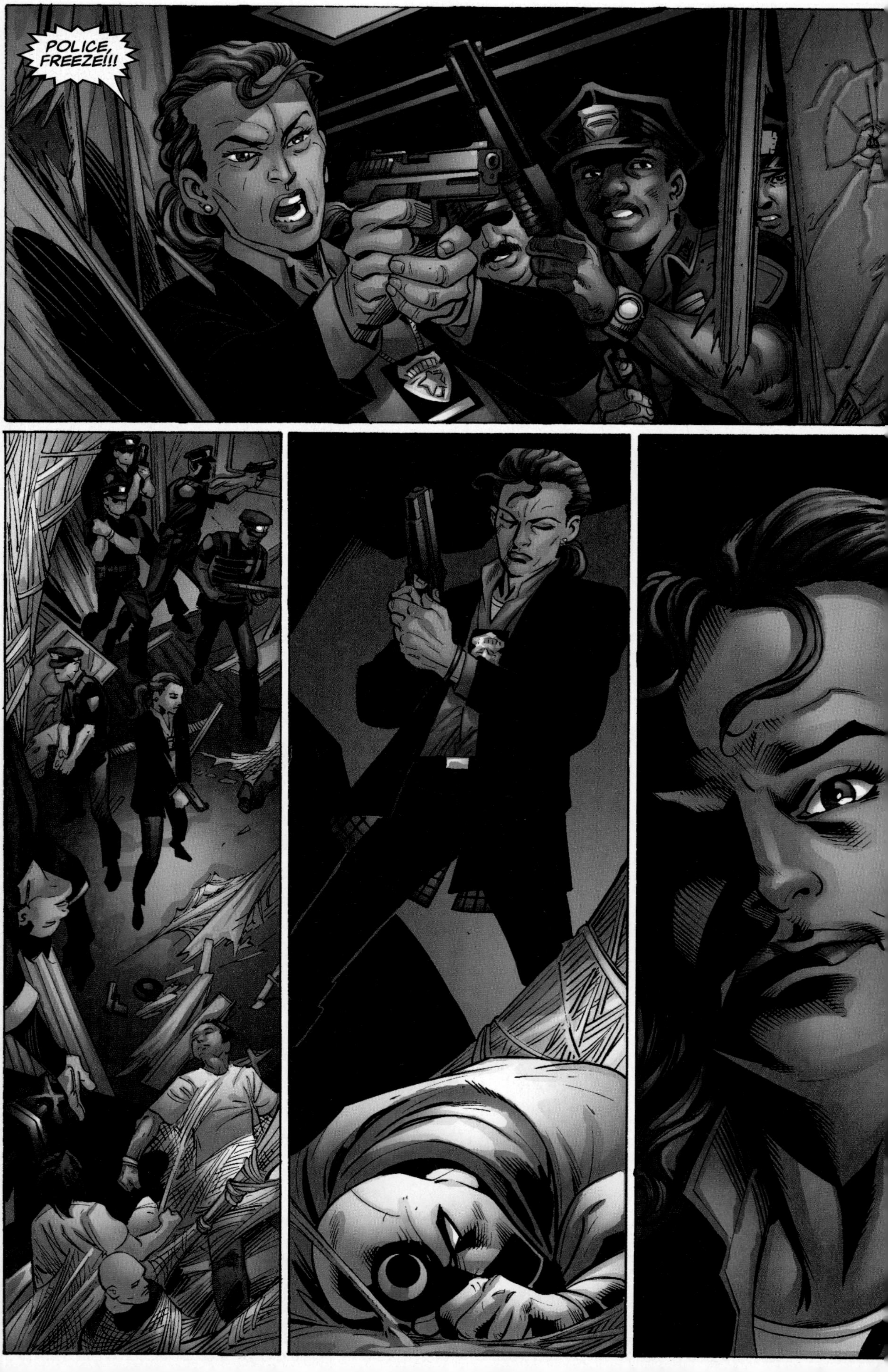
POLICE, FREEZE!!!

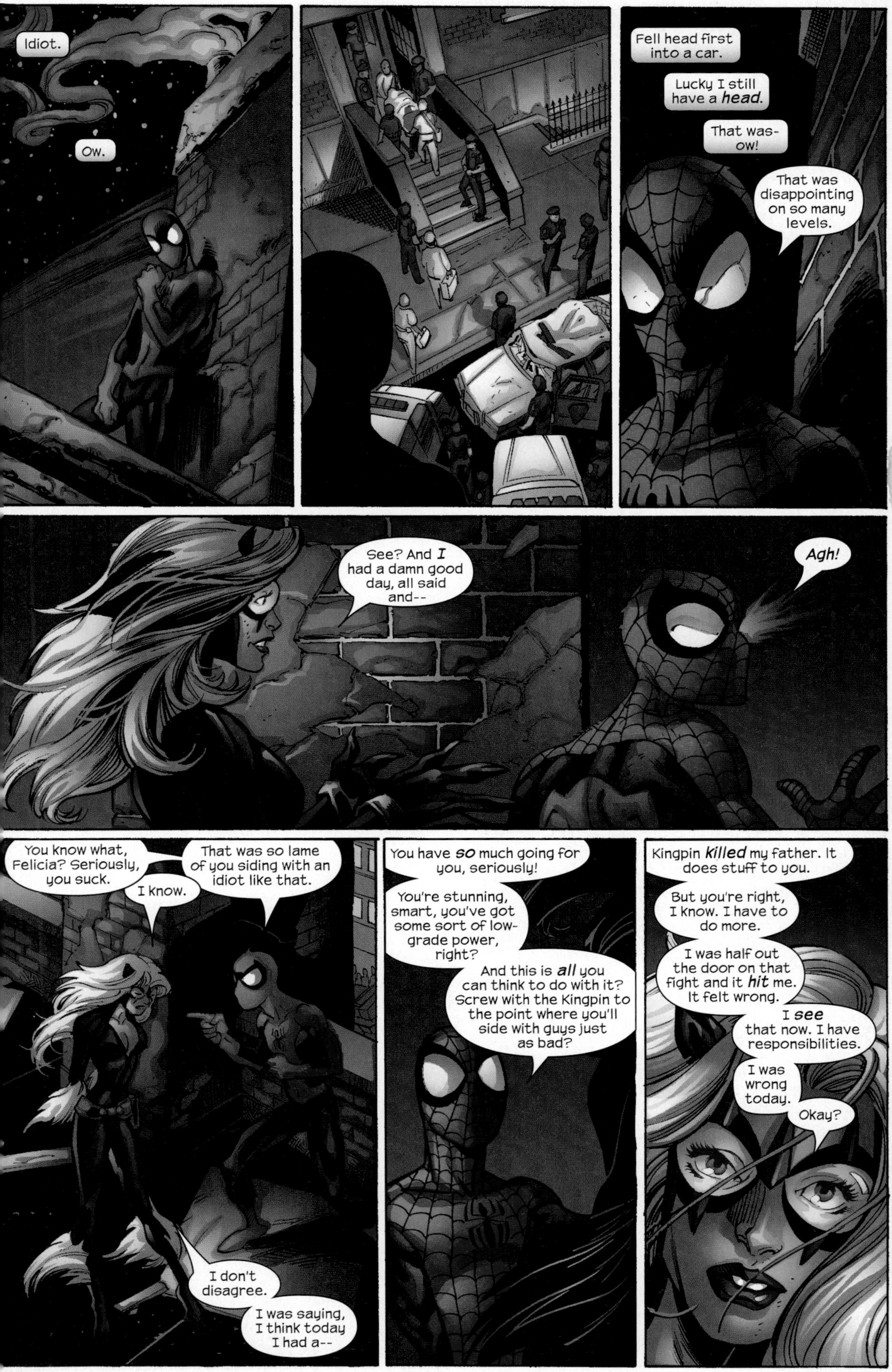
Idiot.
Ow.
Fell head first into a car.
Lucky I still have a head.
That was-- ow!
That was disappointing on so many levels.
See? And I had a damn good day, all said and--
Agh!
You know what, Felicia? Seriously, you suck.
I know.
That was so lame of you siding with an idiot like that.
I don't disagree.
I was saying, I think today I had a--
You have so much going for you, seriously!
You're stunning, smart, you've got some sort of low-grade power, right?
And this is all you can think to do with it? Screw with the Kingpin to the point where you'll side with guys just as bad?
Kingpin killed my father. It does stuff to you.
But you're right, I know. I have to do more.
I was half out the door on that fight and it hit me. It felt wrong.
I see that now. I have responsibilities.
I was wrong today.
Okay?

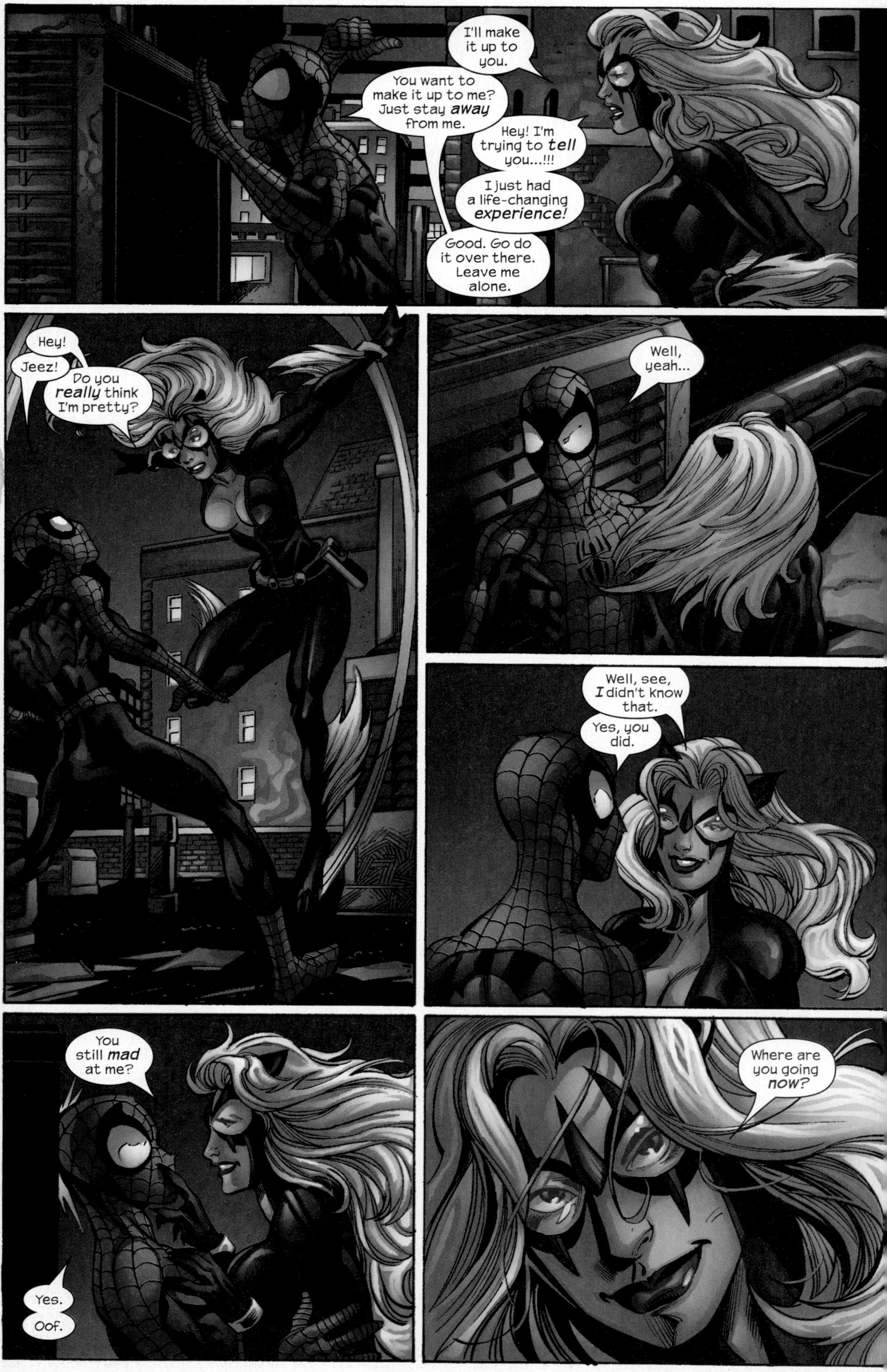

I'll make it up to you.
You want to make it up to me? Just stay *away* from me.
Hey! I'm trying to *tell* you...!!!
I just had a life-changing *experience!*
Good. Go do it over there. Leave me alone.
Hey!
Jeez!
Do you *really* think I'm pretty?
Well, yeah...
Well, see, *I* didn't know that.
Yes, you did.
You still *mad* at me?
Yes.
Oof.
Where are you going *now?*

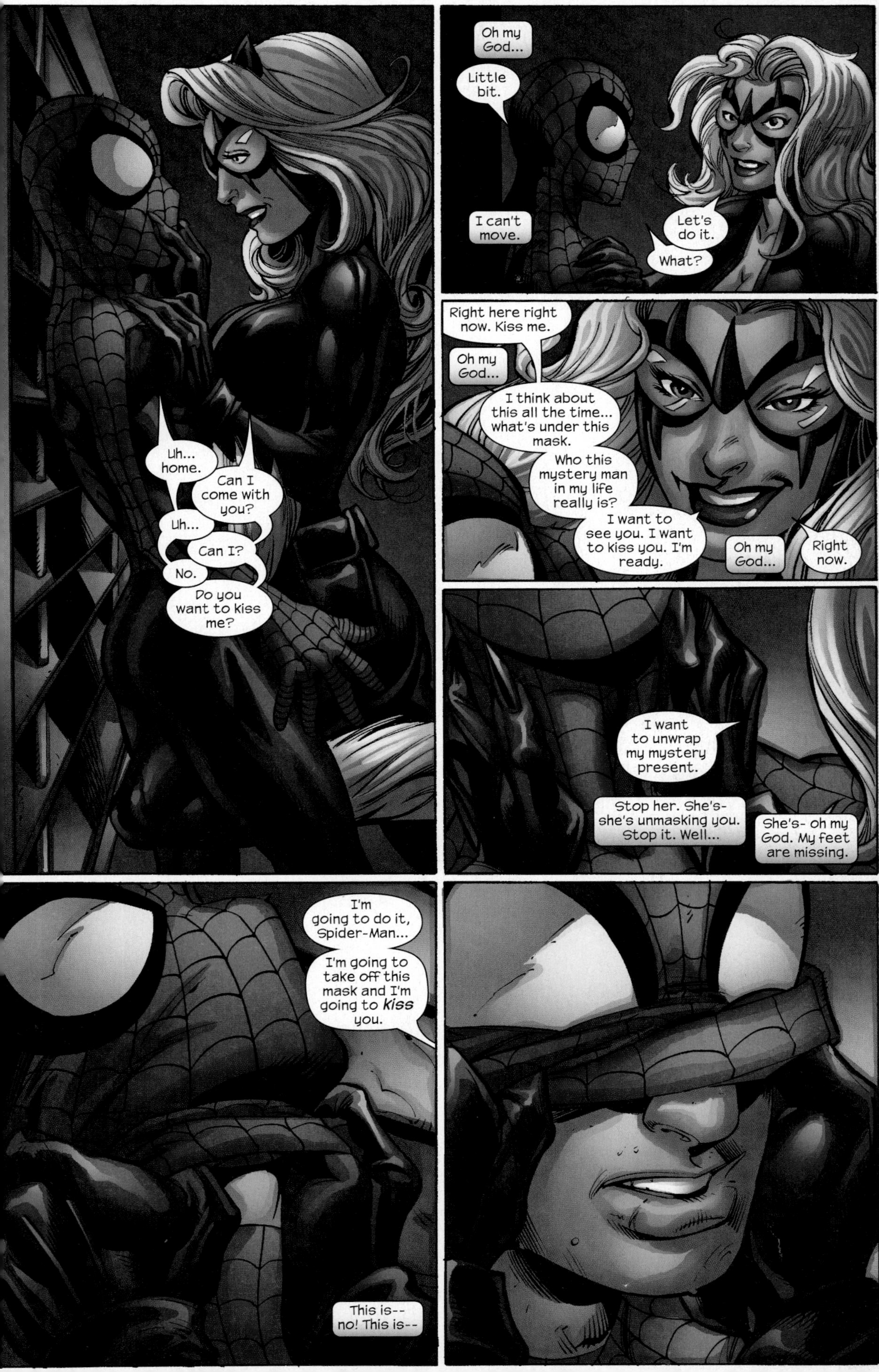
Uh... home.
Can I come with you?
Uh...
Can I?
No.
Do you want to kiss me?
Oh my God...
Little bit.
I can't move.
Let's do it.
What?
Right here right now. Kiss me.
Oh my God...
I think about this all the time... what's under this mask.
Who this mystery man in my life really is?
I want to see you. I want to kiss you. I'm ready.
Oh my God...
Right now.
I want to unwrap my mystery present.
Stop her. She's- she's unmasking you. Stop it. Well...
She's- oh my God. My feet are missing.
I'm going to do it, Spider-Man...
I'm going to take off this mask and I'm going to *kiss* you.
This is-- no! This is--

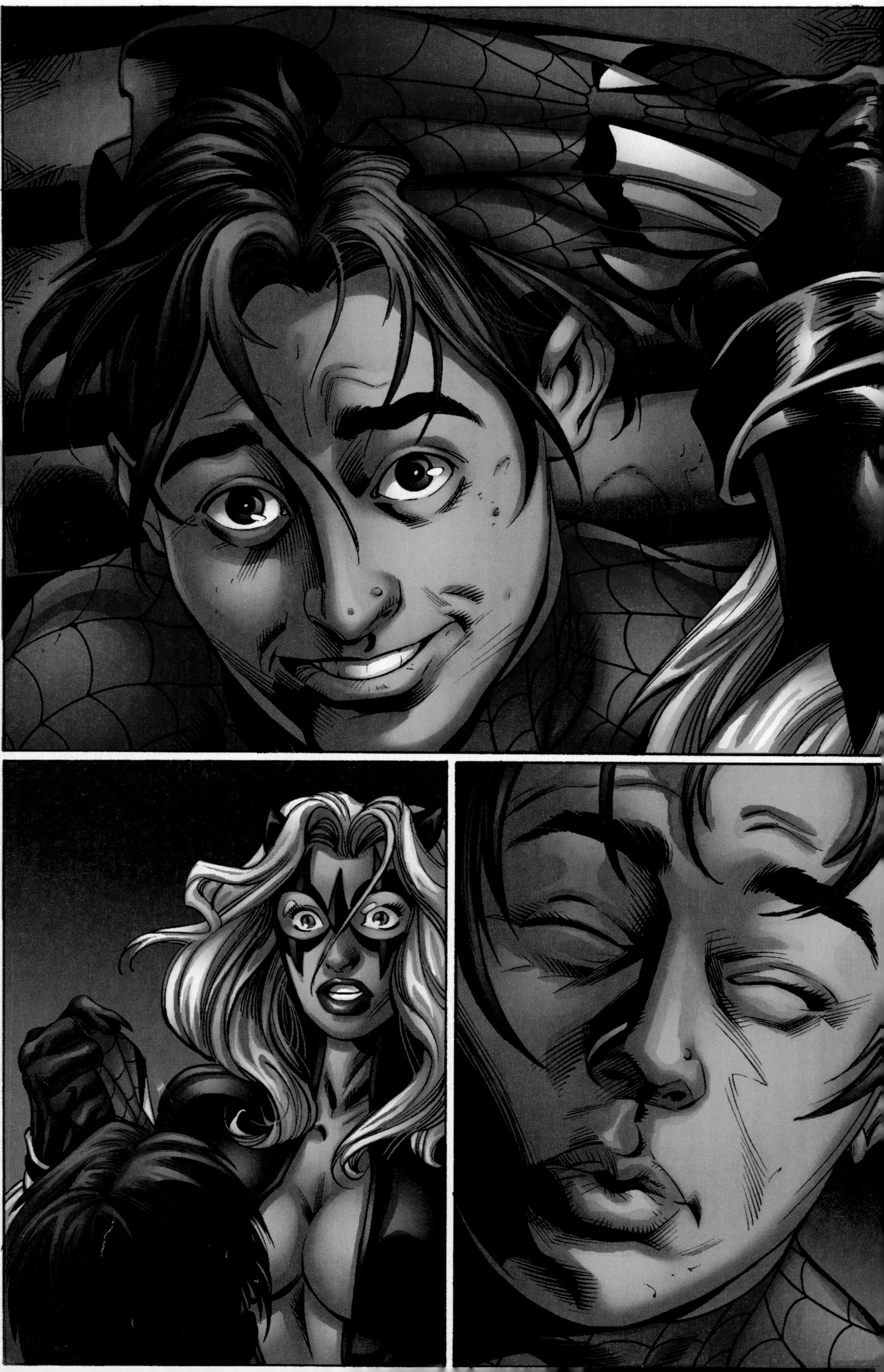

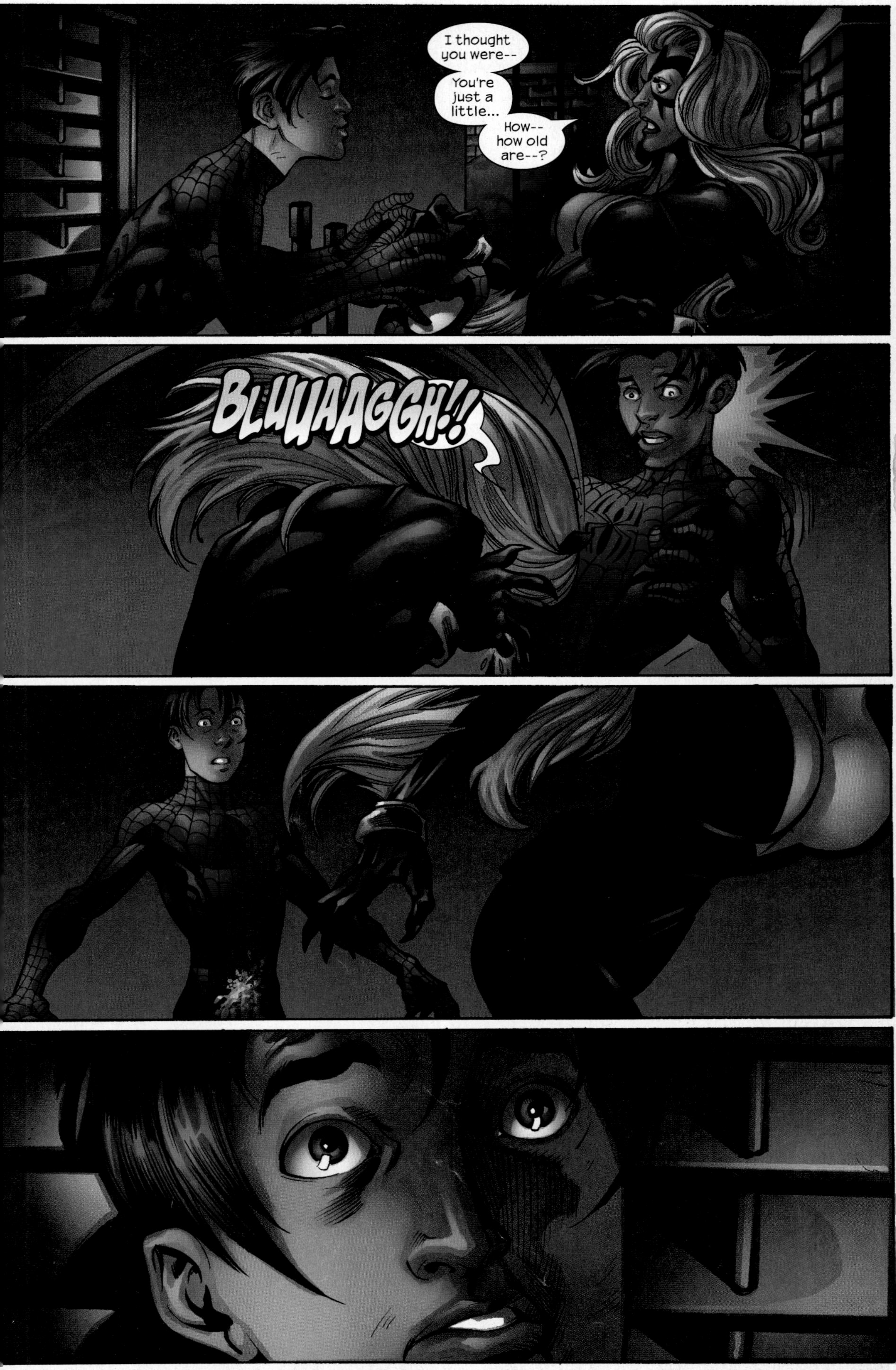
I thought you were--
You're just a little...
How-- how old are--?
BLUUAAGGH!!

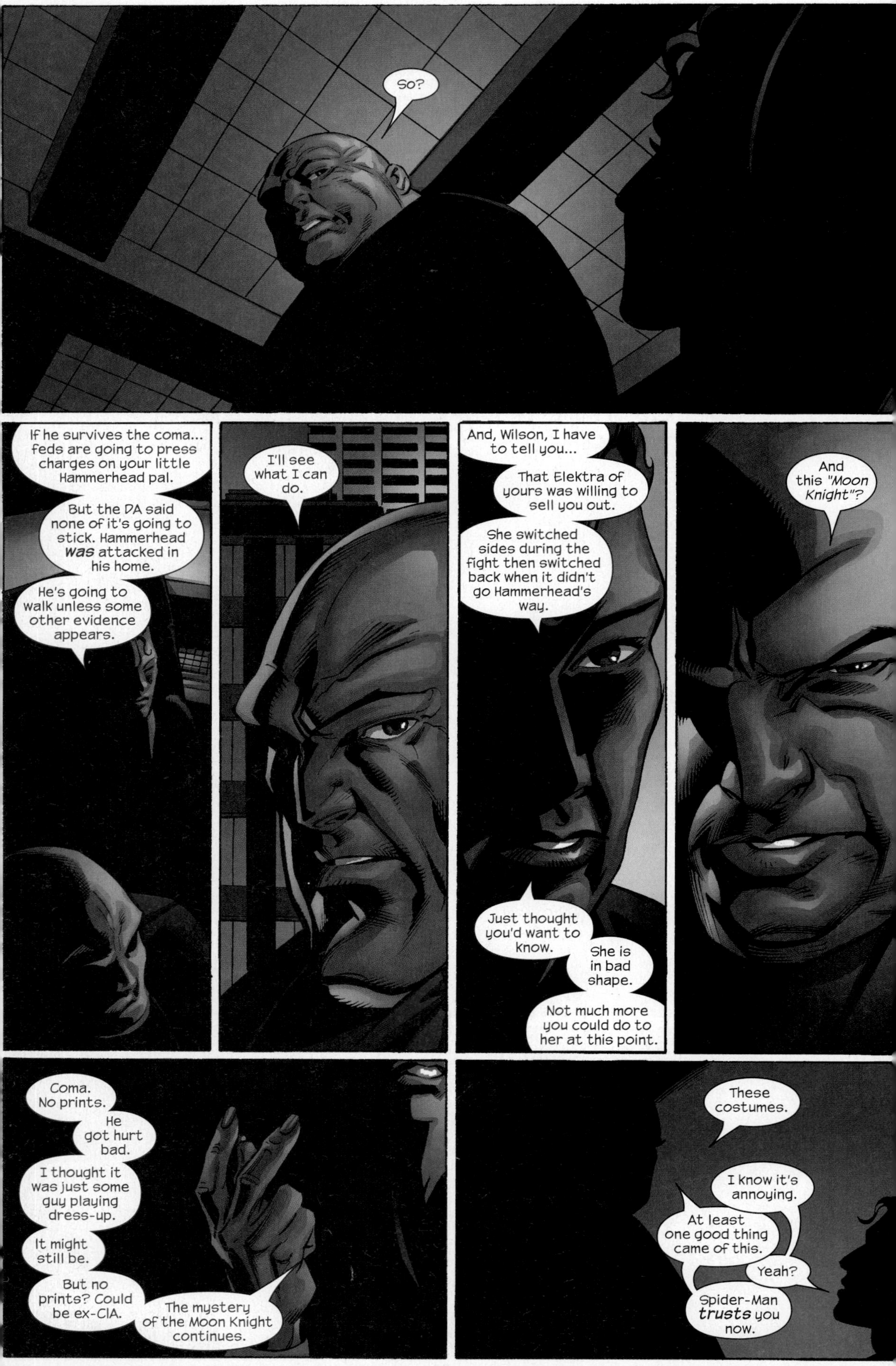

So?
If he survives the coma... feds are going to press charges on your little Hammerhead pal.
But the DA said none of it's going to stick. Hammerhead *was* attacked in his home.
He's going to walk unless some other evidence appears.
I'll see what I can do.
And, Wilson, I have to tell you...
That Elektra of yours was willing to sell you out.
She switched sides during the fight then switched back when it didn't go Hammerhead's way.
Just thought you'd want to know.
She is in bad shape.
Not much more you could do to her at this point.
And this *"Moon Knight"*?
Coma. No prints.
He got hurt bad.
I thought it was just some guy playing dress-up.
It might still be.
But no prints? Could be ex-CIA.
The mystery of the Moon Knight continues.
These costumes.
I know it's annoying.
At least one good thing came of this.
Yeah?
Spider-Man ***trusts*** you now.

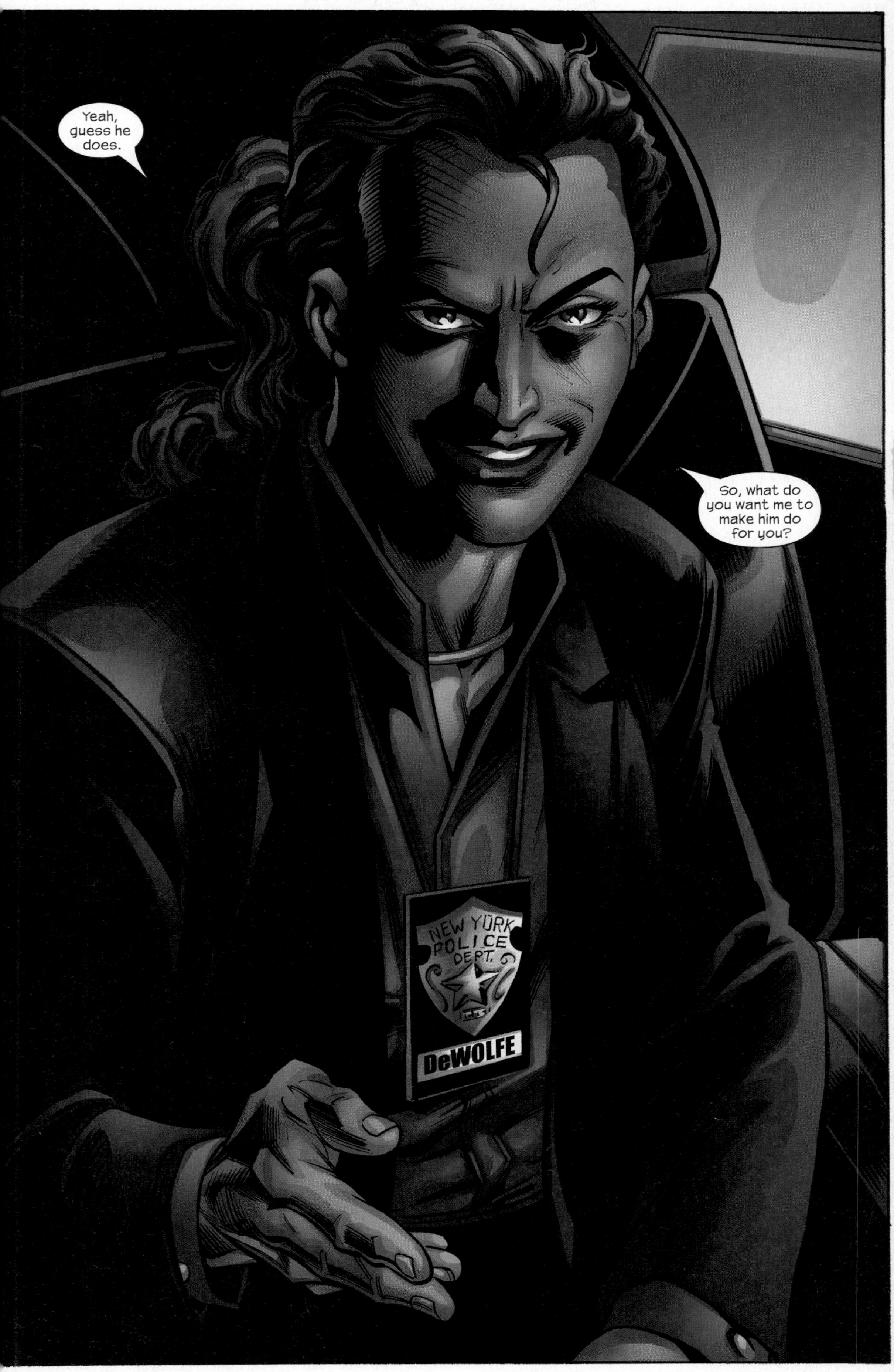

Yeah, guess he does.
So, what do you want me to make him do for you?
NEW YORK POLICE DEPT.
DeWOLFE

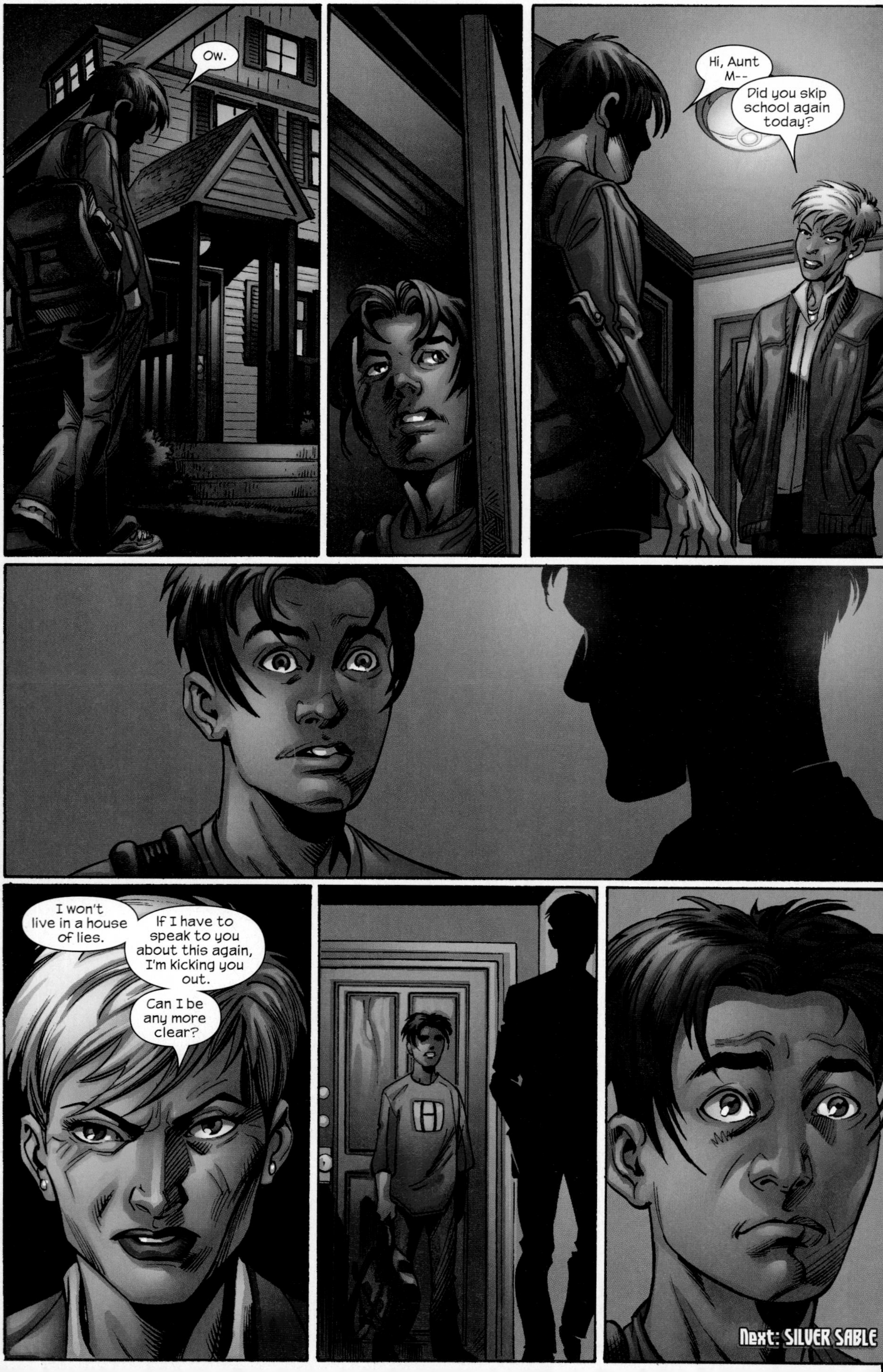
Ow.
Hi, Aunt M--
Did you skip school again today?
I won't live in a house of lies.
If I have to speak to you about this again, I'm kicking you out.
Can I be any more clear?
Next: SILVER SABLE

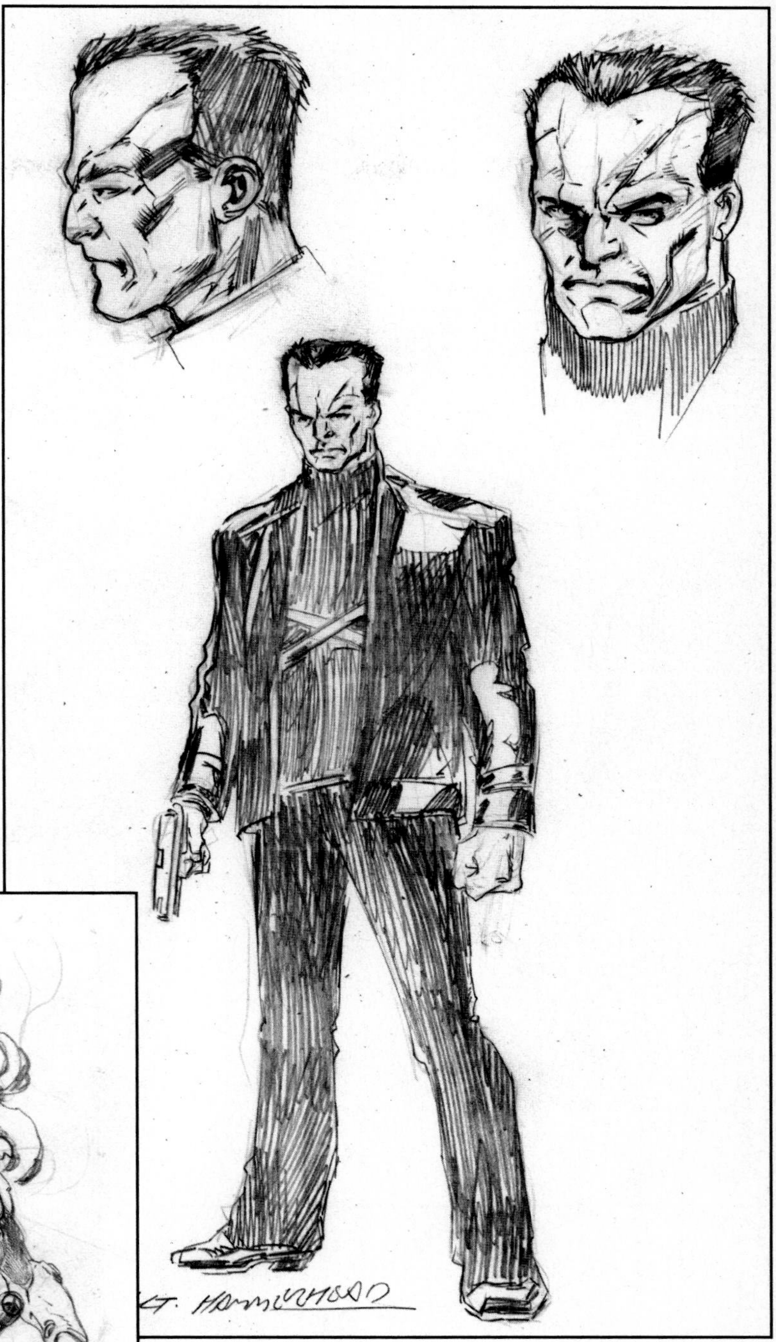

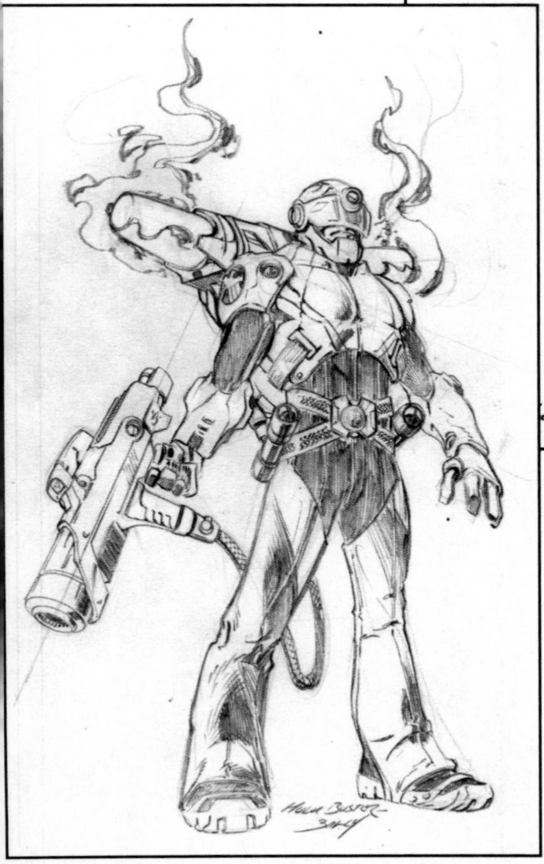

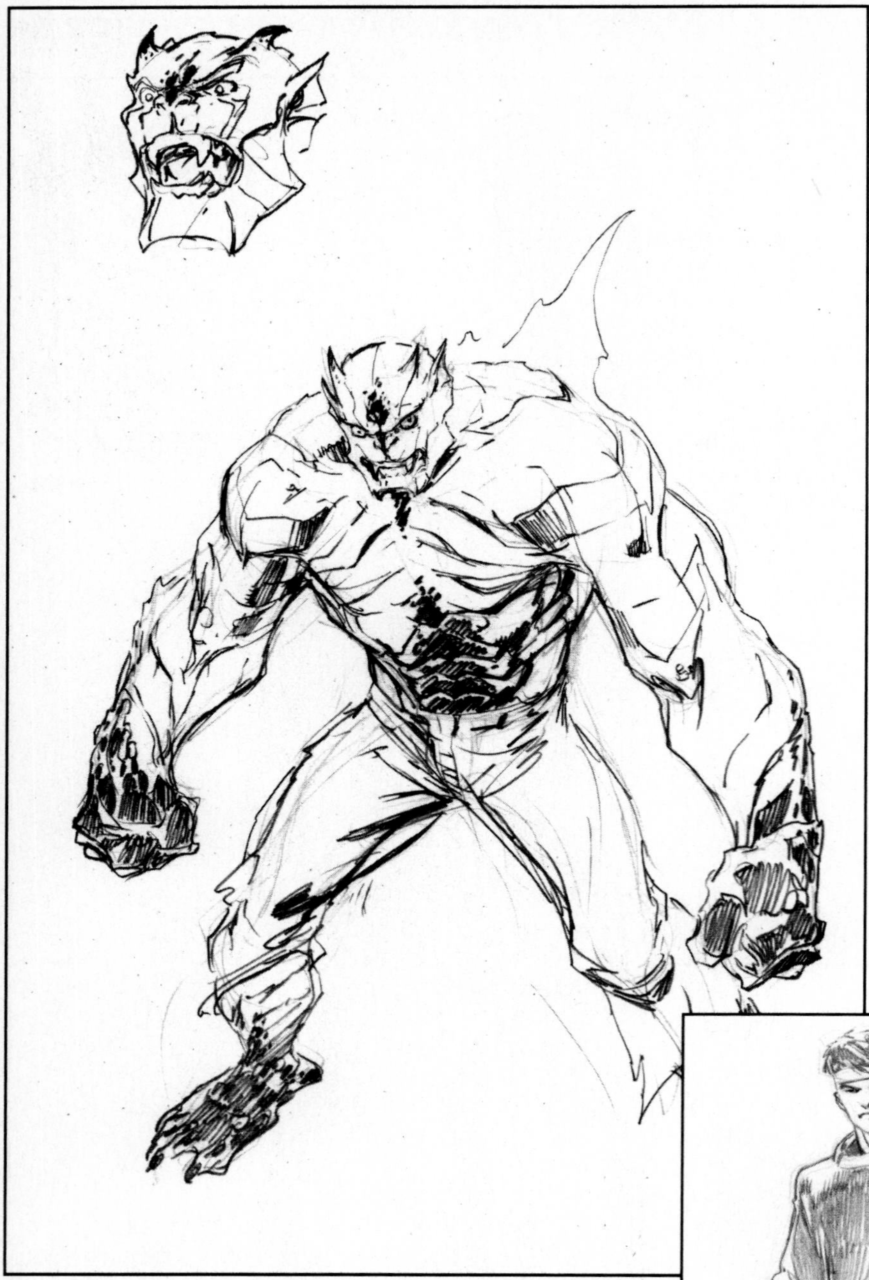

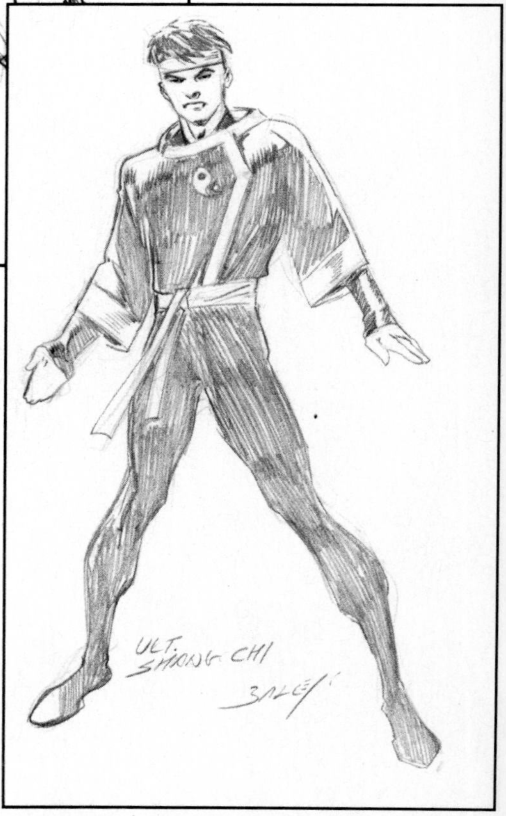
ULT.
SHANG CHI

72

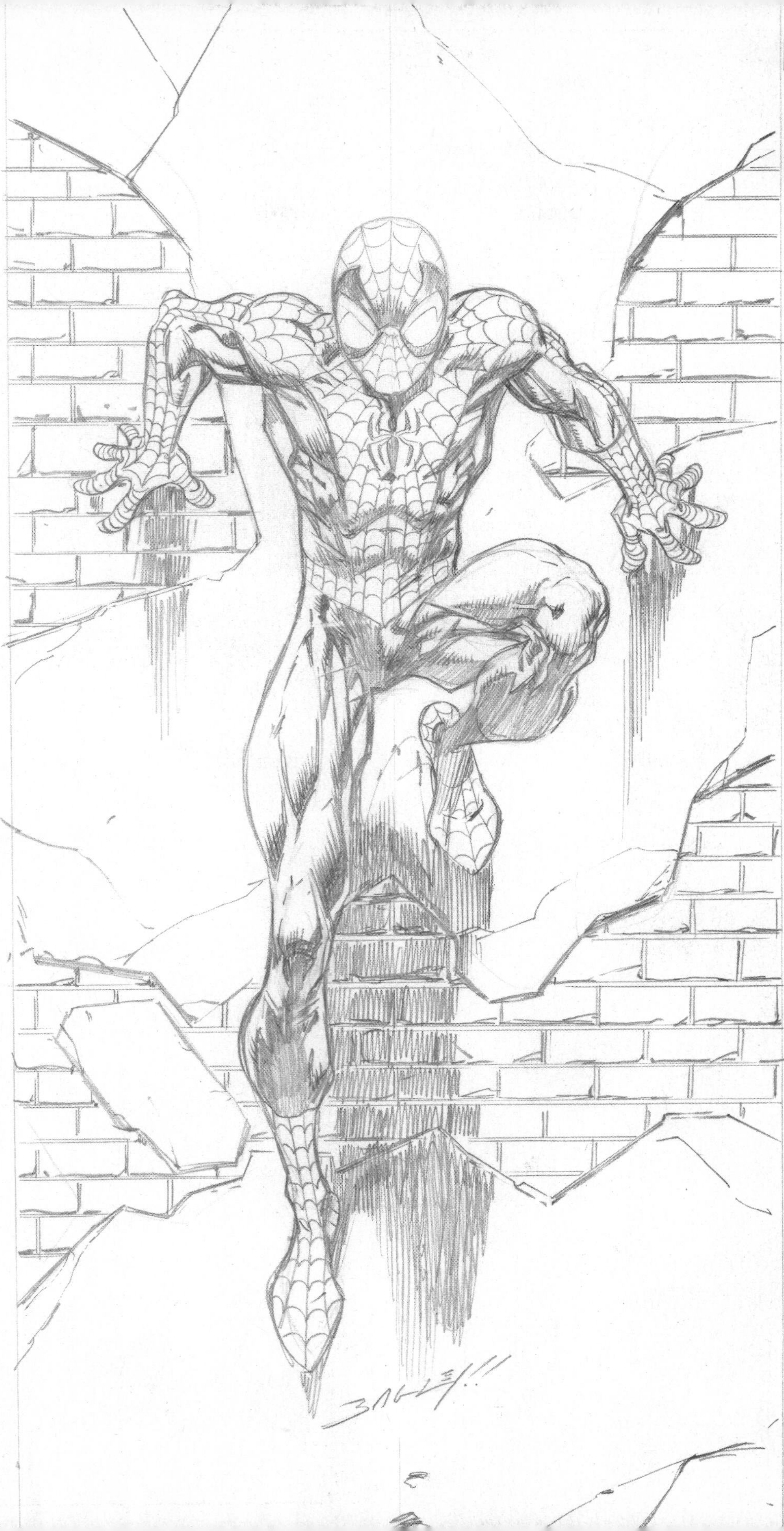

73

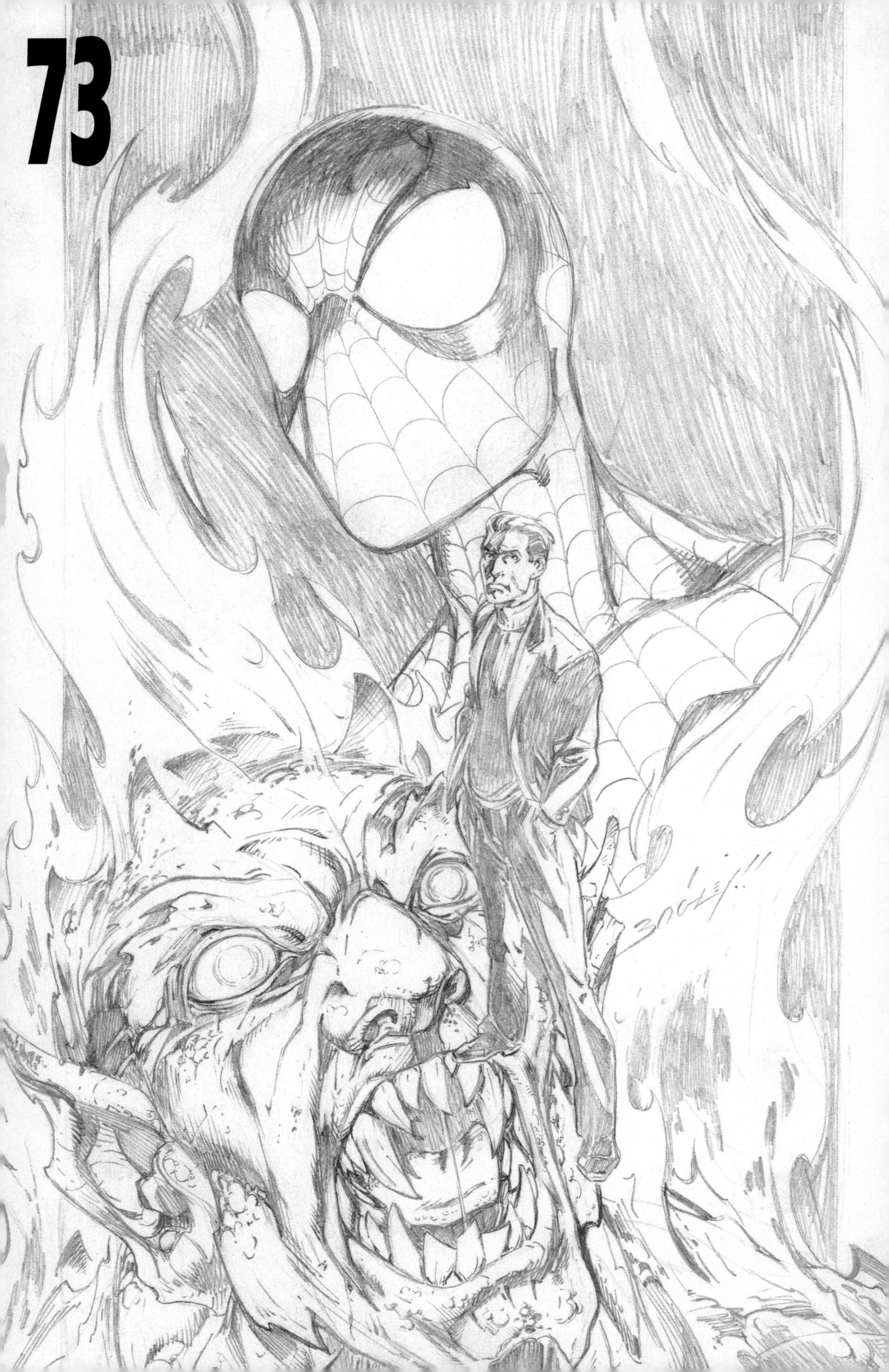

74

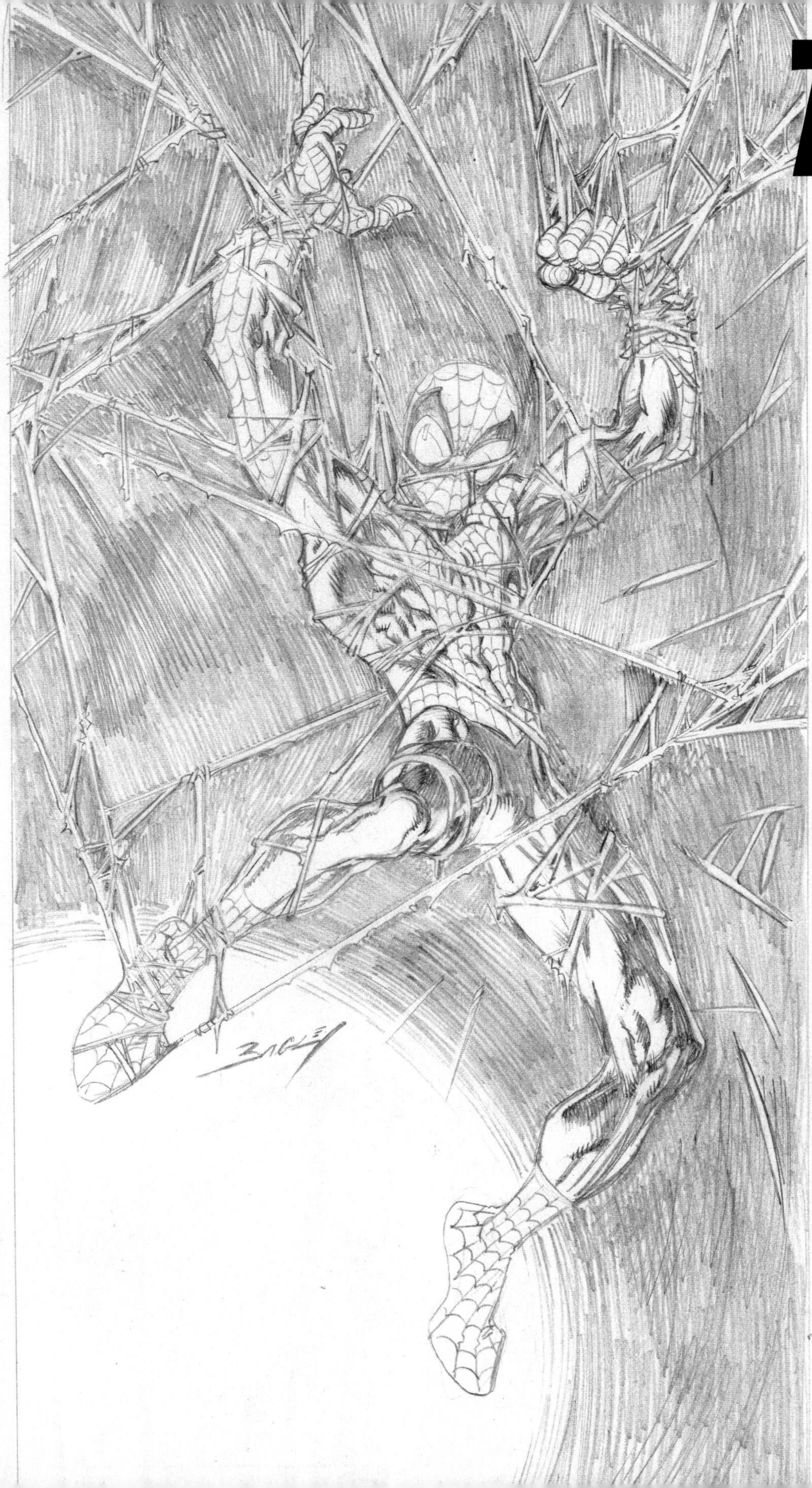

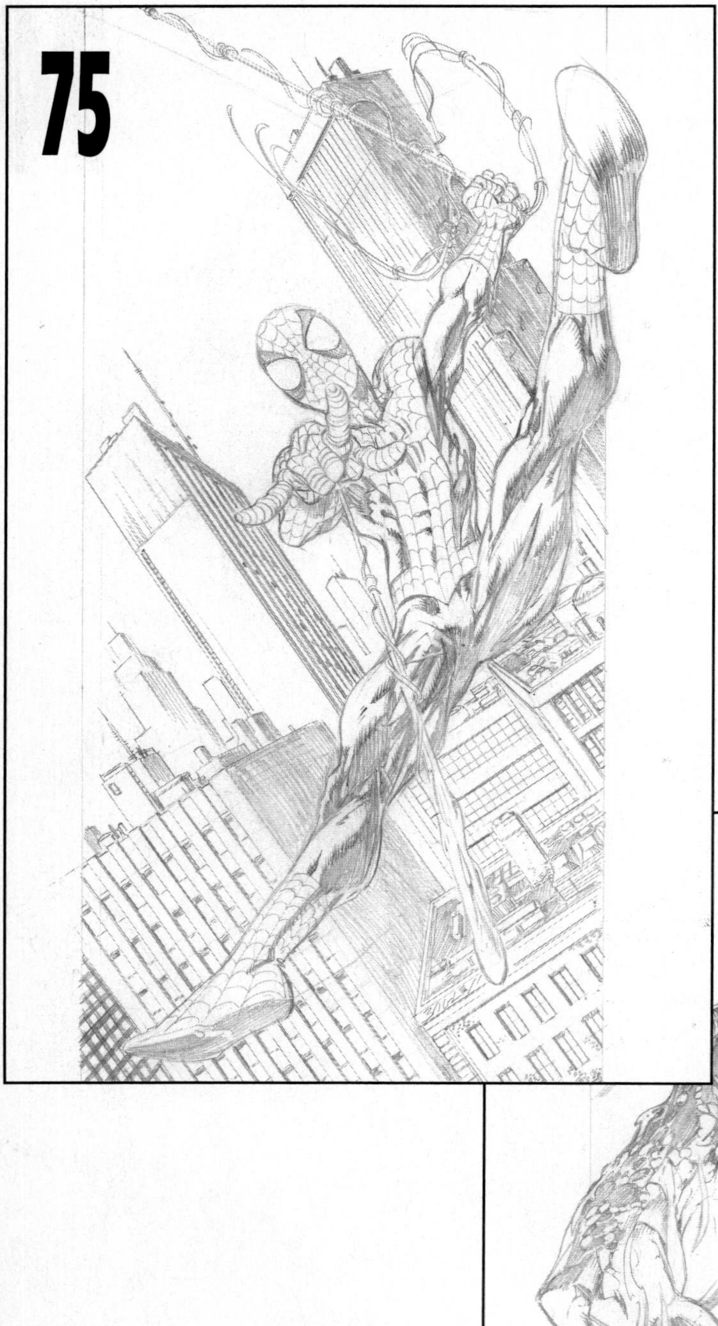
75

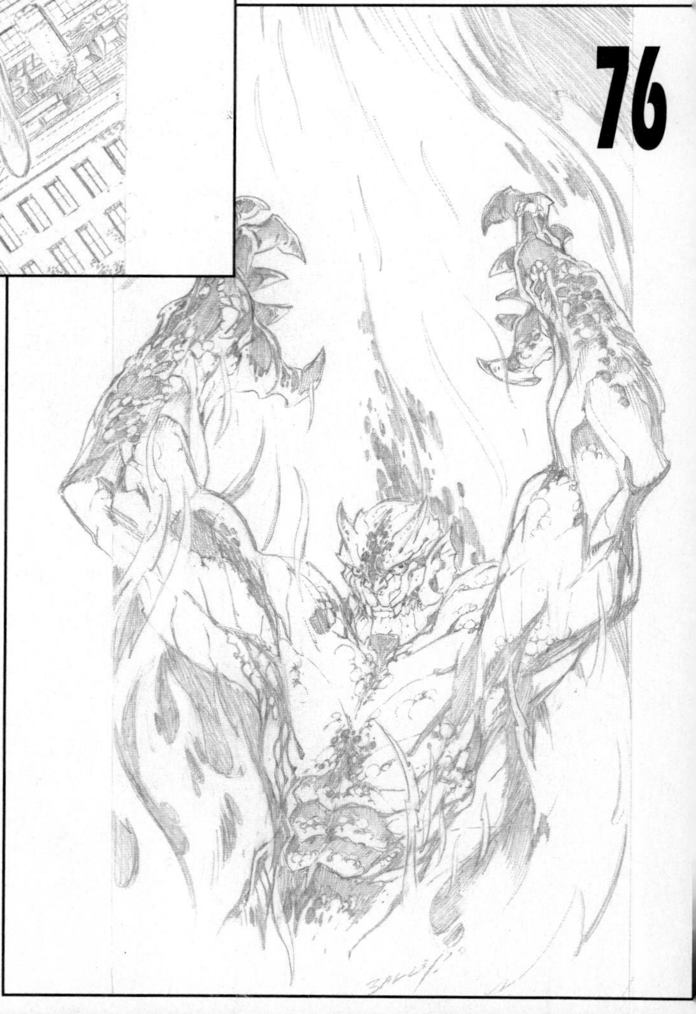
76

77

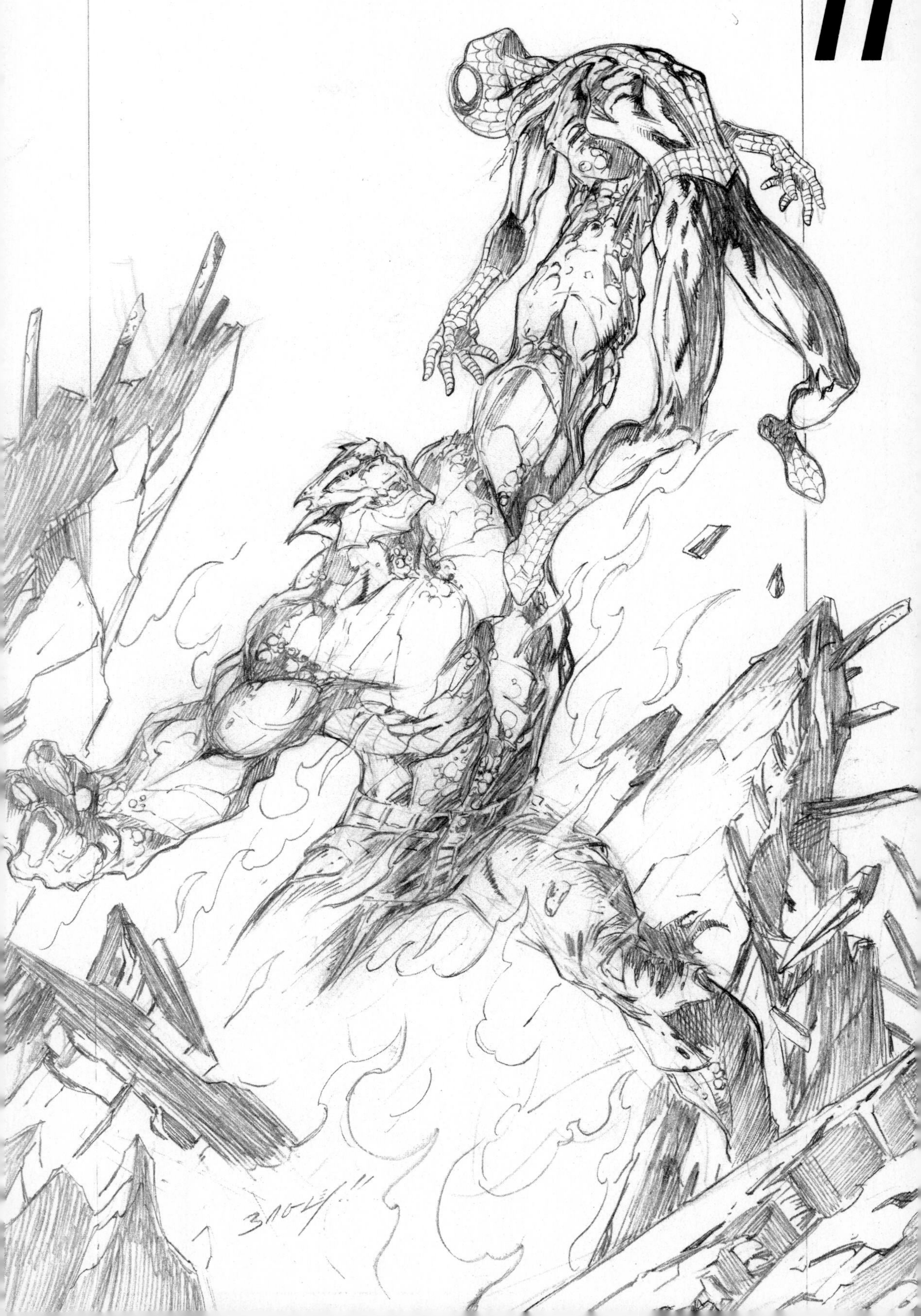

78

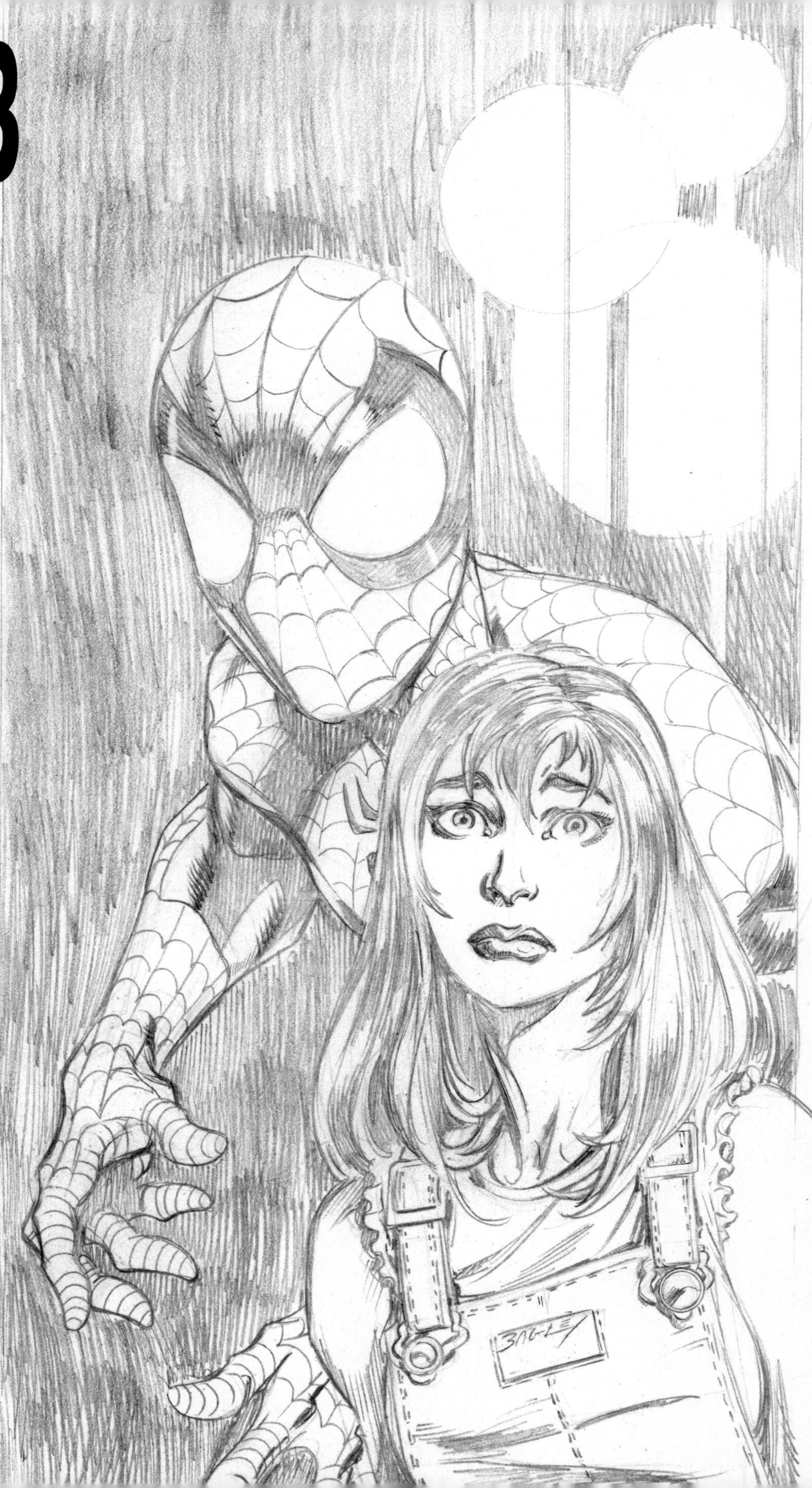

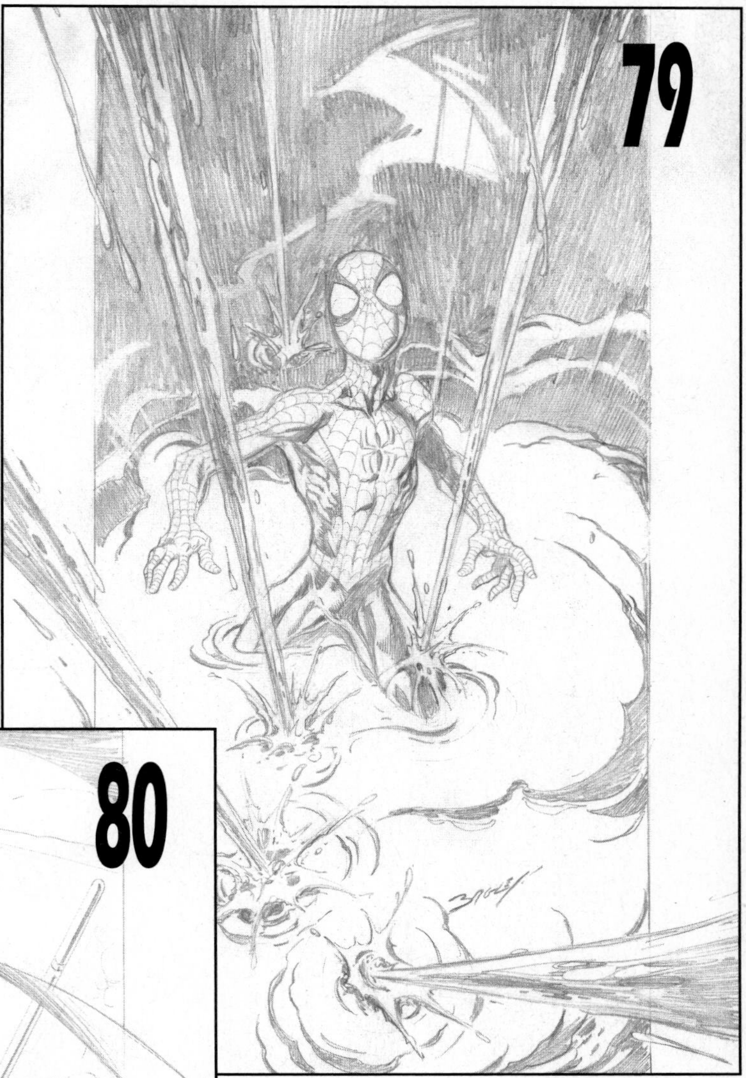
79
BAGLEY

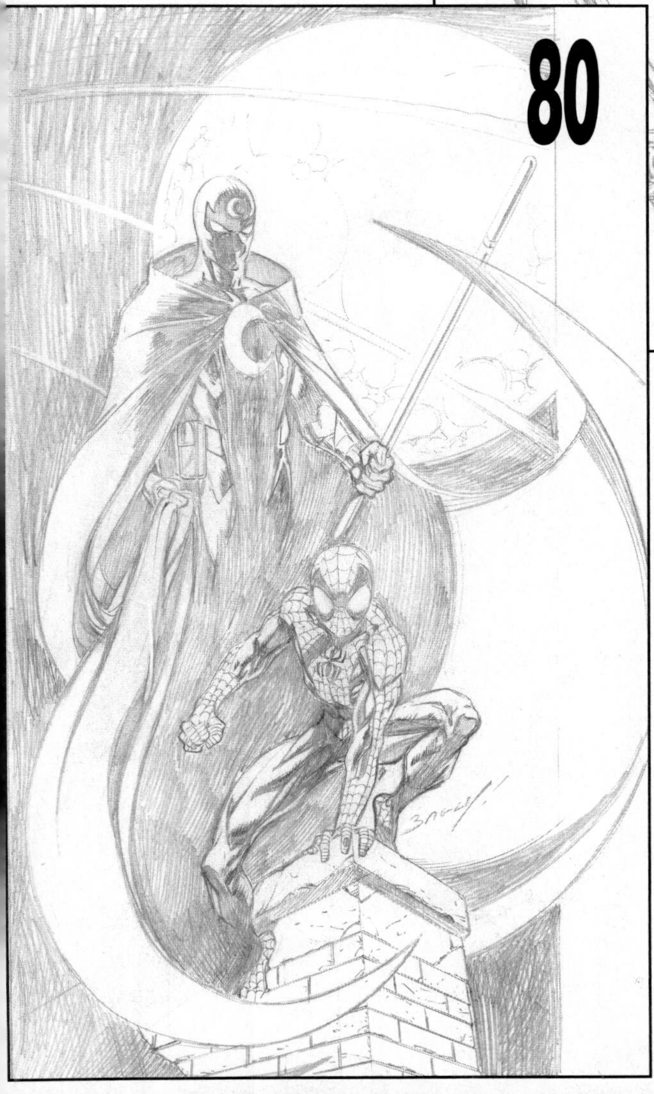
80
BAGLEY

81

B

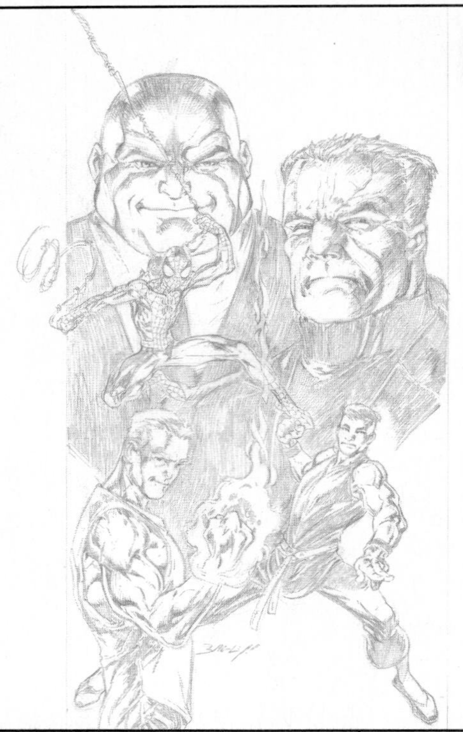

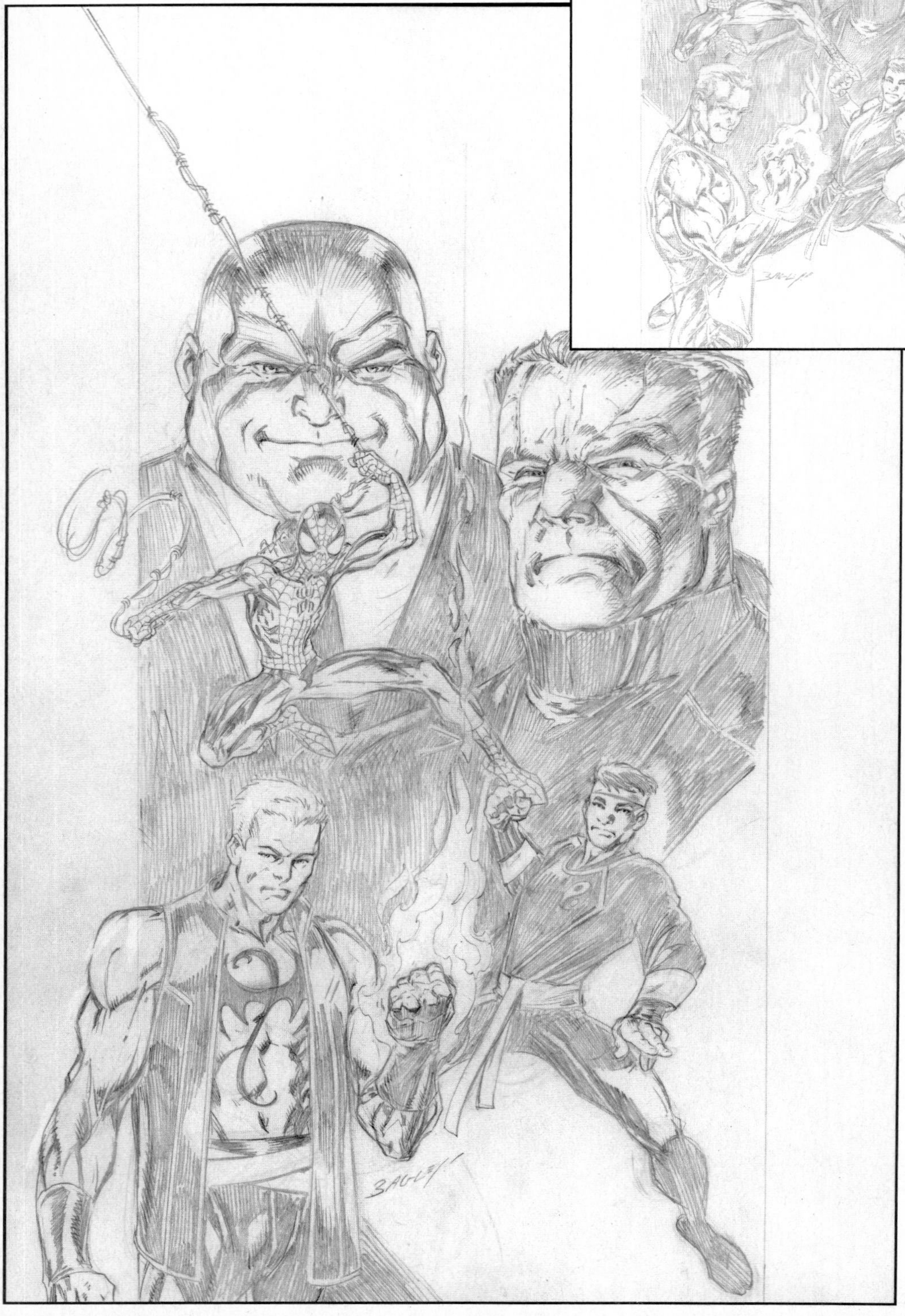

82

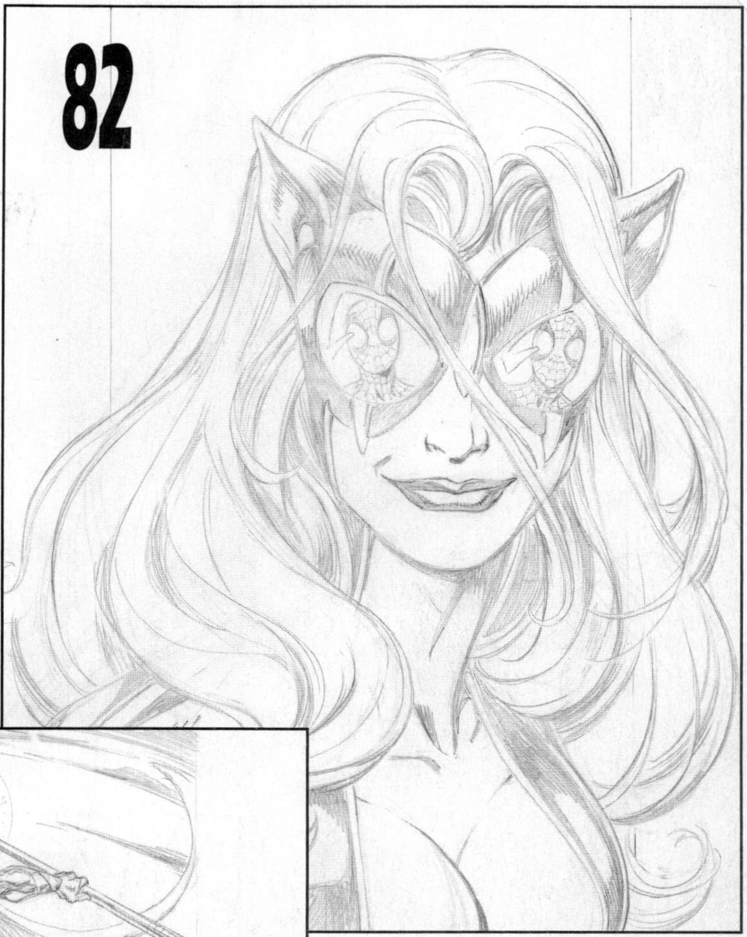

83

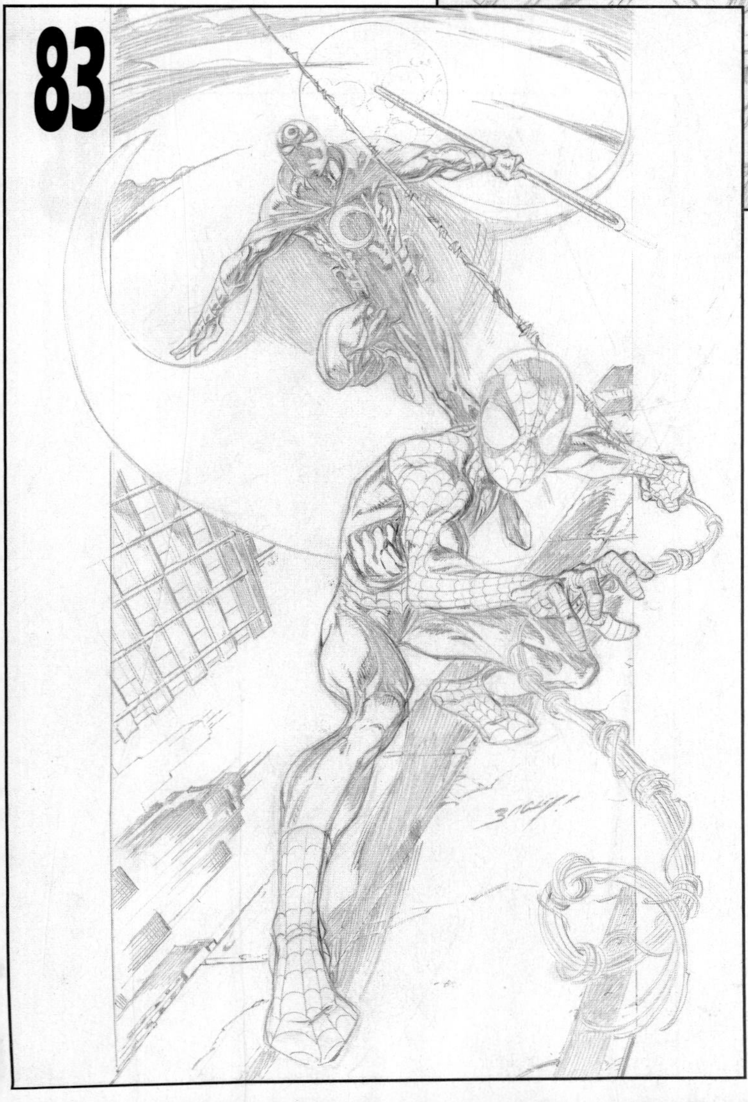

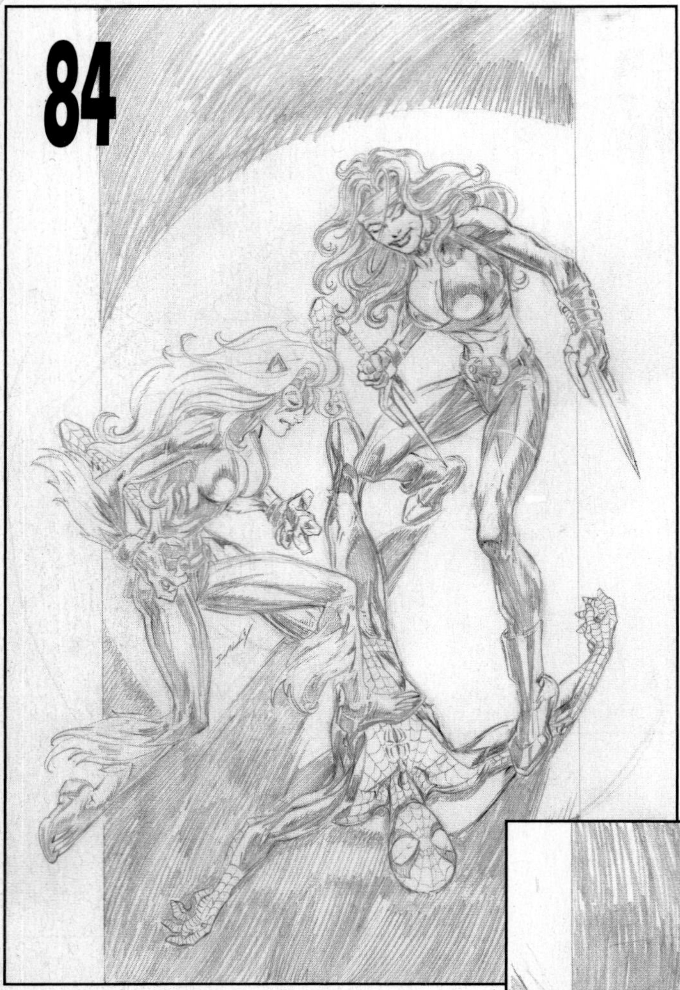
84

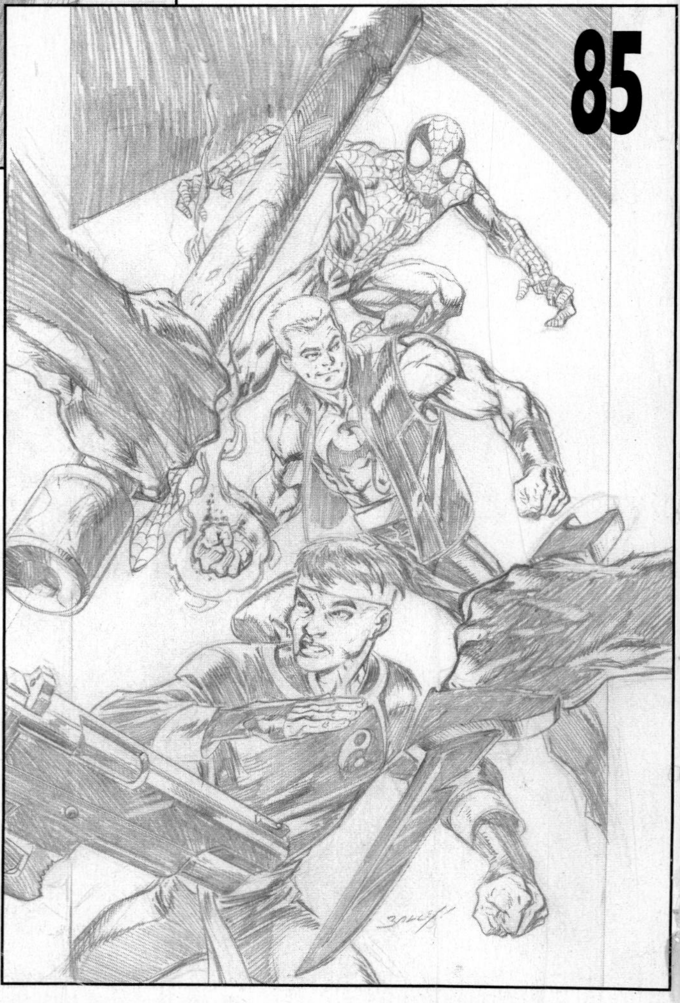
85

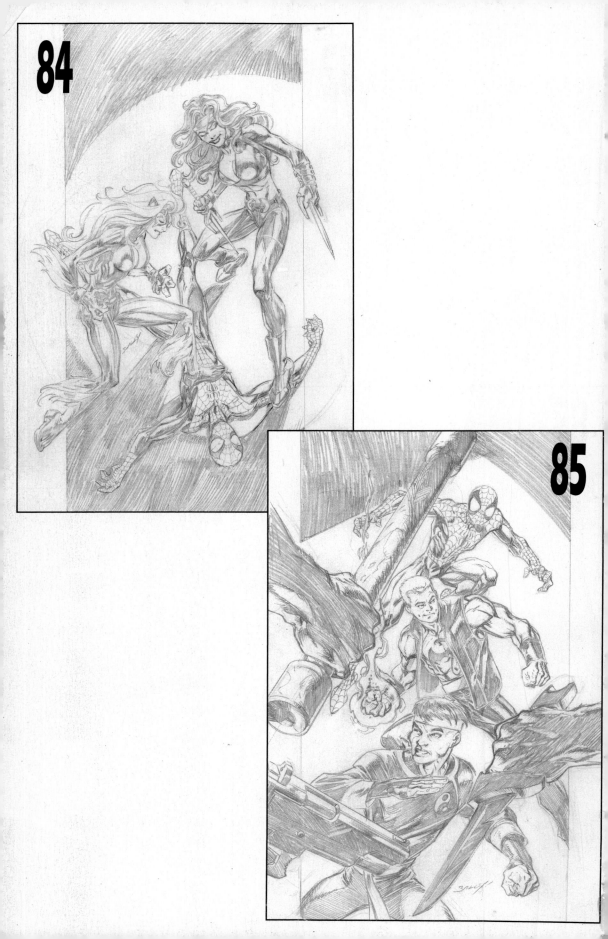